American Lawyers

American Lawyers

RICHARD L. ABEL

New York   Oxford
OXFORD UNIVERSITY PRESS
1989

Oxford University Press

Oxford   New York   Toronto
Delhi   Bombay   Calcutta   Madras   Karachi
Petaling Jaya   Singapore   Hong Kong   Tokyo
Nairobi   Dar es Salaam   Cape Town
Melbourne   Auckland

and associated companies in
Berlin   Ibadan

Library of Congress Cataloging-in-Publication Data
Abel, Richard L.
American lawyers.
Bibliography: p.   Includes index.
1. Lawyers—United States.   I. Title
KF297.A756   1989   340′.023′73   88-22522
ISBN 0-19-505140-8

2 4 6 8 9 7 5 3 1

Printed in the United States of America
on acid-free paper

To Emily

Preface

As will be immediately obvious to readers of this book, I have strongly ambivalent feelings about the American legal profession, of which I have been a member for nearly twenty-five years. It was the idealism of lawyers that originally attracted me. I have a vivid childhood memory of seeing *Inherit the Wind,* a play based on the Scopes trial, and passionately identifying with Clarence Darrow. I came of age during the Civil Rights movement, awed by the courage of blacks who risked humiliation, jail, beatings, and even death to assert their right to equality. I went to law school in 1962, expecting to become a civil rights lawyer. I did research on civil rights law in the summer after my second year, worked for the Lawyers' Committee for Civil Rights Under Law in Mississippi after graduation, and was a legal aid lawyer with New Haven Legal Assistance Association in the early 1970s.

I became an academic lawyer, however, not a legal activist. As a law teacher, I enjoy the privilege of critical distance from the pressing ethical dilemmas of the practicing lawyer and the complex politics of the organized bar. Yet, because I have spent the past nineteen years producing lawyers and will probably continue to do so for the rest of my working life, I am just as deeply implicated in the profession's problems and failings as any practitioner. Of necessity I accept and work within structures that favor certain people in obtaining entry to law school and performing well within it, strongly shape their aspirations and self-image, and direct them into certain careers and jobs. Much of law teaching, like practice, is unreflective routine rather than purposive reform.

All law is inescapably two-faced. It reproduces and justifies existing inequalities and injustices; yet it also embodies ideals and offers mechanisms through which they can be pursued. Lawyers display the same moral ambiguity. The legal profession has constructed and defended an elaborate constellation of economic, social, and political privileges. It propounds an ideology that allows lawyers to escape difficult moral choices by invoking their technical expertise. Most lawyers persist in seeing their daily work as morally neutral and apolitical. Yet many are attracted to the profession precisely because they embrace law as a "transformative vocation" (to use Roberto Unger's eloquent phrase) and wish to dedicate themselves to "struggle against the defects or the limits of existing society." A few remain committed to that ideal throughout their legal careers. If I criticize the American legal profession, therefore, it is only because I measure lawyers against their own impossibly high aspirations, which inhere in the very idea of law.

This book originated with my participation in the Working Group for Comparative Study of Legal Professions. Philip Lewis founded the Working Group in 1979 as part of the Research Committee on Sociology of Law of the International Sociological Association, and I joined him as cochair the following year. We enlisted legal scholars and social scientists in some 20 countries to describe and analyze their legal professions and encouraged another dozen to offer comparative and theoretical observations stimulated by those accounts. After several annual meetings we held a week-long conference in 1984. The University of California Press published the revised papers in 1988 and 1989 under the general title "Lawyers in Society"; the three volumes will cover "The Common Law World," "The Civil Law World," and "Comparative Theories." I prepared the national reports on the United States and on England and Wales. Because of the large quantity of data available and the absence of any contemporary overviews, I expanded those chapters into two books: *The Legal Profession in England and Wales,* published by Basil Blackwell in 1988, and the present volume. Because these volumes share the same analytic framework, their theoretical chapters are similar.

During the more than five years I have been actively engaged in writing this book, I have benefitted from the support and generosity of many people and institutions. Dorothe Brehove endlessly typed and retyped the tables, expertly intuiting the purpose behind my confused notations, imposing order, and designing a clear visual presentation. Other members of the law school secretarial staff also contributed to this difficult task. Two research assistants, David Lehman (a graduate student in history) and Rebekah Parker (a law student) spent many hours in the library uncovering sources I never knew existed. Robert Gordon of Stanford Law School and Terence Halliday of the American Bar Foundation read the entire manuscript and made invaluable comments. I have tried to heed their wise advice, although they still will disagree with some of my conclusions. Many people provided me with unpublished manuscripts, reprints of articles, and copies of books: Robert Bell, Brad Bumsted, Charles Cappell, David Chambers, Anthony Chase, Keith Cox, Steven Cox, Robert Dyer, Robert Fellmeth, William Felstiner, John Flood, James C. Foster, Marc Galanter, John Griffiths, Terence Halliday, Laura Kalman, Thomas Koenig, Herbert Kritzer, Donald Landon, Stewart Macaulay, Kenneth Mann, Martha Melendez, the National Association of Law Placement, Robert Nelson, Michael Powell, Mark Ramseyer, Deborah Rhode, Robert Rosen, Michael Rustad, Terence Shimp, Robert Stevens, Michael Trebilcock, David Trubek, Seymour Warkov, and Robert Weil. The staff of the UCLA Law Library were more than diligent in obtaining obscure books and pamphlets. I am grateful for research support from the Academic Senate and the Law School Dean's Fund of UCLA and the Law and Social Science Program of the National Science Foundation (Grant Nos. SES 81–10380, 83–10162, and 84–20295).

Santa Monica, Calif. R.L.A

Contents

List of Tables

NUMBER OF LAWYERS

CHARACTERISTICS OF LAWYERS

SELF-REGULATION

DIFFERENTIATION WITHIN THE LEGAL PROFESSION

American Lawyers

1

Introduction

Nearly 800,000 American lawyers constitute the largest legal profession in the world, both in absolute numbers and in proportion to population. They are also the wealthiest, particularly at the upper extreme but also on average. They may be the most politically powerful, dominating legislatures and executives, both national and state, more strongly than in any other country. Even culturally they are among the most prominent, ranging from mythic figures like Abraham Lincoln to the morally more ambiguous but perhaps even better known characters in the mass media, such as the television serial *L.A. Law*.

For these reasons among others (including our nation's political, economic, and cultural hegemony), American lawyers have become a model for, and a powerful influence on, legal professions in many other countries. The large law firm, pioneered in the United States at the beginning of the twentieth century, is rapidly proliferating throughout most other advanced capitalist societies (partly in response to competition from the foreign branch offices of large American firms). Because the size of the American legal profession has made it a highly attractive market for computerization, American lawyers have been in the vanguard in embracing developments in information technology, which everywhere is revolutionizing the storage and retrieval of legal knowledge, the organization and presentation of complex factual evidence, and the drafting of legal documents. The internationalization of law practice is fostered not only by the growth of the world economy but also by profound changes in the functions lawyers perform. Until recently, most lawyers devoted the bulk of their energy to litigation. As a result, professions were national (and even local)—centered on the courts in which lawyers appeared. The archetypes were the British barrister, the French avocat, the German Rechtsanwalt, the Japanese bengoshi. Today, an increasing proportion of lawyers devote more of their time to counseling and negotiating for clients who transcend national boundaries, interact with foreign trading partners, and require the approval of foreign governments. The elimination of all internal trade barriers, promised by the European Economic Community in 1992, will create a multinational European legal profession with striking parallels to contemporary American multistate practice.

American lawyers are just as prominent when the comparison is to other professions within our own country rather than lawyers abroad. The legal profession has experienced unprecedented growth over the last twenty years, a trend that seems likely to continue for several more decades. Competition to enter law school remains intense. The starting salaries of law graduates and the profits shared by senior partners in large firms elicit awe and envy from most observers. Lawyers are highly visible participants in virtually every newsworthy event: the Iran-Contra affair, the effort to oust General Noriega from Panama, the AIDs tragedy, litigation and legislation concerning surrogate motherhood, corporate takeover battles, and insider trading scandals, to offer just a few examples. Popular movies, television series, and best-selling novels highlight lawyers. Newspaper advertisements and television commercials have made lawyers much more familiar to the American public, whether the response they evoke is positive or negative.

Most observers of American lawyers—even (perhaps particularly) those who deplore their numbers, prominence, and alleged litigiousness—tend to take for granted the profession's exalted social, economic, political, and cultural standing. Yet no one looking at American lawyers as recently as a hundred years ago would have predicted this triumph. Compared to their counterparts throughout the common law and civil law worlds, nineteenth-century American lawyers were severely disadvantaged. Legal professions in other countries had evolved over long periods of time and could invoke tradition to justify contemporary practices. American lawyers, however, have twice suffered serious ruptures with their past—the revolutionary break with England at the end of the eighteenth century and the egalitarian attack on privilege that lasted from Andrew Jackson's election in 1840 until well after the Civil War. European legal professions were closely associated with other powerful social institutions: the established church (from whose clerics some legal professions were descended), the crown (whose courts lawyers staffed), and the aristocracy (whose property lawyers managed). None of these institutions existed in America. Because many European lawyers belonged by birth to the aristocracy, the landed gentry, or the rapidly growing commercial, financial, and industrial bourgeoisie, they conferred some of their ascribed status and power on the legal professions they joined. But in nineteenth-century America these social classes were either entirely absent or far smaller and, in any case, were less likely to send their sons to law. In Continental Europe and in Latin America law was one of the first university faculties, and it long remained one of the most prestigious. Yet very few American lawyers studied law at university until the twentieth century. English and Continental European lawyers early displayed some of the traits that define professional status—engaging in self-regulation and performing public service (the barrrister's dock brief for an indigent accused or *pro deo* service by European advocates). There is no evidence that their nineteenth-century American contemporaries shared those aspirations or actions.

Nineteenth-century American lawyers were disadvantaged in seeking professional status in comparison not only with their counterparts abroad but also with other professionals at home. Perhaps most important, they could not claim exclusive possession of an esoteric body of knowledge. In contrast with practitioners of the rapidly maturing natural sciences—medicine, physics, chemistry, and the numerous branches of engineering—lawyers appeared to be distinguished only by their unusual "gift of gab." Many saw them as unproductive parasites. Whereas medicine fosters the unqualified good of physical health and technology expands industrial production, law is morally ambiguous. In every controversy one side always loses, and few laypersons enthusiastically accept the defense lawyer's vigorous advocacy on behalf of those accused of crime. Other professions could justify restrictions on entry as a means of ensuring minimum standards of expertise. But it was more difficult for lawyers to deny admission when each new immigrant or underprivileged group saw the legal profession as both the most promising route of social mobility and an essential means for redressing individual and collective grievances.

These historical disadvantages have left an imprint on the contemporary American legal profession that continues to shape its development. The long and arduous task of constructing a profession has been filled with setbacks and reversals. This history helps explain why American lawyers are still struggling to reconcile the tension between their search for professional identity and their pursuit of economic success. It illuminates their deep-seated and enduring status anxiety: the soul-searching visible in the constant writing and rewriting of ethical rules, the acerbic self-criticism by some of their own most prominent members (such as Warren Burger, former Chief Justice of the U.S. Supreme Court, and Derek Bok, president of Harvard University and former dean of Harvard Law School), and repeated (if fruitless) efforts by professional associations to improve their public image. American lawyers appear deeply insecure about their entitlement to the extraordinary wealth and power they enjoy today.

Contrasting the situation of the American legal profession during its formative years in the last third of the nineteenth century with its present circumstances a hundred years later can give us some appreciation of the incredible distance the profession has traveled, its continuing dilemmas, and the resources it can mobilize. In doing so, we will encounter many of the issues that recur throughout this book: barriers to entry, rates of growth, the composition of the profession, restrictions on competition, the distribution of legal services, self-regulation, structures of practice, stratification and other internal divisions, and mechanisms for allocating lawyers to professional roles and socializing them within those roles.

Nineteenth-century American lawyers prepared almost exclusively through apprenticeship, and even that requirement was only loosely enforced. Many jurisdictions did not ask for any formal education, none demanded a college degree, and few entrants possessed much formal legal education. Today, virtually all entrants must complete nineteen years of formal schooling, including four years of college and three of law school. Competition to enter law school is intense, and schools are ranked in a clear and steeply graduated hierarchy. An increasing number of jurisdictions require practitioners to engage in continuing education. Many nineteenth-century jurisdictions had no bar examination; those that did delegated it to local judges, whose inquiries into the competence of candidates (often acquaintances) were brief, perfunctory, and oral. All contemporary jurisdictions have statewide written bar examinations (which draw heavily on a national multistate examination). Although these vary in length (from one to three days) and difficulty (the proportion passing ranges from fewer than half to almost all), most law students treat them as substantial obstacles, preparing with postgraduate cram courses that last one to three months.

Between 1880 and 1980 the number of lawyers increased ninefold while the population grew less than half that fast. The legal profession's growth during the period was highly variable. It grew rapidly at the end of the nineteenth century and especially during the 1920s, reflecting the proliferation of part-time law schools that charged low tuition and accepted virtually all applicants. Growth slowed considerably between 1930 and 1960 as state bars severely tightened entry requirements (insisting on prelegal education, excluding graduates of law schools not approved by the American Bar Association, and making bar examinations more difficult) and the Depression and World War II took their toll. In the last twenty years growth has greatly accelerated again as the number of college graduates rose, the postwar economic boom stimulated demand for legal services, many more women and minorities aspired to become lawyers, and rising salaries and idealism attracted entrants. As a result, the population per lawyer fell by almost a third from 1850 to 1900, was still at the same level in 1950 as it had been in 1900, and subsequently fell by half.

Despite the absence of significant entry barriers, the nineteenth-century American profession consisted almost exclusively of native-born Anglo-Saxon white Protestant males. Explicit, sometimes de jure, ethnoreligious, racial, and sexual discrimination (by law schools, bar examiners, bar associations, and employers) contributed to this homogeneity. As the number of southern and eastern European immigrants multiplied around the turn of the century and their sons sought to become lawyers, the profession tried to preserve its homogeneity and superior social status by requiring citizenship and imposing "character" tests. But despite these efforts, ethnoreligious minorities became proportionally represented (even overrepresented) within the profession, although employer discrimination relegated many to government and solo and small-firm practice. In the last twenty years courts have struck down the citizenship requirement and some of the more abusive interpretations of "character," while the civil rights and feminist movements have greatly augmented entry by racial minorities and women (if neither group has achieved proportional representation). But because the successful attack on some ascriptive barriers (ethnicity, religion, race, and gender) has coincided with heightened competition for law school places, the class background of new lawyers has narrowed, growing even more privileged.

Nineteenth-century American lawyers operated in a relatively free market, competing vigorously with both each other and laymen. Only in the courtroom was their monopoly protected from outsiders. Admission to the bar was no obstacle, and entry to the market required neither a significant capital investment nor membership in some larger productive enterprise (such as a law firm or corporation). Advertising and solicitation were unrestrained and pervasive. As generalists, all lawyers were potential competitors against each other. Because American lawyers belonged to a single fused profession they did not enjoy the protection afforded by the English division between barristers and solicitors or the even more numerous functional divisions found within civil law systems. The localism of political, economic, and social life, however, tended to create natural monopolies, particularly outside the few large cities.

As the rapidly growing number of lawyers suffered the sharp decline in demand caused by the Depression, they sought to restrict not only entry but also competition from both outside the profession and within. Unauthorized practice of law committees secured the enactment and enforcement of rules designed to limit the activities of court clerks, real estate agents, and banks and trust companies. Bar associations concluded agreements with organizations of lay competitors, dividing the market between them. Faced with law graduates and practitioners who wished to migrate in response to demand, state bars imposed residence requirements. State and local professional associations prohibited advertising and solicitation and promulgated minimum fee schedules (although enforcement was spotty, serving more to stigmatize low-status practitioners than to restrain competition).

In the last two decades, the rapid proliferation of new entrants, the consumer movement, and widespread ideological commitment to the "free market" combined to erode restrictive practices. Unauthorized practice of law committees were dissolved and market-division agreements rescinded (under threat of judicial nullification). The U.S. Supreme Court ruled that minimum fee schedules violated antitrust laws, prohibitions against advertising (but not solicitation) infringed on constitutionally protected free speech, and citizenship and residence requirements breached the privileges and immunities as well as the interstate commerce clauses of the Constitution. And the U.S. Justice Department prevented bar associations from favoring group legal service plans that dampened competition among member lawyers.

Lawyers have responded in different ways to these new opportunities and pressures. Large firms have eagerly entered national and even international markets by establishing branch offices in several states and countries. (Indeed, the production of services is beginning to resemble the manufacture of goods in the degree of international competition.) Legal clinics have aggressively marketed their services through saturation advertising on television and radio. Millions of unionized workers have been enrolled in group plans. And the proliferation of specialization—initially de facto but increasingly prescribed by formal requirements—may create new submarkets within which certified producers are protected from external competition. But most lawyers continue to practice much as they did decades ago: within the same small structures, offering the same range of relatively individualized services.

For most of the last hundred years, lawyers were indifferent, and sometimes even hostile, to efforts to redistribute legal services to those who cannot afford them. This indifference is partly explained by the fact that the relatively free market prevailing before World War II offered legal services to a fairly wide cross section of the population. The rapid growth in supply up through the 1930s, combined with the drop in demand following the Depression, kept prices low. And the entry of ethnoreligious (though not racial) minorities into the profession increased the access of these communities to legal services. But although Reginald Heber Smith, a leading reformer, vividly documented the underrepresentation of the poor as early as 1919, legal aid programs were restricted to a few major cities, depended largely on charitable donations, and were limited in amount and subject matter.

Indigent criminal accused had no constitutional right to legal defense, and most were unrepresented. The organized bar did nothing to encourage lawyers to offer gratuitous or "pro bono" legal services to those who could not pay. Indeed, professional associations disciplined lawyers who contracted with organizations of creditors or automobile owners to represent their members. As late as the 1950s, the American Bar Association condemned the new British legal aid scheme as a form of "creeping socialism," vowing to resist it vigorously in the United States.

The changes in the last twenty-five years have been dramatic. The U.S. Supreme Court has granted most indigent criminal defendants a constitutional right to legal representation (though refusing to extend it to civil litigants). When the federal government began to support civil legal services for the poor in 1965, annual national expenditures increased rapidly from less than $5 million to more than $300 million. Foundations granted millions of dollars to public interest law firms (although funding was difficult to find when foundation support ended). Bar associations authorized "open-panel" group legal services plans (in which any lawyer could participate) and then, under pressure from the U.S. Justice Department, reluctantly permitted "closed-panel" plans (formed by and restricted to particular lawyers). These now enroll millions. Thousands of legal clinics opened throughout the country to serve nonwealthy individuals; two have grown to rival the largest law firms in size. The organized profession repeatedly proclaims its support for pro bono services (although no state or national association requires its members to participate). And the Reagan Administration's attempt to abolish the federal Legal Services Corporation was opposed (successfully) by virtually every bar association in the country, many of which have now allocated the interest on lawyers' client trust accounts to legal services for the poor.

Although all these activities remain grossly underfunded, fail to reach certain populations, and often are of doubtful quality, they clearly have increased access to legal services. It is far less clear, however, whether they do much to stimulate demand for the services of lawyers, many of whom fear that the rapid growth of the profession during the last twenty years has led to overproduction. Nor do they necessarily enhance the profession's image if the public sees them as self-interested make-work rather than altruistic responses to objective needs. And all efforts to create demand risk subordinating lawyers to a third-party paymaster, whether governmental or private.

Although all professions proclaim their distinctiveness and justify their privileges by insisting on their unique qualifications to regulate themselves, American lawyers were very slow to adopt this role. Regulatory authority resides with the states, not with federal or local governments, but few effective statewide bar associations had emerged before the twentieth century. The first national ethical code was drafted by the American Bar Association only in 1908. Professional associations introduced "character tests" in the 1930s, but these seem to have been motivated primarily by ethnoreligious prejudice and were ineffectual in excluding potential miscreants. When bar associations did undertake to discipline their members, penalties were infrequent and light; even the rare lawyer who was disbarred could seek readmission or move to another jurisdiction. Few states established security funds to reimburse clients who lost money because of lawyer bankruptcy or fraud.

Lawyers were virtually immune from malpractice claims. Once lawyers passed the bar examination, nothing ensured their continuing competence during careers that lasted forty to fifty years.

The profession has recently displayed greater interest in self-regulation, devoting considerable energy to repeated revisions of its ethical rules (although this may simply reflect its inability to resolve fundamental ethical dilemmas). But much of the change has been exogenous. Fear of losing its regulatory authority has led the profession to increase both the frequency and severity of disciplinary penalties and to add lay members to regulatory bodies. Increases in the number and success of malpractice claims and in the size of damage awards have caused insurance premiums to skyrocket, compelling the profession to pay greater attention to ensuring competence. A majority of states now require continuing legal education. Virtually all have created client security funds (though inadequately funded and overly restrictive). The courts and administrative agencies in which lawyers appear are becoming increasingly active in punishing misconduct. The large organizations within which a growing proportion of lawyers practice—law firms, corporations, government offices, legal aid programs, clinics, and group plans—also have a stake in ensuring that their members perform ethically and competently. Yet this heightened attention to ethics and quality may also represent a loss of control by the organized profession to the state, laypersons, clients, courts, agencies, insurers, and units of production.

Among the profound changes American lawyers have experienced during the last hundred years, one of the greatest is the transformation in the roles they perform and the structures within which they practice. As late as the 1950s, nearly all lawyers still were independent private practitioners, neither employing lawyers nor employed by them or others, and either working alone or sharing expenses (less often profits) with one or two colleagues (frequently relatives). This statistically dominant work environment also was celebrated ideologically as the prerequisite for professional autonomy.

The late twentieth-century legal profession has abandoned these origins in two respects. First, the hegemony of private practice is waning. Increasing proportions of lawyers are corporate counsel, civil servants, judges, prosecutors, public defenders, legal aid lawyers, or law teachers. These roles are gaining status as well as numbers (although the relative advantages of the private sector in a capitalist economy continue to attract a much higher proportion). As a consequence of both the proliferation of lawyers outside private practice and the expansion of law firms, an increasing proportion of lawyers—nearly half—are employees rather than independent practitioners, and a significant proportion of independent practitioners employ other lawyers. Although the "independence" of lawyers remains an unquestioned shibboleth, it may express nostalgia more than it describes contemporary reality. And the growing heterogeneity of lawyer roles and practice structures also threatens the unity of the profession, greatly complicating efforts to take collective action.

Second, an increasing proportion of private practitioners now work in large firms, which continue to expand. Between 1975 and 1987 the number of firms with at least 100 lawyers multiplied more than fivefold (from 47 to 245) and the number of lawyers in those firms grew nearly eightfold (from 6558 to 51,851). The proportion of lawyers in solo practice declined from 61 percent in 1948 to 33 percent in 1980. Today's large firm differs radically from both its predecessors and its smaller contemporaries. Most have branch offices in other states and often in other countries: among the 100 largest firms, the number of lawyers in branch offices increased sixfold between 1978 and 1987 (from 14 to 19 percent of all lawyers in these firms). Hierarchy within these firms has intensified in two ways. The ratio of associates to partners has multiplied, and firms have revived or created new categories of subordinate: the permanent associate, senior attorney, or salaried partner (who does not share profits); and the staff or contract attorney (who is hired annually and never considered for partnership). Firms also employ more paralegals and use computers to increase the productivity of clerical personnel, thereby reallocating significant amounts of legal work previously performed by lawyers. Many firms have diversified their services by hiring a variety of nonlawyer professionals (e.g., accountants, economists, scientists, and psychologists). The size, internal differentiation, and stratification of these service enterprises demands more bureaucratic structures, often headed by nonlawyer managers. Some firms have invested retained earnings in nonlegal enterprises (such as commercial real estate). And there even is talk of allowing nonlawyers to invest in law firm equity, completing the structural homology between the large firm and the corporations it serves.

Although professions generally pay lip service to an egalitarian ethos (claiming that all their members are at least minimally competent while laypersons are not), American lawyers have never been equals. The colonial profession distinguished those who qualified at the English Inns of Court from those who prepared at home, and some colonies recognized an incipient division between barristers and solicitors. Even during the intensely egalitarian Jacksonian era, identifiable elites served larger commercial interests in major Eastern cities. Until the turn of the century, however, the exclusion of Blacks and women, the absence of ethnoreligious minorities, the relatively small size of most American businesses, the hegemony of solo practice, lawyers' common educational background (almost exclusively apprenticeship), and the opportunities presented by the expanding frontier all minimized intraprofessional differences—especially compared with the formal divisions in England and Continental Europe.

The profession has become increasingly stratified throughout the twentieth century, whether the index is income, prestige, or power. Many variables affect a lawyer's position in this hierarchy, including background (ethnicity, religion, class, gender, and race), education, and legal role (private practitioner, corporate counsel, civil servant, judge, and educator). Each role contains further distinctions, which are especially pronounced among private practitioners: employment versus independent practice, firm size, subject matter and functional specialization, and clientele. Like other social institutions, the legal profession justifies differences in its members' rewards in terms of their ability and effort. Although some ascribed characteristics actually have declined in importance—ethnic and religious background, for instance—the greater heterogeneity of the profession may make it more difficult to justify other differences, such as the overrepresentation of women in roles that demand fewer or less erratic hours and of racial minorities in employment, particularly within the public sector—all positions that pay lower salaries and confer less status.

The principal obstacles to unified action by American lawyers around the turn of the century were geographic dispersion, the multiple jurisdictions within the federal polity, and free rider problems (the ability to enjoy the benefits without paying the costs). The importance of geographic distance declined with the growth of cities and technological advances in transportation and communication. States remained autonomous regulatory authorities but tended to engage in parallel activities, particularly under the tutelage of the American Bar Association. And the spread of compulsory (unified or integrated) state bar associations solved the free rider problem. Contemporary American lawyers face different but potentially more intractable problems in attempting to act collectively. The diversity of lawyers' backgrounds and roles, and the stratification this produces, have spawned numerous unofficial professional associations divided by race, gender, religion, age, politics, clientele, function, and role. Although most lawyers also belong to inclusive state and national associations, they often find their goals and style alien and their leadership unrepresentative. Furthermore, the very compulsion that ensures universal membership (thereby endowing state associations with substantial economic and political resources) can produce paralysis.

The increased differentiation and stratification of the legal profession has required a restructuring of the mechanisms for allocating entrants to legal roles and socializing them within those roles. Until the early twentieth century, virtually all lawyers prepared through apprenticeship for the single role of sole practitioner. The only distributional mechanism was the decisions by practicing attorneys to accept apprentices and help them establish their own practices. Although we know little about this process, it seems plausible that most aspiring lawyers had few options within a limited region and that practitioners chose apprentices based on intensely particularistic criteria, often influenced by kinship or prior acquaintance. When law schools replaced apprenticeship at the beginning of the twentieth century, they assumed part of both functions. Although most law schools (even the elite) accepted virtually all applicants, class origin and ethnoreligious background strongly influenced the student's choice of a law school. Employers hiring law graduates were swayed by the same characteristics and often by personal acquaintance as well. The majority of graduates, who entered solo or small firm practice, were socialized informally by their contemporaries or elders.

In the last two decades these mechanisms have changed radically. Because virtually all graduates begin their careers as employees, the critical decisions occur between application to law school and beginning the first legal job. The nearly 200 law schools approved by the ABA are ranked in a widely known and extremely influential hierarchy. Admission to the most prestigious has become intensely competitive (although background characteristics still help predict who will succeed). Great disparities in starting salaries (ratios of at least 4:1) intensify competition for grades and other distinctions within law school. The labor market has been extensively rationalized, permeating the entire law school experience. Students seek summer jobs after their first and second years to get a foot in the door following graduation. Interviewing severely disrupts instruction during the fifth semester. Postgraduate judicial clerkships have become a further screening device for the most prestigious jobs. Many graduates spend years in a subordinate status—as virtual apprentices—before they gain security of employment and the rewards of higher income and power.

This book seeks to describe and explain the dramatic changes in the American legal profession during the last hundred years. How and why did they occur? What does the profession look like today? Can contemporary trends help us anticipate the future? To answer these questions we need an analytic framework that selects and structures the historical and sociological data while using them to test the empirical generalizations. The next chapter, therefore, presents three strands of social theory that are useful in understanding lawyers. Max Weber emphasized the relationship between producers and consumers of services, identifying the distinctive ways in which professionals (including lawyers) seek to control their market. Karl Marx focused on relationships among those who produce goods and services. His conceptualization of the conflict between capital and labor may help illuminate the nature of lawyers' work and the structure of units within which legal services are produced. Talcott Parsons was concerned with both kinds of relationships: where professionals are located within the system of stratification, how they construct community within mass society, and their potential for altruism and disinterest. I will try to show the contemporary relevance of these theories with illustrations from diverse professions, including law. Although I draw eclectically on all three theoretical strands, my primary concern will be the economic aspects of legal practice because I believe that for most lawyers law is a means of earning a living before it is anything else.

I start my account of American lawyers with a narrative of their efforts to become a profession by regulating prelegal and legal education, requiring a bar examination, limiting admission to United States citizens and state residents, and imposing character tests. Then I turn to the consequences of entry control for the number of lawyers and their characteristics (age, ethnicity, class, gender, and race). Next I look at the ways in which lawyers tried to structure their market, restricting competition both from outsiders (through rules against unauthorized practice and market-sharing agreements) and among themselves (by prohibiting advertising and solicitation, setting minimum fees, and creating protected subspecialties).

In the last two decades, lawyers have also devoted considerable energy to redistributing legal services through state subsidies, private insurance, aggressive promotion, and individual and collective philanthropy, not only for economic reasons (to augment demand) but also out of altruism and anxiety about their public image. I consider the ways in which the legal profession has sought to justify the autonomy it enjoys by regulating its own behavior: promulgating ethical rules, disciplining violations, protecting clients against financial loss, and ensuring lawyer competence. Because lawyers have engaged in these activities to increase their income and enhance their status (among other reasons), I evaluate the success of their efforts by looking at changes in those variables over time.

Since World War II, especially in the last two decades, American lawyers have experienced a radical transformation in the roles they perform and the structures within which they practice. I examine the growing number employed in government, offices of house counsel, the judiciary, and law schools. Then I turn to private practice, which remains the core of the profession, charting the decline of solo and small-firm practice. Finally, I describe the incredible expansion of large firms and their dramatically different structures: the internal hierarchy of lawyers and lay employees, intense interfirm competition in attracting and retaining partners and associates as well as clients, penetration into national and international markets, diversification in the services offered, and the bureaucratization of management.

The increasing heterogeneity of the profession and the differentiation of the roles lawyers perform and the structures within which they practice have greatly complicated their efforts to engage in collective action. These changes have also required the rationalization of mechanisms to allocate heterogeneous entrants to diverse and stratified roles and to socialize them within those roles. I conclude the book by returning to the theoretical framework to see how well it illuminates the changes we have observed, critically examining the recent proposals of a prestigious ABA Commission, and offering my own speculations about the future of American lawyers.

In presenting this historical sociology of the American legal profession I emphasize quantitative data over qualitative accounts. This is not because I believe one is superior to the other but simply because I could not do justice to both perspectives within a single book. In order to trace changes over time, make comparisons across states and among types of practice, and generalize about the national profession, it is extremely useful—often essential—to reduce complex reality to something that can be counted. I have summarized much of these data in the tables at the end of the book, but sometimes the complexity of fifty distinct jurisdictions makes such generalization impossible.

I am the first to admit that quantification frequently sacrifices depth for breadth and subtlety for the memorable but incomplete summary. Furthermore, the construction of a numerical index assumes that the observer knows the meaning of a social practice without asking the actors how they understand their own behavior. I have drawn on interpretive accounts, discussions with lawyers, and my own experience in choosing the questions I have tried to answer quantitatively. I hope others will be stimulated to flesh out this numerical skeleton and to challenge it, using qualitative and interpretative methods.

2

Theories of the Professions

This book seeks to describe and understand American lawyers using the analytic framework of the sociology of professions, a subdivision of the sociology of occupations. I have chosen that framework in the belief that the organization of a profession helps to illuminate its role in society. There is little debate about the importance of the subject: both official spokespersons for the profession and external critics agree that lawyers significantly influence political, economic, social, and cultural life. But anyone wishing to understand lawyers still must choose which questions to ask. This book is a sociology of the legal *profession*, not of lawyers' *work*. My focus is not dictated by the logic of explanation: the relationship between legal work and the social organization of the profession is reciprocal—one is not prior to the other. Rather, I am influenced by what we know. Historical and sociological primary and secondary sources offer rich accounts of who lawyers are, how they are trained and certified, the structures within which they practice and the rules that govern them, how much they earn, how they organize themselves into professional associations, and what those associations do. With some notable exceptions, however, most observers tell us little more about what lawyers *do* than how they allocate their time among different subject matters.[1] One aspiration of the present book, therefore, is that its description of the social organization of the legal profession will enable and stimulate others to undertake the more difficult task of studying the content and form of lawyers' daily work.

It is customary to begin any work of social science by defining the phenomenon being examined—here the legal profession—because the definition is stipulative and implicitly introduces theoretical assumptions. In the adjective "legal" I include all those formally qualified and practicing law, either independently or as employees in the public or private sectors, as well as students preparing to do so and law teachers training them. I exclude the myriad individuals without formal qualifications who perform equivalent functions, such as social workers, tax advisers, police, trade union shop stewards, and accountants. I also exclude those who have qualified but are not practicing law, such as corporate executives. And I touch on judges only briefly. I have drawn these boundaries because of my interest in exploring the relationship between the social organization of the occupational category and how its members perform a set of overlapping tasks.

If this categorization of "legal" occupations is a plausible demarcation, the notion of a profession is more controversial. The study of professions encompasses three principal theoretical traditions: Weberian, Marxist, and a structural-functional approach associated with Parsons but rooted in Durkheim. Because each poses fundamentally different questions about society, they view the professions from radically divergent perspectives. Despite their overlapping interests, therefore, proponents of these different traditions often talk past each other. I outline the three perspectives below and explain why I emphasize the Weberian approach, before I present a more detailed exposition of how each theoretical framework informs my description and analysis of the legal profession.

For Max Weber and others in his theoretical tradition—most notably Eliot Freidson, Terence Johnson, Magali Sarfatti Larson, and Frank Parkin—analysis begins with the sphere of distribution.[2] The central question is how actors seek and attain competitive advantage within a relatively free market—one structured by the state but dominated by private producers. The goals are economic rewards and social status, which is partly a consequence of wealth and partly its legitimation. Market competition constructs categories of adversaries *within* classes.[3] The functional division of labor among occupations is one by-product of this process. But because unrestrained competition is certainly unpleasant, and possibly intolerable,[4] all economic actors seek protection from market forces. Professions are distinguished by the strategies of social closure they use to enhance their market chances. This Weberian tradition has parallels in neoclassical economics (both positive and normative), although the two disciplines rarely communicate.[5] In recent decades, economists have critically analyzed how occupations that have gained professional status (or aspire to it) seek to regulate the market for their services, to the detriment of both competitors and consumers. Thus, neoclassical economists, like Weberians, see the arena of struggle as the marketplace, within which the adversaries are members of the same class.

Marx and his followers start with the production of goods and services, not their distribution. Although the mode of production changes, relations of production have always defined a vertical division between two opposed classes—the bourgeoisie and the proletariat under capitalism. I present this oversimplification to highlight the marginality of professionals, who often seem little more than a historic residue of petty bourgeois artisans. At times, indeed, Marx appears to argue that the petty bourgeoisie are destined to vanish in the progressive polarization of capital and labor. Yet Marx also recognized that the progressive concentration of capital required greater numbers of functionaries to mediate between the two classes.[6] The continuing focus of bourgeois (especially American) sociology on this "middle class," together with its explosive expansion since World War II, has inspired a debate among Marxists over its categorization and future. For Marxists, then, the fundamental question is whether the category to which professionals belong—defined variously as the service class, the professional-managerial class, the "new class," or black-coated or educated workers—is destined to ally with labor or capital or become an independent force within the ongoing class struggle, and what will determine the affiliations of its members.

For Emile Durkheim and the structural functionalists who followed him, the critical question is social order. In a society composed of egoistic individuals lacking common values and unconstrained by such traditional institutions as the family, religion, and locality, what prevents the pursuit of self-interest from degenerating into Hobbesian anarchy?[7] The professions appeared to offer one antidote to the insidious poison of selfish materialism. It was particularly important, indeed, that *they* remain disinterested because of the great potential harm were they to misuse their privileged knowledge.[8] The older professions, notably law and medicine, actually did retain significant vestiges of a precapitalist past.[9] And all professions and professionalizing occupations energetically sought to present themselves as communities within the anomic mass society—altruistic where others were egoistic, self-regulating counterweights to an increasingly monolithic state.

This highly flattering portrayal may be part of the reason why the professions preoccupied the sociology of occupations for so long.[10] Although many observers uncritically accepted this portrait, Talcott Parsons was its best-known and most influential proponent.[11] It is worth quoting him at length, if only to indicate the target at which later generations directed much of their fire.

> [T]he professional complex, though obviously still incomplete in its development, has already become the most important single component in the structure of modern societies. It has displaced first the "state," in the relatively early modern sense of that term, and, more recently, the "capitalistic" organization of the economy. The massive emergence of the professional complex, not the special status of capitalistic or socialistic modes of organization, is the crucial structural development in twentieth-century society.[12]

Parsons's tendency toward categorization was paralleled by the dominant "trait" approach to professions, which demarcated them from other occupations by elaborating their allegedly socially integrative functions into a series of distinguishing characteristics.[13] The rhetorical power of this approach is evident in its influence on the English Royal Commission on Legal Services, which defined "the five main features of a profession" as follows:

> A governing body (or bodies) [that] represents a profession and . . . has powers of control and discipline over its members.
>
>   [Mastery of] a specialised field of knowledge. This requires not only the period of education and training . . . but also practical experience and continuing study of developments in theory and practice. . . .
>
>   Admission . . . is dependent upon a period of theoretical and practical training in the course of which it is necessary to pass examinations and tests of competence.
>
>   [A] measure of self-regulation so that it may require its members to observe higher standards than could be successfully imposed from without.
>
>   A professional person's first and particular responsibility is to his client. . . . The client's case should receive from the adviser the same level of care and attention as the client would himself exert if he had the knowledge and the means.[14]

The preamble to the American Bar Association Model Rules of Professional Conduct is similar, if somewhat less systematic:

> A lawyer is an officer of the legal system, a representative of clients and a public citizen having special responsibility for the quality of justice. . . .
>
> In all professional functions a lawyer should be competent, prompt and diligent. . . .
>
> As a public citizen, a lawyer should seek improvement of the law, the administration of justice and the quality of service rendered by the legal profession. As a member of a learned profession, a lawyer should cultivate knowledge of the law beyond its use for clients, employ that knowledge in reform of the law and work to strengthen legal education. A lawyer should be mindful of deficiencies in the administration of justice and of the fact that the poor, and sometimes persons who are not poor, cannot afford adequate legal assistance, and should therefore devote professional time and civic influence in their behalf. . . .
>
> To the extent that lawyers meet the obligations of their professional calling, the occasion for government regulation is obviated. Self-regulation also helps maintain the legal profession's independence from government domination. An independent legal profession is an important force in preserving government under law, for abuse of legal authority is more readily challenged by a profession whose members are not dependent on government for the right to practice.[15]

The reduction of sociological analysis to little more than professional apologetics eventually stimulated a critical reaction.[16] This, in turn, has engendered a defense of professionalism, which has attracted its own critics.[17] But critics either embraced the Weberian or Marxist frameworks or remained preoccupied with challenging the traits claimed by the professions and attributed by the structural functionalists. Thus, critical sociologists sought to demonstrate that governing bodies were unrepresentative and ineffective regulators, professions lacked the expertise they claimed, admission criteria bore little relevance to the profession's actual work, ethical rules were motivated by economic self-interest and failed to ensure competence, and professionals repeatedly betrayed clients.

Although I draw on all three theoretical traditions to select, organize, and analyze the data on the legal profession, I find the Weberian approach the most illuminating. Because professions are primarily a category within the horizontal division of labor, they are relatively marginal to Marxism, which focuses on class conflicts.[18] As economic groupings, they are marginal to structural functionalism, which is concerned with community, altruism, and self-governance—issues that preoccupy social movements and voluntary associations but not occupations. Because most lawyers in the common law world are private practitioners, their first concern is, and must be, the market for their services. The Weberian framework (and its parallel within neoclassical economics) offers the greatest insights into the dilemmas of professionals within such a market. Yet because legal professionals are increasingly becoming employers in the private sector and employees in both private and public sectors, Marxist class analysis poses questions that cannot be ignored. And because the construction of community, the encouragement of altruism, self-governance, and the maintenance of ethical standards and competence are not insignificant issues for professionals (even if they usually are subordinated to material survival and advancement), the dialogue between structural functional theory and its critics remains important. I try to make these theoretical frameworks more concrete, vivid, and immediate with illustrations drawn from contemporary debates and events within other American professions.

Weberian Theories of Professions in the Marketplace

Constructing the Professional Commodity

Professions produce services rather than goods. Unlike the farmer, herder, or artisan before the Industrial Revolution or the manufacturer today, the producer of services cannot rely on consumer demand for physical objects to constitute the market. Service providers confront two distinct problems in particularly acute form. First, the consumer must value the producer's services. The perception of value does not seem problematic from the perspective of contemporary medicine or even law. But if we consider the sorcerer in tribal societies or the clergy in many contemporary western societies, the difficulties are immediately apparent.[19] Second, consumers must be convinced they cannot produce the services themselves. Once again, consumer incompetence may be obvious if we reflect on neurosurgeons or corporate lawyers. In practice, however, we doctor and lawyer ourselves much of the time, often resisting advice to consult an expert.

The success of producers in constructing a market for their services turns on several variables. What consumers "need" is a function of cultural beliefs, over which producers have limited influence. All they can do is amplify or dampen demand by connecting their services to fundamental values: relgion with transcendental beliefs, medicine with the desire for physical well-being, and law with justice, security, or the protection of political and economic stability. Structural functional theory tends to treat the demand for professional services as unproblematic—as the consumer's rational acknowledgment of their objective "utility." But professions emerge and thrive with little or no evidence that their services actually benefit consumers; examples include religion at all times, medicine before about 1900, and astrology today.[20] Even established professions must constantly build consumer confidence in the value of what they are selling.[21] Freidson frames the question starkly: "Is professional power the special power of knowledge or merely the ordinary power of vested economic, political and bureaucratic interests?"[22]

Once potential consumers believe in the value of the service, professionals must persuade them to purchase it rather than simply produce it themselves. The division of labor compels this: as producers become specialized, consumers necessarily become generalized and thus dependent on others.[23] But other factors also shape consumer dependence: professional services contain an irreducible element of uncertainty or discretion, a delicate balance between indetermination and technicality, art and science.[24] If there is too much art, consumers lose confidence (as in quack medicine or investment advice); if there is too much science, consumers can provide the service themselves or resort to nonprofessional advisers (do-it-yourself home repairs or divorces).[25]

Other ingredients may help the profession to construct a marketable commodity. The producer's expertise should appear to be objective, not arbitrary or idiosyncratic. For religious believers, the warrant of expertise is often tradition—a sacred text or church hierarchy—although charismatic leaders also contribute. But for most contemporary professions, the most powerful assurance of objectivity is identification with the natural sciences. Despite the efforts of lawyers to portray law as a logically deductive system, the public clearly see it as a human construct and thus a reflection of political power. Professional knowledge must be esoteric, but aside from the cherished residues of Latin and French, together with English archaisms, legal language is just ordinary language used in strange and arbitrary ways. Professional knowledge must reconcile stasis and change, traditional warrants of legitimacy and the innovations that ensure continuing uncertainty. But whereas scientific traditions can invoke the validation of repeated experience, ancient laws may be seen as the heavy hand of history. And whereas scientific novelty is progress—good by definition—law "reform" may be exposed as a concession to special interests. Professional knowledge is standardized; heterodoxy threatens its very foundation—hence the difficulties that medicine encountered until the twentieth century. At least since the triumph of the nation-state, law has been the voice of a single sovereign and thus clearly unitary; but such unity may be resented as tyranny in pluralistic societies (and all societies are somewhat pluralistic).

The construction of a marketable commodity depends on variables other than the nature of professional expertise. The relation between producers and consumers is clearly critical. It is not coincidental that the two most successful contemporary professions, medicine and law, emerged by selling their services to individual consumers (as did their predecessor, the priesthood). Conversely, many occupations that entered the market more recently and sold their services either to existing professions (nurses to physicians, paralegals to lawyers) or large bureaucratic employers (social workers to government, teachers to school systems) never became more than semiprofessions.[26] The commodity must be packaged in units that consumers can afford, which may be one reason why physicians have been relatively more successful than lawyers. And it is very helpful to have exclusive access to a vital arena: the hospital for physicians, the courtroom for lawyers, the document registry for European notaries.

The task of constructing the professional commodity never ends, for it is constantly being undermined.[27] Other bodies of knowledge may challenge the hegemony of professional expertise: natural science has been eroding the authority of religion since at least the Enlightenment, and economics may be displacing law as the foundation of government today. Expert authority may also be unmasked as political domination: the feminist critique of medicine is a contemporary example; but law is far more vulnerable to such demystification.[28] And the ratio of indetermination to technicality may become unbalanced. Art may be revealed as fakery: "lactrile" as a cancer cure, for instance. More dramatically, politicians and the public may lose faith in the ability of economists to forecast or manipulate macroeconomic trends. At the other extreme, technicality exposes professions to competition from paraprofessionals (e.g., dental hygienists setting up independent practices)—a threat that is amplified by developments in information technology.[29]

Pursuing Social Closure

By constructing a marketable commodity, service producers become only an occupation. To become a profession they must seek social closure. This "professional project" has two dimensions: market control and collective social mobility.[30] Although these are inextricably linked in practice, it is analytically useful to distinguish them, dealing with market control here and collective mobility later (see "Closure as Social Mobility"). Markets compel all occupations to compete. This may be advantageous to consumers—that is the market's fundamental justification, after all—but competition is hardly pleasant for producers since it is the classic zero-sum game: a consumer who buys from one producer generally is less likely to buy from another. It is not surprising, therefore, that producers energetically try to escape from that freedom, notwithstanding their professed enthusiasm for markets.[31]

Producers of goods can seek protection from market forces in a variety of ways: through horizontal monopolies or cartels, vertical control over raw materials, and rights to technology and other intellectual inputs (patent, trade mark, and copyright). Because services are not embodied in a physical form, however, their producers have only one option: control over the production of producers. Indeed, the state began to regulate the markets for goods and services at about the same time.[32] Control over the production of producers is not new, and it is certainly not limited to capitalism. Tribal societies in precolonial Africa often limited specialized occupations, such as blacksmith, to a particular lineage or clan; and Indian castes are among the most elaborate systems of market control. Other nonprofessional forms of closure include guilds, trade unions, civil service employment, academic tenure, and employment within large private bureaucracies. Weber suggests some of the permutations of closure:

> Both the extent and the methods of regulation and exclusion in relation to outsiders may vary widely, so that the transition from a state of openness to one of regulation and closure is gradual. Various conditions of participation may be laid down: qualifying tests, a period of probation, requirement of possession of a share which can be purchased under certain conditions, election of new members by ballot, membership or eligibility by birth or by virtue of achievements open to anyone.[33]

The mechanism of closure may be the object of struggle between potential competitors. "Healers" in California have sought to replace credentialing with title licensure, so that everyone could provide medical services as long as they identified themselves as physicians, nurses, chiropractors, osteopaths, podiatrists, or other healers.[34] The medical profession is also concerned that some physicians may patent new procedures, such as human embryo transfer, and charge royalties for their use by others.[35]

In recent years, a number of writers have elaborated this notion of closure.[36] Johnson contrasts collegiate control through guilds or professions with both control by the client (whether an oligarchic, corporate, or individual consumer) and mediation of the producer-consumer relationship (by the state, a corporation, or an insurer).[37] Parkin makes closure his central analytic concept, analogizing it to the earlier asymmetry between capitalist and worker in the ownership of the means of production.[38] And Bourdieu and Passeron also view credentialed expertise as a form of "cultural capital." Indeed, Murphy suggests that capital, like credentials, is merely another form of closure.[39] Others have adopted the framework of political economy, examining the ways in which professions have sought to mobilize political power in order to structure their market.[40] There is ample evidence that academic credentials confer economic advantages: Americans who dropped out of high school earned an average of $693 a month in 1984, while those with professional degrees averaged $3871.[41]

Structural functionalists address this issue from a very different perspective. Closure is not a response to the market, and certainly not the conscious, self-interested strategy of producers, but simply the means by which society ensures that consumers receive quality services.[42] Because it is so difficult for consumers to evaluate either the process of rendering services or the outcome, society maintains quality through input controls.[43] Producers justify their obviously self-interested behavior in the same way. When Los Angeles initiated a campaign against "bandit" taxicabs operating without an annual $690 permit, the City Attorney proclaimed: "We're going to do everything we can to have a full frontal assault to protect our licensees *and to protect the public* [emphasis added]." And the Taxi Industry Council, representing the seven companies that cartelize the permits, denounced the "bandits" for such wrongs as having "actively advertised, solicited, cruised for fares, sat on taxi stands, hailed passengers, placed telephone ads, responded to telephone and radio orders and otherwise sought to do business."[44]

Weber categorically rejected this functionalist interpretation.

> When we hear from all sides the demand for an introduction of regular curricula and special examinations, the reason behind it is, of course, not a suddenly awakened "thirst for education" but the desire for restricting the supply of these positions and their monopolization by the owners of educational certificates. Today the "examination" is the universal means of this monopolization, and therefore examinations irresistably advance.[45]

Parkin is equally emphatic: "Once a professional monopoly has been established, the way then becomes clear for the elaboration of those purely ceremonial conventions by which access to specialised knowledge is carefully monitored and restricted."[46] I can imagine their response to a recent news article reporting that it is virtually impossible to work as a clown in a major American circus today without a diploma from Clown College in Venice, Florida, which admitted only 60 out of the 3000 applicants in 1985.[47]

Adherents of the Weberian position can point to the lack of fit—or at least the failure to demonstrate any empirical correlation—between credentials and the actual work performed, whether the credential is technical and the work manual or the credential is a liberal education and the work white collar.[48] Even if we concede that education may confer technical competence, the credentials required often far exceed the skills demanded.[49] In fact, that the very institution responsible for producing most professionals—the university—chooses its faculty on the basis of credentials that say *nothing* about teaching ability. And it would be hard to argue that the credentials required of lawyers are necessary to the practice of law, given the considerable national variation in legal pedagogy. Lawyers in England and the United States perform many of the same tasks, but legal education in the two countries differs substantially in the degree to which it requires academic study or apprenticeship, is based on lectures or socratic dialogue, demands oral or written performance, uses treatises or casebooks, stresses rules or analytic techniques, occurs in classrooms or clinics, and takes place at the undergraduate or graduate levels.

Indeed, the little we know about what lawyers do suggests that they make scant use of their formal legal education.

> Scottish solicitors explained that on average they would deal with the law, in the sense of technical knowledge, for something around one hour a week. The rest of their time—taken up with handling personal relationships and business negotiations, and with consultations and meetings—involved little legal skills; either they used totally routinised legal knowledge or else they moved out of, or beyond, specifically legal work. Solicitors further confirmed that in their practice, the most important factor in terms of giving clients satisfactions was *not* careful research, technical skills, or even (when a dispute was involved) winning a case, but rather maintaining relationships with clients on proper grounds.[50]

Jerome Carlin's study of sole practitioners in Chicago in the late 1950s came to similar conclusions:

> Time devoted to writing legal briefs and memoranda is at a minimum for all but a very few respondents. Reading legal material either for "keeping up" or on research in connection with some matter at hand accounts for only a small fraction of the individual practitioner's working day—less than a half hour a day, on the average. And only 6 respondents specifically mentioned engaging in any legal research.
>
> *Interviewer:* Do you spend any time reading legal material?
> *Respondent:* I'm ashamed to tell you, not even an hour a week. You can say I get by on cursory knowledge of the law. But it's mostly the same thing, not just bluffing.
> *Interviewer:* Do you spend any time preparing legal documents?
> *Respondent:* Zero. Well, pleadings, yes, but most are in subrogation cases, and I use a form, filling in the date, and so on, so it doesn't take too much time.[51]

To the extent that mandatory education serves purposes other than market control, it confers status through the association of the university with high culture, socializes entrants to their professional roles, and provides warrants of loyalty and discipline.[52]

Physicians are unusually open about their desire for social closure. In 1983, the president of the Union of American Physicians and Dentists declared that:

> now we find ourselves with a glut of doctors in California. In San Francisco, for example, there is one physician for every 187 citizens, or approximately

three times the numbers that are needed to serve the population adequately. Meanwhile, the five UC [University of California] schools of medicine continue to pour thousands of new and unneeded doctors into the state, at a cost that exceeds a billion dollars a year!

Armies demobilize after a war, companies divest themselves of losing enterprises, sunset laws are enacted to end legislation that is no longer needed. Now is the time to close two of the present UC schools of medicine....[53]

The following year the University of California requested no increase in funding for its medical schools, cut their budget by $7 million, and began planning to reduce enrollment between 5 and 7 percent.[54] In 1985, the New York State Commission on Graduate Medical Education proposed a 30 percent cut in the number of residency programs in state hospitals over the opposition of some of them.[55] And in 1986, the American Medical Association (AMA) board of trustees issued a report urging "review" of medical school enrollments and the exclusion of foreign-trained physicians. The chairman of the board noted that physicians were under "tremendous" pressure to lower their fees. As the AMA executive vice president explained "If we are overproducing physicians and they are progressively more competitive, then it becomes a quality issue." Even the editor of the *New England Journal of Medicine* insisted that "there is more pressure on the doctor to maintain his income than is good for the public or the profession."[56] It is ironic to hear professionals denounce competition as degrading quality when economists usually extol it as enhancing quality.

Closure strategies can be exclusionary (directed against equals or inferiors) or usurpationary (against superiors).[57] They may emphasize either training or testing.[58] Credentials may be demanded of individual producers or of the institutions through which producers become qualified or services are delivered. Closure can be achieved through exclusive rights to use a title, registration, or licensing. The degree of closure sought may vary with the market conditions for the professional commodity.[59]

Associations of producers obviously play a critical role in imposing entry requirements.[60] Yet, paradoxically, the elite who typically organize and dominate the professional association and direct the professional "project" stand to gain few economic benefits by controlling the production of producers; they are more concerned with collective status.[61] Closure is negotiated by the profession, the university, and the state. But despite the profession's constant invocation of the shibboleth of "independence," closure ultimately depends on the authority of the state, whose influence increases as it plays a greater role in financing training and reimbursing professionals.[62]

A central question for a Weberian approach, and one of the most difficult, is why some occupations successfully professionalize while others do not. A number of factors may be relevant. Professions differ in the value their services promote: health and justice obviously rank high today, as salvation did in the past (and still does in many communities).[63] Collegial control of the market is easier to attain if the clientele consists of isolated individuals.[64] Furthermore, the homogeneity of the clientele is correlated with that of producers, which in turn affects whether a single profession emerges or several occupations continue to compete. Elite sponsorship can advance the professional project; conversely, professionalization can be hindered if many members of the occupation have disadvantaged social backgrounds (they are ethnic and racial minorities, children from working-class families, or women).[65] Elite universities can be instrumental, as in Continental Europe; but England (and such former colonies as the United States, Canada, Australia, and New Zealand) clearly demonstrates that legal professions can train entrants largely or exclusively through apprenticeship.[66] Many of these themes are explored in the histories of the medical profession in the United States and England.[67]

Social closure is an elusive goal, even for the most successful professions.[68] It must be constantly defended against threats from consumers and potential competitors as well as the consequences of adventitious events. Success intensifies pressure for entry by aspiring professionals, jurisdictional challenges by potential competitors, and consumer complaints about excessive costs. Limitations on American medical school enrollment have driven 12,000 to 15,000 Americans a year to study outside the country, especially in nearby Mexico and the Caribbean, and then seek to have their credentials recognized in the United States. (It was the "threat" to American medical students in Granada that the Reagan Administration invoked to justify the 1983 invasion.) The profession has responded by increasing the difficulty of the examination administered by the Education Commission for Foreign Medical Graduates (whose pass rate fell from 33 percent in 1982 to 14 percent in 1984) and persuading state boards in New York and California to reject the credentials of particular foreign schools.[69] Those unable to obtain the necessary credential can use political pressure to seek an individual exception, purchase a bogus diploma, attend cram courses that use previous tests, steal the examinations, or simply practice without a license—as an estimated 28,000 "physicians" are believed to do.[70] Ideological changes and social movements can render the continued exclusion of disadvantaged groups intolerable. Demographic shifts caused by wars or changing birth rates can alter both supply and demand. Changes elsewhere in the labor market can affect the relative attractiveness of a professional career.[71] And the expansion of education—secondary schooling at the end of the nineteenth century, the tertiary sector after World War II—can lead to the inflation of credentials.[72]

Economic Analyses of the Professions

Sociological theories of professions as closure are paralleled by economic analyses of professions as restraints on an otherwise free market. Although Adam Smith justified the exemption of professions from market forces as a means of ensuring quality, many of his twentieth-century followers have been considerably more skeptical.[73] A strong and growing tradition sees limitations on entry to the profession and on competition among professionals as unfair to potential competitors (both outside the profession and within) and detrimental to consumers.[74] Some economists subsume these objections within the broader critique that regulation is inevitably captured by and benefits producers at the expense of consumers.[75] Although economists concede that licensing can increase the quality of services *delivered*, they emphasize that the quality of services *received* inevitably declines because higher prices depress demand.[76] These theoretical arguments have been tested and generally confirmed by numerous empirical studies of the effects of licensing and other restrictive practices. Most researchers have looked at medicine because of the high value we place on health, the magnitude of overall expenditures on medical care, the rapid rate of inflation, and the expanding role of public and private third-party payors.[77] A few have also dealt with lawyers.[78]

Economics also contains analogies to structural functional theories of the professions. Some economists argue that the allegedly adverse consequences of licensing simply do not occur: physicians do not enjoy monopoly rents when their lengthy working hours are considered, nor do they engage in price discrimination.[79] Others approach structural functionalism more closely by conceding that professions reduce competition but then justifying such reduction on the ground that informational asymmetry between producer and consumer requires producer control in order to ensure quality.[80] Yet such justifications are open to the objection that the professions themselves create the market failure they purport to rectify.[81]

Human capital theory also seeks to justify the price of professional services as representing a reasonable return on the investment in education.[82] Professional credentials are said to tell prospective employers the value of the employee's services.[83] Yet there is no evidence that training correlates with either productivity or quality. Indeed, empirical studies find that the rate of return on the professional credential varies with the height of entry barriers, even when the length of educational preparation is controlled.[84]

Finally, labor economists have noted the similarities between professions and segmented labor markets.[85] Professions are simply a special instance of the dual labor market, although professionals' generalized skills allow them to move between employers.[86] Economists attempt to justify these privileges, too, on the basis of informational inequality; but they remain open to the general critique of segmented labor markets.[87]

Positive economic analyses describe not only how professions distort the market for services but also how those markets are self-correcting. Entry barriers may create monopoly rents in the short run, but these inevitably attract additional entrants who drive down the price of the professional commodity.[88] There is evidence that the rising number of physicians has encouraged some to practice in smaller towns and forced others to reduce their fees.[89] More generally, the use of credentials as a means of securing economic advantage and social status leads to the overproduction of those credentials and their progressive devaluation.[90] If the 1970s were a decade of rapid professional expansion in response to supply shortfalls, the 1980s appear to be ushering in a period in which excess supply discourages entry: professional school enrollment declined in law, medicine, dentistry, and veterinary medicine.[91] Dental school enrollment in 1987 was a third lower than it had been in 1978, applications were down by two-thirds, and three of the 60 dental schools had closed.[92]

Closure as Collective Mobility

The professional "project" is directed not only toward controlling the market but also toward enhancing professional status, an issue that sociologists treat far more extensively than economists. Indeed, some sociologists define professions in terms of status—the quality and degree of respect enjoyed by virtue of an occupational role.[93] Collective mobility appears to be a central objective of American teachers, who long have been organized in unions but now are preparing to seek a national credential based on examinations and apprenticeship. The proposal has been endorsed by the AFL-CIO and both major teachers unions. Albert Shanker, president of the American Federation of Teachers, has stated that teachers must move beyond collective bargaining if they wish to be accepted as professionals. And it is significant that the Carnegie Foundation, sponsor of the Flexner and Reed reports, which were so pivotal in the transformation of the medical and legal professions, also sponsored the recent report on teaching.[94] This interpretation is consistent with the fact that professional elites, whose economic privileges are secure, energetically pursue (and often initiate) efforts to raise the status of the entire occupational category. Even occupations that cannot achieve market control persist in seeking professional status.

The relationship between economic privilege and social respect is complex. Although inequality always requires justification, entrepreneurs seem to view success within the "free" market as self-legitimating, whereas professionals, who visibly control their markets, feel compelled to offer additional explanations. The exhausting training professionals must complete might better be understood not as the inculcation of technical skills but as a conspicuous sacrifice that justifies future privilege; such an interpretation helps to explain the relative poverty endured by students, the tedium of study, the long hours and indignities of apprenticeship, the anxiety inflicted by examinations, and the postponement of full adulthood (including marriage). Medical internships and large law firm associateships are familiar examples.

The status of a profession is affected by two principal factors (aside from its economic rewards): membership and clientele. Limitations on entry—the foundation of market control—inevitably influence the profession's composition as well as its numbers, whether or not this is intended. When American physicians excluded "persons of inferior ability, questionable character and coarse and common fiber" by implementing the reforms ultimately embodied in the Flexner Report, the proportion of women medical graduates declined from 4.3 percent between 1880 and 1904 to 3.2 percent in 1912.[95] Sociologists categorize entry barriers in terms of whether: (1) professional status is ascribed or achieved, (2) the warrant is aristocratic or modern, (3) entry is based on particularistic or universalistic qualities, (4) and mobility is sponsored or contested.[96] Both the classic elite professions (like the English Bar) and those occupations that successfully professionalized only in the nineteenth century (like Scottish accountants) appear to have benefitted from their members' high status by birth.[97] Professions shifted from ascribed to achieved status during the nineteenth and twentieth centuries as higher education, particularly within the university, came to confer prestige.[98] Some professions resisted this transformation, however, fearing that barriers based on achievement would admit entrants from lower social backgrounds.[99] And many have noted that previously male occupations, such as teaching and clerical work, lost status (and pay) when they were feminized during this period.[100] But it is important not to allow meritocratic ideology to conceal the fact that even "achieved" qualifications disproportionately exclude those disadvantaged by class, race, or gender.[101] Whatever mobility does occur tends to be found within the middle class rather than between classes.[102]

Professions also gain and lose status from their clients. The classic professions of law and medicine clearly benefitted from their historical association with aristocratic patrons. On the other hand, the failure of occupations like teaching and social work to professionalize during the twentieth century may be partly a result of their association with low-status clients.[103] Abbott (1981) has argued, paradoxically, that professions gain public status by conferring order on disorder, but strata within professions lose status through their connection with disorder.[104]

Although professions are defined by the fact that the status of their members is collective—conferred on all who enter the profession and enhanced by mobility of the entire professional category—status differences inevitably persist within the profession. These, too, may be a function of the characteristics of the particular member (ascribed or achieved) or of the member's clients. But whereas collective mobility tends to solidify the professional category, intraprofessional mobility can impair it, as lower strata challenge those above them or higher strata seek to immunize themselves from taint by their inferiors.

Controlling Production by Producers

Controlling entry—the production *of* producers—is only the first step in the professional project. An occupation that seeks to professionalize also must control production *by* producers, both to increase its earnings and to enhance its status. This may be difficult: the American Psychological Association, unable to prevent members from seeking publicity or offering "instant therapy" on radio and television, repealed the rule prohibiting such practices.[105]

Weber, again, surveys the range of possible restrictions:

> Closure within the group as between the members themselves and in their relations with each other may also assume the most varied forms. Thus a caste, a guild, or a group of stock exchange brokers, which is closed to outsiders, may allow to its members a perfectly free competition for all the advantages which the group as a whole monopolizes for itself. Or it may assign every member strictly to the enjoyment of certain advantages, such as claims over customers or particular business opportunities, for life or even on a hereditary basis.[106]

Restrictions may be formal or informal, visible or invisible. Although their principal object is to protect members from competition with each other as well as with outsiders, such restraints may also enhance the profession's status by conferring an aura of disinterest.[107] The image of professionals as *honoratiores* is reinforced by such devices as the academic hood (into which students put the fees paid to professors at medieval universities), Pooh-Bah's characterization of bribes as "insults" in *The Mikado,* and the widespread convention that lawyers and physicians do not discuss fees in advance. British barristers are an extreme example: their clerks negotiate their fees, and they cannot sue clients who fail to pay.

Neoclassical economics discussed and criticized these forms of market control (as well as the entry barriers described earlier). Economists have found empirical confirmation for the theoretical prediction that advertising bans, fee schedules, prohibitions on interprofessional partnerships, and other anticompetitive rules increase consumer prices.[108] Recent studies by the Federal Trade Commission, for instance, have shown that commercial optometrists sell contact lenses for about 35 percent less than ophthamologists and that laws in 36 states limiting the number of automobile dealerships cost consumers $3.2 billion in 1985.[109]Competitors may resort to dirty tricks in the struggle over market shares. After their patents expired, pharmaceutical companies sought to defend a $2 billion market against generic competitors by offering gifts to physicians who prescribed proprietary brands, scaring pharmacists about potential malpractice liability for selling generics, sponsoring "independent" studies, and planting "news" articles falsely purporting to show that generics are inferior.[110] A federal district court has found that the American Medical Association, the American College of Surgeons, and the American College of Radiology engaged in "systematic, long-term wrongdoing" to destroy the chiropractic profession through boycotts and defamation.[111] And groups calling themselves "Physicians Who Care" have engaged in public attacks on health maintenance organizations, phrased in terms of quality concerns but actually seeking to suppress competition.[112]

Yet just as professions have found it difficult to construct and defend their monopolies against external attack, so these restrictive practices, too, are very fragile. Psychiatrists and psychologists have been unable to prevent the proliferation of social workers and marriage and family counselors offering psychotherapy, whose numbers multiplied from 43 percent of providers in 1975 to 55 percent in 1985.[113] Subordinated occupations constantly seek to expand their markets and increase their autonomy: pharmacists now can sell drugs that fall within a category intermediate between prescription and over-the-counter medicines; dental hygienists, dental assistants, and denturists have fought to enlarge their authority and gain the right to practice independently.[114] Anticompetitive rules protect those who would do less well within a free market only by disadvantaging others who would fare better.[115] The 59,000-member American Academy of Family Physicians currently is fighting the 47,000-member American College of Surgeons over the latter's rule that only surgeons can provide postsurgical care.[116] And it is difficult to justify restrictive practices, no matter how vigorously the profession may try to stigmatize violators as charlatans or encroachers or argue that the rules are necessary to ensure quality.[117] The two forms of market control—over the production *of* and *by* producers—appear to rise and fall together.

Demand for Professional Services

Theories of professionalism as closure focus on the nature and extent of occupational control over the *supply* of services. This is particularly true of economic analyses, which view demand as an exogenous variable independent of supply. Explanations of demand must be specific to the service, although demographic changes in the size and age distribution of the population affect most services.

Many factors influence the demand for legal services. Because all law is intimately associated with property rights, the demand for lawyers varies with the distribution of wealth and income. Thus, the rise of the bourgeoisie, the diffusion of home ownership, the growth of pension funds, the concentration of capital, and the proliferation of state welfare benefits all affect that demand. Within the private sector, the mix of economic activities (between the production of goods and services, for instance) can influence the level of demand. As portions of the economy are nationalized, administration may displace law and economists or other technocrats may substitute for lawyers.[118] Indeed, when the growth of the state antedates the accumulation of private capital, lawyers become civil servants rather than independent practitioners.[119] Because law is state social control, it varies inversely with other forms of institutional control.[120] Trends such as the increase in geographic mobility, the attentuation of kinship bonds, the declining salience of residential communities, the weakening of class identification, and secularization may augment the demand for legal control. Whenever the state subjects new areas of social life to legal regulation, the demand for lawyers increases—a notable contemporary example being laws that address the dissolution of marriage. Changes in existing law can have the same effect: the 1987 revision of federal income tax law increased demand for accountants by as much as 25 percent.[121] Finally, cultural approval of recourse to law differs among societies and across time.[122]

But demand is not a given to which professions simply react. Economists have argued theoretically and sought to demonstrate empirically that physicians create demand for their own services.[123] One strategy is the development of new capabilities: physicians increase their ability to preserve or restore health or to prolong life by expanding their scientific knowledge and technological armory; and lawyers expand the benefits they can confer with every legal innovation—or complication. More than 80 percent of American dentists now perform "cosmetic" dentistry, which is estimated to earn the profession half its $32 billion in annual revenue.[124] As control over the production of and by producers has eroded, many professions have engaged in promotional campaigns. Local dental associations urge preventive care at schools and in shopping malls, and practitioners send gifts to patients who refer others.[125] Accountants have sponsored a float in the Tournament of Roses Parade, persuaded the U.S. Postal Service to commemorate the centennial of the American Institute of Certified Public Accountants with a stamp, launched a million dollar campaign of institutional advertising, and sought to encourage the production of a television series about accountants.[126] Physicians mail newsletters, open clinics in shopping malls, and accept credit cards.[127] Accountants hold free seminars and distribute brochures.[128] And hospitals facing the high cost of empty beds, unused equipment, and idle personnel are spending more than $1 billion a year to attract customers by advertising, creating walk-in clinics, providing free physician referral services, holding public relations parties in local homes, offering amenities (candlelight dinners, concierge services, and VCR rentals), and being particularly attentive to the physicians who hospitalize patients.[129] Los Angeles hospitals advertise their obstetric services on highway billboards, offer free pregnancy tests (and referrals to those who test positive), and compete in prices, which have been driven down below $800 for a routine delivery (sometimes below cost, in the belief that a satisfied patient will return to the hospital in the future).[130]

Professions also seek to rationalize and expand their markets by using intermediaries in both the private and the public sectors. Private insurance, frequently a benefit of employment or union membership, has dramatically affected the markets for medical services in the United States and legal services in Germany. Public subsidies have been even more important to the professions, particularly when the state reimburses private practitioners rather than employ professionals. Medicare payments to American physicians now exceed $20 billion a year—more than a third of the income of those who participate.[131] The consequences of these forms of "demand creation" extend far beyond the economic benefits they confer on professionals. They create the potential for abuse and fraud. Five physicians, three pharmacists, and three other medical workers were recently convicted of defrauding the Medicaid program of nearly $20 million.[132] A study of medical examinations and tests performed by private physicians for the Social Security Administration estimated that 13 to 33 percent may be unnecessary, wasting $27 million to $69 million in federal funds annually.[133] The Los Angeles County Auditor has charged that physicians were being overpaid a total of $800,000 a year for expert testimony in criminal trials.[134]

In response, those who pay the bills insist on "mediative" control over the production and distribution of professional services, which increases the heterogeneity of consumers, stratifies the profession, and alters the relationship between producers and consumers.[135] The federal gvoernment has been very concerned over Medicare payments to physicians, which grew from $4 billion in 1976 to an estimated $22.9 billion in 1987.[136] A Medicare study concluded that 14 percent of government financed coronary bypass operations were clearly inappropriate and another 30 percent were questionable.[137] And Medicare has drafted a "preferred provider" program, which would reimburse a higher proportion of medical costs if patients consult designated physicians whose charges remain within government guidelines.[138] Physicians deeply resent governmental cost-containment measures that place a ceiling on their fees or circumscribe the care for which they may be reimbursed.[139] Private employers, whose fringe benefits pay for about $100 billion a year in medical care, are requiring second opinions and insisting that many medical procedures be performed on an outpatient basis.[140] Third-party payment may also affect the collective status of the profession, perhaps enhancing it as a larger proportion of the population enjoy the services but also possibly lowering it if demand creation is seen as professional greed.

Marxist Theories of Professions in the Class Structure

If Weberian theories address horizontal relations among occupational categories competing for market shares and social status, Marxist theories are concerned with the location and behavior of professions within the vertical hierarchy of classes defined by relations of production. Marxism makes class relations central because it views class conflict as the principal engine of change and, ultimately, the mechanism through which socialism will displace capitalism. Yet as I mentioned at the beginning of this chapter, Marxists encounter difficulties in placing professionals. They could be capitalists—but they clearly do not own the means of production. They could be workers—but the tasks they perform, the rewards they garner, and their relations with subordinates and superiors are vastly different from those of most workers. And they could constitute a third category—but that would require a fundamental reworking of Marxist theory.

Marx did not devote much attention to the professions, since they were numerically insignificant and seemingly marginal to relations of production. As members of the petty bourgeoisie—neither exploited by capital nor exploiters of labor—they appeared to be a historical residue from an earlier stage of capitalism. Marx seems to have expected the professions either to disappear or to be incorporated into one of the two great class adversaries. At times, however, both he and later Marxists recognized that the increasing concentration of capital would require the expansion of a category of functionaries representing the owners of capital in their interactions with other capitalists, financiers, and workers.[141] Because history did not follow the path initially predicted by Marx, his followers have had to rethink class analysis to include educated workers and professionals, whose numbers have grown so rapidly, particularly during the last two decades. Different theoretical perspectives have been advanced to locate professionals within the class system.

Orthodox Marxism: Professionals and Relations of Production

Marx defined classes in terms of their relationship to the means of production. He argued that all societies have exhibited the opposition of two major classes, one of which exploits the other by extracting surplus value from its labor. Marxists have encountered considerable difficulty deciding whether professions produce surplus value—the prerequisite for exploitation.[142] This criterion leaves the class identity of lawyers as ambiguous as ever. Much of their work involves reproduction rather than production (e.g., family law, inheritance, or the transfer of unproductive property such as homes). Even within the capitalist enterprise, lawyers are more involved in distributing surplus among capitalists (e.g., through struggles over corporate control) than in extracting it from workers. The basic unit for the production of legal services—the law firm—contains both associates who produce surplus value and partners who consume it.[143]

Some authors have construed Marxism in functional terms, distinguishing the "global" functions of capital and labor and assigning members of society to one category or the other on the basis of the function they perform.[144] The global functions of capital include ideological inculcation, political repression, and the management and supervision of the working class.[145] By this definition, physicians and engineers are members of the dominant class.[146] Lawyers are even more intimately associated with such global functions as social control (criminal law), structuring the relations of production (labor law), exchange among capitalists (commercial law), and ownership of capital (corporate law). Yet such an expansive definition of capital subsumes a large proportion of the population, leaving the working class a minority, the outcome of class conflict a foregone conclusion, and history static.

Erik Olin Wright has argued that the Marxist concept of class is structural and therefore cannot be understood in such functionalist terms.[147] Consequently, he and his associates have refined the basic categories by acknowledging that a number of crucial actors occupy contradictory class locations: semiautonomous wage earners (e.g., law firm associates and the lower ranks of house counsel) between the proletariat and the petty bourgeoisie, small employers (e.g., partners in smaller law firms) between the petty bourgeoisie and the bourgeoisie, and managers (perhaps senior partners in larger firms and corporate general counsel) between the bourgeoisie and capitalists.[148] This more nuanced picture highlights the ambiguity of professions in the class system, but in rejecting functionalism it conflates professionals who perform very different roles.

Professional Expertise as Power

Ever since Berle and Means noted the increasing separation of ownership and control within the capitalist enterprise, analysts have had to assess whether the technical expertise acquired by managers (on the job) and professionals (in the academy) renders them servants of power or enhances their autonomy.[149] A large, diverse group of observers embrace the latter conclusion, although they disagree about whether technocrats will use their power for selfish or unselfish ends.[150] Gouldner is most optimistic about the potential role of Western intellectuals, characterizing them as a "flawed" universal class.[151] In sharp contrast, Konrád and Szelényi describe the actual role of eastern European intellectuals in the darkest colors.[152] Frank Parkin equates the acquisition of formal credentials with the ownership of capital as interchangeable indices of ruling class membership: "the dominant class under modern capitalism can be thought of as comprising those who possess or control productive capital and those who possess a legal monopoly of professional services."[153] Gouldner has challenged this analogy, however.[154] Although professional credentials may be used to extract monopoly rents, they differ from capital in two essential respects: credentials do not valorize themselves, producing more credentials as capital produces more capital; and there is no market for credentials as there is for capital. Ehrenreich and Ehrenreich are equally emphatic that the "professional-managerial class"—those who possess specialized skills and use them to reproduce capitalist culture and class relations—is independent of and opposed to *both* capital and labor.[155] Yet if these analysts are correct and professionals do enjoy some autonomy, class analysis tells us relatively little about their behavior.

Working Conditions and the Proletarianization of Professionals

The third variant of Marxist theory predicts that professionals will become members of the proletariat as a result of changes in their working conditions.[156] Just as proletarianization progressively extended from unskilled workers to include skilled artisans during the early stages of the rise of capitalism, so it eventually will affect educated workers. Derber notes the parallel between the nineteenth-century shift from putting out to factory work and the contemporary displacement of the independent professional by the employee.[157] Indices of proletarianization include ever more detailed specialization and specification of tasks, speedups, subordination to external authority, and the entry of disadvantaged categories into the profession.[158] In the private sector, proletarianization is attributable to rising capital investment in service production, which seeks to organize a dispersed clientele and take advantage of technological development in order to reap the rewards of higher profitability.[159] In the public sector, proletarianization is an expression of the fiscal crisis of the state, which increasingly pays for or subsidizes the production of many services.[160] Physicians in Ontario, Canada, have struck to protest provincial regulations limiting their fees to the amounts reimbursed by public health insurance.[161] American physicians, faced with cost-cutting by the 625 health maintenance organizations that enrolled 25.8 million members in 1987, are beginning to unionize and bargain collectively with their employers.[162]

Not all observers agree that these changes are occurring, and even those who perceive them disagree over their significance. Eliot Freidson is most vehement in rejecting the proletarianization thesis, noting that professions have suffered no decline in either their knowledge base or their social status—indeed, both have increased.[163] Derber concurs that it is essential to distinguish between the deskilling and routinization of manual work, which occurred under the banner of Taylorism, and the situation of contemporary professionals, whose heightened specialization may actually enhance their autonomy.[164] But Freidson concedes that professionals have lost control over the organization of their work.[165]

Derber makes a useful distinction between ideological and technical proletarianization.[166] Technical proletarianization reflects the progressive separation of mental and manual tasks, the substitution of computers for workers, and the growth of a reserve labor force. This is the plight of the lower service class, which suffers a concomitant erosion of income and status.[167] Professionals avoid this fate by embracing ideological proletarianization. They remain autonomous in selecting their means but only by allowing others to determine their goals. Extrinsic rewards (pay, career advancement, working conditions), which are often lavish, displace intrinsic satisfaction, which is limited to the exercise of technical skill. I find this account thoroughly persuasive; indeed, the strongest evidence that professionals have relinquished control over the ends for which they work may be their inability to perceive the loss. Lawyers have actually elevated their plight into an ethical mandate: the "cab rank" rule, which requires English barristers to represent any client who seeks their services (and can pay their fees); and the "principle of nonaccountability," which categorically rejects any moral identification of lawyers with the clients they represent.[168] Yet the theory of ideological proletarianization may also be guilty of romanticizing the situation of "independent" professionals, who always embraced the interests of any clients willing to pay them.

What Does Class Analysis Tell Us?

Although Marxist class analysis sometimes deteriorates into mere taxonomy, its avowed purpose is to identify a category of actors who share a common outlook, engage in similar, even collective, political, economic, and social behavior, and thus can be agents of transformation. Several commentators argue that correctly denominating professionals as capitalists, workers, or some intermediate class allows us to predict their behavior. Thus, Frank Parkin maintains that "those who monopolize productive property and credentials share for the most part a broadly similar political and ideological stance."[169] At the other extreme, analysts who conclude that educated workers have been proletarianized predict that they will exhibit a working-class consciousness.[170] There is evidence that educated workers are increasingly discontent with their conditions and rewards.[171] They have joined unions in greater numbers and displayed more militant opposition to private and public employers.[172] At the same time, professionalism also fosters individualism, status consciousness, and preoccupation with technical autonomy, all of which discourage union membership and collective action.[173] While traditional Marxist analysis assimilates professionals into either the capitalist or the working class, "new class" theories emphasize the autonomy of professional ideology. This view is supported by the apparent diversity of lawyers' political attitudes.[174] But if professionals do not constitute a class "for themselves," with a unitary program, then class analysis may not throw much light on the behavior of lawyers.

Structural Functional Theories of Professions and the Social Order

Whereas the problem for Weberians and neoclassical economists is the market and the problem for Marxists is class, the problem for structural functionalists is the social order: what holds together an aggregation of egoistic individuals? At least since Durkheim, professions have been an important part of the answer. Professions play a significant role within the system of stratification, which organizes the extremes of society and explains their inequality. Professions ensure that expertise is deployed in the general interest; they preserve a form of community that was undermined by the Industrial Revolution; and they regulate themselves, thereby offering a counterweight to an increasingly imperial state.

Professions in the System of Stratification

While Marxists conceptualize inequality as dividing society into two discrete and opposed classes defined by a single criterion (relations of production), structural functionalists stress continuous differences along a multiplicity of variables—including wealth, income, occupation, education, religion, ethnicity, race, gender, and parental background—none of which is theoretically preeminent.[175] They strongly reject the notion that professions either can be identified with capital or labor or constitute a coherent "new class."[176] Instead, they emphasize the heterogeneity of the professions in terms of background, training, function, clientele, rewards, and politics. Certainly it would be difficult to conceptualize class in such a way as to subsume within a single category judges, law teachers, government lawyers, house counsel, and private practitioners. And if lawyers identify strongly with their clientele, the extreme diversity of the client population intensifies the heterogeneity of the profession.[177]

The task of social analysis, then, is to locate lawyers within the system of stratification according to some of the many possible criteria.[178] The hierarchic ordering, and the location of professions at or near the top, encourages competing for rewards within the system instead of challenging it. Studies of social mobility, especially through entry to the professions, are essential to ascertain how the relative starting points in the competition affect the outcomes.[179]

Threats to Professional "Autonomy"

An essential foundation of structural functional theories of the professions is the belief that, if protected from outside interference, they will use their expertise for the general good.[180] Talcott Parsons exemplified this approach in writing about lawyers:

> His [sic—read "the lawyer's"] function in relation to clients is by no means only to "give them what they want" but often to resist their pressures and get them to realize some of the hard facts of their situations, not only with reference to what they can, even with clever legal help, expect to "get away with" but with reference to what the law will permit them to do.[181]

The first question raised by such a theory—the extent to which the "independent" professional actually pursues client rather than personal interest and elevates the public interest above both—is rarely investigated empirically.[182] Instead, structural functionalism simply assumes that independent professionals exhibit such desirable traits and then explores the threats to their hypothetical autonomy. The danger most commonly posited is employment, followed closely by third-party reimbursement. For example, Southern New England Telecommunications Company recently negotiated an agreement with 450 of Connecticut's 5000 licensed physicians by which the latter will provide health care at significantly reduced fees to those of the company's 14,000 employees who join the plan.[183] This threat is the functionalist version of what Marxists characterize as the proletarianization of professionals. There can be no doubt that employment is increasing, more rapidly outside the older professions originally organized around independent practice (primarily medicine and law) but also within them.[184]

Typically the problem is framed as a tension or conflict between professionalism (equated with fee-for-service production) and bureaucracy.[185] Social scientists have made this a principal theme in studies of psychiatrists in the military, scientists in industry and government, and physicians.[186] Whether as employers or paymasters, private and public bureaucracies control professionals through decisions about hiring, promotion, and retention and through the allocation of resources, especially technology.[187] Professionals increasingly do find themselves working in bureaucratic settings. Between 1980 and 1985, the number of physicians in group practices increased by 43 percent, while the number in solo practice increased only 18 percent.[188] Other service industries have concentrated much more rapidly: the five largest advertising agencies in the world billed nearly $25 billion in 1985 as a result of recent mergers.[189] A contemporary manual on managing professionals advised companies to allay boredom by encouraging horizontal mobility, create a promotional ladder within technical departments for the unusually gifted, avoid alienation through personal attention, and cushion full-time employees against fluctuations in demand by using part-time technicians.[190]

This literature has stimulated a revisionist reply, which questions the tension between professionalism and bureaucracy.[191] Critics note that the "autonomy" of private practitioners is not only empirically unsubstantiated but also theoretically dubious. First, market pressures to find and retain clients powerfully influence professionals even when they collectively have succeeded in limiting entry and internal competition. Second, professionalism is not "autonomy" but simply another form of control, one that is particularly appropriate when tasks require a high level of technical discretion and work is discontinuous and relatively unpredictable.[192] Professionalism may differ from bureaucracy, but it is no less constraining. If bureaucracy controls work through rules and constant supervision, professionalism does so by selecting those predisposed to comply with authority and then subjecting them to a lengthy socialization process.[193] Third, external authorities, whether bureaucratic superiors or third-party payors, may be concerned with the organization of work and its cost, but they usually leave technical execution to the professional.[194] Some of these disagreements are questions of emphasis—whether independence of goal or technique is more important—and others are empirical questions about the behavior of professionals in different environments.

Professions as Communities

Community remains an attractive but elusive goal in a mass society in which ideologies of individualism, universalism, and efficiency constantly undermine strong, multiplex, enduring personal bonds. It is against this backdrop that structural functionalism sees professions as a powerful and valuable source of community.[195] Members of a profession are united by a common role definition, an esoteric language, and fairly clear social boundaries. Membership is attained only after a long and painful initiation rite, and for most it is a permanent status.[196] Finally, professions do engage in self-governance.

But there are serious problems with the notion of profession as community. Other communities based on kinship, race, ethnicity, class, religion, gender, locality, friendship, or politics are far more salient to most people most of the time. To the extent that professions do become communities, they often secure the loyalty of their members by excluding those disadvantaged by class, gender, or race—forms of discrimination that are no longer acceptable in the workplace. All professions are riven by major internal divisions between practitioners, administrators, and teachers or researchers.[197] And as an increasing proportion of professionals become employees, especially of large private or public bureaucracies, their community tends to be limited to their fellow workers rather than encompassing the entire profession.

Lawyers have even fewer communal characteristics than other professionals. In a nonegalitarian society, professionals necessarily reflect the stratification of their clients.[198] An extreme example within medicine is the social distance between psychiatrists employed by a public mental hospital and those who treat private outpatients, despite the fact that they share common credentials and possess similar expertise.[199] Specialties also diverge dramatically: in 1983, the median income of anesthesiologists was more than twice that of physicians concerned with industrial and occupational health ($150,200 versus $72,000).[200] Even within private practice, the clienteles of lawyers diverge more dramatically than those of physicians, varying from the poorest individual to the wealthiest corporation.[201] The divisions within the legal profession—among employed, employing, and independent private practitioners and between them and judges, prosecutors, civil servants, house counsel, and law teachers—are more numerous and deeper than those within medicine, even disregarding subject-matter specialization. Partly for this reason, and partly because lawyers have traditionally practiced within a single jurisdiction (though this is changing), legal knowledge is more localized and particular than knowledge in other professions, such as medicine.[202] Certainly lawyers agree less about the meaning of their ultimate value—justice—than physicians do about health.[203] Thus, although groups of lawyers may form particular communities, the legal profession as a whole is a weak community.

Self Regulation

If structural functionalism had to distinguish professions by means of a single characteristic, self-regulation would be a prime candidate. Because professions emerge out of the division of labor between producers and consumers, mechanisms are needed to ensure that producers are technically qualified and do not abuse the power they derive from their specialized knowledge. Powerful consumers—aristocratic patrons in the past, large public or private entities today—may be able to command the loyalty and competence of producers.[204] But most consumers must rely on other protections.

Professions are adamant that they, not the state or the consumer, must exercise regulatory authority. In one of his weekly advertisements in the *New York Times*, entitled "Professionalism Under Fire: Power Vs. Knowledge in St. Louis," Albert Shanker, president of the American Federation of Teachers, attacked the use of student performance on standardized tests to rate teachers.[205] School boards have recently battled attempts by religious groups to exclude certain books from the curriculum and to excuse children from classes in which objectionable books are used.[206] Journalists in Latin America have opposed laws requiring them to obtain licenses to work.[207] The president of the American Institute of Certified Public Accountants, between 1972 and 1980, recently boasted of his organization's success in resisting federal regulation: "Congress never laid a glove on us because we worked pretty hard to keep that glove off."[208] And Florida neurosurgeons have refused to treat patients in order to protest increases in medical malpractice insurance premiums.[209]

Professions rest their argument for self-regulation on two grounds. First, they insist that only fellow professionals possess the necessary expertise to judge professional performance. Even if true, this is self-serving, since the profession deliberately constructed the monopoly of expertise in the first place. Second, they point to the profession's independence from the state; but this assumes that the profession is more solicitous than the state of client (and other public) interests and will defend those interests against the state—empirical propositions for which there is little evidence. Furthermore, despite its emphasis on autonomy, the profession necessarily derives its regulatory power from the state.

Professions do not fulfill their regulatory responsibilities very effectively. Although they claim to dedicate their technical skills to serving society, Weber notes that self-interest frequently dampens their ardor for reform.

> Whenever legal education has been in the hands of practitioners, especially attorneys, who have made admission to practice a guild monopoly, an economic

factor, namely their pecuniary interest, brings to bear a strong influence upon
the process not only of stabilizing the official law and of adapting it to changing
needs in an exclusively empirical way but also of preventing its rationalization
through legislation or legal science.[210]

Like all professionals, lawyers also display their altruism by providing gratuitous or low-cost services; but the magnitude of such charity seems to vary with the
publicity it receives—conspicuous production being the necessary complement of
conspicuous consumption.[211] Although professions portray self-regulation as a
means of reducing client uncertainty, they deliberately draft ethical rules in vague
and ambiguous language to preserve the indeterminacy that is a foundation of
professional power.[212] Many ostensibly "ethical" rules serve the Weberian objective
of market control rather than the Parsonian goal of protecting clients and society.
Rules focus on professional technique but ignore the ends to which it is directed.
Enforcement is weak. Client confidentiality is invoked to obstruct external sur-
veillance of professional misconduct.[213] Larger productive units resist professional
control over their members or employees. And the goal of self-regulation often
appears to be to protect the inept members of the profession rather than the society
they ostensibly serve; this has been documented with respect to physicians.[214] Although the number of physician license revocations increased 59 percent between
1984 and 1985, even the 1985 total was only 406 out of 553,000 physicians; in 33
of the 51 jurisdictions fewer than 5 out of every 1000 physicians suffered any other
penalty.[215] Peer review organizations hired by the federal government to oversee
the care rendered to Medicare patients penalized no physicians in 23 states between
1985 and 1987 and only 77 physicians in the remainder, or about one in 10,000.
One reason may be that the AMA compelled the federal government to allow rural
physicians to be reviewed by their rural peers according to local standards.[216]
Behavior that would aggravate the seriousness of a crime were it displayed by
ordinary criminals is offered and accepted as a mitigating circumstance when displayed by professionals—one extraordinary recent example is the defense of alcoholism, with which Michael Deaver, former White House Deputy Chief of Staff,
has responded to the charge that he committed perjury in testifying to a federal
grand jury.[217] One reason for systematic underenforcement of ethical and technical
norms is that control of misconduct and incompetence readily becomes an arena
for intraprofessional conflict, which threatens the very community that self-
regulation purports to symbolize.[218] Consequently, self-regulation may be more
comprehensible as an assertion of status than a form of social control.[219]
    The visible failure of self-regulation, however, could lead to assertions of
control by clients and external bodies, such as legislatures, courts, and administrative agencies.[220] The Federal Trade Commission has announced its intent to
abrogate optometry industry rules and practices that limit the number of branch
offices, ban offices in shopping malls, prohibit the use of trade names, and restrict
employment by drug and department stores and optical chains.[221] Congress has
discussed increased regulation of the scientific research institutes it funds because
of its dissatisfaction with their choice of subjects and results.[222] The American
Institute of Certified Public Accountants is requiring its members to look actively
for financial fraud in every client, partly to protect themselves from the rising

number of malpractice claims.[223] The federal Medicare program has insisted on stricter scrutiny of the quality of services for which it pays and has made some physicians ineligible for reimbursement.[224] State health departments and licensing boards have asserted greater authority.[225] Regulatory agencies have begun to inform potential consumers about the quality of care provided by physicians and hospitals.[226] When physicians threatened to exchange information about prospective patients who had previously sued for medical malpractice, lawyers responded with a threat to provide patients with a list of physicians who had been sued.[227]

Theoretical Frameworks for Understanding American Lawyers

In the chapters that follow, I present a historical sociology of American lawyers, using the theories developed earlier to organize the data and using the data to test and refine those theories. I address the Weberian questions of how lawyers constructed their professional commodity (legal services) and sought to control their market and raise their collective status by regulating the production *of* and *by* producers and stimulating demand. I explore the Marxist question of the class location of lawyers by examining the structures within which legal services are produced. And I pursue structural functional questions about lawyers in the system of stratification, professional autonomy, self-governance, and self-regulation.

3

Controlling the Production
of Lawyers

Lawyers Without a Profession

The American legal profession did not begin to assume its present shape until the end of the nineteenth century. Some of the thirteen colonies had seen the emergence of nascent legal professions that retained their links to England, preserving the division between barristers and solicitors by sending some students to the Inns of Court in London to prepare for call to the English Bar. But these ties were thoroughly disrupted by the Revolution, which also precipitated the departure of many lawyers with Tory sympathies, including some of the most prominent practitioners.

The first hundred years of independence did not provide a favorable environment for the development of the professional configuration. Associations of lawyers were weak or nonexistent and confined to cities or counties, while states were becoming the significant unit of economic and political activity. The egalitarian ideology of the Jacksonian era was hostile to state-supported monopolies, as it was to all forms of inequality. But even before Jackson's election, several states and territories had abolished or greatly abbreviated apprenticeship, then the only requirement for entry to the profession.[1] The frontier constantly beckoned to any lawyer who found it difficult to enter the bar in the more restrictive states or was unable to obtain sufficient business on the eastern seaboard. In 1800, fourteen out of nineteen jurisdictions required all lawyers to complete an apprenticeship, often extending five years (the period then required of most English solicitors); by 1840 only a third of the states did so (eleven out of thirty), and twenty years later the proportion had dropped to less than a fourth (nine out of thirty-nine).[2]

Because formal legal education was little more than an alternative means of satisfying part of the apprenticeship requirement, there were few law schools and they had small enrollments and offered short courses (see Table 21). Havard Law School, founded in 1817, averaged fewer than nine students during its first twelve years and did not enroll 100 students until 1840.[3] In the year preceding the Civil War there were twenty-two law schools; fourteen of the fifteen northern schools had a total enrollment of 720 students, and four of the seven southern schools enrolled 252. Although several schools were substantial, most had no more than a few dozen students.[4] Many private schools founded in the first half of the nineteenth century later closed or were absorbed by universities.[5]

In 1879, only fifteen of the thirty-eight states required formal preparation to enter practice, and only seven required three years of apprenticeship; twelve years later, only nineteen states required preparation.[6] Even when states began raising the entry barriers after the Civil War, they required apprenticeship rather than law school. In 1881, sixteen out of thirty-nine jurisdictions demanded a definite term of pupillage; only six of these allowed entrants to substitute law school, and only one excused more than a year of apprenticeship.[7] Because neither state requirements nor the threat of a bar examination kept students in school, only seven out of forty-three law schools in 1881 had a three-year course (which many students did not complete); even Harvard offered only eighteen months of instruction until 1870 and two years until 1895.[8] Before Langdell arrived at Harvard in 1870, no examinations were required either to enter the law school or to receive its degree.[9]

Starting about the middle of the nineteenth century, law schools began to proliferate, although this growth occurred later and more slowly than the expansion of medical education. Between 1800 and 1910, 450 new medical schools were founded compared with only 171 law schools, and most of the latter did not appear until the last third of the century.[10] The number of schools of pharmacy increased from 2 to 38 between the first and last quarters of the nineteenth century, and the number of medical schools from 12 to 186 between the beginning and end of that century.[11] By 1891, when almost all physicians and most ministers qualified through formal study, 80 percent of lawyers entered practice without *any* law school training.[12] The proportion of Philadelphia lawyers with college educations (most of whom did not study law) actually declined from more than two thirds in 1800 to less than half in 1860.[13] Enrollment in law schools was only three fourths that in divinity schools and a third that in medical schools in 1878; these proportions had declined to a half and a fourth by the end of the next decade.[14]

Yet when academic legal education did begin to expand during the last decade of the nineteenth century, the pace was rapid. The number of law schools doubled in the twenty years between 1889–90 and 1909–10, while the number of law students increased more than fourfold (see Table 21). Equally important, apprenticeship virtually vanished as a mode of entry. A study of 464 eminent Wisconsin attorneys admitted prior to 1898 found that 216 had qualified exclusively through apprenticeship, and another 116 through apprenticeship and law school; no one was known to have dispensed with apprenticeship entirely. In the two decades 1868 to 1888, the majority of students at the University of Wisconsin Law School worked in law offices while they studied, and others did so before or after. Yet the emphasis was shifting. In 1877, 70 percent of Wisconsin graduates had completed a year of law office work as well as a year of university study; sixteen years later, only 30 percent of Wisconsin graduates divided their time in this fashion, the others preferring to spend both years at the university. By 1888, less than a third of Wisconsin students simultaneously were employed in a law office.[15]

Among the 20 to 30 percent of "elite" Chicago practitioners who belonged to the Chicago Bar Association in the last quarter of the nineteenth century, the proportion who had prepared through apprenticeship declined from 89 percent of the cohort admitted between 1831 and 1850 to 12 percent of the cohort admitted in the 1890s, while the proportion who had attended law school increased from 11 percent to 88 percent.[16] Among elite lawyers whose obituaries were published in the American Bar Association (ABA) Reports between 1900 and 1911, only 35 percent of lawyers in the midwestern cities of Cincinnati, Cleveland, Kansas City, and Milwaukee had ever attended law school, though the proportions were higher in larger cities (Philadelphia 42 percent, New York 46 percent, Chicago 56 percent, Boston 89 percent); many of those who attended law school never graduated.[17]

In striking contrast, analysis of the 1182 lawyers admitted to the Illinois bar in 1915 and 1916 revealed that only 9 percent had prepared through office study (4 percent of Chicago residents and 22 percent of downstate residents, which again suggests that the speed of the transformation varied with city size).[18] In New York, 18 percent of those seeking admission to the bar in 1900 had no law school training; nineteen years later the proportion had declined to less than 3 percent. In 1922, only 9 out of 643 people taking the New York bar examination for the first time (1 percent) had no law school training.[19] In California, an average of 5 percent of bar examinees prepared through office study between 1929 and 1931, and an average of 20 percent of them passed.[20] During the next seventeen years, however, only 0.7 percent of bar examinees prepared through office study, and only 8.7 percent of them passed (compared with 59.9 percent of law school graduates).[21]

The speed and thoroughness with which formal education displaced apprenticeship cannot be attributed to legal compulsion. In 1923, *no* state required entrants to attend law school.[22] A dozen years later, forty-four jurisdictions continued to admit those who prepared through law office study (see Table 1). As late as 1951, thirty-five states still permitted entry through law office study, either alone or in conjunction with law school. Yet in the nineteen states for which records are available for 1947, only 112 out of 5777 bar examinees prepared that way (1.9 percent), and only 24.4 percent of them passed (compared to 55.9 percent of all examinees); consequently, law office study accounted for only 0.8 percent of those admitted.[23] Today, entry through law office study is insignificant, although it is still permitted in eight jurisdictions (either alone or in conjunction with law school) (see Tables 1 and 13). In 1984, only 15 of the 34,318 new admittees to the fifty-one jurisdictions had prepared through law office study, and the proportion never exceeded 0.3 percent in the preceding twenty years. Even in California, those who had prepared in the office of a lawyer or judge were only 0.3 percent of July 1986 bar examinees and 0.1 percent of those passing.[24]

The importance of this transformation cannot be exaggerated. For more than two centuries, apprenticeship had been the sole method of qualification (it remains a prerequisite in most other countries). Until the end of the nineteenth century, the study of law in college was more an ingredient of liberal education than a form of professional training.[25] Furthermore, apprenticeship was an extremely effective mechanism for controlling both the number and the characteristics of entrants. In the period immediately after the Revolution, apprentices paid premiums of several hundred dollars—as much as $500 to a leading advocate—for the privilege of working for up to five years without pay; and six states restricted the number of apprentices a lawyer could supervise at a time.[26]

The reasons why academic education eclipsed apprenticeship are numerous and inevitably somewhat obscure. Many lawyers did not accept apprentices. Outside the larger cities, positions may have become scarce: the number of offices in Dane County (where University of Wisconsin law students apprenticed) declined from 59 in 1860 to 54 in 1870.[27] Permanent clerks (men until the turn of the century, increasingly women thereafter) were beginning to assume the tasks previously performed by apprentices, such as drafting and copying documents. Even in larger cities, apprenticeship could not satisfy the pressures for entry. Immigrants and their sons—a large and expanding proportion of those aspiring to become lawyers around the turn of the century—were not likely to be welcomed as apprentices by lawyers of different class, ethnicity, religion, and culture, whose families had been in America longer. Furthermore, the rate of increase was simply too great to be absorbed through apprenticeship: the profession nearly doubled between 1860 and 1880 and then doubled again by 1900 (see Table 22).

Finally, as we will see in greater detail later, the bar examination was introduced during this period. It seems plausible that formal education offered a better chance to surmount this barrier (or at least was believed to do so by those who confronted it). By the late 1890s, 70 percent of those taking the New York bar examination had some law school training.[28] But law schools possessed another advantage over law offices: automatic admission to the bar for their graduates. This perquisite, known as the diploma privilege, was introduced in Virginia in 1842 and enjoyed by nine schools in seven states in 1870. When the University of Wisconsin law school secured the privilege that year, its enrollment jumped from 13 students in 1869 to an average of 28 between 1870 and 1875. When the Wisconsin bar examination was centralized and reduced to writing, enrollment doubled again, from 60 in 1885 to 113 in 1887. Since the law school was open to almost everyone (Wisconsin accepted high school graduates until 1903), relatively inexpensive (informal allowances were made for students who could not pay the fees), and intellectually undemanding (there were no final examinations until after the 1880s), it is not surprising that it rapidly replaced apprenticeship as the mode of entry [29]

The meaning of this transformation for the professional project was ambiguous. From a late twentieth-century perspective, we associate professionalism with formal education. Yet the rise of the law school a hundred years ago actually undermined professional control over the production of lawyers and did little to elevate their status. True, state requirements for entry into the legal profession proliferated: the proportion of jurisdictions requiring some legal study (apprenticeship or academic) doubled during the quarter century ending in 1904 (from little more than one third to nearly two thirds).[30] But law school offered a relatively easy way of satisfying them, for several reasons.

First, law schools demanded little or no previous education: in 1896, only 7 out of 74 schools required even a high school diploma; eight years later the proportion had risen to 51 out of 111 (as high school education became more widespread), but only 3 required a college degree, another 3 insisted on some college, and a quarter still had *no* educational prerequisite.[31] Even at Harvard law was an undergraduate course for the majority: in 1870, 53 percent of the 115 students lacked a college degree.[32] The first entrance examination was introduced in 1875, but by 1891 only about half of all schools had adopted one.[33]

Second, law school itself was brief: in 1870, there were 14 one-year and 17 two-year courses; in 1880, there were 19 one-year, 29 two-year, and 4 three-year courses; a decade later, these numbers were 9, 45, and 7; and by 1900 they were 8, 47, and 47—more than half the courses still were two years or shorter.[34] In 1895, 453 students were enrolled in one-year courses, 4071 in two-year courses, and 4104 in three-year courses (though the third year was often optional).[35]

Third, and perhaps most important, much of the growth of formal education was attributable to mushrooming part-time law schools, which allowed students to work while studying. In 1889–90, before the period of rapid growth, 51 out of 61 schools offered full-time instruction and enrolled 88 percent of all law students. In 1915–16, only 76 out of 140 schools offered full-time instruction and enrolled only 52 percent of all law students.[36] In New York State the change was even more dramatic: the proportion of students studying full time fell from 79 percent in 1890 to 15 percent in 1930. One reason for the dominance of part-time schools was their dramatically higher student:teacher ratios, which permitted more rapid growth. In New York in 1930 that ratio was 15:1 in full-time schools but 50:1 in part-time institutions.[37] Thus, many schools quickly attained high enrollments: in 1901–02, 6 had more than 500 students and another 7 had more than 200; by 1910–11, 5 still had more than 500 students and 20 now had more than 200.[38] The expansion of legal education also reflected the growth of universities: at private nondenominational institutions, the number of law schools increased from 39 in 1889–90 to 55 in 1919–20; at Catholic institutions it rose from 2 to 17; and at public institutions it rose from 19 to 36. But many law schools were not university-affiliated: the YMCA and the Knights of Columbus operated 10 schools in 1919–20, and there were another 29 independent schools.[39] A study of obituaries of the 20 to 30 percent of "elite" Chicago practitioners who belonged to the Chicago Bar Association in the last quarter of the nineteenth century found that, among those who had attended law school, the proportion attending universities fell from 88 percent of the cohort admitted in the 1880s to 50 percent of the cohort admitted a decade later, while the proportion attending independent institutions rose from 8 to 49 percent. Although the "laxity" of law school admission criteria was repeatedly denounced by elite bar associations, they do seem to have opened the profession to disadvantaged categories: 49 to 56 percent of the sons of workers and small proprietors who attended law school lacked any college education, compared with 13 to 32 percent of the sons of lawyers, other professionals, large businessmen, and public officials; and 42 to 48 percent of Jewish and Catholic law students lacked any college education, compared with 22 percent of Protestants.[40]

The Rise of Professionalism

Concern about the multiplication of lawyers unleashed by this proliferation of undemanding law schools was an important stimulus for the re-emergence of professional associations, which began in the last third of the nineteenth century. The first of the new wave of bar associations were established in the major commercial centers: New York City in 1870, Cleveland in 1873, Chicago and St. Louis in 1874, and Boston in 1877.[41] The ABA was founded in 1878 by fewer than 100 men, and its membership remained small well into the twentieth century. Although the legal and medical professions were about the same size, only 3700 lawyers belonged to the ABA in 1910, compared with the 33,000 physicians who had joined the American Medical Association (AMA) by 1914.[42] These disparities persisted: 3 percent of lawyers belonged to the ABA in 1910, 9 percent in 1920, and 17 percent in 1930—far less than the 51 percent of physicians who belonged to the AMA in 1912 and the 65 percent who belonged in 1929 (see Table 32).[43] The AMA adopted a federal structure, which added the strength of state and local associations to the peak organization; the ABA remained a national body, in which state and local associations played a much smaller part. The rival National Bar Association, which *was* federal in structure, survived only from 1888 to 1893. ABA members were disproportionately urban as well as elite: in 1892, 83 percent of New York members came from New York City, 92 percent of Illinois members from Chicago or Evanston, all Louisiana members from New Orleans, and 70 percent of Massachusetts members from Boston. Only a small fraction of ABA members attended its annual meetings—an average of 113 for its first ten years. In 1915, it was estimated that only 35 percent of New York City lawyers belonged to *any* bar association, local, state, or national.[44]

Municipal organizations were no more inclusive. The self-consciously elite Association of the Bar of the City of New York enrolled slightly more than 10 percent of the city's lawyers a year after its founding in 1870; this proportion had doubled by 1895 but dwindled to 10 percent in 1908 and then grew very slowly to 18 percent in 1919, 24 percent in 1926, and 35 percent in 1969.[45] Although approximately 30 percent of Chicago practitioners joined the Chicago Bar Association during its first three decades, membership dropped to 18 percent of the profession over the next twenty years; even as late as 1930 it was less than 40 percent. Furthermore, members were older than the bar as a whole, disproportionately native-born, and more likely to practice in law firms.[46] One can see the inspiration for these organizations in the fact that three of their five original committees were concerned with admissions, legal education, and grievances; 53 percent of the Chicago Bar Association's 1905 budget was devoted to "professional control." The Boston Bar Association contained 36 to 45 percent of practitioners between 1880 and 1920, the Philadelphia Bar Association contained 44 percent in 1900, the Los Angeles County Bar Association 46 percent in 1951, and the Bar Association of San Francisco 43 percent in 1920.[47] When lawyers did participate in voluntary organizations, they invested greater energy in such local bodies: the number of city and county bar associations increased from 168 in 1890 to 258 in 1900.[48] As late as 1920, more lawyers belonged to the Chicago Bar Association (2900) than to the Illinois State Bar Association (2451). In 1960, 84 percent of California lawyers belonged to local groups and 27 percent were active in them, but only 47 percent belonged to the ABA and 5 percent were active in it.[49] In 1983, metropolitan bar associations in 16 major cities enrolled at least three-fifths of the practicing profession, and half enrolled four fifths.[50]

Yet neither municipal nor national bar associations were well placed to influence supply, for control over entry was the responsibility of the states. State associations were slow to emerge, at least outside the eastern seaboard. Although the first county bar association in Wisconsin was founded in 1857 and others soon followed, the state association was established only in 1878 and did not meet regularly until 1890.[51] Nearly three fourths of all state bar associations were established in the last two decades of the nineteenth century.[52] Their early years were full of pitfalls: 11 of the 25 state bar associations launched between 1878 and 1888 failed to survive, and another 7 required reorganization before 1900.[53] Nevertheless, there were 8 state and territorial bar associations in 1878, 20 in 1890, 40 in 1900, and 48 in 1916.[54]

Many, however, were little more than paper organizations. The California Bar Association, founded in 1909, had only 593 members by 1917 (perhaps a tenth of all practitioners), 500 in 1920, and 2600 by 1927.[55] As late as 1948, among the 15 voluntary state associations, 2 contained less than 30 percent of practitioners, 2 had 31 to 40 percent, 2 had 41 to 50 percent, 4 had 51 to 60 percent, 2 had 61 to 70 percent, and just 3 had more than 70 percent. It was only in 1970 that 14 out of the 15 voluntary state associations attracted even half of all practitioners.[56] At least in the early decades of this century, high levels of membership were secured only through the creation of "unified" or "integrated" bars, which required practitioners to join. Six jurisdictions were unified in the 1920s, 15 in the 1930s, 4 in the 1940s, 3 in the 1960s, and 3 in the 1970s.[57] Even in those associations, membership was not synonymous with involvement: in 1960, only 42 percent of California lawyers (all of whom belonged to the integrated bar) had participated in its activities during the preceding two or three years.[58] Nevertheless, as we will see later, the peak years of the integration movement coincided with the increasing success of supply control.

If state bar associations played an important role in professionalization, the primary engine remained the American Bar Association. At the time of its founding, the ABA established a Committee on Legal Education to pursue the project of tightening entry requirements. Fifteen years later it formed a Section of Legal Education and Admissions to the Bar for the same purpose. In 1900, the two groups were joined in this task by the newly established Association of American Law Schools. Rivalry and tension between the three entities produced much discussion but little action.[59] The ABA passed resolutions on the subject of legal education at only nine of its first forty-four annual meetings and took no action whatever between 1908 and 1918.[60]

The pace of activity dramatically accelerated in the 1920s. The ABA Committee was abolished in 1917. The Root Report, recommending formal prelegal and legal education requirements, was accepted in 1921. That year the ABA began to publish a list of the schools complying with its new standards, in the hope that deviant institutions would simply vanish, as had happened when the *Journal of the American Medical Association* named the schools whose deficiencies were revealed by the Flexner Report.[61] The AALS progressively raised its membership criteria, framed in terms of prelegal education requirements and the length and timing of legal instruction.[62] But neither group had coercive powers: nothing compelled a school to satisfy the ABA requirements or join the AALS, and students had little incentive to prefer schools that did so. Indeed, enrollment in AALS-member schools dropped from 52 percent of all law students the year the Association was founded to 35 percent a quarter-century later, even though the number of member schools had more than doubled.[63]

The history of legal education in the first half of the twentieth century, therefore, is largely a story of the struggle by the ABA to persuade state licensing authorities (supreme courts or integrated bar associations) to adopt its entry standards. It is always risky to impute motives, particularly bad motives, to individuals and especially dangerous to impute them to groups or organizations (whose members inevitably disagree). Yet the evidence is overwhelming that lawyers became increasingly anxious about their numbers and status as the twentieth century progressed. One striking example is the conversion of John Henry Wigmore, the extremely influential dean of the University of Chicago Law School. In 1909, Wigmore and a colleague (anticipating the legal realists by several decades) conducted an empirical study of the relationship between prelegal education and law school performance. Their conclusion was unambiguous: "on the whole, and for the vast majority of men, it [further education after high school] appears not to be essentially different in its results on legal scholarship." Yet a mere six years later Wigmore issued a manifesto entitled "Should the Standards of Admission to the Bar Be Based on Two Years or More of College Grade Education? It Should." He urged that the number of lawyers be halved by requiring two years of college, defending this as "a rational, beneficent measure of reducing hereafter the spawning mass of promiscuous semi-intelligence which now enters the bar."[64]

Lloyd Garrison, then dean of the University of Wisconsin Law School, found only local and isolated complaints about "overcrowding" during the 1920s but observed a crescendo of concern among state bar associations after 1929.[65] In 1933, the journal of the National Conference of Bar Examiners reprinted without comment two *New York Times* articles, one describing a German Bar Association resolution demanding closure of entry for three years and the other a decision by the Greek Minister of Justice to regulate entry to practice and forcibly retire some lawyers.[66] Many lawyers naturally reasoned that curtailing entry would improve the lot of those at the bottom. In 1935, the Philadelphia Bar Association polled its members and found that 59 percent of the respondents favored limiting admissions.[67] Partly in response, Pennsylvania authorized county bar associations to set quotas on the number of entrants they would admit each year (often equal to the number of retirements and deaths), a practice that continued until 1949 in some counties.[68] The California State Bar conducted a plebiscite of its members in 1936 on whether graduates of schools not approved by the ABA should be required to complete at least two years of college and a preliminary bar examination before beginning their legal studies; 92 percent of those replying favored the idea.[69] In a 1937 article, Young B. Smith, dean of Columbia Law School, called for the elimination of proprietary law schools:

> During the last ten years, more than 20,000 young men have been admitted to the bar in the city of Greater New York alone which is at least twice as many as the bar of this city has been able to absorb. This group represents 58% of the entire bar of the state of New York. The consequences have been not only disastrous to thousands of the young men, but they also have created a serious menace to the community.[70]

The combination of expanding legal education (the number of law students more than doubled during the 1920s), a growing profession (the 1930 census revealed a 31 percent increase—almost twice the rate of population growth) (see Tables 21 and 22), and a contracting economy following the 1929 crash generated something approaching panic.[71] Lawyers looked enviously at physicians, who were beginning to overtake them in earnings. In 1900, the 160 medical schools had enrolled 25,213 students. The 1910 Flexner Report revealed the inadequacies of many of those schools. The AMA required graduation from high school in 1914, one year of college in 1916, and two years in 1918 (a requirement that only *one* state had imposed on lawyers even twenty years later). As a result, nearly half the medical schools (75) had closed and enrollment had fallen by almost 50 percent (to 13,789) by 1919–20.[72] During the same period the number of law schools and law students had *doubled*. Consequently, the annual rate of production of lawyers in 1920 approximated the annual rate of production of physicians twenty years earlier (see Table 21). In the years following the Depression, the dispersion of income among lawyers was greater than in any other profession, disclosing the economic vulnerability of many practitioners.[73]

Tightening Control Over Supply

Prelegal Education

The battle to control supply was waged on a number of fronts. The first step was to raise the educational prerequisites for entering law school in order to limit the number and restrict the characteristics of those who qualified. We have seen that until the end of the nineteenth century no law school demanded any college education. In 1896, indeed, only 7 out of 76 law schools required even a high school diploma. This minimal prerequisite spread rapidly: in 1903, nearly half the law schools (51 out of 104) accepted only high school graduates, and these schools enrolled almost two-thirds of law students (9314 out of 14,127).[74] Schools were slow to insist on even a year or two of college, however, for fear of reducing their enrollments. Harvard was the first to demand a college degree (in 1895); but more than twenty years elapsed before any law school followed suit (Pennsylvania in 1916) and another five until the next four did so (Stanford, Yale, Columbia, and Western Reserve).[75] As I mentioned before, the 1909 Wigmore and Crossley study of University of Chicago law students between 1895 and 1905 offered little empirical justification for the requirement: although the best students had some college training and the worst did not, most could not be differentiated by prior education.

Nevertheless, the AALS "earnestly hoped" in 1908 that its member schools would require two years of college, and in 1918 the ABA agreed. Full-time schools gradually adopted this recommendation: 7 in 1908, 31 in 1921, and 65 in 1925. But only 16 part-time or mixed schools had done so by the latter year, at which time the majority of schools still did not comply.[76] In 1927, 66 out of the 166 law schools continued to admit students with less than two years of college. Schools that raised their standards risked losing enrollment to these less demanding competitors. The

University of Wisconsin Law School required one year of college in 1905 and a second year in 1906; enrollment, which had varied between 200 and 262 in the years 1895 to 1903, fell to an average of 165 between 1903 and 1913.[77] When Cornell required only a high school diploma in 1899, its enrollment fell from 125 to 62; when the University of Minnesota demanded a year of college in 1909, the student body shrank from 203 to 69; Yale, which insisted on two years of college in 1909 and four in 1911, saw the number of students drop from 438 in 1908–09 to 133 in 1914–15; Georgetown's enrollment almost halved, from 1130 in 1923–24 to 489 three years later, when it switched from a part-time to a full-time program and required two years of college; and George Washington experienced a drop from 1063 to 717 in the same period for similar reasons.[78]

It was clear, therefore, that state compulsion was going to be necessary to achieve uniformly stringent prelegal requirements. But as late as 1927, thirty-two of the forty-nine jurisdictions did not require *any* prelegal education and another eleven accepted graduation from high school.[79] Only Kansas insisted on two years of college.[80] In the next eight years, an additional twenty-one states imposed a prelegal requirement: eight accepted high school graduation, and twelve demanded some college. Even this did not necessarily protect the more elite schools from their less rigorous competitors. When Illinois demanded a high school diploma, John Marshall, a part-time school in Chicago, established its own high school; Portia (in Boston) responded in the same way to the Massachusetts requirement. And Westminster in Denver and Suffolk in Boston created their own colleges when state authorities began to require some college education.[81]

Beginning in 1936, the ABA's annual *Review of Legal Education* included a map highlighting in black those states requiring less than two years of college. Fifteen were blacked that year, eight in 1938 (all in the South), and five in 1942. By 1948, the *Review* concluded that it had won the campaign and dropped the map, although three southern states continued to accept high school graduates as late as 1954, and another two states had no prelegal requirement.[82] By 1970, eight states required a college degree and another thirty insisted on three years of college.[83] Today, only California allows applicants to take an examination in lieu of college; thirty-nine jurisdictions require three years and eleven a college degree (see Table 1).

Changes in the educational backgrounds of practicing lawyers reflected these ABA pressures, mediated by the states and law schools, as well as the general rise in educational levels (see Table 3.a). The prevalence of college educated lawyers actually appears to have declined in the course of the nineteenth century. The proportion of Massachusetts lawyers who had graduated from college fell from nearly 70 percent before 1840 to 58 percent of those admitted between 1870 amd 1890.[84] Among the 20 to 30 percent of "elite" Chicago practitioners who belonged to the Chicago Bar Association in the last quarter of the nineteenth century, the proportion with some college education declined fairly steadily from 77 percent of the cohort admitted in the 1850s to 60 percent of the cohort admitted in the 1890s.[85] In the last quarter of the nineteenth century, some incomplete data indicate that just a fourth or fewer of all law students had college degrees. An elite school like Harvard showed a very different pattern, however: after 1870 more than three fourths of its students were college graduates.[86] And Harvard required a college degree in 1895; although it tolerated some exceptions until 1909, 3439 out of 3488 students enrolled between 1896 and 1910 were college graduates (99 percent).[87]

Other elite schools had much lower proportions of college graduates in the 1890s (Columbia 43 percent, Northwestern 39 percent, Yale 31 percent, and Michigan 17 percent).[88] In nonelite schools the proportion was insignificant: 2 out of 60 students at Washington and Lee in 1894, for instance.[89] In 1895 it varied inversely with the length of the course: 28 percent in the twenty law schools with a three-year course, 15 percent in the thirty-nine with two-year courses, and virtually none in the eight with one-year courses.[90] There were also significant regional variations. Among elite lawyers whose obituaries were published in the *ABA Reports* between 1900 and 1911, 60 percent of Chicago lawyers had college degrees, 63 percent of New York City lawyers, and 74 percent of those in Boston and Philadelphia.[91] It appears that as more aspiring lawyers sought formal legal education rather than (or in addition to) apprenticeship, law school initially displaced college as an undergraduate degree instead of supplementing it as a graduate course.[92] Moreover, even the low proportion of law students who had graduated from college greatly exceeded the proportion among those who qualified through apprenticeship—a majority of new lawyers until the turn of the century.

In the early twentieth century, as enrollment in part-time law schools gradually overtook that in full-time schools, the prelegal education of entrants may have declined further. A questionnaire answered by 300 out of the 900 lawyers admitted to the New York bar in 1925 and still practicing in 1930 indicated that 87 (29 percent) had no college, 33 (11 percent) had only one year, 45 (15 percent) had two or three years, and 135 (45 percent) had a college degree.[93] These aggregate figures were a composite of two distinct streams. Although George Washington University Law School required only a high school education in 1913–14, 36 percent of its students were college graduates and 27 percent had some college education.[94] Yet a quarter-century later, a survey of evening students at a District of Columbia law school (probably also George Washington) revealed that only 28 percent had college degrees, 32 percent had two years of college, and 40 percent had only a high school education.[95] We can see the same contrast in California: in 1924–25, only 21 out of 112 law students at Hastings had college degrees (19 percent); but the following year 115 out of 314 Stanford law students did (37 percent); and the year after that 181 out of 195 Berkeley law students were college graduates (93 percent).[96]

Yet change occurred at all law schools, if more slowly. A study of lawyers practicing in New York City in the 1960s found that half of those admitted before 1920 had less than two years of college and 20 percent had never attended college, while all of those admitted between 1955 and 1960 had some college and only 4 percent had less than two years.[97] Among those accepted by the University of San Francisco Law School in 1933, 77.8 percent had less than two years of college; fifteen years later the proportion had fallen to 28.6 percent. Some California schools continued to admit students with little regard to their prior education, however: between 1936 and 1942, 58.3 percent of those accepted at McGeorge (then an unaccredited part-time school) had less than two years of college, and the proportion remained 54.2 percent in 1946–49.[98] A 1948 survey answered by 107 of the

122 ABA-approved law schools revealed that only two thirds of entering first-year students had even two years of college. And at some schools, the proportion of entering students with that level of education was much lower: less than 20 percent at 5 percent of the ABA-approved schools, 20 to 29 percent at another 7 percent, 30 to 39 percent at 11 percent, 40 to 49 percent at 14 percent, and 50 to 59 percent at 12 percent.[99]

We can distinguish these two streams in the profile of those taking the bar examination. In 1930, 42 percent of examinees had no college education.[100] In August 1932, 16 percent of California examinees had not graduated from high school, another 19.2 percent had no college education, and only 39.9 percent had college degrees.[101] Between 1936 and 1941, the proportion who had not completed high school fell to 3.1 percent, another 8.6 percent had no college education, and the proportion of college graduates increased to 59.8 percent.[102] Furthermore, those who passed the bar examination were considerably better educated: 26 percent had some college education in 1930 and 28 percent in 1932; 53 percent had college degrees in 1932 and 75 percent between 1936 and 1941 (see Table 19).[103] The advantage that prelegal education appeared to give examinees may explain the surprising statistic that 62.9 percent of a sample of New York City practitioners in 1934 were college graduates.[104] Nationwide, the proportion of the profession who had attended college increased from two thirds in 1949 to more than 90 percent in 1970; the proportion with college degrees doubled, from 37 to 73 percent (see Table 3.a).

From our present perspective, the requirements of a high school diploma and a college degree seem neither unreasonable nor exclusionary. It is essential to remember, however, that free secondary education became generally available only in the twentieth century and college education did not begin to expand dramatically until the 1960s. Only 16.3 percent of seventeen-year olds had graduated from high school in 1920, 28.8 percent in 1930, and 49 percent in 1940—years that span the period when high school graduation became a requirement to enter the legal profession. Only 6 percent of all white men had graduated from college in 1940, 10.3 percent in 1960, and just 15 percent as late as 1970. The proportion of college graduates among black men was consistently less than half that of whites (see Table 3.b). Thus, the requirements of prelegal education had a substantial effect on the numbers and composition of the legal profession when they were first imposed, if they are less significant today.

Legal Education

Although prelegal educational requirements may have reduced the pool of aspiring lawyers during the first half of this century, legal education clearly was the central gatekeeper.[105] We have seen that nineteenth-century requirements were very lax: in 1879, twenty-three out of thirty-eight jurisdictions required no legal study whatsoever; and of the fifteen demanding some, only seven insisted on three years.[106] In 1891, sixteen still required no law study, another sixteen required only two years (three for those with no undergraduate education), and only three demanded three years for all entrants.[107] In 1904, just under two thirds of the states required any law study, and nineteen demanded three years.[108] By 1928, forty-one out of forty-nine jurisdictions called for some legal training.[109]

These requirements were tightened in two ways. First, as we have seen, states began to reject the alternative of apprenticeship, although only after formal education had effectively displaced it for different reasons. Other routes to practice also disappeared. California was one of the few states that continued to permit preparation for the bar examination exclusively through private study and correspondence schools as well as through office study (apprenticeship). Among those taking the 1930 bar examination, 7.6 percent had studied through correspondence courses and 0.8 percent had studied privately, but only 8 percent of the former and none of the latter passed, compared with 51 percent of those with law degrees.[110] Consequently, only 43 of the 1182 lawyers admitted to the California bar in the years 1929–31 (3.6 percent) had prepared outside of law school.[111] Among those taking the August 1932 bar examination, 4.5 percent had taken correspondence courses and 1.4 percent had studied privately; but only 12.9 percent of the former and 10.0 percent of the latter passed, compared with 60.4 percent of those with law degrees.[112] Between 1932 and 1948, only 1.2 percent of bar examinees studied privately and 3.4 percent took correspondence courses. Furthermore, their pass rates were only 11.3 and 11.2 percent, far lower than the 59.9 percent among those who had graduated from law school.[113] But though the pass rate of those preparing through correpondence courses or in law offices remains low, it is significant that a dozen or more lawyers continue to enter the California bar through these avenues each year—which at least should inspire some skepticism about the formal educational requirements of other jurisdictions (see Table 20.a).

Few other states have admitted significant numbers of entrants without a law degree in recent decades. As early as 1939, 96 percent of Michigan practitioners had attended law school.[114] In 1951, six states still allowed preparation through private study (though another two had just abolished it). But in 1947 no one sought to qualify this way in four of those states, and only one examinee passed in each of the other two. Ten states allowed qualification through correspondence schools in 1951. But of the six for which statistics were available in 1947, only 3.7 percent of examinees qualified in this fashion, and only 7 percent of these passed, compared with 47 percent of all examinees; thus, correspondence school students constituted only 0.1 percent of new lawyers in these states.[115] Even in California correspondence school students were only 0.7 percent of those taking the July 1986 bar examination and only 0.06 percent of those passing.[116] As a result, the proportion of practicing American lawyers who had attended law school increased from 76 percent in 1949 to 97 percent in 1970, and the proportion holding a law degree rose from 62 to 93 percent (see Table 3.a).

A second means of tightening entry requirements was to lengthen the period of law study. In 1870, seventeen of the thirty-one law schools offered two-year courses and another fourteen taught only a single year; ten years later, four courses were three years long and twenty-nine were two years, while the number of one-year courses had only grown to nineteen. Yet schools lost enrollment by lengthening their courses, as long as shorter alternatives were available.[117] Only a fraction of students completed even a two-year curriculum, often preferring to spend more time in apprenticeship. In 1872, attrition between the first and second years was

43 percent at Yale, 49 percent at Harvard, and 62 percent at the University of Missouri.[118]

As late as 1927, nine jurisdictions still required no law study, two required less than two years, and seven required only two years.[119] Yet even without state compulsion, the number of law schools with courses shorter than three years was declining: from 54 out of 61 in 1889–90 to 8 out of 147 in 1922 and 10 out of 176 in 1927–28.[120] And the number of law students enrolled in such schools dropped from 3186 out of 4486 in 1889–90 (71 percent) to 980 out of 47,320 in 1927–28 (2 percent) (see Table 2).[121] As longer courses became the norm, schools adopting them did not have to fear losing students: among part-time schools that extended their courses from three to four years between 1922 and 1923, enrollment increased 30.1 percent at three, although it shrunk 11.6 percent at another four.[122] Still, the formal curriculum did not necessarily determine the length of a student's legal education: in Georgia in 1950, three fourths of all law students took the bar examination before graduating.[123]

Alfred Reed summarized this transformation during the period of most rapid change. Dividing jurisdictions into technically advanced (requiring consecutive general and legal education), intermediate (requiring both but allowing them to occur simultaneously), and primitive (failing to require one or both), he noted that the proportions in the three categories had been equal in 1927–28, but seven years later twenty-four jurisdictions were advanced, eighteen were intermediate, and only seven were primitive (see Table 2).[124]

Neither the monopoly of law school nor the lengthening of its curriculum to three full years (or their part-time equivalent) effectively controlled the production of lawyers.[125] We have seen that the number of law schools doubled in the last decade of the nineteenth century and the first decade of the twentieth, while enrollments increased fourfold. In the following twenty years the number of law schools increased by almost 50 percent and enrollments doubled again (see Table 21).

This growth was not evenly distributed. First, it was concentrated in a few large cities, notably those with significant immigrant populations. In 1904, there were five law schools in New England (mostly in Boston), four in New York City, six in Chicago, and seven in the District of Columbia.[126] Second, most of the growth occurred through the founding or expansion of part-time schools with minimal entrance requirements. The first was the Columbian Law School, established in Washington, D.C., in 1865 to serve federal employees whose workday ended at 3 P.M.; five years later it was joined in the District by National Law School.[127] Northwestern College of Law opened in Portland, Oregon, in 1884 and Metropolis Law School in New York City in 1888 (later absorbed by New York University).[128] By 1901, New York Law School was the second largest institution in the country; five years later it was the largest, with 1050 students.[129]

In 1889–90, the 51 law schools offering full-time instruction (out of a total of 61) enrolled 88 percent of all law students. A quarter-century later the number of full-time schools had increased by half (to 76), while part-time institutions had multiplied more than sixfold (to 64); consequently, the former enrolled only 52 percent of all students.[130] One reason part-time schools could grow so rapidly was their poor student:teacher ratio—three times higher than that of their full-time counterparts. If we construct two categories—full-time schools with long courses and schools that were either part-time or offered short courses—the 51 schools in the former category in 1889 had dwindled to 24 ten years later, though enrollment remained constant at just under 4000; but the 55 schools in the latter category had multiplied by 50 percent, and their enrollment had doubled to 7631.

The expansion of part-time legal education accelerated in the twentieth century. Suffolk Law School in Boston was founded in 1914 (over the opposition of Harvard); it enrolled 460 students in 1915, 1512 in 1922, 2018 in 1924, and almost 4000 in 1928, when it had become the largest law school in the world.[131] Its proprietor, Gleason Archer, achieved this growth through aggressive promotion, including a weekly national radio broadcast, publication of books and speeches, the construction of a neon sign on the roof of the school building, which could be seen for miles, and extensive advertising.[132] California law schools paid commissions to students and other solicitors for each new enrolee, and a faculty member from one school was hired as dean of another and paid for each student he lured away from his former employer.[133]

A few large part-time schools in major eastern cities produced a disproportionate number of lawyers. In 1928, 56 percent of all part-time students studied in Boston, New York City, Newark, and the District of Columbia; 43 percent attended eight schools in Boston and New York; and just five New York schools accounted for 31 percent.[134] These centers of immigration experienced unprecedented growth in the 1920s: law school enrollment in cities with populations over 200,000 increased 114 percent during the 1920s—47 percent in full-time schools but 142 percent in part-time institutions.[135] In 11 of the 60 American cities with more than 120,000 people in 1930 the profession grew between 20 and 39 percent during the decade.[136] Interstate migration also created demand for legal education. Although California ranked only sixth in population in 1933, it contained the largest number of law schools (twenty), a third more than its nearest competitor (Ohio); and California's 2800 law students were a fifth of its total practicing bar.[137] We can see the dominance of part-time legal education in the fact that among Illinois bar examinees in 1915 and 1916, 59 percent of Chicago residents had studied at Chicago night schools and another 7 percent at Loyola, a mixed school with both full-time and part-time students.[138]

The ABA responded to this explosive growth by seeking to persuade states to restrict entry to graduates of approved law schools while simultaneously raising its accreditation standards. This was an uphill battle, rendered more difficult by the influential Reed Report commissioned by the Carnegie Foundation, which had recommended that part-time schools continue to prepare lawyers for the lower tier of a "differentiated bar."[139] When the ABA first promulgated its minimum standards in 1921–22, only 31 out of 148 schools complied.[140] Among a 1930 sample of New York lawyers admitted in 1925, 70 percent had graduated from unapproved schools.[141] In 1927, unapproved schools outnumbered approved schools by almost 2 to 1 and enrolled more than twice as many students (see Table 21). Furthermore, unapproved schools often received strong support from alumni serving in state legislatures; throughout the 1920s, an average of 25 graduates of Suffolk Law School (the largest in the nation) sat in the Massachusetts legislature.[142]

Nevertheless, the ABA slowly prevailed. During the 1930s, California, Tennessee, Ohio, and Texas all engaged in deliberate campaigns to put the unapproved schools out of business.[143] A committee appointed by the State Bar of California to survey legal education and admissions to the bar issued the following report in 1933:

> Three questions arise: First, can the bar of California absorb this yearly influx [of 600 new lawyers]? . . .
> As to whether the bar of California is overcrowded, every lawyer knows the answer. . . . For every one who gives up a place in the profession there are always two crowding forward to take his place. . . .
> It is evident that as long as 20 schools operate in the state without restrictions, California will continue to be overcrowded with lawyers . . . it seems apparent that some of these 20 schools have but little excuse for existing.[144]

Between 1928 and 1931, enrollment at unapproved schools declined 29 percent while that at approved schools rose 14 percent (some of this shift is attributable to the accreditation of previously unapproved schools).[145] Enrollment in approved schools exceeded that in unapproved in 1936; approved schools outnumbered unapproved the following year; and these differences steadily widened. Yet in 1938, only two of the twelve Tennessee law schools were approved by the ABA; one offered just a single year of instruction, and another three offered two years; consequently, Tennessee had one law student for every three practicing lawyers.[146]

During the Depression and World War II, when demand for legal education fell, attendance at unapproved schools declined and a number were forced to close. Of the forty that were founded between 1930 and 1949 but failed to obtain ABA approval, half had ceased operations by 1950. Indeed, sixty-nine of the seventy schools that closed between 1930 and 1950 were unapproved.[147] Unapproved schools did not share in the postwar recovery, in part because veterans' benefits were available only to those attending approved schools.[148] Yet in Georgia in 1949, unapproved law schools graduated almost twice as many law students as approved schools (340 versus 182).[149]

Lawyers continued to look enviously at physicians. In 1939, all but one of the forty-eight states required physicians to have graduated from an approved medical school, of which there were only sixty-seven. By contrast, only 57 percent of the 180 law schools were approved by the ABA, and they enrolled only 64 percent of all students.[150] Yet by the end of that year enrollment in approved schools was twice that in unapproved; the ratio reached 4:1 during the war, 10:1 in the mid-1950s, and is more than 20:1 today (see Table 21). In 1935, only nine states required entrants to have graduated from an ABA-approved law school; but the number quickly rose to twenty in 1937, twenty-three in 1938, and forty-six in 1979 (see Table 1).[151] By 1949, those who had attended approved schools constituted 64.4 percent of all lawyers listed in the Martindale-Hubbell directory (85.1 percent of those who had attended law school); only 9.7 percent had attended an unapproved law school (though another 1.5 percent had attended unlisted law schools that almost certainly were not approved).[152] In the 1950s a number of unapproved schools were absorbed by approved schools: the Washington College of Law by American University, Columbian Law School by Catholic University, National

Law School by George Washington University (all in the District of Columbia), and Westminster Law School by the University of Denver.[153] Between 1965 and 1984, graduates of unapproved schools accounted for only 3.8 percent of all those passing the bar, and the proportion never exceeded 7.7 percent in any one year (see Table 17).

Although unapproved schools survive (some because they hope to gain accreditation), thirty-five of the fifty-eight schools in 1979 were located in a single state, California, and they enrolled 70 percent of the students in such schools.[154] Yet even California tolerated unapproved schools reluctantly. In 1937, the state bar association was given authority to require those not attending approved schools to take a so-called "baby" bar examination at the end of their first year of law study. It imposed that requirement on all who prepared through private study, law office study, and correspondence schools as well as those attending an unapproved school a specified proportion of whose graduates failed to pass the regular bar examination—30 percent in 1937, gradually increased to 60 percent in 1949.[155] The baby bar was a significant obstacle: in June 1941, all three who prepared through law office work, all three who prepared through private study, and forty-three of the forty-four who prepared through correspondence school failed.[156] Between 1938 and 1947, the pass rate on the baby bar ranged from 20 to 60 percent (and appeared to vary inversely with the number taking it), although graduates of many unapproved schools did much better.[157]

In 1932, unapproved schools prepared 65.8 percent of all law school graduates taking the California bar examination but only 48.9 percent of those passing.[158] Graduates of unapproved schools have consistently had lower pass rates on the bar examination than those of approved schools: 41.9 percent compared with 84.4 percent in 1932 and 51.7 percent compared with 73.8 percent between 1932 and 1949 (see Table 20.a).[159] In 1979, sixteen California law schools were approved by the ABA, another seventeen were approved by the state bar, and fifteen were approved by neither. The last category of school enrolled only 600 students, however, compared with 20,000 in the first two, and only 51 of its graduates passed the July 1982 bar exam compared with 3000 from schools approved by the ABA or the state bar.[160] The largest unapproved school, Western State University College of Law applied for ABA approval in 1986 because it feared the eventual elimination of unapproved institutions.[161] Although the proportion of those passing the California bar examination after preparing at schools not approved by the ABA declined from 46 percent in 1934 to a low of 14 percent between 1948 and 1949, it has fluctuated around 30 percent for the last 40 years (see Table 20.a).

The virtual monopoly of ABA-approved schools has not halted the expansion of legal education. Several schools have gained ABA approval nearly every year since the 1930s; and the pace of accreditation increased at the end of the 1960s— seventeen were approved in the decade 1968 to 1978—with the result that the number of schools presently approved (175) has doubled since 1935. One reason for this expansion is that monopoly carries responsibility as well as conferring power: the ABA fears that a refusal to accredit might stimulate a lawsuit challenging its authority. Thus, it repealed the categorical exclusion of proprietary (profit-making) schools in the 1970s under threat of losing the accreditation power conferred by the U. S. Commissioner of Education, although it still has not approved such a school.[162] More recently, it accredited the O.W. Coburn School of Law at Oral Roberts University, which requires both students and faculty to sign a pledge "recognizing Christ and following his example" and insists that faculty answer questions about their spiritual beliefs and students submit a recommendation from a clergyman.[163] At the same time, there is some evidence that the standards for approval were tightened in the 1960s, with the result that eight institutions thinking of launching law schools decided against it.[164] In 1987 all three schools that applied for accreditation in 1987 were rejected. Old College, Nevada School of Law—the *only* law school in the state—closed as a result; although thirty-eight out of its approximately seventy-five graduates had passed the Nevada bar, they were denied admission because the school lacked accreditation. Western State University in California, which has appealed the ABA decision, claims that it spent $2.5 million to improve its library, remodel its buildings, and hire consultants to guide it through the accreditation process and lost another $2 million in tuition payments foregone when it raised admission standards and cut enrollment. St. Thomas University College of Law in Florida plans to reapply.[165]

The virtual demise of unapproved schools has also meant the decline of part-time law study. The rapid expansion of law schools between 1889 and 1928 had resulted largely from the growth of part-time education. In 1889, 74 percent of law students studied full time; by 1928, the proportion had fallen to 33 percent (see Table 5). The number of full-time students increased almost fivefold during this period, but the number of part-time and mixed students multiplied 28 times. But the Depression seriously reduced the market for part-time study. Between 1928 and 1931, part-time enrollments fell 21 percent while full-time enrollments declined only 2 percent.[166] The difference was particularly pronounced in large East Coast cities: in Boston, part-time enrollment fell 32 percent while full-time enrollment declined only 3 percent; in New York, part-time enrollment fell 44 percent (52 percent by 1932), while Columbia lost only 16 percent of its students; in Newark, part-time enrollment was down 45 percent.[167] Still, 46.4 percent of law school graduates taking the August 1932 California bar examination had studied in evening schools. At the same time, the proportion of part-time law school graduates who passed the examination was only half that of full-time graduates.[168] Nevertheless, about a third of the members of the New York County Lawyers' Association in 1934 were graduates of part-time schools.[169]

The ABA campaign against unapproved law schools disproportionately affected part-time education. In 1936, seventy-five approved schools offered full-time education, eighteen were mixed, and only one was exclusively part time; by contrast, only eight unapproved schools were full time, seventeen were mixed, and seventy-one were exclusively part time.[170] In 1972, thirty-four of the thirty-nine part-time schools were unapproved.[171] Within ABA-approved schools, the proportion of part-time students declined to 13 percent of total enrollment in 1979, and since then it has risen to only 18 percent. Although the proportion of students at unapproved schools who study part time remains high, the absolute number of such students remains very small (see Table 5). Part-time students were concentrated at schools with limited resources and suffered a higher rate of attrition, largely through withdrawals.[172] At an unidentified metropolitan law school in the 1950s, only 3 percent of the full-time students withdrew during their first year, compared with 17 percent of the part-time students.[173] Despite ABA regulation, however, approved and unapproved schools continue to compete by offering part-time education. When ABA-approved Saint Louis University School of Law terminated its night program in 1976, unapproved Laclede School of Law opened in the same city the following year. Having failed to persuade the Missouri Supreme Court to allow its graduates to take the bar examination, it obtained legislation empowering the state board of education to accredit law schools. Saint Louis University responded by reopening its night program in the fall of 1988.[174]

The decline of part-time schools has rendered legal education financially less accessible to students from poorer backgrounds. Evening instruction makes it far easier for students to support themselves by working. More than half the full-time students at an unidentified metropolitan law school in the 1950s did not work at all, and another 36.2 percent worked 30 hours a week or less; by contrast, all the part-time students worked, and 94.2 percent worked more than 30 hours.[175] Part-time schools also charge lower tuition—about half that of full-time schools (although students must pay for a longer period—usually an extra year). Evening students at George Washington University Law School in 1940 spent only 13 percent of their income on tuition and books.[176] In 1948–49, median full-time tuition at all ABA-approved law schools was $324, while median part-time tuition was only $200.[177]

Financial barriers have grown in importance as the cost of law school has risen. At the beginning of the century, public legal education was virtually free: Wisconsin charged no tuition to residents in 1907, just a $10 fee for each semester.[178] By contrast, private school tuition has always been very expensive: Harvard, Yale, Columbia, and Stanford all charged more than $300 a year in the late 1920s.[179] Tuition at a wide variety of schools increased more than tenfold between 1927 and 1984, generally faster than the rate of inflation, and at some it rose thirtyfold (see Table 6). Between 1938 and 1951, tuition increased more than 200 percent at two of the ninety-three ABA-approved schools, 100 to 200 percent at twelve, 75 to 100 percent at nineteen, and 50 to 75 percent at twenty-seven. It increased 233 percent at one of the twenty-nine unapproved schools, 100 to 200 percent at five, 75 to 100 percent at two, and 50 to 75 percent at eight.[180] Between 1940–41 and 1956–57, the median total annual cost of law school jumped from $450 to nearly $1000 for commuting students and from $750 to $1500 for resident students; the latter paid more than $2000 at fifteen of the eighty schools responding.[181] Between 1948–49 and 1954–55, the median tuition at 116 schools increased from $324 to $400. Between 1955 and 1970, median tuition at 76 private law schools increased from $669 to $1705; at public law schools it rose from $229 to $523 for residents and from $537 to $1235 for nonresidents (all in constant 1970 dollars).[182] In the eight years following 1974, tuition increased 60 percent for residents at state schools and 43 percent for nonresidents, but it rose 87 percent at private schools.[183] In 1983–84, the median cost of tuition and living expenses was $7361 for residents at public law schools, $9529 for nonresidents, and $11,929 for law students at private institutions; it exceeded $9000 at almost half the ABA-approved schools.[184] In 1986–87, tuition alone averaged $9399 at a sample of 26 private law schools (up 9.6 percent from the previous year) and $2138 for in-state and $5018 for out-of-state residents at a sample of 26 public law schools (up 10.7 and 7.6 percent, respectively).[185] Because the cost of undergraduate education has risen at a similar pace, the aspiring lawyer must sustain this burden for seven years, not just three.

Financial aid was severely limited until recently. In 1948 49 a sample of 72 law schools spent only $7.04 per student per year; five years later they still spent only $31.15.[186] The total amount of scholarship awards increased from $238,815 in 1948–49 (72 schools reporting) to $1,887,491 in 1956–57 (99 schools reporting) and $2,228,381 the following year (115 schools reporting). Nevertheless, only about 14 percent of all students received scholarship aid in the latter two years, and for students at half the schools the chances of a scholarship were about one in twenty. Furthermore, only about a third of the scholarships were awarded purely on the basis of need.[187] Among the five Pennsylvania law schools in 1952, two (Duquesne and Dickinson) offered no scholarships, Pittsburgh offered the interest on an endowment of $7000 (probably less than $200 a year), Temple offered one scholarship, and the University of Pennsylvania remitted the tuition of about 4 percent of its students.[188] Only 20 out of 127 ABA-approved law schools offered student loans in 1954, and only 6 schools had even $25,000 a year to lend.[189] Two years later, virtually all loan funds still were intended to meet short-term emergencies rather than finance the cost of law school; few schools had more than $10,000 in outstanding loans at the end of 1956–57.[190]

Today, students can pay the extraordinary costs of higher education only by going deeply into debt. Two thirds of all law students applying for financial aid in 1982–83 had already accumulated educational debts of at least $4700; they would leave law school with an estimated median debt of $14,700, but the average debt of 1986 Yale graduates was $23,000.[191] In October 1984, federally guaranteed loans to students at ABA approved law schools totaled $400 million, representing 51 percent of tuition and fees at the 72 public law schools and 45 percent at the 101 private schools.[192] The magnitude of the burden on all student borrowers (not just law students) is suggested by the fact that the federal government expected them to default on $1.09 billion in 1985, or 11.7 percent of outstanding loans.[193] If the cost of entry does not limit the *number* who aspire to become lawyers (since every place at all ABA-approved schools has been filled in recent years), it certainly influences *who* can aspire to do so and their careers after graduation.

The central role of ABA-approved law schools as gatekeepers to the profession has greatly intensified the competition to enter them. The ease with which law schools could be established and the profits that could be earned from them in the 1920s and 1930s (most of the 67 independent unapproved law schools in 1936 were proprietary) ensured that virtually anyone wishing to become a lawyer could find a place in a law school.[194] In 1927–28, Yale was the first law school to adopt a selective admissions policy, limiting its entering class to 100, requiring an undergraduate transcript, recommendations, and an interview, and developing the first aptitude test in 1928. The next year 274 applicants sought one of those 100 places. Columbia followed suit in 1928–29 and was soon joined by Chicago, Northwestern, and Pennsylvania.[195] Nevertheless, 280 of the 409 applicants who took the Columbia entrance examination in 1931 were admitted (68 percent).[196] And Harvard continued to accept every applicant with a bachelor's degree and the ability to pay: this was still the era of the "gentleman's C." As late as 1937–38 it admitted 81 percent of all applicants.[197] In 1940, 29 percent of evening students at a reputable law school in the District of Columbia (probably George Washington) had earned poor grades at college.[198] In 1950, the Lamar School of Law of Emory University in Atlanta, Georgia, accepted students with a college grade point average (GPA) of 1.3 (slightly better than a D).[199]

Although a few law schools had their own entrance examinations before World War II, the Law School Admission Test (LSAT) was not instituted until 1947, and entry to law school became significantly competitive only in the 1960s. In 1948–49, 87 percent of applicants to a sample of 136 law schools met the minimum requirements for admission and 70 percent were accepted (81 percent of those applying to part-time schools).[200] Among California schools that year, Berkeley accepted only one applicant out of three, Stanford two out of five, and USC two out of three, but most others accepted more than four out of every five.[201] The University of Pennsylvania Law School accepted one out of every three applicants in 1953, although the Medical School accepted only one out of sixteen.[202] As late as 1960, Harvard still admitted half of all applicants.[203]

The situation began to change in the 1960s. In response to a 1963 survey, forty-five out of sixty-two full-time schools said they recently had raised their admissions standards, as did sixteen out of twenty-nine mixed schools and all eight part-time schools.[204] By the late 1960s, the ratio of applicants to acceptances had increased dramatically: 3.0 at Berkeley (it had been 1.4 a decade earlier), 3.2 at Columbia, 3.9 at Harvard (also twice what it had been a decade earlier), and 5.1 at Yale. It was high even at less prestigious public institutions: 2.2 at Illinois, 1.5 at Iowa, 2.2 at Minnesota, and 3.1 at Hastings (which had admitted every applicant at the end of the 1940s).[205]

One index of the pressure on places is the ratio of LSAT examinees to law school entrants the following year (although some examinees never apply). This climbed from less than 1:3 in 1947 to 3.4:1 in 1976–77, before declining to 2.7:1 in the last four years (see Table 4). As a result, the median LSAT scores of those admitted rose dramatically: at Harvard, for instance, from 630 in 1960 to 725 in 1974.[206] In 1975, the ninety most competitive ABA-approved schools were as selective as the eighth-ranked school had been in 1961; all 163 ABA-approved schools were as selective in 1975 as the 27 most competitive schools had been in 1961.[207]

High school and college grades also reveal the difficulty of entry. In 1969, 15 percent of college freshmen declaring an interest in law school had earned A averages in high school and 25 percent had earned C averages or lower (compared with a 13 and 33 percent of the total freshman population). In 1981, 34 percent of prelaw students had earned A averages and only 10 percent had earned C averages (compared with 21 and 19 percent of the total freshman population). In 1969, 12 percent of entering law students had college GPAs of A (compared with 20 percent of all graduate students and 30 percent of medical students). In 1981, 41 percent of entering law students had A averages (compared with 29 percent of all graduate students and 60 percent of medical students).[208] At a sample of 23 law schools, the mean undergraduate GPA rose from 2.76 (1964–66) to 3.04 (1971–72) to 3.35 (1975), not all of which can be explained by grade inflation.[209]

Since 1972, the number of students who completed the centralized application forms sent to all ABA-approved law schools has been approximately double the number who entered law school the following year (see Table 4). In 1975–76, about

40 percent of law school applicants were not accepted by *any* ABA-approved school. The absolute number of disappointed applicants increased eightfold between 1962 and 1977.[210] In the fall of 1970, 353 full-time and 306 part-time places remained unfilled in ABA-approved law schools, but the numbers dropped to 52 and 35 the following year, and since then virtually every place has been taken.[211] One indication of the value of academic qualifications is the fact that in medicine, where supply control is even more stringent, an estimated 10,000 practicing physicians hold counterfeit degrees.[212]

Those who gain admission to an ABA-approved law school still must graduate. Until fairly recently, this was a major hurdle. Because of insufficient academic preparation, ability, or interest (perhaps a function of easy entry, low tuition, and uncertain future rewards), a substantial proportion of law students did not earn their degrees. Between 1904 and 1908, 174 Yale students were excluded on academic grounds; and 250 of the 700 students who entered Harvard in the fall of 1926 failed to complete the first year.[213] Between 1920 and 1929, 39 percent of Harvard matriculates and 73 percent of part-time Suffolk Law School students failed to graduate.[214] (By contrast, attrition seemed to disappear when Yale adopted a selective admissions policy in 1926, rejecting two out of every three applicants; a total enrollment of 296 in 1929 suggests that virtually all of the 100 students admitted in each of the previous three years was still attending.)[215] In 1936, first-year attrition was estimated to be one third to one half at the University of Illinois, one third at Minnesota, one fourth to one third at Chicago and Michigan, and one fifth at Northwestern and Wisconsin.[216] Nearly a third of the students entering Harvard in 1937 failed to complete the first year.[217]

Attrition rates remained high even after World War II. A third or more of students entering in 1948 either were dismissed or withdrew during their first year at such prestigious California schools as Stanford (29 percent), Berkeley (32 percent), USC (37 percent), and Hastings (31 percent). And comparable proportions left other schools during the first or second year at Chicago (39 percent), Minnesota (48 percent), NYU (31 percent), Pennsylvania (25 percent), Texas (30 percent), and the University of Washington (46 percent).[218] At the University of Pennsylvania in the early 1950s, 15–20 percent of law students failed to complete the first two years, whereas only 5 percent failed to complete the entire four years of medical school.[219] In the decade 1949 to 1959, law student attrition was 36 percent at full-time ABA-approved schools, 54 percent at full-time unapproved schools, 55 percent at part-time approved schools, and 67 percent at part-time unapproved schools.[220] As admissions became more competitive in the 1950s, however, the situation began to change. Yale, which had been the first to adopt a selective admissions policy in 1926, lost only 1 percent of its students in 1947; by that time attrition at Harvard had fallen to 11 percent.[221] One study found that attrition in 43 law schools fell from 30 percent in 1956 to 14 percent in 1970.[222]

I calculated attrition as the proportion of entrants no longer enrolled two years later (three years later in part-time programs). Both the University of Wisconsin and Harvard experienced an average attrition of 38 percent in the 1920s. Harvard remained at that level until the war, although Wisconsin fell to 22 percent in the 1930s. Wisconsin then returned to its original level throughout the 1950s and 1960s, while Harvard declined to 17 percent in the early 1950s and to 6 percent after 1955, a level Wisconsin reached only in the mid-1970s (see Table 10). All full-time schools show a similar pattern: between one third and one half of the first-year class was gone by the third year between 1937 and the early 1960s, after which attrition gradually declined to less than one tenth (see Table 9).

Part-time students left law school at much higher rates because of personal or financial difficulties, lack of academic commitment or ability, or the lower rewards anticipated from a part-time degree. Only three or four out of every ten De Paul evening students stayed to their fourth year in the 1950s and 1960s, although almost seven out of ten did so in the 1970s (see Table 10). The dropout rate at all part-time schools was about half until the 1970s and now is about one third (see Table 9). Because virtually all third-year full-time students obtain their degrees (one study found only 4 percent attrition during the third year, even in the 1950s), the ratio of graduates to full-time entrants three years earlier (available only since 1970) confirms this picture (see Table 7).[223] Since two thirds of all students studied part time in the 1920s but fewer than a fifth do so today and attrition was much higher at the unapproved schools, which then enrolled more than half of all students, the aggregate attrition rate must have been close to 50 percent in the 1920s and 1930s, but today it is less than 10 percent. For those who gain admission to law school, therefore, graduation no longer is a major hurdle.

Bar Examination

Law school graduates still must be admitted to the bar of the state in which they wish to practice.[224] During the nineteenth century, when bar examinations were casual, local, and undemanding, some states automatically admitted the small number of law school graduates through the "diploma privilege." In 1860, four states recognized the diplomas of six of the twenty-one existing schools; in 1890, sixteen states conferred a diploma privilege on twenty-six of the sixty-one law schools.[225] Law schools were strong supporters because the privilege attracted students: when Columbia lost it in 1882, enrollment fell from 471 the previous year to 345 in 1885–86.[226] But the profession opposed the privilege because it surrendered control over supply to the academy and increased the flood of new entrants. The campaign against the privilege succeeded only slowly, as the chronology of abolition indicates: New York, 1892; Kentucky, 1902; Pennsylvania, 1903; Tennessee, 1903; Missouri, 1905; Michigan, 1913; California, 1917; Minnesota, 1917; Washington, 1920; Arizona, 1925; Oklahoma, 1929; Utah, 1932; Georgia, 1933; Texas, 1935; Nebraska, 1938; South Carolina, 1948; Idaho, 1949; Florida, 1951; Arkansas, 1952; South Dakota, 1957, but reestablished 1973; Alabama, 1961; Louisiana, 1965; and Iowa, 1974.[227] The number of jurisdictions that admitted lawyers through this route fell to fifteen in 1917, thirteen in 1926–27, and eleven in 1938; but because new jurisdictions granted the privilege, the total returned to fifteen in 1949. Thereafter it dropped steadily to five in 1973, the level at which it has remained (see Table 13).[228] Consequently, the proportion of new entrants who did not take a bar examination fell from about one in ten in the 1930s to about one in fifty in the 1960s, where it has stabilized (see Table 13).[229]

Nineteenth-century bar examinations were brief oral exercises, administered by the judge of a local court. The first written examinations were introduced in

New York and in some Massachusetts counties in 1870.[230] Until 1881, Wisconsin candidates could shop around for the most lenient examiner.[231] New Hampshire created the first centralized state examination board in 1878.[232] From its founding, the ABA worked hard to encourage states to adopt centrally administered written examinations. In 1881, only seven jurisdictions required candidates to write their examinations (two only in certain counties), and only one paid its examiners.[233] No one ever failed the examinations in Alabama, and standards were equally low in Tennessee, Kentucky, and Illinois.[234] In 1890, central examining boards existed in only four of the forty-nine jurisdictions; by 1917, however, the number had grown to thirty-seven.[235] Even so, the twenty-seven central examination boards contained an average of only five members in 1904, and nine states still relied on courts to examine applicants.[236] Oral examinations, which coexisted with written tests in California until 1930, lasted an average of 6 to 7 minutes.[237] In 1930–31, the median jurisdiction still had only five bar examiners, who were poorly paid and often unassisted by other readers.[238] As late as 1938, bar examiners remained unpaid in fourteen jurisdictions and received an inadequate per diem of $5 to $25 in twelve others.[239]

Although we lack comprehensive data concerning the difficulty of these examinations during the first third of the twentieth century, some trends seem clear enough. In 1901, the pass rates for both first takers and repeaters were 71 percent in New York, 57 percent in Massachusetts, and 69 percent in Ohio.[240] They rose significantly over the next few years in these states as well as in Illinois and Minnesota (see Table 15). Twenty years later, pass rates had fallen, often sharply; comparing the proportions that passed in 1904–06 and 1922–29, we find that the rate fell from 74 to 47 percent in New York, from 55 to 42 percent in Massachusetts, from 84 to 70 percent in Ohio, from 78 to 51 percent in Illinois, from 76 to 44 percent in Maryland, and from 73 to 45 percent in Connecticut (compare Tables 15 and 16). In contrast with these more urban, industrializing states, the rural, largely agricultural jurisdiction of Kansas passed all fifty-three candidates at its first bar examination in 1904 and remained almost as lenient for half a century: 93 percent passed in 1908, 97 percent in 1922, 88 percent in 1933, and 94 percent in 1948.[241]

During the 1920s, pass rates in most jurisdictions fluctuated widely from year to year, suggesting that examiners initially did not have a clear idea of what standards to impose. In New Hampshire, for instance, the pass rate varied between 38 and 73 percent during the decade, although an article revealingly entitled "New Hampshire Stops the Leaks" boasted that the aggregate pass rate for first takers was only 48 percent and the cumulative pass rate for those who persisted only 62 percent.[242] Nevertheless, some patterns began to emerge.

First, a few states were distinguished by highly stable pass rates, suggesting that their examiners had reached a decision about either minimum standards of competence or the number they were prepared to admit (range and dates are in parentheses): Connecticut (30 to 44 percent, 1923–28), Massachusetts (33 to 48 percent, 1923–27), New York (45 to 54 percent, 1923–29), and Pennsylvania (56 to 64 percent, 1925–29). Second, states tended to fall into two disparate categories. Those with generally low pass rates contained major cities; a substantial and expanding immigrant community, which contributed to rapid growth of the total population; a large legal profession; and many candidates seeking entry (the 1922–29 aggregate is in parentheses): Rhode Island (37 percent), Massachusetts (42 percent), Maryland (44 percent), Connecticut (45 percent), New York (47 percent), New Jersey (48 percent), Illinois (51 percent), Florida (51 percent), the District of Columbia (53 percent), and Pennsylvania (61 percent). Many of these jurisdictions also had highly stable rates, as we just saw, and large numbers of repeaters who persisted in trying to pass the exam. By contrast, jurisdictions on the old frontier, with small homogeneous populations in mostly rural settings, little population growth, small legal professions, and little pressure for entry had very high pass rates: Delaware (100 percent), Vermont (98 percent), Kansas (92 percent), Kentucky (88 percent), North Dakota (87 percent), Washington (85 percent), Iowa (84 percent), Nebraska (84 percent), New Mexico (84 percent), Arkansas (82 percent), North Carolina (82 percent), Wyoming (82 percent), Colorado (77 percent), West Virginia (77 percent), Montana (76 percent), Maine (72 percent), Oklahoma (71 percent), and Tennessee (70 percent).

Stronger trends emerged in the 1930s, as the profession responded to what it saw as the unhappy conjunction of rapid expansion, the entry of increasing numbers of lawyers from immigrant backgrounds, and the contraction of the economy caused by the Depression. In the year following the Crash of 1929, pass rates fell in fourteen of the thirty-six states for which figures are available and rose in only six.[243] This may have been part of a longer secular trend. One source reports a steady decline in the national aggregate pass rate from 59 percent in 1927 to 45 percent in 1934.[244] About three fourths of all states (including most of the larger ones) failed a higher proportion of examinees in 1933 than in 1927. In some jurisdictions the drop was precipitous: California (from 72 to 36 percent), Kentucky (88 to 49 percent), Mississippi (47 to 29 percent), Massachusetts (46 to 31 percent), Missouri (66 to 27 percent), Nebraska (81 to 56 percent), Ohio (86 to 72 percent), Pennsylvania (56 to 40 percent), and South Carolina (75 to 33 percent). In Tennessee, the pass rate fell from 74 percent in 1929 and 75 percent in 1930 to 47 percent in 1931 and then averaged 46 percent through 1935.[245] The distinction between difficult and easy states, noted earlier, survived the general increase in rigor. In 1936, nine jurisdictions with more than 450 examinees a year had pass rates between 38 and 51 percent, whereas most of the other rates were over 50 percent, and some were more than 75 percent.[246] It is possible, of course, that these differences over time and between states represent real differences in the knowledge of examinees, but it seems unlikely that this would have declined so dramatically in just a few years or be so much lower in the larger industrial states than in rural jurisdictions.

In California, the pass rate dropped sharply on the February 1932 examination, from an average of 53.3 percent of first takers on the three previous February examinations to 35.2, and from an average of 30.5 percent of repeaters on the three previous February examinations to 10.8. The Committee of Bar Examiners noted defensively that contemporaneous pass rates in other states were even lower (Utah 25 percent, Rhode Island 26 percent, New York 32 percent, Montana 20 percent, and Massachusetts 19 percent).[247] Nevertheless, a committee appointed by the State Bar to investigate legal education and admissions acknowledged the following:

The grading seems to have been more strict than in previous examinations, influenced perhaps by the fact that at the preceding annual meeting of the State Bar there had been a great deal of talk about overcrowding of the bar, which had produced a considerable sentiment for limitation of numbers. This undoubtedly affected the character of the questions and the attitude of the readers who marked the papers. Bar examinations cannot be thought of as machines which work with mechanical precision under all conditions. As a matter of fact, they are everywhere extremely susceptible to current opinion and are quite likely to reflect the general attitude and sentiment of the bar.[248]

The steady decline to a low of 31.6 percent on the August 1933 examination (dominated by first takers) and to 35 percent for all of 1934 prompted an (unsuccessful) lawsuit by disappointed examinees alleging that the examiners had established a quota.[249]

It is interesting to compare the pass rates of medical students, whose numbers had fallen following the Flexner Report (from 25,171 in 1900 to 21,597 in 1930), with those of law students, whose numbers had multiplied nearly fourfold over the same period (from 12,408 to 46,751) and who were more than twice as numerous as medical students by the end of it.[250] In the five years between 1935 and 1939, medical licensing boards failed only 11.5 percent of the 35,890 examinees, whereas bar examiners failed 52 percent of the 82,650 examinees.[251] One reason for the difference is that selectivity occurred at an earlier stage of the educational process in medicine. In 1932, only half of the applicants to approved medical schools were accepted (6335/12,280), but only 5.7 to 7.7 percent of the graduates of those schools failed the medical licensing board examination between 1928 and 1932.[252]

In the depths of the Depression Charles Clark, the dean of Yale Law School, candidly admitted, "Obviously the bar examiners are applying some sort of quota now as they certainly should and must."[253] Yet pass rates seemed to stop falling as other mechanisms reduced the number seeking entry (including the cumulative effect of the Depression and the rising admissions standards of law schools). The nadir, both in California and nationwide, coincided with the greatest number of examinees, and the rate began to rise as the absolute numbers fell in the second half of the 1930s.[254]

Before the Depression, even the more difficult examinations do not seem to have excluded the persistent. In New York, where pass rates on individual examinations varied between 45 and 54 percent in the 1920s, 87 percent of those first examined between 1922 and 1931 had passed by the end of 1932—96.5 percent of those first examined in 1922 and 1923.[255] In four large states with rigorous examinations, nearly all of those first examined in 1922–24 had passed by 1933: 95 percent in New York, 93 percent in Pennsylvania, 86 percent in Illinois, and 83 percent in California.[256] In Ohio, 95 percent of those first examined between June 1926 and January 1929 had gained admission by January 1932.[257] In Pennsylvania, 87 to 88 percent of those first examined in July 1928 and July 1929 had passed within three years.[258]

Yet repeaters do seem to have encountered greater difficulties in the 1930s. In California, where only 56 percent of first takers passed between 1929 and 1932, repeaters were even less successful: 29 percent passed on the second try, 23 percent on the third, 12 to 13 percent each of the fourth and fifth, and a total of only 7 percent on all subsequent tries.[259] As of February 1932, only 57 percent of those first examined in January 1929 had passed, 67 percent of those first examined in July 1929, 52 percent of those first examined in April 1930, 60 percent of those first examined in August 1930, and 44 percent of those first examined in April or August 1931.[260] Among first takers between 1930 and 1932, the proportion who passed by April 1, 1936, had fallen to 71 percent in California and 72 percent in Florida, although it was still 91 percent in Illinois, 85 percent in Pennsylvania, 96 percent in Michigan, and 89 percent in Oklahoma.[261] Nevertheless, it is significant that throughout the last half century a fairly constant one fourth to one third of those passing the California bar examination have been repeaters, and about a tenth have taken the examination three times or more (see Table 20.a).

From the low levels of the mid-1930s, bar examination pass rates climbed steadily upward. The national aggregate rose from 45 percent in 1935 to 51 percent in 1940 (data are missing for the war years) and then from 58 percent in 1947 to a peak of 76 percent in 1974, before it gradually declined to 64 percent in 1984 (see Table 17).[262] But these national averages obscure marked differences among jurisdictions, which we saw earlier. Among first takers in 1931, for instance, only 36 percent passed in California, but everyone passed in North Dakota (see Table 18). Jurisdictions typifying the extremes of ease and difficulty display striking commonalities. In the easy states, of which North Dakota is the best example, rates remained consistently high: indeed, in half of the last fifty years North Dakota has admitted every examinee. In the difficult states, pass rates rose following the trough of the Depression, particularly during the war years, when examiners seem to have relaxed standards to admit higher proportions of the much smaller cohort of examinees. They declined for a decade or more following the war as supply control was reasserted. Then they began to rise in the 1960s, accelerating in the 1970s. The persistent were also more successful. When asked in 1963 whether 90 percent of their graduates eventually passed the bar exam, sixty-one out of sixty-four full-time law schools answered affirmatively, as did twenty-four out of twenty-six day programs in mixed schools, twenty-three out of twenty-six evening programs in mixed schools, and all eight part-time schools.[263] In 1970, it was estimated that 90 percent of those who persisted in taking the examination ultimately passed.[264]

The latest trend is the fall in pass rates in the 1980s, most notably in California, New York, Michigan, New Jersey, and Pennsylvania (states with large, highly competitive bars). In 1984, there was a marked drop in thirty-two of the fifty-two jurisdictions: 7.1 percent in New York, 15.5 percent in New Jersey, 13 percent in the District of Columbia, and 7.2 percent in California (New York, New Jersey, and California have the three highest numbers of examinees).[265] Although many states have adopted the Multistate Bar Examination in part, they require different passing scores for admission; in July 1985, these varied between 143 in California and 130 in Florida.[266] These interstate variations cannot be explained entirely by differences in the quality of applicants.

There are several possible reasons for the fluctuation in pass rates since the war. First, there has been a decline in the proportion of repeaters, who do far worse than first takers. In 1929 and 1930, repeaters constituted more than 40 percent of examinees in Illinois and Connecticut, more than a third in California and Texas, and a third in Pennsylvania and the District of Columbia.[267] In the 1950s, as many as 36 percent of examinees nationwide were repeaters. That proportion fell steadily to 17 percent in 1974, however, before it rose to 22 percent in 1980–82 (see Table 17).

Second, the prelegal and legal education of examinees improved as prelegal requirements were raised and unapproved law schools closed; and the ability of examinees increased as entry to approved schools became more competitive. In the ten Pennsylvania bar examinations between 1928 and 1931, 60 percent of college graduates passed but only 53 percent of those without a degree.[268] The likelihood of passing the ten Tennessee bar examinations between 1932 and 1937 correlated strongly with the examinee's college education, number of years of law school, and law school quality.[269] In New Hampshire, the proportion of first takers passing the bar examination between 1920 and 1933 declined steadily from 83 percent of those who had graduated from both college and an ABA-approved law school to 17 percent of those who had only two years of college and graduated from an unapproved law school.[270] On the April 1930 California bar examination, the pass rate varied continuously from 73 percent of college graduates to 10 percent of high school dropouts.

Pass rates also correlated with the candidate's legal education. On the April 1930 California bar examination they ranged from none of the five who studied privately to 5 percent of those who prepared through correspondence schools, 33 percent of those who studied part time at either approved or unapproved schools, 57 percent of those who studied full time, and 83 percent of those who studied full time at ABA-approved schools.[271] (It is interesting, however, that the eventual success of California repeaters between January 1929 and February 1932 did not correlate with prelegal education, although it did vary with legal education.)[272] A study of Ohio bar examinations between 1926 and 1932 revealed a similar relationship between graduation from a full-time law school and pass rates for first takers.[273]

These correlations have remained consistently strong in California (see Tables 19 and 20.a). Between 1932 and 1948, 72.3 percent of graduates of ABA-approved law schools taking the bar for the first time passed, compared with 41.0 percent of graduates of unapproved schools; the proportion ranged from 87.9 percent of Stanford graduates to 15.6 percent of graduates of Lincoln.[274] Among first takers, the disparity between the pass rates of graduates of unapproved and ABA-approved schools was 38.5 and 69.4 percent in 1982, 36 and 65 percent in July 1986 (see Table 20.a).[275]

Yet in Massachusetts, the alumni of Suffolk Law School, an unapproved part-time Boston institution, performed very well on the bar examination during the 1920s. Indeed, when 99 percent of Suffolk graduates passed the July 1925 examination, compared with only 62 percent of Harvard graduates, the former were accused of cheating and required to retake the examination—with the result that 99 percent also passed the second time! (anticipating the recent movie *Stand and Deliver*). Nevertheless, when the bar examiners cracked down with the onset of the Depression, the Suffolk pass rate fell to 16 percent in January 1932, well below the 21 percent pass rate for all examinees.[276] When the pass rates of both day and night law school graduates increased dramatically in Ohio in the 1950s, they also converged.[277]

Although virtually all law students today are college graduates, the quality of their college records still correlates with bar passage. When UCLA Law School graduates taking the July 1984 bar examination were dichotomized into those who had entered with a predictive index above or below 1400 (a composite of under-graduate GPA and LSAT score), the pass rates of the two groups were 75 and 29 percent. The correlation with law school performance was just as strong: among UCLA graduates taking the bar examination in 1979, 1980, 1982, and 1984, 94 percent of the top two thirds of the graduating class passed the first time but only 38 percent of the bottom third; 97 percent of the top 80 percent passed within two tries but only 47 percent of the bottom 20 percent. (Interestingly, there is no statistically significant correlation between the number of "bar" courses taken in law school and the likelihood of passing the bar examination.)[278]

Several of the hypotheses suggested earlier also may explain the decline in the pass rate since 1974. First, bar examiners may be tightening entry again in reaction to the phenomenal recent growth of the profession, just as they seem to have done in the 1920s and 1930s. In California, the pass rate among nonminority law grad-uates fell from 55.1 percent in July 1983 to 48.3 percent a year later, most of which was attributable to a decline in the pass rate among repeaters.[279] In the state of Washington, the bar passage rate dropped from 70 percent in July 1984 to 47 percent the following year; on the mandatory professional responsibility portion of the examination it fell from more than 90 percent to 54 percent.[280] Second, the admission of significant numbers of minority law students disadvantaged by their primary, secondary, and tertiary schooling may have reduced the average pass rate. Although the bar examination no longer excludes a substantial proportion of non-minority graduates in most jurisdictions, it still represents a substantial barrier for many minority law graduates (see "Characteristics of Lawyers: Race," in Chap-ter 4).

Citizenship

Three other barriers confronted those who aspired to become lawyers. In 1909, the ABA urged the exclusion of noncitizens—a rule clearly directed at recent immigrants from southern and eastern Europe.[281] Although this ban may not have significantly affected the number of lawyers, it did expose the protectionist character of entry requirements that the profession sought to justify as quality control. By 1946, all forty-eight states and the District of Columbia excluded noncitizen lawyers, although only twenty-five excluded noncitizen physicians and eighteen excluded noncitizen teachers.[282] The ban persisted until the U.S. Supreme Court struck it down as unconstitutional in 1973.[283]

Residence

It was not just the nation that excluded outsiders; each state sought to do so as well by requiring a period of residence before an applicant could be admitted. This discouraged law graduates from seeking admission outside the states in which either they had studied or their parents lived. It imposed even more drastic restrictions on the mobility of established practitioners, who had to relinquish their practices for a period (often lengthy) before beginning again in a new jurisdiction (just as English barristers and solicitors had to do before transferring to the other branch). In 1879, only Texas required six months residence within the state, although California, Massachusetts, and Minnesota required an intent to reside and other states demanded residence within the particular county or circuit.[284] Like so many other entry barriers, residence requirements were raised between the 1930s and the 1960s, but by 1979 they had been relaxed significantly (see Table 14). Although a few state supreme courts had invalidated them, forty-one jurisdictions still were insisting on some residence prior to admission when the U.S. Supreme Court also declared such barriers to be unconstitutional in 1985.[285]

Although the states have complied with this decision reluctantly, at least six have responded by abrogating reciprocity for experienced attorneys from other jurisdictions, requiring them either to demonstrate residence within the state where they seek to practice or to pass that state's bar examination.[286] The U.S. Court of Appeals for the Fourth Circuit has invalidated such a rule in Virginia.[287] Ironically, federal courts impose greater barriers on interstate practice: twenty-four district courts and ten courts of appeals refuse to admit lawyers who belong to the state bar in which the court is located but maintain no office or residence there. The Fifth Circuit Court of Appeals rejected a recent attack on these rules as violating due process, but the U.S. Supreme Court invalidated them in the exercise of its inherent supervisory authority.[288]

Character Tests

The final requirement for admission to practice is the test of character and fitness. These were deliberately introduced in order to exclude immigrants and their sons.[289] During the 1920s, two thirds of the states tightened their review procedures.[290] In Pennsylvania in the 1930s, an applicant had to name three citizen sponsors and a lawyer preceptor when beginning to study law and submit to two character investigations, one at that time and another after passing the bar examination. In the eight years from 1928 to 1935, the Philadelphia Board interviewed 2217 initial applicants (rejecting 51) and 1600 applicants for final admission (rejecting 13); equally important, 97 withdrew at the earlier stage and 6 at the later; between 1936 and 1938, 11 were rejected and 11 withdrew.[291] Although only about 10 percent were excluded in this fashion, the scrutiny may have discouraged others from ever applying; it is noteworthy that the proportion of Jewish applicants dropped by 16 percent during this period, and virtually no blacks applied.[292] In addition, several suburban counties bordering Philadelphia used this power to set a quota on the number admitted to practice each year.[293]

The numbers excluded in other jurisdictions also were low. In Manhattan and Brooklyn, less than 0.5 percent were rejected in 1931 and only 48 out 11,937 applicants between 1926 and 1932 (0.4 percent); in Brooklyn between 1930 and 1948, only 53 out of 15,653 applicants were rejected (0.3 percent).[294] But the proportions were higher at the peak of concern about "overcrowding." In Brooklyn,

3.3 percent were rejected and another 4.0 percent were pending at the end of 1930–31; 2.7 percent were rejected and 5.7 percent pending at the end of the following year; and 1.5 percent were rejected and 6.1 percent pending at the end of 1932–33.[295] Critics of the California procedure acknowledged in 1933 that "It is common knowledge that anyone, no matter how dishonest or unscrupulous he may be, can supply as reference [*sic*] the names of three persons who will vouch for him."[296] In 1948, California investigated the character of only 9 out of 2764 law student registrants, 40 out of 1360 law graduates applying to take the bar examination, and 6 out of 184 out-of-state lawyers taking the attorneys' examination.[297] In 1934, only twenty states had ever rejected an applicant on the ground of character, and the national proportion remained less than 1 percent.[298]

The National Conference of Bar Examiners was founded in 1931, partly to facilitate character investigations of lawyers applying for admission to the bar of another state. In the first 1000 attorney examinations conducted between 1934 and 1939, more than 10 percent were rejected or withdrew, 51 because of bad character reports.[299] These tests may have contributed to the decline in interstate transfers from 618 in 1937 to 471 in 1939.[300] Character tests were also used to exclude political dissidents. For the 45 years between its founding and 1976, the National Conference exchanged information with the FBI, which also provided data to the District of Columbia Bar Association and the Association of the Bar of the City of New York.[301]

Character tests are even less important today than they were in the 1930s. In a 1981–82 survey, 38 jurisdictions reported that a total of 6.5 percent of candidates were investigated and 1.6 percent summoned to a hearing. However, 41 percent of the forty-one jurisdictions responding excluded no one, and the most stringent state excluded only 2 percent. Only 0.2 percent of all applicants were excluded in those forty-one jurisdictions, a proportion that seems to have been relatively constant over the last twenty-five years.[302] Florida presently has one of the more energetic screening programs. In 1983–84, its twenty-four full-time employees, operating with a budget of $1.3 million, scrutinized 2600 applications; a board of unpaid lawyers and laypersons conducted 134 investigative hearings; the process typically rejects 22 to 25 people each year (less than 1 percent).[303] Law schools also engage in some superficial screening but exclude virtually no one for poor character. Both law schools and state bars seem to be interested primarily in prior criminal convictions.[304]

In recent years there have been numerous challenges to both individual exclusions and the investigative process.[305] Nevertheless, political dissidents still encounter considerable hostility. Bernardine Dohrn, a prominent member of the Weather Underground in the 1970s, recently sought admission to the New York bar. She was rejected, despite the fact that she was working in the New York office of a large corporate Chicago law firm and was described by her lawyer as "conservative and not perceptibly different from anybody in her age group with her responsibilities. She's raising children and being a wife . . . she's a consumer."[306] Similarly, the Oregon Supreme Court rejected the 1987 application of David Fine, who had served three years in prison for a bombing seventeen years earlier in which a man was killed. Although Fine testified that the bombing was "totally wrong, morally, politically and every other way," the court found that he continued to misstate the facts concerning his decision to join the conspiracy and the warning time he had given the police after triggering the bomb.[307]

The Trajectory of Entry Control

American lawyers have been extraordinarily successful in constructing and raising entry barriers during the last century and a half. This achievement is particularly remarkable in view of the scanty resources with which they began, especially when compared with their counterparts in both the common law and civil law worlds. Traditions inherited from England and elaborated during the colonial period were sharply disrupted by the Revolution. Any influence enjoyed by the surviving professional elite was undermined by the Jacksonian attack on privilege. There were no strong collegial associations. Universities played hardly any role in training or qualifying lawyers. Although the judiciary controlled entry to practice, authority was dispersed throughout the states and even among local courts within each. Where apprenticeship was required it was not policed. It is not surprising, therefore, that in many jurisdictions during the mid-nineteenth century virtually any white male could become a lawyer.

During the last quarter of the nineteenth century, legal elites established municipal and national associations to enhance the social standing of the profession. One of their early efforts was to formalize bar examinations. A significant, if unintended, by-product was the displacement of apprenticeship by academic education, which excused some law graduates from taking the examination (through the diploma privilege) and helped the others to pass it. But though graduation from a university law faculty may have raised the status of a small elite, the rapid proliferation of independent (often proprietary) part-time law schools greatly increased the numbers entering the profession and the diversity of their backgrounds.

Throughout the first half of the twentieth century, much of the profession's collective energy was devoted to constructing entry barriers that would control both the number of lawyers and their characteristics. For this purpose, it was necessary to strengthen state bar associations, since only the states possessed the power to regulate lawyers. Frustrated by lawyer reluctance to join voluntary associations, many states created unified bars with compulsory membership. National, state, and local organizations then pursued the professional project by demanding more prelegal education, limiting access to legal education, encouraging more rigorous bar examinations, excluding noncitizens and nonresidents, and imposing character tests.

Although some elite law schools, led by the Association of American Law Schools, required applicants to complete high school and college, many others feared the loss of enrollment to less demanding schools. Only in the 1930s did state bars adopt such requirements. For thirty years this significantly restricted entry into the profession. Since the expansion of public higher education in the 1960s, prelegal educational prerequisites no longer limit the number of lawyers, although they remain a barrier for racial minorities, because of their underrepresentation among college graduates.

The shift from apprenticeship to academic education, which began about 1880

and was complete by 1920, had the unanticipated consequence of greatly accelerating the growth of the profession and facilitating entry by immigrants and their
sons. The American Bar Association responded by promulgating standards that
only some law schools could meet and seeking to persuade states to restrict entry
to graduates of approved schools. This campaign, aided by the effects of the Depression and World War II, led to the demise of most unapproved schools by the 1950s
(except in California). Part-time legal education virtually disappeared with them.
The remaining full-time approved schools raised tuition significantly faster than
the rate of inflation, while the financial burden on students was aggravated by the
difficulty of working while studying and the scarcity of grants and loans. Competition to enter law school greatly intensified, although attrition among matriculates
declined. Yet the profession never exercised complete control over the number of
law students. New schools have attained ABA approval since the 1960s, and existing
schools have expanded. Although the federal government never supported legal
education the way it subsidized medical and dental schools, financial aid has allowed
greater numbers of students with more diverse backgrounds to obtain law degrees.
Nevertheless, competition to enter law school, attrition within it, and indebtedness
upon graduation all affect the size of the profession as well as its class and racial
composition.

The bar examination did not become a significant entry barrier until half a
century after it was introduced. Only gradually did states substitute central examining boards for local judges and a lengthy written examination for a perfunctory
oral interview, fail a substantial proportion of examinees, and eliminate the diploma
privilege. The rigor of the examination has varied with lawyer interest in controlling
numbers. Rural agricultural states with small homogeneous bars and slow growth
rates pass a much higher proportion of examinees than urban industrial states with
large heterogeneous bars and rapid growth rates. Historical fluctuations also reflect
the intensity of professional concern to control numbers—a goal the more candid
examiners occasionally admit. Thus, pass rates plummeted as the Depression deep-
ened, then rose steadily (with a dramatic increase during World War II) until the
mid-1970s, and have turned down sharply since then. Yet just as the profession
cannot fully control legal education, so it cannot fully control the numbers passing
the bar examination: as the prelegal and legal education of examinees improved,
so did their ability to pass the examination. But though the persistent always have
had a good chance of ultimate success, the examination continues to limit the
number of minority law graduates who enter the profession.

The profession was even more explicit about its objectives in requiring citizenship, residence, and "good character." The first and last requirements were
intended to restrict entry by immigrants and political radicals (as well as those who
posed a threat to clients). Many more states required citizenship of lawyers than
of physicians or school teachers, although the accident of birth seems equally
relevant (or irrelevant) to all three occupations. And although states excluded only
a few applicants on the ground of "character," the discretion lodged in examining
boards undoubtedly discouraged others from applying. The residence requirement
was an even more transparent attempt by lawyers in one state to protect their
market from out-of-state competitors. All three barriers were erected and strengthened during the first half of this century; all three have been attacked as uncon-

stitutional and struck down or severely restrained by decisions of the U.S. Supreme Court in the last two decades.

The trajectory of entry control during the last century and a half, therefore, is a success story that simultaneously reveals the inherent limitations of the professional project. National and state associations have persuaded government to require lengthy prelegal and legal education, restrict the number of institutions in which lawyers could be trained, and increase the difficulty of the bar examination. Yet the subsequent expansion of public higher education has increased the number and diversity of those who could surmount each of these obstacles. And neither ascriptive barriers nor patently anticompetitive practices could withstand contemporary judicial scrutiny.

4

The Consequences
of Controlling Entry

The Number of Lawyers

We can trace the effect of these institutional changes on the size of the profession in several ways. The longest times-series data record law school enrollments (which, of course, are not identical to rates of entry to the profession). The number of students increased most rapidly—almost tenfold—between 1890 and 1930, when academic legal education was displacing apprenticeship, new law schools were opening, and existing schools were expanding (see Table 21). After this growth peaked in 1927, enrollment declined somewhat erratically through the 1930s, dropped dramatically during World War II, and was swollen only briefly by the postwar surge of veterans before it returned to the level of the 1930s, where it remained throughout the 1950s.

If we compare average enrollment during the 1930s (37,379) with average enrollment during the war years, 1941–45 (11,303), we find a shortfall of 130,378 student years. If we compare the 1930s with the six above-average postwar years, we find an excess of only 22,621 student years. This suggests that the war caused the loss of 107,757 student years, equivalent to the education of about 35,000 law students (at three years of study per student)—about a fifth of the practicing profession. Enrollment was quite stable for the rest of the 1950s, averaging 41,615. This was only 11 percent higher than it had been during the 1930s, even though the legal profession itself was almost 50 percent larger (requiring more entrants just to replace departures) and the economy was enjoying the greatest boom in modern history rather than suffering from the greatest depression.

Sustained professional growth recommenced only in the 1960s. Between 1961 and 1973 enrollments grew 155 percent, an annualized rate of 12.9 percent; from 1973 to 1976 they grew at an annualized rate of 3.0 percent; from 1976 to 1982, enrollments at ABA-approved schools hardly grew at all (an annualized rate of

1.5 percent); and since 1982 enrollment at ABA-approved schools has actually declined.

These figures are consistent with the hypotheses offered earlier. Supply control was gradually tightened during the 1920s and 1930s. This prevented enrollments from growing during the postwar economic boom of the 1950s. In the 1960s, the university law school became the vehicle for rapid expansion, which lost its momentum in the 1980s. At the same time, it is essential to anticipate an important qualification: recent growth has been concentrated at the less elite schools, while supply control has been maintained within elite institutions. Between 1972 and 1981, enrollment at the 20 schools Gourman ranked first grew by only 7.1 percent, compared with an increase of 25.2 percent for all ABA-approved schools.[1]

Although bar admission statistics lack the same historical depth, they provide a better index of professional expansion and contraction, since they are not distorted by the shift from apprenticeship to formal education, attrition during law school, or failure to pass the bar examination. In the first three decades of this century admissions rose at an annualized rate of 10.3 percent, growing nearly fourfold between 1900 and 1928 (see Table 21). This reveals that much of the growth in law school enrollment represented an increase in the absolute number aspiring to become lawyers. Until 1945 new bar admissions then declined in every year but one, at an annualized rate of 5.2 percent, falling to less than a fifth of the 1928 peak. The fact that this pattern is steadier and stronger than the decline in law school enrollment suggests that the bar exam was a significant additional entry barrier during this period.

During the six years when the war significantly affected entry (1942–47), 25,345 fewer lawyers were admitted than had been admitted during the six prewar years (1936–41); whereas admissions during the six postwar years (1948–53) produced an excess of only 23,800, a net shortfall of 1500 lawyers in addition to those lawyers killed or disabled during the war. The fact that this figure is much lower than my estimate of the loss in student enrollment suggests that law schools were failing fewer students and may have graduated some in less than three years.

The next decade (1954–63) was a period of stasis: admissions remained virtually constant, averaging less than 1 percent above the 1930s level. But the growth of law schools quickly produced an influx of new lawyers—increasing admissions 296 percent between 1963 and 1979, at an annualized rate of 18.5 percent. Thereafter growth declined to less than 1 percent a year, and between 1983 and 1984 admissions actually fell an astonishing 21.5 percent.

Law school enrollment and bar admissions both measure entry rather than the number of lawyers. We know little about departures from practice because most American jurisdictions (unlike England) do not require practitioners to take out annual certificates. A study of obituaries of the "elite" 20 to 30 percent of Chicago practitioners who belonged to the Chicago Bar Association in the nineteenth century revealed that only a third spent their entire professional lives as lawyers; but the proportion who did so increased steadily from 11 percent of the cohort entering practice between 1831 and 1850 to 41 percent of the cohort entering in the 1890s.[2] A study of 1065 lawyers admitted to the New York bar in 1925 found that 165, or 15 percent, had left practice by 1930.[3] By contrast, a 1934 survey of New York County lawyers showed that only 113 out of 4960 respondents had given up practice, half since the onset of the Depression five years earlier (but it is likely that a higher proportion of the 70 percent who failed to respond had left practice).[4] A California study found that 45 out of 320 lawyers admitted in 1931 never practiced, which is consistent with the first New York study.[5] In all three investigations, the number of departures may have been augmented by the Depression; those who persevere to the point of gaining admission usually remain in the profession throughout their lifetimes. In the 1970s, lawyers had the lowest rate of attrition of any profession, retaining more than 60 percent of their entrants until death or retirement.[6]

We lack empirical data about retirements and deaths. If we assume that both the retirement age and the life expectancy of lawyers have remained fairly constant during this century, departures would be primarily a function of the size of the cohort that entered some 40 years earlier. This would produce more departures in the late 1960s, reflecting the spurt of entrants in the late 1920s, but fewer in the early 1980s, reflecting the dramatically lower rate of production during World War II. Since both trends run counter to contemporaneous changes in the rate of entry, they should dampen recent fluctuations in the size of the profession. And the more numerous departures to be expected in the twenty-first century (reflecting the higher entry rates after 1960) should slow the growth rate of the profession.

We can observe the net effect of entry and departure on the growth of the profession since 1850 (see Table 22). The figures through 1950 are taken from the census; since then the American Bar Foundation has based its calculations on the Martindale Hubbell directory. The one attempt to check census data against an actual enumeration of lawyers practicing in Wisconsin found, surprisingly, that the census systematically underestimated the number of practitioners: by 10 percent in 1880, 20 percent in 1910, 13 percent in 1920, and 16 percent in 1930.[7] These estimates of the size of the profession are basically consistent with the preceding analysis, with some noteworthy differences. The legal profession grew rapidly in the last three decades of the nineteenth century, even before law schools began to expand, and then much more slowly in the next two decades, despite the significant increase in the number and size of law schools. The impact of law school expansion is visible in the 1920s, however; and the very much lower rates of growth in the 1930s and 1940s reflect the decline in production associated with tightened supply control, the Depression, and the war. The postwar catch-up can be seen in the high growth rate from 1950 to 1963, but then there is a brief lull before the recent explosion, which produced the highest decennial increase ever recorded—53 percent in the 1970s. Since 1980 the rate of growth has declined every year, although it still remains high. A striking aspect of this pattern is the fact that the ratio of population to lawyers was exactly the same in 1950 as it had been in 1900, despite a half century of dramatic social, political, and economic change.[8]

It is interesting to compare the growth of other professions during the last 130 years. Lawyers, physicians and surgeons, clergymen, and the general population grew at roughly the same rates until 1910, when lawyers fell behind, to be joined by physicians in 1920 as a result of the Flexner Report. The unprecedented growth of lawyers during the 1920s, therefore, may be partly a response to slow growth in the first two decades of the century, a reflection of the gradual transition from apprenticeship to law school and the interruption of World War I. The number of lawyers grew almost twice as fast as the general population during the 1920s, but the number of physicians grew at less than half that pace—confirmation that the Flexner Report had significantly advanced their professional project. During the next three decades, the legal and medical professions expanded at about the same rate as the population. During the 1960s, however, lawyers increased twice as fast as the population (while physicians increased only 1.5 times as fast); and during the 1970s lawyers increased eight times as fast as the population (while physicians increased less than five times as fast). One reason for the slower growth rate of physicians is the much faster growth of subordinate health occupations (such as nursing), which multiplied more than fourfold between 1930 and 1980 while physicians increased only 2.7 times. Finally, it is useful to compare the increase of occupations that have never achieved professional supply control, such as social workers and engineers. The former increased fourteen times between 1930 and 1980 and the latter five times (see Table 23).

Influences on the Production of Lawyers

In presenting the data on the production of lawyers and the number of practitioners, I have suggested several explanations for the fluctuations observed. One, obviously, is the availability of people who want to become lawyers. Wars significantly reduce supply. The Civil War had a catastrophic effect on law schools in the South but hardly any on those in the North: the law schools of the Universities of Georgia and Mississippi closed, and that of Virginia almost did; at Columbia, Harvard, Michigan, Pennsylvania, and Yale, however, enrollment showed only slight temporary declines between 1860 and 1865.[9] Indeed, the southern schools, which altogether lost 30 percent of their enrollment between 1859–60 and 1869–70, never recovered; student numbers fell another 15 percent during the 1870s.[10]

Although aggregate law school enrollment increased slightly between 1915–16 and 1919–20 (see Table 21), that figure conceals a decline of 40 percent between the fall of 1916 and the fall of 1917.[11] Ten schools with a combined average enrollment of 2506 students in the years 1915, 1916, and 1917 had only 696 students in June 1918, a drop of 72 percent.[12] One study reported that 53 out of 56 law schools suffered a 60 percent loss of aggregate enrollment between the fall of 1916 and the fall of 1918.[13] In the first year of America's participation in the war, 102 law schools reported an enrollment loss of between 32 and 35 percent; in the first two years, 94 schools lost 69 percent of their students. Because these figures omit schools that closed (some 25 to 30), the overall effect was probably a drop of 40 percent in the first year and 75 percent over two years. It is interesting that the loss was greater in day schools than in mixed or night schools (79.5, 61.7, and 58.5 percent over two years, respectively) and in elite schools than in others—perhaps foreshadowing the explosion of part-time legal education during the 1920s. (Conscription did not begin until the summer of 1917, and men between 18 and 21 were not included for another year.) In two years, enrollment fell from 857 to 66 at Harvard, from 207 to 11 at Pennsylvania, and from 2430 to 291 at the seven schools with the highest admission standards.[14]

As a result of World War II, enrollment dropped from 35,755 in 1938 (the last prewar year for which there are reliable figures) to 6428 in 1943, a decline of

82 percent; the decline was even greater at unapproved than at approved law schools (89 versus 80 percent) (see Table 21). Although there are no figures for the number of lawyers who served in the armed forces during the war, one source reported that 20,000 veterans returned to practice in 1945–46 and (inconsistently) that 31 percent of all the lawyers in practice in 1947 were veterans (or more than 50,000); indeed, it claimed that two thirds of lawyers under thirty-five years old in 1947 had served.[15] Yet the war also increased supply, because the G.I. bill paid for the education of many who would not have been able to afford college or law school.[16] Furthermore, some jurisdictions relaxed entry requirements. New York waived the bar examination for students whose legal studies were interrupted after they had completed at least two years and who graduated from an ABA-approved law school.[17] Similarly, the Korean War may explain part of the decline in law school enrollments in 1950–53 (amplified by the end of the catch-up following World War II); and the Vietnam War probably contributed to slowing law school expansion from 1966–69 (although the prospect of a deferment may have attracted some to law school who otherwise would not have attended).

Changes in birth rates also affect supply: between 1984 and 1993, the number of college graduates is expected to decline 7 percent, and the proportion majoring in the humanities and social sciences (the traditional feeder subjects for law schools) to decline much more rapidly.[18]

Although sudden and dramatic changes in availability obviously affect the production of lawyers, there is no simple relationship between the size of the population and the legal profession.[19] If we think of population as both the supply of those who want to be lawyers and one influence on the demand for legal services, we might expect a fairly constant ratio of population to lawyers. In actuality, that ratio declined steadily and sharply from 1870 to 1900, increased almost as sharply for the next twenty years, declined again in the 1920s, changed little in the 1930s or 1940s, resumed a gradual decline in the 1950s and 1960s, and then dropped at an unprecedented rate in the 1970s, which it continues to do in the 1980s (see Table 22).[20] I can see no pattern in this ratio until 1920 (before which date figures also are suspect; for one thing, paraprofessionals are included in the earlier years but not in the later). Thereafter, the figures are consistent with a loss of supply control in the 1920s, as part-time education expanded, the gradual assertion of supply control in the 1930s and 1940s, which moderated the growth of the profession in the 1950s and 1960s, and finally a flood of entrants in the 1970s.

Although we may be able to offer a plausible interpretation for gross historical variations in the ratio of population to lawyers, the substantial geographic differences in this statistic cast some doubt on its social significance. First, it changes at different rates in different regions.[21] Second, it diverges greatly across regions at any point in time. In the early 1970s, there were 47 people per lawyer in the District of Columbia and 1095 in North Carolina; 140 in New York City and 604 in Jacksonville, Florida; 130 in Miami and 846 in El Paso, Texas (though both cities had 250,000 to 500,000 people); 124 in Albany and 2849 in Garden Grove, California (though both cities had 100,000 to 250,000 people); 109 in San Francisco and 2425 in San Benito (both California counties).[22] Metropolitan areas have consistently lower ratios than suburbs.[23] In 1930, the 93 American cities with more than 100,000 inhabitants contained 29 percent of the population but 48 percent of the legal profession; communities with fewer than 25,000 people contained 60 percent of the population but only 38 percent of the profession.[24] In 1947, one third of all lawyers in the larger states practiced in cities with more than 500,000 people.[25] In California in 1960, 54 percent of the legal profession was concentrated in cities with more than 50,000 people, while only 7 percent worked in cities with fewer than 25,000.[26] (Yet surveys by the American Bar Foundation found that lawyers were consistently underrepresented in cities over 500,000 and overrepresented in communities under 200,000 between 1951 and 1970, see Table 31.) One reason for this distribution may be the strong correlation between lawyer income and city size, in turn a reflection of the relationship between firm size and city size.[27]

Many other factors clearly influence both the desire of people to become lawyers and the demand for legal services that a given population generates. Much of the expansion of the legal profession during the first three decades of this century is attributable to the efforts of recent immigrants, and even more their sons, to attain professional status. Jerome Carlin's interviews with Chicago sole practitioners in 1957 are poignant testimony to the fact that law simply offered the easiest route to professional status:

> Among Jewish people professions are very important. And with my parents, they had little or no education, their children should have professions....
> I was thinking of medicine, dentistry, or even pharmacy.... I didn't get into medical school or dental school. Law was my third choice....
> I considered engineering, but funds were not available for engineering....
> I wanted to be a chemical engineer but my college professors said it was no place for a Jew.[28]

I discuss the ethnic backgrounds of lawyers further below (in the section on "Characteristics of Lawyers: Ethnicity"). Here I want to examine where the new lawyers practiced. Although the population of the 67 largest American cities grew only 20 percent between 1920 and 1930, the legal profession in those cities grew by 41 percent (while growing by only 25 percent in the rest of the country). Consequently, the proportion of the profession practicing in those cities rose from 35 to 42 percent. The major centers of immigrant settlement displayed even greater disparities between the rates of professional growth and population expansion in the 1920s: Newark (75 versus 7 percent), Jersey City (60 versus 6 percent), Boston (35 versus 4 percent), Philadelphia (21 versus 7 percent), the District of Columbia (43 versus 12 percent), Chicago (41 versus 25 percent), and New York (59 versus 23 percent).[29] In states with large immigrant populations, new admissions to the bar increased even more rapidly between 1920 and 1928 than the high national average of 78 percent: 209 percent in New York, 103 percent in New Jersey, 99 percent in Massachusetts, 117 percent in California, and 102 percent in Connecticut. In sharp contrast, bar admissions actually declined during the same period in some states without immigrant populations: 39 percent in Alabama, 48 percent in Arizona, and 37 percent in Idaho.[30]

The second major push by previously excluded groups occurred during the last two decades. Even after legal barriers had been eliminated, cultural norms discouraged women from pursuing careers, particularly as lawyers, and minorities continued to suffer social, economic, and educational discrimination. Both began entering the legal profession in significant numbers, another topic I return to later (in the sections on "Characteristics of Lawyers: Gender, Race"). In all three instances when previously excluded groups gained access to the profession, the availability of education was critical: the spread of free secondary schooling around the turn of the century, the explosion of part-time law schools with undemanding admissions requirements and low academic standards in the 1920s, the expansion of publicly subsidized undergraduate education in the 1960s, and the development of affirmative action programs for racial minorities in the 1970s. The magnitude of these changes can hardly be exaggerated. Between 1960 and 1980, for instance, college enrollment rose from 2.215 million to 7.226 million, the number of bachelor's degrees conferred annually rose from 395,000 to 999,000, the total number of college graduates rose from 7.6 million to 22.2 million, and the proportion of the population over twenty-five years old that had completed college rose from 7.7 to 17 percent.[31]

Law may become not only more accessible to new groups but also more attractive compared with other occupations. Obviously, anticipated economic rewards affect this judgment. One plausible explanation for the surge of interest in the legal profession in the last two decades is the dramatic rise in lawyer incomes. (I discuss the income of lawyers relative to those of other professions in Chapter 8.) One economist maintains that "by themselves, salaries in law and possible alternatives . . . account for over half of the variation in first-year [law school] enrollments."[32] That rise in lawyer income, in turn, was partly attributable to the excess of demand for legal services over the supply of lawyers, caused by the tightening of entry control during the 1930s and 1940s and its persistence during the postwar economic boom. If this interpretation is correct, then supply control will always be ephemeral within any relatively free economy. Although market correction may take years or even decades and introduce new imbalances, supply and demand do respond to each other.[33]

If supply has increased responsively during the last two decades, demand has continued to grow. The production of all services has been expanding more rapidly than the production of goods: 4.0 versus 2.8 percent compound annual growth between 1960 and 1984, 3.6 versus 2.4 percent between 1980 and 1984. And legal services have been growing faster yet: by 4.6 and 6.4 percent during those two periods.[34] Between 1972 and 1982, the gross annual receipts of law firms increased from under $10 billion to $34 billion (240 percent), while the consumer price index increased 130 percent and the index for all services increased 149 percent.[35]

Another explanation for the growth of the legal profession emphasizes idealism rather than materialism. During the 1960s, law came to be seen by many college students as a central mechanism for promoting social change (while still offering activists the perquisites of status, power, and comfort).[36] The production of Ph.D.s and M.S.s increased 300 percent between 1950 and 1970, while the production of law graduates rose only 25 percent; by contrast, first-year law student enrollment increased 44 percent between 1968 and 1971, while the number of B.A.s rose only 27 percent and graduate student enrollment grew only 15 percent.[37]

From both perspectives, law has recently lost some of its glamour. It is no longer in the forefront of social movements, which simultaneously have lost vigor and attract less student interest. Legal education may not offer the highest rate of return on the student's very substantial investment of time, effort, and money. This may explain why law school applications declined steadily from 1982 to 1987, a total of more than 20 percent, even though the number of undergraduate degrees awarded has continued to increase.[38] Indeed, law schools have begun to engage in direct mail advertising, open houses, and cooperative fairs to entice college grad uates.[39] This campaign may be bearing fruit: the number taking the LSAT was up 15.6 percent in June 1987 from a year earlier and up 27.9 percent in October 1987 from the previous year; the number completing Law School Data Assembly Service applications was up 12.3 percent in 1986–87 compared with 1985–86. In February 1988 the number of law school applicants again increased by 18 percent over the previous year.[40]

This cyclic fluctuation is not limited to law: other professions are also seeing potential recruits turn to careers that offer more immediate rewards. Medical school applicants fell 17 percent between 1975 and 1984—11 percent in the four years 1981–85—with the result that the ratio of applicants to places declined from 2.9 to 2.1.[41] Medical school enrollment, which increased 110 percent between 1963 and 1983, actually fell almost 2 percent the next year.[42] The reasons are not hard to find: although physicians enjoy extraordinary incomes, 89 percent of medical students graduate in debt—an average of $29,000 on top of the debts they incurred in college. Applications to schools of veterinary medicine fell 24.5 percent between 1980 and 1984; even enrollment declined in the fall of 1984 after decades of steady growth. In dentistry the drop in applications has been even more extreme—50 percent since the mid-1970s—with the result that the ratio of applicants to places fell from 2.7 in 1975 to 1.3 today; and enrollment itself has declined since 1980.[43]

Demand for legal services fluctuates independently of supply. (I discuss the ways in which lawyers have sought to stimulate such demand in Chapter 6.) Although population may affect demand as well as supply, most legal services are consumed by business enterprises, not individuals.[44] We have already seen that the Depression coincided with a decline in the production of lawyers. This was partly because aspirants could not afford the costs of qualifying. But the decline may also have been a response to the drastic contraction in the demand for lawyers' services. U.S. Department of Commerce statistics for the number of lawyers in private practice (the category most sensitive to fluctuations in the economy) show little growth during the decade following the Depression and a significant decline (to pre-1930 levels) during the war (see Table 24).[45]

The Depression affected the income of all professionals (another index of demand): between 1929 and 1932, the per capita income of lawyers declined 39.9 percent, while that of physicians fell 38.8 percent and that of engineers 38.4 percent.[46] During the same years, two thirds of Wisconsin lawyers suffered a loss of income—half of them losing more than 35 percent.[47] A 1932 survey of 1200 of the 1466 lawyers admitted to California between 1929 and 1931 revealed that 51 percent did not make enough to support themselves in the first year of practice, 37 percent failed to do so in the second year, and 33 percent still did not break even in the third year; their average net income was $978 in the first year of practice, $1602 in the second, and $2078 in the third. A 1937 survey of 336 of the 535 lawyers admitted to California in 1931 found that they had a median net income of $1250 in 1932, their second year of practice.[48] A survey of lawyers admitted to California in 1932 found that 12.6 percent earned none of their living expenses from law that year, 13 percent earned only a fourth, and 17.5 percent earned half; fewer than half lived entirely on what they earned from law. Four years later, a fifth of that cohort still earned less than half their living expenses from their law practice.[49] A survey of New York City lawyers found that their median income dropped from $4535 between 1928 and 1932 to $2990 in 1933.[50] In 1935, 1500 lawyers enrolled in a legal relief project established by the federal Works Progress Administration.[51] Altogether, there is ample evidence that depressed demand following 1929 may have affected the number aspiring to become lawyers.

It is harder to demonstrate the effect of income on entry at other periods. It may be significant, however, that in 1950, a period of slow professional expansion, the starting salaries of employed lawyers were quite low—$20 to $75 a week (as little as $5 for those who had not yet passed the bar examination). Between 1960 and 1967, when growth remained sluggish, the salaries of young attorneys increased more slowly than those of all male professionals. By contrast, the salaries of young attorneys grew much faster than those of all male professionals (21 versus 5 percent) between 1967 and 1969, when the production of lawyers began to increase rapidly.[52] It cannot be coincidental that starting salaries offered by large law firms skyrocketed from about $7000 in the mid-1960s to more than $70,000 twenty years later, during the period when law school enrollment was expanding more rapidly than it had in half a century.

A number of investigators have explored correlations between the level of business activity and demand for legal services. Cross-sectional synchronic studies using interstate comparisons have produced mixed results. An early effort found no connection between per capita wealth and the population:lawyer ratio.[53] But a 1948 comparison did establish a correlation between the size of the legal profession and measures of wholesale transactions, manufacturing and service establishments, corporations, and sales of goods and services.[54] Studies using 1950 and 1952 data also discovered correlations between both individual and corporate income and the number of lawyers.[55] And a contemporary study identified particular economic sectors that generate disproportionately high demand for legal services: advertising, management and consulting services, public administration, transportation, personal services, and finance.[56]

Longitudinal analyses generally confirm these relationships. A historical study of Wisconsin between 1880 and 1933 found a correlation between 18 out of 20 economic indices and measures of legal work, both in Milwaukee and in rural counties, although the economy consistently grew faster than the legal profession.[57] The experience in California between 1910 and 1930 was consistent.[58] Another historical study found a strong relationship between demand for legal services (measured by the number of lawyers) and the real gross national product.[59] The fact that the recent rapid expansion of the profession has coincided with an even more rapid increase in the aggregate income of lawyers— from $6 billion in 1967 to $11 billion in 1972, $19 billion in 1977, and more than $34 billion in 1982—further supports the notion that the supply of legal services responds to demand (these figures are not adjusted for inflation; see Table 40).[60] Yet all of these analyses are flawed by the use of aggregate measures of both supply and demand: lawyers do many different things, and a social, economic or political variable that might explain the demand for criminal defense would not explain the demand for representation in divorce, for drafting corporate reorganizations, or for tax advice.

The Characteristics of Lawyers

Age

Control over the supply of lawyers affects not only the size of the profession but also its composition. Some of these effects are unintentional: fluctuations in the degree of supply control and the consequent rate of entry shape the age structure of the profession. Until the late 1920s, the number of bar admissions increased every year, with the result that the profession grew constantly younger. Because less-experienced lawyers were most threatened by competition from new entrants, especially during a period of economic contraction, it seems likely that they were vociferous and powerful supporters of supply control. The cohort admitted in the 1920s became dominant in the 1950s and early 1960s, by virtue of not only their age (law is a strongly gerontocratic profession, perhaps because legal knowledge changes so slowly) but also their numbers (later cohorts were considerably smaller). This may help explain the intense conservatism displayed by the profession in the early postwar era. The small size of the younger cohort (partly attributable to the war) also made them the beneficiaries of supply control and thus quite content with the status quo.

The rapid expansion of the profession since the mid-1960s has inverted the age pyramid once again. The small cohort admitted between the late 1930s and late 1940s enjoys the status, wealth, and power that accompany age in most professions, certainly in law (where earnings peak between the ages of fifty and fifty-nine).[61] But it must defend those privileges against a large younger cohort experiencing more intense competition. Because the number of lawyers admitted since 1970 already exceeds the number in practice at that time, both the average age and the average experience of the legal profession are the lowest they have been in many years (see Tables 21 and 22).[62]

Empirical studies confirm these inferences. Although the age categories used by successive surveys are rarely identical, it is clear that the profession aged progressively from 1930 to at least 1960 (see Table 25). Lawyers with ten years or less of experience represented 59 percent of the New York County bar in 1934 but 51 percent of the California bar in 1960. Almost a third of American lawyers (32.4 percent) were under thirty-five years of age in 1930, but little more than a fifth (21.2 percent) were this young in 1954. Lawyers under forty-five constituted 61.8 percent of the New York State bar in 1930; only 42.8 percent of the American profession were under forty-five in 1948; but lawyers under forty-five had again become 59.5 percent of the profession in 1980 (see Table 25). In Illinois, the median age fell from 43 in 1975 to 36 in 1982 and the median years of experience from

15.5 to 8.5; the proportion of lawyers with less than ten years of experience rose from a third to 56 percent.[63] The median age of all American lawyers rose from forty-four in 1947 to forty-six in 1954 and 1960, but by 1980 it had fallen again to thirty-nine.[64] The proportion of American lawyers under thirty-six rose from 24 percent in 1960 to 39 percent in 1980. In 1980, half of all lawyers had less than thirteen years of experience, and 42 percent had less than ten. The age profile was even more skewed for women lawyers: their median age in 1980 was thirty-two (compared with forty for men), and 77 percent had less than ten years of experience (compared with 39 percent of men).[65] It seems unlikely that the profession has been so young since 1910, when 60 percent of lawyers were under forty-five as a result of rapid growth within the major cities and less demanding entry requirements.[66]

Obviously, this age profile has begun to change once again, as the number of entrants has stabilized and actually declined. Indeed, the profession may age more rapidly than it gains experience, because entrants themselves are older. A study of 261 students at George Washington University Law School in 1913–14 found 16 percent under the age of twenty-one, 45 percent between twenty-one and twenty-four, 27 percent between twenty-five and twenty-nine, and 11 percent older.[67] By contrast, among male *applicants* to law school in 1984 (who should, on average, be two years younger), only 8 percent were younger than twenty-three, 48 percent were between twenty-three and twenty-five, 24 percent between twenty-six and thirty, and 19 percent over thirty; a higher proportion of women were both under twenty-three and over thirty.[68] This reflects not only the postponement of graduate education and the increasing number of entrants for whom law is a second career but also the aging of the undergraduate population.[69]

This age profile is significant for several reasons. First, it can affect the profession's political orientation toward both internal affairs and the outside world. When (as presently is the case) a small older cohort dominates professional associations that deeply influence the lives of a much larger younger cohort, with very different backgrounds, attitudes, and working lives, considerable intergenerational conflict is likely. This will be aggravated when women and racial minorities are found almost exclusively in the younger cohort because of earlier discrimination. The growth of alternative professional organizations during the 1960s reflects these tensions.[70]

Second, cohorts may differ in their professional aspirations. Although lawyers admitted since 1970 constituted only 42.3 percent of the profession in 1984 and just 38 percent of lawyers employed by private enterprises, they represented 52.9 percent of lawyers in federal government, 63.4 percent of lawyers in state and local government, 58.4 percent of lawyers representing private associations, and a striking 81.9 percent of lawyers in legal aid and public defender offices. These differences suggest that the post-1970 cohort is more strongly oriented toward public interest work, although it will be necessary in the future to disentangle cohort differences from the effects of maturation. Within private practice (where younger and older cohorts are proportionally represented), post-1970 entrants are overrepresented in the larger firms, especially those with more than twenty lawyers.[71] These choices may indicate the areas of most rapid growth within the profession (see Chapter 10).

Ethnicity

Professional associations did not intend to shape the age profile of lawyers. But they did deliberately construct entry barriers to affect the social composition of the profession in other ways. Indeed, supply control may have been as much a project of controlling *who* became a lawyer, in order to elevate the collective status of the profession, as of controlling *how* many did so, in order to enhance their financial rewards—although the two goals are obviously interrelated.[72]

Native-born Americans dominated the profession at the end of the nineteenth century. Only 3 percent of lawyers practicing in Massachusetts in 1870 or admitted to its bar between 1870 and 1890 were born abroad.[73] Among the 20 to 30 percent of "elite" Chicago practitioners who belonged to the Chicago Bar Association during the last quarter of the nineteenth century, the proportion born abroad fluctuated between 8 and 14 percent among the cohorts admitted in the decades from 1850 to 1900, but the proportion who were Protestant declined slowly from 97 percent of the cohort admitted between 1831 and 1850 to 70 percent of the cohort admitted in the 1890s.[74] Nationwide, the proportion of the profession who were native-born white offspring of native-born parents declined only slightly, from 76 percent in 1900 to 74 percent in 1910.[75] In the latter year, another 20 percent were born in the United States, and only 6 percent were immigrants—although 17.8 percent of the white male population was foreign born.[76] Even at that early date, however, the pressure for entry among immigrants and their sons was obvious: in New York City, 36 percent of lawyers had foreign-born parents and 16 percent were themselves immigrants; the proportions were 34 and 14 percent in Chicago and 26 and 7 percent in Philadelphia. Ten years later, native-born children of native-born parents constituted only 45 percent of practitioners in both New York and Chicago.[77]

The profession reinforced the exclusion of immigrants and their sons with every new barrier it erected: increases in the length of prelegal and legal education (especially when many universities discriminated against religious and ethnic minorities), more stringent standards for ABA accreditation, which curtailed part-time education, character tests, and the requirement of a preceptor or sponsor.[78] When the ABA established a committee in 1920 to neutralize the Reed Report and justify professional control over the number and characteristics of entrants, its chairman, Elihu Root, characterized the committee conclusions as a response to the "tens of thousands" of immigrants seeking to become lawyers.[79] Yale College enforced a quota on the admission of Jews between 1922 and 1960.[80] Dean Swan of Yale Law School urged that the children of foreign-born parents be required to complete more years of college before entering law school, and he opposed admission to law school on the basis of college grades because immigrants performed at least as well as the native born.[81]

Yet this attempt to freeze the social composition of the profession failed. In Boston in the first decade of the twentieth century, the number of lawyers increased 35 percent, but the number of lawyers with immigrant parents increased 75 percent, and the number of foreign-born lawyers rose by 77 percent; in New York City the proportions were 35, 84, and 66 percent, respectively; and similar trends occurred in Chicago, Philadelphia, and St. Louis a decade later.[82] Jewish lawyers constituted

26 percent of new bar admissions in New York City between 1900 and 1910, 36 percent between 1911 and 1917, 40 percent between 1918 and 1923, 56 percent between 1924 and 1929, and an astonishing 80 percent between 1930 and 1934; the proportion declined to 50 percent at the end of the 1940s and then stabilized at 65 percent during the 1950s.[83] At Suffolk Law School, an unapproved part-time Boston institution that claimed to be the largest in the nation, virtually the entire student body were members of ethnic minorities: 48.5 percent were Irish, 18 percent Jewish, and 6 percent Italian.[84] In 1947, 1951, and 1956, more than half of the students at an unnamed metropolitan law school with both day and evening divisions had one immigrant parent and more than a quarter had two, though only 3 percent were foreign born.[85]

As a result, foreign-born lawyers constituted more than 18 percent of the profession in New York City in 1930.[86] A 1938 study estimated conservatively that more than half of New York City lawyers were Jewish (at least 11,400 out of 22,000).[87] The proportion of Protestants in the New York City bar declined from 25 percent in 1920 to 10 percent in 1955; in 1960, that bar was 60 percent Jewish, 18 percent Catholic, and 18 percent Protestant.[88] Law continued to be disproportionately attractive to members of minority religions: among college seniors in 1961, 13 percent of Jews, 8 percent of Catholics, and 5 percent of Protestants hoped to become lawyers. Indeed, law was most attractive to Jews whose fathers were lawyers and who had done poorly in college: more than half sought to follow in their fathers' footsteps. (Those with better college records wanted to become doctors!)[89] Jews continue to be overrepresented in law student bodies (at the expense of Protestants; Catholics are proportionally represented), but to a lesser extent: although only 3 percent of the population, they constituted about a fifth of all law students in 1969 and 12 percent a decade later.[90]

This religious realignment also signified a shift in ethnicity. Irish and central Europeans declined from 65 percent of first- and second-generation immigrant lawyers in New York City in 1900 to 25 percent in 1960.[91] Lawyers whose parents were from the United States, Britain, Ireland, or Canada declined from 74 percent of the New York City bar in 1900 to 42 percent in 1960, while lawyers whose parents were from eastern and south-eastern Europe increased from 3 to 40 percent.[92] The proportion of New York City lawyers who were first- or second-generation immigrants rose from 47 percent in 1900 to 69 percent in 1960.[93]

Ethnicity, generation of immigration, and religion affect not only who enters the profession but also what kind of lawyers they become. In late nineteenth-century Massachusetts, lawyers born abroad (typically in Ireland and Scotland) accumulated significantly less property during their professional careers than native-born lawyers.[94] Because education mediates between background and career it is significant that in New York City in the 1930s, nearly half of all Jewish lawyers had not graduated from college (48.6 percent) or attended law school full time, compared with less than a third (31.4 and 31.5 percent) of the entire New York City bar.[95]

Numerous studies have documented the overrepresentation in solo practice and local government of Jewish and Catholic lawyers from entrepreneurial or working-class backgrounds.[96] In New York City in 1938, 61.1 percent of Jewish lawyers practiced by themselves and another 6.8 percent were sole practitioners with lawyer employees; only 15.1 percent were partners, 14 percent associates, and 3 percent employed by corporations. By contrast, 23.7 percent of all New York City lawyers in 1935 were partners and 21.1 percent were associates.[97] The proportion practicing part time was almost twice as high among Jewish lawyers as among the entire New York City bar (17.4 percent versus 10.0 percent).[98] The income of Jewish lawyers in New York City was significantly lower in 1937 than the income of the entire New York City bar had been four years earlier, in the depths of the Depression (medians of $2426 versus $2990; 22 versus 15 percent under $1000; 43 versus 33 percent percent under $2000; the disparity remained when years of experience are controlled).[99]

There is evidence that the type of practice and the income level both reflected ethnoreligious prejudice. More than half of the Jewish lawyers served a clientele that was more than half Jewish; and these lawyers made significantly less than Jewish lawyers who served a clientele more than half non-Jewish ($2150 versus $2593). Nearly four out of five employed Jewish lawyers worked for Jewish employers (79 percent).[100]

The salience of ethnoreligious background for legal careers has clearly declined in the last half-century. It had less influence on large firm hiring in Chicago in 1980 than in 1960.[101] A longitudinal study following a sample who had entered law school in 1961 found that religion and ethnic origin affected the likelihood of receiving a quality rating in the 1985 Martindale Hubbell Law Directory but neither the level of that rating nor whether the lawyer was listed at all.[102] Background variables were correlated with large firm practice only insofar as they predicted undergraduate academic performance, which in turn predicted quality of law school attended.[103]

Furthermore, Jews constituted a third of the student body in the top twenty law schools in 1969 and only slightly less than that in 1979, when they made up only 12 percent of all law students.[104] And a cross-sectional survey found no correlation between religion and allocation to roles within the legal profession.[105] Yet the historical effects of ethnoreligious discrimination persist, at least in a city like Chicago, where those traditions are particularly strong. A 1977 study found that ethnoreligious background strongly influenced the law school attended; this, in turn, had a substantial effect on the first job, which then affected subsequent jobs. The study also found that Jews were overrepresented in solo practice and small firms and underrepresented in large firms, government employment, and offices of house counsel; there was little difference among age cohorts. Protestants represented 36 percent of the securities lawyers but none of the divorce lawyers; Jews represented only 14 percent of the securities lawyers, but 56 percent of the divorce lawyers.[106]

Class

Entry barriers affected not only the ethnoreligious background of lawyers but also their class origins. The American ethic of egalitarianism opposes explicit discrimination on grounds of religion or ethnicity, but we are much more ambivalent about the advantages of class. Despite the ideal of intergenerational social mobility— epitomized in Abraham Lincoln's mythic rise from log cabin to the White House via the legal profession—many American lawyers have always inherited privilege. In Massachusetts in 1840, 70 percent of lawyers who had attended law school were the sons of doctors, ministers, judges, or lawyers; between 1870 and 1890, 80 percent of lawyers who had graduated from college and 60 percent of lawyers who had not attended college were from the business or professional classes.[107] Among the 20 to 30 percent of "elite" Chicago practitioners who belonged to the Chicago Bar Association in the last quarter of the nineteenth century, between 43 and 62 percent of the cohort admitted in each decade were the sons of lawyers, other professionals, major entrepreneurs, and public officials.[108] Among the 296 students enrolled at Yale Law School in 1929, 134 had gone to Yale College, 18 to Princeton, 7 to Cornell, and 6 each to the University of Pennsylvania and Columbia.[109] We saw earlier that the tuition charged by these elite institutions has always excluded much of the population. Even at a part-time school like Suffolk, most students were from the lower-middle class rather than the working class.[110]

In the first half of the twentieth century, however, the profession was relatively open. A 1932 survey of California lawyers admitted between 1929 and 1931 found that only 17 percent were unemployed at the time of admission (and thus presumably being supported by their parents), whereas 57 percent were employed in legal or semilegal positions and 46 percent in lay jobs (some having both kinds). Among Wisconsin men admitted to the bar in 1928 and 1934, 31 percent were entirely and another 37 to 42 percent at least partly self-supporting at the time of their admission.[111] Evening students at a District of Columbia law school in 1941 (probably George Washington) came from relatively modest backgrounds: 34 percent of their fathers were in clerical or commercial occupations, and 25 percent were manual laborers; only 17 percent were executives and 7 percent professionals. Nevertheless, only 12 percent of the students were themselves engaged in manual work (the rest had clerical, executive, professional, or technical jobs), and half already enjoyed incomes that placed them in the top 8 percent of American families.[112]

The class backgrounds of lawyers narrowed with the contraction of part-time legal education in the 1930s and 1940s. A 1975–76 sample of 548 Chicago lawyers found that 52.5 percent of their fathers were in the professional or managerial classes (twice the proportion in the earlier sample) and another 19.6 percent in lower white-collar jobs; only 21.7 percent were working class.[113] Another study of Chicago lawyers a year earlier found that 73 percent of their fathers occupied professional, technical, or managerial positions and only 27 percent had lower occupations.[114] Class also affects which law school a student attends, and this, in turn, influences legal career: the proportion of students whose families earned less than $25,000 was lower at elite than at regional public law schools in 1975–76 (45.5 versus 58.5 percent), while the proportion receiving financial support from their parents was higher at the former (58.7 versus 35.5 percent).[115] Greater mobility still may characterize rural settings, however: in Missouri, 31 percent of the fathers of rural lawyers were clerical or unskilled employees, compared with only 14 percent of the fathers of urban lawyers.[116]

There always has been a great deal of direct occupational inheritance: 23 percent of Indianapolis lawyers in 1940 had lawyer fathers; 30 percent of all American law students in 1949 had close lawyer relatives; 15 percent of law students entering the University of Pennsylvania in 1953 had a lawyer parent, and 29 percent had had a fair amount of contact with a lawyer relative; 18 percent of a sample entering law school in 1961 were sons of lawyers; and among the 1975–76 sample of Chicago lawyers, 15 percent had a lawyer parent and more than half had a lawyer relative.[117] Among the cohorts entering the Chicago bar between 1954 and 1974, a constant 14 percent had a lawyer father.[118]

Cross sectional studies of the class backgrounds of lawyers fail to differentiate among those admitted at various times during a professional career of about 40 years. Disaggregation by cohort strengthens the evidence that class backgrounds are narrowing. Among Chicago lawyers practicing in 1977, 32.3 percent of those admitted before 1960 were the children of fathers in lower-class occupations, compared with 21.6 of those admitted later.[119] The proportion of lawyers whose fathers were in professional, technical, administrative, or sales occupations steadily increased between the cohorts practicing in 1954 and 1974, while the proportion whose fathers were clerical workers, craftsmen, or farmers steadily decreased.[120] A sample of white law students in the class of 1972 in both elite law schools (Yale, Stanford) and nonelite schools (Boston College, University of Iowa, University of Connecticut day and evening sessions) revealed even greater privilege: 83.5 percent of their fathers were in white-collar occupations; 49.5 percent had college degrees, and another 15.9 percent had attended college. In the 1970 and 1972 classes at those schools, only 2.9 percent of the students came from families with annual incomes under $10,000 (compared with 10.3 percent of the population), while 14 percent came from families with incomes over $40,000 (although only 14.7 percent of all American families enjoyed incomes of even $15,000).[121] Stevens found an increase in the socioeconomic status of law students between 1960 and 1970, although Zemans and Rosenblum found no correlation between date of admission and class background.[122]

It seems likely that the class origins of lawyers have become still more homogeneous and privileged as competition to enter law school has intensified, particularly because women are now seeking admission in numbers nearly equal to men. A study of University of Virginia law students found that, although women came from poorer families than men and relied less on their parents for financial support during law school, a much higher proportion of their mothers had advanced degrees.[123] Because there is a strong correlation between family income, scores on the Law School Admission Test, and undergraduate grade point average, admissions criteria tend to exclude lower class applicants.[124] Surveys by the Carnegie Commission for Higher Education found that in 1969 only a fifth of all law students had fathers in blue collar, service, farm, sales, or clerical occupations (compared with 71 percent of the general population in 1970), while half had fathers in high prestige occupations (compared with only 14 percent of the general population); the proportion of law students with fathers in high prestige occupations increased to 60 percent in 1975.[125] Competition has continued to magnify these inequalities. Compared with all other college freshman in 1981, those who identified themselves as prelaw were more than twice as likely to have family incomes over $100,000 and only about half as likely to have family incomes under $10,000; about 50 percent more had mothers and fathers with college and graduate degrees. The direct transmission of professional membership was even more striking: five times as many prelaw students had lawyer fathers, and four times as many had lawyer mothers (although the absolute numbers were small).[126]

Diversifying the ethnic, religious, and gender backgrounds of lawyers, therefore, has also meant narrowing their class origins. Because women still must overcome significantly greater hurdles, those who succeed within the legal profession tend to come from more privileged family environments than those of men lawyers. Within four large Chicago law firms in the 1980s, 53 percent of the women had fathers in professional or technical occupations compared with 36 percent of the men, and only 11 percent had fathers in lower occupations compared with 30 percent of the men.[127] Class background continues to affect the career aspirations of those who become lawyers. In 1962, first-year law students from blue-collar backgrounds in high- and middle-status law schools did not aspire to become law firm partners and gravitated instead toward government employment.[128] If such correlations appear weaker today, the reason may be an increase in class homogeneity rather than greater intraprofessional mobility.[129]

Gender

The entry of significant numbers of women into the profession beginning in 1970 marks a change in its composition even more dramatic than the entry of Southern and Eastern European immigrants and their sons in the first half of this century. Although the first woman was admitted to a law school and a state bar a century earlier, and eleven states admitted women by 1881, a variety of barriers restricted the proportion of women to less than 5 percent of the profession until the 1970s.[130] A study of forty-five jurisdictions at the turn of the century indicated that thirteen had admitted women at the same time as men, two first admitted women in the 1860s, seven did so in the 1870s, five in the 1880s, and six in the 1890s; but ten still excluded them altogether, and another two delegated that power to counties. Furthermore, most jurisdictions had admitted fewer than ten women each, although forty-seven women were practicing in Massachusetts in 1900.[131] Arkansas and Georgia denied women admission to the bar as late as 1911.[132] Law schools continued to discriminate against women until much later: only 41 of the 137 law schools admitted women in 1915–16, although 122 out of 129 did so in 1920. The number of women law students increased from 205 in 1909 to 1171 in 1920.[133] Columbia continued to exclude women until 1928, Harvard until 1950, Notre Dame until 1969, and Washington & Lee until 1972.[134]

Even when women were admitted, hidden quotas and social and cultural barriers kept their numbers small.[135] Women could not join the American Bar Association until 1918 or the elitist Association of the Bar of the City of New York until 1937.[136] Female law students tended to be concentrated at less prestigious schools. During the first third of this century, many (perhaps the largest proportion) were educated at Portia Law School in Boston, a part-time proprietary institution, founded in 1908 exclusively for women, whose enrollment reached 384 in 1924–25. Its bar passage rate was 82 percent in 1924 and 65 percent in 1929, better than those of most other part-time schools.[137] In 1938, however, it admitted men (in response to the admission of women by Suffolk, a local competitor), and the number of women undoubtedly declined.[138] The Washington College of Law, which began as the Women's Law Class in 1896, graduated more men than women for the first time in 1914, and by 1936–37 women were less than a fourth of its 531 students.[139] Although women constituted 16 percent of evening students at a District of Columbia law school in 1940 and higher proportions in unapproved schools, the contribution of such institutions to the production of lawyers was small and declining.[140] In California in 1948, women were 2.6 percent of the students at the seven ABA-approved schools but 4.1 percent at the six unapproved schools; and within each category their numbers varied inversely with prestige.[141]

Only when the number of male students declined precipitously as a result of the two world wars did law schools seek to replace them with women. During World War I, the number of male students fell from 7477 to 2443 (67 percent) between the fall of 1916 and the fall of 1918 in the 41 schools admitting women, while the number of women rose from 397 to 503 (27 percent) and their proportion increased from 5 to 17 percent of total enrollment. Yet even then they were concentrated at the less prestigious schools: their numbers actually decreased in the day schools, but they increased 31.5 percent in the mixed schools and 92.4 percent in the night schools.[142] The Depression affected the entry of women more severely than that of men (as though women lawyers were a luxury society could afford only in flush times). Women constituted between 5.5 and 6.2 percent of entrants in New York City during the years 1925 through 1928 but then declined steadily to 3.4 percent in 1934.[143] World War II again saw the proportion of women rise to a fourth of all law students, but it quickly dropped to its former level at the end of the war (see Table 27). Consequently, women remained between 1 and 3 percent of the profession and less than 5 percent of enrollment in ABA-approved law schools until the 1970s (see Table 27). As late as 1970–71, women constituted a smaller proportion of law students than of medical students (8.5 versus 9.6 percent).[144]

This has changed rapidly in the last two decades. During the five years following 1969, law school applications increased threefold, but women applicants increased fourteen times. Furthermore, acceptances of women remained at a steady 43 percent of applicants, while acceptances of all students fell from 44 to 18 percent (which confirms my earlier contention that the entry of women greatly intensified competition for places among men).[145]

Between 1967 and 1983, the enrollment of women in ABA-approved law schools increased 1650 percent, from 4.5 to 37.7 percent of the total (see Table 27). Indeed, because the absolute number of male law students has not increased since 1973, *all* subsequent growth of law school enrollments is attributable to the entry of women. Whereas women were more likely to be part-time than full-time law students in the 1950s and 1960s and to study at schools not approved by the ABA, the reverse is true today (see Table 28). Indeed, women outnumbered men among full-time students at 19 of the 175 ABA-approved law schools in 1986–87.[146]

Of course, these changes were not confined to law. The proportion of undergraduates who were women grew from 43 percent in 1972 to 52 percent in 1982; 88 percent of the increase in undergraduate enrollment during that period was attributable to the entry of women.[147] Measured by the baseline of baccalaureats, therefore, women remain underrepresented in law school. Their numbers have increased less rapidly in the legal profession than in other service occupations: the proportion of women grew from 27 to 65 percent in the insurance industry between 1970 and 1984, from 14 to 48 percent in advertising between 1960 and 1983, and from 9 to 39 percent in banking and financial management between 1960 and 1983.[148] By contrast, women have become only 10 to 15 percent of the legal profession (current estimates differ, see Table 26).[149] Furthermore, the increase in the proportion of law students who are women has slowed, although it continues to grow because the number of male applicants to law school dropped further than the number of female between 1982 and 1984 (14 versus 9 percent).[150]

One reason for the disparity in the representation of women among law students and lawyers (aside from the fact that it will take a generation to replace the male-dominated bar) may be that a smaller proportion of female law graduates practice. A 1934 survey of New York City lawyers (with a 30 percent response rate) found that women constituted only 1.65 percent of practitioners, although they had been 4.8 percent of entrants during the preceding 10 years and 3.5 percent of the profession according to the 1930 census.[151] Among the 22,500 lawyers admitted in California between 1972 and 1977, 6.5 percent of women were unemployed in 1977, compared with 3.7 percent of men.[152] A 1984 survey by the Women Lawyers Association of Michigan found that the proportion entering practice was 10 percent lower among women than among all law graduates and the proportion leaving law firms in the early years of practice was 10 percent higher among women than men.[153] Among the many reasons for this differential attrition, the survival of sexual harassment and other forms of sexist behavior may be one. In the mid-1970s, law teachers (almost all of whom still were men) treated men and women students differently.[154] A 1983 New Jersey study found that 86 percent of women reported incidents in which female attorneys were treated disadvantageously by male attorneys, and two thirds reported incidents in which they were treated disadvantageously by judges or other judicial personnel.[155] A 1986 New York study also found that male judges and lawyers routinely demeaned and patronized female lawyers.[156]

Entry into the legal profession does not guarantee equality within it. One index of success is income. The median income of women lawyers in New York City between 1928 and 1932 was $2750, just 61 percent of the $4535 median for all lawyers, although the gap narrowed slightly at the depths of the Depression in 1933 ($2050 versus $2990 or 69 percent). In 1949, the median income of women lawyers was just over half that of men. The proportion of self-employed lawyers earning more than $10,000 a year was more than four times as high among men than women (28 versus 6 percent); the proportion of salaried lawyers earning more than that was 8 times as high among men (16 versus 2 percent). A quarter-century later, when the number of women lawyers still remained insignificant, their financial situation had not improved.[157] A 1975 survey of the median incomes of Illinois lawyers revealed that women earned 88 percent as much as men in the Chicago Loop ($30,000 versus $34,000), 42 percent in suburban Chicago ($10,500 and $25,000), and 31 percent in the rest of the state ($10,000 and $32,000).[158] Women lawyers employed by the legislative branch at all levels of government in 1970 earned 65 percent as much as men.[159]

The entry of large numbers of women lawyers since the mid-1970s has not eliminated income inequalities. A 1982 survey of Minnesota lawyers found that women earned less than two thirds the median income of men; even within the 1975–81 cohort of law school graduates they earned 20 percent less.[160] Throughout the nation in the early 1980s, women lawyers earned 71 percent as much as men, enjoying significantly less income equality than women journalists (85 percent), doctors and dentists (80.9 percent), and teachers (80.3 percent).[161] The Census reported that women lawyers earned 55 percent as much as men in 1979 and 63 percent as much in 1986.[162] A 1983 survey of 605 lawyers found that women earned 62 percent as much as men ($33,000 versus $53,000), which was very close to the disparity within the entire workforce.[163] Among members of the University of Michigan Law School classes of 1976 through 1979 surveyed five years after graduation, the average income of women was 80 percent that of men. (Most of this disparity is attributable to the fact that women and men pursued different career paths, although within small firms women still earned less than men).[164] Among lawyers who had graduated from seven northeastern law schools four and eleven years earlier, women earned less than men in virtually every category of job and age, even when income was normalized for the number of hours worked.[165] The one exception was those working in firms with more than 84 lawyers. Yet the starting salaries of men and women law graduates in the class of 1983 were virtually identical.[166] And in 1986, women lawyers averaged $576 a week, which was 88 percent of the incomes of men lawyers. A 1987 survey of 2500 Boston lawyers found that, among those with one to five years of experience at their present jobs, 70 percent of the women but only 44 percent of the men earned less than $56,000, while 11.2 percent of the men but only 3.7 percent of the women earned $76,000 to $100,000; among those with six to ten years of experience, 11 percent of men but only 6.5 percent of women earned $76,000 to $100,000.[167]

Differential ability cannot be the reason for this persistent gap. Just as women applying to college have better high school records than men, so women applying to law school have better undergraduate records than men, a difference that has survived grade inflation.[168] The LSAT scores of women law school applicants were slightly lower than those of men in the late 1960s but slightly higher in 1970–71.[169] Consequently, women applicants were accepted in higher proportions than men in 1975–76.[170] Nevertheless, the representation of women within law student bodies continues to vary inversely with the prestige of the school: they constituted an average of 38 percent of law students at the fifteen most elite schools in 1984, compared with 45 percent at eleven nonelite schools.[171] Women are underrepresented in the top 10 percent of the law school class, on law reviews, and among judicial clerkships, but their pass rate on the bar examination is consistently higher than that of men (see Table 20.b).[172] Compared with their proportion of law school graduates, women were only slightly underrepresented among Supreme Court clerkships in 1987: 29 percent of outgoing and 26 percent of incoming clerks.[173]

Part of the income disparity is attributable to differences in the age profile of female and male lawyers, but even within age cohorts women have not attained equality. They still are expected to shoulder the burdens of childrearing, and almost all mothers do so.[174] Both female and male law students at Stanford Law School in the early 1980s assumed that most of the childrearing tasks would fall on women. Although many employers granted women lawyers short-term maternity leave, few had developed long-term leave policies or permitted part-time work.[175] A later survey of 100 law firms found that only a third offered paid maternity leave, only a fifth had any policies on paternity leave, and nearly half did not allow part-time work; a firm's flexibility in responding to childrearing responsibilities varied directly with its size. A sample of 220 nonprofit organizations was not much more accommodating.[176] The proportion of Michigan employers who granted maternity leave to women lawyers actually declined from 96 percent in 1984 to 69 percent in 1986.[177] More generous leave policies, while allowing more women to return to practice, might actually aggravate income differences, since women are more likely to interrupt their careers (47 percent of women 21 to 64 years old but only 13 percent of men had spent six months unemployed since their twenty-first birthday) and thus less likely to acquire seniority (23 percent of women but 36 percent of men had held their current job more than ten years).[178]

It is not surprising that many women have resolved these conflicts between work and family by postponing marriage: in both 1960 and 1970, 87 percent of all male lawyers and judges were married; the proportion of women fell from 46 percent in 1960 to 41 percent in 1970. A 1987 survey of 2500 Boston lawyers found that 88.5 percent of the men but only 71.5 percent of the women were married; 68.2 percent of the men had children compared with only 29.6 percent of the women.[179] Postponing marriage is more likely to foreclose it for women because men still marry women who are younger, less well educated, and professionally less successful. A survey of census data for 70,000 households found that among college-educated white women the likelihood of marriage was 50 percent for those who had not married by the time they were twenty-five, 20 percent for those unmarried at thirty, 5 percent for those unmarried at thirty-five, and as little as 1 percent for those still unmarried at forty.[180] And, of course, the prospects of procreation run out much faster for women.

Other women sacrifice career advancement to marital and childrearing responsibilities. In 1970, female lawyers and judges on average worked fewer hours per week than men (38.7 versus 45.8); 21.3 percent of women but only 8.9 percent of men worked less than 35 hours; 58.4 percent of men but only 30.7 percent of women worked more than 40 hours.[181] Five years after graduation, all men and childless women in the University of Michigan Law School classes of 1976 through 1979 worked three to four hours more a week than women with children (although even the latter worked forty-nine hours). Among mothers, 69 percent had taken at least three months of full-time or part-time leave, 37 percent at least seven months, and 25 percent at least nineteen months.[182] The Bureau of Labor Statistics reported that 37,000 lawyers and judges were working part time in 1985, probably an underestimate. The New York Attorney General's Office first permitted half-time work in 1982 and presently has 21 such employees; some law firms also allow part-time practice, although this is more likely to mean 60 or even 80 percent of full time. Although these arrangements allow women to continue practicing law, they are likely to prejudice professional careers, particularly the prospects of partnership.[183] Despite these tensions, however, a 1986 survey of the University of Michigan Law School classes of 1976 through 1979 found that women who had combined childrearing and professional careers expressed more career satisfaction than childless women or men with or without children.[184]

Much of the income difference between male and female lawyers reflects career choices by women who may (reasonably) be anticipating employer discrimination as well as seeking positions they can combine more easily with childrearing. As recently as the early 1980s, a leading Atlanta law firm maintained that it was entitled to discriminate against women in selecting partners, until the U.S. Supreme Court found it in violation of the Civil Rights Act of 1964.[185] Women members of the University of Michigan Law School classes of 1976 through 1979 who were working in firms of one to ten lawyers five years after graduation earned only two thirds as much, on average, as their male counterparts in these classes, which may help explain why the proportion of women graduates working in such firms was only half that of men.[186] Women may (correctly) expect government to be less discriminatory, at least in entry-level positions.[187] These expectations were reflected in career patterns more than 50 years ago. In New York City in 1934, smaller proportions of women than men were in private practice (80 versus 85 percent) and larger proportions were employed in industry (15 versus 10 percent) and government (4 versus 3 percent).[188]

As the number of women lawyers has increased, these differences have became more pronounced. According to census data, the proportion of women lawyers working in government has consistently been twice that of men (28 and 14 percent in 1950 and 1960, 37 and 18 percent in 1970).[189] A detailed analysis of the Martindale Hubbell directory reveals similar patterns. A smaller proportion of women lawyers than men has been in private practice (60.6 versus 69.8 percent in 1970; 55.7 versus 69.4 percent in 1980), and higher proportions have been employed by the federal government (7.6 versus 5.5 percent in 1970, 7.0 versus 3.4 percent in 1980), state and local government (6.4 versus 5.0 percent in 1970, 10.2 versus 5.2 percent in 1980), private associations (2.9 versus 0.9 percent in 1970, 1.9 versus 0.7 percent in 1980), legal aid and public defender offices (4.8 versus 1.2 percent), and law schools (1.7 versus 1.1 percent in 1970, 2.0 versus 1.1 percent in 1980).[190] In Michigan, the proportion of government lawyers who were women increased from 12 percent in 1976 to 25 percent a decade later.[191]

Among members of the University of Michigan Law School classes of 1976 through 1979 surveyed five years after graduation, 70 percent of the men but only 44 percent of the women were in private practice; by contrast, higher proportions of women than men were in government employment (15 versus 9 percent), legal services, public defender offices, and public interest law firms (6 versus 2 percent), and offices of house counsel (14 versus 10 percent). Among those who had tried private practice, the proportion of women who had left was twice that of men (33 versus 17 percent). The desire to work in settings where women are more than a token may accentuate these patterns: these women law graduates found only an average of 19 percent of their fellow workers in private practice were women, compared with 32 percent in other settings. There also is some evidence that married men were overrepresented in private practice partly because they felt greater financial responsibilities as the sole or primary breadwinners in their families.[192] A recent study of seven northeastern law schools revealed that the disparity between the proportions of women and men in offices of house counsel actually was increasing (13 versus 9 percent in the cohort who had graduated eleven years earlier, 9 versus 3 percent in the cohort who had graduated four years earlier).[193] Women are only a small proportion of Washington representatives of private interests (12 percent) and an even smaller proportion of lawyer representatives (7 percent).[194]

These career choices also may reflect personal values. Women prelaw undergraduates are politically more liberal than all undergraduates, and men prelaw undergraduates are more conservative.[195] Women were substantially more liberal than men in the University of Michigan Law School classes of 1976 through 1979.[196] Women law students express much stronger preferences than men to work in substantive areas catering to personal client needs and much less interest in becoming corporate lawyers.[197] This helps explain the fact that 13 percent of lawyers employed by the federal Legal Services Program in 1967 were women (when they constituted only about 3 percent of the profession); women also were a fourth of all lawyers employed by the Legal Aid Society of New York in 1967 and a third in 1981.[198] The proportion of those seeking law teaching jobs who were women increased steadily from 16.6 percent in 1980–81 to 22.1 percent in 1984–85.[199]

Gender differences remain even when we partly control for age by limiting comparisons to the cohort who entered practice after 1970.[200] Yet now that women make up about 40 percent of law graduates, their career choices may be converging with those of men. A recent study of seven northeastern law schools found that the disparity between the proportions of women and men in government employment actually had reversed between the cohort who had graduated eleven years earlier (23 versus 10 percent) and the cohort who had graduated four years earlier (12 versus 14 percent).[201] Law firms attracted 38 percent of the women in the Columbia Law School class of 1972 but 58 percent in the class of 1977; the proportion at Harvard rose from 55 to 63 percent (compared with 68 percent of all graduates in 1977).[202] The proportions of women and men nationwide who entered private practice converged between the classes of 1979 (45 versus 56 percent) and 1983 (56 versus 58.5 percent), as did the proportions entering government or taking public interest jobs (from 28.1 versus 17.9 percent to 16.9 versus 12.4 percent).[203] The gap between the proportions of men and women in private practice five years after graduating from the University of Michigan Law School narrowed significantly between 1981 (70 versus 42 percent) and 1986 (79 versus 67 percent), partly because the proportion of women who were working in mid-sized firms (11 to 50 lawyers) had increased to almost that of men.[204]

Within each professional category, women still hold inferior positions. In 1972, women law teachers were concentrated in schools that emphasized political activism and sought to enroll women and minority students but were underrepresented at elite schools. As late as 1979–80, half of all law schools had fewer than three full-time women teachers, 17 percent had only one, and 4 percent had none.[205] Responses from 97 out of 172 ABA-approved law schools revealed that the proportion of the faculty who were women increased from an average of 7.6 percent in 1976 to 12.3 percent in 1981. Their distribution was very unequal, however: women constituted more than 20 percent at eighteen faculties in 1981 but less than 9 percent at forty-three others, including ten that had no women. Although the representation of women did not correlate with the prestige of the school or the credentials of entering students, most elite schools had less than the 1981 average (12.3 percent): Berkeley (10 percent), Chicago (7 percent), Columbia (7 percent), Harvard (5 percent), Michigan (4 percent), Pennsylvania (6 percent), Stanford (7 percent), Virginia (2 percent), and Yale (7 percent).[206]

Among law teachers hired in 1981–82, the proportion of women entering nontenure-track positions was almost twice that of men (54 versus 28 percent). The retention rate is low in such positions and so is the likelihood of moving to the tenure track. Women were overrepresented in the less prestigious subjects: they were twice as likely as men to teach legal research and writing and almost twice as likely to teach family law but far less likely to teach business courses. Women published somewhat less than men and were substantially less likely to be promoted.[207] Preliminary analysis by the Society of American Law Teachers of questionnaire responses by 108 law schools found that the proportion of women had increased from 10 to 16 percent of tenure-track faculty between 1980–81 and 1986–87 and from 14 to 20 percent of all faculty. In the latter year, all the schools responding had at least two women teachers, and half had at least six. Yet it is striking that women constituted 70 percent of contract-status legal writing faculty, a category that is poorly paid, accorded little respect, excluded from governance, and denied security of employment or the possibility of advancement.[208]

Women began to enter the judiciary in significant numbers only in the 1970s; they represented 5.4 percent of the federal judiciary in 1980 and 2.1 percent of all judges nationwide (but 12.4 percent of family court judges in 1977).[209] By 1985, 7.4 percent of the federal judiciary and 7.2 percent of state judges were women. The pace of change has reflected the degree of political commitment to gender equality. President Carter named forty women to the federal bench, 15.5 percent of all his judicial appointments; President Reagan appointed only fourteen in his first term, 8.4 percent of his appointments. In the first five and a half years of Reagan's administration, only 7 percent of his appointees to the Court of Appeals were women, compared with 20 percent of Carter's. At the end of seven years, Reagan had appointed thirty-one women, 8 percent of his federal court appointments. While the appointment of women to the federal judiciary stagnated, however, the number of women state court judges doubled, from 617 to 1356 between 1980 and 1985.[210] In New York in 1986, women represented 9.7 percent of state judges, but nearly half of them sat in New York City Family, Criminal, Civil, and Housing Courts.[211]

Women are also underrepresented in the governance of professional associations. In 1987, only one of the thirty-two members of the ABA Board of Governors was a woman, although the ABA had just appointed a woman as executive officer.[212]

Within private practice, women have always been distributed differently from men. In New York City half a century ago, women were more likely than men to be in solo practice (60 versus 55 percent) and less likely to be law firm partners (18 versus 24 percent).[213] Among the seventeen women lawyers who answered a Michigan questionnaire in 1939, ten practiced by themselves (59 percent).[214] Today, a higher proportion of women than men are still sole practitioners (55.6 versus 48.1 percent), although this difference is slightly less pronounced among those who entered practice after 1970.[215] A 1963 study found that prejudice against women varied inversely with firm size.[216] This still seemed to be true in 1980: women constituted 2.3 percent of partners in 107 law firms with 90 lawyers or more but only 1.9 percent in 218 law firms with 25 to 89 lawyers.[217] When Los Angeles law firms with at least 20 lawyers were dichotomized into those whose associates were more and less than 25 percent women, the former averaged 71.8 lawyers while the latter had only 40.7 lawyers.[218] Women represented 18 percent of firms with fewer than 50 lawyers but 21 percent of firms with more than 100.[219] Women were less likely to be found in any capacity in firms of 2 to 20 lawyers (and also in smaller offices of house counsel). The proportion of women lawyers who worked in large firms was actually higher than that of men (12.0 versus 7.0 percent in 1980, 14.2 versus 8.6 percent among those admitted since 1970).[220] In the law school classes of 1979 through 1983, smaller proportions of women than men continued to enter small firm practice, while higher proportions joined large firms.[221]

The entry of women into large firm practice is a dramatic reversal of their earlier virtually total exclusion.[222] In 1956, only 18 of the 1755 women lawyers in New York City worked for large law firms (1 percent).[223] In 1964, there still were only eighteen women in the twenty largest New York firms. Some fifteen years later, women were 616 of the 3142 lawyers in the thirty-two largest New York firms (20 percent) and 1297 of the 6034 lawyers in the fifty largest firms nationwide (22 percent).[224] Another 1980 study found 1796 women lawyers among the 13,353 who worked in the 107 firms nationwide with 90 or more lawyers (13 percent).[225] Women were only 5 percent of the lawyers hired by four large Chicago firms before 1970 but 24 percent of those hired between 1975 and 1980.[226] Women constituted 23.9 percent of associates in the 100 largest firms in 1981 but 30.5 percent in the 250 largest in 1985.[227] One reason for the increase in women associates may be the surprising finding that large law firm interviewers of both sexes invited more women than men to "call backs" at the firm and the unsurprising finding that male interviewers (who predominated) were more strongly biased in favor of women interviewees.[228] Yet a survey of the University of Michigan Law School classes of 1976 through 1979 found that men and women employees had virtually identical grades within each category of employer, including large firms.[229]

Women may choose larger firms not only because they offer higher starting salaries and greater prestige but also because women associates believe they offer better chances of advancement. Here the picture is cloudier.[230] There was only one woman partner in any large New York City firm in 1964, three in 1968, thirty-four in 1979, and forty-one in 1980.[231] By 1985, just three major New York firms had no women partners.[232] In Los Angeles in 1973, only five of the twenty-nine law firms with at least twenty lawyers had even one woman partner and none had more; ten years later, 60 of the 86 firms that size had women partners, and nineteen had at least two.[233] In 1987, only 4 of the 247 largest law firms nationwide had no women partners.[234] At the 150 largest firms in 1982, women represented 15.5 percent of the lawyers but only 8.3 percent of the partners.[235] At the 50 largest firms, they were 21 percent of associates but only 2.8 percent of partners.[236]

Although firms may be embarrassed to have *no* women partners (and encounter difficulties in recruiting women associates), the proportion of associates becoming partners still seems to be higher among men than women. In the cohort of lawyers who entered private practice after 1970, 71.2 percent of the women remained associates in 1984, compared with only 48.0 percent of the men.[237] In the Los Angeles firms with at least twenty lawyers in May 1983, women were 25.4 percent of the associates but only 4.3 percent of the partners.[238] In the thirty-two New York City firms with more than ninety-five lawyers in 1980, women were 18.7 percent of the associates but only 1.9 percent of the partners.[239] In the 107 firms nationwide with ninety or more lawyers in 1980, they represented 21.5 percent of the associates but only 2.3 percent of the partners.[240]

These disparities can be partly explained by age differences. In the cohort beginning practice between 1970 and 1980, fewer than a fifth of the women but more than two-fifths of the men entered during the first half of that decade.[241] Yet inequalities remain even when we control for age. Among those graduates of the Harvard Law School class of 1974 who entered private practice, the proportion of men who were partners six years later was more than twice that of women (51 versus 23 percent).[242] Among members of the University of Michigan Law School classes of 1976 through 1979 the proportions also were 2:1 five years after graduation (25 versus 13 percent), although they declined to 4:3 during the period 7 to 10 years after graduation (72 versus 56 percent).[243] One reason for this is that women who enter private practice leave it at a higher rate than men. Although a slightly higher proportion of women than men in that same Harvard Law School class entered private practice (61 versus 58 percent), 40 percent of those women left during the next eight years while another 3 percent of their male classmates transferred into it.[244] Among members of the University of Michigan Law School classes of 1976 through 1979 who entered private practice, 70 percent of the men but only 45 percent of the women remained there five years later.[245] Nevertheless, the situation appears to be changing. A comparison between the 100 largest law firms in 1981 and the 250 largest in 1985 shows that the proportion of partners who were women increased from 2.8 to 6.0 percent; furthermore, 17 percent of the new partnerships in those firms between May 1984 and December 1985 were granted to women.[246] By 1987, women constituted 33 percent of the associates and 7.9 percent of the partners at the 247 largest firms, having received 19 percent of new partnerships at those firms between 1985 and 1987.[247]

Race

The last category to enter the legal profession was people of color: blacks who suffered centuries of slavery and another hundred years of de jure discrimination; Indians who received inferior education on reservations after their lands were taken; immigrant agricultural workers who endured conditions of virtual peonage; and recent political and economic refugees from the Caribbean, Latin America, and Asia. These groups were virtually excluded from the profession until the 1960s, and relatively small numbers have gained admission in the last two decades.[248] During the nineteenth and early twentieth centuries, most law schools taught few or no blacks; although we lack data on the racial composition of predominately white law schools, this seems a plausible inference from the founding of ten black law schools between the Civil War and the end of the nineteenth century.[249] Only three of these survived for more than a few years, however, and their limited impact can be seen in the tiny number of black lawyers in the country in 1900— 730 or 0.5 percent of the profession at a time when 11.6 percent of the population was black. Ten years later the number had grown to only 795 and racial underrepresentation had scarcely changed (blacks were 0.7 percent of the profession and 11.1 percent of the population); almost half the states had fewer than ten black lawyers.[250] In Texas in 1890, blacks were 0.3 percent of the legal profession but 22 percent of the population; ten years later they were still only 0.6 percent of the profession.[251]

Until 1935, no law school south of the District of Columbia was racially integrated. Among the twelve Tennessee law schools in 1938, only the unapproved Kent College of Law admitted blacks; it had an enrollment of eleven, and just two of its graduates passed the bar examination between 1933 and 1937.[252] In response to threats of integration, several southern states opened black law schools: North Carolina Central University in Durham in 1939, Texas Southern University in Houston in 1947, and Southern University in Baton Rouge, Louisiana, that same year.[253] Only twenty blacks were admitted to the Philadelphia bar between 1909 and 1945, none between 1933 and 1943; it may not be coincidental that a mandatory photograph identified the race of applicants and examinees.[254] When the ABA inadvertently admitted three blacks in 1914 it "persuaded" them to resign, after which it formally excluded blacks until 1943.[255] Even in a liberal northern state like New York, blacks made up only 0.4 percent of the legal profession in 1930 but 3.3 percent of its population; and only 1.2 percent of the profession in Manhattan was black, despite its large black population.[256]

Even when explicit discrimination diminished, the absolute number of blacks in the profession remained virtually constant and their underrepresentation actually increased. Blacks represented 1.1 percent of the profession (1952 out of 179,567) but 10.2 percent of the population in 1940, 0.7 percent of the profession (1450 out of 212,605) but 10.5 percent of the population in 1950, 0.8 percent of the profession (2180 out of 285,933) but 10.6 percent of the population in 1960, and 1.3 percent of the profession (3236 out of 355,242) but 11.2 percent of the population in 1970.[257] Among the 98 ABA-approved law schools responding to a 1969 questionnaire about racial variation in bar examination pass rates, a "substantial number" reported no minority graduates during the preceding 5 years and "many others" said they had fewer than five.[258]

The few minority lawyers have not been evenly distributed in proportion to the minority population. In 1960, only 17 percent of black lawyers lived in the South, which had 45 percent of the nation's black population; blacks constituted 1.8 percent of the Virginia legal profession but 26 percent of its population.[259] There were only three black lawyers in Mississippi in 1965, less than 1 percent of the 2766 practitioners in 1971, although blacks were 42.1 percent of the state population in 1960 and 36.8 percent in 1970.[260] In California in 1967, people with Spanish surnames represented 0.8 percent of the profession but 14 percent of the population.[261] In Texas, they constituted 4 percent of the profession in 1985 but 21 percent of the population in 1980.[262]

Beginning in the late 1960s, the cumulative effect of the Civil Rights movement and of affirmative action programs in colleges and law schools produced a sharp increase in minority enrollments.[263] In 1965, minority law students were 800 of the 65,000 total—little more than 1 percent.[264] In my own law school class (Columbia, 1965) there was one black out of almost 300 students. By 1983–84, the 12,444 minority law students constituted 9.9 percent of enrollment at ABA-approved law schools (see Table 30).

These gains are impressive, but it is important to put them into historical perspective. Affirmative action has been criticized as a form of reverse discrimination, yet it did nothing more than reopen to racial minorities some of the doors that had been open to ethnic and religious minorities in the early part of this century but subsequently were closed by a legal profession eager to control the number and characteristics of its members. Despite affirmative action programs, entry remains far more difficult today than it had been a half-century earlier because racial minorities suffered greater educational deprivation, law school admissions standards were much higher as a result of the elimination of part-time unapproved schools, and the bar examination was a greater obstacle. As evidence of the historical difference it is noteworthy that seven of the eleven black lawyers practicing in Galveston, Texas, between 1895 and 1920 never attended law school and all but one came from working-class families.[265] The ABA accreditation campaign led to the closing of three black law schools: Freylinghuysen in the District of Columbia in 1927, Virginia Union in 1928, and Simmons in Kentucky in 1932. Even Howard, the preeminent black school, saw its enrollment decline from 135 students in 1923–24 to only 44 in 1932 when it raised standards in order to gain ABA approval (which it secured in 1930) at the same time that the Depression was taking its toll.[266]

During the first third of this century, most law schools admitted everyone who applied and required little prelegal education. Today, a bachelor's degree is virtually a prerequisite, but the proportion who obtain that qualification is lower among minorities than whites. In 1970, at the beginning of law school affirmative action programs, the proportion of white males with a bachelor's degree was double that of blacks (15 versus 6.8 percent; see Table 3.b). A decade later, 83 percent of whites graduated from high school but only 72 percent of blacks; 45 percent of white high school graduates entered college but only 40 percent of blacks; 56 percent of white college matriculates graduated but only 51 percent of blacks.[267] Hispanics fared even worse: in 1980, only 54 percent of those eighteen to twenty-four years old were high school graduates compared with 83 percent of whites; only 7.7 percent of twenty-five-year-old Hispanics had completed college compared with 17.8 percent of whites.[268] Blacks were 12.7 percent of the population in 1976 but 5.3 percent of baccalaureats in 1974; Chicanos were 2.8 and 1.3 percent, respectively.[269] Among those twenty-five years or older in 1985, 20 percent of whites had completed college, compared with 11 percent of blacks and 8 percent of Hispanics.

Minority undergraduate enrollment has fallen since the initial victories of the Civil Rights movement. Blacks (who make up 13 percent of eighteen- to twenty-four-year-olds) were 3 percent of undergraduates in 1972 and 10.3 percent in 1976; but the proportion declined to 9.6 percent by 1982 and 8.8 percent by 1984. The proportion of black eighteen- to twenty-four-year-olds who were enrolled in college declined from 33.5 percent in 1976 to 26.1 percent in 1985.[270] Hispanics, who are 7.1 percent of all those eighteen to twenty-four years old, were 0.6 percent of undergraduates in 1970 and 4.3 percent in 1984. Asian-Americans, who are 1.5 percent of all those eighteen to twenty-four years old, were 1.8 percent of undergraduates in 1976 and 3.1 percent in 1984. American Indians, who are 0.7 percent of all those eighteen to twenty-four years old, were 1.2 percent of undergraduates in 1970 and 0.7 percent in 1982.[271]

It should not be surprising, therefore, that minority law student enrollment has grown slowly and appears to have reached a ceiling. A slightly higher proportion of black than white college graduates enter graduate or professional schools (66 versus 61 percent).[272] Nevertheless, the proportion of minorities in the fall 1979 first-year law school class was smaller than the proportion among baccalaureats the previous spring (9.4 versus 12.7 percent), despite the fact that black college freshman had declared a preference for law in about the same proportion as all freshmen.[273] Minorities clearly have greater difficulty gaining admission to law school: in 1975–76, ABA-approved law schools admitted 59 percent of white applicants, 47 percent of Chicano applicants, and 39 percent of black applicants.[274] One reason for this may be the alleged bias of the Law School Admission Test. Although this issue is hotly debated, it is clear that the test predicts law school performance less accurately for minorities than for whites.[275] Minority law school applicants do have poorer academic records: in 1975–76, the proportion of applicants who had LSAT scores of 600 or better and undergraduate GPAs of at least 3.25 was 20 percent of whites, 4 percent of Chicanos, and 1 percent of black applicants.[276] In 1985, white law school applicants had an average LSAT score of 32.8, compared with 30.6 for Asian-Americans, 26.4 for Chicanos, 21.7 for blacks, and 18.7 for Puerto Ricans; GPAs followed similar patterns, although the differences were smaller.[277]

The continuing social, economic, and educational disadvantages experienced by racial minorities help to explain why their numbers have increased much more slowly than those of women, stopped growing earlier, and have not come as close to proportionality (compare Tables 27 and 38). Indeed, the simultaneous increase in the entry of women (most of whom have been white) makes it much more difficult for racial minorities to gain admission—a source of competition that ethnoreligious minorities did not face during the first half of this century. The number of minority law students increased little more than fourfold between 1969 and 1983, while the number of women increased more than tenfold, even though a higher proportion of law students were women at the beginning of this period (6.8 versus 4.3 percent; compare Tables 27 and 30). It is noteworthy that a much higher proportion of minority than of white lawyers are women—31 versus 13 percent— just as women represent a higher proportion of all minority professionals than of white—66 versus 48 percent.[278] The experience of various minority groups differs: law school enrollments of blacks and Mexican-Americans peaked as early as 1976, but enrollments of other racial minorities continued to grow into the 1980s (the number of "other Hispano-Americans" is still growing, but many come from relatively privileged backgrounds).

If the present static racial distribution is extrapolated until the year 2000, when most of the lawyers admitted before the affirmative action programs of the 1970s will have left practice, the proportion of minorities in the legal profession still will be only *half* that of the population. Educational institutions cannot blame outside pressures for this loss of momentum in correcting past injustices. The U.S. Supreme Court imposed constraints on medical school affirmative action programs only after the enrollment of most minority groups had stagnated, and its decision required no more than minor adjustments in those programs.[279] Black medical school enrollment grew from less than 1 percent in 1948 to a high of 6.3 percent in 1974 before declining to 5.6 percent in 1983. Much of the increase occurred at three predominantly black schools, which enroll a third of all black students. Between 1970 and 1974, when affirmative action reached its peak, the proportion of applicants accepted was higher for blacks than whites (43 versus 35 percent). By 1983 this ratio had been reversed (40 versus 50 percent), despite the fact that the proportion of applicants who were black had increased (from 5.6 to 7.3 percent between 1974 and 1983) and their test scores, although still lower than those of whites, had risen more rapidly.[280] The fourteen medical schools in New York are now trying to remedy the imbalance between minority physicians (4 percent), minority medical school enrollment (8.5 percent), and the state's minority population (20 percent) by recruiting and preparing minority students in high school.[281] The aggregate enrollment of blacks in law, medicine, and dentistry remained a constant 4.6 percent between 1976 and 1982.[282]

Admission to law school is only the first step in qualifying as a lawyer; students must also graduate. The attrition rate has been markedly higher among minority law students than among law students generally (compare Tables 7, 8, 9, and 12). Nine out of ten entering white law students were enrolled in the third year two years later, whereas the proportion was less than eight out of ten for all minority students and less than seven for certain groups. One reason is the inadequacy of prior education. When UCLA minority law students in the early 1970s were dichotomized by means their "predictive index" (a composite of LSAT and undergraduate GPA), 74 percent of the higher group graduated but only 52 percent of the lower.[283] Another reason for attrition is financial difficulties.[284] In a sample of minority law students in 1974, 54 percent were working, 87 percent of those for more than 10 hours a week; 22 percent came from families with incomes of less than $5000, and a further 34 percent of families earned $5000 to $10,000.[285]

The bar examination is yet another obstacle to proportional representation of racial minorities within the legal profession. Although national pass rates among first takers rose above 80 percent in the 1970s (Table 18), these aggregate figures conceal enormous racial differences. On the Pennsylvania bar examination, between 1955 and 1970, the disparity between the pass rates for all students and for black students were 65.1 and 38.3 percent for Temple graduates, 80.2 and 53.8 percent for University of Pennsylvania graduates, and 75.5 and 50.0 percent for Villanova graduates. It is estimated that 98 percent of all those taking the Pennsylvania examination ultimately pass, compared with only 70 percent of black examinees.[286]

The California figures are most complete, and there is no reason (other than the greater difficulty of the examination) to believe they are atypical. Among graduates of ABA-approved California law schools taking the examination for the first time between 1970 and 1973, 70 percent of whites passed, compared with only 37 percent of minorities.[287] Among members of the UCLA classes of 1976 through 1978, 93 percent of white graduates had passed by 1979 compared with only 70 percent of minority graduates.[288] Among all first-takers of the July 1978 California bar examination, 67.8 percent of whites passed but only 53.4 percent of Asians,

30 percent of Latinos, and 18.1 percent of blacks; the differences were just as marked among repeaters.[289]

The situation has not improved as overall pass rates have fallen: in July 1984, 48.3 percent of whites passed the California examination, 30 percent of Asians, 18.1 percent of Latinos, and only 11.6 percent of blacks.[290] Among all first takers in July 1986, 64.0 percent of whites passed but only 44.5 percent of Asians, 29.0 percent of Latinos, and 25.0 percent of blacks; the differences were just as marked among repeaters (except that Asians did better than whites).[291] Among UCLA law graduates, 83 percent of those admitted entirely on the basis of LSAT scores and undergraduate GPAs passed but only 26.5 percent of those admitted through the "diversity" program. During the five years from 1982 to 1987, blacks constituted 3 percent of those passing the bar examination, Latinos 4 percent, Asian-Americans 4 percent, and other minorities 1 percent (see Table 20.b). Although several lawsuits have been filed alleging racial discrimination by bar examiners, none has succeeded.[292]

Thus, not only have affirmative action programs been inadequate to achieve proportionality between minority law student enrollments and minority representation in the general population but even the limited number of minority law graduates is not reflected in the production of practitioners.[293] In California in 1975, the disparity between racial minority representation in the population and the legal profession was almost as great as it had been before affirmative action began: Asian-Americans were 1.8 percent of the population but 0.97 percent of the profession, blacks were 6 and 1.4 percent, Chicanos 15.4 and 1.4 percent, and Native Americans 0.43 and 0.02 percent.[294] Throughout the nation in 1980, minorities were 16.8 percent of the population but only 5 percent of the legal profession.[295] Blacks constituted 4.6 percent of lawyers and judges nationwide in 1981 but 11.8 percent of the population.[296] In the law school class of 1983, a significantly smaller proportion of minority graduates than of whites were employed the following year.[297]

Minority students who surmount all the hurdles and gain admission to the bar pursue career paths different from those of white lawyers, either out of choice or because of real or anticipated discrimination. Among second- and third-year black law students at the University of Michigan in the spring of 1971, more than half intended to work for the federal government, the public defender, or legal aid, and another quarter intended to become private civil rights lawyers; none expected to enter corporate practice.[298] Among the UCLA class of 1974, 19 percent of minority graduates but only 2 percent of white graduates took jobs in legal aid; 19 percent of minority graduates but only 10 percent of white graduates entered government; by contrast, 47 percent of white graduates but only 25 percent of minority graduates joined law firms.[299] In 1978, the National Association for Law Placement reported similar disparities between all graduates and minorities in first jobs: private practice (53 versus 28.2 percent), government (15.5 versus 28 percent), and public interest law (5.9 versus 17.2 percent).[300]

These differences in career aspirations may be declining. The first jobs of minority and white law school graduates became more similar between 1979 and 1983. In 1979, 22 percent fewer minority graduates than all graduates entered private practice (32.2 versus 53.8 percent); four years later, the difference had shrunk to 13 percent (45.7 versus 58.9 percent). The proportion of minority graduates obtaining judicial clerkships rose from only half that of whites in 1979 to near parity in 1983 (9.8 versus 11.4 percent). In 1979, the proportion of whites who went to work for corporations was a third higher than that of minority graduates; four years later the proportions were equal. The proportions of both minority and white graduates starting work in government or public interest firms dropped by about half between 1979 and 1983, although minority graduates were still about twice as likely to choose these jobs. One reason for the shift toward the public sector is undoubtedly its greater material rewards. Minority graduates entering private practice or corporations in 1983 made nearly 50 percent more than those entering government and nearly 100 percent more than those in public interest jobs.[301]

Until the 1970s, most black lawyers were government employees or sole practitioners.[302] A 1966 national survey mailed to 2000 black lawyers (of whom 38 percent responded) revealed that 73 percent of those in private practice were sole practitioners, compared with 50 percent of the entire profession. Black private practitioners served a clientele composed largely of individuals (87 percent) and almost entirely of blacks.[303] Their career choices were more limited than those of whites despite the fact that higher proportions of black lawyers had some college education (82 versus 64 percent) and law degrees (95 versus 87 percent).[304] The 253 members of the Mexican American Bar Association of Los Angeles revealed a similar distribution in 1986: 42 percent were sole practitioners, and another 24 percent practiced in firms with three or four lawyers.[305]

Geraldine Segal found that *all* black lawyers admitted to the Philadelphia bar between 1890 and 1920 either began to practice by themselves, joined black firms or entered the government; among the cohort admitted between 1938 and 1954, by contrast, 15 percent began practice in white firms and 9 percent were employed by corporations. A higher proportion of the younger cohort still were in white firms and corporations in the late 1970s, and a smaller proportion were in solo practice.[306] These cohort differences appear to represent an ongoing trend.[307] In the law school classes of 1979 through 1983 nationwide, minority graduates were substantially less likely than whites to begin as sole practitioners.[308]

The underrepresentation of minority entrepreneurs makes it difficult for minority law firms to establish and expand the business clientele they need in order to grow. To overcome this obstacle, ten major Chicago corporations pledged to give business to a newly opened Hispanic firm for at least two years.[309] But even though the senior partner of the best-known black firm in Baltimore was an acquaintance of the city's mayor, it merged its seven lawyers with the preeminent 176-lawyer Piper & Marbury.[310]

Like women lawyers, minority lawyers are drawn to the larger firms both because they offer greater material and intangible rewards and because they appear to hire and promote solely on the basis of technical competence.[311] In 1963, the degree of prejudice against blacks varied inversely with firm size.[312] In 1979, there were virtually no blacks in white firms with three lawyers or fewer in New York, Chicago, the District of Columbia, Atlanta, and San Francisco; blacks constituted 1.5 percent of lawyers in the most prestigious large firms but only 0.4 percent in those with fewer than thirty lawyers.[313] In the law school classes of 1979 through

1983 nationwide, the proportion of minority graduates who joined small or medium-sized firms (with fifty lawyers or fewer) was only about half that of whites, but almost equal proportions of the two groups entered the larger firms.[314]

Yet minorities clearly were not welcome in large firms until very recently. Law review experience is often a prerequisite to being hired by a large firm, but no black or Latino served on the *Virginia Law Review* until it adopted an affirmative action program in 1987—the first southern law school to do so.[315] None of the older cohort of black Philadelphia lawyers belonged to a firm with more than ten lawyers, whereas 42 percent of firm lawyers in the later cohort did so, and ten out of thirty-one belonged to firms with more than fifty lawyers.[316] One commentator has asserted that only forty-five white law firms contained *any* black lawyers in 1963. A decade later, the ten largest New York City firms still contained only 25 blacks among their 1504 associates (1.7 percent) and just one black and one Puerto Rican partner.[317] In a 1972 survey of forty-four law firms with more than thirty lawyers, located in nine midwestern cities, blacks were 12 out of 976 associates (1.2 percent) and 1 out of 1249 partners (0.1 percent).[318] In 1979, only 12 out of 3700 partners in the fifty largest U.S. firms were black.[319] A study of large firm interviewing at UCLA found that minority students in the first three quartiles of their class encountered greater difficulty than nonminority students in obtaining a "call back" to the firm after an on-campus interview.[320]

The increasing number of minority law graduates is gradually being reflected in the composition of the large firms. Among a 1980 sample of 107 firms with ninety lawyers or more, 192 out of 7757 associates were black (2.5 percent) and 19 out of 5596 partners (0.3 percent); the proportions were slightly lower in another 214 firms with 25 to 90 lawyers; interestingly, a higher proportion of women associates than of men in the larger firms were black.[321] The next year the proportion of partners who were black had grown to 20 out of 4251 (0.5 percent), while the proportion of associates had remained constant at 151 out of 6408 (2.4 percent).[322] Yet in 1983, two thirds of the largest U.S. firms still had no black partners, and a sixth had no black lawyers at all; more than three quarters had no Hispanic partners, and half had no Hispanic lawyers at all.[323] Two years later there were only seven black partners in major New York City firms.[324] Among 247 of the 250 largest firms in 1987, 27 had no black lawyers, 88 had no Asian-Americans, and 98 had no Hispanics; more than half had no black partners, 76 percent had no Asian-American, and 79 percent had no Hispanic.[325] It may not be coincidental that the Reagan administration's opposition to affirmative action was paralleled by a decline in black representation in larger firms. In the 100 largest firms nationwide 2.3 percent of associates were black; in the 250 largest firms only 1.95 of the associates were black in 1985 and 2.1 percent in 1987; the proportion of partners who were black rose from 0.5 to 0.7 to 0.8 percent. Hispanics have done slightly better, increasing from 0.6 to 1.1 percent of associates between 1981 and 1985 (the proportion remained the same in 1987) and from 0.25 to 0.33 percent of partners between 1981 and 1985 (0.38 percent in 1987).[326]

The proportion of minority lawyers has grown more rapidly in other legal careers. Among the 5325 lawyers employed by the Legal Services Corporation in 1980, there were 565 blacks (10.6 percent) and 512 Hispanics (9.6 percent). In the mid-1950s there was only one full-time black lawyer teaching outside a black law school; in 1981–82 there were 224 blacks out of the approximately 5000 law teachers at ABA-approved schools (about 5 percent).[327] Among those seeking teaching positions, the proportion who are minority lawyers has grown very slowly, from 4.1 percent in 1980–81 to 6.8 percent four years later.[328] In 1985, 6 percent of full-time law teachers in ABA-approved law schools, 5 percent of part-time teachers, and 6 percent of deans and librarians were minority.[329] If minority law schools are excluded, the proportions are even smaller. Preliminary analysis by the Society of American Law Teachers of questionnaire responses from 108 law schools found that blacks had increased only from 2.8 to 3.7 percent of all faculty (tenure-track and others) between 1980–81 and 1986–87, while Hispanics had remained a constant 1 percent. More than a quarter of the schools still had *no* black or Hispanic faculty members, three fifths had fewer than two, and 83 percent had fewer than three. Although there were no differences in the rate at which minority and nonminority faculty were granted tenure, a higher proportion of minority faculty left before the tenure decision was made.[330]

Blacks were 226 out of the 1946 judges in sixteen major American cities in 1981 (11.6 percent) and 31 out of the 212 judges in federal district and circuit courts (14.6 percent).[331] In 1985, 7.2 percent of the federal and 3.8 percent of the state benches were black; 3.1 and 1.2 percent were Hispanic; and 0.4 and 0.6 percent were Asian and Pacific Islander. The gain by blacks within the federal judiciary is attributable largely to President Carter, who appointed thirty-seven of the fifty sitting in 1985—14.3 percent of his judicial appointments. President Reagan, by contrast, only appointed two blacks in his first term—1.2 percent of his appointments; during the first year and a half of Reagan's second term, he appointed twenty-eight whites but no minorities to Courts of Appeals. During his first seven years, Reagan appointed six blacks (1.6 percent of his judicial appointees), two Asian-Americans (0.5 percent), and fourteen Latinos (3.8 percent). Even so, minorities have had a better chance of reaching the bench through appointment than through election.[332]

The allocation of minority lawyers across professional roles strongly affects their incomes. The black sole practitioners surveyed in 1966 earned very little, even less than black lawyers employed in government—a reversal of the relationship among white lawyers.[333] A 1975 survey of Illinois lawyers found that whites made 28 percent more than blacks in the Chicago Loop and 52 percent more in suburban Chicago.[334] Just as racial minorities have greater difficulty entering the profession than either earlier immigrant groups or women, so they appear to have greater difficulty attaining the most desirable positions within it. Nevertheless, starting salaries of minority and white law graduates in the class of 1983 were virtually identical.[335]

The divergent ways in which women and minorities have been incorporated into the legal profession are reflected in their different relationships to professional associations. Once women were admitted to the profession, during the last third of the nineteenth century, they were readily accepted by state and local professional associations, which they joined in the same proportions as men (although their absolute numbers were much lower). Although a National Association of Women Lawyers was formed in 1899 (originally as the Women Lawyers' Club) because the ABA did not admit women until 1918, the proportion of women lawyers it enrolled declined from 21 percent in 1951 to a mere 2 percent in 1980. Women clearly have decided that male-dominated organizations offer them more than sex-segregated groups, even though they have not yet achieved positions of leadership within the former.[336]

Blacks were admitted to the profession earlier than women. The Reconstruction amendments ended de jure exclusion, and black lawyers were needed to serve the newly freed black population. As we have seen, however, the ABA excluded black lawyers until 1943, and the Chicago Bar Association continued to do so until after World War II. Blacks responded by forming their own organizations: the National Bar Association in 1925 and local groups even earlier—the Cook County Bar Association was founded in Chicago in 1914.[337] Because the racism of the larger society was inevitably reproduced by the profession—first as segregation and then in more subtle forms of discrimination—black lawyers join black bar associations in at least as high proportions as they belong to integrated associations. In 1945, the National Bar Association said it enrolled a quarter of all black lawyers; in 1981 it claimed two thirds (8000 out of an estimated 12,000).[338] Although assisted by federal government grants in the past, it is now self-financing from membership dues.[339] A 1970 survey found that 41 percent of black respondents belonged to the ABA, 38 percent to the NBA, 64 percent to local integrated bar associations, and 54 percent to local black associations.[340] Ten years later, a study of black Philadelphia lawyers revealed that 88 percent belonged to the Philadelphia Bar Association and 83 percent to the Barristers' Club (the local affiliate of the NBA) but only 55 percent to the ABA.[341] Other minority groups have also formed thriving local and national bar associations. The continued vitality of these groups is strong evidence of the racial disunity of the profession.

Demographic Change

The theory of professions as social closure, advanced in Chapter 2, found support in the history of entry barriers in Chapter 3. The present chapter offers additional evidence that these barriers significantly influenced both the number and the background characteristics of lawyers. All three quantitative measures—law student enrollment, bar admissions, and the number of practitioners—fluctuate in a pattern consistent with the gradual tightening of professional control over entry followed by the erosion of that control. The shift from apprenticeship to academic education coincided with dramatic expansion: law student enrollment increased tenfold between 1890 and 1930, bar admissions increased fourfold between 1900 and 1929, and the practicing profession nearly doubled between 1890 and 1930. The efforts to control supply gradually succeeded during the next thirty years, assisted by such extraneous events as the Depression and the war. Law school enrollment declined after 1927 and did not return to that level until 1961 (except for a brief postwar bulge). Bar admissions declined after 1928 and did not significantly exceed that level until 1964 (with the same exception). And the population:lawyer ratio was the same in 1950 as it had been in 1900, perhaps the same in 1960 as it had been in 1885. The third phase saw rapid expansion: law school enrollment grew nearly threefold between 1961 and 1981, bar admissions increased nearly fourfold between

1963 and 1978, and the population:lawyer ratio fell by almost half between 1950 and 1984. Since the early 1980s, law school enrollment and bar admissions have fallen, and the growth rate of the legal profession has stabilized. The fluctuations in the size of other professions followed similar patterns, although medicine has always been more successful in regulating its numbers.

Thus, the evidence in this chapter strongly suggests that the profession's efforts to control entry were highly effective, even if it could not suppress market forces entirely. Many other variables also affected the number of lawyers, however. Wars—the Civil War, the two world wars and the Korean and Vietnam wars— reduced supply, at least temporarily, and entry control hindered postwar recoupment of these losses. But though population affects both the supply of lawyers and the demand for their services, large geographic variations in the population:lawyer ratio make it clear that other forces are operating. Notwithstanding the professional project, the market remains at least somewhat self-correcting: tighter control over supply increases the imbalance with demand, driving up the price of legal services and intensifying pressures for entry. At times, recruits have also been attracted by more altruistic motives. In the twentieth century, the profession found it increasingly difficult to justify exclusions based on ethnoreligious background, race or gender. Finally, cross-sectional and longitudinal studies confirm that the supply of lawyers responds to major fluctuations in demand, such as the contraction of economic activity during the Depression, variations between rural and urban environments, the postwar boom, the growth of the service sector, and the emergence of national and international markets.

Entry barriers affect the composition of the profession as well as its size. Sometimes this is largely inadvertent, as when variation in the size of entering cohorts alters the age profile of lawyers. Even if unintentional, this can affect the degree of competition within a cohort and the balance of power between cohorts, which may differ in ideology and culture. Thus, it is not insignificant that the constriction of entry between 1930 and 1960 caused the profession to age, rendering it politically more conservative, while rapid growth during the next two decades introduced a large diverse younger cohort, considerably more receptive to change. The slackening of growth since 1980 may cause the profession to begin aging once again, possibly curtailing opportunities for newer entrants.

Entry barriers influence *who* become lawyers—their ethnoreligious background, class origin, gender, and race. At the beginning of this century, the professional elite were quite open about their desire to exclude Jewish and Catholic Eastern and Southern European immigrants and their sons, whose entry into the profession had been greatly facilitated by the shift from apprenticeship to academic training. The introduction of prelegal educational requirements, the attack on unapproved and part-time law schools, the requirement of citizenship, and the introduction of "character" tests were all directed toward this end, in whole or part. Yet the effort failed completely: the proportion of Jewish and Catholic lawyers whose families came from eastern and southern Europe soon exceeded their representation in the population. Discrimination by elite universities and law firms only served to relegate ethnoreligious minorities to solo and small firm practice and government employment. Even these forms of discrimination and self-selection have greatly diminished in recent cohorts.

Nevertheless, these barriers continue to narrow the class background of lawyers, whose origins have grown even more privileged. Educational prerequisites, the elimination of part-time law schools, and the increasing difficulty of bar examinations in the first half of this century all tended to constrict the class composition of the profession. The expansion of public higher education since the early 1960s somewhat broadened access. But the entry of women during that period nearly doubled the competition for admission to law school. As a result, lawyers still come from highly privileged backgrounds, and a significant proportion have lawyer parents. Within this homogeneous category, family background continues to influence which college and law school a future lawyer attends, and this, in turn, affects the lawyer's first job and subsequent career.

It is a constant of contemporary society that family privilege reproduces itself across generations through the medium of academic education. Attitudes toward other forms of inequality are more ambivalent. During the nineteenth century, the law prohibited both women and blacks from becoming lawyers. The Reconstruction amendments ended the de jure exclusion of blacks, and most states had admitted women to practice by the early twentieth century. But law schools, bar associations, and employers continued to discriminate openly against both groups until well after World War II. Those who managed to gain entry were channeled into government employment, legal aid, and solo practice. Since the 1960s, the assimilation of these two groups into the legal profession has diverged markedly, reflecting important differences between institutional sexism and racism.

The proportion of law students who were women increased rapidly after 1967, peaking at about 40 percent by the mid-1980s; indeed, the absolute number of male law students has not increased since 1973. Female lawyers come from more privileged backgrounds and have better college records than men, and they do equally well in law school. Yet they are found in different legal careers: overrepresented in government employment, public interest work, and teaching and underrepresented in private practice. Within each category they remain disadvantaged: teachers are off the tenure track or at nonelite schools, judges serve in lower courts, and private practitioners are associates or salaried partners in law firms rather than profit-sharing partners. Some of this difference can be explained by age, preference, and residual discrimination. But much of it is attributable to the fact that women bear children and continue to shoulder primary responsibility for rearing them. Consequently, women lawyers must either forego families or interrupt their professional careers, limit their hours, and often work part time. The partial assimilation of women into the legal profession, nevertheless, has weakened their own professional associations, although women still are underrepresented in the governance of predominately male associations.

Because racial minorities, unlike women, are socially and culturally segregated and economically disadvantaged, their incorporation into the legal profession has been much less complete. Even after de jure and de facto exclusion had ended, members of racial minorities found it difficult to enter law school, graduate, and pass the bar examination. Affirmative action programs begun in the late 1960s helped to increase their representation within law student bodies, but growth effectively peaked by 1976 (a decade before it did for women) at only half their proportion of the population (compared to four fifths for women). Indeed, the entry of nonminority women may have made it more difficult for minorities to gain admission. And efforts by the profession to reassert control over numbers by lowering the bar examination pass rate have disproportionately excluded members of racial minorities, who remain disadvantaged by their earlier education.

Racial minorities are not only more seriously underrepresented within the legal profession but also more segregated. Their concentration in government employment and legal aid reflects both ideological preference and fear of discrimination. They have had greater success in penetrating such visible and politically responsive sectors as the judiciary and the law faculties than in entering private practice. Within the latter category, they remain overrepresented in solo practice and small minority firms; although some have become large firm associates, few have been granted partnerships. Within each category their incomes are lower than those of their white counterparts. Given the persistence of disadvantage and discrimination within the profession, as well as their very different collective biographies and cultures, it is not surprising that minority lawyers devote most of their organizational energies to their own professional associations rather than accept minority status within the overwhelmingly white groups.

Thus, the legal profession has exercised significant control over entry, but it has not been able to suspend market forces entirely. After vigorously resisting entry by and assimilation of ethnoreligious minorities, it has reluctantly accepted them as equals. It appears willing to treat some childless women as honorary men, but those who insist on performing the maternal role (which men collude in assigning them) must accept the subordinate status that goes with their lesser commitment to a legal career. The profession has been accessible to those from lower-class backgrounds largely to the extent that disadvantaged minorities have managed to enter—ethnoreligious minorities in the 1920s and 1930s and racial minorities since the 1970s. But the latter face persistent discrimination and the consequences of economic disadvantage, cultural difference, and residential and educational segregation.

5

Restrictive Practices:
Controlling Production by Producers

Chapter 3 narrated the legal profession's growing influence over the number of lawyers. But control over the production *of* producers is only part of the professional project of market control; control over production *by* producers is equally important. These two elements are necessarily sequential: it makes no economic sense to impose restrictive practices on members of one's profession while the number of producers is unregulated. Restrictive practices also presuppose that the profession enjoys extensive powers of self-regulation—ideally through an integrated bar, but otherwise through a state supreme court and legislature that are responsive to practitioners. As American lawyers secured these two prerequisites in the early decades of the twentieth century they began to assert control over production *by* producers.

Defining the Monopoly

The first and most important step was defining the lawyer's monopoly and defending its boundaries against lay competitors. Until 1870, the legal profession was concerned primarily with establishing its exclusive rights in the *courts,* against challenges by both lay representatives and court personnel (such as clerks).[1] Even this minimal claim encountered strong opposition from populist adversaries: laypersons could represent parties in Justices of the Peace and Police Courts in California as late as 1933.[2] The real threat, however, was neither clients nor the ideology of self-help but other occupations. During the last quarter of the nineteenth century and the first quarter of the twentieth, professional associations sought to ward off incursions by title insurance companies, credit and collection agencies, banks and trust companies, accountants, automobilie clubs, mortgage and insurance companies, and lay representatives seeking to appear before administrative agencies.[3]

In response, the Chicago Bar Association (CBA) established a Committee on Persons Assuming to Practice Law without a License in 1905, and the New York County Lawyers' Association followed in 1914 with its unauthorized practice committee.[4] Yet the former received so few complaints (eighteen in 1908, two in 1909, nine in 1913) that it urged the CBA to create the machinery that would allow it to pursue criminal prosecutions on its own.[5] In 1930 the ABA created the Special Committee on Unauthorized Practice of Law, which began publishing the *Unauthorized Practice News* in 1933, to coordinate the activities of state and local bar associations. By 1940, 400 of the those associations had functioning unauthorized practice committees.[6] Between 1933 and 1977, twenty-four articles on the subject appeared in the *American Bar Association Journal* and 358 in state and local journals.[7]

Bar associations used a variety of tactics in this fight. First, they sought legislation that would define their monopoly as expansively as possible to include giving legal advice, drafting wills, collecting assigned claims, transferring title, drawing up deeds, and appearing before administrative agencies; 17 laws were enacted between 1870 and 1920 and another 12 between 1920 and 1960.[8] No other legal profession claims such a broad territory, except those in a few Canadian provinces. Then bar associations negotiated agreements with competing occupations, dividing the market with each. The first of these was concluded with the New Haven Corporate Fiduciaries Association in 1925, and by 1934 there were similar agreements in 14 cities and 9 states. The first national agreement was reached with the trust division of the American Bankers' Association in 1933, and by 1958 there were agreements with national organizations of accountants, banks, collection agencies, insurance adjusters, life insurance underwriters, publishers, and realtors.[9] The profession also sought to oust lay competitors from practice before administrative agencies, especially after these began to expand during the New Deal.[10] Finally, the profession initiated legal action against individuals or groups, seeking injunctions, citations for criminal contempt, and criminal convictions; 58 reported cases were filed before 1920, 149 between 1921 and 1934, and 190 between 1935 and 1958.[11] The California Statewide Committee on Unauthorized Practice, founded in 1947, had investigated some 500 complaints by 1956, 89 in the year 1952–53 alone.[12] These concerned property transactions, commercial and corporate law, advice, and advocacy.[13] A 1953 survey of members of the Ohio State Bar Association found that nearly a fifth believed that laypersons performed at least 20 percent of the legal work in the state, and another fifth thought they performed 10 to 20 percent. Not surprisingly, these beliefs were more pronounced among younger lawyers with lower incomes practicing in larger cities.[14]

The substantial energy the profession devoted to this campaign and the success of particular initiatives should not conceal the fact that lawyers encountered substantial opposition and lost many battles. In California, with its strong populist tradition, an 1872 law limited the professional monopoly to the courts, explicitly allowing laypersons to perform any other legal function. Collection agencies were able to take assignments of debt and sue to recover them without a lawyer until 1939. The profession unsuccessfully sought legislation regulating unauthorized practice in 1913, 1915, and 1917. In 1921, when it finally obtained a law restricting the activities of banks and trust companies, the latter launched a referendum campaign, which repealed the enactment the following year. Independent claims adjusters who bought personal injury actions from tort victims and then sued on their behalf were protected from professional attack, although the lawyers who worked for them were disciplined.[15]

Nevertheless, the state bar did begin to win some victories. In 1932 it persuaded the automobile club to represent members only in small civil matters, not in criminal cases. In 1933 it sued the two most powerful banks, which responded with an electoral initiative that would have amended the constitution to allow free legal advice. Two years later these groups reached an agreement in which the banks promised not to draft wills, appear in court except through lawyers or advertise legal services. Yet the following year the bar signed a treaty with the California Land Title Association conceding the latter's right to fill in forms and thereby losing the extremely profitable market for residential real estate transactions. The bar failed to reach an agreement with claims adjusters or to exclude lay representatives from administrative tribunals. A 1951 ethical ruling prohibiting lawyers from working for collection agencies led to an agreement with the latter two years later. Yet conflict with notaries public and certified public accountants continued without any resolution.[16]

The tide began to turn against the profession in the 1960s. Although it always invoked client interests when defending its monopoly, *all* complaints about unauthorized practice came from lawyers, not clients.[17] As the consumer movement encouraged clients to become more aggressive in asserting their real interests, the profession's rationalizations lost credibility. But the principal actors in the attack on restrictive practices were not consumers but competing occupations, whose economic interests were far more concentrated. In 1962, Arizona realtors responded to a judicial decision limiting their activities by launching an inititative to amend the constitution, which passed easily.[18] Virginia title insurers overcame state bar opposition to win the right to conduct title searches.[19] The ABA ceased publishing *Unauthorized Practice News* in 1977. The California State Bar dissolved its committee on unauthorized practice.[20] When the U.S. Justice Department began investigating California market division agreements, the State Bar promptly rescinded all twenty.[21] And at its February 1980 meeting, the American Bar Association anticipated similar attacks by repudiating its agreements with architects, professional engingeers, the American Land Title Association, and publishers.[22] One irony of this struggle is that political conservatives, usually close allies of the legal profession, followed their ideological commitment to laissez-faire economics to its logical conclusion by attacking rules against unauthorized practice.[23] Indeed, Reagan's appointee as chairman of the Legal Services Corporation recently argued that the Corporation could and should be abolished if only the legal profession would abandon its rules against unauthorized practice![24]

Some jurisdictions have acceded to the pressures from clients and lay competitors.[25] The California legislature recently adopted a form for wills simple enough to allow many testators to draft their own.[26] It has been estimated that as many as 20 percent of California divorces are conducted pro se.[27] The Michigan Supreme Court recently permitted laypersons to represent employers at contested unemployment compensation hearings.[28] And nonlawyers routinely appear before the Patent and Trademark Office and the Social Security Administration.[29]

Yet the profession certainly has not relinquished its claim to a monopoly. The New York County Lawyers' Association sued to prevent publication of Norman Dacey's book, *How to Avoid Probate*.[30] The Florida State Bar Association attacked a notary public and former legal secretary who was charging clients a nominal fee for assistance in filling out forms for routine legal transactions, such as adoptions, name changes, uncontested divorces, and personal bankruptcy protection. Although the Bar secured a criminal contempt conviction against her for violating an injunction, the governor granted a pardon soon after she began serving the thirty-day sentence.[31] The Oregon State Bar obtained an injunction against another paralegal in 1982, prohibiting her from accompanying clients to court, drafting legal documents, or giving legal advice.[32] Courts in both Texas and Florida have sustained the prohibition against laypersons helping immigrants to fill out federal forms.[33] The Unauthorized Practice of Law Committee of the Texas Supreme Court has investigated the activities of HALT (Help Abolish Legal Tyranny), an organization launched in the District of Columbia in 1978 to publish forms and books enabling laypersons to conduct real estate transactions, probate estates, and handle other matters by themselves.[34] Texas courts continue to enjoin the publication and sale of legal forms to laypersons, even when sellers offer no advice about completing the forms.[35] Although the profession may be in retreat, many lawyers clearly are determined to continue fighting rearguard actions in defense of their territory.

They will not be greatly encouraged by a study of the actual self-help activities of laypersons seeking uncontested divorces and personal backruptcies in Phoenix, Arizona, between 1980 and 1985, commissioned by the ABA Special Committee on the Delivery of Legal Services. This report found that the incidence of self-help varied inversely with complexity: the proportion of divorces completed without legal representation was three to six times as high as that of bankruptcies; self-help divorces doubled during the period while self-help bankruptcies increased only 50 percent; both the presence of children and the duration of the marriage reduced the likelihood of self-help in divorces, just as assets exceeding $5000 reduced the incidence of self-help in bankruptcy.[36] Although court personnel believed that self-help often harmed litigants and caused more work for the court, examination of the case files fails to support these charges.[37] Indeed, one Superior Court Commissioner noted that self-help divorces typically take *less* judicial time because they are uncontested.[38] The report concluded with a strong recommendation to encourage and facilitate self-help rather than obstruct it (perhaps reflecting the fact that one of the authors was an economist, not a lawyer!).

Defending the Turf Against Other Lawyers

To control the production of services *by* producers, it is almost as important for the profession to exclude other lawyers from the jurisdiction as it is to suppress lay competition. A lawyer usually can appear in an individual matter *pro hac vice*, without being admitted to the jurisdiction, although this courtesy is being curtailed. Admission to federal court generally follows automatically from admission to any state bar, although here, too, new barriers are being imposed. But because states regulate the practice of law, lawyers must be admitted to each one in which they regularly practice. Comparisons of occupations confirm that interstate mobility varies inversely with both state licensure and the denial of reciprocity.[39]

Interstate mobility has been restricted in two ways. First, lawyers may have to take additional bar examinations; although these are unlikely to exclude most of those who have surmounted one such hurdle, they do demand a sufficiently substantial investment in preparation to discourage anyone expecting to practice less than full-time in the new jurisdiction. In 1930–31, only five out of forty-nine jurisdictions required out-of-state attorneys to pass their bar examinations. The other forty-four admitted lawyers on motion as long as they had practiced for a specified period in a state that granted reciprocity; virtually every applicant was admitted.[40]

As states tightened their entry requirements for new lawyers, they significantly curtailed interstate mobility as well. California was a favorite destination of migrating attorneys. Between 1905 and 1909 more than two thirds of the lawyers admitted by the District Court of Los Angeles entered by motion.[41] In 1929 and 1930, one out of every four interstate admissions entered California, and one out of every two entered California, Illinois, or the District of Columbia.[42] Between 1920 and 1930, the 1656 lawyers admitted to California on motion were almost a third of those admitted by examination.[43] California responded in 1931–32 by imposing a character test, a separate attorneys' examination, and a $100 fee; this reduced out-of-state admissions from an annual average of 169 between 1921 and 1931 to 43 between 1932 and 1935 and from an average of 30 percent of all admissions to 8.5 percent.[44] Between 1933 and 1942, the proportion of admittees who had previously practiced elsewhere ranged from 4.2 to 11.6 percent, an aggregate of 7.8 percent for the decade.[45] Of the 956 out-of-state lawyers who took the attorneys' examination between 1943 and 1948, only 45 percent passed.[46] As the number of applicants increased, particularly after the war, the pass rate fell and the length of the examination was increased by 50 percent.[47]

Pass rates for attorneys seeking admission to other states during this period were also low: 49.5 percent in Florida, 21.6 percent in Nevada (which had no law school), 65.5 percent in New Jersey, 57 percent in Washington state, and 61 percent in New York.[48] The National Conference of Bar Examiners began conducting character examinations of migrating attorneys at the request of the admitting jurisdiction three years after it was established in 1931. Twenty-two states were using the service by 1937, and thirty-five by 1947.[49] The number of investigations grew rapidly, from 69 in 1935 to 1354 in 1948.[50] Of the first 1000 attorneys examined, 104 either were denied admission or withdrew their applications, and the rate of exclusion subsequently rose.[51] Many jurisdictions increased the number of years out-of-state attorneys had to practice before they could seek admission on motion. By 1952, thirteen states required three years, twenty-two required five years, and two required ten years. Twelve jurisdictions admitted on motion only those out-of-state attorneys who had completed the legal education demanded of in-state entrants, and ten required evidence that the in-state prelegal educational prerequisites also had been fulfilled.[52]

Protectionism intensified after the war. The number of states examining migrating attorneys nearly doubled between 1948 and 1982 (from twelve to twenty-three).[53] It is ironic that this development coincided with the introduction of the

200–question multiple-choice Multistate Bar Examination in 1972 and its adoption (in whole or part) by all fifty jurisdictions. Five states and the District of Columbia have also expressed interest in a Multistate Essay Examination, which was introduced in July 1988.[54] In 1986, only twenty five jurisdictions admitted out-of-state lawyers on motion, and most of these required the applicant to have practiced for at least five years. Florida explicitly sought to discourage retiring out-of-state lawyers from launching a new practice in the Sunshine State, even though lawyers previously admitted elsewhere constituted a quarter of its bar.[55] Although the number of lawyers admitted on motion has risen steadily over the last thirty years, the proportion of total admissions attributable to interstate migration has remained constant, and the absolute number recently declined (see Table 13). Furthermore, about two thirds of those admitted on motion today actually are qualifying for federal practice in the District of Columbia.

The second barrier to interstate mobility is the residence requirement: a lawyer who must establish residence in a new jurisdiction for a significant period before being admitted may have to abandon an existing practice, which often is a substantial financial sacrifice. (The nineteenth century English rule that solicitors and barristers wishing to transfer to the other branch had to cease practicing for several years served a similar purpose in a jurisdiction that was geographically unitary.) By 1954, thirty-nine states had imposed a residence requirement.[56] In 1985, forty-one states required residence of all applicants, both new admittees and experienced practitioners. However, seven states already had struck down such rules in response to applicant challenges.[57] And in the spring of that year the U.S. Supreme Court nullified all such rules on constitutional grounds.[58]

This decision probably will have the greatest effect on offices of house counsel, whose staff can now qualify more easily in multiple states, thereby diminishing the corporation's need to retain outside counsel. Even before the Supreme Court's ruling, the highest rates of interstate mobility were found among house counsel, the next highest among government lawyers, and the lowest among private practitioners.[59] The American Corporate Counsel Association, with 7000 members, is one of the strongest proponents of eliminating barriers to interstate mobility. So are multistate law firms, which seek to move their lawyers across jurisdictional lines, thereby threatening the market position of local firms (see Chapter 10, "The Rise of the Large Law Firm").

Several states have already responded to the ruling with new forms of protectionism. Arkansas abrogated reciprocity for experienced practitioners, requiring *all* foreign attorneys to take the bar examination.[60] Virginia insists that foreign lawyers declare their intent to practice full time in that jurisdiction, abandoning work in any other state.[61] The U.S. Supreme Court has already abrogated a federal district court rule in the Eastern District of Louisiana requiring members of the state bar who seek admission to the federal court to live or have an office in the district; it has also agreed to hear a challenge to the Virginia rule, which has been adopted in at least six other states.[62] Local lawyers remain extremely hostile to those they see as carpetbaggers. When California lawyers Melvin Caesar Belli (son of the famous trial lawyer) and Richard Brown (an associate of Belli senior) set up an office in the Dallas-Fort Worth airport hotel two days after the crash of the Delta Boeing 747 flight from New Orleans and filed the first suit in that disaster four days later, the Unauthorized Practice of Law Committee of the State Bar of Texas immediately began an investigation.[63] This hostility extends to lawyers qualified to practice in other countries. The New York bar now requires foreign lawyers to obtain a license merely to advise New York clients about *foreign* law; of course, they still cannot appear in court; four other state bars are considering similar proposals.[64]

Price Fixing

Excluding lay and professional competition is only the first step in controlling production *by* producers. Lawyers still must restrict competition *among* licensed practitioners. A favorite device was the minimum fee schedule, introduced during the Depression.[65] The Chicago Bar Association established its Committee on Professional Fees in 1930.[66] The prevalence of this mechanism can be seen in the 26 state and nearly 700 local bar association fee schedules compiled by the ABA in 1964 and again in 1966, in order to encourage others to promulgate such schedules and urge all associations to update and coordinate their minima.[67]

There is considerable evidence that schedules actually influenced lawyer behavior. In 1966, three fourths of all Florida lawyers believed that a statewide fee schedule would benefit them, although only 6 percent identified local schedules as the factor they considered most often in setting fees.[68] A 1967 survey of Colorado Bar Association members found that 22 percent used the schedule as the predominant means of setting fees.[69] A 1969 survey of South Carolina lawyers found that 29 percent used the minimum fee schedule as the most common means of setting fees, and another 20 percent identified it as the second most important factor.[70] A 1971 survey of 2000 practitioners in eight states (40 percent of whom responded) found that 90 percent used the minimum fee schedule; of the 10 percent who never did so, two thirds practiced in California, which had no state schedule and local schedules in only some cities and counties. Use varied with the degree of competition; it was greatest among lawyers with little experience who practiced alone or in small firms and earned low incomes.[71] Empirical studies of fees charged by Florida lawyers in 1966, South Carolina lawyers in 1969, and Maryland lawyers in 1974 found very little variation in either hourly fees or total fees charged in most matters.[72] Furthermore, there was a statistically significant relationship between use of the fee schedule and both the level of fees and lawyer income.[73]

Despite the obvious antitrust implications of such activities, they were uncritically condoned for decades, until the first attack convinced the Supreme Court to strike them down in 1975.[74] Yet a careful longitudinal study of lawyer pricing practices in North Carolina suggests that the effects of the decision were mixed. The schedules had affected fees for settling estates before 1975, and prices dispersed and dropped thereafter. Yet even before the Supreme Court's decision, fees generally were lower than the schedule demanded, both because probate court clerks helped lay executors settle estates without the assistance of any lawyers and because the fee schedule was complex and hard to apply. There is even some evidence that abolition had a perverse effect, cutting fees for large estates but raising them for small ones, which larger estates previously had subsidized.[75] In two other states where fee data have been studied since 1975, there is little evidence of competitive pricing. In Arizona in 1976, for instance, 42 percent of lawyers charged between $45 and $54 a hour, while only 16 percent charged less than $35 or more than $64.[76]

Perhaps more important than external restraints on the power of professional associations to fix minimum fees is the legislative imposition of maximum fees in medical malpractice cases. More than half the states have enacted such ceilings, which have been upheld by both state and federal supreme courts when challenged by bar associations. Although the profession occasionally makes pious noises about maximum fees—"A lawyer's fee shall be reasonable"—no effort is made to prevent abuses.[77] When the immigration law was amended in 1986 to allow some aliens to obtain permanent resident status, lawyers charged these particularly vulnerable applicants up to $3000 for work that nonprofit agencies were doing for $100.[78] Indeed, a U.S. Justice Department threat forced the ABA to state explicitly that the adjective "reasonable" was not meant to preclude free or low-fee services.[79]

Advertising and Solicitation

Even in the absence of explicit price fixing, it is difficult for lawyers to compete if they cannot communicate with potential consumers. The first ethical code promulgated by the ABA in 1908 prohibited lawyer advertising, although it was widespread in the nineteenth century and seems to have been generally accepted.[80] The Chicago Bar Association established a Committee on Inquiry in 1917 to investigate lawyer publicity and initiate disciplinary proceedings.[81] During the next sixty years, much of what passed for professional self-regulation actually was preoccupied with limitations on what lawyers could do to promote themselves.[82] Yet the construction and implementation of these restrictions was complicated by the very different problems confronting the two principal professional strata in seeking to acquire and retain clients.

Large law firms establish ongoing relationships with their corporate clientele, which are constantly reinforced and extended through social interaction. Sometimes the promotional objectives are patent. The Texas firm of Vinson and Elkins made former Senate majority leader Howard Baker a partner, paying him an estimated $700,000 to $800,000 a year for part-time work as a "rainmaker" while allowing Baker to continue practicing with his old Tennessee firm and earning additional income on the lecture circuit.[83] The New York firm of Finley, Kumble, Wagner, Heine, Underberg, Manley, Myerson & Casey hired retiring U.S. Senators Paul Laxalt of Nevada and Russell B. Long of Louisiana at incomes over $1 million each, with the expectation that their excellent contacts would generate substantial business.[84] Rarely do large firms have to engage in illegal behavior in order to attract business, although the chief legal counsel and vice-president of Bekins Moving and Storage Co. pleaded guilty to accepting kickbacks from outside counsel for channeling business to them.[85]

Large firms traditionally cemented client loyalty by encouraging partners to accept positions on the boards of the corporations they advised. In the decade between 1974 and 1984, however, a study of 633 corporations found a decline in the proportion of directors who were law firm partners (from 39 to 27 percent of the board) and an increase in the proportion consisting of outside lawyers (from 28 to 34 percent). There were at least two reasons for this change: corporations sought advice untainted by self-interest, and law firms feared civil liability for corporate misconduct when a firm member served on the board.[86] Even large firms now are turning to commercial marketing strategies: the membership in the National Association of Law Firm Marketing Administrators grew fivefold in the two years following its inception in 1985.[87]

But it is the sole or small-firm practitioner, serving individuals with sporadic discrete needs for legal services, who confronts the real problem of attracting clients. Until recently, the only way such lawyers could make themselves known to potential clients was by joining organizations whose members might need legal services, running for political office, or registering with lawyer referral services or law lists.[88] The last two mechanisms, although officially endorsed by the profession, were generally ineffective. Some lawyers flouted the restrictions on self-promotion, gaining a competitive advantage over their more law-abiding fellows by employing chasers or paying intermediaries to obtain criminal defense and personal injury cases.[89]

The enormous increase in the production of lawyers during the 1970s greatly strained the profession's restraints on advertising and solicitation. Opinion polls revealed that younger lawyers eager for business favored their relaxation or abolition, while older lawyers with established clienteles wanted them retained.[90] Finally, a legal clinic established by two young Arizona practitioners deliberately flouted the rules and, when disciplined, persuaded the U.S. Supreme Court to declare such commercial speech partly protected by the First Amendment.[91]

This has not been the end of the matter, however. Although the ABA proposed a substantial liberalization of the kinds of advertising permitted, many states continue to be far more restrictive, leading to repeated challenges and Supreme Court rulings that have gradually widened the ambit of protection to include direct-mail advertising but not commercial solicitation.[92] The lack of any principled criteria is visible in the recent decision of the Iowa Supreme Court (on remand from the U.S. Supreme Court) reaffirming its earlier ruling prohibiting television advertisements containing background sound, visual displays, more than a single, nondramatic voice, or self-laudatory statements.[93] State appellate courts in New York and New Jersey have permitted virtually all forms of print advertising and direct mailings to former clients by lawyers who have left the firm.[94] At the same time, the State Bar of Texas has launched an investigation of solicitation by plaintiffs' personal injury lawyers, and the Association of Trial Lawyers of America has inquired into alleged violations of a 1986 resolution against solicitation in the aftermath of the San Juan Dupont Plaza Hotel fire on New Year's Eve 1986.[95] Nor are courts and lawyers the only ones imposing restrictions. Two Arizona newspapers and one in Michigan refused a Michigan lawyer's advertisement targeting families of the victims of a Northwest Orient Airlines plane that crashed on a flight from Detroit to Phoenix.[96]

Lawyers have been slow to take advantage of even this limited expansion of competitive tactics. A survey of 1400 bar association members in a midwestern and an eastern state in the year following the Supreme Court's liberalization found that

53 percent opposed advertising in print; 99 percent opposed radio and television advertising; 53 percent thought only bar associations should be permitted to advertise; 69 percent opposed price advertising (and 32 percent feared that prices would drop as a result); 57 percent thought that demand might increase, but only 16 percent thought it would be sufficient to provide jobs for the new lawyers entering the profession; 60 percent thought public confidence would be impaired; and 85 percent thought stringent regulations would have to be imposed. The attorneys who intended to advertise were younger, practiced alone or in small firms, and represented individuals.[97] A higher proportion of younger attorneys also favored including detailed information in advertisements, even prices.[98] A second study shortly thereafter, comparing 500 bar association members and potential clients in an eastern state, found the latter much more favorable toward advertising; the two groups diverged even more sharply over price advertising.[99] Nevertheless, nearly two thirds of a 1978 sample of potential consumers never had seen an advertisement for legal services, and fewer than 1 percent indicated they would rely on advertising to select a lawyer.[100] Almost a decade after the Supreme Court decision, only 7 percent of individual clients were selecting lawyers through advertisements.[101]

The behavior of lawyers has reflected this skepticism. When the unified Wisconsin Bar Association assessed members a \$35 fee to pay for a public relations campaign in 1978, several lawyers successfully petitioned the Wisconsin Supreme Court to prohibit the charge. There was similar opposition when the voluntary Maryland Bar Association voted the following year to require its members to pay \$40 for the same purpose, and 491 members (7 percent of the total) refused to make the payment, quitting by the association.[102]

Lawyers initially were not much more enthusiastic about individual advertising. Two years after the Supreme Court decision only 3 percent engaged in any; after four years, national expenditures were just \$6 million. Yet by 1983 about one lawyer in seven was advertising.[103] ABA surveys found that the proportion had risen to 24 percent by 1986.[104] A 1982 study of Wyoming lawyers found that 29 percent advertised.[105] The 20 largest television advertisers increased their budget from \$81,000 in 1977 to \$38.3 million in 1985 and spent \$21.8 million in the first half of 1986, but just two legal clinics accounted for a fifth of the 1984 total.[106] (I will return to the phenomenon of legal clinics in Chapter 6.)

Even larger firms are turning to advertising. Forty of them now employ non-lawyer in-house marketing directors, and many others hire public relations firms to produce brochures and newsletters.[107] A 250–lawyer Pittsburgh firm has aggressively promoted its Techlex Group to high-tech clients.[108] And an international trade firm in Chicago has persuaded the state to publish and distribute its guide to doing business in Illinois, which has been translated into Chinese and Japanese.[109] Personal injury lawyers have taken the next step, cooperating with unions in offering free medical tests to those exposed to asbestos, who may have claims against manufacturers and employers.[110]

There is considerable evidence that advertising affects the price of legal services. Studies by both the Federal Trade Commission and academic economists found that the amount of advertising varied directly with the liberality of state rules, while the price for routine services like wills, personal bankruptcy, and uncontested divorces varied inversely with the amount of advertising.[111] Yet the survival of restrictions on advertising, together with the reluctance of lawyers (like most entrepreneurs) to engage in price competition, has meant the perpetuation of uniform (and high) prices. A study of 350 lawsuits found that half the lawyers charged hourly rates between $40 and $59, and the spread was even narrower within geographically bounded markets.[112] Pricing practices appear to reflect a reputational premium.[113] Thus, the increase in the number and heterogeneity of lawyers following the erosion of professional control over the production *of* producers may have reduced professional control over production *by* producers, but it certainly did not lead to free competition.

Specialization: Recapturing Control by Redefining the Market

Specialization by lawyers increases in response to many factors, including the quantity and complexity of legal knowledge and the size of producers and consumers of legal services. But it also is a mechanism by which some lawyers seek to reassert market control in the face of intensifying competition. Specialization is largely a postwar phenomenon. In 1938, thirty out of a sample of fifty Connecticut lawyers said they did not specialize, even though that was defined merely as repeating the same type of work.[114] In the late 1940s, 78 percent of respondents to a Pennsylvania survey characterized themselves as general practitioners, while only 16 percent did not.[115]

Yet by 1960, 24 percent of a sample of California practitioners described themselves as specialists, and another 33 percent called themselves generalists with a special emphasis; only 41 percent claimed to be true generalists. Much of this specialization still was limited to lawyers employed in government or in commerce and industry, 73 percent of whom styled themselves specialists, compared with 15 to 16 percent of firm lawyers and only 9 percent of sole practitioners.[116] In 1967, 56.6 percent of all private practitioners called themselves specialists; they earned 57.7 percent of their receipts from their primary specialty and 11.7 percent from other specialties. Lawyers who described themselves as specialists also reported higher earnings.[117] In the 1960s, three fifths to two thirds of lawyers devoted half or more of their time to a single field: 62 percent in Florida in 1966, 63 percent in South Carolina in 1969, and 59 percent in Colorado in 1967.[118] By the late 1970s specialization had progressed much further: 22 percent of a sample of Chicago lawyers worked exclusively in one field and another 39 percent spent more than half their time there; a total of 70 percent considered themselves specialists.[119] A 1982 survey found that 57 percent of all practitioners characterized themselves as specialists.[120]

The degree of specialization, however, remains unequally distributed among substantive fields and practice structures. Complete specialization is found among half of all prosecutors, 40 percent of patent attorneys, and 22 percent of corporate tax lawyers, but not among more than 5 to 6 percent of those concentrating in most other fields.[121] If we define specialists by a less stringent criterion—as lawyers who devote half or more of their time to a single field—the proportion ranges from 70 percent of prosecutors, 69 percent of patent attorneys, 56 percent of union lawyers, and 44 percent of management lawyers at one extreme to 18 percent of lawyers doing general corporate work, 17 percent doing probate, 16 percent doing personal real estate, 12 percent doing family law, and 11 percent doing commercial work at the other.[122]

These differences in the degree of actual specialization influence lawyer attitudes toward formalizing the practice. Not surprisingly, large-firm lawyers who already are highly specialized favor formalization, while generalist small-firm lawyers oppose it.[123] The first such scheme was established by California in 1973; twelve years later a dozen states had operative plans.[124] Because of hostility from the majority of lawyers, who fear the loss of business, most plans have been compromises that allow self-designation, admit older lawyers under "grandfather" clauses, or demand minimal prerequisites of those who wish to call themselves specialists. Such a plan, like that in Florida, enrolls six times as high a proportion of the profession as the one in California, which requires more rigorous proof of competence. The Iowa legislature considered a proposal that would have required lawyers seeking specialist certification to devote at least 25 percent of their time to the subject for three years, take twenty hours of continuing legal education for each of three years, obtain references from five lawyers, and submit to a reevaluation every five years. Both the Iowa Bar Association and the Association of Trial Lawyers of America successfully opposed it, after polling their members and confirming that rural lawyers overwhelmingly disliked the proposal, although urban lawyers favored it.[125]

Despite lawyer hostility, some jurisdictions have erected substantial obstacles to the attainment of specialist status, thereby restricting supply. The Judicial Conference of the United States (the policymaking body for the federal courts) accepted the recommendations of its King Committee to increase "competence" by requiring examinations, trial experience, student practice, and peer review. Thirteen out of ninety-one federal districts already impose some such requirement on federal litigators as a result of the recommendations of the Devitt Committee in 1979: four have created a two-tier bar, and nine have experimented with mandatory continuing legal education and an additional bar examination.[126] Thus far, only two states have established examinations of specialist competence, and only a tiny minority of lawyers have attempted to pass them: 1.7 percent in California and 7.4 percent in Texas in 1982.[127] Nevertheless, we can see the emergence of state-regulated specialties as a means by which segments of a profession that has lost some control over its market seek to demarcate submarkets in which they can reassert control.

The Rise and Fall of Restrictive Practices

We saw in Chapter 2 that the professional project has two distinct components. Members of an occupational category within the division of labor first must control entry; American lawyers sought to do this primarily through apprenticeship, academic education, and professional examinations. Only when social closure is well advanced can a profession turn to the second element: restricting competition. Clearly it would be economic suicide for members of a profession to limit their own competitive activities while outsiders are free to compete. The promulgation and enforcement of restrictive practices also presupposes a mechanism for collective action (the professional association), a minimal level of economic comfort (to permit the sacrifice of short-term benefits for long-term gains), and a fair degree of internal homogeneity. Furthermore, though the profession is unified by efforts to exclude outsiders, it is frequently divided by efforts to restrict internal competition. For these reasons, among others, the trajectory of professional control over production *by* producers differs from that of control over the production *of* producers. Restrictive practices emerge later, are never as complete, and succumb more readily to internal divisions and external attacks.

The legal profession's efforts were initially directed toward defining and defending its monopoly. Although lawyers early displayed their resentment toward court personnel who helped laypersons represent themselves, the battle against the "unauthorized practice of law" by other occupational specialists became more vigorous as the legal profession succeeded in limiting entry while its market contracted during the Depression. Professional associations established committees on unauthorized practice, concluded agreements dividing the market with other occupations, and policed violations of both the legal monopoly and interoccupational treaties. Yet some competitors refused to sign treaties, and courts occasionally rejected the profession's expansive definition of its monopoly. These rebuffs became more frequent in the 1960s and 1970s, with the rise of the consumer movement and the growing obsession with the "free market." Embarrassed by its highly visible protectionism, the legal profession abrogated all market division agreements and dissolved some of its unauthorized practice committees. But the core of the monopoly remained intact, and state and local associations continue to mount a rearguard action against external competitors.

Until the 1930s, lawyers admitted in one state encountered few impediments in practicing in another, and many migrated in response to economic opportunities or personal preferences. But as state bars raised the barriers to entry, they also sought to protect their markets from out-of-state lawyers. Some increased the number of years a lawyer had to practice before being admitted on motion; others insisted that all entrants take a bar examination (which became progressively more difficult); and most required that attorneys establish residence in the state before seeking admission, which often meant relinquishing all professional income for a considerable period. The Supreme Court struck down that last barrier as unconstitutional in 1985. This easing of interstate mobility will be particularly important to house counsel and multistate law firms. But states have responded by eliminating reciprocity and requiring a commitment to full-time practice within the jurisdiction. Furthermore, they have continued to restrict practice by foreign lawyers and to scrutinize severely out-of-state lawyers who appear in individual cases, especially personal injury matters.

Although courts in many common law and civil law countries regulate legal fees, American lawyers have always been free to charge whatever they wished, in accord with America's strong laissez-faire ideology. But few entrepreneurs are really enthusiastic about price competition, and lawyers are no exception. Because the legal profession entered the Depression with its numbers enlarged by historically lax restrictions on entry, lawyers rightly feared that competition for diminishing business would drive down prices. State and local professional associations responded by promulgating minimum fee schedules and punishing price cutting as an ethical offense. This helped maintain a floor below prices until the Supreme Court invalidated the schedules in 1975 as violations of the Sherman Act. Nevertheless, most lawyers continue to refrain from aggressive price competition. At about the same time, many state legislatures imposed a ceiling on prices for the first time, in response to the medical malpractice "crisis." The ongoing controversy about the tort liability "crisis" may generalize this to all contingent fees.

Professions are deeply ambivalent about seeking business. On one hand, it aggravates internal divisions and is thought to diminish public respect. On the other, restrictions on advertising and solicitation (like all cartelized restraints) are difficult to enforce because they require some market participants to refrain from seeking profits at the expense of others. Lawyer advertising appears to have been unrestricted and widespread well into the twentieth century. Enforcement of the ban became more frequent during the Depression. Elite lawyers supported the prohibition because it enhanced the profession's image without significantly hindering their own promotional activities, which occurred largely through social contacts. Most nonelite lawyers favored it because they preferred to see business spread evenly rather than concentrated. Those who opposed it were able to seek business through the less visible means of personal solicitation, knowing they were unlikely to be disciplined in the sporadic campaigns against ambulance chasing. The profession encountered greater difficulty in restraining advertising as it expanded and diversified in the 1970s. Indeed, it was an appeal from a state disciplinary proceeding against young lawyers seeking to reach new clients through innovative marketing strategies that led the Supreme Court in 1977 to invalidate the total ban on lawyer advertising as a violation of the First Amendment. This decision has not freed the market from all professional restraint, however. State bars continue to limit advertising and prohibit solicitation. Most lawyers take little advantage of what is allowed, prices remain tightly clustered, and clients prefer personal recommendations to impersonal advertisements. Still, advertising has contributed to concentration within the market for individual clients by allowing clinics and other mass producers to generate the volume of business necessary to support their extensive advertising budgets.

As each restrictive practice has come under attack in recent decades, lawyers have turned increasingly to another response to competitive pressures: specialization. This is simply an elaboration of the division of labor, which originally spawned the profession. In this as in so much else, lawyers have followed physicians. For the first half of this century the vast majority of lawyers were, and considered themselves, generalists; today, most acknowledge and indeed boast of their specialization. But although the exclusion of nonlawyers from the profession and the professional market united lawyers, the exclusion of generalists from specialties and specialist markets has seriously divided them. Thus far most state bars have opted for a compromise allowing most lawyers to call themselves specialists. But this is unlikely to satisfy either the generalists or the specialists for long.

We saw in Chapter 3 that the academy has superseded the profession as the principal locus of control over the number and characteristics *of* producers of legal services. Similarly, courts, legislatures, and administrative agencies have displaced the profession as the principal agents controlling production *by* producers.[128] Unauthorized practice rules have been attacked and relaxed, the residence requirement has been struck down, minimum fee schedules have been abolished, and the blanket prohibition on advertising has been abrogated. These restrictive practices were vulnerable for several reasons. Entry controls unite the profession, but restraints on competition tend to divide it. As entry control eroded in the 1970s and large numbers of young lawyers from more diverse backgrounds began to practice, these internal divisions intensified. And although meritocracy and quality assurance can be invoked to justify entry control, neither the economic well-being of lawyers nor the enhancement of their status offers a persuasive defense of restrictive practices. Nevertheless, the lawyers' monopoly survives, if in narrowed form, states continue to protect their bars against external competition, few lawyers engaged in price competition, the most effective forms of promotion remain illegal, and specialization offers new havens from intraprofessional competition.

6

Demand Creation: A New Strategy in the Professional Project?

The legal profession's struggle for market control, which began in earnest in the last quarter of the nineteenth century, was directed almost exclusively toward regulating supply—the production of and by producers of legal services. Lawyers came closest to achieving that goal during the two decades after World War II, when enrollment in ABA-approved schools remained relatively constant, most unapproved schools had closed, and restrictive practices were accepted and enforced. But supply control gradually eroded as pressure for admission intensified (especially among previously excluded categories such as women and racial minorities), additional law schools obtained ABA approval, approved schools expanded, and both newly qualified lawyers and consumers attacked restrictive practices. In response, the profession turned to a different strategy: demand creation. Efforts to create demand simultaneously serve several very different purposes: they offer lawyers the hope of new business; they promise to enhance the legal profession's reputation for altruism; and they reaffirm a fundamental premise of liberal legalism—"equal justice under law."

Of course, there is nothing new about creating demand: lawyers do it whenever they devise new legal forms—the current flurry of innovations generated by the flood of corporate takeovers is an example.[1] But both the level of professional interest and its direction have changed since the war. I do not want to overstate this argument. Most lawyers were initially very suspicious of demand creation, and many remain skeptical. A 1967 survey of the Colorado bar revealed that 59 percent favored an annual legal checkup, but those who did so had lower incomes than those who opposed the idea ($14,515 versus $17,400).[2] Even more than supply control, demand creation aggravates tensions within the profession. And it is im-

possible to disentangle motives: many lawyers are genuinely interested in redistributing legal services to promote both formal and substantive justice, not just to
enhance their own material well-being and the legitimacy of both the profession
and the legal system. Among the legal reforms recommended by a sample of
Chicago large firm lawyers, for instance, only 6 percent would have expanded their
practices.[3] Despite the motivational ambiguities, however, I think it is impossible
to understand the postwar history of the American legal profession without ana-
lyzing its efforts to redistribute legal services.

The Rediscovery of Legal Need

Lawyers have long been cognizant of the gross inequalities that characterize the
distribution of legal services. Reginald Heber Smith depicted them eloquently in
Justice and the Poor some seventy years ago.[4] His proposal that bar associations
establish law offices for people of moderate means was discussed extensively in the
1930s, under the combined stimulus of overproduction and falling demand.[5] But
the profession rejected his call for nearly half a century. Only the National Lawyers
Guild sponsored the creation of neighborhood law offices in Philadelphia in the
1930s.[6]

World War II drastically reduced supply, and professional controls limited
postwar production during a period of rapid economic expansion. Consequently,
the profession did not seriously embrace the strategy of demand creation until the
1960s. Before the initiation of federal support during the War on Poverty, legal
services to the indigent were limited to the grossly inadequate legal aid programs
funded by private philanthropy and municipal government and the even more
exiguous pro bono activities of private lawyers (both discussed later).

Although the few empirical studies of lawyer use conducted in the 1940s and
1950s confirmed that most people had little or no access to professional services,
those findings went unheeded.[7] In the 1960s and 1970s, however, the pace of
research increased, culminating in a massive study of "legal needs" jointly sponsored by the American Bar Association and the American Bar Foundation. This
quantified what the profession had always known, if not admitted. Individuals rarely
consulted lawyers: 36 percent of the sample had never used a lawyer; another 44
percent had done so only once. Even the nearly two out of three who had seen a
lawyer had done so an average of only 2.15 times. And lawyer use varied strongly
with gender, age, race, income, and education.[8]

A superficial reading of these data might suggest an "unmet need" for legal
services and thus support an argument for governmental or philanthropic efforts
to subsidize lawyers for the poor. But further analysis reveals that the relationship
between consumers and lawyers is more complex. There are enormous differences
in the extent to which the various aspects of social life have been subjected to legal
regulation. Not surprisingly, lawyers have made their services available to paying
clients whenever they hope to profit, which generally means whenever significant
amounts of property are involved (although people also will pay substantial sums
to preserve their freedom).[9] In the population sampled by the American Bar Foundation, 25 percent of those who used lawyers had done so in real estate transactions,

another 25 percent had arranged the distribution of estates, 13 percent had dissolved marriages (and divided marital property and custody over children), and 7 percent had probated wills.[10] The vast majority of people without significant amounts of property are likely to have little use for lawyers, even if the latter are subsidized, as long as lawyers continue to provide the conventional services they have rendered to propertied interests in the past.[11] The American Bar Foundation study confirms this: defining legal problems as those matters lawyers routinely legalize, it concluded that its respondents had encountered a mean of only 4.8 problems.[12] Use of lawyers is an acquired habit; most people never surmount the barriers of fear, ignorance, and unfamiliarity.[13] Thus, although legal need studies laid the foundation for demand creation, the prospects of that project were dubious from the start.

The Limitations of Professional Charity

Lawyers always have offered some charity to those unable to pay for legal services. Although we know nothing about the magnitude of such "pro bono" services before the 1970s, a higher proportion of lawyers may have represented clients at reduced fees than do so today because more lawyers practiced alone or in small firms and were relatively accessible to the needy. Willingness may be inversely related to accessibility, however. A 1967 survey of Colorado lawyers revealed that slightly more than half (55 percent) believed pro bono services were a professional obligation; because those who did so were more experienced and earned higher incomes they also were less likely to encounter indigent clients.[14]

Charitable services are severely limited in quantity and available to only certain categories of needy people. Lawyers assist those they expect to become paying clients in the future, at the behest of intermediaries who can perform reciprocal favors, such as referring paying clients. These motivations tend to exclude the very young and very old, members of racial minorities, and others unconnected to influential people.[15] Lawyers also reject clients who appear deviant in character or behavior.[16] The lawyer's goal is to satisfy both the client and the intermediary with a minimum of effort. Consequently, most matters are handled by a telephone call or letter; almost none are litigated.[17] Lawyers direct most of their charity toward individuals; most of the organizations they represent are charitable, artistic, and educational institutions that do not challenge the status quo.[18] Even so, the conservative Washington Legal Foundation recently investigated pro bono activity by the top 20 District of Columbia law firms to uncover whether they are "creating a body of legal precedent that is adverse to the business community. . . . If firms do things that hurt the free enterprise system, their clients should know about it."[19]

Not only are the neediest often excluded, but the overall quantity of services delivered also is disappointing. An unscientific 1951 survey of state "correspondents" found that eight out of twenty-five did not consider it unprofessional to refuse to represent indigents who otherwise would remain unrepresented, and 13 out of 25 did not consider it unprofessional to refuse to represent indigent criminal defendants.[20] In the early 1970s about one third of all lawyers performed no pro bono services, and those who rendered any spent an average of 27 hours a year handling three cases.[21] A 1978 survey of 183 large law firms containing more than

5500 lawyers found that their members devoted a median of 30 hours a year to *all* charitable, community, and civic endeavors, most of which did not help poor individuals.[22] A survey of 224 lawyers in four large Chicago firms in the early 1980s found that they gave an average of fifteen hours of year to pro bono activities.[23] A 1982 survey of Illinois lawyers reached similar conclusions: a third had rendered no pro bono services, another third had devoted fewer than five hours a month, and only 14 percent had spent more than ten hours a month.[24]

In recent years, law firms, professional associations, and the Legal Services Corporation have become involved in delivering pro bono services.[25] Yet in the fall of 1984, only 12 percent of all lawyers were participating in projects sponsored by the organized bar.[26] A 1985 ABA survey found that 30 percent of lawyers donated less than 25 hours a year, 22 percent donated 25 to 50 hours a year, and only 20 percent donated more.[27] In 1986, 88,000 lawyers were participating in 450 programs in 52 jurisdictions, about the same proportion of the profession (just over 10 percent) that had been involved two years earlier.[28]

Efforts to use compulsion to increase the amount of pro bono services and equalize the burden within the profession have had little success. In the late 1970s the American Bar Association and the Association of the Bar of the City of New York both considered requiring pro bono services, but each retreated in the face of member resistance.[29] One state supreme court recently decided that the government could not compel lawyers to render services without compensation.[30] A fifty-one-lawyer New Orleans firm has refused a court appointment to represent an accused murderer facing the death penalty on the ground that it lacks the necessary expertise.[31] And lawyers have denounced mandatory pro bono programs as "latent fascism."[32]

Nevertheless, state bar associations in Colorado, South Carolina, and Wyoming as well as the Chicago Bar Association have all issued guidelines for what constitutes a minimum amount of pro bono work. A Manhattan Civil Court judge has written the fifty largest New York City firms asking them to send at least one attorney to represent tenants when she sits in Housing Court. Finally, local bars in Illinois, Wisconsin, and Florida and courts in Arkansas, New York, and Texas have established compulsory pro bono programs affecting about 7750 lawyers (about 1 percent of the profession). Yet even these impose minimal burdens (perhaps two cases a year); about half the attorneys are allowed to buy out of their obligation (for nominal payments of about $100); other lawyers purchase substitutes without any official sanction; and outright resistance is simply overlooked.[33] Although pro bono activities undoubtedly help the particular recipients and ease the consciences of lawyers, they do relatively little to fulfill the promise of equal justice and, of course, almost nothing to create paying business for the profession.

Institutionalizing the Right to Legal Defense in Criminal Cases

That legal representation is a right, not a gift dependent upon the charitable impulses of lawyers and philanthropists, was first established in criminal cases, where the coercive power of the state is most obvious. The U.S. Supreme Court granted the constitutional right to counsel to criminal defendants in federal courts in 1938, extending it to felony defendants in state courts in 1963 and to all those at risk of imprisonment in 1972.[34] But though the later expansion of defendants' rights coincided with the accelerated production of lawyers, private practitioners experienced little increase in demand. To satisfy the new constitutional requirements, most jurisdictions created government-supported public defender offices staffed by salaried employees.

Their numbers grew slowly before World War II—there were five in 1917 and twenty-eight in 1949—but quickly thereafter; by 1973 there were 163 public defender programs, a third of which had been established since the 1963 Supreme Court decision.[35] As recently as the 1960s, New York and Los Angeles together had fewer than 100 full-time public defenders; by 1980, Los Angeles alone had more than 400.[36] State subsidized counsel were representing 65 percent of all felony defendants in 1973; indeed, one observer characterized private defense counsel as "a dying breed."[37] In 1967, state governments spent $17 million and the federal government $3 million to provide legal representation for indigents accused of felonies; four years later the combined total had increased to $178 million, and by 1977 it had reached $403 million.[38]

There can be no doubt that state subsidies for criminal defense help to foster an image of equal justice—law and order proponents even argue that the system is biased in favor of defendants. Indeed, it is hard to imagine today how the premises of liberalism were ever reconciled with the prosecution of unrepresented criminal defendants. But it is unclear whether the legal profession derives significant benefits, material or intangible, from such state intervention. Certainly its claim to altruism is undermined by state payment for representation. (French lawyers strongly opposed the creation of government legal aid in the 1970s for just this reason.)[39] And lawyers gain neither compensation nor enhanced prestige when state courts order them to represent criminal accused but legislatures refuse to appropriate money to pay them.[40]

Even when payment is made, however, the vast majority of lawyers obtain no business because the tendency in recent years has been to increase the number of salaried public defenders at the expense of court appointment of private practitioners (except when the public defender has a conflict of interest) in order to reduce costs and improve quality. Even conservatives ideologically committed to privatization have been disappointed with the experience of contracting out defense services to private law firms.[41] Although 6 percent of counties have experimented with such arrangements, some have found the quality of representation very poor, because the lawyers either are incompetent or try to inflate their profits by stinting on time.[42]

State payment of private criminal defense lawyers has numerous drawbacks. Rates of pay are so low that the work attracts only the least successful lawyers. Where payment levels are high enough to make the work profitable, judicial favoritism can affect which lawyers benefit.[43] The system encourages abuses that erode its legitimacy: in Los Angeles, for instance, three lawyers billed the county $352,000, $301,000, and $278,000, respectively, during a sixteen-month period.[44] The incentive for fraud is high: Los Angeles County spends $25 million a year for private criminal defense.[45] Although limits were subsequently imposed on hourly and daily billings, the county auditor later found overpayments of $340,000 to some sixty-four attorneys.[46] A West Virginia lawyer billed the state for as much as 75 hours of work on a single day and claimed separate reimbursement for travel for each of twenty-two clients he represented in a single court; he justified his behavior on the ground that he was paid only $20 to $25 an hour for such work.[47] Finally, judges can manipulate the structure of rewards to shape the tactical decisions of private defense counsel, encouraging plea bargains rather than trials.[48] Thus, state support for criminal defense creates little demand for the private bar, and what work it does generate undermines professional autonomy and public respect.

The Contested Terrain of Civil Legal Aid

Civil representation of indigents is an even more problematic strategy of demand creation. The criteria for equal civil justice are much less clear than the minimum conditions of due process in criminal prosecutions.[49] The difference is visible in the refusal of both state and federal courts to recognize a constitutional right to legal representation in civil matters. State courts have granted representation only in certain numerically insignificant situations, which resemble criminal cases, such as prisoners defending civil actions, putative fathers in paternity suits, or parents threatened with losing rights to their children.[50] Indeed, the U.S. Supreme Court recently held that Congress actually can *prohibit* the appearance of counsel at administrative hearings to preserve their informality.[51]

In the absence of constitutional compulsion, efforts to provide civil representation for indigents have been inadequate and erratic. Because legal aid societies supported by local charities and municipal governments were the only source of assistance until 1965, representation was severely limited in amount and often poor in quality.[52] The vast majority of lawyers had nothing to do with these programs: a few local bar leaders served on the boards of legal aid programs, and the profession made derisively small financial contributions.[53] The leading local lawyers, businessmen, and religious and philanthropic notables who dominated the boards of legal aid societies expressed the prevailing ambivalence about civil representation for the indigent, often prohibiting programs from filing bankruptcies (to protect business creditors) or divorces (to avoid offending the church).[54] Private practitioners were particularly concerned to ensure that these salaried lawyers never represented clients who might possibly be able to afford a fee.[55] The programs were staffed by those unable to find other jobs, either because they attended low-status law schools, had poor academic records, and lacked connections or because they suffered discrimination against women and racial and ethnoreligious minorities.[56]

The profession did not even contemplate more adequate representation for nearly three quarters of a century after these programs were initiated. Indeed, when England established the first national legal aid scheme in 1949, American bar leaders denounced it as "socialistic."[57] In 1965, however, when Lyndon Johnson launched the War on Poverty, it included a federally funded legal services program almost as an afterthought. The ABA board of governors supported it unanimously, although local bar associations and private practitioners continued to fear both the loss of business and the threat to engrained habits posed by the energetic advocacy of young, well-trained legal services lawyers.[58] (As a lawyer with New Haven Legal Assistance Association in 1971–72, I can add my personal experience of this hostility.) Federal intervention rapidly expanded the legal aid budget from less than $5 million a year to a peak of $321 million in 1980–81, which supported some 6000 lawyers.[59]

Yet civil representation for the poor remains a hotly contested issue. Legal aid lawyers generally have shunned the politically exposed role of community organizer, preferring to devote most of their efforts to conventional strategies in routine matters.[60] Nevertheless, under the guise of protecting the Legal Services Corporation (LSC) from political interference, the Nixon administration prohibited its grantees from representing undocumented workers and draft resisters, handling cases concerning abortion, school desegregation, and voter registration or employing such strategies as lobbying, picketing, demonstrations, strikes, and electoral initiatives.[61] The Reagan administration went even further, seeking to abolish federal legal services entirely.

By 1980, however, the legal profession (if not the courts) had come to view civil representation as essential to the liberal ideal of equal justice under law. Lawyers also may have feared that their pro bono obligation would become more burdensome if the federal government no longer paid the tab: the State Bar of California has had to take responsibility for some 36,000 case files abandoned by the Southeast Legal Aid Center in Compton when it closed in 1983 following the Reagan budget cuts.[62] As a result of concerted efforts by bar association leaders and others, the administration was prevented from doing more than reducing the LSC budget by a third in 1981. Since then expenditures have returned to the 1980 dollar level (although seriously diminished by inflation).[63] Furthermore, state bar associations have begun to collect the interest on lawyer trust accounts (so-called IOLTA funds), applying some of the proceeds to legal aid programs. The first of these schemes was established in Florida in 1978, and by 1985 they existed in thirty-five states and had survived constitutional challenge.[64]

Nevertheless, the Reagan administration continued its attack on the Legal Services Corporation (which still provides the bulk of funds for local programs) by appointing deeply conservative board members, who have initiated audits by teams including a National Rifle Association lobbyist, a former Immigration and Naturalization Service official, and a retired executive of the American Farm Bureau.[65] In 1987, the chairman of the Legal Services Corporation himself urged its abolition, arguing that laypersons could adequately represent the poor if the bar would just abolish the rules against unauthorized practice.[66]

If lawyers see civil legal aid as both indispensable to the legitimacy of the legal system and a protection against public demands for more pro bono services, they also have become increasingly interested in it as a source of business. Fears among private practitioners that legal aid would intensify competition were allayed as lawyers realized that aggressive representation of the poor creates *more* work for those representing creditors, landlords, and employers. Partly because American lawyers were ideologically opposed to what they saw as state incursions into professional autonomy, they initially missed the opportunity to benefit more directly from state subsidies. The legal aid programs in every other country in the world expend all or most of their funds on payments to private lawyers representing needy

clients.[67] In the United States, by contrast, civil legal aid was delivered exclusively
through salaried employees, until very recently.

As the budget of the Legal Services Corporation spiraled upward, American lawyers began to rethink their attitude toward state support and seek to divert federal money to private practitioners. Their economic interests coincided
with the political agenda of conservatives, who wished to restrain the aggressive
advocacy of legal services lawyers and redirect resources away from law reform
toward routine representation. As a result, the 1974 Legal Services Corporation
Act required the Corporation to examine various ways of delivering legal services to the poor, including the payment of private practitioners under "judicare" programs. This study confirmed the fears of activists that private lawyers
were far less innovative in seeking to assert and extend the rights of their
clients.[68] Another study sympathetic to the use of private practitioners found
that many were either incompetent to practice poverty law (because they lacked
expertise) or uninterested in doing so (because they derived greater rewards
from their paying clients); consequently, referral networks quickly concentrated
judicare work in a few offices despite efforts to disperse demand.[69] The Reagan
administration, nevertheless, required the Legal Services Corporation to devote
10 percent of its budget to cooperation with the private profession, some of
which funds are spent on judicare programs. Even so, the vast majority of private practitioners earn far less from the civil representation of indigents than
from their criminal defense.

Public Interest Law

If state subsidies for legal representation have been a mixed success in legitimating
the legal system and insignificant in creating demand for private practitioners,
private philanthropy has been even more marginal. We saw earlier that the pro
bono activities of lawyers have always produced minimal amounts of service; private
lawyers' financial support for legal aid programs, never significant, dried up entirely
when the federal government began providing funds. Starting in the 1920s, lawyers
and political activists also created public interest law firms to advance particular
substantive goals. The best-known examples are the American Civil Liberties Union
and the NAACP Legal Defense and Education Fund, Inc.[70] In the late 1960s and
early 1970s, greatly increased foundation support, the growth of social movements,
and the political commitment of law students combined to produce an explosion
of firms advocating on behalf of civil rights and liberties, environmental and consumer protection, feminism, the disabled, education, the mass media, health care,
and welfare.[71] Some of the most highly qualified recent law graduates competed
intensely for jobs that would pay them substantially less (at least 20 percent) than
they could earn in the private sector.[72]

Public interest firms encountered problems similar to those that troubled legal
aid programs, but in more acute form. First, their legitimacy was even more ten-
uous. Donors concerned to protect their tax-exempt status insisted that recipients
restrict their lobbying activities.[73] Most firms, in any case, were eager to concentrate
on litigation to the exclusion of other strategies, partly because their clients lacked

political muscle and partly because few lawyers possessed the skills and contacts required for political campaigns.[74] Even in the courtroom public interest lawyers could not easily assume the comfortable ethical posture of the hired gun because they often began by identifying a social problem and then went looking for clients willing to assert a grievance. Paradoxically, the apolitical image sought by progressive lawyers also has allowed conservatives to create their own "public interest" law firms, enjoying the same advantages of enhanced legitimacy and tax-free status.[75]

Second, and for similar reasons, funding for public interest law always has been limited and insecure. Even at its peak in the early 1970s, there were only 75 to 100 firms employing 500 to 700 lawyers with a budget of $35 million to $50 million.[76] By contrast, governmental expenditures on criminal and civil representation exceeded $700 million, and the private sector spent tens of billions of dollars on legal services. Virtually all the income of public interest law firms came from foundations, 80 percent from the Ford Foundation alone.[77] But foundations are inherently fickle; competition among them and careerism within them both contribute to the rapid turnover of causes; consequently, most have reduced their commitment to public interest law.[78] Firms have found it difficult or impossible to establish an independent financial base. Client fees are limited by the firm's tax-exempt status. Membership dues generate little income. Court-awarded fees are rarely available under American law; when granted they are paid only years later, if ever. The U.S. Supreme Court has continued to limit the situations in which fees may be recovered.[79] And conservatives are attacking even these limited provisions, seeking to have such fees eliminated or at least curtailed.[80]

In addition to the beneficiaries of foundation largesse, some 50 to 100 private law firms, often organized as collectives, support themselves from client fees while devoting a substantial portion of their energies to political work.[81] Both kinds of public interest law firm offer an essential outlet for the altruism of the small number of activist lawyers and confer important benefits on their clients, but they do little to enhance the legitimacy of the legal system or the legal profession and nothing to create demand for lawyers' services.

Expanding the Middle-Class Clientele

Lawyer Referral

Government and private philanthropy are not responsible for all redistributions of lawyers' services. Some reflect market innovations that extend representation to workers and the middle class. For many years professional associations have operated lawyer-referral services that inform potential consumers about local lawyers.[82] The Wisconsin statewide Lawyer Referral Information Service, established in 1979, expected 40,000 telephone inquiries in 1981 and hoped that a third of the callers would become paying clients.[83] These services may allocate demand randomly, thereby reducing intraprofessional competition, but they augment demand only for potential clients discouraged merely by the difficulty of identifying a lawyer.

Furthermore, just 2 percent of a national sample had ever used a lawyer-referral service—only 5 percent of those who said they knew of the service.[84] This is not surprising: individuals seeking services, including legal representation, strongly prefer the recommendations of friends and relatives to impersonal referral mechanisms.[85]

Group Legal Services

Group legal services seem more promising as a stimulus of demand. These plans were created more than fifty years ago by merchants and physicians seeking to collect debts and automobile owners anxious to ensure representation in criminal and personal injury cases while traveling.[86] Like the medical profession, the organized legal profession opposed these innovations, fearing that lawyers who served such groups would gain a competitive advantage—though of course the professional associations couched their objections in terms of the "threat" that lay intermediaries posed to the lawyer-client relationship.[87] Unions and other voluntary associations won the right to refer their members to sympathetic lawyers only in the 1960s, when the U.S. Supreme Court extended First Amendment protection to such activities.[88]

Even then the profession did not capitulate. Group plans can be categorized by means of two variables. Members of insurance plans pay a substantial premium entitling them to a prescribed range and quantity of legal services; subscribers to referral schemes make a nominal payment for access to a list of participating lawyers, who offer a free initial consultation (as do most other lawyers) and may reduce their fees for some matters. Members of open-panel plans can choose among a wide range of lawyers—sometimes the entire local bar; those who join closed-panel plans can consult only lawyers (sometimes a single firm) who belong to the plan and have agreed to accept a schedule of fees, generally below the market price. Just as the medical profession preferred the "Blues" and opposed health maintenance organizations such as HIP and later Kaiser, so the American Bar Association preferred open-panel referral schemes to closed-panel prepaid plans, promulgating "ethical" rules that favored the former and discouraged or prohibited the latter.[89] The ABA abandoned such discrimination only under threat of a federal antitrust prosecution.[90]

The legal profession first began to display significant interest in group plans when its control over supply had been seriously eroded, half a century after these schemes were introduced. Yet they have not fulfilled lawyers' hopes for increased business. Lawyers have sought to spread subscriber demand broadly, just as they promoted lawyer referral services and favored institutional advertising over advertising by individual lawyers, advertising over solicitation, court-appointed counsel over public defenders, and judicare over staffed-office legal aid programs. But demand has inevitably become concentrated among a few providers. Subscribers naturally prefer closed-panel plans, which often negotiate lower fees for their members and also reduce the psychological and economic costs of choosing a lawyer. For the latter reason, even members of open-panel plans seek referrals to particular lawyers, which narrows the range of providers.[91] This competitive advantage is sometimes improperly obtained: two Philadelphia lawyers have been indicted for giving kickbacks to Roofers Union Local 30–30B in exchange for being retained by the union prepaid plan.[92]

Group legal service plans not only concentrate business, but the amount they generate also has been disappointing. As a fringe benefit, legal services have received a very low priority among union negotiators, who have been suffering major reductions in their bargaining power as a result of national recessions and international competition. Furthermore, unions represent less than a fifth of the workforce. As late as 1978, group plans enrolled only a million subscribers. Individuals have displayed little interest in purchasing insurance for legal costs: a 1974 national survey found that among the third of the adult population who had never used a lawyer, 55 percent were unwilling to subscribe to a prepaid plan that cost even $3 a month, 76 percent were unwilling to subscribe at $6 a month, and 94 percent were unwilling to subscribe at what probably was the most realistic estimate of $12 a month.[93] Midwest Legal Services, the largest marketer of prepaid plans, estimated that 60 to 80 percent of employees choose such coverage when it is offered within a "cafeteria" benefit plan, and about 20 percent ultimately subscribe to a voluntary plan. Furthermore, participating lawyers generally must discount their fees significantly.[94]

Coverage has nevertheless continued to expand.[95] An estimated 7 million employees belonged to group plans negotiated by their unions in 1984, 15 million in 1986, and 17 million in 1987.[96] That year, the AFL-CIO offered nearly half of its 12.8 million members a no-premium legal services plan entitling participants to a free initial consultation at designated law firms and a 30 percent discount on subsequent legal services.[97]

Private entrepreneurs have also begun to direct their marketing capacity to enrolling members in prepaid plans. Some 30 companies were doing so at the end of 1987, many of which found their business doubling annually.[98] Amway (which sells soap, vitamins, and other products) uses its one million distributors to promote the Ultimate Legal Network, a $160 package of advice. Montgomery Ward, one of the nation's largest retailers, is marketing a prepaid plan to its one million credit card holders, offering advice and limited drafting for $81 a year; 200,000 subscribers had enrolled by early 1987.[99] Prepaid Legal Services, Inc., is an open-panel scheme that reimburses clients for significant litigation costs in return for an annual premium of about $200 a year; it had attracted more than 300,000 members by early 1987.[100] And a syndicator has persuaded a million subscribers to pay $90 a year for an unlimited number of seven-minute telephone consultations with a panel of lawyers as well as telephone calls and letters by those lawyers.[101]

Finally, lawyers themselves have initiated schemes. Hyatt Legal Services, the nation's largest clinic, created LawPlan, offering free advice and some drafting (but not representation) for an annual fee of about $100, which it has begun marketing to 1.25 million holders of Citibank credit cards.[102] Jacoby & Meyers, the second largest clinic, offers "Legal Advantage" to the 6.7 million subscribers to Compu-U-Card.[103] Although consumers never will be persuaded that legal insurance is as indispensable as medical insurance, it can generate a significant amount of new business for some lawyers.

Legal Clinics

Legal clinics may be a more successful device for tapping the potential demand of working-class and middle-class consumers. Clinics are private law offices that attempt to cut costs by attracting a large clientele, routinizing services, and replacing lawyers with paraprofessionals who use forms and word-processing equipment.[104] When the first clinics were established in the early 1970s, the organized profession responded with unqualified hostility, disciplining participating lawyers for using the word "clinic," giving interviews to the media, and, of course, advertising.[105] Only when the U.S. Supreme Court protected clinics from these attacks by extending the First Amendment to some forms of commercial speech did they begin to expand.[106] The ABA responded by establishing a clinic that somehow would not compete with other lawyers; not surprisingly, the enterprise was a commercial failure.[107]

There were 8 clinics in 1974, 800 in 1980, and more than a thousand by 1984.[108] All of them seek to concentrate business previously dispersed across a large number of sole practitioners and small firms; a few have grown into exceedingly large enterprises. In 1984, Hyatt Legal Services was the ninth largest firm in the country and Jacoby & Meyers the ninety-fifth. The following year, Hyatt was *second,* with 550 lawyers (up 45 percent from 1984) in 174 offices in 29 cities in 17 states; Jacoby & Meyers was forty-first with 236 lawyers (up 50 percent from 1984) in 150 offices in 5 states.[109] A year later Hyatt had grown 23 percent to 674 lawyers in 192 offices while Jacoby & Meyers had jumped to thirty-first place with 297 lawyers.[110] In 1987, however, both had fallen back: Hyatt to fifth place (having lost 38 lawyers) and Jacoby & Meyers to forty-first (although it added 5 lawyers) (see Table 46, note a).[111] That year Hyatt was only nine years old and Jacoby & Meyers twelve. In 1984, Hyatt was planning to spend $4,475,000 for advertising and expecting to attract 18,000 new clients a month.[112] In the first six months of 1985, Hyatt spent $2.9 million on television advertising and Jacoby & Meyers increased its television budget 228 percent.[113] Jacoby & Meyers subsequently brought its advertising in-house, spending $5 million a year on television.[114] These efforts clearly paid off: Hyatt was seeing 300,000 clients a year and Jacoby & Meyers 175,000.[115]

Yet the actual impact of clinics on both the image and the pocket of the legal profession is uncertain. Defenders claim that clinics demystify the law, rendering it more accessible to ordinary people; their detractors respond that clinics commercialize the profession, undermining public respect. Clinics insist that the majority of their clients would never use conventionally marketed legal services; sole practitioners and small firms maintain that clinics merely concentrate existing business, competing unfairly through massive advertising budgets and misleading discounts, only to raise their prices once they capture the market. Certainly the clinic form (like the public interest law firm) is not the exclusive possession of one side of the adversary process; it can be adapted to serve business clients as well as individuals. The Los Angeles clinic of Katz and Block represents landlords seeking to evict tenants, handling more than 300 cases per month—twice as many as any other firm and perhaps 10 percent of all evictions in the city; two thirds are resolved out of court, and 85 percent of the cases filed are settled before trial.[116] Clinics claim to raise the quality legal services by eliminating careless errors; their competitors deplore the routinization and lack of lawyer-client contact.[117] Critics have also noted that low salaries cause rapid turnover, preventing lawyers from acquiring experience and creating discontinuities in representation.[118] Jacoby & Meyers replied that its average lawyer salary was a respectable $47,500 in 1986, and more than a dozen of its 297 lawyers earned over $100,000.[119]

Is Demand Creation an Effective Means of Market Control and Status Enhancement?

It is impossible to prove conclusively that the profession deliberately embraced new strategies of market control and status enhancement during the last two decades, but the coincidence of events is certainly striking. For more than a century lawyers had been largely indifferent to the needs of the unrepresented poor, although their plight was repeatedly publicized beginning in 1919. Pro bono activities were individual, sporadic, and extremely limited. Large-firm lawyers who expressed a slightly greater sense of obligation were comfortably protected from actual demands by poor clients. The organized profession condemned government support for civil legal aid as creeping socialism. It condoned state prosecution of unrepresented criminal accused until the 1970s. It prohibited advertising and solicitation, periodically waging highly visible campaigns against violators. It opposed group plans as threats to the lawyer-client relationship.

Then, starting in the late 1960s, professional control over the production *of* and *by* producers of legal services seriously eroded. The number of lawyers grew at an unprecedented rate, their backgrounds became more diverse, the profession suffered incursions into its monopoly, interstate mobility increased, and courts struck down prohibitions against unauthorized practice, price cutting, and advertising. Lawyers responded by sponsoring major studies of "legal need," endorsing federal support for legal aid, defending the Legal Services Corporation against political attack, seeking to divert government funds from salaried lawyers to private practitioners, organizing and promoting pro bono activities, embracing group plans, devoting substantial resources to institutional and then individual advertising, employing more paraprofessionals and word processors, establishing high-volume clinics, and cutting prices to reach new clients.

Yet it is far from clear that these new strategies will achieve either goal of the professional project. They may impair the profession's image rather than strengthen it. Studies of legal need may demonstrate the impossibility of achieving equal justice. Pro bono activities may lower rather than enhance status: among Chicago lawyers, prestige correlated *inversely* with reputation for altruism.[120] For most lawyers, the individual economic interest in avoiding pro bono obligations clearly outweighs any collective desire to improve professional prestige. In any case, state-supported legal services have partly supplanted and greatly overshadowed pro bono activities. Private lawyers appear less "independent" when paid by state funds rather than clients. Educated by health care scandals, the public rightly suspects professionals of overcharging third-party payers, whether government or private insurers.[121] Lawyers serving the poor—especially indigent criminals—become associated with the characteristics and alleged immorality of their clients.[122] Lawyers subsidized by government or philanthropy are less able to justify their actions by reference to the market or the adversary system and consequently appear more explicitly political. Staffed-office legal service programs highlight the parochial interests served by private practitioners. At the same time, the heavy caseloads of legal aid lawyers and public defenders amplify differences between the quality of legal services purchased in the market and those subsidized by the state. And efforts to expand the middle-class clientele expose the fundamentally commercial nature of law practice.

Demand creation may be no more successful in relieving the economic pressures created by excess supply. Although political conservatives may have ideological preferences for paying private practitioners to represent the poor, fiscal conservatism favors salaried legal aid lawyers and public defenders, who deliver services at costs that are lower and more easily controlled.[123] A striking illustration can be found outside legal aid programs. In 1984 and 1985, federal agencies spent some $50 million on private lawyers, at rates sometimes exceeding $200 an hour, even though the government already employed more than 17,000 lawyers. In response, the Reagan administration sought to legislate a ceiling of $75 an hour on the fees paid to private lawyers representing the government. Ironically, one stimulus for this curb was the $472,000 bill submitted by the private practitioners who represented Attorney General Edwin Meese during his ethics investigation.[124]

Lawyers employed or reimbursed by the state will never enjoy the economic rewards of private practice. In any case, state welfare expenditures are contracting, not expanding, when adjusted for inflation. Foundations also have reduced their support for public interest law. Even at their high point, however, governmental and philanthropic legal services budgets were never more than 1 or 2 percent of private sector expenditures. Efforts to stimulate demand by individuals (whether legal aid clients or members of group plans) are likely to be frustrated by the facts that substantive law, as presently constituted, is rarely useful to those without substantial property and that almost everyone is extremely reluctant to become involved in legal disputes (63 percent of survey respondents uninterested in joining a group plan explained that they needed legal services too infrequently).[125]

The limitations on the strategy of demand creation are located not only in the larger social, political, and economic environment but also within the profession itself. Efforts to control supply united the profession against an external enemy composed of potential entrants and lay competitors (although some lawyers had higher stakes in this project than others). Attempts to stimulate demand, however, necessarily pit lawyers against each other. Salaried lawyers in legal services and public defender offices compete with private practitioners; public interest lawyers confront private interest lawyers; those who contribute pro bono services resent those who do not; lawyers who serve a group plan compete with lawyers outside it; and clinics compete with sole practitioners and small firms. Indeed, many strategies of demand creation—preeminently advertising, solicitation, price cutting, and specialization—directly undermine professional control over production *by* producers. Hence the profession is constantly torn between the desire to generate demand effectively and the desire to dampen competition by distributing new clients randomly through judicare schemes, court-appointed criminal defense counsel, pro bono obligations, lawyer referral, and open-panel group legal services plans. Intra professional competition will nevertheless continue to intensify and to increase concentration in the production of legal services for individuals.

7

Self-Regulation

The Promulgation of Ethical Rules

One of the hallmarks that distinguishes a profession from other occupations is the power and practice of self-regulation. We saw in Chapter 5 that the legal profession used this privilege largely to dampen competition, until its restrictive practices were struck down by external authorities. The content of the ethical code and the nature of its enforcement both reflected jockeying among lawyers for competitive advantage.[1] Self-regulation also helped stave off state regulation. Despite the importance of self-regulation to the professional project, however, lawyers were in no hurry to construct the necessary institutional framework. In the nineteenth century, the profession was organized in groups that were sufficiently localized and small (outside the major cities) to ensure conformity through informal sanctions.[2] The ABA first adopted an ethical code only in 1908. Thereafter, concern with the content of ethical rules became a major preoccupation of professional associations—perhaps also a surrogate for doing anything about the behavior prescribed. Complete revisions of the ABA rules were proposed or adopted in 1928, 1933, 1937, 1954, 1969, and 1982.[3] The reporter for the last revision now has coauthored a gloss on those rules that is nearly 900 pages long.[4] Numerous books and journals offer moral instruction about the dilemmas of lawyers.[5] The sense of unease appears to have intensified, for immediately after its latest recodification of the Rules of Professional Conduct, the ABA created a Commission on Professionalism, which devoted two years to producing a report entitled *In the Spirit of Public Service: A Blueprint for the Rekindling of Lawyer Professionalism.*

The profession defines the ethical dilemmas of lawyers as matters of individual choice and maintains that exhortations, properly phrased, will discourage delinquency. Its response to the Watergate scandal, which involved an embarrassing number of lawyers from the President on down, exemplified this strategy: the ABA compelled approved law schools to require instruction in professional responsibility, and many states also made it a separate subject on the bar examination.[6] Nearly all law schools today insist that students take a course in professional responsibility, even though empirical studies repeatedly have shown that these measures have no effect on behavior.[7] Indeed, there is evidence that law school makes students *more* cynical about legal ethics.[8]

The Disciplinary Process

The suspicion that professional associations promulgate ethical rules more to legitimate themselves in the eyes of the public than to engage in effective regulation is strengthened by the inadequacy of enforcement mechanisms. State and local bar associations did not take their responsibility for discipline seriously until well into the twentieth century. The Association of the Bar of the City of New York established a Committee on Grievances at its founding in 1870 but heard no complaints for the next fourteen years.[9] The 1912 report of the Standing Committee on Grievances of the State Bar Association of Ohio may illustrate the organized profession's attitude toward misconduct. Here it is in its totality: "This committee has never found it necessary to even have a meeting. If any of the members of the Ohio State Bar Association have any grievances against each other they have not made it known to this Committee." To which President Taft of the Bar Association replied: "Some man from Cincinnati has a grievance against a lawyer who has been dead for several years. I do not know what the grievance is, but it is here, and we will turn it over to the Committee. It may make interesting reading."[10]

Such levity notwithstanding, ethical rules are not self-enforcing. Surveys repeatedly show that lawyers are ignorant of many rules and fail to internalize those they do know.[11] For example, forty-six of the fifty states prohibit fee-splitting: one lawyer may not compensate another for forwarding business. Yet when a random sample of 600 lawyers were questioned in September 1984, 40 percent thought that forwarding fees were permitted and another 27 percent did not know; 62 percent approved of forwarding fees if the amount was reasonable and it was disclosed to the client; and even among those who thought forwarding fees were *not* permitted, nearly half thought they were appropriate.[12] A thoroughly unscientific 1951 inquiry among twenty-five state "correspondents" found that seven did not consider forwarding fees unprofessional and nineteen believed they were a common practice.[13] A careful investigation of litigators (1000 in Michigan and another 1500 in large firms across the nation) confirmed that the lawyers were ignorant of ethical rules, failed to internalize them, and consistently violated their precepts.[14] For instance, only 57 percent of the Michigan litigators and 75 percent of the national sample felt obligated to ask a client to correct a clearly false statement concerning a material issue in a deposition; and nearly half of both samples felt entitled to use and aggravate delays in litigation to obtain a more favorable settlement. Lawyers consistently abuse pretrial proceedings to frustrate the legitimate goals of their adversaries.[15] A reporter posing as an accident victim found that five out of thirteen randomly chosen New York personal injury lawyers encouraged her to lie in order to hold Consolidated Edison liable for her slip and fall.[16]

More disturbing, most lawyers never even perceive moral dilemmas in their practice. Only 16 percent of a sample of 224 lawyers in four large Chicago firms in the late 1970s had ever refused work because it conflicted with their personal values.[17] The proportion was twice as high (31 percent) among Washington lawyers in the early 1980s, but among house counsel to private interests or trade associations it was even lower than among independent counsel in Chicago.[18] A survey of Florida practitioners found that few rejected cases on moral grounds, and even those did so only out of reluctance to accuse a fellow lawyer of malpractice or to take a civil rights matter.[19] Neither clients nor lawyers expect the latter to assume the role of independent counselors.[20] Indeed, lawyers have condoned and even encouraged misconduct by their corporate clients in a significant, and perhaps growing, number of instances.[21] One reason for this apparent lack of autonomy may be the fact that, although large law firms rarely earn more than a small percentage of their income from any one client, *individual* lawyers in those firms typically devote a third or more of their billable hours to a single client.[22] Consequently, a client that is insignificant to the firm may be indispensable to the lawyer. Yet if lawyers are excessively loyal to those who can pay, their record of representing politically unpopular clients has often been disappointing.[23]

Whatever the situation may have been in the nineteenth century (or still may be among the small proportion of lawyers practicing in rural settings), contemporary urban lawyers suffer few informal sanctions for violating ethical rules; peers may even encourage misconduct.[24] Nor is the formal disciplinary process much more effective. Individual clients who might be motivated to complain about lawyer misconduct are ignorant of the content of ethical rules and poorly situated to perceive most lawyer misbehavior. Furthermore, many ethical violations actually advance rather than injure client interests. In any case, only 13 percent of a sample of clients knew of the existence of professional disciplinary procedures.[25] Lawyers, who are somewhat better informed about the rules and more likely to observe violations, are reluctant to turn in their colleagues, perhaps recognizing that they themselves have committed similar infractions and might suffer retaliation. In a sample of Missouri lawyers, only 34 percent of rural and 71 percent of urban practitioners said they would report ethical infractions, and the proportions who actually had done so were even smaller (11 and 27 percent respectively).[26] In fact, professionals file fewer than a tenth of all grievances.[27]

This gentleman's agreement may be breaking down, however. Lawyers often complain to gain a tactical advantage over adversaries or punish them for seeking such an advantage. Cadwalader, Wickersham & Taft urged the U.S. District Court for the Eastern District of Virginia to remove another New York firm, Skadden, Arps. Slate, Meagher & Flom, as bankruptcy counsel for A.H. Robins Co. Inc. because it also represented Aetna Life and Casualty Co., a creditor in the case.[28] Milbank, Tweed, Hadley & McCoy has filed a grievance against Sullivan & Cromwell, accusing it of bribing witnesses in a contest over the $500 million Johnson estate.[29] In another case involving the proceeds of a trust, the Appellate Division of the New York State Supreme Court, responding to charges by Patterson, Belknap, Webb & Tyler, found that Sullivan & Cromwell had obtained essential documents by improper means, including deceit, and disqualified the firm from further representation in the matter.[30]

The disciplinary process also supports the status hierarchy within the legal profession.[31] The Chicago Bar Association deliberately focused discipline on lawyers representing personal injury victims and (unsuccessfully) sought legislation that would have imposed prison sentences on lawyers who solicited clients and authorized the state attorney to seek injunctions against such practices.[32] More than 80 percent of those disciplined in California, Illinois, and the District of Columbia in 1981–82 were sole practitioners, and none practiced in a firm with more than 7 lawyers, even though sole practitioners represented fewer than half of all private practitioners in the nation (48.6 percent) and firms with more than seven lawyers contained almost exactly the same proportion (47.2 percent).[33]

Starting from a population of complaints that already overlooks most misconduct, the disciplinary process then displays extraordinary lenience. Throughout the first half of this century (1903 to 1949), Kansas disbarred or suspended only 55 lawyers—little more than one a year—although more than 2000 were practicing in the state in 1940. Half of those disbarred (28) were subsequently reinstated, although a quarter of these were disbarred a second time.[34] One reason for the infrequency of punishment may be the inadequacy of enforcement mechanisms. In 1935, sixteen integrated state bar associations had authority to discipline and another fourteen state supreme courts had established their own procedures; but in nineteen jurisdictions, voluntary bar associations could only recommend action to the state supreme court. Furthermore, grievance committees were empowered to issue subpoenas and administer oaths in only twenty-eight jurisdictions.[35]

During the prewar period, most jurisdictions were insufficiently concerned with discipline to keep any records of their actions; a 1948 ABA survey found that twenty-eight states either had no records or failed to furnish them, and the others had incomplete data.[36] Only the three largest jurisdictions—New York, California, and Illinois—maintained reasonably complete statistics. Between 1905 and 1920, the Association of the Bar of the City of New York investigated more than 8500 complaints (a small fraction of those received), but New York courts ultimately sanctioned only 260 lawyers (3 percent of the complaints investigated and just 16 lawyers a year in a bar that contained more than 15,000).[37] Between 1925 and 1935, the Association received 22,800 complaints, held 900 hearings (3.9 percent of complaints), found 314 lawyers guilty (1.4 percent), and prosecuted 275 before the Appellate Division of the Supreme Court (1.2 percent); the latter dismissed 43 cases, allowed 69 lawyers to resign without a final decision, suspended 39 (0.2 percent), and disbarred 108 (0.5 percent).[38] In 1948–49, the Association received 1529 complaints, held 85 hearings (5.6 percent), and recommended prosecution in 31 cases (2.0 percent); the Appellate Division dismissed the charges against 7, censured 2, suspended 4 (0.3 percent), and disbarred 4 (0.3 percent).[39] Throughout the first half of this century fewer than 1 percent of New York City lawyers accused of misconduct received a significant punishment. In the fifteen years from 1958–59 to 1972–73, 30,810 complaints were filed, 663 were tried (2 percent; one year missing), 178 were disbarred (0.6 percent; 55 of these after felony convictions), and 200 were suspended (0.6 percent) (see Table 36). In 1983, 8766 complaints were filed against lawyers; 38 percent were dismissed or withdrawn; another 34 percent were rejected after a preliminary investigation; and a further 12 percent were sent to other agencies. The disciplinary committees cautioned 4.6 percent, admonished or reprimanded 0.3 percent, and forwarded 491 complaints to the court, which alone could impose significant penalties. Among the 299 cases decided by the court that year (including some from previous years), 65 lawyers were disbarred (0.7 percent), 86 suspended (1.0 percent), and 12 censured. The New York bar then contained more than 80,000 lawyers.[40]

In 1927 California established a unified bar with compulsory membership and regulatory power. During the next eight years it suspended or disbarred *sixty* times as many lawyers as it had during the seventy-seven years between the state's admission to the Union and 1927 (apparently a total of *three!*).[41] But that says more about the lenience of the first eight decades than about the severity of those that followed. During its early years, the unified California bar appears to have conducted a preliminary investigation of most complaints: 7965 out of 8335 between 1927 and 1939 (96 percent). Yet it issued only 1425 notices to show cause (17 percent of complaints) and found support for the charges in only 596 cases (7 percent). It ultimately administered 84 public and 77 private reprovals and recommended harsher discipline in only 278 cases (3 percent of complaints). However, the Supreme Court rejected its recommendation in 44 of the 119 cases appealed, with the result that just 159 lawyers were suspended (1.9 percent of complaints) and 92 disbarred (1.1 percent)—only slightly higher proportions than those in New York. Between August 1, 1938, and July 31, 1939, the State Bar received 680 complaints; this time it conducted only 299 preliminary investigations (44 percent of complaints) and issued only 83 notices to show cause (12 percent). Between 1929 and 1948, the annual number of preliminary investigations declined by a factor of more than ten (from 1531 to 148) while the profession nearly doubled in size (see Table 34.a).[42]

Attrition during the later stages of the disciplinary process in California almost equals that in New York City. Between 1928 and 1948, four out of five complaints investigated were dismissed without a hearing. Two thirds of those heard were dismissed without any punishment. Only 2.5 percent of lawyers investigated were suspended, 1.5 percent were disbarred, and another 1.4 percent were allowed to resign (most without prejudice to applying for readmission) (see Table 34.a).[43] Furthermore, though the frequency of punishment increased during the 1930s and early 1940s, it declined after 1944. The California Supreme Court reduced sentences of disbarment in about a quarter of the cases in which it was proposed, although the court slightly increased the number of suspensions. If we make the generous assumption that half the complaints were investigated during the latter part of this period, then only about 2 percent of those accused were suspended or disbarred— perhaps twice the proportion in New York City but nothing to boast about. Furthermore, those punished each year were an insignificant proportion of the entire profession—about 0.05 percent. In California in 1984, 8329 complaints were filed against the more than 80,000 practicing lawyers, but only 48 received private reprimands, 23 public reprimands, 81 suspensions (1.0 percent of complaints), and 11 disbarments (0.1 percent)—just 0.1 percent of the bar was punished.[44]

In the third of these jurisdictions, Illinois, the Chicago Bar Association (CBA) was responsible for discipline in Cook County, while the Illinois State Bar Association oversaw the rest of the state. Complaints to the CBA gradually increased from 100 in 1902 to 245 in 1914, while the annual total of disbarments and resignations ranged between 6 and 35.[45] In the early 1950s, the CBA received almost one complaint a year for every ten Chicago lawyers, compared with 0.15 for every ten downstate lawyers.[46] Of the approximately 18,000 complaints filed between 1928 and 1948, the CBA referred fewer than half (8622, or 47 percent) to its Committee on Inquiry, which held hearings in only 1005 cases (5.6 percent of complaints) and recommended discipline in 301 cases (1.7 percent). The state Supreme Court disbarred 214 (1.2 percent of complaints) and suspended 45 (0.2 percent).[47] The number of complaints investigated annually declined drastically during the 1940s, from a high of 952 in 1933–34 to an average of 174 between 1942 and 1948, as it did in California.

The Illinois State Bar Association held 566 hearings between 1928 and 1948, recommending discipline in only 28 cases (5 percent of hearings, compared with 30 percent of the cases heard by the CBA); the Supreme Court actually disbarred 17 lawyers and suspended 9 (4.6 percent of hearings and undoubtedly a much smaller proportion of the complaints filed).[48] As in California, the state Supreme Court generally reduced the severity of punishment: in another 81 cases in which the state bar had recommended 75 disbarments and 6 suspensions, the court imposed 35 disbarments and 18 suspensions, dismissing 28 cases.[49]

There is no evidence that the situation has improved since the 1940s.[50] The small number of complaints filed still do not reflect the quantity of misconduct. Between 1975 and 1979, the total number of complaints nationwide ranged between 30,836 and 37,548, averaging 33,186 (see Table 33). In the early 1980s, 32,000 complaints were filed in a twelve-month period, or about one for every fifty practicing lawyers.[51] Recently the numbers have increased, from 39,356 in 1984 to 54,152 in 1985 and 54,600 in 1986—at a faster rate than the growth of the profession.[52] Yet in California, the number of complaints per 100 practitioners remained incredibly stable, varying only between 9 and 11 between 1973 and 1986.[53]

Disciplinary procedures still dismiss more than 90 percent of complaints with little or no investigation.[54] There is reason to believe that this expresses the solicitude practicing lawyers feel for each other. When disciplinary authority over Chicago lawyers was transferred from the CBA to the independent Attorney Registration and Disciplinary Commission, the proportion of complaints dismissed without investigation fell from 83 percent in 1969–70 to 57 percent in 1974–75 while the proportion of formal hearings increased from 3.5 percent in 1969–70 to 13.5 percent in 1983.[55]

Light penalties are imposed on most of the few found guilty: in California, 60 percent are merely reprimanded.[56] Other studies have found that fewer than 1 percent of those accused received court-imposed sanctions, generally synonymous with suspension or disbarment.[57] The total number of lawyers disbarred in the decade between 1974 and 1983 was less than 0.5 percent of those practicing during that period and the total suspended only about 1 percent (see Table 33). Indeed, between 1975 and 1979, the number of serious punishments (disbarments, disbarments by consent, and suspensions) never exceeded 2 percent of the complaints (see Table 33). Jurisdictions vary greatly in the punishments they inflict for similar offenses, although the ABA Center for Professional Responsibility has proposed common standards. Only New Jersey and a few other states automatically disbar lawyers who have stolen client funds.[58] Because disciplinary proceedings generally remain secret except in the rare instance when a serious penalty is imposed, potential clients cannot learn about prior complaints. Only in Oregon are they a matter of public record from the moment of filing.[59] However, New Jersey publishes an annual report with the names of all publicly disciplined attorneys and a description of their misconduct, and the West Virginia Supreme Court has invalidated a bar rule preserving the confidentiality of disciplinary procedures.[60]

Both the lawyers who administer discipline and the judges who hear appeals from convictions are extremely solicitous of excuses for misbehavior—such as marital troubles, alcohol or drug abuse, or financial difficulties—which would be aggravating rather than mitigating circumstances in most criminal prosecutions.[61] Furthermore, courts are very reluctant to discipline lawyers for such extraprofessional misconduct. In the 1970s, these grounds accounted for less than 4 percent of disbarments, suspensions, and resignations (excluding automatic disbarments following a felony conviction).[62] Among the 107 lawyers disbarred for nonprofessional activity in California, Illinois, and the District of Columbia between 1967 and 1981, 101 had committed felonies.[63] Indeed, the Oregon Supreme Court recently decided that "attempted possession of cocaine" was not an act of moral turpitude justifying any professional discipline, although the dissent noted the widespread cocaine abuse among lawyers and the fact that the prosecution had allowed the defendants to plead guilty to a misdemeanor.[64] By contrast, the New Jersey Supreme Court publicly reprimanded three young lawyers for cocaine possession, warning that it would issue suspensions in the future.[65] Even lawyers who commit felonies may continue to practice for years before being disbarred.[66] Harry E. Clairborne, Chief Judge of the U.S. District Court for Nevada, was found guilty of failing to report $107,000 on his 1979 and 1980 tax returns, jailed for seventeen months, impeached, and removed from office. Nevertheless, the Nevada Supreme Court rejected the State Bar's disciplinary recommendation and imposed no sanctions. He continues to practice law.[67]

The few lawyers suspended or disbarred usually are readmitted by the disciplining jurisdiction or gain admission to other jurisdictions.[68] In California between 1928 and 1948, 48 of the 86 petitions for reinstatement were granted by the State Bar; the state Supreme Court reviewed 19 of the 38 rejected and granted another 5. Not all of those punished were rehabilitated: 56 of those suspended were again found guilty of misconduct after they reentered practice. In New York during the same period, 15 of the 215 suspended were found guilty of misconduct a second time. And in Illinois, 12 lawyers who had been disbarred and reinstated were subsequently disciplined. The number of recidivists who escaped detection undoubtedly was much higher.[69] In Michigan in the 1980s, 44 percent of the attorneys against whom complaints were filed had been the object of earlier complaints.[70] In New Jersey between 1948 and 1982, 27 percent of attorneys who were disciplined for stealing client money but not disbarred were found to have stolen again.[71] Between 1974 and 1983, the total number of reinstatements was 88 percent of the total number of disbarments; reinstatements actually exceeded disbarments in five of these ten years (see Table 33). Lawyers admitted in multiple jurisdictions who are disbarred in one often continue practicing in the others.[72]

Lack of resources is one reason for this poor regulatory record. The Chicago Bar Association spent 25 percent of its 1910 budget on its Grievance Committee, but the proportion declined steadily to 1 percent in the middle and late 1920s.[73] Between 1975 and 1979, total annual disciplinary expenditures nationwide ranged from \$7,054,368 to \$9,397,190, or \$13.26 to \$20.80 per lawyer.[74] They varied from \$116 per lawyer in Hawaii to \$12 in South Carolina in 1984, from \$180 in Alaska to less than \$10 in South Carolina in 1986.[75] California, which spent \$72 per member in 1984 and budgeted an additional \$840,000 in 1984 and 1985 to hire seven more investigators, nevertheless had a backlog of 5000 uninvestigated complaints, 2800 of which were more than six months old.[76] A year later, the backlog had grown to 6000, of which 3700 were more than six months old.[77] California disciplinary expenditures increased from \$2.8 million in 1981 to \$6 million in 1986.[78] Yet in 1987, California lawyers voted to reject a \$25 dues increase, precluding the implementation of necessary reforms.[79] At the beginning of 1988 the president of the State Bar sought a dues increase from \$275 to \$450, pledging to use the approximately \$17.5 million additional revenues for discipline, but the State Bar discipline monitor insisted that this still was not enough.[80] Although the outgoing director of discipline in Minnesota sought a 64 percent increase in his budget (noting that sixty-two practitioners were delinquent in paying their state taxes), the bar approved only a 30 percent increase and rebuked him for overzealous enforcement.[81]

Although laypersons have been involved in the disciplinary process in thirty-three jurisdictions, they are everywhere outnumbered and overshadowed by lawyers.[82] But external critics are becoming impatient with the laxity of professional discipline. The California legislature temporarily refused to authorize the State Bar to collect its 1986 dues because of its inefficient discipline and 5000–case backlog; criticism of the bar united such perennial adversaries as the conservative Republican Governor George Deukmejian and the liberal Democratic Assembly Speaker Willie Brown (both lawyers).[83] This growing anger may explain why professional associations have been stripped of disciplinary functions in eighteen states and the District of Columbia, play only a limited role in nineteen others, and control discipline in just thirteen.[84]

The California legislature became sufficiently discontent with the regulatory performance of the Bar to appoint a law professor as State Bar Discipline Monitor in 1986. His two reports are a detailed indictment of professional discipline and have prompted some changes. The Monitor found that although the State Bar had a toll-free number for client inquiries, it was unpublicized and unknown because the Bar was reluctant to augment the existing backlog of 5000 to 6000 complaints. Even so, those who called the number in early 1987 encountered a busy signal 62 to 72 percent of the time. By the middle of the year, efforts had been made to publicize the number, and it was engaged only 30 to 45 percent of the time.[85] Many local bar associations "accepted" complaints without informing clients that they lacked both investigative and disciplinary authority and would seek only to mediate the dispute.[86] The Bar was uninterested in complaints from nonclients (suggesting that its purpose was to minimize consumer dissatisfaction, not lawyer misconduct).[87]

Written complaints elicited a form acknowledgment in thirty to sixty days but no further contact for another twelve to eighteen months (since cut to four months). If the complainant did not respond to this inquiry or a single follow-up letter, the case was closed for insufficient facts; 80 percent of complaints ended this way. All complaints concerning fees or unauthorized practice were also dismissed, even though the Bar's own audit showed that 14 percent of these merited further investigation.[88] The Bar used volunteer attorneys to clear files, although many failed to perform their duties, others conducted superficial investigations, and some knew the lawyers they were investigating. The program was terminated in 1987.[89] The Bar paid poorly both lay intake officers and lawyer investigators, which caused high turnover.[90]

Multiple complaints against a single lawyer often were assigned to different investigators.[91] Bureaucracy further hampered investigation. Every expenditure of funds required approval by a superior; so did every interview with another client of the accused attorney, with the result that only 30 such interviews were requested in disposing of 9000 complaints in 1986.[92] Investigators were denied access to Legal Services Trust Fund records concerning misappropriation, the transcripts of moral fitness hearings, and even the newly mandatory attorney disclosures of criminal convictions or malpractice suits.[93] State prosecutors began to refer matters to the Bar for investigation only in the middle of 1987.[94] All investigations were abated whenever a criminal or civil proceeding was brought against the attorney, and until 1987 there was no mechanism for reviving the investigation when the proceeding terminated.[95] The Office of Trial Counsel (OTC) lacked any capacity to initiate an investigation on its own or to handle complex cases.[96] It began using its own computerized records to detect patterns of repeated misconduct only in the middle of 1987; until then, indeed, the OTC routinely shredded two thirds of its files.[97] All proceedings remained secret unless and until the OTC sent the accused a notice to show cause; even then the information disclosed to those who inquired was often incomplete or inaccurate.[98]

It took as long as five years for the OTC to issue a notice to show cause; in 1986, the State Bar Court took another nineteen months to decide the average case.[99] The State Bar Court consisted of 448 lawyers (volunteers until 1987) and 80 laypersons; but the vast majority of cases were heard by a single lawyer rather than a three-person court including a layperson.[100] Legislative pressure on the Bar to clear the backlog has had mixed results: the proportion of complaints leading to a notice to show cause actually declined from about 10 percent to 2 to 4 percent, and many complaints were reclassified as "inquiries."[101] Still, the backlog remains high—more than 2500 complaints pending for more than six months—and the caseload is three times what an investigator can reasonably handle (see Table 34.b).[102] More than 90 percent of complaints are still dismissed at the investigative stage, and only 2 percent lead to serious penalties (disbarment, resignation, or suspension) (see Table 34.b). The California experience offers little reason to believe that even the most vigorous and independent outside monitor can transform a professional association into an effective disciplinary mechanism.

Protecting the Client Against Financial Loss

One of the most serious forms of lawyer misconduct is the loss or misuse of client money. A New Jersey study found that it accounted for 53 percent of all public sanctions imposed on lawyers between 1948 and 1982.[103] Only six states proactively review trust accounts, and only New Jersey requires banks to report overdrafts to the Office of Attorney Ethics.[104] Until recently, clients had no recourse except to pursue the lawyer, who may have absconded or declared bankruptcy; in the early

1960s, only twenty-one jurisdictions had client security funds. All states now have such schemes, usually funded by the interest on lawyer trust accounts.[105] Yet they remain only partial solutions. Many jurisdictions have ceilings of $5000 to $20,000 per claim. In some, a claim is not paid unless the lawyer has been disciplined. Fewer than half the claims are paid, and fewer than two thirds of these are compensated in full.[106] Until compelled by its Supreme Court, California, like many other states, did not admit the victimized claimant to the hearing (although it allowed the accused lawyer to appear with an attorney) and gave no reason for its disposition.[107] The number of claims appears to be rising—from 530 to 696 between 1979 and 1980 nationwide (31 percent)—an increase that may require formalization of the claims procedures.[108] California alone paid $1,093,887 to 200 claimants from 1981 to 1983 but nearly three times as much ($2,917,358) to more than twice as many claimants (448) from 1984 to 1986.[109]

Ensuring Professional Competence

Professions claim the privilege of self-regulation on the ground that they not only correct misconduct but also ensure the quality of the services they render. Indeed, clients are far more concerned with courtesy, cost, responsiveness, speed, and, of course, success than with lawyer obedience to most of the ethical rules.[110] Competence can be enhanced by monitoring input, process, or outcome.[111]

Input Measures

We saw in Chapter 3 that the profession erected numerous entry barriers during the first half of this century. But almost no effort has been made to validate these input measures by testing their relationship to quality, and there is little reason to assume such a relationship. As competition for admission has intensified during the last two decades, law schools have rejected applicants just as qualified as those accepted. The Law School Admission Test, a major determinant of entry, acknowledges a measurement error of plus or minus 70 points—a spread larger than the entire range of scores of those admitted at many schools. Because most law graduates pass the bar examination, it no longer functions as a guarantee of quality; nor have bar examiners ever have sought to ascertain whether the score attained has any connection with later competence in practice. Furthermore, such background variables as parental income, social status, and education correlate strongly with college attended, college grades, LSAT scores, law school attended, law school performance, and passing the bar examination.[112] One interstate comparison found that the restrictiveness of entry correlated directly with peer review ratings in Martindale-Hubbell and inversely with the size of legal malpractice premiums and the number of formal disciplinary actions, but the authors conceded that none of these was a reliable index of quality.[113] Furthermore, although everyone would agree that the academic ability of law students has increased in recent years, the number of lawyers disciplined annually has been rising faster than the size of the profession.[114]

Finally, it is absurd to pretend that any test of competence administered to someone at the age of twenty-five, no matter how well constructed, can ensure quality throughout a fifty-year career. Lawyers have lagged behind physicians in mandating continuing education, perhaps because medical expertise changes much more rapidly than legal. Minnesota and Iowa were the first jurisdictions to require further training in 1974.[115] By the end of 1986, twenty-two states and thirteen federal district courts demanded some continuing education. Private providers have been attracted to the field by the fact that practicing lawyers (unlike law students) have ample resources and can claim a tax deduction for their educational expenses.[116] The ABA has endorsed continuing education, and a large majority of lawyers surveyed in Colorado and Minnesota felt it had enhanced their competence.[117] Occasionally, however, a lawyer will acknowledge that compulsory lectures are an inefficient instructional method and that continuing legal education can easily degenerate into a tax-deductible junket.[118] Specialization also has potential as a means of quality control, but thus far it is little more than a form of self-certification allowing those already advantaged by experience to protect themselves from competition from more recent entrants (see Chapter 5, "Specialization").

Process Measures

The second way in which professions maintain quality is by overseeing lawyers as they render services. The degree of variation in lawyer behavior was revealed by a reporter who posed as a potential client and described a very simple problem to nine New York legal clinics; he received nine very different recommendations, with fee estimates ranging between $45 and $2122.[119] Compared with entry barriers, process controls are more likely to affect quality, but they are also far more difficult to operationalize. Large law firms train associates and monitor their performance for years before deciding whether to admit them to partnership. Yet they admit some on the basis of business-getting skills rather than technical competence; those rejected continue to practice law in other settings; and the majority of lawyers presently practicing never experienced such supervision, nor will many who enter practice in the future. Some law firms are extending peer review to partners, both to anticipate problems that might lead to malpractice and to ensure that clients are satisfied; the review also can affect the division of earnings.[120]

External reviews of process are even more difficult to institutionalize. Individual clients rarely complain, seek a second opinion, or change lawyers.[121] Although the vast majority of client complaints involve matters of competence (see Table 35), professional disciplinary bodies generally reject charges of incompetence as outside their jurisdiction. Among the 531 complaints that the Illinois State Bar Association dismissed between 1928 and 1948 (94 percent of all those filed), most concerned competence: failure to keep the client informed (28 percent of those dismissed), fees (20 percent), insufficiently vigorous advocacy (17 percent), failure to follow the client's instructions (8 percent), and fraud or overreaching (6 percent).[122] The only clients who can effectively police the quality of representation they receive are large corporations, which increasingly are using in-house counsel to supervise the quality and cost of services rendered by law firms (see Chapter 10, "House Counsel").

The forums in which lawyers appear can review and control advocacy, although not the vast majority of activities that lawyers perform outside of litigation. Courts can hold lawyers in contempt, but only for egregious errors or misconduct committed in the course of litigation.[123] Nevertheless, judges are becoming more active in identifying misconduct and more creative in devising remedies. A Cook County Circuit Court judge recently cut almost in half the nearly million dollar fee claimed in an estate matter by Kirkland & Ellis (a leading Chicago firm) and rebuked the firm for overstaffing, duplication of effort, representation of multiple parties, and lack of good faith.[124] A New York Supreme Court justice ordered a plaintiff's personal injury lawyer to return $237,853 he had received for representing a minor, finding that the lawyer had sought to increase his fee at the expense of the child's recovery.[125] The Appellate Division of the New York State Supreme Court removed Sullivan & Cromwell from representing one party in a lengthy bitter dispute over a family trust, finding that its lawyer used "clandestine," "deceptive," and "covert" methods to obtain critical documents. When the firm sought a rehearing or appeal, the court reprimanded it for making such a "frivolous" motion and sent the matter to the disciplinary committee of the Association of the Bar of the City of New York.[126] A U.S. District Court judge in Boston has ordered lawyers on both sides of a lawsuit to attend a day-long continuing legal education seminar on federal practice because of their carelessness in drafting pleadings.[127] And a U.S. District Court judge in San Diego has entered a default judgment against a party whose lawyer deliberately failed to produce a witness an adversary had sought to question.[128]

A 1983 amendment to Rule 11 of the Federal Rules of Civil Procedure gives federal judges considerably more control over attorney behavior.[129] Federal trial judges, and to a lesser extent their state court counterparts, are imposing substantial fines on lawyers whose actions they find to be frivolous, dilatory or unfounded.[130] In two separate cases, a U.S. District Judge in Houston has fined lawyers $167,850 and $250,000 for filing frivolous lawsuits.[131] A Florida circuit judge jailed a criminal defense lawyer for refusing to represent an accused murderer who, the lawyer claimed, insisted on committing perjury.[132] The chief U.S. District Court judge in Connecticut imposed costs on the City of Bridgeport when its attorney used peremptory challenges to exclude blacks from the jury in three civil actions.[133]

Parties also can seek the imposition of sanctions on lawyers representing their opponents. Salt Lake City has invoked the civil provisions of the federal Racketeer Influenced and Corrupt Organizations Act against a Dallas law firm representing a debtor of the city who declared bankruptcy.[134] Recent changes in federal law allow prosecutors to monitor the activities of defense counsel in white-collar, racketeering, and drug cases, requiring them to disclose cash payments over $10,000 and to disgorge fees paid by defendants from the proceeds of illegal transactions.[135] Lawyers who regularly collect consumer debts now are regulated by the federal Fair Debt Collection Practices Act and may be liable to debtors for statutory damages.[136] The Pennsylvania Supreme Court recently allowed a lawyer to sue opposing counsel for libel contained in a letter that the latter sent to the former.[137]

Agencies are increasingly proactive in policing lawyers who appear before them or file papers with them: between 1950 and 1954, the SEC disbarred one lawyer, the NLRB suspended one, and the Patent Office suspended one and reprimanded two; half the proceedings against lawyers initiated by the SEC between 1935 and 1980 were begun after 1975.[138] In addition, lawyers and nonlawyer employees increasingly are subject to insider-trading rules and prosecution for using or leaking information about clients.[139]

Outcome Measures: Legal Malpractice

The third means of monitoring performance is measuring the outcomes lawyers achieve. The market does not do this effectively because clients must choose lawyers *before* they render services, and most clients are not repeat players. Although the contingent fee (where allowed) would seem to create an identity of interest between lawyer and client in maximizing recovery, it actually introduces strong incentives for the lawyer to betray the client by settling early.[140]

Dissatisfied clients can sue their lawyers for malpractice, but until recently such suits were rare and difficult to win. As late as 1950 almost no claims were made, and few lawyers carried malpractice insurance, even though it was inexpensive. In 1959, a Minnesota lawyer could buy a $5000 insurance policy with no deductible for only $21; ten years later the premium had tripled and the deductible was $500.[141] By 1967, 65 percent of sole practitioners and 83 percent of firm lawyers in Philadelphia carried malpractice insurance.[142] In Illinois in 1982, 65 percent of sole practitioners and all lawyers in firms of five or more had such insurance.[143] Even some 10 percent of judges have bought malpractice insurance to protect themselves against lawyers' fees in administrative hearings of complaints.[144]

The annual rate of claims per 100 lawyers increased from 1.8 in 1973 to 10 in 1979.[145] The proportion of California lawyers being sued for malpractice doubled in the six years between 1978 and 1986 (from 7 to 14 percent); in Illinois in 1982, by contrast, only 5 percent of lawyers had ever been sued.[146] The Attorneys' Liability Assurance Society Ltd., which covers 350 law firms, reported that only one of its insured out of every hundred is sued annually, but other insurance companies report a rate of 4 out of 100, and rates as high as 15 out of 100 have been reported in California.[147]

Analysis of 25,290 claims handled by malpractice insurers disclosed that lawyers in small firms (of two to five) are overrepresented among defendants (43.6 percent of claims versus 22.4 percent of lawyers), whereas sole practitioners are underrepresented (35.6 versus 48.6 percent), as are lawyers in large firms (with more than thirty) (2 versus about 10 percent). Plaintiff's personal injury and real estate lawyers together constitute more than half of all defendants. Experience is no defense: lawyers with more than ten years of experience constitute 57.7 percent of the profession but are the object of 65.5 percent of claims.[148] More than half of all claims arise out of litigation, and more than a quarter concern the lawyer's failure to file the action within the statute of limitations; calendaring alone accounts for one claim in five, errors of substantive law for two in five, and problems with client relations for one in eight.[149]

Clients are winning a higher proportion of the larger number of cases they are filing—67 percent of jury trials according to one source.[150] Yet insurance companies report that clients sue in only a third of the claims; more than half of these suits are dismissed; and insurers pay anything in only a third of all claims. Although the size of recoveries is also growing, 70 percent of all claims still were resolved for less than $1000 in 1985, and fewer than 5 percent of clients obtained more than $25,000.[151] Average insurance company payouts doubled from $5622 in 1973 to $11,936 in 1975.[152] Ten years later, a survey found that damage awards following trial ranged from $8000 to $1,870,608, with an average of $43,575 (excluding verdicts over a million dollars).[153]

If most payments remain modest, lawyers also have suffered some staggering malpractice judgments in recent years. The actress Doris Day won a $26 million verdict against her lawyer of 18 years.[154] The eminent New York firm of Rogers & Wells paid $40 million to settle a $100 million claim arising out of the bankruptcy of its client J. David & Co., the San Diego investment firm. It still faces additional claims that may total another $10 million; and three other firms have settled claims in the same matter for a total of $12.4 million.[155] The highly respected Baltimore firm of Venable, Baetjer and Howard has paid $27 million to resolve claims brought by the State of Maryland following the collapse of the state's $9 billion savings and loan industry; two partners resigned, and the managing partner stepped down from that position.[156] Legal advice to a real estate investment firm that subsequently declared bankruptcy led to malpractice charges against two Chicago law firms, which have been settled for payments totaling $9.2 million.[157] The New York firm of Cadwalader, Wickersham & Taft took the unprecedented step of naming another New York firm—Fried, Frank, Harris, Shriver & Jacobson—as codefendant in claims of more than $50 million arising out of the Ivan Boesky scandal.[158] The former Seattle firm of Houghton Cluck Coughlin & Riley has paid $7.25 million to settle claims arising out of the default by the Washington Public Power Supply System on bonds used to build its nuclear power plants.[159]

As claims and recoveries have increased in both number and size and invest-ment income has fallen with declining interest rates, malpractice insurance pre-miums have skyrocketted, growing four to five times in California (nine times for some Los Angeles firms) and three times in the District of Columbia.[160] The in-surance carrier for Michigan lawyers recently raised its premiums 456 percent, backing down only under threat of a lawsuit by the Michigan bar; even then it terminated the coverage of twenty nine firms and altered the policies of nineteen others. The carrier for 6500 Los Angeles lawyers indicated that it would not renew any policies after October 1, 1985, partly because the claims rate of 14 per 100 lawyers was twice the national average. Half the primary malpractice liability in-surance carriers have stopped writing policies for lawyers in the last two or three years.[161] In New York, small firms without prior claims are paying $1500 for a policy with a $1000 deductible, and large firms are paying $10,000 for each $1 million in excess coverage—ten times as much as they did until recently.[162]

In response to the high cost and increasing unavailability of insurance, lawyers are beginning to form their own "captive" insurers: seven states or localities have done so since 1978, and others are considering such schemes.[163] One such firm, Attorneys Liability Assurance Society Ltd., now insures 40 percent of all firms outside New York City with more than forty lawyers. Two large New York City firms have convened separate consortia to seek mutual insurance for themselves, as have consortia in Los Angeles and San Francisco.[164] The Association of Trial Lawyers of America launched a captive insurer for its members in July 1987, and the Attorney Liability Protection Society offered insurance to lawyers in ten to twelve smaller states at the end of that year.[165] Other lawyers are "going bare"— an estimated one fourth of smaller California firms and even some of the largest according to one source, half of all California private practitioners according to another.[166] Because a fourth of all lawyers still have no insurance, Oregon made it compulsory in 1978, and five other states are thinking of doing so. Yet the presence of insurance has the perverse effect of increasing the frequency, size, and success of claims.[167] Oregon, where insurance is compulsory, reports that its annual rate of claims—one for every five lawyers—is twice the national average.[168] Although there is little evidence that malpractice claims stimulate professionals to take greater care, some insurers are now advising insureds on ways to limit exposure to liability.[169]

The Record of Self-Regulation

Despite periodic scandals and persistent public criticism, there is little evidence that the legal profession has engaged in more effective regulation of misconduct or incompetence in recent years. It has revised the rules of professional conduct with increasing frequency, required law students to study them, and tested the knowledge of applicants for admission. But practitioners remain ignorant of many ethical constraints and reluctant to acknowledge their obligation to obey those they know. Clients, who may have the incentive to complain, are poorly placed to observe misconduct and uninformed about the disciplinary process. Lawyers are far more knowledgeable but strongly opposed to tattling. Although the number of complaints has risen faster than the number of lawyers, it still represents a small fraction of client discontent and attorney misconduct. The single empirical study of this question found that only 2 percent of the dissatisfied clients of English solicitors complained to the Law Society.[170]

Disciplinary bodies dismiss the vast majority of complaints as outside their jurisdiction or unfounded. They punish a small fraction of those accused (an even smaller fraction of practitioners), favoring reprimands and warnings over suspensions and disbarments. Many of those punished return to practice in the same jurisdiction or another. Large backlogs of pending cases and inefficiencies in enforcement are attributable to inadequate budgets, which belie the profession's vocal commitment to self-regulation. Despite the fact that financial misconduct is a major cause of discipline and client disaffection, the profession has done little to police accounting practices, and client security funds fail to reimburse all losses. The legal profession has been even slower to take responsibility for ensuring competence, lagging well behind the medical profession in requiring continuing education and excluding complaints of incompetence from the jurisdiction of disciplinary bodies.

Perhaps in response to this laxity, external controls over lawyer behavior have proliferated. Courts are increasingly concerned to monitor both the content and length of the law school curriculum and have considered imposing postgraduate entry requirements on litigators.[171] Both courts and agencies are more active in policing the behavior of lawyers who appear before them. Prosecutors are more aggressive in criticizing and attacking what they view as the obstructive behavior of criminal defense attorneys, particularly in the areas of organized crime and drug-related offenses.[172] Private practitioners seek strategic advantage in litigation by filing grievances with disciplinary bodies and complaining to judges about opposing counsel. Clients may remain cynical about disciplinary proceedings, which benefit them little, but they are increasingly interested in suing their lawyers for malpractice, and courts are more willing to award damages. Malpractice insurers have become essential participants in the regulatory process, aided by high premiums, a shrinking number of underwriters, and compulsory coverage, although the growth of "captives" may return some control to practitioners.

Although thirty out of thirty-three unified state bars and fifteen out of twenty-three voluntary statewide associations issued ethics opinions in 1980, fear of violating antitrust laws moved three states to transfer that function to the state supreme court, which is exempt from federal scrutiny.[173] In any case, ethical opinions were binding on disciplinary authorities in only five out of thirty-three states. Criticism of excessively lenient discipline led Illinois and Wisconsin to shift responsibility from the bar association to the supreme court.[174] There is evidence that independent disciplinary authorities investigate complaints more thoroughly. The California legislature has ordered performance audits of the State Bar and has threatened to deny the latter authority to collect its annual dues until it does something about disciplinary inactivity. The bars of seven states and the District of Columbia have placed nonlawyer members on their governing boards.[175] Through its inaction the organized bar may be losing a hallmark of professional status—the right to engage in self regulation.

8

How Successful Was
the Professional Project?

During the last hundred years, American lawyers have been quite successful in controlling the production *of* producers and *by* producers of legal services. It has become progressively more difficult to enter the profession, and competition from laypersons and among lawyers has been significantly dampened. An integral part of this professional project was the attempt to construct an image of the lawyer as a professional by defining who could become lawyers and by shaping their behavior. In the last two decades, the legal profession has adopted another strategy—demand creation—to enhance the status of lawyers, bolster the legitimacy of the legal system, and generate more work for their growing numbers, as well as to express lawyers' altruistic impulses and commitment to social change. In this chapter I examine the very fragmentary and often inconclusive evidence concerning two measures of the success of the professional project: the income of lawyers and public opinion about lawyers.

The Income of Lawyers

It is extraordinarily difficult to determine whether supply control enabled the profession to extract monopoly rents (prices for its services exceeding what would be paid in a freely competitive market). The data are incomplete, and it is impossible to exclude the influence of many extraneous variables. In particular, it is hard to separate the impact of supply control from exogenous fluctuations in demand (over which lawyers exercised little influence). Even though the economy had begun to recover from the Depression by the late 1930s, for instance, the average number of cases docketted in the Michigan Supreme Court fell 21 percent between 1931–34 and 1936–39; and the number of cases docketed in the Circuit Court, the Superior Court for Grand Rapids, and the Recorders Court of Detroit fell 18 percent from

1931 to 1938.[1] I will present several kinds of income data: changes over time (and comparisons with other professions), differences within the profession (between salaried and independent professionals, sole practitioners and large firms, rural and urban lawyers, and young and old lawyers), and geographic variations. But I fear the results are no more than suggestive.

The most complete data describe lawyer income over time, especially during periods of rapid fluctuation. The theory of professionalism as market control makes several predictions. Lawyers lost significant supply control during the first third of the twentieth century as a result of the expansion of legal education, particularly in part-time institutions. Combined with the impact of the Depression, this should cause lawyer income to fall. Then the profession achieved progressively more effective control over the production *of* and *by* lawyers between the 1930s and the late 1960s, assisted by the effects of World War II. Combined with the impact of the postwar economic expansion this should cause lawyer income to rise. Finally, the rapid increase in the production of lawyers during the last two decades combined with the repeated recessions should again depress lawyer income.

These predictions are generally confirmed. Lawyer income fell precipitously during the early 1930s. Median lawyer income declined 8 percent between 1929 and 1933, the low point of the Depression.[2] In 1935, 1500 lawyers took a pauper's oath in order to apply to a legal relief project under the Works Progress Administration.[3] A 1941 survey of 2353 New Jersey lawyers reported a dramatic fall in earnings between the late 1920s and late 1930s: beginning practitioners, who had earned an average of $2850 in 1925, earned only $950 in 1937; lawyers with fifteen years of experience, who had grossed $10,425 in 1928, grossed only $4850 in 1938.[4] A 1940 survey of 900 Michigan lawyers found that 46 percent suffered a loss of professional income during the Depression, while only 3 percent enjoyed an increase.[5] A 1939 Michigan study found that substantial proportions of those qualified to practice were not doing so: 11 percent of lawyers admitted in 1936 through 1939, 17 percent of those admitted in 1931 through 1935, and 23 percent of those admitted in 1921 through 1930—rates of attrition much higher than those experienced in periods of economic prosperity.[6] The median income of private practitioners—who were the vast majority of the profession at the time and also the most severely affected by competition and declining demand—fell 13 percent in the decade following the Depression.[7] The aggregate gross income of private practitioners was only 9.6 percent higher in 1941 than it had been in 1931 (11.7 percent higher than it had been in 1929); while the number of practitioners had increased 13.3 percent (23.1 percent since 1929), average gross income had fallen 3.9 percent (10.3 percent) and average net income 5.8 percent (13.4 percent).[8]

Before the legal profession began to expand at the end of the nineteenth century, its members appear to have been much better off than physicians. A study of Massachusetts professionals in the 1870s revealed that lawyers had accumulated twice as much wealth as physicians.[9] Lawyers suffered more from the Depression than did physicians, however. Part of the reason, undoubtedly, is that fluctuations in economic activity have a greater effect on demand for legal services, but part may also be the greater control that physicians exercised over supply as a result of the Flexner Report. The ratio of physicians to population fell during the 1930s, while the ratio of lawyers to population actually rose, notwithstanding declining demand.[10] Thus, although the median income of lawyers exceeded that of physicians in 1930, the latter drew even by 1940 and was almost twice that of lawyers by the 1950s; indeed, lawyers also fell behind dentists by 1955.[11]

Between 1929 and 1951, average annual earnings in all industries increased 131 percent, while those of employed lawyers rose only 77 percent. Among independent professionals, the earnings of physicians and dentists increased 157 and 83 percent, respectively, but those of lawyers rose only 58 percent. Because the consumer price index climbed 52 percent during that period, real lawyer income was virtually stagnant.[12] After falling to a low point in 1933, lawyer income remained flat until 1939 and did not regain its predepression level until 1942 (partly as a result of the departure of many lawyers for military service and the precipitous drop in admissions); by contrast, physician income began climbing again in 1933, rapidly after 1940.[13] Between 1929 and 1948, net lawyer income rose only 47 percent, while net physician income rose 125 percent; from the low point of 1933, lawyer income rose 110 percent and physician income 298 percent.[14] Although the income of all full-time workers had increased 112 percent between 1920 and 1951 and that of all those producing medical services had increased 157 percent, the income of all those producing legal services had increased only 58 percent.[15]

In the first two postwar decades, the legal profession more than regained the ground it had lost during the Depression. Although returning veterans briefly swelled the production of lawyers, demand for legal services significantly outpaced supply. During the 1940s, demand grew 86 percent and supply 12 percent; in the following decade the disparity was 76 and 35 percent.[16] This imbalance was reflected in rising lawyer earnings. Starting salaries in Kansas City law firms increased from about $100 a month between 1936 and 1941 to $200 a month in the immediate postwar years.[17] The median income of Colorado lawyers increased from $5413 in 1949 to $7312 in 1955, $10,000 in 1961, and $13,512 in 1966.[18] Between 1947 and 1954, lawyer income throughout the nation rose faster than the consumer price index and accelerated toward the end of this period.[19] Between 1950 and 1978, the income of all those involved in producing legal services increased 544 percent, compared with 498 percent for all those producing medical services and 338 percent for all full-time workers. Personal consumption expenditures for legal services, which had barely increased at all between 1929 and 1940 (from $402 to $423 million, an annualized growth of 0.5 percent) jumped to $8612 million in 1976 (an annualized growth of 51 percent), outstripping the growth of total consumption expenditures in every decade except the 1940s. As a result, legal services increased from 0.5 percent of total personal consumption expenditures in 1929 to 0.78 percent in 1976.[20]

When the legal profession began to expand again at the end of the 1960s and American economic growth slackened, the material circumstances of lawyers worsened, at least relatively. The mean income of Michigan lawyers fell from $36,738 in 1972 to $21,974 in 1976, measured in constant 1972 dollars (presumably depressed by the low earnings of recent entrants).[21] Maryland lawyers earned less in 1974 than in 1967, when incomes are adjusted for inflation.[22] And Illinois lawyers were worse off in 1981 than they had been in 1975, again after adjustment for inflation.[23] The median starting salary of law firm associates did not keep up with inflation in 1984 or 1985.[24] Excess supply does not seem to have hurt the medium-sized or larger law firms, however; a survey of 150 firms containing 5000 lawyers found that profits per lawyer and the incomes of both associates and partners increased at approximately the same rate as the consumer price index between 1975 and 1985.[25] A similar study found that between 1975 and 1984 after-tax spendable income in 1975 dollars increased 13 percent for associates but only 2 percent for partners, and it actually declined 3 percent for lawyers employed by corporations.[26] Median income of large firm partners rose only 3 percent between the high inflation years of 1982 and 1983, from $197,065 to $203,610.[27]

Income differences among lawyers offer further evidence of the relationship between supply control and economic well-being. The magnitude of these differences is striking and suggests the difficulty lawyers encountered in controlling supply. In Boston in 1870, the ten wealthiest lawyers had accumulated nearly twenty times as much property as the median lawyer.[28] Throughout the nation in the 1920s, the median income of lawyers with thirty years of experience was nearly five times that of lawyers with less than five years, whereas the ratio in medicine was about three to one. Among respondents to a 1930 survey of the Harvard Law School class of 1911, five reported incomes of at least $100,000 and another fourteen earned $50–100,000, while two earned only $2500 or less and another eleven $2500 to $5000.[29] Among practitioners in New York County in 1933, the 19 percent who enjoyed median incomes of $8750 or more earned 63 percent of total lawyer income, while the 68 percent who had median incomes of $4000 or less earned only 24 percent.[30] In 1943, the dispersion of incomes was greater within the legal profession than in any other.[31] In Ohio in 1952, lawyers in the lowest decile received 1.1 percent of total lawyer income, while those in the highest received 33.3 percent; those in the lowest fifth received 4 percent while those in the highest received more than half.[32] A 1984 ABA survey of 3000 respondents found that 6 percent earned less than $15,000, 13 percent earned $15,000 to $25,000, 26 percent earned $25,000, to $40,000, 18 percent earned $40,000 to $55,000, 14 percent earned $55,000 to $75,000, 9 percent $75,000 to $100,000, 11 percent $100,000 to $200,000 and 3 percent earned over $200,000.[33]

As the profession asserted increasing control over supply, the dispersion of lawyer incomes declined steadily from 1936 to 1948 and from 1950 to 1954.[34] The pattern of income differences is also consistent with a theory of market control. In 1941, the dispersion was greater among independent practitioners, who are most exposed to market forces (41 percent earned less than $2500), and least among salaried lawyers (only 17 percent earned that little). Between 1936 and 1941, the median income of independent practitioners rose only 11 percent, while the median income of salaried lawyers rose twice as fast.[35] Physicians (and most professionals) earned more in independent practice than in salaried positions in 1951, but the reverse was true for lawyers.[36] And between 1967 and 1974, Maryland lawyers in private practice lost 10 percent of their income (adjusted for inflation), while house counsel and government lawyers lost only 3 percent.[37]

Even in a profession like law, in which earnings always have risen steeply with age, the least experienced lawyers suffered unusual economic privation during the Depression, when weak market controls exposed them to intense competition for declining demand. In New Jersey, the income of beginning lawyers fell 67 percent between 1925 and 1937, while the income of those with fifteen years experience fell 53 percent between 1928 and 1938.[38] In New York County in 1933, a third of all lawyers made less than $2000; but only a tenth of those who had practiced for ten to thirty-three years earned this little. Nearly half of all Wisconsin lawyers made less than $2000 in 1932; two years earlier, only a fifth of lawyers in practice for ten to twenty-nine years had earned that little. In Michigan, 38 percent of the respondents to a 1940 survey said that they had been unable to make a living during at least one of the years between 1929 and 1934.[39] Within the cohort of California lawyers who began practicing in 1932, nearly a third earned less than $500 their first year, a fifth did so in their second, and 14 percent in their third; after five years of practice, 9 percent still earned no more.[40] In 1941, the mean income of lawyers older than fifty-five was higher than that of physicians the same age, but this relationship was reversed among younger professionals, and lawyers under the age of thirty-seven made less than their age mates who were dentists.[41]

As the legal profession tightened its control over supply, younger lawyers appear to have benefited most: the median income of all lawyers increased 36 percent between 1947 and 1954; but lawyers who were thirty years old in 1947 earned 114 percent more in 1954, not all of which can have been due to their greater experience.[42] Conversely, the dramatic expansion of the profession in recent years has been most detrimental to younger lawyers. Within the Illinois bar, only lawyers who had practiced for eleven to twenty years were relatively exempt from the general deterioration in market conditions between 1975 and 1982. And younger lawyers were most critical of the "overcrowding" of the profession.[43]

The influence of market control on income can also be seen in the relative vulnerability of lawyers in different practice situations. The 1937 income of Jewish lawyers in New York City varied strongly with principal client, from $7604 for the fifty-one who mainly served banks to $1281 for the thirty-one mainly engaged in criminal defense.[44] Within the Illinois bar in the late 1970s, nearly half of all sole practitioners and lawyers sharing office space complained that they had too little work, compared with only 4.5 percent of lawyers in firms with ten or more; and changes in economic well-being varied directly with firm size.[45]

For the same reason, incomes are less dispersed in rural environments than in cities: rural lawyers generally earn higher incomes than the least successful urban lawyers but much less than the most successful.[46] Lawyers in St. Louis and Kansas City suffered greatly from the Depression between 1929 and 1933, but the rest of the Missouri bar reported little effect.[47] Similar urban–rural differences were found in New Jersey.[48] Perhaps because of the intensity of competition, the 1943 median income of New York City lawyers was below that of the nation, although lawyer income generally varied directly with city size.[49] Among Arizona lawyers in 1976, the proportion who complained about insufficient work was higher in Phoenix and Tucson than in smaller communities.[50] And rural Illinois lawyers were exempt from the worsening economic conditions that affected the urban bar between 1975 and 1982.[51]

Interstate comparisons offer yet another test of the relationship between market control and lawyer income. The first of these studies found a statistically significant negative relationship between bar examination pass rates and lawyer income.[52] The next attempt, which used the demand for entry (measured by the number taking the bar examination) as an indirect index of lawyer income, also found an inverse correlation with pass rates.[53] A third study confirmed the statistically significant inverse relationship between lawyer salaries and both the total number holding LL.B. degrees and the number of degrees awarded annually.[54] But the two latest studies have been somewhat more cautious. One found that the inverse correlation between number of bar examinees and pass rates disappeared when the investigators controlled for the overall differences in income levels between jurisdictions. They concluded that the theory was valid only if there were nonmonetary incentives for practicing in the jurisdictions that displayed excess demand.[55] The latest also found a negative correlation between bar examination pass rates and profitability, even when many other variables were introduced, but it was not statistically significant.[56]

The Status of Lawyers

The energy lawyers have devoted to raising entry barriers, suppressing competition, redistributing legal services, and engaging in self-regulation appears to be motivated partly by a desire to improve the profession's public image and social status.[57] As early as 1927 the Chicago Bar Association created a Committee on Publicity and Public Relations, which devoted substantial resources to "creating a more favorable attitude on the part of the public toward the bar."[58] Although all professions are concerned with these matters, lawyers seem to be obsessed: almost half of all practitioners worry that they are less highly regarded than other professions.[59] This collective insecurity appears to have been a historical constant.[60] Lawyers exaggerate public distaste, displaying an almost paranoid belief that people view them as tricky, evasive, manipulative, overbearing, greedy, and cold.[61]

These fears are not entirely unfounded. In a 1963 survey, lawyers ranked eleventh among a list of occupations, the equals of chemists and dentists. The relative status of lawyers appears to have improved consistently since 1925, when they first began to enjoy the fruits of the professional project of supply control and collective mobility.[62] Nevertheless, a 1973 Harris Poll found that a smaller proportion of the public (18 percent) had confidence in lawyers than in garbage collectors, police, or business firms. In 1978, public respect for law firms was at the same low level as that for Congress, organized labor, and advertising agencies and below that enjoyed by eighteen other organizations.[63] A 1986 poll placed clergy, doctors, and teachers well ahead of lawyers in the respect these professionals elicited.[64] Between 1976 and 1985, 27–30 percent of the respondents to the Gallup Poll rated the honesty and ethical standards of lawyers low or very low. A poll conducted by the ABA Commission on Professionalism found that 68 percent of corporate legal clients and 55 percent of federal judges noted a decline in "professionalism."[65]

These survey data are difficult to interpret because of differences in the populations sampled and the questions asked. Nevertheless, it is at least suggestive that lawyer status appears to have risen during the half century when the professional project was enjoying its greatest success and to have declined as entry barriers were breached, members of low-status groups gained admission, competition intensified, and the profession lost some regulatory power. Yet it is a mistake to treat the profession as an undifferentiated whole: just as there are enormous disparities in lawyer income, so it seems plausible to expect considerable variation in public opinion. We know that lawyers themselves accord significantly different prestige rankings to their fellows, putting those representing large corporations at the top and those handling the dirty work of individuals at the bottom.[66] Future studies of public respect will have to probe these distinctions and others if they are to depict accurately the contradictory concept of professional status.

The reasons for public suspicions about the legal profession are complex. The public is convinced that the legal system is biased: 60 percent agree that lawyers do not work as hard for poor clients as for rich, and 59 percent feel that the legal system favors the rich.[67] The profession's efforts to create demand are accurately seen as self-interested: 82 percent of the public believes that lawyers seek to monopolize many matters, such as estate planning or tax advice, that could be handled more cheaply and just as effectively by nonlawyers, such as tax accountants and trust officers of banks; 30 percent also feel that lawyers needlessly complicate their clients' problems.[68] People also retain a low opinion of lawyers' ethics and competence: about two in five believe lawyers would engage in unethical or illegal activities to help a client and that the profession does nothing about misconduct; and between 40 and 60 percent feel that lawyers are dilatory, fail to keep clients informed or to ensure that clients understand the situation, take on work for which they lack experience, and overcharge.[69]

These numerous and disparate grievances can be subsumed under a single heading: lawyers abuse their professional privileges. Clients dislike having to depend on lawyers rather than on themselves or on cheaper, less threatening service providers. They suspect lawyers do not actually possess the expertise they claim and, at best, construct a semblance of technicality by means of obfuscation. Clients resent the monopoly rents lawyers are able to charge. And they do not believe the pretensions to altruism and effective self-regulation by which lawyers justify their monopoly. It is noteworthy that client feelings of neglect intensify with exposure to lawyers, although the belief that lawyers overcharge or are unethical declines.[70] Not surprisingly, the most privileged segment of society, white males, have the highest expectations of lawyers and therefore are most disappointed by their performance.[71] At the same time, the least privileged—undocumented immigrants—have a far more negative image of lawyers than whites, Asian Americans, or Hispanics.[72] These problems of lawyer image are structural and not readily solved through cosmetic reforms in the distribution of legal services or the regulatory apparatus.[73] The mass media accurately captures public ambivalence about lawyers: they are both virtuous protectors who loyally represent clients against overwhelming odds and also outsiders and troublemakers; they are the intimates of money and power, with all the good and bad connotations that these central symbols evoke for Americans; and they reinforce a social order that is essential but also oppressive.[74]

The Varying Fortunes of Lawyers

Variations in both external measures of the success of the professional project—income and status—are consistent with the narrative presented in the preceding chapters. Lawyer income fell during the Depression (when growing numbers encountered declining demand), rose rapidly after the war (when demand fueled by the economic boom outstripped static supply), and leveled off or declined again as numbers expanded despite the recurrent recessions of the 1970s and 1980s. The incomes of lawyers always have been dispersed more widely than those of physicians (although part of the difference can be explained by the fact that lawyers serve both individuals and businesses, whereas physicians serve only individuals). Incomes are more dispersed among independent practitioners, who are more exposed to market forces, than among salaried lawyers; and when supply control was weakest, the former actually earned less than the latter—a reversal of the usual relationship. Because younger lawyers suffer more from competition than those with greater experience, they experienced the greatest economic losses during periods of weak or eroding control over supply and the greatest gains when that control was tightened. For the same reasons, weak supply control has greater consequences for urban than for rural lawyers, and for sole and small-firm practitioners than for those in large firms. Although interstate comparisons are complicated by the effects of extraneous variables, they generally confirm the correlation between supply control (measured by bar examination difficulty) and lawyer income.

Although lawyers often appear even more obsessed with their collective status than with their incomes, it is considerably more difficult to assess the success of this component of the professional project. Because of theoretical and methodological disagreements over how to measure status, readings taken at different times often are not comparable. And the high (and increasing) degree of differentiation and stratification within the profession make a mean or composite measure almost meaningless. There is little evidence, therefore, that the periodic moral campaigns by the organized profession—to exclude undesirables, punish miscreants, or perform exemplary acts of altruism—have any lasting effect on public opinion.

Measures of income and status reveal both the transitory success of the professional project and its ultimate limitations. Lawyers can influence the production of and by producers of legal services and even the level of demand, but they cannot *control* the market. Indeed, their very efforts to do so inevitably stimulate corrections: increased pressure to enter the profession, competition within it or from other occupations, and consumer resistance. Lawyers can respond to the public's (justified) skepticism about the profession's claims of disinterested service by loudly condemning individual misconduct (as in the Watergate scandal) and publicizing pro bono activities. But the profession cannot redress the fundamental and widely recognized inequality of access to justice, disguise the lack of technicality in much legal work (which makes it appear superfluous to the public), or eliminate the moral ambiguity of the lawyer's role as hired gun.

9

Differentiation Within
the Legal Profession

National legal professions differ in both the nature of their internal divisions and the distribution of lawyers among those categories. In most European legal professions, graduating law students make career choices that are fairly irrevocable, whereas American lawyers move between categories throughout their professional lives. Furthermore, European private practitioners are only one category among others—judges and prosecutors, civil servants, and lawyers employed by business—all of which tend to be equal or greater in size and in the material and intangible rewards they enjoy. In the United States, by contrast, private practice has always attracted the vast majority of lawyers and offered the highest income and considerable prestige (see Tables 37 and 38). Yet the changes in the nature and extent of market control described previously have been accompanied by, and have contributed to, changes in the division of labor within the American legal profession and in the structures within which its members produce legal services.

We lack comprehensive and reliable data about the distribution of lawyers across professional roles before World War II. Yet studies of both beginning and established practitioners in a wide variety of states consistently agree that more than 80 percent and perhaps as much as 90 percent of the profession was engaged in private practice (see Tables 37.a and b). The small number of employed lawyers were divided approximately equally between the public and private sectors. After World War II the proportion of lawyers in private practice declined steadily, from a high of nearly nine out of ten to the present low of two out of three. At the same time, the proportion of lawyers employed by private enterprise more than doubled, as did the proportion in education. A recent survey of the graduates of seven northeastern law schools found that 59 percent were in private practice, 18 percent in the public sector, 18 percent in business, and 5 percent in education or other occupations; this varied surprisingly little with status of school; those who graduated earlier generally were less likely to be in private practice or the public sector and more likely to be in business or education (except for those who graduated earliest, twenty-six years previously).[1] In this chapter, I examine the growth of lawyers at the periphery of the profession—those employed in government, business, the judiciary, the academy, and politics—before turning to changes within the core of the profession, private practice.

The Professional Periphery: Employed Lawyers

Government Lawyers

Despite an endless refrain of complaints about our bloated government, the judiciary has remained a constant proportion of the profession for more than three decades, and the proportion of lawyers employed in government has grown much more slowly than that in commerce and industry—hardly at all in the last twenty years (see Tables 37.c and d). Furthermore, despite the mythology about the centralization of power within the federal bureaucracy, the proportion of lawyers employed in state government has grown more rapidly than that employed by Washington (although the proportion in local government has declined), with the result that state and local government lawyers outnumber federal lawyers three to two.

Government employment has grown so slowly partly because it is financially less rewarding than other alternatives. In 1954, the average nonjudicial salary for government lawyers was $7920, compared with $13,770 for lawyers in industry.[2] In Arizona in 1976, house counsel in public utilities and private corporations earned $30,000 and $27,000, respectively, about half as much again as their counterparts in government.[3] In 1981, starting salaries in New York City were $21,000 to $38,000 in law firms (depending on firm size) and $21,400 to $25,000 in corporations but only $20,400 in government; lawyers with six years of experience earned $36,100 to $57,800 in firms and $44,600 to $46,200 in corporations but still only $35,000 in government.[4] A 1984 survey found that law graduates started at $21,300 in state and local government but at $30,000 in private corporations and $31,000 in law firms; government and corporate employees with the same experience earned $35,900 and $53,000, respectively; the chief legal officer earned $45,000 in state and local government but $150,134 in private corporations. A sample of firm lawyers who acted as Washington representatives for private interests earned a median of $137,000 in the early 1980s—two to four times as much as the government lawyers they sought to influence. Median salaries are higher in state than in local government and highest in the federal government.[5]

The differential in starting salaries may explain why the proportion of law graduates beginning work in government declined from 16.2 percent in 1974 to 10.9 percent in 1984.[6] The lack of material rewards for experience also discourages lawyers from remaining in government: the earnings ratio of law firm partners to associates in 1983 was 2.48; the earnings ratio of corporate chief legal officers to nonsupervisory attorneys in their departments in 1984 was 2.45; but in some 368 state and local government departments in 1984 the earnings ratio of chief legal officers to nonsupervisory attorneys in their agencies was only 1.25.[7] In 1984, recent law graduates earned only 1.4 times as much in corporations as in government, but chief legal officers earned 2.9 times as much in the private sector as in the public.[8] Among the graduates of seven northeastern law schools, government employees fell progressively further behind their age mates as the years passed: in the cohort that graduated four years before the study, they earned less than those in firms with more than nine lawyers; in the cohorts that graduated eleven and sixteen years earlier, they earned less than all but sole practitioners; and in the cohort that graduated twenty-six years earlier, they had been passed by sole practitioners.[9] In the federal government in 1981, most lawyers began at $23,566, but only a few could ever expect to exceed $60,689.[10]

Furthermore, the notorious "revolving door" allows those who have gained government experience to turn around and sell it at a premium to private employers or clients.[11] Studies of federal lobbyists in the 1950s and the 1980s (not all of whom were lawyers) found that half had been employed by the federal government.[12] A third of Washington representatives in the early 1980s had law degrees, and half of these had worked for the federal government.[13] Among the graduates of seven northeastern law schools, 13 percent of those who had graduated four years earlier were in government legal positions, but the proportion declined steadily to 3 percent of those who had graduated twenty-six years earlier.[14] Although the Depression seems to have motivated some lawyers to move from private practice to both government and corporate employment during the 1930s (see Table 37.a), today most lateral mobility is in the other direction. Among Chicago practitioners between the ages of thirty and seventy-five in 1975, only 32.5 percent of those who had begun their legal careers in government still worked there; by contrast, 77.9 percent of those who had begun with a firm of more than thirty lawyers still worked for such a firm. *No* one had moved into government from a large or medium firm, and only small proportions had done so from small firms (6 percent) and solo practice (10 percent).[15] Neither those who leave nor those who stay see anything wrong with this movement. One government lawyer responded: "I have no qualms about changing sides. Will I be comfortable defending [businesses] in front of the [agency]? I can hardly wait! Certainly there are two sides to every story."[16]

Yet even if government has not significantly increased its share of the profession, there has been growth in both absolute numbers and the size of the units within which government lawyers practice. In 1952, one of the largest municipal law offices was the Law Department of the City of New York, with 125 lawyers.[17] By the late 1970s, the Los Angeles County District Attorney's Office had 500 employees, and its counterpart, the public defender, had 400.[18]

House Counsel

The number of lawyers employed by business has grown much faster than those in government: their proportion of the profession has more than tripled since 1948 and nearly doubled since 1951—another indication that legal resources, like all others in American society, remain firmly in the hands of the private sector (see Table 37). Although there was a slight downturn in the 1970s, the absolute number of lawyers in private employment increased from 12,631 in 1951 to 59,100 in 1980, or nearly fivefold (see Table 37).[19] As lawyers accumulate experience, they move out of government but into private employment. Among the graduates of seven northeastern law schools, the proportions holding legal and nonlegal positions in business rose from 6 and 5 percent, respectively, of those who had graduated four years earlier to 9 and 14 percent of those who had graduated twenty-six years earlier.[20]

Several explanations have been offered for this growth. Some commentators have characterized it as a response to greater government regulation.[21] But the most careful study to date found little support for that hypothesis. The ratio of employed lawyers to real gross product actually declined in the most heavily regulated industries between 1940 and 1970 while remaining constant in many non-regulated industries. Still, the number of lawyers employed by a particular company is related to the extent of government regulation.[22] And clients who used Washington representatives to intercede with the federal government tended to rely much more heavily on employees than on outside counsel for all tasks except litigation.[23] House counsel also may be preferred because they are wholly loyal to their employer, while outside counsel must respond to conflicting demands and like to claim at least a modicum of independence. One general counsel asserted: "I always feel I have one hat, and this is: I am a corporate officer who is a lawyer."[24]

The use of in-house counsel also varies among economic sectors; it is most common in finance, insurance, real estate, transportation, communications, public utilities, and manufacturing—a distribution that has changed little in the last three decades.[25] Corporations that are publicly owned, produce services (especially financial services), and employ a highly educated work force generate greater demand for legal services.[26] Lawyers are most likely to be CEOs in public utilities, life insurance companies, transportation, and diversified financial companies.[27] This suggests that businesses engaging in large numbers of fairly routinized legal transactions prefer to rely on employed lawyers rather than outside counsel.

In-house counsel make the greatest contribution to cost cutting when they can achieve significant economies of scale.[28] Thus, their increasing numbers appear to reflect the accelerating concentration of capital. Half of all the lawyers employed by business are found in the Fortune 500 largest industrial companies or the Fortune 50 largest financial corporations.[29] In 1982 (before divestiture), the largest law office in the world was the corporate counsel of AT&T, which had 909 lawyers, more than twice as many as the largest law firm; GE, with 410, was almost as large as the largest law firm.[30] A 1985 survey of 388 offices of house counsel found that their size varied directly with total corporate sales, from an average of 2.7 attorneys in companies selling less than $250 million annually to 63.0 attorneys in companies selling more than $7 billion.[31]

Offices of house counsel have expanded in all companies. A 1949 survey of 2048 corporations found that 1301 of them employed lawyers, yet these offices tended to be very small: almost 60 percent contained only a single lawyer, another 23 percent employed two, 8 percent employed three or four, 6 percent employed five to nine, 3 percent employed ten to twenty-four, and less than 1 percent employed more.[32] A survey of 500 large corporations thirty years later found that just under half had fewer than six lawyers, 28 percent had six to fifteen, 10 percent had sixteen to twenty-five, 8 percent had twenty-six to forty-five, and 5 percent had over forty-five; more than half of those with anuual sales of at least $2 billion employed at least twenty-seven lawyers.[33] Many large companies have greatly enlarged their law departments in recent years. By 1978, Exxon had grown to 400 (from 200 in 1968), Dow to 100 (from 15 in 1963), GM to 135 (from 80 in 1968), Bank of America to 130 (from 70 in 1974), American Express to 49 (from 26 in 1973), J.C. Penney to 110 (from 66 in 1973 and 25 in 1965), and Aetna Life & Casualty to 75 (from 20 in 1968).[34] In 1980, 7 percent of privately employed lawyers worked in departments with more than 200 lawyers, 12 percent worked with 100 to 199, 13.4 percent worked with 50 to 99, and 11.9 percent worked with 25 to 49.[35] Between 1977 and 1982, 183 corporate law departments grew an average of 29 percent, although industrial companies with sales under $1 billion still averaged only 4 or 5 lawyers.[36] Nevertheless, most offices remain small: a New York consulting firm found that the average size of all house counsel had grown from three lawyers in 1978 to only eight in 1986.[37]

The repeated recessions of the recent decades and heightened international competition have compelled all American companies to cut costs. Because employed lawyers cost corporations about half as much as outside counsel and also monitor the quality and price of the latter's work, Xerox was able to cut its payments to outside counsel from $25 million in 1976 to $5 million in 1981. Playboy Enterprises more than halved its expenditures on outside counsel between 1978 and 1980 while simultaneously reducing the cost of its in-house capacity by 18 percent.[38] In 1984, the hourly cost of house counsel was about $100—approximately half what a senior law firm partner might charge.[39] Indeed, a 1986 survey of 200 large firms revealed that lawyers in 67 of them billed at $250 an hour or more and lawyers in 22 billed at $300 or more; furthermore, some firms were turning to "value billing" and "premium billing" to extract even higher fees in large transactions.[40] A year later, lawyers in 92 out of 167 large firms surveyed billed at more than $250 an hour, and lawyers in 31 billed at more than $300.[41]

An important function of house counsel, therefore, is to decide what work to send outside and where to send it, while also monitoring law firm bills.[42] A recent book entitled *The Terrible Truth About Lawyers*, advising corporations how to cut legal costs, garnered praise from the CEOs of Playboy, Atlantic Richfield, H.J. Heinz, and Rockwell International.[43] Most larger companies spread their legal work widely: only 10 percent of a sample of major corporations gave more than half their business to a single firm.[44] Medium-sized law firms have sought to take work away from their larger competitors by aggressively marketing their services to in-house counsel.[45] Although in-house counsel still tend to specialize in such matters as patents, securities, trade mark, and taxation, an increasing number are assuming some responsibility for litigation, which will allow them to take over even more tasks from outside counsel.[46] House counsel account for about two thirds of corporate expenditures on legal advice and representation, nearly half even in the area of litigation.[47] Yet the expansion of house counsel may be slowing now that corporations have reduced the use of outside counsel as far as possible and are seeking to cut expenses elsewhere.[48] A survey by the American Corporate Counsel Association found that a majority of corporations hired *no* lawyers in 1984.[49]

The availability of eager recruits has contributed to the growth of house counsel. Corporate employment has been particularly attractive to those groups whose representation within the profession has been expanding rapidly in recent decades. It appears to offer more regular hours to women and to exhibit less bias against both women and racial minorities. Since the mid-1970s, a fairly constant 10 percent of law graduates have been starting their legal careers as house counsel.[50] Average starting salaries approach those offered by law firms ($30,000 and $32,500 in 1984), and salary levels do not fall behind significantly for five to ten years.[51] Cantor & Co. found that the average starting salary was $34,088 in 1986.[52]

Nevertheless, corporations still prefer to hire more experienced lawyers.[53] Among the 850 employers sending interviewers to law schools in 1984, only 30 were corporations. Just 3 percent of Harvard law students who graduated after 1980 were in offices of house counsel, compared with 10 percent of those in the classes of 1959 to 1980. Only 47.6 percent of Chicago house counsel in 1975 had begun as house counsel, whereas 77.9 percent of lawyers in Chicago firms with thirty or more lawyers had begun practice in large firms.[54] A 1985 survey of 388 house counsel found that about half the attorneys previously had worked in law firms, and most of the rest had worked in other corporations or government; few were hired directly out of law school.[55]

Retention of house counsel is high. The proportion terminated by employers was small in 1983 and 1984, although it may be rising.[56] Among the graduates of seven northeastern law schools, those who began as house counsel were more likely to remain in that position than those who had taken any other first job.[57] This loyalty persists even though the income of house counsel gradually falls behind that of their age mates in private practice because most reach their highest positions after twelve to fifteen years.[58] The same study found that house counsel who had graduated four and eleven years earlier earned as much as those in firms with fewer than eight-five lawyers, but house counsel who had graduated sixteen and twenty-six years earlier earned little more than those in firms with fewer than nine lawyers.[59] Still, the financial rewards of seniority are substantial. In 1984, the mean salaries of lawyers employed by business were $67,989 for supervising attorneys, $76,456 for managing attorneys, and $94,449 for chief legal officers. All three categories varied greatly by industry and size of employer: the chief legal officer in companies with 25,000 employees or twenty-five lawyers earned more than $200,000.[60] One 1986 survey found that the average income of chief general counsel was $174,000; another reported that the salary of general counsel in the largest law departments was $259,785.[61] In 1985, general counsel with at least fifty subordinate attorneys earned an average of $321,110.[62]

House counsel can be a route to power as well as wealth. A study of 1185 CEOs who had served nearly 800 of the largest American corporations found that 15.4 percent were lawyers; of these 182, more than half had worked for law firms and another 11.5 percent for government.[63] A 1987 survey of the CEOs of the 1000 largest corporations found that 117 had law degrees and 81 had practiced law.[64] Yet the influence of lawyers within the corporation may be declining as it seeks to separate governance from legal advice, both to ensure the independence of the latter and to avoid SEC regulations requiring the disclosure of legal fees paid to corporate directors. The proportion of companies whose boards included an attorney who provided legal services declined from 51.7 percent in 1973 to 35.1 percent in 1979; the proportion of the Fortune 50 largest industrial corporations with in-house counsel on their boards declined from 31 percent in 1969 to 13 percent in 1979.[65]

Judges

The judiciary occupies a paradoxical position in the American legal profession and state. On one hand, it enjoys extraordinary power and prestige because of the prominent law-making role of American judges. Performance of this function both requires that judges elicit respect from the citizenry and makes it unusually difficult for them to do so. On the other hand, the process by which judges are selected does not inspire respect. In most civil law countries, the judiciary is a distinct branch of the civil service, which attracts many of the most talented law graduates and retains them throughout their careers, those who demonstrate the greatest ability being elevated to higher courts. In England and several of its former colonies, the judiciary is appointed from among the most successful members of the "senior" branch of the profession, the Bar, and draws luster from their high social standing (both ascribed and achieved).[66] But in the United States, a long tradition of direct democracy from the Jacksonian era through the progressives has challenged the authority of the bench and sought to make it responsive to the people through the election and recall of judges.[67] Because lower state and municipal court judgeships pay poorly and confer limited prestige, they have become political favors that allow the party in power to repay debts. Even the higher levels of the judiciary are visibly politicized. One example was the (successful) campaign to defeat three members of the California Supreme Court standing for reelection—most prominently Chief Justice Rose Bird—which occupied the headlines throughout much of 1985 and 1986. Another is the political litmus tests employed by the Reagan administration in appointments to the federal judiciary and the protracted bitter battle over the confirmation of a replacement for Lewis Powell on the Supreme Court.

The judiciary has remained a fairly constant proportion of the profession over the last three decades (see Table 37). This 3 percent should be compared with the 15 to 20 percent in many civil law countries; the disparity may explain the acute and worsening problems of court congestion and delay confronting American litigants.[68] During the 1970s, the federal judiciary grew much faster (205 percent) than the state (63 percent), although the latter remained six times as large as the former.[69] States have been supplementing their permanent judiciaries by hiring lawyers part time: half the states now appoint judges pro tem, and forty-one states hire lawyers as arbitrators, referees, and commissioners.[70] The size of the judiciary is determined by legislative decisions, but the quality of judges is affected by salary levels, which have fallen well behind what many appointees could earn in private practice, although the higher judiciary continues to confer extraordinary prestige, as well as generous pensions.[71]

Law Teachers

The professoriate rapidly changed in both size and structure with the expansion of law schools. In 1860, no school had more than three full-time instructors; Michigan hired its fourth in 1866, and Columbia and Harvard did so in 1874. Most instructors were paid a proportion of the fees collected; only Virginia, Harvard, and Michigan had salaried professors in 1860, though they were joined by Columbia in 1878, Cornell in 1887, Pennsylvania in 1888, NYU in 1889, Northwestern in 1891, North Carolina in 1899, and Yale in 1904.[72] All law teachers at the University of Wisconsin were actively engaged in practice during the three decades following its founding in 1868, but the introduction of the case method in the 1890s soon was accompanied by the emergence of full-time academics.[73] An 1897 survey of 81 law schools identified 75 full-time and 274 part-time teachers (of whom 35 were judges). Some of these schools were still extremely small: the University of the South and the University of South Carolina each had a single instructor, the University of Georgia and Cumberland University each had two. Perhaps because of this, full-time teachers were paid very well: an average of $2564 for the 68 reporting. Harvard assistant professors earned $2250 and full professors as much as $5000.[74] At the University of Wisconsin Law School at the turn of the century, law teachers earned $3000 to $3500, which exceeded the incomes of all but the most successful private practitioners.[75] Yet when Charles Evans Hughes tried teaching at Cornell in 1891, he found the work too hard to warrant sacrificing the $13,500 he had been earning in private practice for a salary of $3000, and he left after a year.[76]

The 293 law teachers in the fall of 1887 had multiplied to more than 2000 in the fall of 1948.[77] Their proportion of the profession doubled between 1957 and 1970 (from 0.6 to 1.2 percent) (see Table 37.c). Although the legal profession as a whole grew only 117 percent between 1950 and 1977, and law school enrollments grew 171 percent between 1947 and 1977, the number of part-time teachers grew 194 percent during the latter period and the number of full-time teachers 291 percent.[78] The ratio of full-time to part-time teachers has not changed significantly, however: full-time teachers were 67 percent of the professoriate at AALS law schools in 1930, 64 percent in 1940–41, 58 percent at ABA-approved schools in 1948, and 61 percent in 1984.[79] Nevertheless, full-time instructors taught an average of 84 percent of class hours and a median of 91 percent by 1956–57.[80] The differentiation of teaching and practice, initiated by Harvard's 1873 appointment of James Barr Ames—the first instructor without any experience in practice—was far advanced. Among full-time teachers at AALS schools in 1930, 22.5 percent lacked any practical experience, another 40 percent had less than five years, and only 22 percent had ten years or more; by contrast, 77 percent of part-time teachers had practiced for at least six years.[81]

The size of individual faculties has also multiplied several times. In 1936–37, eighty-one of the ninety-four ABA-approved schools had a total of 989 faculty (full-time, part-time, and administrators), an average of 12 per school, although thirty-eight schools had fewer than 10.[82] In the winter of 1940, a survey of 99 of the 108 ABA-approved schools found that 21 had ten or more full-time teachers (an average of fourteen), 39 had six to nine (an average of seven), and 39 had five or fewer (an average of four).[83] In 1940–41, the 93 schools belonging to the AALS had an average of 11.6 full-time and part-time faculty.[84] In 1948, the 111 ABA-approved schools had an average of nine full-time instructors: 77 had fewer than ten, 28 had ten to nineteen, and only 6 had more than twenty. Among the 34 unapproved schools reporting, none had more than seven full-time instructors; of those that had any, the average was three.[85] In 1982, the average faculty of the 173 ABA-approved schools contained twenty-six full-time instructors: only 2 had fewer than eleven, 48 had eleven to twenty, 79 had twenty-one to thirty, 28 had thirty-one to forty, 12 had forty-one to fifty, and 4 had fifty-one to sixty.[86] The mere growth in the size of law faculties has accentuated the differentiation between academic and practicing lawyers.

Until recently, lawyers earned about as much in teaching as they could in private practice: a median of $5333 at 103 law schools in 1949, $6850 at 119 schools in 1953–54.[87] Median salaries ranged from $3000 for assistant professors to $5250 for full professors in 1940–41 and from $6000 to $8928 in 1956–57.[88] Salaries varied greatly by school size, however, from an average of $3500 in schools with five full-time teachers or fewer in 1940 to $6600 in schools with ten or more.[89] Between 1955 and 1970, the median salary at 90 of the 115 ABA approved schools increased 65 percent.[90] By 1972–73, however, the median base salary of law teachers was $23,300, significantly below the $27,400 average for all male lawyers, even though most law teachers had academic records that would allow them to command much higher incomes.[91] Many professors may feel amply compensated for their lower salaries by the greater control they enjoy over their time.[92] Yet the growing disparity between law teacher salaries and the rewards of private practice may be draining away talent from teaching and encouraging those who remain to devote more time to consulting.[93]

Although law teachers are increasingly differentiated from practitioners, most still are not scholars. In 1956–57, teachers spent an average of 7.54 hours per week in the classroom, another 41.9 hours in activities related to teaching, 3 hours in administrative duties, and 13 hours in research and reflection.[94] A 1973 survey of 350 professors found that they worked 39.7 hours a week—significantly less than most lawyers. The vast majority thought of themselves primarily as teachers (78.8 percent) and administrators (17.8 percent), not scholars, and they devoted less than a fifth of their time to research.[95] A study of 118 teachers who entered tenure-track positions in 1975–76 disclosed that a fifth wrote *nothing* in the following eight years, another fourth wrote only one article, and fewer than a third wrote three.[96] A study of publications by tenured faculty in the early 1980s revealed that 44 percent had published nothing in the last three years, and the median number of publications was only one.[97] Another study found that productivity (measured by pages per faculty member published in twenty-three respected law journals within a thirty-three-month period in the early 1980s) averaged thirty pages at the ten most productive schools but only nine at the schools that ranked thirty-six to forty-five.[98]

Law schools also differ from other academic departments in their relatively low standards for granting tenure. Responses from 97 of the 172 ABA-approved law schools in 1981 indicated that more than half had denied tenure to no one in the preceding five years.[99] Several studies suggested that until recently attrition among teachers, either through tenure denial or voluntary departure, was very low—20 to 30 percent per decade. That may be changing. The proportion of the cohort that had left within ten years of entering increased from 27 for the 1965–74 decade to 37 percent for the 1970–79 decade and 45 percent for the 1975–84 decade.[100]

Perhaps because university hiring and promotion is relatively meritocratic, law school teaching has been particularly attractive to Jewish law graduates, who constituted 27 percent of all law professors in 1969 and 22 percent a decade later, when ethnoreligious discrimination in law firms had significantly diminished.[101] Both for this reason and because law teachers enjoy greater control over their time, the proportion of women is higher than in the profession. Women were 16.9 percent of full-time and 17.4 percent of part-time teachers in ABA-approved schools in 1984, though they were still overrepresented among law librarians (47.6 percent of deans and librarians, but almost none were deans).[102] Women were 3.7 percent of new appointments in 1965, 4.3 percent in 1970, 18.9 percent in 1975, and 20.1 percent in 1980.[103]

Lawyer Politicians

Lawyers involved in politics do not require a legal qualification for that work and generally do not perform legal functions. Yet they differ from law graduates who pursue other nonlegal careers in that lawyers dominate American politics to a degree unequaled in any other country.[104] This has been true ever since the Revolution: twenty-five of the fifty-two signers of the Declaration of Independence were lawyers. And it has remained fairly constant despite dramatic changes in the numbers, background, training, and role of lawyers. They were 54 percent of U.S. Senators in 1789, 86 percent in 1845, 60 percent in 1895, and 64 percent in 1945.[105] From the Revolution until 1930, lawyers constituted two thirds of the Senate, a third of the House of Representatives, two thirds of state governors, and significant proportions of southern state legislatures.[106] From 1937 to 1968, lawyers represented between 57 and 74 percent of the Senate and betweeen 55 and 59 percent of the House.[107] They also have dominated the federal executive: more than 70 percent of presidents, vice-presidents, and cabinet members between 1877 and 1934 were lawyers.[108] Although not a majority, they are the largest single occupational category in state legislatures; they are more prominent in upper than in lower houses of bicameral legislatures and especially common in leadership positions as speakers of lower houses and presidents of senates.[109] In 1949, twelve of the forty California state senators and twenty-five of the eighty assemblymen were lawyers, as had been six of the last eleven governors.[110] The reasons for this dominance have been debated endlessly.[111] Although lawyers have lost political influence in other countries following the rise of labor parties (which distrust them) and the emergence of technocrats (who seem to possess more useful expertise), the United States has no labor party, and its lawyers may have postponed obsolescence by acquiring competence in economic analysis.[112]

Lateral Mobility among Legal Careers

Although each of the categories of lawyers just discussed is a distinct career line in civil law countries, chosen on graduation from university and rarely changed thereafter, American lawyers move quite freely among them. Among Chicago practitioners thirty to seventy-five years old in 1975, the proportions working in the sector where they began were: 32.5 percent of government lawyers, 47.6 percent of house counsel, 53.3 percent of those in firms with fewer than ten lawyers, 56.4 percent of sole practitioners, 63.0 percent of those in firms with ten to twenty-nine lawyers, and 77.9 percent of those in firms with more than twenty-nine lawyers. Higher proportions remained in some form of private practice, although they varied by first job: 81.1 percent of sole practitioners, 85.6 percent of those who began in small firms, 84.8 percent of those who began in medium-sized firms, and 92.2 percent of those who began in large firms.[113] Indirect evidence of lateral mobility can be drawn from comparisons among age categories in 1980, though it is impossible to distinguish between cohort effects (generational differences) and maturation effects (changes within a life cycle). Although private practice remained a fairly constant 70 percent of each age category until lawyers began to retire in their sixties, lawyers in industry increased from 7.9 percent of recent graduates to 13.4 percent of those forty-five to fifty-four years old, membership in the federal and state judiciaries increased from 1.3 percent of thirty-year-olds to 13.4 percent of those fifty-five to sixty-four, and teachers were three times as large a proportion of those forty to forty-four as of those under thirty. By contrast, the proportion in federal and state and local governments dropped from 13.5 percent immediately after graduation to little more than half of that (7.1 percent) among those fifty-five to sixty-four, and the proportion in legal aid or public defender offices declined even more dramatically, from 3.6 percent of recent graduates to 0.3 percent of those fifty-five to sixty-four.[114]

Lateral mobility follows fairly clear patterns. Several years of experience as a law firm associate has been the natural path to employment with a corporation, although some lawyers are now reversing this sequence by putting their corporate expertise to use in specialist "boutique" firms. Government has been a training ground for criminal defense lawyers as well as large firm lawyers with a regulatory practice, and senior partners often spend short periods in high government positions when their party is in power.[115] The judiciary is an honor that accrues after years of private practice or government service (sometimes assisted by donations to the appropriate political party), and most judges serve out their lifetime appointments, although some have returned to private practice to enhance their incomes. Although most law teachers used to be private practitioners, who often continued to practice part time, few today have any experience other than a judicial clerkship and perhaps a year or two in government or a large firm, and few do more than occasional consulting. More senior professors occasionally leave the academic world for government or the judiciary. Thus, although the legal profession is differentiated into categories that perform very diverse tasks, there is considerable mobility among them. To the extent that the direction of actual movement indicates relative prestige, private practice has a higher status than employment in government or business (except at the very highest levels), academia parallels private practice, and the higher judiciary outranks everything else.

Has the Periphery Moved toward the Center?

Compared to their counterparts in the civil law world, common lawyers employed outside private practice are marginalized; they are relative newcomers within the profession, few in numbers, poorly paid, and lacking prestige. A third of all law graduates in many northern European countries are employed in commerce and industry, but a far smaller proportion are house counsel in the United States. And although the best graduates of European law faculties frequently seek to become judges, prosecutors or civil servants, government jobs in the United States often are the refuge of those with lower grades from less prestigious law schools, and judgeships reward political service rather than recognize professional excellence.

This has been changing in the last hundred years, however, particularly since World War II. The proportion of lawyers employed outside private practice has increased from one out of ten to one out of three (though this still is only half the proportion in many European countries). Some of this growth represents the differentiation and expansion of new branches of the profession. Law teaching emerged with the displacement of apprenticeship by academic education at the end of the nineteenth century and became a distinct subdivision only when full-time teachers replaced part-time and academic performance replaced practical experience as a criterion for faculty hiring (though it is noteworthy that law professors are far more concerned with teaching and administration and far less involved with scholarship than other university faculty). House counsel are an even more recent phenomenon and have multiplied much more rapidly in response to the growth of government regulation, the concentration of capital, and competitive pressures to cut legal costs. By contrast, the number of judges and lawyer civil servants has grown much more slowly, as might be expected in a country highly suspicious of "big government."

It is not accidental that the growth of the periphery coincides with the entry of disadvantaged groups into the legal profession. Even before the 1960s, women and ethnoreligious and racial minorities were overrepresented in that sector. All three groups are attracted by the hope that hiring and promotion will be more universalistic because appointments are more visible, the sector has a stronger ideological antipathy to discrimination, private clients wield less influence, and competition for jobs is less intense. Growth in the size of units—house counsel, government legal departments, prosecutorial offices, public defenders, law faculties, and judiciaries—tends to strengthen universalism. Women are also attracted by their greater control over working hours and the possibility of part-time work and leaves of absence.

Yet though the proportion of lawyers employed outside private practice has grown substantially, they remain peripheral. Indeed, their numbers have expanded largely because private practice has been unable to absorb the nearly threefold increase in the annual number of new admittees. Public and private employment thus remains a safety valve reducing competition among private practitioners. The financial gap between private practice and employment has widened: judges and teachers used to earn salaries comparable to those of the median private practitioner, but they have fallen considerably behind. Civil servants must accept a standard of living far below that of most lawyers. In a society in which almost all values are expressed in money, the prestige of employed lawyers tends to reflect their incomes rather than their authority or the importance of their work.

In civil law countries, law students choose at graduation between private practice, employment in commerce and industry, the civil service, the judiciary, and teaching and remain in that sector for life. The result is strong collegiality within each sector but considerable friction and misunderstanding between them. The high lateral mobility of American lawyers reduces the centrifugal tendencies accentuated by increasing differentiation. At the same time, however, it expresses and reinforces the hierarchy among legal careers. Many law graduates enter government only to gain expertise they can sell to private clients. The American civil service is notorious for its short career ladder, which offers few rewards for loyalty and continued productivity. Even the brief periods of public service by law firm partners simply confirm the centrality of private practice. Thus, employment outside private practice may have expanded numerically, but its composition, rewards, and career structure continue to affirm its professional marginality.

The Core of the Profession: Private Practice

The growing proportion of lawyers employed in government, business, the judiciary, and the university naturally has meant a decline in the proportion engaged in private practice. This is a reversal of earlier trends. With the end of the Depression and the cumulative success of the project of supply control (aided by the war), the proportion of lawyers in private practice increased from 67 percent in 1930 to 71 percent in 1940 and 83 percent in 1948.[116] They were drawn to private practice by the possibility of higher incomes. Although a greater proportion of private practitioners than salaried lawyers earned less than $5000 in 1947 (25 versus 6 percent), a greater proportion also earned more than $20,000 (6.2 versus 3.1 percent); seven years later these differences remained roughly the same (25 versus 5 percent below $4000; 6.7 versus 3.5 percent above $25,000).[117] A 1976 Arizona survey found that the median income of private practitioners was 30 percent higher than that of salaried lawyers ($26,000 versus $20,000).[118] In Florida seven years later, a survey of 5600 lawyers revealed that the median income of private practitioners was 58 percent higher than the median for all lawyers ($68,000 versus $43,000).[119]

Yet analysis of the Martindale Hubbell directory found that the proportion of lawyers in private practice declined from nearly nine out of ten in 1948 to slightly more than two out of three in 1980 (see Tables 37.c and d).[120]. These upward and downward trends (as well as the movements by individuals charted in the previous section) both suggest that private practice is the career of choice for American lawyers, who turn to public or private employment only when supply exceeds demand.

Although the proportion of the profession in private practice in the United States today remains higher than in any other country and sufficiently high for private practitioners to dominate the profession politically, economically, and symbolically, the postwar change has been dramatic.[121] The third of those who possess law degrees and call themselves lawyers but do not practice privately have concerns very different from those of private practitioners. They are not particularly interested in controlling the supply of lawyers, maintaining restrictive practices that dampen competition, stimulating demand, or enhancing the status of the private bar. The proportion of employed lawyers who belong to established professional associations is significantly smaller than the proportion of private practitioners. And private practitioners often find themselves subordinated to other lawyers: judges and agency administrators before whom they appear or who review disciplinary proceeedings, legislators who regulate the professions and appropriate funds for unified bars, and teachers who train lawyers. These internal divisions undermine the capacity of the profession to take united action at the same time that the decline in the relative size and influence of private practitioners diminishes their autonomy.

The Eclipse of the Paradigm of the Independent Professional

Not only has private practice shrunk as a proportion of the profession, it also has been transformed internally. Ideologically, the paradigmatic lawyer remains the independent practitioner, who neither is employed by another nor depends on employees; the British barrister is the model. The proportion of lawyers working alone may actually have increased during the Depression, when the lack of business presumably discouraged law firms from taking on partners or associates. A 1937 survey found that the proportion of lawyers in solo practice rose fairly constantly from 69.6 percent of those admitted in 1929 to 74.1 percent of those admitted in 1936.[122]

The relative number of sole practitioners has fallen drastically over the last three decades, however, from six out of every ten lawyers in 1948 to one out of three in 1980 (see Table 37.c; but Table 37.a suggests lower proportions of sole practitioners in the 1930s).[123] A recent survey of graduates of seven northeastern law schools found that the proportion in solo practice rose steadily from 6 percent of those who had graduated four years earlier to 12 percent of those who had graduated twenty-six years earlier.[124] The proportion of total lawyer receipts earned by sole practitioners fell from 45 percent in 1967 to 25 percent ten years later (see Table 40; some of this may be due to the reclassification of sole practitioners as professional service organizations and to the rising incomes of large firms). A 1975 study of Chicago lawyers found that only 16 percent practiced by themselves.[125] Throughout Illinois, the proportion practicing alone or sharing office space (but not income) declined from 21 percent in 1975 to 16 percent in 1982; indeed, the proportion of private practitioners working alone declined from 24 percent to 13 percent during these seven years. Furthermore, only 21 percent of private practitioners with four to six years of experience were practicing alone or sharing office space, compared with 26 percent of those with twenty-one to thirty-five years of experience.[126] The proportion of law graduates beginning their careers as sole practitioners declined from 4.5 percent in 1979 to 3.9 percent in 1983. Because the proportion of women and minority graduates entering private practice in recent years has been consistently lower than the proportion of men and white graduates, the growing numbers in the former categories are likely to accentuate these trends.[127]

While the relative number of sole practitioners has declined, the proportion of private practitioners employed as associates has doubled, making it the fastest growing category within that sector (the proportion of partners has increased only slightly). While sole practitioners were *twice* as numerous as firm practitioners in 1948, the first category now is smaller than the second. Even if sole practitioners and partners are grouped together as independent practitioners (a dubious conflation), they represent only 60 percent of lawyers, down from 85 percent in 1948.

The paradigm of the independent professional is not restricted to sole practitioners but clearly encompasses small firms as well. But these are also being eclipsed by increasing concentration within private practice, as larger firms expand in number and size and the proportion of lawyers practicing in small firms diminishes. Given the magnitude, speed, and visibility of this trend, it is easy to forget just how recently large firms emerged. In 1872, only 14 firms in the entire country had even four lawyers; by 1915, there were 439 such firms.[128] As late as 1947, the average firm contained only 1.64 lawyers. Among firm practitioners that year, 55.8 percent were associated with just one other lawyer, 18.5 percent with two, 7.9 percent with three, 12.8 percent with four to seven, and only 4.9 percent with more.[129] In Pennsylvania between 1946 and 1949, 47.9 percent of firm lawyers practiced with one other, 14.6 percent with two, 10.4 percent with three, 16.7 percent with four to seven, and only 10.4 percent with more. Among firms with associates, 45 percent employed only one, 30 percent employed two to five, 20 percent employed six to ten, and only 7 percent employed more.[130] Throughout the nation in 1954, more than a fifth of private practitioners had no lawyer employees, three fifths had only one, and less than a fifth had even two. Among firm lawyers, 51.0 percent practiced with one other, 22.5 percent with two, 9.1 percent with three, 11.1 percent with four to seven, and only 6.3 percent with more.[131]

The postwar changes have been dramatic. In 1947, more than half of all firm lawyers (55.8 percent) practiced with just one other; in 1980, the proportion had fallen to less than a third of its former level (17.2 percent). In 1947, nearly three fourths (74.3 percent) of all firm lawyers practiced with fewer than three others; fewer than a third (29 percent) did so in 1980. In 1980, the proportion of firm lawyers practicing with fewer than three others (37.6 percent) was less than half what it had been in 1947 (82.2 percent). And in 1980, the proportion of lawyers in firms with more than ten (38.8 percent) was more than seven times the proportion who had practiced in firms with more than eight in 1947 (4.9 percent).[132] Even in the 1960s, it was clear that lawyer income correlated strongly with firm size. In Florida in 1965, median lawyer income increased from $16,000 in two-person firms to $33,500 in those with more than eight lawyers.[133] In Colorado in 1967, median lawyer income varied from $15,000 in two-person firms to $32,000 in firms with sixteen to twenty lawyers.[134]

The decline in the proportion of lawyers practicing in small firms is a concomitant of the geographic shift within the profession from rural to urban environments, where firms are larger (see Table 31). A recent study of Missouri lawyers found that county size varied inversely with the proportion in solo practice and directly with the proportion practicing with five or more colleagues.[135] The preferences of recent graduates also are likely to accelerate the tendency toward concentration: lawyers who graduated after 1970 were more likely than those who graduated earlier to be found in firms with more than five lawyers, especially in firms with more than twenty, and less likely to be in firms with two to five lawyers.[136] In Illinois in 1982, 44 percent of private practitioners with four to six years of experience were in firms with ten or more lawyers, compared with 21 percent of those with twenty-one to thirty-five years of experience; 19 percent of the former were in firms with two to four lawyers, compared with 35 percent of the latter.[137]

Before I turn to the larger firms that attract so much professional and public attention, however, I want to stress that they still represent only a small minority of lawyers. The average law office contained just 2.3 lawyers in 1972 and 2.7 in 1977; even if we exclude sole practitioners, these averages were only 4.7 and 5.4. Although increases of this magnitude in a mere five years are significant, the units within which legal services are produced remain quite small in comparison with other economic sectors, even within service industries.[138] In 1980, nearly half of all private practitioners worked alone, almost another fourth worked with four colleagues or fewer, 15 percent practiced in firms with five to nineteen other lawyers, 6 percent in firms with twenty-one to fifty lawyers, and only 7.3 percent in firms with more.[139] In Arizona in 1976, 20 percent of private practitioners worked alone, 36 percent with three colleagues or fewer, 13 percent in firms with ten to twenty-five lawyers, and only 14 percent in larger firms.[140] In Illinois in recent years, the proportion of private practitioners associated with one to three others remained constant (26 percent), although the proportion associated with four to eight others increased from 17 to 20 percent, and the proportion associated with more rose from 25 to 33 percent.[141]

Throughout the country, sole and small-firm private practitioners derive their income from just a few kinds of work: real estate transactions, intergenerational transfers of property (drafting wills and trusts and distributing estates), personal injuries, and corporate and commercial law for small businesses. Despite their greater notoriety, divorce and criminal law generate a much smaller proportion of lawyers' work.[142] Demand for many of these subjects is uncertain and likely to decline: real estate agents, title companies, mortgage lenders, and escrow agents all seek to perform land transactions; most people can draft their own simple wills and probate smaller estates; no-fault automobile insurance and caps on damage awards threaten personal injury plaintiffs' lawyers; do-it-yourself divorce is available to couples without children or substantial property; and public defenders represent most criminals. Furthermore, high-volume clinics can cut costs and spend large amounts on advertising (see Chapter 6, "Legal Clinics"). And some subjects, such as property settlements in divorce matters, are becoming too technical to be handled by the general practitioner.[143]

Although the American legal profession never exalted solo practice to the level of a mandate or even an ideal, as barristers did in Britain and other common law countries and advocates did in the civil law world, the paradigmatic American lawyer did practice alone until quite recently. The decline of the sole practitioner has been dramatic: from three out of every four new entrants in 1936 to three out of five lawyers in 1948 to only one out of three in 1980. The reasons are varied: the growing complexity of law and the need to specialize, the correlation between law firm size (particularly the associate:partner ratio) and profitability, the shift from rural to urban practice, the disinclination of recent entrants to practice alone (because they lack practical skills or entrepreneurial inclination or because, as women and minorities, they fear they will be unable to attract the clientele), and growing competition from legal clinics and nonlawyers. But the decline has slowed and never equalled that in Britain, where only one out of ten solicitors now practices alone. And there are reasons why it may halt or even reverse: computers may restore the profitability of solo practice, which once again may become the refuge of recent graduates unable to find jobs elsewhere.

The Rise of the Large Firm

Only a small proportion of lawyers practice within large firms: in 1980, 5 percent of all lawyers worked in firms with fifty or more and 9.2 percent in firms with more than twenty.[144] Nevertheless, such firms have become the most conspicuous feature in the American legal landscape. Furthermore, they are virtually unique to the United States, although firms are growing in England, Canada, and Australia, some Latin American countries, and most recently in Europe.[145]

Numbers.   Until the late nineteenth century, even law firm "partners" did not always pool their income; and law clerks often were unsalaried, depending for their income on their own clients or on family support while they qualified through apprenticeship.[146] Among the "elite" 20 to 30 percent of Chicago practitioners who belonged to the Chicago Bar Association in the last quarter of the nineteenth century, the proportion who practiced exclusively in a firm was only 21 percent of the cohort admitted in the 1850s, and though it rose steadily it reached only 39 percent of the cohort admitted in the 1890s.[147] The large firm as we know it today began to emerge in the last quarter of the nineteenth century: in 1872, only 3 law firms in the nation contained as many as five lawyers (partners and associates) and only 1 had six; by 1898, 35 firms contained five lawyers and another 32 had more; and by 1915, 104 firms contained five lawyers and another 136 had more. In New York, Chicago, and Boston between 1900 and 1915, firms with more than four lawyers grew much faster than the profession as a whole (6.7 versus 1.7 percent annually). Firms with at least five lawyers became more strongly institutionalized over time: less than half (47 percent) of those in 1893 still had that many in 1904; but nearly three fourths (71 percent) of those in 1915 remained at least that large in 1924. In 1915, the five largest American cities contained 27 "law factories" (firms with a minimum of either seven partners or ten partners and associates); nine years later they contained 101, almost a fourfold increase; furthermore, the number of lawyers in these firms grew more than fivefold, from 237 to 1303.[148]

During the next six decades, large firms expanded and consequently changed character at the same time that they enlarged their market share. Four large Chicago firms remained relatively constant between 1940 and the mid-1950s, grew slowly for the next decade, and then took off in the early 1960s.[149] The twenty largest New York City firms grew 16 percent between 1957 and 1962, while the profession as a whole grew only 13 percent between 1957 and 1963. The seventeen largest firms outside New York grew 47 percent between 1951 and 1961, while the profession as a whole grew only 29 percent (see Table 22).[150] Four of the largest Chicago firms each grew fourfold in the 1960s and 1970s.[151] In 1959, there were only 32 firms with more than 50 lawyers; in 1979, the 200 such firms contained 22,000 lawyers, and 90 had more than 100.[152] Texas had only four firms with more than 25 lawyers in 1960 but thirty-six in 1979, four of which had more than 100 lawyers. Nationwide in 1979, thirty firms were as large as the single largest firm had been eleven years earlier, and eighty-two were as large the twentieth largest firm had been.[153] The ten largest Chicago firms in 1979, which had an average of 148 lawyers, had a median of only 23 lawyers in 1935 (see Table 45.a). The average number of lawyers in the fifty largest U.S. firms rose from 44 in 1950 to 188 in 1979 (see Table 45.b). In the eleven years from 1968 to 1979, the average size of the twenty largest U.S. firms nearly doubled (from 128 to 234); in the nine years from 1979 to 1987, it more than doubled again (to 527) (see Table 45.c).

The pace of growth has been accelerating, if anything. The twenty-five largest law firms in 1982 had expanded a total of 37 percent in the preceding three years, whereas the profession as a whole grew less than 10 percent between 1980 and 1982. Between 1979 and 1982, the median size of the twenty-five largest firms grew from 194 to 288, while the average rose from 221 to 303.[154] Three years later, these figures had increased again (from 288 to 375 and from 303 to 374); if we exclude the two largest (which were not really firms), the median of the next twenty-five was 305 and the average 355.[155] The largest firm in the nation in 1970 was Shearman & Sterling, with 164 lawyers; in 1985, Baker & McKenzie (really a collection of quasi-independent firms) had 755 lawyers, Hyatt Legal Services (a chain of clinics) had 550 (having begun with three lawyers in 1977), and the largest real firm, Finley, Kumble, had 520; Shearman & Sterling (then in eighth place) had 432.[156] The average size of the 200 largest firms increased from 105 lawyers in 1978 to 144 in 1982 and 216 in 1987.[157] Baker & McKenzie broke the 1000 lawyer barrier at the end of 1987.[158] Table 46 displays the growth of the 200 largest firms from 1975 to 1987. Mean and median firm size nearly tripled during this period, as did the total number of lawyers. Although no firm had more than 200 lawyers in 1979, forty firms were larger than that in 1987. The large firm has spread outside the major commercial centers. In 1978, the 100 largest firms were concentrated in eighteen cities, seven of which contained 77 of them; by 1987, twenty-four cities had at least one of the 100 largest firms (see Table 47).

As large firms have grown in size and numbers, their market share has also increased. Baker & McKenzie, the largest of all, expected to gross $140 million in the fiscal year ending June 30, 1986.[159] The proportion of firms with receipts over $1 million doubled between 1972 and 1977; in the latter year the 2.6 percent of all firms in that bracket earned 36.4 percent of all receipts in private practice. At the same time, the proportion of firms with receipts less than $50,000 declined from 46.2 to 35.0 percent, and their market share fell by nearly half, to a mere 5.4 percent (see Tables 41.b and c). In 1987, more than twenty firms had gross revenues over $100 million, and thirteen had net pretax incomes over $50 million, compared with only four such firms a year earlier.[160]

Firms grow for many reasons, including economies of scale, the magnitude and diversity of their clients and their clients' problems, and the enhancement of partner profits (see the section on "Extending and Intensifying Capitalist Relations of Production"). Size permits diversification while protecting individual partners from the threat that their human capital will depreciate if their specialty becomes obsolete.[161] Many firms have recently felt the need to add such specialties as pension funds (ERISA) and immigration law.[162] Firms grow by attracting rainmakers away from competitors.[163] Size also becomes an important surrogate for quality when consumers are unable to evaluate technical competence.[164] Gaston Snow & Ely Bartlett, a 230–lawyer Boston firm, issued a press release in 1987 proclaiming that it had "just completed the most successful financial year in its history," grossing about $70 million, up 25 percent from the previous year. Its chief operating officer explained that clients "like to know a firm has control of its destiny" (even while they pay the bills).[165] Law firm growth has also been fueled by the pace of corporate mergers and acquisitions: 5489 in 1986, involving companies worth $276.4 billion; 2056 in the first five months of 1987, involving companies worth $106.3 billion.[166]

It is not clear, however, that larger firms are significantly more efficient.[167] Twenty and thirty years ago, the proportion of gross income consumed by overhead did not vary greatly with firm size.[168] In 1985, the proportion of gross receipts distributed to lawyers as income was virtually the same whether the firm had two to eight lawyers (56 percent) or more than seventy-four (58 percent).[169] Profitability varies greatly among firms of similar size: overheads are 75 percent of gross income among the bottom quartile of sole practitioners but only 42 percent among the top quartile.[170] Between 1976 and 1986, partners in mid-size and smaller firms actually enjoyed greater increases in earnings (118 and 99 percent, respectively) than those in larger firms (78 percent).[171]

Some firms have found other ways of cooperating without actually merging. Six medium-sized firms in Chicago, Philadelphia, Atlanta, Minneapolis, Phoenix, and Providence have joined to form the United Law Network, sharing resources (and perhaps mutual referrals) without pooling profits—much the same as sole practitioners share office space and expenses.[172] When two firms in Denver and Dallas discovered that each independently had created a high-tech law department by merging with a patent law firm, they formed the TechLaw Group to produce and market their services nationally; firms in Indianapolis, San Francisco, Minneapolis, Boston, Pittsburgh, and Atlanta have since joined.[173]

Success and Failure in the New Marketplace.   Competition is intense and fortunes are unstable in the large-firm market today.[174] Clients feel less loyalty to their firms, and clients themselves are changing.[175] A survey of companies that went public in 1986 found that 25 percent changed law firms or retained an additional firm.[176] New firms have emerged out of nowhere: Finley Kumble was founded in 1968 with six partners and three associates. By acquiring all or part of other firms, it grew to 57 lawyers a decade later, to 98 by 1980, and to 684 in September 1987.[177] It was approached two or three times a week by firms interested in merging; and it doubled the number of cities in which it had offices, from six to twelve, between 1985 and 1987.[178] Two firms specializing in corporate takeovers grew just as rapidly: Skadden, Arps from 18 lawyers in 1967 to 818 in 1987, and Weil, Gotshal & Manges from 13 in 1951 to 443 in 1987. Their growth was fueled by the anxiety of corporations to pay each firm a substantial annual retainer ($50,000 to $100,000) just to ensure that it would be on their side in the event of a takeover battle. Skadden, Arps is reported to have 200 such retainers and to charge two to three times its regular rates when participating in such a fight. The Chicago firm of Katten, Muchin, Zavis, Pearl, Greenberger & Galler began in 1975 with 22 lawyers specializing in health care law; twelve years later it contained nearly 200 lawyers, many of whom specialized in mergers and acquisitions.[179]

The largest merger thus far, between the 500 lawyers of Jones, Day, Ravis & Pogue in Cleveland and the 75 of Surrey & Morse in Washington, D.C., has created the second largest law firm in the country (after Baker & McKenzie) with 828 lawyers in 1987; it also combines the 6 American offices of Jones Day with the foreign offices of Surrey & Morse in Paris, London, and Riyadh and its practice in China.[180] Mergers are difficult to consummate, however, and some fail after a short trial or lead to the departure of key partners.[181] Don H. Reuben left the Chicago firm of Kirkland & Ellis in 1977, taking a number of partners and associates with him to form Reuben & Proctor. In 1986, the new firm merged with Isham, Lincoln & Beale; in the months following, half the original Isham firm and a fourth of Reuben & Proctor departed; by the end of 1987, only 35 of the 125 original Isham lawyers remained at the firm, and many of these were talking about leaving.[182]

Not all firms grow, of course.[183] When the New York firm of White & Case lost a major client (Seagrams), it had to let go 7 percent of its lawyers; Kutak, Rock & Huie, specializing in tax-exempt finance, dropped 30 of its 216 lawyers. Boutiques—small firms offering a few specialties—are common in many areas: entertainment law, communications, litigation, international trade, taxation, plaintiff's antitrust actions, and even divorce. The situation is highly fluid, with large firm departments breaking off to become boutiques and boutiques joining large firms to provide the full range of services many clients demand.[184]

Junior partners and associates, dissatisfied with earnings or advancement, leave to form their own firms. Gelberg & Abrams was founded in 1979 by ten partners from Kaye, Scholer, who wanted to practice in a small-firm setting; although it grew to fifty-one lawyers, it eventually dissolved when four partners decided to return to a large firm.[185] And partners may be asked to leave if they are generating insufficient billings, as were six members of Wilkie, Farr & Gallagher in the late 1970s.[186] An increasing number of firms are making partnership compensation reflect business acquired or work performed rather than mere seniority.[187] The New York firm of Milbank, Tweed, Hadley & McCoy did so in 1986, electing a five-partner committee to readjust shares on a sixteen-step scale ranging from about $200,000 a year to about $600,000; some partners were advanced or demoted as much as three steps, or about $100,000.[188] The success of younger partners at the New York firm of Kaye, Scholer, Fierman, Hays & Handler in generating business is related to the fact that their compensation is influenced by billings.[189]

Linking remuneration to performance can have adverse effects, however. At the 112–lawyer Minneapolis firm of O'Connor & Hannan, an associate or limited partner who obtains a new client receives 20 percent of gross payments by that client for all work performed by *any* firm lawyer during a period continuing five years after the lawyer dies or retires; the result has been intense competition for new business and numerous departures.[190] A Washington, D.C., firm dissolved over controversies arising out of the enormous differences in partnership shares based on overhead costs, billable hours, and business secured.[191] There is considerable controversy over whether profit-sharing based on seniority or "productivity" better preserves the unity and efficiency of the law firm.[192] Nixon, Hargrave, Devans & Doyle, of Rochester, New York, doubled in size to 232 lawyers in five offices between 1982 and 1987, making it the 78th largest firm in the country; it attributes its success to the retention of a "lockstep" system of remunerating partners solely on the basis of seniority.[193]

Differences over management practices can also divide firms.[194] In 1985, internal divisions led to lawsuits between former partners in at least two New York and two California firms.[195] When a name partner and three others left the 51–lawyer New York firm of Gelberg & Abrams to join the 275–lawyer New York firm of Proskauer Rose Goetz & Mendelsohn, litigation arose over whether the event was a defection or dissolution.[196] The departure of two equity partners, a junior partner, three associates, and a paralegal from a Boston personal injury firm led to extensive litigation about the division of fees, especially those contingent on the outcome of cases not yet resolved at the time of departure.[197] Some 30 to 40 lawyers out of about 125 left the prominent Philadelphia firm of Dilworth, Paxson, Kalish & Kaufmann in 1985 and 1986, under conditions of considerable acrimony.[198]

Departures and fissions are aggravated by the difficulty of dividing accumulated partnership earnings and pension rights. Firms may seek to discourage disloyalty by withholding some benefits until a partner reaches retirement. A 1984 Altman & Weil study of firms with seventy-five lawyers or more found that 88 percent had written retirement policies, 40 percent of which rewarded loyalty.[199] At the same time, lateral mobility is encouraged by the movement of major firms into new markets, where they attempt to secure a foothold by hiring local talent at premium prices: New York firms moving to Los Angeles have been willing to pay 50 percent more than the local pay scale or partnership share.[200]

The large firm market has become so unstable that rumors can have a serious effect, just as they do in the stock market or among advertising agencies. When nearly a quarter of the more than sixty lawyers left the Washington, D.C., firm of Wald, Harkrader & Ross, it felt obligated to make a public announcement that the departures had been amicable.[201] One of the nation's largest firms, the 650–lawyer Finley, Kumble, felt compelled to make a public announcement that it was *not* suffering defections or breakup in mid-1987, in response to rumors concerning dissatisfaction with management. To demonstrate its good health, it even gave the *New York Law Journal* five years of financial statements, which revealed that it expected to earn nearly $60 million on a gross of $200 million in 1987 and to pay two top partners $1.275 to $1.550 million and another four partners $800,000 to $1,000,000.[202] After Finley, Kumble did dissolve at the end of 1987, an even larger firm, Jones, Day, Reavis & Pogue, reassured clients in its newsletter that its own organizational structure and financial condition were entirely different, notwithstanding similarities in the two firms' rate and method of growth.[203]

Some major firms actually have closed: Greenbaum, Wolff & Ernst in June 1982, and a month later Marshall, Bratter, Green, Allison & Tucker, which once had almost 100 lawyers.[204] Rifkind & Sterling, with fifty-five lawyers in offices in Beverly Hills, Santa Barbara, and New York, has also dissolved.[205] Herrick & Smith, a 79–lawyer Boston firm founded in 1916, which grossed more than $14 million in 1985, dissolved in March 1986 as a result of the steady erosion of both partners and clients.[206] The 70–lawyer Miami firm of Arky, Freed, Stearns, Watson, Greer & Weaver, which was the ninth largest in the state, dissolved when accusations of financial misconduct against its founding partner led to his suicide.[207] The Washington, D.C. firm of Bergson, Borkland, Margolis & Adler, founded in 1951, declined from a peak of forty-five lawyers in 1980 to close in 1986 because the Reagan administration's lenient enforcement of antitrust laws left it with too little business.[208] Even though 1986 was its best year, a 78–year old New York general practice firm dissolved when 16 lawyers left for Rogers & Wells and 11 others for Mudge Rose Guthrie Alexander & Ferdon; and a Boston firm that lost the Hunt family as a client has had to dissolve.[209]

The rise and fall of the Los Angeles firm of Memel, Jacobs & Ellsworth illustrates the rewards and risks in this overheated market. Beginning with 5 lawyers practicing mainly health law in 1975, it grew to 144 in six cities in just ten years. But the rate of expansion and financial difficulties stimulated a rapidly increasing number of defections starting in 1985. A major reorganization in 1986 sought to halt the hemmorhaging, but on February 1, 1987, the remaining 30 partners voted to dissolve and put the firm into state court receivership.[210] Kadison, Pfaelzer, Woodard, Quinn & Rossi of Los Angeles, which had more than 100 lawyers at its peak, also dissolved in 1987 after twenty years of practice, following departures by 43 of its 45 partners and the failure of a merger with Nutter, McClennen & Fish of Boston.[211]

The trajectory of Finley, Kumble offers another cautionary tale. Founded in 1967, it had grown to include 47 lawyers in 1975 and 60 in 1978, which made it the 173rd largest law firm. Thereafter, growth was more rapid: 80 lawyers in 1979, 99 in 1980, 182 in 1981, 223 in 1982, 332 in 1983, 462 in 1984, 520 in 1985, 597 in 1986, and 684 in 1987. In each of these last three years it was one of the five largest firms. But this growth concealed enormous problems. It was financed in part by a debt burden that had grown to $83 million, borrowed to pay the huge partnership draws of those it had hired as rainmakers. The addition of nearly a hundred lawyers a year since 1980 had created rivalries and management problems. Marshall Manley, who became comanaging partner in 1983, left the firm three years later (although he remained of counsel, earning $1.3 million in 1987). Founding partner Steven Kumble effectively lost control of the New York office to Harvey Meyerson in February 1987. Despite its protestations of financial success, the firm stopped distributing profits to partners early in 1987. At the end of 1987, following the defection of at least a dozen partners, it appeared that 130 lawyers in the four Florida offices would secede to form their own firm; the remainder probably would divide into two other firms. Hugh Carey, former governor of New York and the firm's spokesperson, said that hiring "high-powered, affluent lawyers may be the worst mistake ever made." He has become executive vice-president of W.R. Grace & Co. and of counsel to Carey & Normile, a muncipal bond firm established with other former partners. Another founding partner is taking several lawyers to join the real estate department of Whitman & Ransom. Part of the Chicago office is being absorbed by the New York firm of Kelley Drye & Warren. The dissolution was final at the end of 1987, but litigation over assets and liabilities is likely to drag on for years.[212]

These accounts illustrate the instability of the large-firm market, although there still are no systematic studies. Among the 250 largest firms in 1987, 63 either engaged in mergers or hired partners laterally, and nearly half lost at least one partner to another firm or to business.[213] We do know somewhat more about the lateral movement of individual lawyers, however. A 1975 study of Chicago practitioners found that 70 percent had held, or probably would hold, at least two jobs during their legal careers.[214] The National Association of Legal Search Consultants stated that a lawyer with good credentials moves an average of three times before the age of thirty-five.[215] Graduates of seven northeastern law schools had held an average of 2 jobs, ranging from 2.5 for those who had graduated twenty-six years earlier to 1 for those who had graduated only four years earlier.[216]

A more indirect index of the frenetic pace of lateral movement is the fact that legal recruitment firms or "headhunters," which first emerged in the late 1960s in response to a shortage of junior associates in New York, had multiplied to 83 in 1983, 109 in 1984, 145 in 1985, and 167 in 1987.[217] These firms expected aggregate billings of about $30 million in 1984, calculated as 25 to 30 percent of the first-year salary of each lawyer placed.[218] This would represent about a thousand placements a year, assuming the lawyers started at the conservative average of $100,000. In 1985, search firms placed more than 500 lawyers in Los Angeles alone, a majority in law firms with at least fifty lawyers and another 16 percent in house-counsel departments. One firm now mails the monthly newsletter *Legal Exchange* to 9500 Los Angeles law firm associates and house counsel; it contains classified advertisements from law firms seeking employees.[219] Another firm has formed a separate company to advise law firms interested in mergers or acquisitions. And in 1984, about fifty placement firms established the National Association of Legal Search Consultants, which has been trying to draft a code of conduct and improve the image of the industry.[220] Law firm demand for lateral hires strongly encourages the growth of the placement industry: a number of the largest law firms now host regular meetings with recruiters to encourage them to send applicants to their firms.[221]

Regionalizing, Nationalizing, and Internationalizing Law Practice.   Intensified competition also has meant attempts to capture new clients or retain old ones by establishing branch offices. This is a very recent phenomenon. The twelve largest Chicago firms in 1979 had only two branch offices in 1960 and four as late as 1970, but they had twenty by 1980.[222] Although there were virtually no branch offices in Washington, D.C., in 1970, within the next ten years 178 out-of-town firms had established such offices, employing 1800 lawyers; seven of these branches had grown to rank among the 25 largest firms in the District.[223] By 1983, 247 out-of-town law firms had Washington branches.[224] Among the 100 largest firms, the proportion of lawyers located in branch offices rose from 13.8 percent in 1978 to 23.7 percent in 1982 and 34.8 percent in 1987.[225]

My own calculations reveal similar growth (see Table 50). The number of lawyers practicing in branches in the 100 largest law firms increased nearly sixfold between 1978 amd 1987; their proportion of all lawyers in those firms rose from 12 to 31 percent. The proportion of firms with fewer than two branch offices fell from half in 1978 to only 11 percent in 1987; the number with more than three branch offices increased more than fivefold during this period (from twelve to sixty-one). The proportion of firms with fewer than 10 percent of their lawyers in branch offices declined from nearly two thirds to just a sixth; the proportion with more than 30 percent of their lawyers in branch offices jumped from just a tenth to nearly half.

Yet branching is restricted to a tiny fraction of firms in a relatively few locations. In 1980, 90 percent of all firms had an office in just one community, 7 percent had offices in two, and just 2 percent had offices in more. Only 516 (1 percent) of the

38,482 firms were multistate. The incidence of branching obviously varies directly with firm size. The proportion with offices in more than one community increased steadily from 14.3 percent of six- to ten-lawyer firms to 62.4 percent of firms with more than fifty lawyers. The proportion with offices in more than one jurisdiction increased from 2–4 percent of six- to twenty-lawyer firms to 47 percent of firms with more than fifty lawyers. Three out of every five lawyers in the ten largest firms practice in branches, one out of three in the 100 largest, and one out of five in the next 200.[226] Branching also varies with location: 39 percent of District of Columbia firms were multistate and 7 to 10 percent of those in Virginia, Maryland, and Alaska; but in no other state was the proportion more than 5 percent. Two thirds of all multistate firms had offices in the District of Columbia, and nearly a third had them in New York City.[227] Large national firms can attract business even in cities where they have no branches: a survey of corporate consumers of legal services in twenty-nine large and medium-sized cities found that firms with no local office increased their market share from 0.5 percent to 3.6 percent between 1984 and 1987.[228]

Many branches are located in sunbelt states or suburban high-tech industrial parks to continue serving retired individuals or corporate clients that have acquired subsidiaries in areas of rapid economic growth.[229] Between 1974 and 1980, twenty-nine New York firms opened branch offices in Florida.[230] The New York firm of Kelley Drye & Warren recently merged with the established Miami firm of Smathers & Thompson to form a 330–lawyer firm, which was one of the twenty largest in the country.[231] A New York firm established the first Los Angeles branch office in 1972; by late 1986, thirty-seven New York firms and at least fourteen from other cities had Los Angeles offices; thirteen of these contained more than twenty-five lawyers, and another eighteen had at least ten.[232] Finley, Kumble of New York opened a Beverly Hills office in 1978; by 1986, it contained 133 lawyers, and the firm's San Diego branch had another 21.[233]

New York can be colonized as well as colonizer: Morgan, Lewis & Bockius of Philadelphia was one of the first to open a New York office in 1972; by 1986 it had seventy-five lawyers, and the firm expected it to surpass the home office. That year another seven firms from Los Angeles, Chicago, Cleveland, and Richmond, Virginia had New York offices containing more than twenty-five lawyers.[234]

An increasing number of major firms have branch offices outside the United States.[235] And Japan has just concluded reciprocity agreements that will admit American lawyers for the first time since the Occupation; thirteen firms have established offices there.[236] The largest American firm, Baker & McKenzie, is a truly international operation. In 1987, only 297 of its 946 lawyers were located within the United States, in such international trading centers as Chicago, New York, Washington, D.C., San Francisco, Dallas, and Miami. The remaining two thirds were in twenty-four other countries. It recently opened a branch office in Hungary, the first American law firm in a communist country (other than China).[237] Since then Coudert Brothers of New York has decided to open an office in Moscow.[238] Even if we exclude Baker & McKenzie (and Hyatt Legal Services, a legal clinic), twenty out of the next twenty-five largest American firms had a total of forty-eight foreign offices in eleven different countries.[239]

Expansion through branching is not confined to the largest firms in the largest cities. One suburban Chicago firm specializing in personal injury defense has opened a ring of offices around the city because that is where tort actions are being filed, especially medical malpractice claims against hospitals.[240] The rapid pace of real estate development in Orange County, California, between 1980 and 1987 stimulated a 50 percent growth in the number of lawyers (7000) working in firms of over 100, many of them branches of Los Angeles and even out-of-state firms.[241] The two largest St. Louis firms, which had 32 and 65 lawyers in 1975, grew to 141 and 237 in 1986. The former expanded regionally, with offices in St. Charles, Missouri, and Belleville, Illinois, as well as Washington, D.C.; the latter, partly in response to its principal client (McDonnell Douglas), became national and international, with offices in Washington, New York, Los Angeles, Phoenix, London, and Riyadh.[242] In 1985 and 1986, the largest Indiana firm, based in Indianapolis, opened an office in Fort Wayne, the second largest city; contemporaneously, the second largest firm in the state (also based in Indianapolis) merged with a Fort Wayne firm. Two Fort Wayne firms responded by merging (to become the largest in the city) and opening an office in Indianapolis; a number of partners were encouraged to make lateral moves.[243] In 1986, firms in both Durham and Charlotte, North Carolina, merged to become the largest in the state, with 108 lawyers in those two cities as well as Raleigh, focused on the "Research Triangle" created by three state universities and neighboring high-tech companies.[244] The second largest firm in Providence, Rhode Island, with 91 lawyers, merged with a 25–lawyer Boston firm and planned to establish offices in all the major New England cities: Hartford, Connecticut, Portland, Maine, and a New Hampshire city.[245]

Overall, the number of out-of-state branches tripled between 1978 and 1983; by the latter year, 93 of the 100 largest U.S. firms had branches; these contained 25 percent of their lawyers—up from 13 percent five years earlier.[246] In 1980, one law firm out of ten had offices in two communities, and 516 firms had offices in at least two states; among firms with 50 lawyers or more, nearly half had offices in at least two states. Among multistate firms, two thirds had an office in the District of Columbia and a third had an office in New York.[247]

Multistate practice has its own problems, however. To dampen resentment against carpetbagging, colonizing firms usually hire several local attorneys to work with those dispatched by the home office, or they acquire a local firm.[248] But branch office lawyers may be less loyal to the firm and more likely to defect, taking valuable clients with them (partly because the home office may not treat branch office lawyers as equals); and billing rates, salaries, and work styles in the home office may create tensions elsewhere.[249]

Extending and Intensifying Capitalist Relations of Production.   One of the distinguishing characteristics of large firms is their internal composition and especially their reliance on subordinate personnel: associates, paralegals, clerical workers, and experts in other fields. We saw earlier ("The Eclipse of the Independent Professional") that the proportion of the profession who were associates doubled between 1948 and 1980, whereas the proportion who were partners barely changed (see Table 37). Between 1972 and 1977, the number of associates increased 37.1 percent, while the number of partners increased only 30.0 percent (see Table 43).

In absolute terms, the number of associates increased nearly fivefold between 1951 and 1980 (from 10,194 to 47,714), while the number of partners increased less than threefold (from 51,412 to 142,600), so that the ratio of all associates to partners grew from 0.21:1 to 0.36:1. In Illinois, the proportion of private practitioners who were associates increased from 20 to 33 percent between 1975 and 1982, while the proportion who were partners actually declined from 48 to 46 percent.[250] Since most lawyers remain associates for only a small fraction of their careers, the proportion of entrants who pass through that status is much higher than these figures suggest. More than half of a sample of Chicago lawyers who graduated between 1971 and 1975 began practice as associates.[251]

Aggregate statistics tell only part of the story because associates are not equally distributed across law firms. First, there is geographic variation: California has the highest ratio of associates to partners, and the South has the lowest—possibly a function of the rate at which law firms in those two regions have been growing. Second, the associate:partner ratio varies directly with firm size. Firms with fewer than nine lawyers have the lowest ratio (0.48 nationwide), and firms with more than seventy-four have the highest (1.11), although the relationship is not unilineal in the middle of the spectrum.[252] In 1967, the ratio increased steadily from 0.3 in firms with three lawyers to 1.3 in firms with fifty or more.[253] In Illinois in 1975, the ratio was 0.3 in firms with two to four lawyers but almost twice as high in firms with ten or more; seven years later the disparity was 0.44 and 0.83.[254] A national survey found that the ratio increased smoothly from 0.06 for firms whose annual receipts were less than $50,000 to 0.83 for firms with annual receipts over $1 million.[255]

Several firms have much higher ratios: large New York firms such as Davis Polk & Wardwell (3.29 in 1984) and Cravath, Swaine and Moore (3.8); rapidly growing New York firms such as Skadden, Arps (3.7 in 1978, 2.6 in 1984) and Weil, Gotshal & Manges (3.1 in 1984); and even a smaller New York firm such as Herzfeld & Rubin (3.3) or a Philadelphia firm like Liebert, Short, Fitzpatrick & Lavin (3.2).[256] The ratio also has been increasing over time: from 1:1 in the fifty largest U.S. firms in 1975 to 1.6:1 in 1979; this growth is even more pronounced in New York (see Table 48).[257] One large Chicago firm had twice as many partners as associates in the early 1950s and still had one and a half times as many as late as 1970.[258] All of these patterns are shown in Table 49: the ratio increased significantly between 1975 and 1987, it is significantly higher in New York than in other cities and in the 50 largest firms than in those ranking 150 to 250 in size order.

At least one reason for these high ratios is the indispensable contribution of associates to the extraordinary incomes large firm partners enjoy. No lawyer personally could generate the billings necessary to produce net partnership distributions that now approach, and increasingly exceed, half a million dollars a year. Even a partner billing 2000 hours a year at $300 dollars an hour (both of which figures lie at the outer limits of physical and economic possibility) would generate only $600,000, a good proportion of which would be consumed by overhead. A 1980 study by Price Waterhouse found that median partnership income in twelve of the largest New York firms was $242,685, although the median gross fees generated by all lawyers in those firms were only $184,000.[259] And at the ten most profitable law firms in 1986, profits per partner (not actual partnership draws) ranged from $520,000 to $1,440,000.[260] Such astronomical profits cannot be merely a reasonable rate of return on capital investments, for these are trivial. In 1967, capital expenditures in all law firms with four employees or more were only 1.8 percent of total receipts.[261] In Michigan that year they averaged $8000 per lawyer.[262] In 1985, the median capital investment ranged between $11,000 and $18,000 per partner, depending on firm size.[263] In 1986, firms with up to twelve lawyers reported an average capital investment of $25,478 per lawyer.[264]

In fact, partnership incomes reflect the surplus value law firms extract from associates—the disparity between the rate at which associate time is billed to clients and the salaries associates are paid—traditionally a ratio of about three to one.[265] This practice is neither new nor accidental. Shortly after World War I, the managing clerks of the leading New York law firms entered into an agreement to fix the starting salaries of associates and not to hire associates away from each other—an agreement that lasted until the 1960s.[266]

Although firms naturally try to conceal information about levels of exploitation, it is possible to attempt a crude reconstruction. Let us assume that beginning associates are expected to bill 1600 hours a year at $50 an hour, earning $80,000 for the firm. These are very conservative estimates. Even in far less competitive environments, all lawyers bill nearly that number of hours: a median of 1500 in South Carolina in 1969, 1450 in Florida in 1966, and 28.2 hours a week in Colorado in 1967 (or 1410 for a fifty-week year).[267] A 1976 Price Waterhouse study found that Wall Street associates billed an average of 1667 hours annually.[268] A 1985 survey of 150 medium-sized and larger firms found that the number of hours an experienced associate was expected to bill had reached 1760, a 17 percent increase since 1975.[269] Yet in April 1985, when billing rates had also risen, the average associate starting salary was $26,000 and the median $25,000—less than a third of the income an associate generated.[270]

If we make the more realistic assumption that starting associates are billing 2000 hours annually at $75 an hour, they easily earn the firm more than three times their salaries, even though these now start at more than $50,000 at some firms. A 1982 survey found that associates were billing an average of 1700 hours, but those at Cravath, Swaine & Moore billed an average of 2100.[271] A 1985 survey found that associates in firms with more than ten lawyers billed 40 hours a week (2000 hours for a fifty-week year) at $80 an hour, generating $160,000 a year in firm income.[272] Another 1985 survey found that the upper quartile of associates were billing between 1908 and 2045 hours at rates ranging between $70 and $110 an hour, thereby producing nearly $200,000 in firm income but earning only $38,700 to $64,909 (depending on their years of experience).[273] Altman & Weil found that associates billed 1694 hours in 1976, 1794 in 1985, and 1814 in 1986.[274] And a survey of graduates of seven northeastern law schools found that all lawyers in private practice work a median of about fifty hours a week (though they billed fewer hours); this varied little by firm size, although smaller firms displayed more variation among lawyers, and it declined relatively little during the first sixteen years of practice.[275]

Although partners do bill at higher rates than associates, the difference is not nearly enough to account for their much larger incomes. In Maryland in 1974, partners in firms with fewer than nine lawyers billed at $50 an hour, while associates billed at $38–50 an hour; in firms with more than nineteen lawyers, partners billed at $60 and associates at $40.[276] Nationwide in 1976, billing rates at firms with two to six lawyers ranged from $34 to $60, depending on experience; in firms with forty lawyers or more the range was $36 to $85.[277] In 150 medium-sized and larger firms in 1975, senior partners billed at only twice the rate of beginning associates but earned 5.4 times as much while working fewer hours; virtually the same relationship prevailed in 1985.[278] A 1984 study found that the median maximum billing rates were $87 for associates and $134 for partners.[279] The following year, senior partners billed at only 1.5 the median rate of associates but enjoyed median incomes 4.3 times higher.[280] In firms with seventy-five lawyers or more, these ratios were 2.1 and 4.8.[281] A national survey that year revealed even smaller differences: billing rates of $75 and $99 for all firms (1.3) and $80 and $116 for those with more than ten lawyers (1.4).[282] A 1986 survey of the ten major cities suggested that large firm partners rarely billed even twice as much per hour as associates and often considerably less than that.[283] In firms with forty-one to seventy-four lawyers in 1986, the average hourly rate of partners with at least twenty years of experience was less than twice that of associates with fewer than two years of experience; in firms with two to eight lawyers the ratio was less than 1.5:1.[284] A 1987 survey of large firms revealed that partner billing rates consistently were less than twice those of associates.[285]

Partners obviously have considerable interest in motivating associates to bill as many hours as possible. Firms require associates to keep more accurate time sheets than those of partners, and larger firms are more scrupulous about this than smaller.[286] As clients have begun to resist further inflation of associate billing rates and competition to hire highly qualified graduates has driven up associate salaries, firms have resorted to other devices to increase hours billed. A Los Angeles firm pays a base salary to all associates and then adds a bonus for each hour billed above 1800.[287] Two New York firms have tied annual bonuses to billable hours.[288]

As a result of both these incentives and intense competition for partnership, associates do bill more hours than partners. In Maryland in 1974, associates billed a mean of 1761 and partners 1668.[289] In 178 large firms in 1978 the medians were 1620 and 1530.[290] A 1985 survey found that the median declined steadily from 1715 to 1799 for associates with less than ten years of experience to 1170 to 1634 for partners with ten to forty years of experience.[291] A 1985 survey revealed that both partners and associates expected the latter to bill about 100 hours more a year.[292] And Altman & Weil found that these expectations were accurate: the difference was 1694 versus 1549 in 1976 and 1794 versus 1685 ten years later.[293] A detailed study of four Chicago firms found that, within each firm and specialization, associates averaged 76 more hours per year than partners (while all the lawyers averaged 2097 billable hours).[294]

The degree of associate exploitation rather than differences in the quality of legal services (for which there is no evidence) must be part of the reason why partner income varies directly, and strongly, with firm size. Cravath, Swaine & Moore illustrates this clearly. It had 57 partners in 1986, only 4 of whom had joined the firm since 1983; these derived a significant portion of their profits from the work of more than 200 associates (a ratio of 3.6:1). Because few associates had any chance of making partner, twenty to twenty-five percent left each year; the average tenure declined from 5 years in the mid-1970s to 3.7 years in 1986. Cravath has consistently been the first New York firm to raise associate starting salaries (perhaps since it held out such little hope of partnership). It could well afford to do so. When it increased them $12,000 in 1986, its partners had to absorb about $3 million a year in additional expenses without raising their billing rates. But since Cravath partners were estimated to earn an average of $700,000 to $800,000 annually, the $50,000 burden on each was tolerable.[295]

Numerous studies in a wide variety of settings have confirmed the relationship between firm size and partnership income. In downtown Chicago in 1975, average income ranged from less than $40,000 for lawyers in three- to four-person firms to more than $60,000 for those in firms with over fifty lawyers.[296] A survey of all Illinois lawyers six years later found a continuous relationship between firm size and lawyer income, ranging from $26,000 for sole practitioners to $89,000 for lawyers in firms with ten or more.[297] The 1982 Altman & Weil Survey of Law Firm Economics found that average earnings per partner increased from $67,184 in firms with two to six lawyers to $118,173 in firms with forty or more.[298] Three years later that survey reported a range from $85,953 in two- to eight-lawyer firms to $104,873 in nine- to twenty-lawyer firms and $144,120 in firms with more than seventy-four lawyers.[299] An April 1985 survey found that median partner income ranged from $48,000 in two-lawyer firms to $129,200 in firms with more than ten.[300]

This relationship between firm size and partnership income cannot be explained entirely by differences in partner billing rates. Although these were 42 percent higher in the largest firms than in the smallest, the income disparity was much greater.[301] In 1985, partners in firms with two to eight lawyers earned 2.3 times as much as associates, whereas partners in firms with seventy-five lawyers or more earned 2.9 times as much; partners in firms with two to eight lawyers billed at rates 1.4 times that of associates, whereas partners in firms with seventy-five lawyers billed at rates 1.9 times as high.[302] Nor can the relationship be explained by differences in hours billed. Although lawyers in firms with twenty to forty lawyers billed an average of 200 hours more than those in firms with fewer than nine (1688 versus 1487 hours), the difference was not nearly enough to explain the earnings disparity.[303] Even in the Chicago firm of Kirkland & Ellis, where partners bill 2100 hours (more than associates), they would have had to charge an average of about $240 an hour to generate the earnings of $380,000 that equity partners enjoyed in 1984, allowing a conservative one third of their gross for overhead.[304]

Although associate salaries also vary directly with firm size, they do not consume all the additional surplus generated by the higher ratio of associates to partners in larger firms. In 1976, median associate starting salaries ranged from $12,000 in firms with fewer than seven lawyers to $17,000 in those with forty or more.[305] A 1984 ABA survey found that median associate salaries varied from $18,940 in two-lawyer firms to $31,000 in those with more than ten lawyers; the following year they ranged from $22,000 to $32,200.[306] A 1981 survey of New York firms found that first-year associate salaries ranged from $20,000 in firms with fewer than ten lawyers to $38,000 in those with 100 or more; seventh-year associate salaries ranged from $36,100 to $57,800.[307] A 1985 survey found that associate salaries increased steadily from $32,000 in firms with two to eight lawyers to $45,600 in those with more than seventy-four.[308] Partnership earnings in firms with annual receipts over

$1 million were twice as high as the median, whereas associate salaries were only 1.2 times the median.[309]

To extract the maximum surplus from employed lawyers, firms have lengthened the period associates must serve before they are considered for partnership, reduced the proportion who become partners, and created (or revived) the status of permanent associate or salaried or nonequity partner.[310] A survey of 150 medium-sized and large firms found that the tenure of an associate before becoming partner was 20 percent longer in 1985 than it had been in 1975.[311] Another 1985 survey found that the average time to partnership was five years, but it was six years for women, six to seven years in firms with more than ten lawyers, and eight to nine years in 13 percent of the cases.[312] In 1975, the length of time to partnership was longer in Baltimore than in the less urbanized portions of Maryland and longer in firms with nine lawyers or more than in those with just two.[313] A 1987 survey of the five largest firms in each of seven major cities found that the length of time to partnership was more than six years in all but one, more than seven years in twenty-nine of the thirty-five, and more than eight years in four of the five New York firms.[314] There is evidence, however, that the length of associateship in Chicago declined steadily from 7.5 years in the 1950s to 5.6 years for those who became partners between 1976 and 1980.[315]

Shorter tenure as an associate may indicate higher turnover rather than earlier partnership. The likelihood of becoming a partner varies directly with the firm's rate of growth and inversely with the ratio of associates to partners. Before 1960, about 35 percent of associates remained in their firms at least four years; after 1960, the proportion was only 20 percent.[316] In nineteen of the twenty largest Chicago firms in 1979, 35.3 percent of associates hired after 1970 had left without becoming partners, staying an average of 2.3 years.[317] The proportion of associates leaving their firms in the single year 1982 ranged from 12 percent in Chicago to 19 percent in San Francisco.[318] In 1983, half of all Los Angeles associates and four fifths of New York associates left their firms without becoming partners.[319] A 1987 survey of the five largest firms in each of seven major cities found that the proportion of associates who became partner was less than half in 31 of the 35, less than a third in 20, and just 10 to 17 percent in four of the five New York firms. A contemporaneous study found that eleven of the thirty largest New York firms granted partnerships to less than 15 percent of their associates.[320]

Firms that rely most heavily on associate billings to generate partner profits have sought to control this attrition in several ways. Some withhold a significant amount of associate compensation, awarding it as a discretionary year-end bonus, both to encourage greater effort (qualitative and quantitative) and to motivate associates to stay. In 1986, seventh-year associates received 25 percent of their compensation as a bonus at Shearman & Sterling, 23 percent at Milbank, Tweed, 20 percent at Paul, Weiss, 19 percent at Fried, Frank, up to 16 percent at Weil, Gotshal, and 16 percent at both Cravath and Davis Polk.[321] Latham & Watkins of Los Angeles uses another technique: after two years, most of an associate's compensation is based on the firm's earnings.[322]

Ideally, of course, firms would like to keep associates in that status forever, and several have found ways to do so. The New York firm of Davis Polk abandoned its "up or out" policy in 1980 and now has eleven "senior attorneys"; several firms in New York and other cities have followed suit.[323] Only half of the 112 partners in Kirkland & Ellis share in the firm's equity.[324] A 1985 survey of 150 medium-sized and large firms found that about a fourth had nonequity partners, 50 percent more than in 1975.[325] Half of a 1986 sample of firms with seventy-five lawyers or more had at least two classes of partners, the lower of which enjoyed only limited rights to share in profits and management.[326]

Some large firms have also created a second tier of associates, known as staff attorneys, who are given yearly contracts and told unequivocally that they never will be considered for partnership: Jones, Day hired thirty-six staff attorneys in 1985 at $30,000 a year, when they were paying new associates $52,000.[327] Even less secure are the lawyers hired through temporary employment agencies for periods ranging from a day to several months. A Chicago placement service charges law firms $35 to $70 an hour—less than the employing lawyer will bill the client but more than the agency pays its employees. Temporary lawyers are between jobs, seeking experience, or, most commonly, women trying to balance career and family.[328]

The growing disparity between partners and other lawyers in terms of their relative numbers, remuneration, job security, and participation in governance, combined with the progressive refinement of these distinctions, have increased the structural homology between large law firms and the corporations they serve. The competitive pressures generating these changes are likely to intensify. As law firms seek to cut costs to retain corporate clients with growing in-house capabilities, their reliance on subordinate personnel can only increase. Yet rising associate salaries have squeezed partnership earnings, particularly in the larger firms. Partnership earnings declined from half of gross fees in 1972 to little more than a third in 1980.[329] Partnership profits increased only 3 percent between 1984 and 1985, while associate starting salaries rose 6 percent and paralegal salaries 9.5 percent.[330] Associate salaries increased 128 percent between 1976 and 1986, but partnership earnings increased only 78 percent (well below the 93 percent increase in the consumer price index).[331] It is unclear whether large firms will be able to halt, much less reverse, falling profitability by exploiting subordinate lawyers more intensively or extensively.

Associates are not the only subordinates. Lawyers have always relied on large numbers of clerical workers (see Tables 43 and 48). The advent of word processing and other office equipment (which more than tripled from 4 percent of law firm capital in the 1970s to 13 percent in 1987) has made such personnel more specialized and more efficient, but it has not necessarily replaced them.[332] Responses from 188 of the 500 largest law firms in 1987 revealed that virtually all used a computer time and billing system, 170 had a separate word processing department, 70 percent of all secretaries used a word processor (up from less than 50 percent two years earlier), and the number of lawyers with their own or shared work stations more than doubled from 2858 (12 percent) in 1986 to 5872 (26 percent) in 1987.[333] Yet there was virtually no difference between the ratio of support staff to lawyers (approximately 1:1) in 1976 and 1986, and it may even have grown in the largest firms.[334] The salaries of nonprofessional employees constitute an important element of overhead; and, unlike that of associates, their time generally is not billed to clients. Indeed, personnel expenses were at least 58 percent of overhead for law firms with more than three employees in 1967, and another 24 percent may be partly attributable to payroll.[335] Because the production of legal services is a labor-intensive process, capital investment is low, as we have seen. Nonsalary overhead also is relatively low—20.5 percent of gross receipts in 1976,[336] 20 to 25 percent in 1985, depending on firm size.[337] Efforts to keep salaries down have encouraged clerical employees to unionize, and a group of unionized employees recently engaged in the first strike against a law firm—ironically one that represented unions.[338]

The last decade or so has seen the multiplication of a relatively new category of employee, the paralegal, whose time is billed to clients, which *generates* profits rather than consuming them as overhead.[339] A 1976 survey of Arizona lawyers found that 43 percent billed paralegal time separately and 48 percent included it in the bill for lawyers' services.[340] In Illinois, the proportion of lawyers who billed the time of paralegal employees separately increased steadily from 24 percent of sole practitioners to 92 percent of firms with ten lawyers or more.[341] Paralegals perform routine tasks, such as reviewing and indexing documents and doing limited amounts of legal research and drafting. By replacing secretaries (which many paralegals have been), they transform overhead into billable time; since legal secretarial salaries in 1984 averaged $17,520 ($21,168 on the West Coast), this can be a significant savings.[342] By replacing associates, they dramatically cut salary costs and may allow the firm to increase its market share by lowering its fees. Unlike associates, furthermore, they need never be considered for partnership.

In the early 1980s, there were an estimated 30,000 to 45,000 paralegals in the United States.[343] The U.S. Census Bureau found that their numbers more than doubled between 1972 and 1977 (see Table 43). Rather than follow clerical workers by unionizing, they have aspired to the professional status of their employers by forming voluntary associations, one of which promulgated an ethical code in 1975 and established an examination and certification program the following year. But like most subordinate occupations, they have failed to professionalize. Neither of the two rival associations enrolled more than a fraction of all paralegals in 1982 (5000 belonged to the National Federation of Paralegal Associations and 1600 to the National Association of Legal Assistants). A paralegal has little incentive to acquire the certification offered by the latter association, since it confers few advantages in hiring or promotion. The ABA has also sought to assert control over paralegals by accrediting training schools, but this effort to institutionalize subordination has been equally inconclusive, for only 57 out of the more than 300 institutions are accredited.[344] One reason for the difficulty of professionalizing paralegals is that most are women in their twenties, who remain in the position three years or less before leaving to enter law school, begin other careers, or have children.[345]

The use of paralegals, like that of associates, varies with firm size. In a 1984 sample, 61 percent of firms employed paralegals, averaging 9.6 paralegals per firm. However, only 24 percent of two-lawyer firms had paralegals (an average of 1.5), compared with 48 percent of firms with three to ten lawyers (an average of 2 paralegals) and 93 percent of firms with more than ten lawyers (an average of 14.2 paralegals).[346] In Illinois in 1982, the proportion of lawyers employing paralegals ranged from 14 percent of sole practitioners to 76 percent of firms with more than nine lawyers.[347] In the largest 200 firms, the number of paralegals nearly doubled between 1975 and 1978 and the ratio of lawyers to paralegal fell from 7.6 to 5.3.[348] In 1987, the twenty-five largest firms contained 2800 paralegals; even at this rarified level the number of paralegals per partner varied greatly, from 2.24 at Skadden, Arps to 0.35 at Baker & Hostetler.[349] A 1984 survey of 450 law firms found a ratio of 3.4 lawyers per paralegal, down from 4:1 the previous year.[350] The ratio of paralegals to partners in the fifty largest firms more than doubled between 1975 and 1987, nearly tripling in New York; it was significantly higher in those firms than in firms ranked 200 to 250 in size (see Table 49).

Although firms are little more forthcoming about the profits they extract from paralegals than they are about the exploitation of associates, it is possible to trace the general parameters of the relationship. The 1984 survey found that paralegals billed a median of 30 hours a week at $30 an hour. A 50–week year would generate $45,000 in revenue for the law firm. Median paralegal salaries began at about $17,000 and peaked at about $25,000.[351] A 1985–86 survey reported a median paralegal salary of about $20,000.[352] Thus, paralegals generate between two and three times as much income for their firms as they cost in salary (and require less overhead than associates). If paralegal time was billed at $50 an hour, as another study found, they would earn between three and more than four times their salary for their firms.[353] In 1985, paralegals billed a median of 1344 hours annually at a median of about $40 an hour, generating $53,760 a year for their employers while earning a median salary of $22,030.[354]

Some support for the proposition that paralegals generate surplus value can be found in the relationship between their use by law firms and lawyer profits. The largest number of lawyers earning more than $75,000 a year employed one paralegal for every four to six lawyers, whereas the largest number of lawyers earning $35,000 or less used no paralegals (although the two categories had the same number of clerical workers per lawyer).[355] Law firms with gross receipts below $50,000 had one paralegal for every 34.3 partners; those with gross receipts over $1 million had one for every 7.2 partners; by contrast, the ratio of partners per clerical employee ranged from 1.6 to 0.4.[356] In Arizona, the median income of lawyers who employed paralegals was $50,000, compared with $28,000 for those who did not.[357]

Law firms have begun to hire yet another kind of employee—the nonlawyer expert—in order to diversify their functions and expand their markets.[358] The number and variety of such entrepreneurial activities is very impressive. Heron, Burchette, Ruckert & Rothwell, of Washington, D.C., employs more "government relations advisers" as lobbyists than any other law firm.[359] The California firm of Lillick, McHose & Charles recently bought the top Sacramento lobbying firm and retained its seven employees.[360] And the Miami firm of Sparber, Shevin, Shapo & Heilbronner has hired former Representative Louis A. "Skip" Bafalis, a nonlawyer who served ten years in Congress and several terms in the Florida legislature and ran unsuccessfully for governor.[361]

The Philadelphia firm of Pechner Dorfman Wolffe Rounick & Cabot has formed a consulting company to advise corporations on personnel practices.[362] The Washington, D.C., firm of Arnold and Porter has created two subsidiaries: the Secura Group (led by the former chairman of the Federal Deposit Insurance Corporation), to advise banking clients, and APCO Associates, now a 50–person real-estate advisory group.[363] The Memphis firm of Borod and Huggins established one subsidiary firm of investment bankers and another that provides educational services to lawyers.[364] A small Chicago firm has created Operations Management Associates to advise its labor law clients on industrial engineering and cost and quality control.[365] Kaye, Scholer, Fierman, Hays & Handler, of New York, established China Business Consulting Group Ltd. Hogan & Hartson of Washington, D.C., joined the Lash Group, which advises health care providers. It also has agreed with the former superintendent of the District's public school system to create an educational consulting firm.[366] Howrey & Simon of Washington, D.C., formed Washington Economic Research Consultants to assist in antitrust, tort, and international trade matters. Sutherland, Asbil & Brennan joined Energy and Environmental Consultants Ltd., which has a former assistant secretary of energy as general partner and employs both lawyers and engineers.[367]

Alston & Bird of Atlanta created Peachtree Benefit Consultants.[368] The Los Angeles firm of Paul, Hastings, Janofsky & Walker has founded Leasehold Technology Group, in which it owns a 75 percent interest, to handle real estate brokerage for major commercial tenants.[369] The Atlanta firm of Asbill Porter Churchill & Nellis has opened an investment bank.[370] The Washington, D.C., firm of Leftwich, Moore & Douglas has formed a joint venture with engineers and accountants to advise municipalities on problems associated with asbestos abatement.[371] Van O'Steen, a partner in the legal clinic that won the right of lawyers to advertise, has launched an enterprise that sells advertising and marketing skills to lawyers.[372] A Houston firm specializing in product liability has hired an engineer to expand its expertise.[373] The Los Angeles firms of Manatt, Phelps, Rothenberg, Tunney & Phillips and Mitchell, Silberberg & Knupp have invested some of their undistributed earnings in an office building, both for the prestige it confers and the income it earns.[374] Although rules of professional conduct prohibit lawyers from entering into partnerships with nonlawyers for the purpose of practicing law, competitive pressures may encourage lawyers to seek their repeal. Both the District of Columbia and North Dakota have considered doing so.[375]

Bureaucratizing Management.   The changes in the structure of large firms, traced here, have increasingly compelled them to adopt the bureaucratic forms of their corporate clients. Until recently, even very large firms tended to be quite casual about internal governance, sometimes doing without formal partnership agreements.[376] But only small firms can still afford this luxury. In 1966, 37 percent of Florida firms with fewer than ten partners had partnership agreements, compared to 87 percent of those with ten partners or more.[377] Because most Arizona firms still were quite small in 1976, only 39 percent had written agreements.[378] Today, all larger firms have drafted such agreements.[379]

The growing complexity and size of law firms—the number and variety of employees, the magnitude and technological sophistication of the physical plant, and the size of the budget—have convinced many to hire professional managers, who may not be lawyers, to assume some of the tasks of the managing partner and executive committee.[380] Full-time managers now administer nearly all large and medium-sized firms; some 5000 of them have formed the Association of Legal Administrators.[381]

The final step in the transformation of the law firm from an association of professional peers to a bureaucratic, hierarchic capitalist enterprise would be the further separation of ownership and control through the sale of equity interests to nonlawyers. Both the District of Columbia and North Dakota have considered changing their ethical rules to allow this, although economists are divided over whether such a form would be feasible.[382]

Assimilating the Professional Firm to the Corporate Client.   The large law firm emerged only a few decades after the corporations it serves. But it attained prominence within the legal profession long after the large corporation came to dominate the national economy, and its hegemony remains less complete. As late as 1947, 83 percent of firm lawyers practiced with just one or two others; by 1980, the proportion had shrunk to only 29 percent. In the last 20 years, both the number of large firms and their size have grown at accelerating rates. Many of the largest firms were founded within that period. Several now have gross annual incomes over $200 million, and their market share is expanding rapidly. Although there is reason to believe that costs of coordination have long since outweighed economies of scale, further growth is stimulated by mergers and acquisitions among clients, specialization, profitability, and status competition. Yet it is essential to reiterate that the visibility and preeminence of large-firm lawyers greatly exceed their numbers: in 1980, firms with more than fifty lawyers contained only 5 percent of the profession.

The marketplace served by large firms today is far more volatile than it used to be, when lawyers and clients remained loyal to a firm forever. Some of the most spectacular growth has been attained through lateral hiring and mergers (which have spawned a whole new industry of search firms), but these unions are often very fragile. Although corporations do not change law firms the way they switch advertising agencies, the loss of a major client can compel major retrenchment and even dissolution. That ephemeral quality "reputation" crucially affects a firm's fortunes, attracting lawyers and clients when it is rising but producing panicked flight when it is declining. Firms seek to strengthen lawyer loyalty by withholding compensation for retirement; but tying compensation to productivity and business acquisition increases intrafirm tensions, and partners who are not pulling their weight may even be asked to leave.

Until 1970, nearly all law firms consisted of a single office; only a few of the largest had a second small office in Washington. By 1987, a third of the 100 largest firms had multiple offices. Although most were in New York and Washington, branch offices had proliferated throughout the major American cities, across regions, in suburbs, and outside the United States. These moves were a response to the growth of governmental regulation, the concentration of capital, the nationalization and internationalization of the economy, and the market advantages associated with name recognition. There is every reason to expect this trend to continue and even accelerate. Yet branching carries serious risks: coordination becomes qualitatively more difficult (and expensive), and unity and loyalty are severely attenuated.

Although increased profitability is not the only reason for law firm expansion, it certainly is one of the most important. The extraordinary incomes of large firm partners cannot be explained by their capital investments (which are small), their billing rates (which are not that much higher than those of associates), or their billable hours (which are lower than those of associates). Rather, they are attributable in large part to the portion of associate billings (approximately a third) not consumed by associate salaries or overhead. Partnership incomes therefore are a function of firm size, specifically the ratio of associates to partners, which has been inflated by the rapid expansion of the profession during the last twenty years. Firms seek to extract more profits from associates in a number of ways: lengthening the period of associateship, distributing some compensation as year-end bonuses, tying other compensation to productivity, reducing the number of associates offered partnership, and creating a category of permanent associate. To do this, however, they must constantly increase associate starting salaries and offer comparable raises to more senior associates, which is squeezing partnership earnings—perhaps another example of the falling rate of profit. Firms have responded by adding lower tiers of employees: law graduates with poorer academic records from less prestigious schools, who will never qualify for partnership; and paralegals, whose services can be billed to clients at several times their salaries (displacing both the more expensive labor of lawyers and the overhead of secretaries, whose time cannot be billed). To the extent that women are overrepresented among associates, who leave without becoming partners or remain as senior attorneys, and even more among paralegals (almost all of whom are women), their entry into the work force has enhanced (or at least preserved) the earnings of male lawyers.

Just as firms have grown in order to offer a full range of legal specialties and have established branch offices to serve geographically dispersed clients and appear before federal agencies, now they also are beginning to diversify outside of law practice in order to provide related services: financial advice and banking, real estate development, management consulting, and technological innovation. This dramatically illustrates the enterpreneurial character of American lawyers (especially when compared with other legal professions) and their growing interest in creating demand rather than merely responding to it. These efforts are too recent to assess; but their success would run the risk of submerging lawyers within large multiservice firms, which they no longer control.

The size, geographic dispersion, and vertical stratification of large firms have compelled them to adopt more bureaucratic structures of governance. Lawyers have accepted these constraints so compliantly—indeed, eagerly—that they cannot even see them. A leading partner in a large Chicago firm insisted "there really is a great deal of personal freedom. . . . There is no problem of a lack of individual freedom except in the case of the crazy person."[383] Informal understandings have been replaced by detailed partnership agreements. Partners have hired professional managers, often nonlawyers, to run the firm as a business enterprise. Several jurisdictions are even considering allowing law firms to sell equity interests to nonlawyers.

Given its size, the number and hierarchical organization of its employees, their importance in generating profits for partners, the diversification of tasks, the proliferation of branch offices, the greater importance of capital investments from undistributed profits, the bureaucratization of management, and the progressive separation of ownership and control, the large law firm increasingly resembles its corporate clients far more than the traditional ideal of the independent professional.

Professional Stratification

We saw earlier that a profession composed almost exclusively of private practitioners has fractured into a minority of independent professionals and a majority divided among half a dozen distinct categories of employed lawyers, each of which has little in common with any of the others. Now we see that even the professional core, composed of independent practitioners, has fissioned into what Heinz and Laumann call two hemispheres.[384] These diverge markedly along every conceivable dimension.

Despite the myth of the lawyer as generalist, lawyers have actually been specializing for many years, though the degree of specialization varies greatly. In the early 1960s, Joel Handler found that only 17 percent of the lawyers in a small midwestern city devoted at least half of their time to a single area of practice, and only 5 percent devoted three fourths of their time.[385] By contrast, Jerome Carlin reported that 70 percent of New York City lawyers were 50 percent specialized and 40 percent were 75 percent specialized.[386] Some 20 years later, Donald Landon discovered significant differences in the degree of specialization when he compared lawyers in Springfield, Missouri (pop. 150,000), with those in the more rural communities of that state; one reason was that 87 percent of the latter practiced alone or in two- or three-person firms.[387] Similarly, in Arizona in 1976, the proportion of lawyers reporting a specialty was greater in Phoenix (65 percent) than in communities with fewer than 300,000 people (27 percent).[388]

The New York figures are not untypical of urbanized environments: comparable levels of specialization characterized California in 1960 and Chicago in the 1970s.[389] One study found that 87 percent of Chicago lawyers devoted at least 25 percent of their time to a single field.[390] A second investigation reported that 15.5 percent of Chicago lawyers worked exclusively in one area, and another 14.4 percent did significant work in two, whereas less than a fourth performed significant work in more than three.[391] Yet even within a large city like Chicago, specialization varied dramatically with firm size: the proportion doing significant work in just one field ranged from 4.5 percent of sole practitioners to 17.3 percent of lawyers in firms of fifty or more; the proportion doing significant work in five fields or more ranged from 11.1 percent of lawyers in firms with fifty or more to 37.5 percent of sole practitioners.[392] Nationwide in 1972, the proportion of lawyers who derived at least 25 percent of their income from a single field was three times as high among those in large firms (with receipts over $1 million) as among those in small firms (with receipts of $50,000 to $99,000); five years later it was more than five times as high among those in large firms as among those in very small firms (with receipts of $30,000 to $49,000) (see Tables 41.b and c).

Lawyers are divided not only by the degree of specialization but also by its content. They specialize in both clients and subjects.[393] In 1967, sole practitioners with no lawyer employees derived 64.8 percent of their receipts from individuals and only 19.6 percent from businesses; by contrast, firms with twenty to forty-nine lawyers derived only 6.0 percent of their receipts from individuals and 77.6 percent from businesses; this gulf persisted throughout the 1970s and actually widened for most categories of practice (see Table 44).[394] Eighty-five percent of rural Missouri lawyers, almost all of whom practiced alone or in very small firms, earned more than half their income from individual clients.[395]

There is little overlap between the two hemispheres: only 56 of the 699 respondents in the 1975 Chicago study (8 percent) devoted more than 25 percent of their time to personal business *and* more than 25 percent to corporate practice. Chicago securities lawyers derived 61 percent of their business income from major corporate clients, but divorce lawyers earned only 4 percent.[396] Nationwide, law firms with receipts over $1 million derived 59.9 percent of their 1972 income from specializing in banking and commercial law, corporations, insurance law, personal injury defense, patent, trademark, and copyright, real estate, taxation, and wills, estate planning, and probate—all matters that concern businesses or wealthy individuals; firms with receipts of $50,000 to $99,000, by contrast, earned only 13.2 percent of their income from such specialties; five years later the proportions remained 56.0 and 12.8 percent—only 8.2 percent for firms with receipts of $30,000 to $49,000 (see Tables 41.b and c). Furthermore, the sole practitioners and small-firm lawyers, who disproportionately represent individuals, do not specialize: firms with receipts of $50,000 to $99,000 in 1972 earned only 5.1 percent of their income from specializing in criminal law, domestic relations or personal injuries; five years later the proportion was virtually the same (5.2 percent), and just 3.9 percent for firms with receipts of $30,000 to $49,000 (see Tables 41.b and c).

The shift during the last half-century from solo to law firm practice, and the growth in the size of those firms, has constituted a redistribution of legal services from individuals to businesses. Nonsalaried lawyers earned 48.5 percent of their gross income from individuals and 52.1 percent six years later; because individuals generally pay lower fees than businesses, the proportion of lawyer time devoted to individuals was even higher.[397] Between 1947 and 1949, Pennsylvania lawyers earned 70 percent of their income from personal legal services to individuals.[398] But the proportion of effort devoted to individuals quickly began to decline. In 1947, 71 percent of all lawyers earned more than half their fees from individuals; seven years later the proportion had fallen to 67 percent.[399] In 1972, the proportion of its income a firm earned from individual clients varied inversely with its size (as measured by total receipts): firms earning up to $30,000 received 80 percent of their income from individuals, but firms earning more than $1 million received only 20 percent.[400] Between 1972 and 1982, the proportion of total fees private practitioners earned from individual clients declined from 52.3 to 44.7 percent.[401]

Today, the two categories of clients represent approximately equal investments of effort—hence their characterization as hemispheres. In 1975, Chicago lawyers devoted 47 percent of their time to corporations and 45 percent to individuals and small businesses (see Table 44). The latter category, however, remains a composite; defined more narrowly as the response to "personal plight," legal services to individuals represent only 18 percent of total lawyer effort.[402] Even these proportions are somewhat misleading, because the time invested by lawyers serving corporate interests must be multiplied by the greater productivity achieved by their more numerous support personnel, sophisticated office equipment, and greater specialization.[403]

Of course, even lawyers who represent individuals generally serve only the more privileged strata. In 1960, only 5 percent of New York City lawyers served a clientele whose median income mirrored that of the general population; 70 percent served a clientele whose median income was twice as high and 46 percent a clientele with four times the median income.[404] In Chicago in 1975, the clientele of lawyers devoting more than 25 percent of their time to securities matters contained no blue-collar workers, but that of lawyers devoting more than 25 percent of their time to divorce was 38 percent blue collar.[405]

Lawyers also specialize by subject matter: family and criminal law, torts, and house sales in one hemisphere; corporations, taxation, trusts and estates, and commercial real estate in the other.[406] In the mid-1930s, most Wisconsin lawyers indicated that their predominant work was in substantive areas of interest to individuals: probate (12 to 13 percent), negligence (7 to 8 percent), domestic relations (6 to 7 percent), and title work (6 to 7 percent); only small proportions of lawyers identified their predominant work as subjects primarily relevant to businesses, such as foreclosures (9 to 11 percent) and collections (7 to 11 percent).[407] In the late 1950s, Jerome Carlin found that 45 percent of New York City lawyers earned the largest part of their income from business law, whereas 51 percent earned the largest part from probate, personal injury, real estate, matrimonial, criminal, workers' compensation, and individual taxation.[408] Studies in Florida, Pennsylvania, and New Jersey in the 1960s found that 70 percent of lawyer income was derived from probate, real estate, and personal injury work.[409]

Lawyers in these two hemispheres also differ in the number of clients they serve and the duration of the lawyer-client relationship. In 1975, Chicago public utilities lawyers represented a median of just 3 clients a year, whereas plaintiffs' personal injury lawyers served 151 victims.[410] In Illinois in 1982, only 12.4 percent of lawyers concentrating in the personal sphere devoted more than 25 percent of their time in the previous year to a single client, compared with 50.6 percent of lawyers concentrating in the corporate sphere.[411] In the early 1980s, rural Missouri lawyers handled a median of 400 matters a year, some as many as 800.[412]

Partly as a consequence, these two categories of lawyers relate differently to their clients. Because the clients of large firms are repeat players, who provide a constant and significant share of the firm's business (and an even larger share of the work of individual lawyers), because corporate executives and wealthy individuals are as highly educated as their lawyers and their social equals or superiors, and because corporations often have house counsel who can oversee the work of outside lawyers, clients are the dominant actors in this relationship. A 1980 study of 224 lawyers at four large Chicago firms found that 84 percent had never refused any client or task on moral grounds.[413] Interviews with thirty-three attorneys in large Boston firms revealed only two moral objections: to a weapons manufacturer and to a school board engaged in laying off teachers (from a lawyer married to a schoolteacher).[414] By contrast, numerous accounts of sole and small-firm practitioners have demonstrated the ways in which they dominate their one-shot individual clients, who generally are experiencing crises, legally naive, of lower social status, and unlikely to bring additional business.[415] Statements by two personal injury lawyers vividly illustrate the character of the latter relationship:

> Because the client is ignorant, I don't let my clients think. If you look for guff from your clients you'll get it.

> I tell the client that I will do all the worrying about the case—period! . . . A little education is a dangerous thing. Just let the client know that the problem is in the hands of an extremely competent counsel.[416]

Even legal services lawyers display this kind of paternalism, despite the fact that it violates their ideology:

> [We] preach client autonomy, but in reality, it's a little impractical when the client isn't educated or doesn't know the system so she can make choices. After the 450th case, where all the clients make the same kind of decision, you've been through it, you feel that you might as well make the decision for the next client. . . .[417]

Lawyers in the two hemispheres perform different functions for their clients. In Missouri, rural lawyers spend 64 percent of their time conferring with clients, whereas urban lawyers spend 30 percent of their time in researching and preparing briefs, 25 percent negotiating, and only 15 percent conferring with clients.[418] Chicago lawyers specializing in securities work never appear in state court, whereas Chicago divorce lawyers make 15 appearances a month.[419]

The structure of practice is also very different. Within the Chicago bar in 1975, 61 percent of divorce lawyers practiced alone and none practiced in a firm with as many as thirty lawyers, but three fourths of securities lawyers practiced in firms with thirty or more lawyers, and none was a sole practitioner.[420] In Illinois in 1982, 43 percent of lawyers concentrating solely on the personal sphere practiced alone and 56 percent merely shared offices (but not profits), whereas 64 percent of those concentrating exclusively on the corporate sphere practiced in firms with at least ten lawyers.[421] Solo practice was a very small business, indeed: in 1967, 58 percent of sole practitioners had no employees at all, and another 39 percent had fewer than four.[422]

The hemispheres differ markedly in the origins of their lawyers and the prestige they enjoy. Only 15 percent of Chicago securities lawyers attended local law schools, compared with two thirds of divorce lawyers; 45 percent of securities lawyers attended elite law schools but no criminal lawyers.[423] Jews were 14 percent of securities lawyers but 56 percent of divorce lawyers; Catholics were 9 percent of divorce lawyers but 53 percent of criminal lawyers.[424] Professional prestige (as ranked by lawyers) varied inversely and strongly with the amount of time lawyers spent on pro bono matters and the number of individual clients they served—both of which were higher for sole and small-firm practitioners. The law firm emerged during the first half of this century largely in response to client demands for office work, with the result that the amount of time lawyers devoted to litigation may have decreased; but litigation has been a growth area within large-firm practice in recent years and one that enhances the prestige of both the firm and the litigator.[425] This may partly explain why house counsel, who traditionally referred complex litigation to outside firms, enjoyed less prestige, although both the practice of referrals and the relative ranking may be changing (see "House Counsel").[426]

Prestige varies directly with several other characteristics associated with large firm practice: intellectual challenge and technical expertise, the rate at which legal rules change, the reputation for ethical conduct, membership in the Republican Party, graduation from an elite law school, stability of clientele, and degree of specialization. Prestige varies inversely with such characteristics of solo and small-firm practice as the lawyer's freedom of action (paradoxically, since this is a measure of professional autonomy) and the proportion of lawyers who are Jewish.[427] Andrew Abbott has advanced the generalization that professional prestige is a function of professional purity and thus varies inversely with the degree to which the professional is contaminated by direct contact with social problems.[428]

There is an enormous range of variation in lawyer income (which also correlates with prestige, if sometimes weakly).[429] Indeed, as we saw in Chapter 8, incomes are dispersed more broadly among lawyers than in any other profession. The great divide separates sole and law firm practitioners. Even within the Harvard Law School class of 1911, partners reported earning 2 to 3 times as much as sole practitioners ten to twenty years after graduation.[430] In 1933, law firm partners in New York earned 2.8 times more than sole practitioners ($6490 versus $2310); 37 percent of sole practitioners but only 17 percent of firm lawyers earned less than $2000; the proportions earning more than $10,000 were 9 percent and 36 percent.[431] In 1935, law firm practitioners made twice as much as those in solo practice; as the economy began to emerge from the Depression two years later the ratio was more than 3:1.[432] Although sole practitioners averaged $7200 in 1952, 19 percent earned less than $3000 and only 4 percent more than $20,000.[433]

Even at the height of the postwar boom, many sole practitioners barely eked out a living. In 1967, more than nine out of ten earned gross receipts of less than $30,000: 17.6 percent less than $5000, 12.9 percent from $5,000 to $9,999, 11.9 percent from $10,000 to $14,999, 11.3 percent from $15,000 to $19,999, 16.3 percent from $20,000 to $24,999, and 20.4 percent from $25,000 to $29,999. By contrast, half of all principals in firms with at least four employees earned more than $32,000.[434] Five years later, three fifths of sole practitioners with at least one employee still grossed less than $50,000: 4.4 percent less than $10,000, 11.7 percent from $10,000 to $19,999, 16.1 percent from $20,000 to $29,999, and 29.4 percent from $30,000 to $49,999.[435]

Lawyer income varies even more strongly with number of employees and firm size.[436] In 1954, lawyers in firms of nine or more earned five times as much as sole practitioners.[437] In Virginia in 1961, partners in firms with six to seven lawyers earned 2.4 times as much as sole practitioners ($29,604 versus $12,224).[438] In 1967, the top decile of partners in law firms with at least four employees enjoyed net incomes nine times higher than those in the bottom decile. In 1967, partners in firms with fifty or more earned 1.55 times as much as sole practitioners with at least four employees; in the top decile of each category the disparity was more than 4 to 1; in the bottom decile it was almost 10 to 1.[439] Income also varies directly with other characteristics of large-firm practice, such as a high degree of specialization and a predominantly business clientele.[440] A recent survey of graduates of seven northeastern law schools found that median income increased steadily: from $25,000 for sole practitioners to $46,000 for those in firms with more than eighty-four lawyers, in the cohort who had graduated four years earlier; from $35,000 to $123,000 in the cohort graduated eleven years earlier; from $41,000 to $160,000 in the cohort graduated sixteen years earlier; and from $60,000 to $200,000 in the cohort graduated twenty-six years earlier.[441] Income also varies with city size, but this variable is probably a surrogate for firm size, since the larger firms are located in the larger cities.[442] Of course, income is also a function of both age and experience.[443]

Because income varies directly with both firm size and age, it is the senior partners in the largest firms who earn the truly astronomical incomes. According to one source, four or five partners in each of the fifty largest firms earned $200,000 to $500,000 in 1972.[444] Another claimed that senior partners in the largest New York firms averaged $161,000 in 1978.[445] The two named partners in the New York firm of Shea and Gould each took $646,000 in partnership earnings in 1982.[446] And a 1984 ABA survey found that the median income for partners in all firms with more than ten lawyers was $129,200 and the average $162,400.[447]

Few move between the two hemispheres of private practice. Among Chicago lawyers surveyed in 1975, only 9 percent of those who began in firms with fewer than ten lawyers had moved to larger firms (only 3.6 percent to firms with thirty or more), and only 12 percent of lawyers who began in firms with thirty or more had moved to smaller firms (only 6.5 percent to firms with fewer than ten).[448] A study of graduates from seven northeastern law schools found that within each cohort (graduates of four, eleven, sixteen, and twenty-six years), retention rates were higher at the two extremes of firm size than in the middle.[449]

Although historians and sociologists have found evidence of the continuous stratification of the legal profession from the colonial period to the present, the two hemispheres are more differentiated and polarized today than ever before. Their members vary greatly in the degree to which their practice is specialized. Some lawyers serve a clientele of working-class and middle-class individuals, and others serve businesses and wealthy individuals, but few serve both categories. The growth in the size of law firms parallels a shift in the distribution of legal services from individuals to businesses. Lawyers serving these different clienteles specialize in different subject matters. Some provide brief, transitory representation or advice to many clients, whom they tend to dominate; others form enduring relationships with a few, who tend to dominate them. The two categories perform different functions and appear in different courts and agencies. These divergences in the content of legal practice closely reflect variations in structure: both between sole and firm practitioners and among firms of different sizes. Family background and prelegal and legal education influence who enters each hemisphere. Background variables and practice structure, in turn, affect lawyer prestige and income, which are increasingly polarized. In what other profession do some members earn fifty times more than others? Once a lawyer has entered one hemisphere it is virtually impossible to move to the other.

One Profession or Many? The Dilemmas of Collective Action

The fission of the legal profession—into employers, employees, and the self-employed; public and private sector employees; teachers, judges, and practitioners; and firms differentiated by size, status, income, clientele, subject matter, and function—creates serious obstacles to collective action. For more than a hundred years, the American Bar Association has been the only instrument through which the profession could speak with a single voice. As we have seen, however, membership is not compulsory and the ABA exercises no authority either directly over lawyers or indirectly over those state bars that do regulate the profession. The ABA *never* has attracted even half of all lawyers, in sharp contrast to the English Law Society and General Council of the Bar, which enroll virtually all private practitioners and a substantial proportion of employed lawyers (see Table 32).[450] Furthermore, the historical conservatism of the ABA hardly induces newer entrants to join.[451] Local associations engender the same suspicions. Between 1954 and 1974, a higher proportion of the Chicago Bar Association than of the practicing bar were the children of fathers in the professions (particularly law) and technical occupations, had attended elite law schools, were firm practitioners (rather than in solo practice, government or house counsel), and were white.[452]

As women and racial minorities have overcome legal and social barriers to enter the profession in significant numbers and as the proportion of younger lawyers has grown with the erosion of supply control, these new recruits have invested their energies in other voluntary associations that express their interests more forcefully. The National Bar Association enrolled 8500 black lawyers in 1985 and had gained economic self-sufficiency after a period of relying on federal government grants.[453] Younger lawyers have always been less interested in the established professional associations: in 1934, lawyers with less than five years of experience were 28 percent of the New York bar but only 17 percent of the New York County Lawyers' Association; those with less than ten years of experience were 59 and 42 percent, respectively.[454]

Not only demographic changes split the professional associations; the growing structural and functional divisions among lawyers also create sharply divergent interests. Within both the ABA and state and local bar associations, these differences are expressed as tensions over governance, which has never been representative of the organizational membership, much less of the profession as a whole.[455] The ABA leadership is dominated by older lawyers at the expense of younger, law firm partners at the expense of sole practitioners, graduates of elite law schools, and private practitioners at the expense of lawyers employed in the public sector.[456] In 1986, its thirty-six-member Board of Governors included no minority lawyers and only one woman.[457]

As the Chicago Bar Association absorbed an increasing proportion of local practitioners, the selection of its governing body became more oligarchic: it began as direct nomination and election at the annual general meeting, then limited members to voting on an official slate chosen by the Nominating Committee, and finally abandoned the charade of an election when the official slate was unopposed. It became virtually impossible for insurgents to attain office.[458] Not surprisingly, leadership positions in the Chicago Bar Association were held disproportionately by graduates of elite law schools and lawyers earning high incomes; 20 percent of securities, patent, and public utilities lawyers had held such positions, compared with only 5 percent of criminal defense and personal injury lawyers.[459] A detailed study of the CBA Board of Governors between 1950 and 1974 revealed that the average age (fifty years) was much higher than that of the profession, 71 percent of the governors were the sons of parents both of whom had been born in the United States, 56 percent were the sons of fathers who were professionals or managers, 20 percent were members of the fifteen largest firms (which contained only 6 percent of the local bar), and only 10 percent were employed in business or government (about half the proportion of the local bar).[460] The unrepresenta tiveness of governance was explicitly recognized (and perhaps entrenched) by the reservation of seats for relatively powerless categories: beginning in 1936, 20 percent of all committees (except the pivotal Candidates Committee) was reserved for those under thirty-six years of age (who then constituted more than 50 percent of the profession!); one of the forty-four seats on the Board of Managers was set aside for a black in 1956 and another for a woman in 1959.[461]

One response to unrepresentative governance within a professional association is apathy. ABA membership among Virginia lawyers in 1961 varied from 41 percent of those earning less than $5000 a year to 92 percent of those earning more than $30,000.[462] Active participation in state bar associations is very limited. In 1973, only 3 percent of Wisconsin lawyers served on committees of the unified (i.e., mandatory) state bar association (2 percent in 1981) and just 15 percent attended the annual meeting; only 25 percent participated in the activities of local voluntary bar associations.[463] Involvement varies with status. The proportion of California lawyers who had participated actively in the (mandatory) state bar association in the two or three years preceding 1960 varied from 33 percent of lawyers employed in government or business to 39 percent of sole practitioners, 41 percent of law firm associates, and 53 percent of partners.[464]

Another response to unrepresentative governance is the formation of rival associations. Less than ten years after the founding of the Chicago Bar Association in 1874, a group of younger, better-educated attorneys from ethnic and religious minorities established the Law Club of Chicago.[465] The New York County Lawyers Association represents sole and small-firm practitioners, whereas the Association of the Bar of the City of New York represents larger firms. The St. Louis Bar Association split into two groups, one dominated by the plaintiffs' personal injury bar and the other by lawyers representing insurance companies and corporations.[466] The membership of the Chicago Bar Association differs significantly from that of the Chicago Council of Lawyers (founded by younger attorneys in 1969), in politics, ethnicity, religion, age, income, law school attended, and type of practice.[467] On a national level, the Association of Trial Lawyers of America claims 65,000 members, most of whom represent plaintiffs in personal injury matters; its positions on legal ethics, damages, and tort liability often differ widely from those of the ABA.[468] The Defense Research Institute serves lawyers on the other side in personal injury cases. The American Corporate Counsel Association, created in 1982 by lawyers employed in corporations, had enrolled 7000 members by 1987. The National Association of Criminal Defense Lawyers had 5000.[469] And there are associations of judges, law teachers, and government employees.

Bar associations seek to avoid controversial political issues: integrated bars because compulsory membership may violate freedoms of association and expression; voluntary bars because they fear the loss of members. Thus, the Chicago Bar Association embraced a position of legalism in response to both the anticommunist attack on civil liberties during the McCarthy era and the subsequent movement for civil rights.[470] Internal divisions forced the Wisconsin State Bar Association to withdraw from the judicial selection process as early as 1963 and to refund dues money that had been spent on other political activities.[471] The Chicago Bar Association and the Chicago Council of Lawyers have clashed over the evaluation of judges running for election.[472] The conservative Washington Legal Foundation has sued both the ABA and the U.S. Department of Justice to curtail the ABA's role in judicial selection.[473] Similar controversies over the permissible scope of bar association activities have arisen in Michigan, New Mexico, Idaho, and the District of Columbia.[474] Courts have limited the power of the Florida and California Bars to use compulsory dues for purposes other than "improving the administration of justice."[475] In response, lawyers have created voluntary Political Action Committees (LAWPACs) in Arkansas, Illinois, Minnesota, Ohio, Wisconsin, Michigan, South Dakota, Utah, and Washington, to separate professional and political activities.[476] There is every reason to expect further proliferation of voices and heightened disharmony.

The legal profession may be divided not only by political ideologies but also by economic self-interest. As more lawyers become employees or dependent on government to pay their fees, professional associations may retreat into economism or be displaced by trade unions. The latter already have emerged in legal aid organizations, among government employees, and even in private law firms.[477] Indeed, it is particularly ironic that the California State Bar's thirty-three lawyer employees who investigate and prosecute disciplinary cases belong to the Service Employees International Union and recently struck for 23 days to demand higher wages, thereby paralyzing the already backlogged regulatory process.[478] Union representation of employee interests can engender employer retaliation and heighten class consciousness. A legal services lawyer described negotiations between her union and the program: "during bargaining sessions we were treated like shit by management, at the table and in the office. . . . People began to say 'They think we're workers!' And then they realized that we *were* workers."[479]

American lawyers have encountered repeated difficulties in speaking with a single voice. The first obstacle was geography: the size of the country, the dispersion of its population, and regional differences all made organization difficult. Thus, the earliest professional associations emerged within the major cities, and counties often organized before states, whose bar associations remained weak until they acquired the power to compel membership, starting in the 1920s. The American Bar Association was not only geographically remote from most practitioners and unable to mobilize government coercion to require membership but also only loosely articulated with the state associations, which were either self-regulating or positioned to influence the state legislatures and supreme courts that had regulatory power.

As the nation urbanized and integrated both economically and politically, distance ceased to be a major obstacle to collective action. But voluntary associations still failed to attract significant segments of the profession. Younger lawyers may feel unrepresented or preoccupied with career pressures. As the generation gap widened in the 1960s and 1970s, they formed alternative organizations in the major cities. Women and racial minorities, particularly the latter, have also responded to their sense of exclusion by creating associations in which they are not mere tokens. Lawyers at the lower end of the prestige and income hierarchy have always remained either outside the established associations or uninvolved in their activities. In some cities they have created rival groups.

Just as the membership of local, state, and national associations is unrepresentative of the profession, so their governance also is unrepresentative of the membership and thus doubly unrepresentative of the profession. Older white males from privileged backgrounds, who graduated from elite law schools and practice in large firms are overrepresented.

Even when organizational structures exist, professional differences of background, practice setting, income and prestige, and ideology inhibit collective action. Potentially powerful inclusive organizations are paralyzed by internal divisions, lapsing into the passivity of the lowest common denominator either out of fear of lawsuits from members smarting under compulsion or defections by those who belong voluntarily. Organizations that are relatively exclusive and homogeneous may be able to attain the unity of purpose essential to action but lack the political or economic resources to be effective. The other organizational form is illustrated by the narrow economism of trade unions of lawyers employed by government and specialist associations pursuing parochial interests. If American lawyers today are less divided by geography and federalism than they were 100 or even 50 years ago, they are more divided by stratification, heterogeneity of background, and differentiation of practice environment.

10

Reproducing the Profession

Law School Socialization

The extensive differentiation within the legal profession requires a mechanism for allocating law graduates to roles and socializing them within those roles. The law school has performed both functions ever since it emerged as gatekeeper to the profession at the beginning of this century. In recent years, it has grown in importance as a device for distributiong an ever more diverse student body among increasingly varied careers, with dramatically different rewards. At the same time, these first jobs have acquired greater influence as informal apprenticeships socializing novices into particular professional subcultures.

At first glance, law school appears to be a powerful socializing agent. It has been extraordinarily uniform and changeless since the case method triumphed shortly after the turn of the century and part-time schools were eliminated several decades later.[1] In 1925–26, first-year students at such major law schools as Chicago, Michigan, Yale, Columbia, and Harvard all were instructed in large sections (median 152, mean 148), just as they are today.[2] The casebook, consisting largely of appellate decisions, is the dominant reading matter in first-year courses, and some variant of the Socratic method prevails everywhere.[3] Even when Yale Law School was most vehement about situating law in a social context, a 1948 study found that 70 percent of the student body took the basic courses that prepared them for a business law practice, while fewer than 20 percent took the remaining 65 to 70 courses and seminars offered each year.[4]

Teachers and texts present the law as a coherent, comprehensive system of rules produced by an invisible process of democratic consensus that strips them of all political content. These rules provide unambiguous answers to all questions. Uncertainty, where acknowledged, is resolved by "balancing" equally legitimate values. Rules are criticized, if at all, only in terms of ostensibly apolitical criteria, such as the Cons'itution, the legal process, and now economic concepts of market efficiency.

Most students experience law school, particularly the first year, as intellectually monolithic, emotionally overwhelming, and personally transformative. Numerous empirical studies have found heightened symptoms of obsessive-compulsion, anxiety, depression, and hostility, beginning in the first six months of law school and persisting throughout the entire three years, even influencing the first two years of practice.[5]

Yet there are reasons to doubt that the long-term effect of law school is as great, or as uniform, as students protest and fictional accounts continue to insist. If the resources devoted to legal education are any index of the intensity of the socialization process, it is an extremely diffuse experience. The number of students per faculty member has always been very high. At Harvard, it grew from 40 in 1895 to 78 in 1925. In that latter year it was even higher elsewhere: 103 at Columbia, 112 at Dickinson, 150 at Albany, and a staggering 283 at Buffalo.[6] At Cumberland University Law School, the largest institution in Tennessee in 1938, there was one full-time law teacher for every 217 students and one teacher for every 72.[7] A 1940 survey of 99 of the 108 ABA-approved schools found that the annual expenditure per student ranged from $251 at the smaller schools to $374 at the larger.[8] At all law schools in 1948–49 there were 52 students for each full-time teacher and 36 students per teacher (if part-time teachers are included as one-fourth of a full-time teacher); the mean annual expenditure per student was $293.[9] In 1956–57, there was an average of 16.5 students per full-time teacher and a median of 22; the average first-year class was 60 students and the median 51.[10] These numbers strongly suggest that most students interact with faculty only in large groups, although institutions also socialize students in other ways, such as peer pressures.

Students encounter law school only after they have been thoroughly imbued with some variant of American culture for at least twenty years.[11] Legal education presents only one of the many images of the law to which they have been exposed through the mass media—although most have had less direct experience of law than medical students have had of medicine, notwithstanding the fact that a sixth of all law students have a lawyer parent and half have a lawyer relative.[12] Law students may be a self-selected group who emphasize thought over emotion or are tough-minded rather than tender-minded, but their basic moral values do not seem to change significantly during the three years.[13] Furthermore, the increasing diversity of the law student body, particularly the presence of older students (many with advanced degrees and extensive career experience), women, and racial minorities—who together constitute more than half of the enrollment—renders the culture of the law school less monolithic.[14] When members of the University of Michigan Law School classes of 1976 through 1979 were questioned five years after graduation, 10 percent of the women but only 3 percent of the men said they had entered law school with a strong determination to work in government or legal services and remained faithful to that ideal.[15] Perhaps the most significant effect of law school is to convince those who enter without a commitment to practicing law (about 20 percent of a 1961 sample) to decide to become lawyers.[16]

The strongest reason for questioning the influence of law schools, however, is their inability to immerse students in what Goffman calls a total environment.[17] Law schools are permeated by external pressures, most notably the bar examination and the job market. Despite the fact that bar examination pass rates rose steadily from the 1930s to the early 1980s, law students continued to choose their courses in anticipation of what would be examined, spending 85 percent of their three years on "bar" subjects.[18] An analysis of the curricula at smaller law schools found that they correlated strongly with the subjects examined on the bar examination in thirty-six of the forty-eight institutions; even at Yale, reputed for its innovation, 75 to 90 percent of student time was devoted to traditional subjects.[19] Students also exert pressure on their teachers (through course evaluations that influence tenure, promotion, and self-respect) to focus on what students expect the bar examination to test. At the same time, the fact that bar examination cram courses are widely available (major cities offer several competitors) and almost universally taken allows students to reduce their investment in law school, particularly after the first year. Thus, the shadow of the bar exam pervades law school from the first day, reminding both students and faculty that the true purpose of legal education is the memorization of rules that can be regurgitated and quickly forgotten.

The Rationalization of the Labor Market

The influence of the job market is more recent but probably more powerful. It may be difficult from our present perspective to remember that "jobs" for lawyers are a mid-twentieth-century novelty. Samuel Williston asserted that no one in his Harvard Law School class of 1888 could obtain a paying position in the year after graduation.[20] Significant numbers of graduates used to set up practice on their own, perhaps sharing space with another lawyer.[21] The proportion of new admittees who began practice as employees of other lawyers was only 39 percent among New York lawyers with one to four years of experience in 1935, 32 percent among California lawyers with one to two years of experience in 1933, and 24 percent among Wisconsin lawyers with one to two years of experience in 1936 (which suggests that it varied inversely with the degree of urbanization).[22] Among the 1119 California lawyers admitted in 1929, 1930, and 1931, slightly fewer than half (555) worked as law firm employees; even among those who did, a fifth of the total (222) were allowed to retain all the fees they collected from clients, and only 9 kept none.[23] Among college seniors who hoped to attend law school in the fall of 1961, 43 percent expected to be self-employed.[24] As late as 1969, three fifths of law students expected to be self-employed and only a fourth anticipated jobs; yet just six years later the proportions were reversed.[25] One reason for this change was that jobs became both more available and more attractive.[26] Today, virtually every graduate expects to start as an employee: in the decade 1974–84, less than 4 percent of the 90 percent of graduates who began work immediately after law school started as sole practitioners; in 1985, less than 3 percent did so.[27] Thus, the job market has become the central preoccupation of law students.

Until recently, job-hunting occurred at the very end of the 3–year course and took place outside law school. It certainly did not resemble a freely competitive labor market; positions were obtained primarily through personal contacts. Among those admitted to the Wisconsin bar in 1934, 38 percent secured their first positions through family and friends, 31 percent through individual initiative, 7 percent through previous work experience, and very few through relatively universalistic means: just 14 percent through their law schools and *none* by answering advertisements.[28] Among the 555 California lawyers who were admitted between 1929 and 1931 and began their careers as law firm employees, half used personal contacts (191 had social connections and 84 had business connections). Although the California State Bar Association created a clearinghouse for young attorneys seeking jobs, and many graduates registered, only *one* law firm ever even inquired, and it hired no one.[29] Similarly, when the New York County Lawyers' Association and the Association of the Bar of the City of New York collaborated to create a Lawyers Bureau in 1947, there were 8.9 job seekers for every potential employer.[30] In response to a 1950 questionnaire asking law firms across the country whether they had openings for young lawyers, 63 percent said they had none and only 20 percent answered affirmatively.[31] A contemporaneous survey of 3300 Virginia lawyers found only *eleven* firms interested in hiring recent graduates.[32] As late as the 1960s, third-year students sought jobs primarily by knocking on law firm doors during the Christmas vacation. Harvard did not even have a placement office in 1947.[33] In 1949, thirty-six law schools spent a total of $80,600 on their placement offices, an average of only $2239 per school.[34]

But as contacts and personalistic criteria succumbed to the combined effect of enormous increases in numbers (of both applicants and employers), law firm demands for greater technical competence fostered by heightened competition, and law student attacks on discrimination, the hiring process was rationalized and institutionalized within the law school. Harvard's placement office arranged visits for sixty-four potential employers in 1950–51; Michigan's hosted 697 in 1984, more than ten times as many at a school that was slightly smaller and less prestigious.[35] Today, the fall semester of the third year is consumed by on campus interviews and "call-backs." At Michigan, the total number of interviews increased from 7000 in 1974 to 14,000 in 1984 (at least 20 per student if the entire second- and third-year classes participated); about 75 percent of students report that they obtained their jobs through this process. The number of interviewers at the University of Virginia increased from 292 in 1971 to 782 in 1984. Second-year students averaged twenty-three on-campus interviews apiece, and some attended more than fifty.[36] Columbia has a computer data base of hundreds of law firm resumes, which are constantly updated, and it is thinking about extending its services to alumni seeking lateral moves.[37] Indeed, recruitment has become so disruptive of the educational process that some law schools suspend classes for a week during the fall semester in order to make time for that activity.[38] Some students are taking advantage of their market power to combine interviewing with vacations, when they have little or no interest in working for the firm paying the bill.[39]

Law ultimately may follow medicine in taking the next step toward rationalizing its labor market: a central computerized clearinghouse. Canadian law students seeking articles (a mandatory postgraduate apprenticeship) with 113 Toronto law firms participated in such a program for the first time in the fall of 1986; and a Cambridge, Massachusetts, placement firm has tried to organize something similar in Boston.[40] Law firms are beginning to cooperate on their own: five large firms from New York, Philadelphia, Phoenix, Chicago, and Baltimore hired Human Resource Services Inc. to interview 394 candidates at 18 non-Ivy League schools.[41] And consortia of law firms in Phoenix and Philadelphia have dispatched joint interviewing teams to promote their cities as good places to live.[42] The Association of American Law Schools has joined with the National Association of Law Placement Inc. to create a proposal for regional job fairs to replace both on-campus interviewing and call-backs.[43]

To attract law students and get to know them better before offering them positions as associates, law firms have also been employing clerks during the summer after their second year, at least since the 1960s. Large firms pay clerks extraordinary salaries, up to $1000 a week in 1984, while entertaining them royally and giving them interesting work and light workloads.[44] In 1986, Shearman & Sterling paid summer clerks $15,500 for ten weeks.[45] A very high proportion of second-year summer clerks are offered jobs on graduation: 88 percent at the twenty-five largest firms in 1987, ranging from 73 to 100 percent at individual firms. About half the clerks accept such offers (the percentage ranges between 40 and 78 percent at different firms), and more return after judicial clerkships.[46] An annual survey of large-firm summer associates consistently confirms that they are strongly attracted by the combination of high salaries, stimulating work, and an active social life.[47] As a result, second-year students now participate as actively as third-year students in the fall hiring season. Many students even find legal jobs at the end of their first year—almost 75 percent at Michigan—although some of these are unpaid. Consequently, the job market now permeates the consciousness of first-year students as well.

Since World War II, only a tiny proportion of law students have formally studied part time in order to work full time; but a large proportion actually do work during the term in order to earn money, gain experience, and get a headstart on job hunting. In a 1956–57 survey of eighty-five law schools, twenty-four (28 percent) reported that fewer than 25 percent of their students worked during the term, forty-one (48 percent) reported that 25 to 49 percent worked, seventeen (20 percent) reported that 50 to 64 percent worked, and three reported higher proportions.[48] More than half of the 1960 graduates of several elite schools (except Yale) had worked while students, though not necessarily in legal jobs; the same was true of 1970 graduates (except at Pennsylvania), although the proportion had declined somewhat.[49]

A more detailed investigation of student employment in 1975–76 found that a third of all students were employed at any given time (and many more at *some* point during their three years in law school); two thirds of these worked in law-related jobs. The proportion employed varied inversely with law school status, however: 19 to 25 percent at elite schools, compared with 41 to 47 percent at regional public institutions. Nearly a third of these students worked more than fifteen hours a week, which significantly reduced the amount of time they spent on their studies.[50] A survey of University of Utah law graduates of the 1970s and early 1980s disclosed that 55 percent had held nonlegal jobs while attending law school and 90 percent had held legal clerkships either during the term or in the summers between terms; of the latter, 87 percent of the graduates surveyed and 76 percent of the current students had clerked during an academic semester. The largest proportion (86 percent) of those clerking did so to gain practical experience (although they actually spent most of their time on library research and obtained little feedback from their employers). A plurality agreed that "by comparison to clerking, law school was boring" (47 versus 35 percent). Nearly half (43 percent) reported that the clerkship led directly to a permanent job offer.[51] Among alumni of seven northeastern law schools, 18 percent were hired after graduation by an employer for whom they had worked during law school, and the proportion was greater among more recent graduates.[52]

Allocation to Roles

Within the opportunity structure defined by the job market, law schools continue to play a significant role in allocating students to positions and simultaneously shaping student values. The first step in the sorting process is the admission of applicants. The kind, status, and quantity of formal education lawyers attain has always affected their subsequent careers. A study of New York lawyers between 1928 and 1932 found that college graduates enjoyed average incomes almost 50 percent higher than nongraduates ($5220 versus $3570). Similarly, those who studied law full time earned incomes more than 50 percent higher than those who studied part time ($5140 versus $3355). Fewer than half of college graduates were sole practitioners, compared with almost two thirds of nongraduates (46 versus 63 percent), and the difference between full- and part-time law students was almost as pronounced.[53] A 1939 Michigan study found that sole practitioners were twice as likely as law firm associates to have attended a part-time law school and significantly more likely to have attended and graduated from college.[54] Among Jewish lawyers in New York City in 1937, the 498 who had attended schools at the bottom of the hierarchy (St. Johns or Fordham) enjoyed a median income of $1357; the 1761 who had attended middle-status schools (New York Law School, NYU or Brooklyn Law School) earned a median income nearly twice as high ($2389); and the 491 who had attended elite law schools (Yale, Cornell, Harvard, or Columbia) had a median income nearly three times as high ($3784).[55]

A 1948 study found a strong correlation between the kind of legal education lawyers acquired and their prior educational attainments. The proportion with some college education declined from 82 percent of graduates of ABA-approved law schools to 56 percent of graduates of unapproved law school and only 25 percent of lawyers who had not attended law school. In the same three categories, the proportion who had graduated from college was 52, 23, and 4 percent, respectively.[56] Law school, in turn, had a significant influence on later careers. In 1928, the alumni director of Suffolk Law School, an unapproved part-time Boston institution, surveyed its graduates, eliciting a response from 450 out of 1516. None belonged to the elite State Street firms; a few worked in local politics or for businesses, and many remained in the nonlegal jobs they had held before they studied law, but the vast majority were in solo practice or small firms. In 1930, members of the Harvard Law School class of 1911 reported an average income of $27,732 ($41,634 for those in partnerships); by contrast, a national income survey the previous year found that all lawyers averaged only about a third as much after fifteen and twenty years of experience ($7654 and $9682, respectively).[57] These differences persisted half a century later: in the decade 1972–82, 70 percent of the associates hired by the top thirteen Boston firms were from Harvard and only 4 percent were from Suffolk.[58]

Among the lawyers listed in the 1949 Martindale Hubbell Law Directory, the proportion who had not attended law school declined from 29 percent of sole practitioners to 17 percent of lawyers employed in government or business and 14 percent of law firm partners. The school a lawyer attended was equally significant: 42 percent of Harvard Law School graduates but only 17 percent of Brooklyn Law School graduates were law firm partners, and there were similar differences in the proportions who were associates (11 versus 2 percent) and sole practitioners (43 versus 79 percent).[59] In both 1957 and 1962, 71 percent of the partners in the twenty largest Wall Street firms were graduates of Harvard, Yale, or Columbia Law Schools.[60] A 1969 study found that law school status varied inversely with the proportion of graduates in solo practice and directly with the proportion in law firms, firm size, and lawyer income.[61] A study of Chicago lawyers in the late 1970s found that among high-status securities law specialists, 45 percent had graduated from elite law schools and only 14 percent from low-status local schools; among divorce practitioners, by contrast, the proportions were 11 and 65 percent, respectively.[62] A 1982 survey of lawyer income that divided law schools into four status categories found that graduates of the top schools earned 36 percent more than those in the bottom category at the beginning of their careers ($34,000 versus $25,000) and 18 percent more after seven years in practice ($53,300 versus $45,000).[63]

Graduation from a prestigious law school is not the only predictor of career success. Grades have become the consuming preoccupation of almost all students. This is not a new phenomenon. A 1935 survey found a significant correlation between the law school grades and subsequent incomes of University of Wisconsin law graduates between 1904 and 1931.[64] In Colorado in 1967, lawyers who claimed to have been in the top quarter of their classes reported a median income 24 percent higher than the rest of their classmates ($17,680 versus $14,233).[65] The comparison with medical school is instructive. Although it has long been more difficult to enter medical school than law school, competition is less intense among medical students than law students. At the University of Pennsylvania in 1952, 19 percent of medical students but 74 percent of law students reported experiencing a great deal of competition.[66] Grades have become so important that law students have begun to lie about their records, compelling some employers to demand official transcripts.[67] The Illinois Supreme Court recently disbarred a University of Michigan Law School graduate who had falsified his transcript to obtain a job at Kirkland & Ellis and apply for a teaching position at DePaul University College of Law.[68]

Judicial clerkships have become a further selection device—a one- or two-year elite apprenticeship mediating between law school performance and subsequent career—which absorbed 12 percent of graduates in 1985.[69] Federal clerkships are the most valued postgraduate credential: the editors-in-chief at fifteen of the twenty leading law reviews began clerkships after graduating in 1986.[70] Competition is intense, and applications must be completed by the spring of the second year. Harry T. Edwards of the District of Columbia Circuit, whose clerks have gone on to clerk for eight Supreme Court Justices, receives 500 to 1000 applications a year and interviews 20 to 40 students for three positions.[71] Virtually all of the thirty-one clerks who began work at the Supreme Court in 1987 had completed a clerkship with a lower federal court judge; more than a third had graduated from Yale or Harvard. Two thirds entered large firms on leaving the Court, three began to teach, three joined the government, and two did public interest work.[72]

Academic performance strongly affects student career choices because those who do well can aspire to the extraordinary financial rewards of large-firm practice. The New York firm of Cravath, Swaine & Moore, which has been a bellwether in the past, paid 1986 law school graduates $65,000 to start—$99,000 for those who had served as clerks to U.S. Supreme Court justices.[73] Rosenman, Colin, Lewis & Cohen, which had denounced the Cravath move and initially refused to follow, publicly caved in six weeks later, and at least fifteen comparable firms followed.[74] A mid-sized New York firm soon upped the ante to $70,000.[75] A year later two of the leading Chicago firms raised their starting salaries to $60,000, although Los Angeles remained almost $10,000 lower.[76] In the fall of 1987, starting salaries at the 250 largest firms averaged $65,600 in New York, $57,600 in Washington and Chicago, $53,200 in Boston, $52,700 in Los Angeles, $52,400 in Philadelphia, $51,300 in Atlanta, $51,100 in Dallas, and $50,000 in Houston and San Francisco.[77] Cravath raised its 1987 starting salary to $71,077.[78]

Firms also compete for graduates by touting partner contact, paralegal support, childcare, immediate litigation experience, public interest opportunities, and vacation condominiums.[79] A Minneapolis firm has bucked the trend of demanding long hours in exchange for high wages by allowing associates to work two thirds of the year for 60 percent of their usual salary.[80] When starting salaries increase, those of senior associates also must be raised: in 1986, seventh-year associates in the highest-paying New York firms earned between $130,000 and $140,000, including bonuses of more than $30,000.[81] One reason for the inflation of associate salaries is that large law firms now must compete with investment banks, not only in lateral hiring but also in filling first jobs, and they are losing significant numbers of the best law graduates to the prospect of engineering major deals and earning salaries that are two to three times what large law firms pay.[82]

Given the material rewards and status of large-firm practice, it is hardly surprising that most law students quickly lose interest in subjects like criminal and family law or in jobs with a government agency, prosecutor's office or public defender.[83] When members of the University of Michigan Law School classes of 1976 through 1979 were surveyed five years after graduation, only 10 percent of women and 15 percent of men reported that they had entered law school intending to work in firms of fifteen lawyers or more; by graduation, however, 36 percent of the women and 44 percent of the men had such plans; of the large number who entered law school without any career plans, half had chosen large firm practice by the end of their three years.[84] Between 1977 and 1982, the proportion of Stanford Law School graduates beginning practice in firms with more than fifty lawyers ranged between 36 and 46 percent.[85] More than half the 1986 UCLA Law School graduates who had full-time legal jobs by the end of their third year were going to work for firms with more than fifty lawyers, and more than 70 percent were entering firms with more than twenty-five lawyers. By contrast, only 3 of the 256 UCLA Law School graduates of 1987 who responded to a survey at the end of their third year (1.2 percent) had taken public interest jobs.

The last decade and a half has seen a secular decline in the proportion of law graduates entering public interest work. Although 21.5 percent of 1974 graduates took government or public interest jobs, only 14.6 percent of 1983 graduates did so, a drop of almost a third, while the proportion entering private practice increased from 52.2 percent to 60.4 percent; there was little change two years later. The proportion of graduates entering firms with more than fifty lawyers increased from 7 percent in 1979 to 19 percent in 1985 (although these firms contained only 5 percent of all lawyers in 1980). In the class of 1985, the fifth of graduates who were over thirty years old were more than twice as likely as all graduates to enter government (26.6 versus 12.7 percent).[86] The proportion of University of Michigan Law School graduates entering private practice increased from 65 percent of the classes of 1971 and 1972 to 89 percent of the classes of 1983 and 1984, while the proportion entering government or legal services fell from 17 to 5 percent. Much of the decline was attributable to changes in women's careers: 67 percent of women in the class of 1981 were in private practice five years after graduation, compared with 42 percent of those in the class of 1976.[87] Among the alumni of seven northeastern law schools, the proportion of those who began working for legal services programs declined from 11 percent of those who had graduated sixteen years earlier to 4 percent of those who had graduated four years earlier.[88] A survey of second- and third-year law students at Chicago, Georgetown, and NYU in 1986 and 1987 revealed that at least 89 percent rated geographical location, type of practice, reputation of employer, nice people, and atmosphere and salary as very important or moderately important in selecting an employer, but only 24 percent rated pro bono practice very important, and 43 percent rated it moderately important.[89]

If law graduates are attracted to large firm practice by high salaries, they are discouraged from taking low paying government and public interest jobs by the substantial debts they have accumulated during seven years of postsecondary education. In 1975–76, just under a million undergraduates or recent graduates owed more than $2 billion in student loans; ten years later, more than 4 million students and graduates owed more than $9 billion (both in constant 1985 dollars); law graduates owed an average of $25,000.[90] Members of the University of Michigan Law School classes of 1971 and 1972 graduated with an average college and law school debt of $3100; members of the classes of 1980 and 1981 owed an average of $9400, and those in the class of 1987 an average of $19,100.[91] Among Harvard law graduates in 1986, the average indebtedness for legal education alone was $27,200; for those with undergraduate debts, the total was $32,800. In 1978, Harvard offered students who took low-paying jobs a two-year moratorium on loan repayments. Ten years later it agreed to assume all legal education loan repayments for graduates who earned less than $20,000 (a fairly safe bet!) and all payments above 6 percent of the lawyer's income for those earning $20,000 to $29,000. But though several elite schools have established similar programs, few graduates have taken advantage of them.[92]

One reason may be that income differentials are too great to be ignored by any but the most dedicated (or the independently wealthy). A 1973 study concluded that lawyers sacrificed $8840 a year (28 percent of their income) to work in a public interest law firm and $18,410 (44 percent) to work in a legal services office.[93] This gap has yawned wider in the last fifteen years. Starting salaries were $16,000 in large New York firms, $13,300 in the federal government, and $12,500 in the District Attorney's Office or Legal Aid in New York in 1972; but fourteen years later large New York firms were starting associates at $65,000, while the federal government was paying only $27,000, the District Attorney and Legal Aid only $25,000, and some public interest law firms the same.[94] The average salary for all first law jobs in 1985 was $29,224; New York firms with more than 100 lawyers offered $49,027, and large firms in other major cities were not far behind, but public interest jobs paid only $19,976; there were 14,328 entry-level jobs in law firms but only 787 in public interest careers.[95]

The Revival of Apprenticeship

Law school thus plays an important role in justifying the allocation of graduates among careers that offer very different rewards. The vast majority of graduates remain in law-related jobs throughout their working lives. A 1975 Chicago survey found that law retained a higher proportion of entrants than almost any other profession, at all ages: 84 percent at age thirty-five, 67 percent at forty-five, and 56 percent at fifty-five.[96] A survey of seven northeastern law schools found that 87 percent of their graduates remained in law, decreasing from nearly 90 percent of those only four years after graduation to little more than 70 percent of those who had graduated twenty-six years earlier.[97]

Given the nonprofessional content of much legal education and the enormous variation among legal careers, further socialization must occur within the first job (and at the beginning of each subsequent job). We know very little about this process in many sectors of the profession, such as teaching or employment in government or industry, although accounts of solo practice, legal aid, and prosecutors' offices sometimes discuss the early years.[98] A 1975 survey of a variety of large employers revealed that they had regularized procedures governing apprenticeship and career advancement. Most used formal evaluations in deciding whether or not to retain and promote lawyers: 72 percent of the Fortune 500 corporations, 83 percent of the 105 largest law firms, 90 percent of federal agencies employing at least thirty lawyers, and 70 percent of both state attorneys general and city attorneys of the fifty largest municipalities.[99]

We do have anecdotal information about the experience of being a law firm associate.[100] And since more than half of all 1983 law graduates were employed in private practice (almost two thirds of all those employed and almost three fourths of those employed in law), and more than a third were employed in firms with more than ten lawyers, the position of law firm associate represents a significant environment for postgraduate socialization.[101] Furthermore, although 70 percent of Chicago lawyers held at least two jobs during their legal careers, there was a strong relationship between first and subsequent jobs, and large firms retained a higher proportion of their entrants than any other category: 77.9 percent remained within large firms and 91.2 percent within private practice.[102]

Although the best law students enjoy a seller's market, carefully comparing the blandishments law firms offer (summer clerkships, starting salaries, and fringe benefits), associates are much more the captives of those firms, passively accepting the raises and bonuses subsequently awarded as clues to the progress they are making toward partnership. (The increase in lateral mobility among firms and between private practice and corporate counsel, aggressive headhunting by search firms, the proliferation of branch offices, and the possibility of launching a boutique firm may be encouraging greater assertiveness among associates.) The enormous difference between associate salaries and partnership shares (sometimes more than 10:1) symbolizes both the subordination of the former and the rewards that follow from accepting it gracefully. A study of associates at four large Chicago firms found that they received less than a fifth of their work from client contact and more than four fifths from a superior in the firm; partners, by contrast, received 60 percent of their work directly from clients.[103]

Associates remain in this status for many years: a median of 6.7 in 320 firms across twelve cities, 7.6 in New York, and as long as 10 in some firms (but perhaps less than 5 in those with fewer than three lawyers).[104] Therefore, associates do not acquire significant responsibility for either intrafirm governance or clients' affairs until their early thirties or even later. Furthermore, the prize of partnership is elusive. In the more selective firms, only one or two out of every ten beginning associates become partners.[105] At the New York firm of Dewey, Ballantine, Bushby, Palmer & Wood, only 1 percent of the associates hired in 1973 and 1974 were partners in 1984; at Cadwalader, Wickersham & Taft the proportion was only 9 percent; but in other New York firms it was 40 percent.[106] In 1983, associates in firms with 100 lawyers or more had a 52 percent chance of becoming a partner.[107] And across the nation, a survey found that 77 percent of associates become partners: 80 percent in firms with fewer than eleven lawyers, 74 percent in those with fifty or more.[108]

Those not offered partnerships often remain indebted to the firm for help in obtaining positions in the office of house counsel of a client or in a smaller firm that represents the same clients; and some are invited to remain as permanent associates—27 percent of those denied partnership.[109] Robert Nelson traced the careers of ninety-one lawyers who left four Chicago firms with more than fifty lawyers between 1970 and 1979 (45 percent of all who left): forty-one of these (45 percent) still practiced in law firms (twenty-one in firms of two to nine lawyers, ten in firms of ten to twenty-nine lawyers, and ten in larger firms); twenty-nine (32 percent) were house counsel; and only twenty-one (23 percent) had other positions (ten sole practitioners, seven government employees, and four law teachers).[110] Thus, the long and painful postgraduate apprenticeship in the law firm teaches the associate that extraordinary rewards will be granted by those in absolute power to some of those who display total obedience and work compulsively. Not surprisingly, 85 percent of the partners at four large Chicago firms were committed to practicing there for the rest of their careers (compared with only 51 percent of associates).[111]

For many, however, those rewards are not enough. Research is just beginning to uncover the considerable dissatisfaction among private practitioners. The National Association for Law Placement found that one out of four associates surveyed expected to change jobs within two years, including many who were very satisfied or somewhat satisfied, primarily because they saw insufficient potential for advancement. Women were much less satisfied than men, largely because they felt they were not respected (they also made much less money). Dissatisfaction was highest among those in firms with three or four lawyers and lowest in medium-sized firms with twenty-one to sixty lawyers.[112] An ABA survey confirmed that dissatisfaction was greatest among lawyers in very small or very large firms: the former complained of insufficient intellectual challenge and financial rewards, the latter of political intrigue, too little time for themselves, and the absence of a warm personal atmosphere.[113] Among the graduates of seven northeastern law schools, more than three fourths had left their first jobs, a third of these because of job dissatisfaction; movement was significantly more frequent among those who began in law firms.[114] Career counselors report that lawyers are more dissatisfied than other professionals and often seek to leave law altogether.[115]

The Institutionalization of Reproduction

As recently as a hundred years ago the legal profession reproduced itself through a simple, informal process: an apprentice worked in a lawyer's office until he felt ready to set up practice on his own. In recent decades, however, the increasing heterogeneity of entrants, the differentiation and stratification of legal roles, and the greater technicality and specialization of legal work have required a much more elaborate complex of institutions, both to socialize lawyers and to allocate them to positions within the professional hierarchy. As law schools displaced apprenticeship at the turn of the century, they became the primary socializing agent. Their very homogeneity allowed them to prepare lawyers for what effectively was a single role—solo or small-firm practice. By the 1940s, the two strata of law schools that Alfred Reed described and applauded in the 1920s had been replaced by a monolithic uniformity arrayed across a hierarchy of status differences: all schools taught virtually the same curriculum in large classes using the Socratic method to analyze appellate cases and ranking students by means of written examinations that tested their ability to spot issues in complex factual hypotheticals.

Law students today experience their schooling, particularly the first year, as personally transformative, to a degree unparalleled among undergraduate or graduate students. Nevertheless, empirical research shows little change in basic values, which is consistent with the diffuse atmosphere of the large classroom, the lengthy socialization law students have already undergone, the considerable influence of the media in shaping conceptions of law, and the effect of self-selection and competitive admission in narrowing the range of entrants. At the same time, the women, racial minorities, and older students—who together now constitute a majority of law students—may be more resistant to the culture of this alien environment. Furthermore, the socializing effects of law school are now permeated by the threat of the bar examination (which strongly shapes what professors teach and students learn) and the job market (which defines what careers are worth pursuing).

If law school has declined in importance as a socialization mechanism, it has grown in importance as a device for allocating graduates to roles. This is a fairly recent development: until World War II, at least two thirds and perhaps as many as three fourths of all law graduates went directly into practice by themselves; clients, not employers, determined their career success. Today, a mere 3 percent of graduates begin to practice alone, while all the rest seek jobs (or continue their education). Consequently, the labor market has become an overwhelming influence on law students. Well into the 1950s, graduating students sought employment through personal contacts, individual initiative, and chance. Today, placement offices are a central law school institution, well-endowed with resources; and law firms (if not all other employers) devote extraordinary time and energy to recruitment. Law firms are beginning to pool their resources in order to interview as widely and effectively as possible. There still is little cooperation among law schools, despite abortive efforts to agree on a process for selecting judicial clerks. But it seems likely that law school placement will ultimately be rationalized along the lines of medical internships. The search for jobs already consumes almost the entire fifth semester of law school; with the proliferation of summer clerkships it has permeated the second year as well; and many first-year students now spend a good part of their second semester seeking legal jobs for the following summer, even foregoing salaries to get them. Although the ABA had virtually eliminated part-time legal education by the 1950s, most full-time students now engage in legal work at some point during their law school careers to help pay the ever-higher tuition, obtain experience, and gain an entree to jobs after graduation.

Although it is employers who ultimately select employees, law school remains an essential intermediary. Even fifty years ago there was clear evidence that the status of the law school attended correlated strongly with the graduate's subsequent practice environment and income. Law schools performed this allocating function partly by selecting among applicants on the basis of the college attended and undergraduate record and partly by ranking student performance. Law students experience the competition for grades as fiercer and more destructive than anything in their prior education; by contrast, entry to medical school is more competitive and learning within it is less so. Judicial clerkships now provide yet another sorting mechanism, perhaps necessitated by the growing number of highly qualified graduates with virtually indistinguishable credentials. The impetus for this intense competition is the extreme stratification of professional careers in terms of income and status, ranging from the largest law firms at the apex to solo practice and perhaps local government employment at the base. These poles have diverged further in recent years. Salaries were perhaps 30 percent higher in law firms than in public interest jobs in the late 1960s, but today they are 150 to 200 percent higher. And students graduate far deeper in debt. The Reagan administration's campaign to deregulate and privatize also has reduced the number of public interest jobs available. It is not surprising, therefore, that students who declare an interest in public service when they enter law school quickly develop a fascination for corporations, taxation, commercial law, and real estate finance by the time they leave, resulting in a dramatic reduction in the proportion who take public interest jobs.

Although law school undoubtedly continues to play an important role in socializing students (if they exaggerate its impact) as well as allocating them to roles, the growing diversity of professional careers has required employers to assume these functions as well. In effect, we have seen the revival of apprenticeship following academic education—a sequence found elsewhere in both the common law world and some civil law countries. Law faculties, government departments, and offices of house counsel all relegate new employees to a probationary status. But the best-known and most extreme example is the large firm. The inferiority of associates is symbolized by their dramatically lower salary, status, and responsibility compared with those of partners; they must accept five to ten years of insecurity; and only a few receive the prize of partnership. Although accounts of this experience remain anecdotal, it seems to have much greater potential for socializing future lawyers than law school. Given the high level of mobility during the early stages of a legal career, these initial employers are also extremely influential in directing those employees who leave to more permanent positions within the professional hierarchy. Thus, the law school and the legal employer have developed into a complex institutional structure that allocates diverse entrants to equally varied positions and socializes them to their new roles.

11

The Future of the Legal Profession

In this concluding chapter I want to do three things: recapitulate what we know about the formation of the American legal profession during the last hundred years, use that knowledge to test and refine the theories of professionalism presented in Chapter 2, and speculate about the future of American lawyers.

There is sharp theoretical disagreement over the conditions under which an occupation becomes and remains a profession. Weberians argue that occupations consciously pursue social closure in order to enhance both their earning power and their collective status. Structural functionalists reply that entry barriers are merely the necessary and sufficient conditions for ensuring the quality of professional services. Economists mirror this sociological division: some see professions as blatant cartels seeking to extract monopoly rents from unorganized consumers; others believe that the long years professionals invest in their education explain and justify their high incomes.

The emergence of the American legal profession seems to support the more cynical view. Professional elites formed municipal, national, and ultimately state bar associations in the last quarter of the nineteenth century expressly to raise entry barriers. Their first step was to introduce bar examinations. Because academic legal education excused graduates from the examination in "diploma privilege" states and prepared them to pass it in others, adoption of this hurdle accelerated the decline of apprenticeship. Yet because the unanticipated, and undesired, consequence was to stimulate the rapid proliferation of inexpensive, accessible, part-time law schools, bar associations next sought to require formal education and simultaneously to restrict its availability. They increased prelegal educational requirements at a time when only a tiny elite graduated from college, and they waged a campaign that ultimately persuaded almost all states to admit only graduates of law schools approved by the American Bar Association. Combined with the effects of the Depression and World War II, this led to the demise of most unapproved schools, drastically curtailing part-time legal education. Although the bar examination initially was more a symbol of the profession's dedication to quality than an exclusionary device, the dramatic and widespread decline in pass rates following the onset of the Depression is hard to explain except as an attempt to reduce the supply of lawyers in the face of falling demand for their services. The profession was even more explicit about other barriers: the citizenship requirement and "character and fitness" tests were intended to exclude both ethnoreligious minorities and political dissidents; and residence requirements protected in-state lawyers from out-of-state competition.

Although it is difficult to prove the motives of individual lawyers, much less of the entire profession, the consequences of their actions still seem unambiguous. The first third of the twentieth century witnessed a dramatic expansion of the profession: a tenfold increase in law student enrollment between 1890 and 1930, a fourfold increase in bar admissions between 1900 and 1929, and a near doubling in the number of lawyers between 1890 and 1930. Thereafter, heightened prelegal educational requirements, restrictions on access to law schools, and tougher bar examinations took their toll, assisted by the Depression and World War II. Law school enrollment did not regain its 1927 level until 1961, and bar admissions did not achieve their 1928 level again until 1964. More telling, the ratio of population to lawyers was the same in 1950 as it had been in 1900—perhaps the same in 1960 as it had been in 1885!

Weberians acknowledge that social closure is difficult to sustain, just as economists insist that the market eventually is self-correcting because monopoly rents increase pressure by outsiders to enter. Several independent factors have helped to erode the legal profession's control over supply. Undergraduate education expanded enormously in the 1960s, subsidized by both state and federal governments. As better-educated students sought admission, bar examination pass rates rose. New law schools met the criteria for ABA approval, and older schools enlarged their enrollments. Courts struck down citizenship and residence requirements and invalidated vague "character" criteria. Most important, racial minorities and women sought and obtained entry. Law school enrollment grew nearly threefold between 1961 and 1981, bar admissions nearly fourfold between 1963 and 1978. Consequently, the ratio of population to lawyers fell by almost half between 1950 and 1984.

Larson argues that the "professional project" seeks social status as well as material rewards. Although wealth confers status, particularly in American society, it alone is an insecure foundation, as likely to engender envy as respect. Furthermore, the close identification of lawyers with the characters and activities of their clients may undermine rather than enhance professional status. Consequently, it has been particularly important for lawyers to control the composition of their profession as well as its size. Structural functional theory, by contrast, argues that technical competence is the only criterion for admission to a profession. At the same time, it sees professions offering their members the possibility of community in an otherwise anonymous mass society, conveniently ignoring that this community is grounded on exclusion as well as inclusion. Economists also have difficulty accounting for discrimination, which appears to impair efficiency by disqualifying potentially productive professionals but is attributable to neither imperfect information nor an officious state.

Once again, the data strongly support the Weberian interpretation. The historical record clearly demonstrates that bar associations actively sought to exclude ethnoreligious minorities during the interwar period (if with little success), erected "universalistic" barriers that disadvantaged those from lower-class origins, and took for granted the virtual exclusion of racial minorities and women (while profiting from their absence). Since the 1960s, the civil rights and feminist movements have succeeded in overcoming centuries of racism and patriarchy. The proportion of women has risen from less than 5 percent of law students to nearly half, and their first jobs increasingly resemble those of their male age mates, although women remain overrepresented in government employment, public interest law, and teaching. But their primary responsibility for childrearing continues to disadvantage them within the most competitive legal careers. Because racial minorities are still socially and culturally segregated and economically disadvantaged, their proportion of new lawyers remains less than half of their representation in the population. The entry of nonminority women may have increased the difficulty minority applicants encounter in obtaining law school places. And the recent drop in bar examination pass rates (coinciding with widespread professional and social concern about "oversupply") has disproportionately affected racial minorities. Those minority graduates who become lawyers are overrepresented in government employment and legal aid; within private practice most work alone or in small minority firms; and the few in larger firms tend to be associates rather than partners. Because the entry of women has nearly doubled the competitiveness of law school admissions, and because women still must overcome social barriers that men do not confront, the class backgrounds of nonminority lawyers have become even more privileged. Consequently, the collective status of the legal profession has not been adversely affected by the changing composition of law school enrollments during the last two decades. Most lawyers still come from privileged backgrounds, and the professional elite remains predominantly male and white. Furthermore, this distribution of wealth, prestige, and power across variables of class, race, and gender appears to be the outcome of either "meritocratic" decisions (law school admission, grades, and bar examination passage) or personal "choice" (of careers and childrearing responsibilities).

Weberian theory argues that professionals also seek to control production *by* producers. Again, the goals are multiple: increasing material benefits for lawyers by excluding external competitors, protecting the inept (who would suffer from internal competition), constructing and preserving colleagiality, and, paradoxically, enhancing collective status by appearing to disavow pecuniary motives. This phase of the professional project necessarily presupposes effective control over the production *of* producers: professionals would commit economic suicide were they to limit their own competitive activities while outsiders competed freely; and collective comfort and internal homogeneity are essential before some professionals can be persuaded to relinquish the advantages they could attain through free competition with their less effective colleagues. Because the profession is united by efforts to achieve control over the production of producers but divided by efforts to achieve control over production by producers, the latter goal is more difficult to attain, never as completely achieved, and succumbs more readily to internal and external attacks. Structural functionalism sees professional limitations on external and internal competition as selfless assurances of quality, which would only be undermined by market pressures. Economists display similar disagreement: those with greater faith in the market denounce restrictive practices on behalf of consumers; others point to the market imperfections caused by informational asymmetry, justifying professional restraints as unavoidable paternalism.

The early efforts of lawyers to control production by producers were directed toward defining, expanding, and defending the professional monopoly. Although the profession justified these actions in the name of consumer protection, it offered no evidence that lawyers performed the restricted tasks better than others, much less that lawyers alone displayed minimal competence. (The implausibility of these claims is suggested by the fact that only in the United States and a few Canadian provinces do lawyers monopolize legal advice.) By the time lawyers had begun to establish effective control over the production of producers in the 1930s, the market for their services was contracting under the influence of the Depression. Lawyers responded by intensifying control over production by producers. Professional associations established committees on unauthorized practice, concluded market division agreements with organized competitors, and sought prosecutions and injunctions against unorganized intruders. They protected their markets from the incursions of out-of-state lawyers by increasing the number of years such lawyers had to practice before being admitted on motion, requiring them to establish residence (which often meant relinquishing all professional income for a considerable period), and compelling all entrants to take a bar examination (which became progressively more difficult). They promulgated minimum fee schedules and punished price cutting as an ethical offense. And they proscribed advertising and solicitation, periodically waging highly publicized, if largely ineffective, campaigns against flagrant offenders.

Since the 1970s professional control over the production of producers has eroded, numbers have multiplied, heterogeneity has increased, and restrictive practices have been attacked by both the consumer movement and free market ideologues. Many anticompetitive rules have been struck down or weakened. Competing occupations challenged the lawyers' monopoly, both in court and before the electorate, leading the profession to terminate market division agreements and reduce the visibility of its attacks on lay competitors, although it continues to mount rearguard actions. The Supreme Court struck down the residence requirement in 1985, although jurisdictions still discriminate against out-of-state lawyers in other ways. The Court invalidated minimum fee schedules in 1975, although most lawyers still scrupulously refrain from price competition. The Court abrogated the blanket ban on advertising in 1977, in response to younger lawyers who sought to reach new markets by mass producing routine services at reduced prices. Yet state bar associations continue to prohibit solicitation and limit advertising, with Supreme Court approval. And most lawyers take little advantage of what competition is allowed.

These attacks have produced two responses. Just as the profession originally emerged as one manifestation of the growing division of labor, so lawyers now are refining that division through further specialization. But although the campaign to exclude nonlawyers from the professional market united all lawyers, proposals to exclude generalists from the specialist market divide them. Consequently, most bar associations have allowed lawyers freely to designate themselves as specialists. This unstable compromise is unlikely to satisfy either generalists or specialists. Second, the regulatory vacuum left by the withdrawal of professional controls is being filled by other agencies. Although market choices by individual consumers remain ill-informed, collective consumers (corporations, trade unions, large employers, and private and public third-party payers) may obtain satisfactory quality and price through an unregulated market. Government regulation is increasing simultaneously—state legislation limiting maximum contingent fees, for instance, or Federal Trade Commission review of restrictive practices.

In seeking to shape the market for their services, professions try to influence demand as well as supply. Weberian theories offer two explanations for this behavior. From an economic perspective, demand creation is simply an obvious effort to enlarge the profession's market share and thus is most likely to occur when professional control over supply is weakening (economists themselves are divided about the capacity of professionals to engender demand). Sociologists stress the profession's interest in legitimating its privileges and ameliorating the grossly unequal distribution of services produced by market forces; consequently, demand creation is most energetic when the profession enjoys the greatest material security. Structural functional theories, by contrast, see efforts to redistribute services as the spontaneous expression of altruistic impulses that are released when a profession is freed from market pressures by its control over the production of and by producers; such altruism should increase as professionals perfect their control over the market.

Although it is impossible to obtain the kind of information about professional consciousness that would allow us to choose confidently between these theories, historical fluctuations in professional interest in redistributing legal services strongly favor the Weberian view. Until quite recently, the organized profession remained indifferent or even hostile to redistribution. It was unmoved by Reginald Heber Smith's disclosures in 1919 that poor people lacked access to legal services. It accepted without demurrer a criminal justice system that prosecuted and punished unrepresented accused until the U.S. Supreme Court extended constitutional protections to state criminal defendants in the 1960s and 1970s (although English barristers early felt obligated to accept "dock briefs" without pay for those accused of serious crimes). It promulgated and policed rules against advertising and solicitation, denying citizens information about both their legal rights and the availability and identity of lawyers who could help protect them. It did little to encourage lawyers to give more than token pro bono services. It denounced government support for legal aid as creeping socialism. And it condemned and attacked group legal service plans as threats to the lawyer-client relationship. Although many lawyers would maintain, nostalgically, that their "professionalism" reached an apex in the 1950s, that achievement clearly failed to release the predicted flood of altruistic activity.

The mood of the organized profession has changed quite dramatically since the mid-1960s. It rediscovered "unmet legal need," sponsoring the most extensive study ever conducted of the actual use of legal services by individuals. It devoted considerable energy to encouraging lawyers to perform pro bono services (contemplating compulsion, although ultimately losing nerve) and even more to publicizing the profession's good works. Lawyers enthusiastically embraced group plans. The ABA unanimously endorsed the OEO Legal Services Program in 1965 and was joined by virtually all state and local bar associations in defending the Legal Services Corporation against Reagan's attacks in the 1980s. Professional associations launched public relations campaigns, and individual law firms and clinics aggressively sought new clients.

Although this about-face was startling, its meaning is difficult to interpret. First, much of the impetus for change originated outside the profession, which acquiesced only with great reluctance. The federal government, not the organized bar, launched the nearly hundredfold expansion of legal aid, initially engendering strenuous and protracted opposition from many local associations. The Supreme Court had to order bar associations to stop outlawing group plans, favoring open-panel plans over closed panels, and preventing lawyers from advertising or cutting prices. Second, it is very unclear whether these redistributional efforts were motivated by material interests, status enhancement, or pure altruism. It can hardly be coincidental that lawyers turned to demand creation just when their control over the production of and by producers was significantly eroding or that those most enthusiastic about advertising, group plans, and judicare also were those most exposed to market forces—lawyers without established clienteles, serving individuals in solo practices or small firms. The professional elite, by contrast, neither needed nor sought individual clients but may have felt most uncomfortable about the unequal distribution of legal services and their own extraordinarily privileged economic, social, and political position; they were most interested in redistributions that would enhance the profession's status and legitimacy: pro bono activities, public interest law, and staffed office legal services programs. And even though altruism cannot explain all this activity, its significance cannot be denied, especially as manifested by groups previously excluded from the profession, such as women and racial minorities.

Lawyers encounter serious obstacles in pursuing each of these multiple, potentially conflicting, goals. Government support for legal aid is likely to remain constant or decline in the face of enormous pressure to reduce the federal budget deficit. Furthermore, political conservatives who might favor delivering legal services to the poor by reimbursing private practitioners also tend to be fiscal conservatives who prefer the greater budgetary control government exercises over salaried employees. Even vigorous promotional activity is unlikely to persuade many middle- or low-income individuals to join prepaid plans or consume cut-price legal services, since most facilitative law concerns the acquisition and preservation of property (which they lack) and they share the universal dread of litigation. Furthermore, strategies of demand creation inevitably deepen professional divisions over how that demand should be distributed: between salaried legal services lawyers and public defenders on one hand and private practitioners reimbursed by judicare programs and through court appointments on the other (as well as among private practitioners paid by public funds); between open- and closed-panel legal services plans (and among members of open-panel plans); between institutional advertising that benefits the entire profession, individual advertising that benefits primarily the advertiser (but may have limited spillover effects for other producers), and solicitation that generally benefits only the firm soliciting.

Demand creation may be equally unsuccessful in enhancing the prestige or legitimacy of the profession. Documenting the unequal distribution of legal services may also reveal the impossibility of equalizing it. Pro bono and legal aid activities identify lawyers with poor and often outcast clients facing apparently trivial problems; such public contamination may endanger rather than elevate professional status. And the patent self-interest of lawyers in judicare schemes, group legal services, advertising, and legal clinics belies their protestations of altruism. Third-party payment (whether public or private) also appears to compromise the lawyer's independence. Finally, those seeking to promote social change by serving the unrepresented may be frustrated by the institutional constraints on their actions and the inherent limitations of the legal form.

Structural functional theory makes self-regulation a central element in the definition of professions. Self-regulation is necessary because professional knowledge is so esoteric that only one member can judge another's performance. And it is acceptable because professional status ensures that regulatory powers will be deployed in the public interest. Weberian theory is far more cynical. It expects professions, like other status groups, to pursue their collective self-interest at the expense of outsiders, seeking regulatory powers largely to immunize themselves from external scrutiny. It also expects intraprofessional divisions to structure the regulatory process: high-status practitioners will scapegoat those with lower status while seeking protection within their own large productive units.

The actual record of professional self-regulation tends to support the cynical view. Lawyers claimed professional status long before they displayed any interest in self-regulation. They have devoted far more energy (and publicity) to drafting and redrafting ethical norms than to enforcing them. Whereas much social control by police and regulatory agencies is proactive—intrusive patrolling and investigating, assisted by mandatory record-keeping and reporting—professional self-regulation is resolutely reactive. But the lawyers and judges, who are best situated to perceive misconduct, are discouraged from reporting by communal solidarity (except when complaining might enhance the lawyer's status, competitive advantage, or litigation strategy). And clients are either ignorant of lawyer behavior and ethical norms or defeatist about the consequences of filing grievances. Perhaps they are merely realistic. Disciplinary bodies refuse to review charges of incompetence or discourtesy, which constitute the vast majority of client complaints. They dismiss at least 90 percent of all accusations with little or no investigation. Inadequate funding (for which the profession itself is responsible) impedes and slows the investigatory process. Most of the small number penalized receive slaps on the wrist. Even the few suspended or disbarred often return to practice, in the same jurisdiction or another. The profession also has been dilatory and ungenerous in responding to clients injured by the financial misconduct of lawyers.

If the test of self-regulation is its capacity to convince outsiders to keep their hands off, then the legal profession may be failing. Courts and agencies scrutinize the behavior of lawyers who appear before them with increasing stringency, summarily punishing misconduct. Clients file a rapidly growing number of malpractice suits. Malpractice insurers themselves shape lawyer behavior through the availability, cost, and content of the policies they offer. Several state bar associations have relinquished to independent bodies their authority to discipline lawyers and issue ethical opinions. Others have coopted laypersons onto disciplinary boards. State supreme courts and legislatures take much greater interest in the regulatory performance of bar associations. If self-regulation is the hallmark of professionals, lawyers may be losing that status.

Weberian theory sees the profession as a "project," whose fortunes constantly fluctuate. Although professional associations seek to control their markets, they can never do so completely. As economists note, the very success of the project intensifies competitive pressures, which threaten different segments of the profession to varying degrees. Although professions seek to enhance their collective status, some segments may benefit at the expense of others. Furthermore, the very content of professional work simultaneously confers social status and endangers it (lawyers are particularly involved with crises, deviance, and other forms of social "dirt"). Structural functional theory sees the material and social rewards of professions as both more stable and more uniform. Stability allows professions to pursue the public interest rather than be preoccupied with self-aggrandizement. And uniformity preserves and strengthens the professional community.

The material fortunes of the legal profession have fluctuated quite dramatically during the twentieth century, reflecting both its varying control over supply and exogenous changes in the demand for legal services. Lawyer income declined during the Depression, when imperfect supply control coincided with falling demand; it rose rapidly in the 1950s and 1960s, when effective supply control coincided with the postwar boom; and it leveled off in the 1970s and 1980s, as expanding numbers coincided with an economy that was growing slowly if at all. Indeed, the stringency of postwar supply control, which rapidly drove up starting salaries, helped to attract increased numbers of entrants, gradually correcting the imbalance between supply and demand. But aggregate income data conceal almost as much as they disclose because incomes are more widely dispersed among lawyers than in any other profession. Lawyers differ greatly in their exposure to market forces and thus in the way they perceive and participate in the professional project.

Similarly, a profession that contains such diversity—large firm corporate lawyers, self-promoting personal injury lawyers, sole practitioners relying on court appointments to defend indigent criminals, house counsel, salaried legal aid lawyers, federal cabinet members and local government clerks, Supreme Court justices and municipal judges, and law professors—cannot have a *collective* status. Despite this (or perhaps because of it) the legal profession has been obsessed with its public image. But the highly visible activities through which lawyers hope to bolster professional status, such as moral campaigns against ethical misconduct or pro bono representation in major cases, are likely to do little more than enhance the image of elite private practitioners at the expense of other lawyers. These activities cannot overcome the fundamental sources of popular discontent: unequal access to legal services, excessive technicality (at best a form of make-work, at worst the obstruction of justice), and the moral ambiguity of the lawyer's role as hired gun for often unattractive clients or practices.

All theories of the professions emphasize the environments within which services are produced. Structural functionalists argue that professionalism requires complete autonomy, which is threatened whenever the professional is subordinated to an employer, embedded within a bureaucracy or even reimbursed by a third party. Therefore, they view private practice—archetypically solo practice—as the ideal environment and employment within the public or private sector, practice within large firms, and third-party payment as potentially dangerous deviations. Weberians see bureaucracy as the structural expression of rationality in Western societies and therefore as a necessary constraint upon the exercise of power (although Weber himself was deeply ambivalent about the desirability of this development). Economists also expect productive units to grow in size and diversify in response to competitive forces. Marxists maintain that professions engaging in productive activities inevitably generate surplus value and thus conflict over who shall enjoy it. Therefore, they predict that capitalist relations of production will emerge within professional work, leading to progressively more intensive and extensive exploitation of subordinates. These increasingly proletarianized jobs will be filled disproportionately by workers who encounter social and cultural barriers to attaining full professional status—primarily racial minorities and women. Heightened consciousness of exploitation together with aggregation within large employers will lead to collective action, generally expressed as trade unionism.

The postwar history of the American legal profession bears out the fears of structural functionalism, the predictions of Weberians and economists, and the warnings of Marxists. At least until the New Deal, the legal component of the state apparatus was insignificant. State and federal judiciaries were shockingly understaffed by European standards. Few corporations had significant legal departments until very recently. Law faculties were small. Consequently fewer than one lawyer in ten was employed outside private practice. Even "large" law firms were small by today's standards. All this has changed quite dramatically. House counsel have multiplied rapidly, law faculties have grown, and the number of lawyer civil servants and judges have also increased, although at a slower pace. Now one lawyer in three is employed outside private practice. And all these productive units are much larger and more bureaucratic.

Yet the structural functional ideology still prevails: private practice remains the core of the profession, while other forms of employment occupy the marginalized periphery, characterized by lower status and income. Growth of that periphery reflects the production of law graduates in numbers larger than private practice could absorb, among other factors. These jobs continue to be filled disproportionately by lawyers excluded from private practice by social, economic, and educational disadvantage or childrearing responsibilities: graduates of nonelite law schools, racial minorities, and women. Law graduates enter government to obtain experience and contacts they can sell to private practice. Corporate counsel hire law firm associates who are not offered partnerships. The gap continues to widen between the incomes of private practitioners and the salaries of most employed lawyers.

The core of private practice has undergone an equivalent transformation. The proportion of lawyers in solo practice, which structural functionalism identifies with the ideal of professional autonomy (as do the bars of Great Britain, some other common law jurisdictions, and many civil law countries), shrank by nearly half between 1948 and 1980 (from three lawyers out of five to one out of three). Similarly, the proportion of lawyers practicing with one or two colleagues dropped from more than eight out of ten in 1947 to less than three out of ten in 1980. Solo and small-firm practice will continue to contract in response to the growing complexity of the law and the need to specialize, as well as competition from legal clinics and nonlawyers. And though private practice continues to enjoy higher status than public or private employment, contemporary law graduates clearly prefer to take jobs as large firm associates rather than face the entrepreneurial risks and demands of launching their own practices, alone or with a few colleagues. The professional ideal no longer is the "autonomy" of being one's own boss but the material security afforded by the large enterprise, notwithstanding—or perhaps precisely because of—its bureaucratic nature.

In the last few decades, the large firm has come to symbolize law practice, both inside and outside the profession, even though only 5 percent of all lawyers worked in firms with more than fifty lawyers in 1980 and only 9 percent in firms with more than twenty. The large firm violates the structural functional ideal of professionalism in many ways. Rather than being insulated from market forces, it increasingly must compete for clients with other firms, nationally and internationally, as well as with offices of house counsel. Internal colleagiality has been strained as members jockey for power (on the executive committee) and lock horns over the division of profits. Membership used to be a lifetime commitment, but lateral movement of both associates and partners is increasingly common today; firms may even oust those who attract insufficient business or bill too few hours. To keep existing clients and attract new ones, firms are establishing branch offices throughout the United States and abroad. But geographic dispersion enlarges the bureaucratic apparatus necessary to achieve coordination (particularly essential among lawyers confronting potential conflicts of interest).

Law firms grow for many different reasons: specialization, the needs of increasingly diversified corporate clients, geographic coverage, heightened name recognition, and the identification of both size and growth with success. But one of the most significant pressures is that emphasized by Marxist theory—the exploitation of subordinate labor to inflate partnership incomes. Competition among firms and with house counsel places a ceiling on what corporate clients will pay. Profits can be increased only by extracting more surplus from the labor of employees. The dramatic increase in the number of law graduates (and the willingness of firms to hire from a broader cross-section of family backgrounds and law schools) has greatly expanded the pool of potential associates. Because the extraordinary income and prestige enjoyed by large firm partners strongly motivates associate effort, firms have been able to extract more surplus from them by lengthening the period of associateship, raising expectations about billable hours, tying compensation to productivity, and expanding the category of permanent associates. But firms can employ and retain associates only by holding out some prospect of partnership. Consequently, firms must constantly expand, conferring partnerships to attract associates and hiring associates to swell partnership earnings. Firms also have added lower tiers: graduates with lesser academic credentials, who will never be considered for partnership; and paralegals, who can cut labor costs while simultaneously billing their time to generate surplus value. All these subordinate positions (associates who leave before partnership, permanent associates, law graduates never considered for partnership, and paralegals) are disproportionately filled by women, reflecting the connections between patriarchy and professional hierarchy.

In response to both competition from outside the profession and the need for continuous expansion, law firms have begun to diversify their services beyond the practice of law. These innovations display the entrepreneurial energy of American lawyers (in sharp contrast to the more conservative European legal professions, which have lost considerable business to other occupations). But diversification also threatens to submerge the professional identity of lawyers within large service firms, which they no longer control. Finally, the growing size, geographic dispersion, functional diversity, and internal hierarchy of large firms have compelled them to replace informal understandings and colleagial control with bureaucratic forms, even adopting the structures of their corporate clients by hiring nonlawyer managers and contemplating the sale of equity interests to nonlawyers. A vast array of autonomous individual professionals is being displaced by a dwindling number of large, diversified, national or multinational, bureaucratic capitalist service firms.

For structural functional theories, it is almost as important that professions be communities as that they engage in self-regulation. Indeed, the former is a precondition for the latter. Furthermore, as Durkheim particularly stressed, professional communities form one of the few structures intermediate between the individual and the state in contemporary mass society. As communities, they satisfy the need for collegiality and express the collective identity of their members. Other sociological traditions are more skeptical of community, noting both that groups often achieve internal cohesion through exclusion and that they still contain internal differences, which find expression in stratification, oligarchy, apathy, and fission. Finally, the Marxist tradition identifies distinct classes within the legal services industry (defined by the relations of production) and expects their irreconcilable interests to produce conflict, initially in the form of trade unionism.

American lawyers have deviated sharply from the ideal professional community, as epitomized by the English Bar, for at least a century (and probably much longer). Unlike physicians, lawyers serve dramatically varied clienteles. As those clienteles have grown more distinct with the accumulation and concentration of capital, professional stratification has polarized into what Heinz and Laumann call the two hemispheres of the legal profession. Lawyers from relatively modest backgrounds attend nonelite local law schools, generally becoming sole and small-firm practitioners (or entering government employment). Those in private practice serve lower- and middle-class individuals and small businesses, offering routine services (primarily minor litigation in local courts but also the transfer of property between individuals and generations). They tend to dominate their lower-status clients, with whom they have relatively transient relationships. At the other extreme, lawyers from more privileged backgrounds attend elite national law schools, generally joining larger firms serving wealthy individuals and larger corporations or offices of house counsel. Most of their work is facilitative, but they also handle nonroutine litigation in state appellate or federal courts. They tend to be dominated by their upper-status clients, with whom they have relatively enduring relationships. The two hemispheres differ dramatically in prestige and income; in few other professions do some members earn fifty times more than others or some subcategories (such as Supreme Court justices) bask in popular adulation while others (such as criminal defense, personal injury, and divorce lawyers) are ranked with garbage collectors. And there is virtually no movement between the hemispheres.

Whereas structural functionalism sees voluntary associations as spontaneous expressions of the communitarian sentiments inherent in professionalism, other analytic frameworks (particularly those drawn from economics) stress the difficulty of overcoming intergroup antagonism and individual indifference. During the professional revival of the last third of the nineteenth century, a major obstacle to organization was the geographic dispersion of lawyers across a large, predominantly rural country. (English solicitors encountered similar difficulties in forming a national association, especially in contrast to the Bar, which was concentrated in London.) Professional associations emerged first in cities and counties; state organizations remained weak and unstable until many turned to governmental compulsion after the 1920s, in order to ensure that they could speak on behalf of all lawyers and would have the means to do so effectively. Although the American Bar Association purported to represent the entire profession, it was remote from most practitioners, unable to compel membership, and only loosely articulated with the state associations enjoying regulatory power or influence. It never has enrolled more than half of all lawyers.

As urbanization, political and economic integration, and technological advances in transportation and communication have lowered the geographic barriers to collective action, new obstacles have emerged with the increasing differentation of lawyer backgrounds and practice settings. Younger lawyers always have been less involved in established organizations; as their numbers multiplied in the 1960s and 1970s, they formed alternative organizations in the major cities. Although the first women to enter the profession created their own organizations, these attract a declining fraction of women lawyers today. By contrast, a very high proportion of minority lawyers join minority organizations—testimony to the persistence of professional segregation. Lower-status private practitioners have separate organizations in some larger cities. Lawyers united by strong political beliefs or religious convictions have formed their own associations. And lawyers outside private practice—house counsel, government employees, teachers, and judges—also have independent organizations, rarely joining state or national bar associations. Although some lawyers in public employment have formed trade unions and even engaged in industrial action, those employed by corporations or law firms appear to have been dissuaded from such class treachery by the promise of upward mobility and equal membership in the professional community.

Professional differentiation not only makes it impossible for all lawyers to unite within a single organization, it also creates problems of governance and collective action within any organization that claims to speak for a large constituency. Just as the memberships of national, state, and local bar associations are unrepresentative of the lawyer populations they serve, so governance of those associations is also unrepresentative of the membership (and thus doubly unrepresentative of the profession). Their executive bodies have disproportionately few women, minorities, younger lawyers, employed lawyers, graduates of nonelite law schools, and sole and small-firm practitioners. Internal divisions manifested in lawsuits or membership defections reduce political activity to the lowest common denominator. Professional associations have been no more successful than any other collectivity in resolving the contradiction that power is gained through inclusion, but exclusion is necessary to agree on and pursue a focused political agenda.

Whereas Marxist theories of inequality focus on the irreconcilable antagonisms between those who produce surplus value and those who control and consume it, structural functional theories of inequality map the continuous variation of income and status, stressing the legitimacy of this hierarchy and its contribution to social integration. The latter theories direct our attention to the ways in which new lawyers are screened, allocated to positions within the profession, and socialized in their ultimate locations. A hundred years ago, the relative homogeneity of entrants and the limited number of legal roles required only very simple mechanisms of professional reproduction: young men apprenticed with a lawyer (often a relative or family acquaintance) until they felt ready to practice on their own. The displacement of apprenticeship by the law school around the turn of the century preserved significant elements of this process: anyone could attend law school; and most graduates still entered practice by themselves until after World War II. Market forces (shaped by professional controls) influenced the success or failure of those who hung out their shingles.

Today, by contrast, only 3 percent of graduates embark directly on solo practice; the rest enter employment (a few continue their education). The increasing heterogeneity of entrants, the differentiation and stratification of legal roles, and the progressive specialization of legal knowledge all require more elaborate mechanisms of allocation. The law school has assumed this responsibility—indeed, some would say that allocation, not education, is its raison d'être. Law schools perform this task in several ways. First, the limited number of places excludes many aspirants and narrows the class backgrounds of those who gain admission. Second, the steep hierarchy of law schools classifies students at the moment of entry. Third, and most important, schools rank their students. The fact that almost all schools teach the same curriculum through the same pedagogical method and evaluate student performance through the same kind of examination facilitates the comparison of class rank across schools. This ranking not only informs potential employers but also profoundly structures student conceptions of their own worth and just desserts.

As late as the 1950s, the minority of students who sought jobs after graduation (rather than beginning practice on their own) used personal contacts and pounded the pavement. Today, the law school's second most important function is placement (only slightly less significant than determining class rank). This now consumes the entire fifth semester (even forcing some schools to close for a week); the search for summer jobs strongly permeates the second year; and even first-year students seek summer positions, volunteering if necessary. Judicial clerkships have become a further filter, differentiating among the students with the best academic records. The increase in lateral movement has created a market for headhunters, who facilitate movement up and down the hierarchy for another five or ten years after graduation. Competition for position within the stratified profession has been intensified by the growing divergence of rewards: starting salaries that differed by some 30 percent twenty years ago now vary by 300 percent, and the divergence increases with age.

In stressing the functions of reproducing and legitimating stratification among lawyers, I do not mean to deny that the academy and the profession also educate and socialize entrants. Here, too, there have been significant changes. Students experience law school as transformative—more so even than college or graduate school. Its one undeniable effect is to persuade most of those who get good grades that they want to work for large firms, no matter what originally drew them to law school. But the first job may have displaced law school as the most significant socializing agent as a result of the growing diversity of law practice and specialization of legal knowledge. Most graduates spend several years in a probationary status— as judicial clerks, lower civil servants, untenured law teachers, and especially law firm associates. This revival of apprenticeship not only confers technical competence but also acculturates the novice through a combination of heavy (often crushing) work demands, total subordination to superiors expressed through obedience to authority, dramatically lower income and status, and prolonged job insecurity, and intense competition for lifetime entitlement to the professional perquisites of wealth, power, and status.

What does the history of the American legal profession during the last hundred years suggest about its future? Prediction is always risky. Just twenty-five years ago who would have foretold the rate of growth, the entry of women and minorities, the attack on restrictive practices, the shift from private practice to employment, or the expansion and restructuring of law firms? In extrapolating current trends, I will try to identify alternative paths. I also will relate them to the recent report of the American Bar Association's Commission on Professionalism, which illustrates the leadership's conception of the problems facing the profession and the appropriate solutions.[1]

Although the rapid increase in the number of lawyers during the last two decades was stimulated by external factors—the expansion of undergraduate education, the feminist and civil rights movements, and the postwar economic boom— the profession did not lose all control over supply. Even at maximum rates of production only about half of those who applied to law school were admitted. Pressure for further expansion of law school enrollments has eased as women have gained nearly equal representation, the number of minority students has peaked at half their representation in the population, undergraduate enrollments have stabilized, and the material and intangible rewards of business and finance have begun to overshadow those of law. Yet the difference between rates of entry into the profession and of departure (through retirement and death) will produce continued growth for another forty years. At the present rate of approximately 27,000 additional lawyers annually, the profession will nearly triple in size.

Although this prospect clearly frightens lawyers, their response is much more guarded today than it was half a century ago. The ABA Commission welcomed the decline in student applications and admonished law schools (whose interests differ from those of practitioners) not to lower admission or graduation standards to maintain enrollment, warning that such actions might lead to loss of accreditation. It also displayed ill-concealed satisfaction about the recent drop in bar examination pass rates and discouraged any lowering of examination "standards" to keep them from falling further. Yet it was anxious that bar examiners not appear to be manipulating pass rates to reduce entry and fearful that tighter law school admissions policies might hurt affirmative action programs and exclude minority candidates.[2]

I doubt that tinkering with entry requirements will significantly influence the production of lawyers. Furthermore, labor supply responds to fluctuations in demand only after a considerable lag. Consequently, lawyers must expect their numbers to continue rising despite relatively flat demand, which will inevitably intensify internal competition.

The composition of the legal profession has changed dramatically during the last twenty years, but neither women nor minorities have gained full equality. Although women now enter the profession in almost the same numbers as men, they leave earlier, and those who stay are channeled into different careers. The profession has made little effort to smooth the interruptions of pregnancy and childbirth and even less to equalize the childrearing burdens of men and women lawyers. The practice of law (as opposed to the composition of the profession) has not been significantly feminized. Minority law student enrollment virtually stopped growing more than ten years ago, and recent cutbacks in student loans, increases in undergraduate and law school tuition, and drops in bar examination pass rates all inhibit further expansion. Not only is the proportion of minorities in the legal profession less than half that in the population, but minority lawyers also are far less well represented across legal roles than are women. The ABA Commission did not feel that these issues were sufficiently germane to the "rekindling of lawyer professionalism" to be worth mentioning.

Professional control over production *by* producers has eroded even more dramatically than control over entry. Growing size and heterogeneity have intensified competition. Political conservatives, the traditional allies of professional privilege, today also are free market ideologues, who join consumer advocates in attacking restrictive practices. As business clients have expanded and individual clients have been organized in group plans, market relations between producers and consumers of legal services have become more equal. Local markets have been opened to regional, national, and even international competition.

The ABA Commission openly expressed lawyers' fears that "the economic pressure is likely to become even greater in the future as the anticipated 50% increase in the number of lawyers between now and the year 2000 intensifies the competition."[3] Yet its response again was muted and equivocal. Thirty years ago the ABA vigorously promoted minimum fee schedules to curtail competition.[4] Now, however, it was embarrassed by lawyers who openly pursue material self-interest—for instance, by defending the borders of their monopoly against proposals to deprofessionalize routine matters. "[P]arochial and shortsighted efforts to garner additional income for lawyers generally, or groups of lawyers, through special interest legislation, can only decrease public esteem."[5] Nevertheless, it supported "rigorous" licensing standards for paraprofessionals and insisted that "unauthorized practice committees of bar associations have a place" when "abuses of clients occur."[6] The Commission reported the anger of some at lawyers who aggressively seek personal injury clients, endorsed disciplinary action against those who disseminate false, fraudulent, or misleading advertising, and condemned public relations brochures highlighting the influence of firm partners or suggesting an ability to obtain particular results. Yet it then conceded lamely that "it is principally lawyers—not clients—who are concerned about the style and message of certain legal advertising."[7] The Commission would require lawyers who wish to advertise a specialty to pass an examination in the subject but still allow all lawyers to practice in the area.[8] But lawyers will never succeed in regaining market control through professional rules, although they may continue to dampen competition by means of informal understandings (about fees or "dignified" advertising). In the struggle between generalists (who want continued access to the entire market) and specialists (who want protection within a more limited arena) the outcome is less predictable.

Since the mid-1960s, lawyers have displayed growing enthusiasm for stimulating demand and redistributing legal services. Yet they have been unable to resolve the central contradictions underlying these strategies: whether their motive is greed or altruism, how to engage in promotional campaigns that inevitably concentrate demand while simultaneously distributing that business broadly and evenly among lawyers, how to reconcile third-party payment by public or private entities with claims of professional independence, how to allay the public's deep-rooted fears about lawyers and litigation, and how to overcome fiscal conservatism and political anxiety on the part of government funding sources.

All of these contradictions surfaced in the Commission's report. It recommended replication of the American Bar Foundation study of the legal needs of the public, confident that this would confirm that "the lack of access of the middle class to affordable legal services" is "one of the most intractable problems confronting the legal profession today."[9] (The Commission did not consider that lack of access to legal services by the *poor* might be a more important *social* problem.) The Commission attributed limitations on access to the fact that "costs generally have risen for lawyers as they have for everyone else" rather than to the monopoly rents lawyers are able to extract.[10] It urged the profession "to educate members of the public about their rights and obligations" through television, "dial a law" telephone information services, and "lawyer in the classroom" programs; but, as we have seen, it was acutely uncomfortable about individual promotional activities.[11] It endorsed lawyer referral services, even suggesting that clients be matched with lawyers specializing in their problem.[12] Yet it was highly defensive about widespread corporate and media criticism of the litigation crisis.[13] It responded by scapegoating plaintiffs' personal injury lawyers who actively seek clients and by entertaining the possibility of no-fault reforms.[14] At the same time, it waxed enthusiastic about alternative dispute resolution as a means of rendering litigation cheaper and more palatable—so that there would be *more* of it rather than less.[15]

The very title of the report reiterated Roscoe Pound's claim that "public service is the primary purpose" of the legal profession, which only "incidentally" is a means of livelihood; and it encouraged the bar to "increase the participation of lawyers in *pro bono* activities and . . . resist the temptation to make the acquisition of wealth a primary goal of law practice."[16] But it refused to recommend mandatory pro bono activities because that would be "antithetical to the tenets of public service."[17]

I see no reason to expect either a spontaneous surge of lawyer altruism or a dramatic rise in middle-class demand for legal services. But I do believe that the organized profession could campaign more actively to increase government support for legal services for the poor, especially since per capita expenditures in the United States are far below those in less wealthy countries, such as Britain, the Netherlands, some Australian states, and some Canadian provinces.

Although self-regulation is an essential element in the definition of a profession, lawyers often appear to be more interested in creating the semblance than the reality. They have been preoccupied with formulating norms rather than enforcing them; they have responded passively to client complaints rather than initiating investigations themselves; and they have imposed few serious penalties. Disciplinary proceedings often reflect divisions within the professional hierarchy or struggles for advantage in the course of litigation. This sorry record has stimulated increasing external regulation by legislatures, courts, and administrative agencies.

Although the Commission reiterated the ideology of professional self-regulation, it trivialized the actual task. It began by conceding that "many [ethical] questions do come down to matters of carefully weighed personal choice."[18] Having characterized the problem as individual rather than structural, the Commission's logical response was the liberal panacea, education: prelaw reading lists, law school courses in ethics and professionalism, professors who can serve as role models, student conduct codes, bar examination essay questions on ethics, films and videotapes on ethical and professional issues, discussions of ethical issues among lawyers, and ethics advisory committees within law firms.[19] It also urged the profession to exclude those likely to violate ethical rules by requiring law schools to report student misconduct; it recommended more adequate funding so that character and fitness committees could engage in spot checks; and it contemplated reviving the system of preceptors for apprentice lawyers.[20] Although it exhorted judges and lawyers to report misconduct, it conceded ruefully that few did so and even fewer were disciplined for their silence.[21] Finally, it addressed a major source of client discontent—fees—by reprimanding lawyers for overcharging and endorsing mandatory fee arbitration.[22]

There is no reason to expect that these proposals would either reduce lawyer misconduct or increase public confidence in the regulatory process. Instead, outside institutions staffed by legal professionals—courts, legislatures, and administrative agencies—are likely to become increasingly aggressive in circumscribing the behavior of private practitioners and penalizing transgressions.

Lawyers have always been obsessed and mystified by the apparent lack of respect for their calling. The ABA, indeed, asked the Commission to investigate how legal services "are *perceived* to be performed."[23] The Commission, in turn, expressed profound self-doubt: "Has our profession abandoned principle for profit, professionalism for commercialism?"[24] It conducted a study that confirmed its worst fears:

> [O]nly 6% of corporate users of legal services rated "all or most" lawyers as deserving to be called "professionals." Only 7% saw professionalism increasing among lawyers; 68% said it had decreased over time. Similarly, 55% of the state and federal judges . . . said lawyer professionalism was declining.[25]

But the Commission's responses were wholly incommensurate with the nature of public discontent. People believe that lawyers are hired guns, willing to do virtually anything a client asks; the Commission answered: "in the end, it is the responsibility of individual lawyers to ensure that abuses do not occur."[26] People believe that lawyers make work for themselves at the expense of clients; the Commission answered that the profession should "encourage innovative methods which simplify and make less expensive the rendering of legal services."[27] And people believe that lawyers enjoy unjustifiably high incomes; the Commission answered that the profession should "resist the temptation to make the acquisition of wealth a primary goal of law practice."[28] No one is likely to be convinced.

Change in the structures within which legal services are produced is a central element in the transformation of the profession, comparable in importance to the rapid increase in the rate of growth and the entry of women and minorities. Indeed, all three are intimately related. Erosion of professional control over the production of and by producers has made it increasingly difficult for lawyers to extract monopoly rents from clients. To preserve their economic and social privilege, lawyers have had to intensify their exploitation of subordinate labor, who are disproportionately women and minorities. I believe that each of these structural trends will persist and that, cumulatively, they represent a qualitative change. Unfortunately, the Commission had little to say about them, beyond expressing its discomfort and nostalgia.

Employment in the public and private sectors will increase: even the Reagan Administration was unable to freeze, much less significantly shrink, the federal regulatory apparatus; court congestion is likely to lead to more judges, not less litigation (just as traffic jams lead to more highways rather than fewer cars); and corporations will continue to enlarge their in-house legal staff. This will challenge the dominance of private practice, confuse the identity of the legal profession, and reduce its capacity for collective action. Employment also tends to undermine the lawyer's claim to independence. The Commission was deeply concerned about this threat to professional ideology.

> Lawyers should exercise independent judgment as to how to pursue legal matters .... Ideally, clients should recognize this duty....[29]

> The lawyer has an obligation to the legal system in his capacity as an officer of the court to dissuade the client from pursuing matters that should not be in court in the first place, and from using tactics geared primarily to drain the financial resources of the other side.[30]

But the Commission did not appear to appreciate the intractability of the problem. It seemed surprised that "the candid citation by counsel of opposing case precedent is rare."[31] And its only solution to excessive lawyer loyalty to corporate employers (or clients) was formal guidelines by the latter urging lawyers not to abuse the legal system.[32] These are not likely to resolve the contradiction between the economic imperatives of the market and the moral restraints of legal professionalism.

Private practice not only has lost some of its numerical superiority (though not its economic or social preeminence), it also has been structurally transformed. Heightened competition has increased concentration at both ends of the professional hierarchy. This trend is likely to continue, although conflict of interest rules probably will prevent large law firms from merging into the small oligopoly found within accounting; and geographic convenience, the value placed on personal relationships, and market imperfections probably will preserve some solo and small-firm practices. But individual lower- and middle-class clients will turn increasingly to legal clinics and group plans, attracted by assurances about price and quality. Consequently, employment will displace entrepreneurship for most private practitioners.

At the upper end of the hierarchy, competition among firms and with house counsel will encourage continued growth in firm size and lawyer specialization, the proliferation of branches, and the bureaucratization that all this requires. More firms will diversify into nonlegal services. Although the Commission "views the [last] trend as disturbing and urges the American Bar Association to initiate a study to see what, if any, controls or prohibitions should be imposed," any attempt to turn back the clock is doomed to fail.[33] Lateral mobility among both associates and partners will increase as firms seek to enhance profitability and individual lawyers strive to increase income and power. Partners will augment the number of associates and paralegals while replacing other subordinate employees by information processing equipment that raises labor productivity. But hiring and retaining associates reinforces the vicious circle that demands expansion of the partnership. The cumulative effect of these changes will be to transform the professional firm into a capitalist multiservice corporation, characterized by hierarchy, bureaucracy, the extraction of surplus value from workers by partners, and even the progressive separation of ownership from daily control (through the hiring of a nonlawyer business manager and perhaps even the sale of firm equity to nonpartners).

At various times and places, the legal profession has offered its members the attractions of membership in a community. But the homogeneity enjoyed by small town bars and elite big city associations vanished long ago. The profession has grown increasingly diverse in terms of background (race and gender, if not class), structure (employment and private practice, large firms and small), and function (litigation, legislation, advice, negotiation, teaching, research, and judging), with a concomitant divergence of interests. Yet the Commission could not even see that it was championing the special interests of the professional elite against those of sole and small firm practitioners by maintaining that

> it is hard to justify how opposition to legislation aimed at simplifying the handling of uncontested matters—clearly in the public interest and aimed at holding down fees—should ever properly be opposed by groups of lawyers.[34]

Diversity has multiplied the professional associations representing special interests. Concentration among producers of legal services has led to the emergence of collectivities intermediate between the individual lawyer and the profession—government departments, offices of corporate counsel, law schools, judicial benches, and law firms—whose importance the Commission recognized when it recommended the creation of law firm ethics committees.[35] But there are no solutions to the classic dilemmas of democratic representation—the choice between inclusive, compulsory legally recognized organizations paralyzed by the divergence of membership interests and exclusive, voluntary, unofficial organizations disempowered by their small memberships, lack of political and economic resources, and inability to form coalitions. Despite the Commission's misinformed Anglophilia, the "American Inns of Court, founded in 1980, which seeks to create intimate, local societies of judges and lawyers, law students, and law professors who meet on a regular basis and discuss ethical issues and the quality of legal advocacy in America" are wholly irrelevant to the fundamental problem.[36]

When lawyers learned their trade through apprenticeship and began practice by hanging out a shingle, the market served as the primary mechanism for allocating entrants to roles. The increasing diversity in the backgrounds of lawyers and the roles open to them has demanded new mechanisms. The law school early assumed a central position, and its responsibilities have expanded in recent decades, to the point that they distort and disrupt its educational mission. But even law schools cannot justify the enormous disparity in economic rewards that different lawyers enjoy, or explain why these appear to reflect the lawyer's race, gender, and class background. Furthermore, just as the law school relinquished preparation for the bar examination to an unregulated market of proprietary crammers, so it plays no role in the lateral reshuffling that continues for ten years or more after graduation. Similarly, the increasing specialization of both legal knowledge and role expectations has magnified the importance of first employers as socializing agents, at the expense of law schools. Here, again, the unity of the profession, symbolized by educational institutions sharing common curricula and examinations, has dissolved as individual employers assume the task of hiring and socializing graduates, just as they confer wealth, status, and security, offer community, engage in self-regulation, and defend their collective interests.

Having criticized the recommendations of the ABA Commission on Professionalism, I feel an obligation to offer my own views on how the legal profession should prepare to enter the twenty-first century. I also feel presumptuous in doing so, not because I am an academic rather than a practitioner but because I write as an individual. Changes of the magnitude I propose are conceivable only if formulated and pursued collectively.

The profession should begin by opening its doors to all those desiring to become lawyers, both to allow them to pursue their personal dreams and to increase access to legal services. Every existing barrier should be thoroughly scrutinized and razed or lowered unless there is convincing evidence that it is necessary to ensure some minimum level of quality in legal services. We presently have no data relating *any* barrier to lawyer performance. Law school should be opened to all who want to attend through increased financial aid, the development of alternative admissions criteria (supplementing or replacing undergraduate grades and LSAT scores), compensatory education for those from disadvantaged backgrounds, and flexible hours and part-time programs for those with work or family obligations. The profession should actively seek to equalize the opportunities of men and women. Formal leaves for pregnancy and childbirth (with generous salary allowances and rights to return) are necessary but not sufficient. Men will have to *choose* to assume equal childrearing responsibilities, interrupting their careers as often and for as long as women in order to fulfill them. This might equalize gender roles sufficiently that the values in which women are socialized would become just as influential as those of men within the legal workplace and legal process. Employers as well as law schools must adopt affirmative action programs designed to attract, retain, and advance minority graduates in more than token numbers.

The profession must subject its control over production *by* producers to the same scrutiny as its control over the production *of* producers, eliminating every restrictive practice unsupported by convincing evidence that it is necessary to protect the public against incompetence, fraud, or other abuse. Legal protection of the professional monopoly should be narrowed greatly, if not eliminated altogether. Lawyers should be free to practice across state, and perhaps even national, boundaries (constrained only by their own awareness of limited competence, notice to clients of their education and experience, and fear of malpractice liability). The profession should encourage other occupations to advise, negotiate, draft, and represent, offering the supervision of lawyers but not requiring it. Lawyers should stop taking the public's name in vain: if laypeople and clients are offended by advertising, solicitation, price competition, or closed-panel group plans *they* will complain. Although the profession should encourage the growth of specialized legal knowledge and develop mechanisms for ascertaining who possesses it, specialization should not become an excuse for erecting new protectionist barriers around submarkets.

Lawyers' self-interest in creating demand should be harnessed to the task of increasing the quantity and quality of legal services while reducing their price. Lawyers must be free to compete even when that will concentrate business by rewarding some producers at the expense of others. Freer competition will encourage individual rather than institutional advertising, solicitation as well as advertising, and closed- rather than open-panel group plans. At the same time that the profession frees private practitioners to stimulate demand among middle-class individuals and businesses, its collective efforts should be devoted toward the poor. Pro bono service is not an act of charity but an obligation to make some return for the state's protection of the professional monopoly, the nearly two decades of subsidized education all lawyers receive, and the extraordinary economic and social privileges they enjoy. Because it is an obligation it must be made mandatory: altruism is strengthened by seeing others do their duty and weakened by widespread shirking. Even the trivial burden of two cases a year, were it to be borne by all 700,000 lawyers, would more than double the representation presently offered by the Legal Services Corporation. At the same time, the organized profession must use its moral authority and political clout to increase government expenditures for legal services, at least to the per capita levels found in less wealthy nations.

Lawyers loudly criticize the failure of self-regulation among other occupational groups: police, politicians, physicians, environmental polluters, manufacturers of dangerous products, and employers. It is about time they acknowledged the weakness of their own performance. The regulation of lawyer incompetence and misconduct must be entrusted to an institution wholly independent of both the organized bar and private practitioners. It must be staffed by a career civil service whose salary and status are sufficiently high to attract and retain good law graduates. The bar should not control the budget, although there is ample justification for taxing lawyers to pay for their own discipline. Lawyers should be required to keep and disclose records of transactions likely to involve misconduct, particularly those involving client funds. The regulatory agency should not passively rely on complaints by judges, lawyers, and clients—all of whom have strong, if different, reasons for silence—but mount its own aggressive investigations. The profession should acknowledge the virtual impossibility of predicting who will commit misconduct before they enter practice and concentrate instead on identifying lawyers who *have* deviated, making sure they do not repeat and discouraging others from beginning. The profession must recognize that its members are unusually prone to substance abuse and promptly suspend abusers from practice while seeking to rehabilitate them. And lawyers should acknowledge that the most common sources of client discontent—fees, discourtesy, and delay—are the by-products of market imperfections for which the profession itself is responsible; freer competition among lawyers and with other occupations is the most effective remedy.

Lawyers constantly bemoan the fact that they are misunderstood and undervalued. But they will never increase public respect through conspicuous acts of altruism or sporadic crackdowns on ambulance chasing. People are not fools; lawyers must change who they are and what they do if they want to change how they are perceived. All the reforms I propose will help to improve public opinion; let me indicate just a few of those linkages. If entry into the profession and success within it were equally open to all without regard to sex, race, ethnoreligious background, or class, the dominant meritocratic ideology would help to justify the privileges of all lawyers and of elites within the profession (although the enormous disparities of income, status, and power would have to be greatly reduced before they could be explained by "merit" or effort). And if lawyers actively encouraged client self-help and the activities of competing occupations, the public might more readily see the limited services lawyers do perform as essential rather than mere make-work.

Yet the greatest obstacle to public respect may not be the profession's efforts to attain social closure but rather the widespread identification of lawyers with the flawed character and reprehensible actions of their clients. The profession's response has been to invoke the shibboleth of "independence," emphasizing the lawyer's countervailing obligations to the legal system and society. No one is convinced. Lawyers *are* hired guns: they know they are, their clients demand that they be, and the public sees them that way. As more lawyers are employed by or represent increasingly powerful clients, this identification grows even stronger. Lawyers must stop denying the identification and embrace it. Instead of seeking to justify their actions by reference to process values that allegedly produce truth and justice, lawyers must concede—indeed, affirm—that they actively promote the objectives of their clients and justify their own behavior in terms of the substantive justice of their clients' goals.

Lawyers are uneasy about the transformation of productive relations—the displacement of independent practitioners by employers and employees trapped within large, bureaucratic institutions that increasingly resemble the corporations they serve. Although I have criticized professional rules that seek to hold back this tide, I am just as unhappy about the restructuring, if for different reasons. I do not believe that economic efficiency requires centralized control, bureaucracy, capitalist relations of production, gross inequalities of income and status, or an extreme division of labor. In the interests of efficiency, therefore, as well as human autonomy, equality, and community, I believe that law firms should decentralize their operations, reduce hierarchy, curtail the division of labor, equalize income, and democratize governance.

Advanced capitalist societies confer on their more privileged members high levels of material security and personal autonomy. But even the few who enjoy such advantages acutely suffer from the lack of community. The workplace can, and should, be an important environment for the construction of community. But true community can be achieved only through inclusion, not exclusion. The legal profession must welcome its newer entrants, transforming *itself* to celebrate their differences instead of expecting them to assimilate. It must openly recognize the existence of divergent subcommunities, strengthening them so that they can meet as equals within the large occupational category. It must narrow the extreme inequalities of status and income that generate subordination and envy. And it must create unity through common efforts to realize the social ideals embodied in law.

Only if American lawyers are prepared to make these fundamental changes will they be entitled to claim, with Roscoe Pound, that the legal profession is "a group . . . pursuing a learned art as a common calling in the spirit of public service."[37]

Tables

Table 1.   State Educational Requirements for
Admission to Bar, 1935 and 1984

	Number of States	
	1935	1984
Prelaw		
None	11	0
High-school diploma	19	0
Two years of college	17	1[a]
Three years of college	0	39
College degree	1	11
Law		
Law office study (three to four years)	44	4
With one year of law school	0	0
One year with two years of law school	0	3
One year with three years of law school	0	1
Two years of law school or less	10	0
Law school approved by ABA	9	48
Diploma privilege	11	2
Correspondence school	1	1
Postlaw office study	0	3
Lawyer admitted in other U.S. jurisdictions		
Admitted on motion (residence and reciprocity may be required)		29
Attorney's exam		8
Regular exam		15

Note: a.   California allows examination in lieu of
two years of college

Source: Review of Legal Education (1935; 1984)

Table 2. Total Length of Prelegal and Legal Education of Law Students, 1889-90 to 1938

Year	Full-time Schools Requiring: >5 Years #	%	5 Years #	%	3 or 4 Years #	%	Part-time Schools Requiring 3 or 4 Years #	%	Mixed Schools #	%	Schools Requiring Less Than 3 Years #	%	Total Number	Distribution of Schools Requiring at Least 3 Years Percentage FT	PT/M
1889-90	0	0	0	0	1,192	27	108	2	0	0	3,186	71	4,486	27	2
1899-1900	761	6	0	0	3,992	32	2,251	18	704	6	4,676	38	12,384	38	24
1909-10	1,741	9	751	4	5,946	30	4,787	25	1,963	10	4,310	22	19,498	43	35
1919-20	3,407	14	2,326	9	4,799	20	9,338	38	3,087	13	1,546	6	24,503	43	51
1920-21	3,733	14	2,570	9	4,977	18	11,049	40	3,567	13	1,417	5	27,313	41	53
1921-22	4,201	13	3,241	10	5,164	16	11,814	37	7,082	22	711	2	32,213	39	59
1922-23	4,394	12	4,121	11	4,736	13	12,746	35	9,504	26	729	2	36,230	36	61
1923-24	4,531	11	5,143	13	4,214	11	13,964	35	11,114	28	816	2	39,782	35	63
1924-25	4,811	11	5,617	13	4,600	11	15,208	36	11,658	27	849	2	42,743	35	63
1925-26	5,068	11	8,158	18	1,675	4	16,160	36	12,365	28	914	2	44,340	33	64
1926-27	6,288	13	8,034	17	1,385	3	15,706	33	14,927	32	980	2	47,320	33	65
1927-28	6,531	13	8,188	17	1,065	2	16,767	34	15,284	31	758	2	48,593	32	65
1928-29	6,796	14	9,129	19	349	1	16,669	34	15,229	31	770	2	48,942	34	65
1929-30	7,770	17	8,284	18	283	1	16,220	35	13,418	29	761	2	46,736	36	64
1930-31	7,694	18	7,925	18	324	1	14,577	34	12,019	28	784	2	43,323	37	62
1931-32	8,220	19	7,539	18	168	1	14,366	34	11,145	26	727	2	42,165	37	60
1932-33	8,521	21	7,304	18	176	1	13,584	33	10,708	26	860	2	41,153	39	59
Fall 1935	8,763	21	6,775	16	50	1	11,343	27	14,212	34	777	2	41,920	37	61
Fall 1936	9,013	22	6,135	15	45	1	10,264	26	14,075	35	686	2	40,218	37	61
Fall 1937	9,374	24	5,416	14	11	1	9,386	24	14,606	37	462	1	39,255	38	61
Fall 1938	9,492	25	5,197	14	12	1	7,846	21	14,407	39	452	1	37,406	39	60

Source: Review of Legal Education

Table 3a. Effect of Educational Requirements:
Education of Practicing Lawyers, 1949–70

Year	Percentage Attended College	Percentage College Degree	Percentage Attended Law School	Percentage with Law School Degree
1949	66.0 78.8[a]	37.1 45.1[a]	76.4 92.6[a]	61.5 74.7[a]
1952	73.9 82.6[a]	44.0 49.2[a]	84.6 94.6[a]	72.0 80.5[a]
1955	78.3	49.1	88.6	77.8
1958	81.1	52.1	90.8	80.1
1961	83.9	58.0	92.6	84.5
1963	86.5	62.6	94.2	87.3
1966	88.7	67.1	95.5	89.6
1970	91.3	73.3	96.8	92.7

Note: a.   Source of these figures is Blaustein

Sources: Sikes et al. (1972: 8); Blaustein
          (1950: 374; 1952: 1054)

Table 3b. Effect of Educational Requirements:
Education of American Population, 1870–1970

| | | White Males | | | Black Males | | |
Year	High School Graduates, as % of 17-yr.-olds	% who completed years of college 1-3	4	Median years completed	% who completed years of college 1-3	4	Median years completed
1870	2.0						
1880	2.5						
1890	3.5						
1900	6.3						
1910	8.6						
1920	16.3						
1930	28.8						
1940	49.0	5.2	5.8	8.4	1.6	1.4	5.4
1947		6.9	6.5	9.0	2.0	2.3	6.6
1950	57.4						
1952					3.3	2.0	6.8
1960	63.4	9.1	10.3	10.6	4.4	3.5	7.9
1964		9.4	12.3	11.9	4.9	5.6	8.7
1970	75.6	11.3	15.0	12.2	6.2	6.8	9.8

Source: U.S. Dept. of Commerce (1975: 379–80)

Table 4. Number Taking LSAT, Completing LSDAS, and Entering Law School, 1947-48 to 1986-87

Year	First Year Enrollment	Number Taking LSAT	Ratio of LSAT to Number Entering Following Year	Number Completing LSDAS	Ratio of LSDAS to Number Entering Following Year	Number of Reports to Law Schools	Ratio of Reports to LSDAS Completions
1947-48		6,882	0.3				
1948-49	23,963	7,655	0.4				
1949-50	21,542	8,037	0.4				
1950-51	19,461	6,748	0.4				
1951-52	17,295	6,588	0.4				
1952-53	14,700	7,557	0.5				
1953-54	14,458	8,653	0.6				
1954-55	15,729	10,158	0.6				
1955-56	16,137	11,755	0.7				
1956-57	16,771	12,770	0.8				
1957-58	15,842	14,846	0.9				
1958-59	16,169	17,374	1.0				
1959-60	17,105	20,903	1.2				
1960-61	17,031	23,800	1.3				
1961-62	17,698	25,878	1.3				
1962-63	19,746	31,691	1.4				
1963-64	22,930	32,598	1.5				
1964-65	25,515	39,503	1.5				
1965-66	26,508	45,268	1.7				
1966-67	26,720	47,458	1.8				
1967-68	25,746	50,793	1.7				
1968-69	30,719	60,503	1.7				
1969-70	36,642	77,900	2.1				
1970-71	37,538	107,147	2.8				
1971-72	37,724	121,871	2.9	80,364	1.9	468,377	5.8
1972-73	41,810	122,702	3.0	81,913	2.0	517,876	6.3
1973-74	40,683	136,106	3.3	85,999	2.1	500,908	5.8
1974-75	41,217	135,094	3.1	83,100	1.9	553,964	6.7
1975-76	43,044	134,720	3.2	82,243	1.9	504,124	6.1
1976-77	42,704	133,078	3.4	70,717	2.0	491,180	6.2
1977-78	39,676	125,257	3.1	81,366	2.0	482,199	5.9
1978-79	40,479	111,235	2.7	72,529	1.8	433,361	6.0
1979-80	40,717	112,675 / 112,446[b]	2.7	76,689	1.8	392,355[a]	5.1
1980-81	42,296	111,373 / 107,373[b]	2.6	79,669	1.9	378,253[a]	4.7
1981-82	42,521	113,272 / 118,565[b]	2.7	82,636	2.0	390,300[a]	4.7
1982-83	42,034	111,620	2.7	82,145	2.0	388,079[a]	4.7
1983-84	40,747	104,621	2.6				
1984-85	40,796	95,019					
1985-86	40,195	95,129		68,806			
1986-87				77,301			

Notes: a. Actual applications
        b. Source of these figures is AALS Syllabus

Sources: T. White (1984: 373); Vernon & Zimmer (1985);
          Metaxas (1986); 18(4) AALS Syllabus 8 (December 1987)

Table 5. Full-time and Part-time Law Students, 1889-90 to 1985[a]

| | ABA Approved Schools | | | Unapproved Schools[b] | | | | |
Year	Number full-time	Number part-time	Percentage part-time	Number full-time	Number part-time	Percentage part-time	Number of schools responding	Total percentage part-time
1985	99,985	24,107	19					
1984	98,735	21,112	18					
1983	99,884	21,317	18	266	1,488		12	
1982	100,649	21,142	17	445	814		8	
1981	99,714	21,165	18	750	1,659		4	
1980	98,396	21,105	18	1,146	2,398		7	
1979	97,880	15,230	13	1,328	2,662	67		15
1978	95,685	20,465	18	1,986	3,313	63		
1977	92,990	20,090	18	2,946	4,536	61	15	
1976	91,782	20,590	18	3,012	4,517	60	15	
1975	90,268	20,779	19	1,735	3,745	68	6	
1974	85,610	20,098	19	2,050	7,116	78	11	
1973	81,851	19,824	19	3,078	5,520	64	23	
1972	79,289	18,753	19	997	3,089	76	13	
1971	73,919	17,306	19	532	2,250	81	8	
1970	62,376	15,963	20	311	3,606	92	13	
1969	50,307	11,896	19	169	3,380	95	10	
1968	47,353	12,145	20	1,000	4,661	82	21	
1967	49,183	16,243	25	1,167	4,631	80	19	
1966	47,154	12,082	20	653	4,874	88	17	
1965	44,014	12,496	22	622	4,566	88	16	
1964	39,235	11,844	23	608	4,743	89	20	
1963	35,332	11,334	24	468	4,218	90	21	
1962	31,099	10,910	26	695	2,799	80	17	
1961	28,460	10,434	27	397	2,821	88	20	
1960	27,355	10,360	27	436	3,423	89	21	
1959	26,069	9,700	27	385	3,161	89	25	
1958	26,854	9,832	27	246	3,104	93	23	
1957	26,606	9,666	27	298	2,997	91	26	
1956	26,579	8,659	25	513	3,227	86	26	
1955	24,950	8,455	25	267	4,091	94	33	
1954	23,979	8,378	26	298	3,714	93	29	
1953	23,721	8,145	26	658	3,720	85	29	
1952	24,540	8,793	26	715	4,613	87	30	
1951	27,518	9,216	25	1,042	6,610	86	39	
1950	32,918	8,657	21	1,250	7,381	86	41	
1949	35,972	7,085	16	2,072	8,606	81	48	
1948	37,994	6,878	15	1,891	7,949	81	53	
1947	26,640	5,800	18	986	5,914	86	37	
1944	2,292	1,920	46	21	1,226	98	35	
1938	17,029	5,410	24	1,115	9,494	89	67	
1937	17,037	5,580	25	1,637	12,394	88	86	
1936	16,872	3,948	19	2,043	13,929	87	94	
1935[a]	16,778	3,046	15	2,585	14,913	85	106	
1931[a]	13,621	3,382	22	1,190	20,744	95		
1928[a]	12,994	2,390	16	2,084	28,929	93		68

| | All Schools | | | |
| | Full-time | | Number | Number |
Year	Number	Percentage	part-time	mixed
1926-27[c]	14,906	33	15,750	14,705
1925-26	15,090	34	16,818	12,365
1924-25	15,272	36	15,813	11,658
1923-24	14,177	36	14,491	11,114
1922-23	13,515	37	13,211	9,504
1921-22	12,820	40	12,311	7,082
1920-21	11,764	43	11,982	3,567
1919-20	11,185	46	10,231	3,087
1909-10	9,948	51	6,036	3,444
1899-1900	7,384	60	3,477	1,523
1889-90	3,325	74	1,027	134

Notes: a. Students enrolled for first degree; excludes graduate and special students
       b. Only a tiny proportion of unapproved schools report enrollment figures in recent years
       c. Fall enrollment; if mixed are allocated between full- and part-time, full-time students are 42% of total

Sources: Review of Legal Education; Reed (1928: 120); Smith & Rogers (1932: 568)

Table 6. Law School Tuition (selected institutions and years)[a]

Law School	1905[e]	1927	1935	1950	1960	1979	1984
Univ. of California, Berkeley		10C (225)	102 (227)	70 (370)	135.50 (636.50)	800 (3,200)	1,437 (5,000)
Univ. of Southern California	50	245 (180)[c]	300	530	500	5,040	9,842
Yale University	150	310	460	750	1,200	5,400	9,900
University of Idaho		51 (111)	36 (96)	150	250	754 (2,254)	1,290 (3,290)
Harvard University	150	307	410	630	1,000	4,580	9,185
University of Michigan		118 (138)[d]	124 (144)	210	400 (880)	2,083 (4,383)	4,091 (8,591)
Ohio State University	60	108 (213)	117 (267)	105	369 (744)	1,350 (3,000)	2,482 (5,728)
University of Toledo		b	108	190 (228)	N.A.	1,332 (2,787)	2,074 (4,108)
University of Oregon	60	86.25 (236.25)	79.50 (199.50)	30	270 (525)	1,594 (2,510)	2,705 (3,953)
Nashville YMCA		50	75	250	250	b	b
University of Texas		30	57	25 (150)	100 (400)	418 (1,426)	209 (639)
University of Wisconsin	50	35 (159)[a]	80 (280)	140 (440)	240 (620)	1,237 (3,871)	1,789 (5,323)
University of Wyoming		42	60 (82.50)	42 (112)	245 (507)	434 (1,720)	721 (2,231)
Consumer Price Index[f]				72.1	88.7	116.3	237.1[g]

Notes:
a. Figure in parenthesis is tuition for out-of-state students
b. School closed
c. Evening
d. 109 and 129 for women
e. 24 law schools $100 to $160/yr.; 16 schools $75 to $99;
   24 schools $50 to $74; rest less than $50
   (1 American Law School Review 311–12 [1905])
f. 1967 equals 100
g. May 1982

Sources: Review of Legal Education (1926 and 1927; 1935; 1950; 1960; 1979; 1984)

256

Entry Barriers: Table 7

Table 7. Proportion of Students Enrolled at ABA–Approved
Law Schools Graduating Three Years Later, 1963–85

Year	First-year Enrollment Three Years Earlier	J.D. & LL.B. Degrees Awarded	Percentage of First-year Class Graduated in Three Years[a]
1963	15,607	9,638	62
1964	16,489	10,491	64
1965	18,346	11,507	63
1966	20,776	13,115	63
1967	22,753	14,738	65
1968	24,167	16,077	67
1969	24,077	16,733	69
1970	24,267	17,183	71
1971	23,652	17,006	72
1972	29,128	22,342	77
1973	34,713	27,756	80
1974	36,171	28,729	79
1975	35,131	29,961	85
1976	37,018	32,597	88
1977	38,074	33,640	88
1978	39,038	33,317	85
1979	39,996	34,590	86
1980	39,676	35,059	88
1981	40,479	35,598	88
1982	40,717	34,846	86
1983	42,296	36,389	86
1984	42,521	36,887	86
1985	42,034	36,829	88

Note: a.   Distorted by fact that part-time students
graduate in four years and number of ABA
schools varies from year to year

Sources: Review of Legal Education (1979; 1983; 1985)

Table 8. Law School Attrition, Aggregate Enrollment, 1922–41

Year	First Year	Second Year	Third Year	Fourth Year	Total[a]	Number of Schools Reporting	Third Year as Percentage of First Year Two Years Earlier[b]
1922	13,403	9,517	6,560	779	30,259	130	
1923	14,764	10,363	8,444	1,236	34,807	154	
1924	14,854	10,184	8,223	1,682	34,943	138	61.4
1925	14,428	10,434	8,513	1,397	34,772	143	57.7
1926	16,865	11,110	9,358	1,685	39,018	142	63.0
1927	16,157	12,949	10,296	1,868	41,270	160	71.4
1928	15,515	11,642	10,507	1,985	39,649	166	62.3
1929	15,497	12,769	10,330	2,430	41,026	170	63.9
1930	13,387	11,096	9,567	1,992	36,042	182	61.7
1931	14,164	10,501	9,995	2,156	36,816	179	64.5
1932	13,919	10,194	8,383	1,658	34,154	166	62.6
1933	13,884	10,336	8,279	1,576	34,075	171	58.5
1934	14,088	10,223	8,074	1,456	33,841	171	58.0
1935	15,781	11,231	9,116	1,547	37,675	172	65.7
1936	15,339	10,743	9,197	2,025	37,304	172	65.3
1937	13,390	10,113	9,073	2,117	34,713	162	57.5
1938	12,458	10,022	8,947	2,065	33,492	166	58.3
1939	11,231	9,420	8,770	2,361	31,782	166	65.5
1940[c]	10,355	8,185	8,243	2,112	28,895	171	66.2
	10,166	8,025	8,150	2,112	28,453	169	65.4
1941[c]	7,569	5,658	6,242	1,623	21,092	164	55.6
	7,507	5,612	6,207	1,594	20,920	162	55.3

Notes: a. Excludes graduate, special, unclassified, and summer
             school students and those from other departments

        b. Distorted by fact that number of schools changes

        c. Different years give different figures

Source: American Law School Review

Table 9. Attrition at ABA-Approved Law Schools, Full-time and Part-time, 1937-86

	Full-time			Part-time		
Year	First-year enrollment two years earlier	Third-year enrollment	Percentage remaining[a]	First-year enrollment three years earlier	Fourth-year enrollment	Percenta remainir
1937	7,152	4,907	68.6			
1938	6,959	4,857	69.8	1,343	714	53.2
1939	6,884			1,458		
1940	6,913			1,748		
1941				1,817		
1942						
1943		530			299	
1944						
1945	1,044					
1946				829		
1947		8,683			577	
1948		9,784			1,206	
1949	15,932	9,768	61.3		1,101	
1950	16,500	9,984	60.5	2,650	1,202	45.4
1951	14,381	8,465	58.9	3,032	1,289	42.5
1952	12,652	7,442	58.8	2,963	1,568	52.9
1953	10,638	6,789	63.8	3,759	1,406	37.4
1954	9,655	6,083	63.0	3,829	1,422	37.1
1955	10,002	6,320	63.2	3,456	1,295	37.5
1956	10,722	6,743	62.9	3,302	1,367	41.4
1957	11,145	7,346	65.9	3,486	1,532	43.9
1958	11,649	7,809	67.0	3,495	1,726	49.4
1959	10,615	6,866	64.7	3,672	1,636	44.6
1960	11,103	7,530	67.8	4,138	1,822	44.0
1961	11,082	7,632	68.9	4,023	1,764	43.8
1962	11,324	7,882	69.6	3,979	1,780	44.7
1963	12,264	8,669	70.7	4,283	1,847	43.1
1964	13,770	9,559	69.4	4,225	1,820	43.1
1965	15,981	11,420	71.5	4,576	1,989	43.5
1966	17,611	12,893	73.2	4,795	2,030	42.3
1967	18,854	14,078	74.7	5,142	2,244	43.6
1968	19,318	14,457	74.8	5,313	2,282	43.0
1969	19,923	12,216	61.3	4,759	2,219	46.6
1970	18,931	14,776	78.1	4,344	2,402	55.3
1971	23,149	19,296	83.4	4,721	3,108	65.8
1972	27,684	24,373	88.0	5,979	2,983	49.9
1973	29,080	25,485	87.6	6,778	3,495	51.6
1974	28,448	25,376	89.2	7,091	3,763	53.1
1975	30,202	28,308	93.7	6,683	4,014	60.1
1976	31,347	28,885	87.6	6,816	3,920	57.5
1977	32,184	29,204	90.7	6,727	3,881	57.7
1978	33,149	30,527	92.1	6,854	4,135	60.3
1979	33,308	31,116	93.4	6,847	4,187	61.2
1980	34,118	31,326	91.8	6,368	4,246	66.7
1981	34,632	31,220	90.1	6,361	4,263	67.0
1982	35,329	33,249	94.1	6,085	4,346	71.4
1983	35,826	32,149	89.7	6,967	4,435	63.7
1984	35,334	32,524	92.0	6,695	4,249	63.5
1985	34,568	31,448	90.9	6,700	4,286	64.0
1986	34,125			6,591		
1987				6,622		

Note: a. Distorted by fact that number of schools changes

Source: Review of Legal Education

Table 10. Attrition at Selected Schools, 1924–84 (third-year students
          as percentage of first-year students three years earlier)

Year	University of Florida	DePaul[a] University	Boston University	Harvard University	University of Wisconsin
1924	46		67	57	59
1925	53	(78)	132	64	61
1926	83	(63)	88	58	63
1927	70		96	61	64
1928	71		83	56	63
1929	94		83	58	78
1930	71	90	81	59	82
1931	76	89	87	58	103
1932	110[c]	33	87	62	74
1933	77	31	84	61	77
1934	82	92	81	64	77
1935	64		76	67	83
1936	77	(27)	85	69	90
1937	97	(30)	86	62	80
1938	107[c]	(27)	81	60	70
1939	82	(26)	88	74	79
1940	52	(48)	86	70	73
1941	36	(39)	74	58	59
1950	35		68	82	68
1951	35	44	63	81	63
1952	36	33	46	81	62
1953	45	32	62	86	62
1954	45	32	62	83	52
1955	53	39	59	83	57
1956	61	43	72	91	51
1957	60	46	48	91	52
1958	50	41	46	90	59
1959	43	23	56	90	48
1960	63	34	61	92	50
1961	68	40	53	92	69
1962	70	50	54	95	73
1963	72	41	57	92	72
1964	61	44	68	91	59
1965	66	50	69	98	64
1966	61	40	76	96	50
1967	64	45	79	96	71
1968	38[b]	67[b]	75[b]	92[b]	67[b]
1969	64	53	64	71	48
1970	54	51	65	91	70
1971	71	48	80	97	78
1972	69	72	90	104[c]	85
1973	72	67	93	100[c]	93
1974	70	55	91	102[c]	97
1975	67	67	90	93	95
1976	37?	82	89	98	100[c]
1977	75	57	91	96	102[c]
1978	67	65	88	95	94

Table 10.   Attrition at Selected School, 1924–84 (third-year sudents
a percentage of first-year students three years earlier) (continued)

Year	University of Florida	DePaul[a] University	Boston University	Harvard University	University of Wisconsin
1979	91	64	88	99	92
1980	103[c]	74	92	95	99
1981	99	72	92	99	88
1982	75	75	95	96	91
1983					
1984	136	82	94	95	94

Notes: a.   DePaul is a mixed school--hence the percentage
              is fourth-year students as proportion of part-time
              first-year three years earlier; when this is not
              available, figure in parenthesis is all third-year
              students as percentage of all first-year students
              two years earlier

         b.   Sudden drop probably due to Vietnam War

         c.   Presumably due to the return of students who
              had dropped out earlier or to transfer students

Sources: American Law School Review; Review of Legal Education

Table 11. Attrition of Male and Female Law Students, 1971-72 to 1985-86

	Full-time						Part-time					
	All Students			Women Students			All Students			Women Students		
Year	First year	J.D. and LL.B.	No. of degrees as % of first yr. 2 yrs. earlier[a]	First year	J.D. and LL.B.	No. of degrees as % of first yr. 2 yrs. earlier[a]	First year	J.D. and LL.B	No. of degrees as % of first yr. 3 yrs. earlier[a]	First year	J.D. and LL.B.	No. of degrees as % of first yr. 3 yrs. earlier[a]
1985-86	34,304			13,885			6,492			2,655		
1984-85	34,125	31,993	91	13,567	12,342	91	6,622	4,836	72	2,666	1,777	72
1983-84	34,568	31,615	89	13,468	11,749	88	6,591	5,072	73	2,581	1,837	74
1982-83	35,334	31,712	90	13,596	11,525	90	6,700	4,677	77	2,540	1,535	73
1981-82	35,826	30,499	88	13,332	10,145	89	6,695	4,347	68	2,479	1,349	66
1980-81	35,329	30,708	90	12,779	10,052	89	6,957	4,835	76	2,493	1,460	76
1979-80	34,632	30,486	92	11,399	9,258	93	6,035	4,575	67	2,091	1,311	55
1978-79	34,118	30,316	91	11,286	8,561	92	6,351	4,274	62	2,056	1,184	64
1977-78	33,308	28,546	89	9,995	7,504	87	6,358	4,771	71	1,933	1,131	69
1976-77	33,149	29,059	93	9,347	6,780	92	6,847	4,581	67	2,007	881	73
1975-76	32,184	28,116	93	8,627	5,575	91	6,854	4,476	67	1,845	663	68
1974-75	31,347	25,737	90	7,367	4,086	90	6,727	4,234	60	1,639	460	59
1973-74	30,202	25,674	88	5,107	3,147	94	6,816	3,653	54	1,357	300	48
1972-73	28,448	24,415	88	4,529	2,079	71	6,633[b]	3,341	56	979[b]	202	48
1971-72	29,080	19,537	84	3,351	1,397	83	7,091	2,805	59	775[b]	166	50

Notes: a. Distorted by fact that number of law schools change
        b. In 1974, first-year part-time enrollment four years earlier includes mixed schools

Source: Review of Legal Education

Table 12. Attrition of Minority Students in
ABA-Approved Law Schools, 1971-72 to 1985-86[a]

Year	Black	Mexican-American	Puerto Rican[b]	Other Hispano-American	American Indian	Asian/ Pacific Islander	Total[c]
1971-72	68.3	69.4	62.1	100	40.9	56.7	70.8
1973-74	70.3	67.2	65.3	79.7	62.0	79.5	70.7
1974-75	69.7	70.4	80.8	97.9	82.3	96.6	74.1
1975-76	74.7	75.5	100.0	86.2	77.1	87.8	77.3
1976-77	77.9	81.5	88.2	70.6	68.2	88.1	79.5
1977-78	73.7	78.7	93.8	83.5	76.3	97.0	78.7
1978-79	73.9	86.3	88.1	79.5	93.2	82.2	78.5
1979-80	73.9	80.1	77.5	72.8	73.0	88.8	77.1
1980-81	75.8	82.2	76.6	78.5	73.8	84.9	78.3
1981-82	79.7	84.4	67.4	97.3	72.5	84.2	81.5
1982-83	75.7	74.5	66.5	90.8	67.5	87.7	78.0
1983-84	76.5	76.8	80.5	81.9	83.8	88.9	79.4
1984-85	76.0	77.4	71.9	81.9	72.1	82.1	77.6
1985-86	79.7	77.9	65.1	104.1	73.4	87.5	82.5

Notes: a. Third-year students as a percentage of first-year
            students two years earlier overestimates success
            because of steady increase in number of schools
        b. Excludes students in Puerto Rican law schools
        c. Includes other

Source: Review of Legal Education

Table 13.   Admissions to Bar on Motion and by Diploma Privilege, 1920-85

	Admissions on Motion		Admissions by Diploma		
Year	Number	Percentage of total admissions	Number	Percentage of total admissions	Number of jurisdictions admitting
1985	3,471	8.2	549	1.3	
1984	2,229	6.5	679	2.0	5
1983	1,685	3.8	795	1.8	5
1982	1,716	4.0	654	1.5	5
1981	2,197	5.2	940	2.2	5
1980	3,100	6.9	892	2.0	5
1979	3,350	7.3	853	1.9	5
1978	2,795	6.7	767	1.8	5
1977	2,504	6.9	839	2.3	5
1976	2,741	7.8	790	2.3	5
1975	2,104	6.0	786	2.3	5
1974	1,758	5.3	882	2.6	5
1973	1,603	5.2	804	2.6	5
1972	2,099	8.4	639	2.5	6
1971	1,379	6.7	507	2.5	6
1970	1,324	7.4	528	2.9	6
1969	1,272	6.7	467	2.4	6
1968	931	5.4	508	2.9	6
1967	851	5.3	428	2.7	6
1966	847	5.8	401	2.7	6
1965	830	6.3	356	2.7	6
1964	867	7.2	347	2.9	7
1963	736	6.8	430	4.0	7
1962	754	7.0	592	5.5	8
1961	758	7.1	551	5.1	8
1960	704	6.7	513	4.9	8
1959	665	6.2	602	5.6	8
1958	635	6.1	770	7.4	8
1957	587	6.1	777	8.1	9
1956	534	5.7	799	8.5	12
1955	549	5.7	841	8.8	13
1954	631	6.4	960	9.7	12
1953	725	6.6	1,280	11.7	13
1952	555	4.7	1,435	12.1	14
1951	498	3.8	1,573	12.0	15
1950	475	3.9	1,626	11.9	14
1949	573	4.3	1,571	11.8	15
1948	708	6.3	1,418	12.5	13
1947	1,027	13.2	628	9.3	
1946	1,128	19.0			
1945	588	21.5			
1944	449	19.5			
1943	331	10.0			
1942	399	5.7			
1941	401	4.9			
1940	431	5.1	528	6.6	
1939	471	5.2	429	5.0	
1938	591	6.3	692	7.9	
1937	618	6.5	945	10.6	

Table 13.   Admissions to Bar on Motion and by Diploma Privilege, 1920–85 (continued)

	Admissions on Motion		Admissions by Diploma		
Year	Number	Percentage of total admissions	Numer	Percentage of total admissions	Number of jurisdictions admitting
1936	502	5.5	976	11.4	12
1935	601	6.3	822	9.2	12
1934	775	7.8	854	9.4	12
1933	678	6.8	764	8.3	
1932	624	6.3	566	6.1	
1930	586[a]	5.5	567	5.9	
1929	765	6.9	630	6.3	12
1928	731	6.4	617	5.9	12
1927	876	8.0	553	5.2	12
1926	877	8.4	526	5.5	12
1925	829	9.2	490	6.0	13
1924	957	10.9	542	6.9	14
1923	922	11.5	467	6.6	14
1922	869	10.9	511	7.2	14
1921	970	14.4	441	7.6	14
1920	984	14.1	469	7.8	14

Note: a.   Incomplete data

Sources: Bar Examiner; Stason et al. (1960); 1936 Review of Legal
           Education 31; Stevens (1983: 174 n.27); Brenner (1932b);
           Friedman & Kuznets (1945: 38); 1 Bar Examiner 310 (1932)

Table 14.   Residence Required Before Application,
Examination, or Admission (number of states)

	1938	1954	1960	1979
None	6		5	10
At time of application, examination, admission	16	16	16	23
One month prior	0	0	0	4
Two months	0	1	2	3
Three months	2	5	4	6
Four months	0	0	1	2
Six months	9	10	14	3
Nine months	0	1	1	0
Twelve months or more	2	7	6	0

Sources: Review of Legal Education (1938; 1960;
1979); Blaustein & Porter (1954: 211-12)

Table 15. Bar Examination Results, Selected States, 1902-07

State	1904		1905		1906		1904-06		1902-07	
	Number taking	Percentage passing	Number taking	Percentage passing	Number taking	Percentage passing	Number taking	Percentage passing	Number taking	Percentage passing
New Jersey										
Attorney	155	54	156	55	147	44	458	51	815	55
Counsellor	164	52	92	56	108	50	264	53	452	56
New York	1,297	69	1,350	76	1,176	77	3,823	74		
Pennsylvania	303	68	310	68	267	66	880	66		
Massachusetts	484	61	431	52	535	55	1,470	55		
Connecticut	68	77	67	72	68	72	203	73		
Illinois	440	73	398	80	419	81	1,257	78		
Ohio	373	72	280	87	291	92	944	84		
Minnesota	59	48	48	58	54	76	161	60		
Maryland	123	81	107	72	104	76	334	76		
Total[a]	3,302	68	3,147	72	3,061	73				

Note: a. Excludes N.J. Counsellors
Source: ABA Committee (1907: 570-72)

Table 16.   Bar Examination Results by States, 1922-29

Number Taking/Percentage Passing

	1922	1923	1924	1925	1926
Alabama			33/61	63/75	46/33
Arizona [a]		18/45	22/41		28/29
Arkansas					
California		295/69	22/33		421/72
Colorado		58/75	83/85	83/79	96/83
Connecticut	81/40	193/38	83/30	144/44	140/39
Delaware					
Dist. of Columbia			455/53		485/50
Florida				132/84	755/48
Georgia		75/55	79/70	70/39	55/64
Idaho				12/33	15/73
Illinois		319/64	184/40	220/45	751/58
Iowa			123/83	117/78	
Kansas		71/87	64/96	78/88	70/93
Kentucky		82/88	117/91	58/92	
Louisiana			25/68	82/79	
Maine			25/88	20/75	20/75
Maryland			183/57		
Massachusetts		614/48	623/46	211/48	1,088/46
Michigan		206/57	290/63	185/76	472/81
Minnesota	240/95	26/95	224/57	173/62	157/72
Mississippi		34/71	7/29	29/72	37/73
Missouri		256/73	207/67	289/60	507/64
Montana		3/67	4/100	4/100	2/50
Nebraska		42/89	29/94	52/83	77/81
Nevada		33	2/100	4/0	13/39
New Hampshire [b]		22/60	30/44	22/36	21/33
New Jersey		144/52	334/59	346/50	444/37
New Mexico		26/66	10/100	8/100	2/100
New York		1,057/46		1,986/46	1,560/54
North Carolina			122/57	95/63	135/80
North Dakota		100	19/100	21/77	18/95
Ohio		494/41	327/66	562/79	661/80
Oklahoma			64/72	94/66	78/79
Oregon	68/75		79/76		
Pennsylvania			300/75	360/64	354/56
Philippine Islands			643/31		1,055/21
Puerto Rico			9/45		13/38
Rhode Island		15/53	28/29	33/31	36/15
South Carolina			15/33	5/40	12/75
South Dakota			20/80		21/53
Tennessee [c]		138/86	257/72		
Texas		c.25	79/51		184/50
Utah			18/73		
Vermont			9/100	10/80	
Virginia			322/39		176/44
Washington			64/82	49/80	54/82
West Virginia			49/71	21/52	71/39
Wisconsin		122/68	164/57	201/63	
Wyoming			6/100	9/45	18/89

Entry Barriers: Table 16 (continued)

	1927	1928	1929	Total 1922-29	Number Passing
Alabama	58/57		36/50	236/59	133
Arizona a	32/75	32/57	49/14	181/52	94
Arkansas	32/82			32/82	26
California		576/57	235/48	1,549/62	955
Colorado	55/75	63/64	75/79	513/77	397
Connecticut	227/42		140/52	1,008/45	458
Delaware			2/100	2/100	2
Dist. of Columbia	391/60		385/50	1,716/53	906
Florida	261/51	79/51	64/32	1,291/51	658
Georgia	63/58	74/57	62/70	478/58	279
Idaho	8/62	16/75	13/69	64/64	41
Illinois		288/41	682/48	2,444/51	1,250
Iowa	123/89	124/93	106/79	593/84	499
Kansas	48/94	52/100	63/94	446/92	412
Kentucky	59/88	108/86	44/70	468/88	413
Louisiana	122/70	65/45	73/70	367/67	247
Maine		27/78	60/50	152/72	110
Maryland	157/31			340/44	151
Massachusetts	498/33		829/40	3,863/42	1,619
Michigan	408/85	143/70		1,704/74	1,260
Minnesota	166/59		144/62	1,130/60	677
Mississippi	45/47		30/80	182/65	119
Missouri		249/67		1,508/71	1,066
Montana	3/33	5/80	4/100	25/80	20
Nebraska		44/80	49/88	293/84	247
Nevada	13/70		5/80	37/54	20
New Hampshire b		27/59	28/50	150/52	78
New Jersey			634/50	1,902/48	920
New Mexico	12/33	12/75	10/70	80/84	67
New York	1,747/49	1,401/45	2,499/45	10,250/47	4,853
North Carolina	115/69	120/70	126/83	713/79	564
North Dakota	42/90	11/55	17/100	128/88	113
Ohio	623/85	192/75	297/55	3,156/70	2,201
Oklahoma		110/77	89/65	435/71	311
Oregon	92/66	90/60		329/66	225
Pennsylvania	470/56	250/64	417/57	2,151/61	1,309
Philippine Islands	545/34		272/57	2,515/30	750
Puerto Rico		14/72		36/53	19
Rhode Island	53/32	54/21	54/31	273/37	102
South Carolina		10/80	17/59	59/58	34
South Dakota	23/57	10/40	19/32	93/54	50
Tennessee c	184/54	105/60	228/74	912/70	635
Texas			126/48	389/50	193
Utah			11/37	29/59	17
Vermont	13/100		15/94	47/98	46
Virginia		161/55	225/48	884/45	395
Washington		92/96	68/78	327/85	277
West Virginia	25/48	31/42	20/65	217/74	160
Wisconsin	215/60		145/49	847/59	499
Wyoming	23/87			56/82	46

Notes: a. Years 1927 and 1928; 6 out of 18 districts
        b. From 1903 to 1923, 400 took the exam and 247 passed,
            for a rate of 62%
        c. From 1918 to 1923 about 60% passed

Sources: 1(6) Law Student 3 (May 15, 1924); 2(6) Id. 3 (May 15, 1925);
             3(2) Id. 3 (Nov. 11, 1925);
          3(6) Id. 3 (May 15, 1926); 4(3) Id. 3 (January 1, 1927);
             5(6) Id. 2 (May 1, 1928);
          6(5) Id. 2 (May 1929); 7(5) Id. 2 (May 1930)

Table 17. National Bar Examination Results, 1927-85

		% First Takers Passing	% Repeat Takers Passing	Repeat Takers as % of Total	First Takers					Number Qualifying by Office Study
					Number taking	Passing				
Year	% Passing					Number	Number ABA approved[a]	Number unapproved[a]	Percentage unapproved[a]	
1927	59				14,958	8,825				
1928	54				17,288	9,276				
1929	51				18,305	9,387				
1930	48				19,830	9,445				
1931	48				19,019	9,129				
1932	45				19,470	8,774				
1933	46				18,314	8,494				
1934	45				17,958	8,245				
1935	48				16,812	8,149				
1936	47				16,435	7,651				
1937	48				16,629	7,989				
1938	48				16,789	8,105				
1939	51				15,985	8,102				
1940	51				14,581	7,414				
1947	58				9,743	5,656				
1948	60	68	34	26	16,273	9,835				
1949	61	66	44	32	19,296	11,773				
1950	60	64	45	33	20,113	12,017				
1951	59	64	42	33	19,691	11,568				
1952	59	67	40	35	17,871	10,465				
1953	60	65	44	33	16,217	9,696				
1954	56	66	37	36	15,945	8,968				
1955	59	68	40	36	14,813	8,746				
1956	59	68	37	33	14,540	8,651				
1957	61	67	41	31	14,732	8,818				
1958	60	68	43	33	16,079	9,695				
1959	60	67	43	32	16,682	10,142				
1960	62	71	43	35	16,001	9,992				
1961	63	72	44	31	16,033	10,178				
1962	65	73	45	28	15,585	10,192				
1963	65	72	43	28	16,051	10,361				
1964	67	75	45	26	17,347	11,676				
1965	68	76	48	25	18,703	12,763	9,373	332	3.4	27
1966	68	75	44	24	21,001	14,236	9,985	423	4.1	32
1967	68	76	41	24	22,986	15,579	10,219	236	2.3	14
1968	68	76	43	24	25,292	17,256	14,516	549	3.6	53
1969	70	78	46	23	26,470	18,656	14,119	596	4.1	24
1970	70	79	46	25	24,667	17,394	14,069	609	4.1	7
1971	72	80	44	23	27,904	20,004	15,767	367	2.0	5
1972	74	82	44	20	32,916	24,447	17,736	136	0.8	9
1973	76	82	45	22	39,508	29,903	24,722	642	2.5	7
1974	76	83	46	19	43,798	33,358	27,329	882	3.1	4
1975	74	82	40	20	46,414	34,144	27,289	1,482	5.2	13
1976	70	74	36	21	49,099	34,951	27,232	1,514	5.3	19
1977	70	81	36	23	51,970	36,514	28,486	2,543	7.9	16
1978	67	78	33	23	53,980	36,434	28,638	2,802	8.9	23
1979	69	79	39	27	57,671	39,631	30,582	2,781	8.3	27
1980	67	78	35	25	58,040	38,972	30,305	2,054	6.3	25
1981	66	75	32	24	59,307	39,088	30,499	1,334	4.2	18
1982	65	78	34	26	63,339	41,313	31,897	1,138	3.4	23
1983	66	78	36	28	64,877	42,913	29,607	1,719	5.5	23
1984	64	78	45	27	64,419	41,517	33,996	307	0.9	15
1985	66				66,861	44,225	32,260	271		108

Note: a. Some states do not report breakdown;
percentage calculated from those that do

Sources: Bar Examiner; Friedman & Kuznets (1945: 38)

Table 18. Bar Examination Results for First Takers (F) and
Repeaters (R), Selected States, 1931-85

Year		CA	CT	DC	HI	IL	MA	MI	NJ	NY	ND	OH	PA	TX	UT	VT
1985	F	57	81	82	89	92	87	80	79	77	84	90	--	60	87	66
	R	24	40	25	42	47	38	27	41	38	--	44	--	42	43	25
1984	F	56	85	75	95	87	81	85	67	74	96	93	77	78	92	55
	R	15	36	16	80	42	34	34	30	33	50	80	2	48	28	55
1983	F	60	83	80	97	90	81	81	81	77	84	86	88	80	93	51
	R	23	43	37	25	57	48	48	58	44	69	60	36	47	78	62
1982	F	59	82	76	97	90	80	87	72	73	81	83	87	90	88	91
	R	24	44	28	83	47	32	44	48	39	25	51	37	44	89	86
1981	F	42	76	70	90	92	87	87	72	NA	96	81	85	89	94	50
	R	22	28	28	65	46	36	35	41	NA	82	43	35	32	67	49
1980	F	63	72	76	98	92	92	83	66	NA	81	88	85	92	96	60
	R	24	42	42	100	56	50	35	43	NA	75	48	37	60	43	51
1979	F	65	89	74	93	82	90	82	55	76	99	92	87	91	93	74
	R	31	73	28	52	53	51	50	27	58	--	64	33	39	65	84
1978	F	62	73	81	94	85	90	NA	66	78	100	88	91	NA	NA	73
	R	25	71	35	57	43	42	NA	29	56	--	29	50	NA	NA	42
1977	F	66	NA	81	86	92	90	89	76	78	99	93	90	91	93	61
	R	25	NA	31	68	60	60	46	36	55	50	45	36	45	44	61
1976	F	67	95	82	81	90	84	92	73	78	96	92	89	94	90	75
	R	25	81	33	46	50	38	52	26	57	100	48	50	47	89	27
1975	F	70	83	78	87	89	82	91	81	78	83	97	85	94	93	83
	R	29	71	41	56	55	31	60	42	57	--	46	16	49	40	33
1974	F	71	85	77	88	86	82	94	86	77	100	91	94	92	94	83
	R	37	60	43	76	59	46	52	66	49	--	25	52	53	100	64
1973	F	63	75	76	89	85	69	98	82	78	100	96	95	94	99	83
	R	34	62	31	57	69	15	64	42	49	--	84	50	61	88	4
1972	F	67	70	82	91	79	74	94	90	78	100	86	98	93	73	84
	R	33	17	51	50	63	45	57	64	44	--	70	92	65	33	84
1971	F	66	85	75	92	81	75	92	82	78	100	77	92	92	99	84
	R	35	61	53	43	62	46	30	45	45	--	69	74	57	100	3
1970	F	66	86	63	87	76	70	90	87	78	100	75	85	90	95	9
	R	38	52	70	30	66	28	49	46	54	--	67	63	66	75	5

Table 18. Bar Examination Results for First Takers and
Repeaters, 1931–85 (continued)

Year		CA	CT	DC	HI	IL	MA	MI	NJ	NY	ND	OH	PA	TX	UT	VT
1969	F	62	84	61	90	81	77	91	80	76	100	88	81	88	92	88
	R	36	60	49	70	65	37	66	37	56	75	80	62	57	100	100
1968	F	60	79	56	98	76	67	82	74	77	92	84	83	93	89	94
	R	35	61	55	58	68	40	60	29	52	--	60	59	78	100	67
1967	F	58	90	72	83	75	64	88	77	75	90	91	76	92	96	89
	R	28	33	60	42	60	32	56	38	54	--	61	53	78	100	100
1966	F	61	88	62	85	77	60	84	66	73	100	89	81	89	94	90
	R	30	80	69	38	62	37	64	35	53	100	74	46	69	38	100
1965	F	68	62	67	65	72	63	86	68	71	100	78	85	91	94	100
	R	44	58	43	25	48	32	52	30	52	--	66	85	66	50	50
1964	F	60	90	70	69	80	65	90	67	69	94	90	72	89	95	88
	R	33	48	60	11	55	35	58	38	50	--	60	71	74	100	100
1963	F	63	67	69	70	77	67	81	60	67	98	77	69	87	96	83
	R	29	62	52	29	64	32	48	40	48	--	62	61	64	67	--
1962	F	71	89	59	58	74	71	81	61	65	100	88	69	92	94	88
	R	45	55	45	45	60	37	49	34	43	100	54	34	66	25	0
1961	F	62	84	58	54	71	70	87	54	63	92	88	69	88	91	100
	R	41	41	41	29	43	31	46	37	44	--	81	73	54	100	--
1960	F	62	86	64	51	76	66	84	62	57	100	83	64	NA	88	92
	R	35	60	40	--	56	30	52	45	44	100	74	54	NA	100	0
1959	F	60	81	52	72	69	64	84	64	55	98	69	65	NA	89	100
	R	33	62	38	56	49	41	56	48	43	--	60	60	NA	25	--
1958	F	61	76	55		77	64	81	59	54	100	79	56	NA	89	92
	R	34	50	48		53	21	48	44	44	--	53	58	NA	80	0
1957	F	61	66	53		73	73	78	64	53	100	77	58	NA	87	87
	R	40	45	43		50	33	45	39	41	--	56	41	NA	100	0
1956	F	61	81	60		69	63	83	63	60	100	65	60	NA	94	100
	R	42	64	47		43	32	52	39	36	--	46	41	NA	67	25
1955	F	64	75	64		71	67	77	81	57	96	NA	56	NA	92	63
	R	42	41	48		41	46	53	58	36	100	NA	39	NA	67	100

Table 18. Bar Examination for First Takers and
Repeaters, 1931–85 (continued)

Year		CA	CT	DC	IL	MA	MI	NJ	NY	ND	OH	PA	TX	UT	VT
1954	F	60	81	60	70	57	73	68	56	73	NA	54	85	89	85
	R	35	59	42	47	19	26	49	35	--	NA	51	61	100	100
1953	F	67	57	62	70	59	80	55	56	100	NA	55	NA	96	79
	R	49	15	44	57	24	42	35	51	100	NA	46	NA	64	--
1952	F	60	73	58	69	49	69	68	56	91	NA	62	NA	90	91
	R	52	59	32	58	26	35	46	31	67	NA	50	NA	50	0
1951	F	44	68	68	70	43	74	49	57	95	NA	57	NA	81	94
	R	31	62	51	60	34	54	33	41	100	NA	44	NA	80	67
1950	F	54	74	69	67	28	NA	51	53	70	NA	69	NA	74	83
	R	34	70	59	56	38	NA	27	44	100	NA	51	NA	92	50
1949	F	62	84	61	66	54	NA	50	52	98	NA	63	NA	76	89
	R	39	77	51	51	29	NA	34	43	--	NA	47	NA	68	67
1948	F	68	68	67	69	48	NA	56	54	97	NA	64	NA	70	76
	R	31	54	34	39	34	NA	15	35	--	NA	33	NA	46	100
1943	F	86	65	48	72	54	83	54	64	100	93	63	60	61	75
	R	19	71	35	35	47	47	17	47	--	48	60	78	66	--
1942	F	60	61	NA	76	41	81	62	67	100	93	62	42	80	100
	R	31	47	NA	41	36	51	29	50	--	71	63	80	57	100
1941	F	56	54	NA	78	29	79	68	54	94	85	63	32	54	85
	R	26	44	NA	41	23	42	30	44	--	54	52	75	100	100
1940	F	59	73	NA	75	31	67	65	53	100	78	61	26	62	78
	R	37	31	NA	39	25	41	45	41	--	52	61	68	43	67
1939	F	47	60	NA	80	35	69	63	52	100	70	44	39	75	100
	R	16	41	NA	55	34	31	34	42	--	48	46	55	78	--
1938	F	57	46	NA	67	46	74	47	46	100	62	58	24	64	100
	R	32	29	NA	47	28	45	26	43	--	33	45	48	14	0
1937	F	45	36	NA	61	47	67	57	51	100	70	44	22	73	100
	R	26	42	NA	39	36	42	27	42	--	50	36	36	71	100
1936	F	57	70	NA	55	46	68	46	47	94	63	47	8	75	86
	R	43	67	NA	28	31	35	35	42	100	40	36	38	29	100

Table 18. Bar Examination Results for First Takers and
           Repeaters, 1931–85 (continued)

Year		CA	CT	IL	MA	MI	NJ	NY	ND	OH	PA	TX	UT	VT
1935	F	52	80	64	42	75	51	49	100	73	53	5	67	56
	R	30	26	35	24	43	27	44	100	60	42	43	42	100
1934	F	47	66	59	46	73	47	47	84	78	55	3	58	100
	R	23	46	42	39	45	29	40	100	56	45	39	31	100
1933	F	49	54	54	39	NA	NA	42	68	NA	47	NA	46	73
	R	19	36	45	24	NA	NA	41	--	NA	31	NA	40	--
1932	F	56	50	63	32	NA	NA	41	100	NA	60	19	35	NA
	R	22	23	35	19	NA	NA	39	--	NA	46	40	10	NA
1931	F	36	58	65	18	NA	NA	40	100	76	44	NA	50	NA
	R	11	19	31	19	NA	NA	31	--	37	52	NA	0	NA

Source: Bar Examiner

Table 19. Relationship Between Prelegal Education and Bar Examination
Results in California, 1930, 1932, 1936-41

Preparation	1930			August 1932			1936-41		
	Percentage of Takers	Percentage of Passers	Pass Rate (%)	Percentage of Takers	Percentage of Passers	Pass Rate (%)	Percentage of Takers	Percentage of Passers	Pass Rate (%)
High School									
none	5.7	1.7	12	2.1	0	0	3.1[a]	0.7[a]	12[a]
2 years	4	2.1	22	14	7.2	29			
3 years									
2-4 years graduate	33	22	29	19	12	34	8.6	4.1	25
College									
1-2 years	11	9.2	34	15	17	61	16	12	40
3-4 years	47	64	57	9.7	11	61	10	9	46
degree				40	53	73	60	75	67
	N=1251	N=521		N=677	N=371		N=3238	N=1726	

Note: a. Not a high school graduate

Sources: Committee of Bar Examiners (1930: 351-52); State Bar of California (1932: 293-95);
McClain et al. (1949: 40)

Table 20a. California Bar Examination, 1932-87:

First Takers/Repeaters and Legal Education: Number Passing/Percentage Passing

Year/Month	Total	First Takers	Second Takers	Third or More Takers	California ABA	California Other	Out-of-State ABA	Corresp. Schools	Law Office Study	Private Study
1932/Feb.	105/20	70/36	27/16	8/5	45/62		21/47	4/12	2/11	1/11
1933/Feb.	216/42	123/56	86/69	113/68	36/97		30/83	8/24	7/32	3/27
1933/Aug.	263/32	243/46	15/12	6/3	122/72		25/48	2/5	5/20	0/0
1934/Feb.	159/28	49/33	86/40	24/12	40/57	82/24	22/51	9/18	1/6	1/6
1934/Aug.	249/42	237/51		12/9	137/70	85/30	21/39	2/7	1/17	1/11
1935/Feb.	146/35	45/35	77/42	24/23	42/66	69/29	20/51	5/18	2/14	0/0
1935/Sept.	267/46	232/57	18/25	17/17	137/58	104/43	16/43	4/15	2/13	1/8
1936/March	187/48	64/43	87/58	36/41	78/66	61/37	36/84	3/12	3/21	1/12
1936/Sept.	295/54	259/63	18/26	18/28	162/69	89/44	26/59	2/7	3/33	8/50
1937/March	114/30	49/34	50/36	15/16	49/46	30/19	27/53	4/13	1/8	1/11
1937/Sept.	261/47	225/56	20/25	16/20	143/66	84/37	24/38	4/16	4/36	0/0
1938/March	136/39	55/40	66/46	15/18	49/56	49/32	32/58	1/4	1/25	3/38
1938/Sept.	307/53	270/63	17/21	20/22	177/77	90/40	32/50	3/14	0/0	3/21
1939/March	87/28	41/35	37/31	9/13	32/46	37/29	13/21	1/6	2/17	0/0
1939/Oct.	254/35	227/50	13/12	14/9	178/59	37/18	32/31	3/7	1/8	0/0
1940/Oct.	417/50	297/59	81/52	39/22	261/74	86/34	55/42	4/12	1/7	5/20
1941/Oct.	334/45	261/56	48/37	25/17	227/75	50/24	40/45	1/3	1/12	4/21
1942/Sept.	209/46	145/60	37/39	27/24	110/70	54/36	22/50	2/9	1/17	0/0
1943/Oct.	118/34	86/48	15/28	17/15	65/61	22/22	9/29	3/12	2/29	1/11
1944/Oct.	141/40	91/51	28/44	22/20	65/87	32/56	8/57	1/5	1/17	1/10
1945/Oct.	154/35	123/51	16/22	15/12	66/64	24/26	9/29	0/0	0/0	0/0
1946/April	99/27	53/37	27/27	19/16	23/40	12/17	8/36	0/0	0/0	0/0
1946/Oct.	176/37	107/45	36/42	33/22	54/55	25/31	37/32	3/19	0/0	2/33
1947/April	137/40	78/56	29/32	30/27	52/67	9/22	20/59	1/12	0/0	0/0
1947/Oct.	243/48	192/62	12/24	39/26	122/80	25/34	21/43	1/8	1/20	1/12
1948/April	221/57	192/69	17/29	12/23	148/84	5/33	35/48	0/0	0/0	1/25
1948/Oct.	475/63	433/68	25/39	17/30	318/78	15/30	95/58	4/80	0/0	0/0
1949/April	414/61	313/68	90/52	11/23	281/79	11/26	84/55	0/0	1/33	
1949/Oct.	490/53	431/58	33/30	26/32	341/67	46/39	75/50	0/0	1/25	
1950/April	193/38	89/43	93/41	11/14	119/54	27/29	29/33	0/0	0/0	
1950/Oct.	519/53	457/57	27/30	35/37	392/69	57/33	51/41	0/0	1/50	
1951/April	260/44	131/42	104/45	25/44	139/58	42/31	35/41	1/50	1/100	
1951/Oct.	391/38	349/45	27/18	15/14	307/53	35/18	29/28	0/0	0/0	
1952/April	463/61	/59			/87	/48	/46			
1952/Oct.	507/53	/61			/76	/38	/33			
1953/April	433/63	196/71	146/57	91/59	211/82	88/50	45/61	0/0	0/0	
1953/Oct.	509/58	449/66	27/32	33/30	336/76	64/41	40/45	1/33	1/50	
1954/Spring	323/47	143/53	112/51	68/36	140/80	71/68	30/48	1/12	0/0	
1954/Fall	458/51	413/63	22/24	23/16	329/72	45/29	31/39	1/33	2/100	
1955/Spring	348/57	133/59	129/59	86/51	136/79	84/53	29/47	1/20	1/25	
1955/Fall	466/54	430/66	17/20	19/16	325/76	60/36	32/40	2/67	1/20	
1956/Spring	301/57	129/59	111/61	61/48	115/84	73/48	26/60	2/50	2/40	
1956/Fall	432/52	400/61	23/23	9/12	317/76	26/19	38/58	0/0	1/100	
1957/Spring	312/53	129/56	129/58	54/41	125/82	57/39	34/67	3/38	0/0	
1957/Fall	482/54	451/63	18/23	13/13	371/76	24/19	34/53			
1958/Spring	313/46	144/50	127/49	42/29	119/70	48/33	33/47	1/14	0/0	
1958/Fall	614/56	572/65	19/21	23/19	464/78	37/22	51/47	3/33	0/0	
1959/Spring	281/44	117/47	127/47	37/30	116/72	44/27	41/55			
1959/Fall	643/55	595/64	24/20	24/20	479/73	46/27	67/58	0/0	0/0	
1960/Spring	346/40	118/44	152/50	76/26	172/72	48/22	43/43	3/15	0/0	
1960/Fall	774/56	660/67	53/36	61/25	515/77	70/27	90/69	6/22	0/0	
1961/Spring	437/56	136/58	178/63	123/47	162/79	95/46	52/60	10/42	0/0	
1961/Fall	702/52	641/63	30/26	31/14	488/70	60/25	73/60			
1962/Spring	451/55	144/59	207/66	100/38	182/76	93/44	56/72	11/31	1/100	
1962/Fall	908/63	800/73	44/40	64/28	588/78	98/40	112/75	4/16	1/100	
1963/Spring	304/39	134/50	117/44	53/22	146/65	36/20	37/52			
1963/Fall	838/55	749/66	36/30	53/20	576/70	78/28	100/66	9/32	1/100	
1964/Spring	400/45	138/55	194/57	68/24	186/68	77/31	52/58	9/35	0/0	
1964/Fall	899/51	816/61	42/34	41/14	623/64	62/23	116/62	6/25	0/0	
1965/Spring	602/57	180/63	306/71	116/35	302/76	104/43	58/60	7/21	0/0	
1965/Fall	1103/60	1009/69	43/35	51/19	776/76	105/31	131/66	7/18	0/0	
1966/Spring	412/42	/53			/66	/33	/67			
1966/Fall	1184/53	1069/63	44/26	71/18	843/67	109/25	153/68	4/10	2/67	

Table 20a. California Bar Examination, 1932-87:
First Takers/Repeaters and Legal Education: Number Passing/Percentage Passing (continued)

Year/Month	Total	First Takers	Second Takers	Third or More Takers	California ABA	California Other	Out-of-State ABA	Corresp. Schools	Law Office Study	Private Study
1967/Spring	454/37	145/45	250/48	59/16	225/55	79/21	55/53	8/19		0/0
1967/Fall	1224/49	1094/60	41/24	89/18	891/64	105/21	147/60	8/15		0/0
1968/Spring	570/41	150/44	329/55	91/19	293/61	119/27	59/48	8/17		0/0
1968/Fall	1541/53	1320/63	78/36	143/26	970/70	200/41	219/68	6/9		0/0
1969/Spring	660/44	178/49	361/56	121/24	296/66	137/28	84/49	17/26		0/0
1969/Fall	1675/55	1461/63	82/39	132/24	1069/72	198/37	231/66	11/18		2/67
1970/Spring	867/51	303/61	430/59	134/27	364/80	190/43	113/69	16/28		0/2
1970/Fall	1974/56	1586/67	71/33	137/22	1167/66	177/34	252/71	9/18		0/0
1971/Spring	708/41	272/53	336/50	100/18	367/48	78/23	81/52	7/11		0/0
1971/Fall	2130/59	1820/68	105/43	205/31	1542/68	179/35	228/70	15/25		0/0
1972/Spring	826/48	277/59	398/56	151/27	448/55	124/31	83/58	12/21		1/100
1972/Fall	2213/57	2071/68	60/27	82/13	1638/72	156/43	253/67	11/20		1/33
1973/Spring	1001/50	400/64	446/55	155/27	507/54	182/33	107/58	9/18		0/0
1973/Fall	2519/55	2325/64	79/30	115/17	1916/64	185/25	275/64	11/22		1/50
1974/Spring	1274/51	437/60	630/57	207/32	710/59	241/37	128/60	9/20		0/0
1974/Fall	3317/62	3050/73	106/31	161/19	2467/72	337/34	313/72	17/35		0/0
1975/Spring	1136/43	522/59	447/46	167/21	574/50	256/31	122/55	10/23		0/0
1975/Fall	3550/61	3225/72	115/34	180/18	2523/71	493/39	335/69	11/24		2/40
1976/Spring	1176/38	636/54	434/41	106/12	547/43	309/29	121/51	9/20		2/33
1976/Fall	4002/59	3644/70	130/26	228/21	2663/72	807/41	365/70	7/15		4/40
1977/Spring	1493/44	746/63	545/44	202/20	634/51	489/35	133/58	7/16		1/20
1977/Fall	3959/54	3690/67	108/21	161/12	2442/66	489/35	357/65	14/25		3/30
1978/Spring	1622/38	735/53	671/44	216/16	683/47	587/31		9/19		0/0
1978/Fall	3906/51	3561/64	115/20	230/15	2537/64	498/32	287/30	4/10		6/43
1982/Spring	1492/31	613/45	540/36	339/18	631/36	413/21	134/44	9/19		1/12
1982/Fall	3624/48	2956/63	211/28	457/21	2450/60	502/24	417/63	3/7		0/0
1983/Spring	1332/28	556/42	500/33	276/14	662/33	270/15	123/38	6/12		3/30
1983/Fall	3773/49	3112/64	214/29	447/21	2595/61	411/21	426/65	4/8		3/21
1984/Spring	1202/30	552/45	449/33	231/15	570/35	237/16	127/47	7/13		0/0
1984/Fall	3074/42	2707/56	123/19	244/13	2192/52	247/15	387/56	6/12		1/10
1985/Spring	1555/33	616/48	718/41	221/14	826/40	250/17	139/43	1/2		1/11
1985/Fall	3484/46	2815/57	193/30	476/22	2256/54	396/23	475/57	7/13		2/12
1986/Spring	1332/28	551/44	589/34	192/11	613/32	200/14	174/45	1/2		4/21
1986/Fall	3466/44	2835/59	187/26	444/19	2243/55	377/21	498/53	2/4		5/23
1987/Fall	3780/50	3212/65	178/28	390/20	2442/62	373/23	598/61	5/9		1/6

Table 20b. California Bar Examination, 1932-87:
Gender and Race: Number Passing/Percentage Passing/Percentage of Passers

Year/Month	Men	Women	White	Black	Hispanic	Asian	Other
1978/Fall	2811/50/72	1095/54/28	3630/56/93	39/13/1	90/24/2	105/42/3	42/23/1
1982/Spring	973/30/65	519/34/35	1291/35/87	49/13/3	83/24/6	43/24/3	26/19/2
1982/Fall	2340/47/65	1284/49/35	3252/53/90	88/18/2	121/25/3	123/42/3	38/20/1
1983/Spring	866/27/65	466/29/35	1143/31/86	50/12/4	63/17/5	59/28/4	17/12/1
1983/Fall	2314/47/61	1459/53/39	3415/55/91	79/16/2	120/25/3	131/40/3	28/15/1
1984/Spring[a]	429/23/64	246/25/36	548/27/81	42/14/6	43/16/6	27/17/4	15/13/2
1984/Fall	1839/41/61	1181/43/39	2767/48/92	54/12/2	89/18/3	110/31/4	19/12/1
1985/Spring	926/32/60	614/35/40	1318/38/86	56/15/4	69/20/4	67/28/4	20/14/1
1985/Fall	2106/45/61	1315/46/39	3111/51/90	68/14/2	124/24/4	123/36/4	33/18/1
1986/Spring	820/28/62	506/29/38	1147/33/87	42/11/3	68/17/5	54/23/4	14/9/1
1986/Fall	2086/45/61	1351/44/39	3070/51/89	86/16/3	112/20/3	133/36/4	35/19/1
1987/Fall	2179/49/58	1566/52/42	3309/56/88	81/17/2	151/29/4	155/45/4	50/24/1
Percentage of passers 1982-87	62	38	89	3	4	4	1

Note: a. Repeaters only

Sources: California State Bar Journal; Committee of Bar
Examiners, State Bar of California, unpublished reports

Table 21. Number of Law Schools, Enrollments, and Bar Admissions, 1840-1986

	Law School Enrollment					No. of law schools				Bar Admissions		
Year	Total[a]	Annual percentage change	ABA approved	Un-approved[a]	Unapproved as % of total	ABA approved	unapproved[b]	Total	Enrollment: as % of profession	Total[b] new	Annual percentage change	Admissions as % of profession
1840	345											
1850	400											
1860	1,200											
1870	1,653											
1878	3,012							31	3			
1879	3,019	0.2						39				
1880	3,134	3.8						43				
1881	3,227	3.0						41(51)				
1882-83	3,079	-4.6						41				
1883-84	2,686	-12.8						38				
1884-85	2,744	2.2						34				
1885-86	3,054	11.3						39				
1886-87	3,185	4.3						40				
1887-88	3,667	15.1						46				
1888-89	3,906	6.5						47				
1889-90	3,517	-10.0						50				
1889	4,486	27.6						45				
1890	4,518	0.7						61				
1895								67	5			
1899	12,408 / 12,384											
1900	12,516							102	11	2,750		2.5
1904	15,000							108				
1909	19,498							116(124)	17	4,125		3.6
1910	19,567							137				
1915-16	22,993											
1919	24,503							143	17	6,004		4.9
1920	20,992											
1920-21	27,313											
1921	27,100					31	117	148		5,777	-4	
1922	32,111					38	109	147		7,058	22	
1923	36,211	13				48				7,106	1	
1924	39,782 / 36,639	1				55				7,846	10	
1925	42,743 / 38,412	5	15,384	31,103		64				8,211	5	
1926	44,273 / 42,042	9			67					9,576	17	
1927	44,341	5				64	112	176		10,026	5	
1928	42,323	-5				66	99	165		10,685	7	
1929	43,876	4				71	107	178		10,397	-3	
1930	41,426 / 39,013	-11				75	105	182	24	10,012	-4	6.2

Table 21. Number of Law Schools, Enrollments, and Bar Admissions, 1840–1986 (continued)

	Law School Enrollment						No. of law schools				Bar Admissions		
Year	Total[a]	Annual percentage change	ABA approved	Annual percentage change	Un-approved[a]	Unapproved as % of total	ABA approved	unapproved[b]	Total	Enrollment as % of profession	Total new	Annual percentage change	Admissions as % of profession
1931	39,868	2	17,483		21,934	56	81	101	182		9,676	-7	
1932	37,259	-7					82	103	185		9,340	-3	
1933	37,057	-1					84	106	190		9,258	-1	
1934	37,872	2					84	109	193		9,099	-2	
1935	41,418	9	20,430		21,490	51	88	107	195		8,971	-1	
1936	40,529	-2	22,094	8.1	18,124	45	94	96	190		8,591	-4	
1937	38,056	-6	24,029	8.8	15,226	39	97	88	185		8,934	4	
1938	37,406[d]	-2	23,827	-0.8	13,579	36	101	79	180		8,797	-2	
	35,755	-6											
1939	34,539[d]	-8	22,661[d]	-4.9	11,878[d]	34	102	78	180		8,531	-3	
	33,508	-6	25,578	7.3	8,961								
1940	30,830	-11 / -8	24,047	+6.1 / -6.0	5,989		108	68	176	17	7,942	-7	4.4
1941	21,943e	-29	17,274[e]	-28.2	4,669	21	108	68	176		7,706	-3	
	22,033	-29	18,394	-23.5									
1942	17,671[c]	-20	13,768[c]	-20.3	3,903[c]	22	109	50	159		6,591	-14	
	9,839	-55	7,871	-57.2	2,148								
1943	6,332[d]	-64	4,797[d]	-65.2	1,535[d]	24	111	48	159		2,973	-55	
	6,428	-35	4,803	-39.0	1,625								
1944	7,465	18 / 16	5,619	17.1 / 17.0	1,874		112	55	167		1,853	-38	
1945	10,752	44	9,466	68.5	2,134		114	54	168		2,142	16	
1946	38,331	257	33,904	258.2	5,871		120	47	167		4,815	125	
1947	51,015	33	43,719	28.9	8,674 / 7,296	14	124	40	164		6,782	41	
1948	56,914	12	46,647	6.7	10,267	18	126	42	166		11,299	67	
1949	57,759	1	46,645	0	11,114	19	127	41	167		13,344	18	6.4
1950	53,025	-8	43,685	-6.3	9,340	18	128	39	166	25	13,641	2	5.9
1951	47,610	-10	39,626	-9.3	7,984	17	129	39	166		13,141	-4	
1952	41,276	-13	35,634	-10.1	5,642	14	129	38	166		11,900	-9	
1953	39,339	-4	34,423	-3.4	4,916	12	130	30	160		10,976	-8	
1954	39,565	1	35,015	1.7	4,550	11	132	31	159		9,928	-10	4.1
1955	40,347	2	35,792	2.2	4,555	11	134	29	159		9,587	-3	
1956	41,888	4	37,949	6.0	3,939	9	135	27			9,450	-1	
1957	42,271	1	38,883	2.5	3,438	8					9,592	2	3.6
1958	42,645	1	39,144	0.7	3,502	8					10,465	9	
1959	43,507	2	39,631	1.2	3,876	9					10,744	3	
1960	43,695	0.4	40,381	1.9	3,314	7				15	10,505	-2	3.6
1961	45,012	3	41,499	2.8	3,513	8					10,729	2	
1962	48,663	8	44,805	8.0	3,858	8					10,784	1	
1963	54,433	12	49,552	10.6	4,881	9				18	10,788	0	3.6

Table 21. Number of Law Schools, Enrollments, and Bar Admissions, 1840-1986 (continued)

	Law School Enrollment						No. of law schools			Enrollment as % of profession	Bar Admissions		
Year	Total[a]	Annual percentage change	ABA approved	Annual percentage change	Un-approved[a]	Unapproved as % of total	ABA approved	unapproved[b]	Total		Total new	Annual percentage change	Admissions as % of profession
1964	59,813	10	54,625	10.2	5,548	9	135				12,023	11	
1965	65,057	9	59,744	9.4	5,313	8	136				13,109	9	
1966	68,121	5	62,556	4.7	5,565	8	135			22	14,637	12	5.0
1967	70,332	3	64,406	3.0	5,926	8	136				16,007	9	
1968	68,562	-2	62,779	-2.5	5,783	8	138				17,764	11	
1969	72,032	5	68,386	8.9	3,646	5	144				19,123	8	
1970	86,028	19	82,041	20.0	3,987	5	146			24	17,922	-7	
1971	95,943	12	93,118	13.5	2,825	3	147				20,510	14	7.0
1972	105,245	10	101,664	9.2	3,581	3	149	40	189	29	25,086	22	
1973	114,800	9	106,102	4.4	8,698	8	151	47	198		30,707	22	
1974	116,517	1	110,713	4.3	5,804	5	154	43	197		33,358	9	
1975	122,542	5	116,991	5.7	5,551	5	164	65	229		34,930	5	8.1
1976	125,010	2	117,451	0.4	7,559	6	163	62	225	27	35,741	2	
1977	126,085	1	118,357	0.9	7,528	6	168	69	237		37,302	4	
1978	126,937	1	121,506	2.6	5,331	4	168	64	232		39,086	5	
1979	126,915	0	122,360	1.0	4,055	3	169	58	227		42,756	9	
1980	128,983	2	125,397	2.1	3,586	3	171	57	228	24[f]	41,997	-2	7.7[f]
1981	129,739	1	127,312	1.5	2,427	2	172	46	218	23[f]	42,382	1	7.4[f]
1982	129,124	0	127,328	0.4	1,296	1	172	48	220	22[f]	42,905	1	7.2[f]
1983	128,742	-1	127,195	-0.5	1,547	1	173	46	219	21[f]	41,684	-3	6.7[f]
1984	N.A.	N.A.	125,698	-1.1	N.A.	N.A.	174	48	222		42,630	2	6.6[f]
1985	N.A.	N.A.	124,146	-1.2	N.A.		175				42,450		
1986	N.A.	N.A.	123,277	-0.7	N.A.		174						

Notes:
a. Enrollment figures for unaccredited law schools incomplete
b. Excludes admission of out-of-state attorneys on motion
c. Spring 1942
d. May be inflated because it includes graduate and other studies
e. Second figure from Committee on Trend of Bar Admissions, 1942
f. Size of profession estimated

Sources: Reed (1921: 442; 1928: 529); Rutherford (1937: 66-67); Carnegie Foundation (1915; 1917); Woodworth (1973: 497-500); Leary & Douty (1958); ABA Committee on Legal Education (1895: 315); 1 American Law School Review 265 (1904); Committee (1891: Appendix B); Review of Legal Education; Bar Examiner; Hobson (1986: 108-09).

Table 22. Size of Profession and Population, 1850-1984

	Lawyers			Population		Population per Lawyer		
Year	Number	Decennial % change	Annualized % change	Number	Decennial % change	Ratio	Decennial % change	Annualized % change
1850	23,939[b]			23,191,876		969		
1860	34,839[b]	46		31,443,321	35.6	903	-6.8	
1870	40,736[b]	17		39,818,449	26.6	947	+4.9	
1880	60,626	49		50,155,783	26.0	827	-12.7	
1890	85,224	41		62,947,714	25.5	739	-10.6	
1900	109,140	28		75,994,575	20.7	696	-15.8	
1910	114,704	5		91,972,266	21.0	802	+15.2	
1920	122,519	7		105,710,620	14.9	863	+7.6	
1930	160,605	31		122,775,046	16.1	764	-11.5	
1940	179,567	12		131,669,275	7.2	733	-4.1	
1948	169,489		-0.7					
1950	212,605	18	12.7	150,697,361	14.5	709	-3.3	
1951	221,605		4.2			696		-1.8
1954	241,514		3.0			672		-1.1
1957	262,320		2.9			653		-0.9
1960	285,933	35	3.0	178,464,236	18.4	632	-10.9	-1.1
1963	296,069		3.5			637		+0.3
1967	316,856		1.8			621		-0.6
1970	355,242	24	4.0	203,302,031	13.4	572	-9.5	-2.6
1972	358,920		5.2					
1977	462,000		5.7					
1980	542,205	53	5.8	226,545,805	11.4	418	-26.9	-1.7
1981[a]	569,000		4.9			403		-3.6
1982[a]	595,107		4.6			390		-3.2
1983[a]	622,000		4.5			377		-3.3
1984[a]	649,000		4.3			364		-3.4

Notes: a.   Estimates
          b.   Includes abstractors, notaries, and justices of the peace

Sources: Segal & Fei (1953: 114); Blaustein (1950: 370); Sikes et al.
(1972: 6); York & Hale (1973: 1 n.3); Schwartz (1980: 1270 n.1);
Curran (1985)

Table 23. Lawyers and Other Professions and Subordinate Occupations, 1850-1980

	Legal Occupations		Medical Occupations				Religious Occupations				
Year	Lawyers	Abstractors, notaries, and justices of the peace	Physicians and surgeons	Healers	Dentists	Trained nurses	Clergy	Religious, charity, and welfare workers	Social workers[c]	Engineers	Population
1850 Number	23,939		40,765[a]				26,842				23,191,876
1860 Number	34,839		55,159[a]				37,529				31,443,321
% change	46		35				40				35.6
1870 Number	40,736		62,448[a]				43,874				39,818,449
% change	17		13				17				26.6
1880 Number	60,626	3,511	85,671				54,698				50,155,783
% change			37				47				26
1890 Number	85,224	4,406	104,805				88,203				62,947,714
% change	40	25	22				36				25.5
1900 Number	109,140	5,320	132,007[a]				111,638				75,994,575
% change	28	21	26				27				20.7
1910 Number	114,704	7,445	151,132	6,834	39,997	82,327	118,018	15,970		88,755	91,972,266
% change	5	40									21.0
1920 Number	122,519	10,071	150,007	14,774	56,152	149,128	127,270	41,078		136,121	105,710,620
% change	6.8	35.3	-0.7	116.2	40.4	81.1	7.8	157.2		53.3	14.9
1930 Number	160,605	11,756	159,920[b]	17,640	71,055	294,189	148,848	31,290	31,241	226,249	122,775,046
% change	31.1	16.7	6.6	19.4	26.5	97.3	17.0	-23.8		66.2	16.1
1940 Number	177,643		170,656[b]	19,555	70,121	355,786	136,597	34,672	69,677	245,288	131,669,275
% change	10.6		6.7	10.9	-1.3	20.9	-8.2	10.8	123.0	8.4	7.2
1950 Number	180,461		206,543[b]		72,310	398,534	160,694	41,431	75,487	518,781	150,697,361
% change	1.6		21.0		3.7	12.0	17.6	19.5	8.3	111.5	14.5
1960 Number	209,684		234,388[b]		87,110	590,568	200,776	57,370	96,395	869,716	178,464,236
% change	16.2		13.5		19.6	48.2	24.9	38.5	27.7	67.6	18.4
1970 Number	277,695		280,557		92,776	848,182	222,478	35,450	222,493	1,256,935	203,302,031
% change	32.4		19.7		6.5	43.6	10.8	-38.2	130.8	44.5	13.4
1980 Number	524,806		431,418		124,772	1,266,801	280,965	48,830	442,970	1,382,095	226,545,805
% change	89.0		53.8		34.5	49.4	26.3	37.7	99.1	10.0	11.4

Notes: a.   Includes healers
b.   Includes osteopaths (1930: 6117; 1940: 6007; 1950: 14,596; 1960: 4C81)
c.   Social workers categorized separately for the first time in 1930

Sources: 1930 Census: vol. 5--Population: Table 3; 340 Census: vol. 3--Population, Pt. I--U.S. Summary: Table 58; 1950 Census: vol. 2--Characteristics of the Population, Pt. 1--U.S. Summary: Table 124; 1960 Census: Population: Subject Reports: Occupational Characteristics: Table 1; 1970 Census: Population: Subject Reports: Occupational Characteristics: Table 1; 1980 Census: Population: Subject Reports: vol. 2--Occupations by Industry: Table 4; Reed (1921: 422); Review of Legal Education (1923: 43-45)

Table 24. Number of Private Practitioners, 1929-47

Year	Number
1929	104,000
1930	108,000
1931	113,000
1932	114,000
1933	116,000
1934	119,000
1935	120,000
1936	122,000
1937	124,000
1938	126,000
1939	128,000
1940	128,000
1941	117,000
1942	107,000
1943	107,000
1944	110,000
1945	130,000
1946	135,000
1947	140,000

Source: Weinfeld (1949: 19)

Table 25. Age Distribution of Lawyers, Selected Jurisdictions, 1930-80 (percent)

1930[a]

Age	U.S	N.Y. State
≤24	4.5	8.0
25-34	27.9	31.5
35-44	24.1	22.3
45-54	20.5	18.5
55-64	14.3	10.7
65-74	6.7	4.4
≥75	1.8	1.1

1934[b]

Years of experience	New York county
≤4	28.3
5-10	30.8
11-16	11.6
17-23	10.1
24-34	12.8
≥35	6.5

1939[i]

Age	Michigan
≤29	12.8
30-39	39.5
40-49	22.8
50-59	14.7
60-69	8.0
70-79	2.0
80-89	0.3

1939[j]

Years of experience	Michigan
≤4	14.6
5-9	21.0
10-19	35.0
≥20	28.0
N.A.	1.4

1941[c]

Age	U.S.
≤29	3.8
30-34	14.7
35-39	19.2
40-44	13.9
45-49	10.4
50-54	11.6
55-59	8.5
60-64	8.1
≥65	10.3

1947[d]

Age	U.S.
≤29	2.9
30-34	14.9
35-39	18.9
40-44	18.7
45-49	11.9
50-54	9.3
55-59	7.6
60-64	5.7
≥65	10.3

1948[e]

Age	U.S.
<34	11.6
34-43	31.2
44-53	25.3
54-63	16.7
64-73	10.5
>73	4.7

1951[f]

Age	U.S.
<37	24.8
37-46	28.8
47-56	21.9
57-66	13.8
67-76	7.8
>76	3.0

1954[g]

Age	U.S.
≤29	5.7
30-34	15.5
35-39	14.0
40-44	14.6
45-49	15.5
50-54	12.0
55-59	7.2
60-64	6.1
≥65	9.4

1960[h]

Years of experience	California
<1	5
1-5	23
6-10	23
11-20	18
21-30	15
31-40	9
≥41	4
N.A.	3

1960[i]

Age	U.S.
≤35	23.6
36-45	25.1
46-55	23.7
56-65	15.7
≥66	11.9

1970[i]

Age	U.S.
≤35	26.5
36-45	24.6
46-55	19.5
56-65	16.3
≥66	13.1

1980[i]

Age	All U.S.	Male	Female
≤29	14.9	13.2	34.9
30-34	20.6	19.9	18.0
35-39	14.9	15.1	12.8
40-44	9.1	9.4	5.9
45-49	8.2	8.6	4.1
50-54	7.7	8.1	3.5
55-59	6.7	7.0	2.9
60-64	5.0	5.3	2.3
65-69	4.4	4.6	2.0
70-74	4.1	4.3	1.7
75-79	2.5	2.6	1.1
≥80	2.0	2.1	0.9

Sources:
a. New York County Lawyers' Association (1936: 46)
b. Ibid. 30% response rate
c. Denison (1943: 26)
d. Weinfeld (1949: 22)
e. Blaustein (1950: 375)
f. Blaustein (1952: 1054)
g. Liebenberg (1956: 33, 36)
h. Field (1960: 3)
i. Curran et al. (1985: 7-8)
j. Platt (1980: 633, 646)

Table 26. Women Lawyers, by Source, 1870-1986

Year	Epstein		Sikes		Fossum		Halliday; Pear		Curran	
	No.	%	No.	%	No.	%	No.	%	No.	%
1870[a]							5	0.01		
1880[a]							75	0.1		
1890[a]							208	0.2		
1900[a]							1,010	0.9		
1910	558	1.1					558	0.5		
1920	1,738	1.4					1,738	1.4		
1930	3,385	2.1					3,385	2.2		
1940	4,447	2.4					4,187	2.4		
1948			2,997	1.8						
1950	6,348	3.5					6,256	3.6		
1951			5,059	2.5						
1954			5,036	2.3						
1957			6,350	2.7						
1960	7,543	3.3	6,488	2.6		3.5	7,434	3.5		
1963			7,143	2.7						
1966			8,068	2.8		4.0				
1970	13,000	4.7	9,103	2.8	13,403		13,964	5.1		
1971					14,634	5.0				
1972					16,197	5.2				
1973					18,478	5.4				
1974					21,925	5.9				
1975					26,471	6.6				
1976	38,000	9.2			32,709	7.6				
1977					40,370	8.7				
1978					49,005	9.8				
1979					58,924	11.0				
1980	62,000	12.0					72,312	16.0	43,918	8.1
1984									83,072	12.8
1985										13.1
1986								15.0		

Note: a.   Includes semiprofessions

Sources: Epstein (1981: 4); Sikes et al. (1972: 5); Fossum (1980b: 904-06); Halliday (1985); Pear (1987); Curran (1985)

Table 27.   Women Students in ABA-Approved Law Schools, 1940-86

Year	Enrollments No.	% of total	Degrees[a] No.	% of total
1940	690	4.3		
1942	678	11.7	110	3.7
1943	929	21.9		
1944	1,048	21.8		
1947	1,405	3.3		
1948	1,376	2.9		
1949	1,268	2.7		
1950	1,364	3.1		
1951	1,420	3.6		
1952	1,483	4.2		
1953	1,456	4.2		
1954	1,418	4.0		
1955	1,370	3.8		
1956	1,169	3.1		
1957	1,302	3.4		
1958	1,274	3.3		
1959	1,392	3.6		
1960	1,429	3.5		
1961	1,497	3.6		
1962	1,818	4.0		
1963	1,883	3.8		
1964	2,183	4.0		
1965	2,537	4.2		
1966	2,678	4.2		
1967	2,906	4.5		
1968	3,704	5.9		
1969	4,715	6.8		
1970	7,031	8.5		
1971	8,914	9.4		
1972	12,173	11.9	1,563	7.0
1973	16,760	15.8	2,281	8.2
1974	21,788	19.7	3,447	11.8
1975	26,737	22.9	4,546	15.2
1976	29,982	25.5	6,238	19.1
1977	32,538	27.4	7,661	21.5
1978	36,808	30.3	8,635	25.9
1979	38,627	31.4	9,745	28.2
1980	42,122	33.6	10,569	30.1
1981	44,902	35.3	11,607	32.7
1982	47,083	36.8	11,494	33.0
1983	47,980	37.7	13,060	35.9
1984	48,499	38.6	14,038	36.2
1985	49,038	39.5	14,119	38.6
1986	49,557	40.2		

Note: a.   J.D. and LL.B.
Sources: Review of Legal Education;
         Gulliver (1943: 10)

Table 28. Distribution of Women Students in ABA-Approved and Unapproved
Full-time and Part-time Law Schools, 1943-44 to 1985

| | ABA Approved | | | | | | Unapproved[a] | | | | | |
| | Full-time | | | Part-time[b] | | | Full-time | | | Part-time[b] | | |
Year	Women	Total	%	Women	Total	%	Women	Total	%	Women	Total	%
1943-44	564	2,292	24.6	365	1,920	19.0	6	21	28.6	235	1,217	19.3
1950	887	32,918	2.7	372	8,657	4.3	37	1,250	3.0	370	7,381	5.0
1960	879	27,355	3.2	417	10,360	4.0	29	436	6.7	182	3,383	5.4
1970	5,527	62,376	8.9	1,178	15,963	7.4	30	311	9.6	394	3,606	10.9
1980	33,779	98,396	34.3	7,055	21,105	33.4	334	1,146	29.1	865	2,398	36.1
1984	38,750	98,735	39.2	8,129	21,112	38.5	N.A.	N.A.		N.A.	N.A.	
1985	39,184	97,862	40.0	8,302	20,838	39.8	N.A.	N.A.		N.A.	N.A.	

Notes: a.   Only a small proportion of all schools report statistics
         b.   Includes afternoon, evening, and mixed enrollments

Source: Review of Legal Education

Table 29. Law Teachers in ABA-Approved Schools and
Proportion of Women, 1947 to 1985-86

Year	Law Teachers						Deans and Librarians		
	Full-time			Part-time					
	Total	Women	% women	Total	Women	% women	Total	Women	% women
1947	992			868					
1950[b]			0.4[c]						54.5[a]
1960[b]			0.7[c]						47.1[a]
1961									
1962									
1963									
1964									
1965									
1966									
1967									
1968									
1969-70	2,873			1,520					
1970-71	3,139		2.2[c]	1,691					35.3[a]
1971-72	3,426			1,910					
1972-73	3,643	253	6.9	2,243	149	6.6			
1973-74	3,218	234	7.3	1,643	125	7.6			
1974-75	3,584	319	8.9	1,777	109	6.1			
1975-76	3,702	335	9.0	1,875	204	10.9	485[b]	97[b]	20.0[b]
1976-77	3,875	411	10.6	2,156	230	10.7	344[b]	32[b]	9.3[b]
1977-78	3,957	429	10.8	1,907	168	8.8	337[b]	33[b]	9.8[b]
1978-79	4,146	498	12.6	2,020	154	7.6	465[b]	96[b]	20.1[b]
1979-80	4,225	517	12.2	2,255	205	9.1	465[d]	96[d]	20.1[d]
1980-81	4,261	582	13.7	2,328	273	11.7	472[d]	90[d]	19.1[d]
1981-82	4,476	661	14.8	2,514	306	12.2	491[d]	107[d]	21.8[d]
1982-83	4,451	712	16.0	2,530	337	13.3	503[d]	121[d]	24.1[d]
1983-84	4,461	754	16.9	2,862	497	17.4	1,473	701	47.6
1985-86	4,881	934	19.1	3,117	569	18.3	1,652	795	48.1

Notes: a. Law librarians only

        b. Deans and administrators who teach

        c. Full- and part-time combined

        d. Deans and librarians who teach

Sources: Fossum (1980b: 904-06); Review of Legal Education

Table 30. Minority Students in ABA-Approved Law Schools, 1969-70 to 1985-86

Year	Black	Mexican American	Puerto Rican[a]	Other Hispano-American	Asian/Pacific Islander	American Indian	Total[b] Minority	Minority as % of Total Enrollment
1969-70	2,128	412	61	75		72	2,933	4.3
1971-72	3,744	883	94	179	480	140	5,568	5.9
1972-73	4,423	1,072	143	231	681	173	6,730	6.6
1973-74	4,817	1,259	180	261	850	222	7,601	7.2
1974-75	4,995	1,362	272	392	1,063	265	8,372	7.5
1975-76	5,127	1,443	333	406	1,099	295	8,712	7.4
1976-77	5,503	1,588	335	538	1,324	301	9,589	8.1
1977-78	5,305	1,564	350	617	1,382	363	9,580	8.1
1978-79	5,350	1,649	423	716	1,424	390	9,952	8.2
1979-80	5,257	1,670	441	706	1,547	392	10,013	8.1
1980-81	5,506	1,690	442	882	1,641	414	10,575	8.4
1981-82	5,789	1,756	396	1,037	1,755	402	11,134	8.7
1982-83	5,852	1,739	418	1,249	1,947	406	11,611	9.1
1983-84	5,967	1,744	450	1,302	1,962	441	11,866	9.3
1984-85	5,955	1,661	407	1,439	2,026	429	11,917	9.9
1985-86	6,052	1,635	412	1,632	2,153	462	12,357	10.4

Notes: a.   Excludes ABA-approved law schools in Puerto Rico;
              1,711 enrolled in 1980-81
         b.   Includes other

Source: Review of Legal Education

Table 31. Geographic Distribution of Lawyers and Population, Percentage
by City Size, 1948-70

Year	Lawyers					Population		
	<50,000[a]	50,000–200,000[a]	<200,000	200,000–500,000	>500,000	<250,000	250,000–500,000	>500,000
1948			48.8	11.7	39.5			
1951			47.5	13.6	38.9	15.5[d]	17.3[d]	67.2[d]
1954			47.7	13.8	38.5			
1957	30.7	16.4	47.0	14.0	39.0			
1960	29.4	16.3	45.7	14.5	39.8	14.4	14.8	71.6
1963	28.9	17.3	46.2	14.6	39.2			
1966	29.1	17.8	46.8	14.2	38.9			
1970	28.7	20.3[b]	49.0[c]	11.5	39.4	12.2	14.2	73.6

Notes: a. State listings (exclude lawyers not listed)
        b. 50,000–250,000
        c. <250,000
        d. 1950

Sources: American Bar Foundation, Lawyers Statistical Survey; Census

Table 32. ABA Membership, 1895-96 to 1984

Year	ABA Membership	No. of Lawyers	Percentage of Profession Belonging to ABA
1895-96	1,393		
1900-01	1,720	109,140	2
1905-06	2,606		
1910-11	4,701	114,704	3
1911-12	5,584		
1912-13	8,049		
1913-14	9,872		
1914-15	9,626		
1915-16	10,651		
1916-17	10,898		
1917-18	11,010		
1918-19	10,691		
1919-20	11,959		
1920-21	15,181	122,519	12
1921-22	17,447		
1922-23	19,899		
1923-24	22,073		
1924-25	23,368		17
1925-26	24,939		
1926-27	26,287		
1928	27,332		
1929	27,411		
1930	28,667	160,605	18
1931	27,578		
1932	29,795		
1933	27,748		
1934	25,951		
1935	27,178		
1936	28,228		
1937	29,452		
1938	30,820		
1939	33,954		
1940	31,626	179,567	18
1941	30,834		
1942	30,601		
1943	30,968		
1944	32,000		
1945	34,134		
1946	36,484		
1947	40,209		
1948	41,262		
1949	40,926		
1950	43,000	212,605	20
1951	45,628	221,605	21
1952	48,077		
1953	50,000		
1954	52,624	241,514	22
1957	88,396	260,320	34
1958	93,604		
1959	94,872		
1960	97,996	285,933	34
1961	101,520		
1962	109,979		
1963	115,358	316,856	38
1964	116,462		
1965	124,500		
1966	120,492	316,856	38
1967	129,222		
1968	136,553		
1969	139,084		
1970	143,962	355,242	41
1971	148,974		
1972	157,162	358,920	44
1973	168,338		
1974	182,564		
1975	207,990		
1976	210,541		
1977	219,404	462,000	48
1978	234,500		
1979	258,732		
1980	275,725	542,205	51
1984	301,000	649,000	46

Sources: Reed (1926: 702; 1928: 32); Melone (1977: 44); ABA Reports

Table 33. State Disciplinary Sanctions, 1974-86[a]

	1974	1975	1976	1977	1978	1979	1980	1981	1982	1983	1984	1985	1986
Number of complaints[b]		32,122	37,548	33,454	30,836	31,972					39,356	54,152	54,600
Disbarments	113	131	128	141	147	136	129	172	212	192	210	236	} 1,147
Disbarments by consent	61[d]	93[d]	98[d]	91[d]	10	18	96	100	158	146	157	212	
Suspensions	179	266	297	321	374	387	412	505	555	639	621	627	} 1,696
Less severe penalty[c]	66	269	388	362	326	430	532	829	856	918	1,190	1,263	
Public reprimand	66	113	166	137	136	180	146	214	227	283	320	332	
Probation					25	50	52	90	80	78	128	157	
Fines, costs, restitution					138	149	265	381	433	468	622	653	
Resignation					58	98	82	35	33	25	49	36	
Reinstatement	65	93	135	190	153	152	144	112	117	137	137	134	
Number of lawyers[b]		391,949	409,816	395,908	451,842	612,858							615,000
Discipline budget[b]		$7,054,368	$7,710,726	$7,340,631	$9,397,190	$8,117,323							$43,600,000

Notes: a. Successive reports give different figures for same year; latest report used. Includes District of Columbia
b. Incomplete figures, missing following number of states: 1975: 15; 1976: 15; 1977: 8; 1978: 12; 1979: 9
c. Includes retaking professional responsibility examination and other
d. Includes resignations

Sources: ABA Standing Committee on Professional Discipline (1978-1986); Wall Street Journal, p. 1, col. 1 (November 13, 1986); Cook (1986b); Middleton (1987e)

Table 34a. Outcomes of Disciplinary Proceedings in California, Numbers (percentage of previous action): 1928-48

	1928	1929	1930	1931	1932	1933	1934	1935	1936	1937	1938	1939
Preliminary investigations	1072	1531	960	941	750	490	394	444	626	247	160	287
Notices to show cause	367 (34.2)	132 (8.6)	178 (18.5)	84 (8.9)	75 (10.0)	77 (15.7)	123 (31.2)	101 (22.7)	77 (12.3)	85 (34.4)	73 (45.6)	86 (30.0)
State Bar actions												
dismissed	337 (91.8)	90 (68.2)	125 (70.2)	58 (69.0)	45 (60.0)	36 (46.8)	76 (61.8)	55 (54.5)	42 (54.5)	51 (60.0)	37 (50.7)	54 (62.8)
privately reproved	0	3	14	8	7	10	6	7	5	6	6	7
publicly reproved	12	20	11	4	3	3	8	7	8	5	3	5
suspension recommended	7	7	15	10	13	17	20	19	14	11	12	8
disbarment recommended	11	12	13	4	7	11	13	13	8	12	15	12
Supreme Court actions												
dismissed	0	0	0	4	0	1	1	2	2	1	2	1
reproved	0	0	0	1	1	1	0	0	0	0	0	0
suspended	0	15	16	18	12	13	23	19	15	12	11	11
disbarred	0	14	8	5	3	8	9	9	14	10	5	13
Suspension & disbarment as % of investigations	0	1.9	1.6	2.4	2.0	4.3	8.1	6.3	4.6	8.9	10.0	8.4
Resignations												
voluntary	1	2	7	2	7	9	6	6	11	10	6	1
with prejudice	0	0	0	0	0	0	4	3	1	4	2	5
Suspended or disbarred following conviction	3	4	2	5	7	9	8	3	10	8	14	8

Table 34a. Outcomes of Disciplinary Proceedings in California,
Numbers (percentage of previous action): 1928–48 (continued)

	1940	1941	1942	1943	1944	1945	1946	1947	1948	1928-48
Preliminary investigations	382	302	158	190	122	128	171	181	148	9684
Notices to show cause	105 (27.5)	57 (18.9)	37 (23.4)	51 (26.8)	27 (22.1)	26 (20.3)	30 (23.4)	48 (26.5)	19 (12.8)	1858 (19.2)
State Bar actions										
dismissed	66 (62.9)	30 (52.6)	7 (18.9)	26 (51.0)	12 (44.4)	7 (26.9)	21 (70.0)	33 (68.8)	10 (52.6)	1218 (65.6)
privately reproved	3	3	2	6	1	4	3	0	1	102
publicly reproved	7	3	4	2	3	5	2	5	1	121
suspension recommended	17	8	17	9	10	8	2	3	7	234
disbarment recommended	12	13	7	8	1	2	2	2	0	191
Supreme Court actions										
dismissed	0	7	1	0	1	1	1	0	1	25
reproved	0	0	0	0	1	0	0	0	0	4
suspended	12	12	12	10	9	8	5	4	7	244
disbarred	5	16	5	8	4	2	0	3	0	141
Suspension & disbarment as % of investigations	4.5	9.3	10.8	9.5	10.7	7.8	2.9	3.9	4.7	4.0
Resignations										
voluntary	6	5	4	4	2	2	0	0	2	103
with prejudice	3	5	2	0	0	1	0	0	0	30
Suspended or disbarred following conviction	5	9	6	0	1	3	0	0	5	110

Source: Blaustein & Forter (1954: 256)

Table 34b. Outcomes of Disciplinary Proceedings in California,
Numbers (percentage of previous action): 1981-86

	1981	1982	1983	1984	1985	1986
Office of Investigation						
Complaints received	6,946	7,779	8,094	8,329	7,981	8,574
Closed					7,287	7,791
Not sufficient facts					7,128	7,715
Admonition a					N/A	59
Office of Trial Counsel						
Resignations accepted with charges pending					34	58
Admonitions					152	59
Office of State Bar Court						
Disbarments	17	17	13	18	25	38
Resignations	6	15	9	12	34	69
Interim suspensions	18	23	30	29	36	25
Suspensions	75	88	83	95	82	86
Public reprovals	27	21	17	23	23	25
Private reprovals	43	53	29	48	59	19
Admonitions	20	21	17	21	29	13
Dismissals	43	54	30	31	56	37
Complaint pendency: total (percent)					6,109	6,222
≤6 months					2,345 (38)	3,653 (59)
7-9 months					899 (15)	750 (12)
10-12 months					838 (14)	442 (7)
13-21 months						874 (14)
>21 months					2,027 (33)	503 (8)

Note: a. OI authorized to issue admonitions in April 1986
Source: Fellmeth (1987a: Exhibits 18, 29)

Table 35. Complaints Against Lawyers to the Committee on Grievances of the
Association of the Bar of the City of New York, by Subject, 1958-59 to 1972-73

Year[a]	Negligence	Fee Dispute	Misuse of Client Funds	Personal Business Transaction	Threats, Abuse	Perjury	Crime	Misc.	Attorney in Other Jurisdiction	Requests for Advice
1958-59	617	263	60	25	13	36	2	241	48	129
1959-60	655	310	110	79	14	34	3	221	59	146
1960-61	660	363	117	86	21	30	5	280	75	144
1961-62	849	350	94	121	27	40	1	320	76	99
1962-63	880	378	80	116	30		5	361	75	159
1963-64	563	363	126	100	55	16	55	529	112	267

Year[a]	Offense Against Client	Offense Against Colleague	Direct Advertising	Offense Against Admin. of Justice Bribery	Fraud	Misc. Prof. Offense	Nonprofessional Offense	Crimes and Minor Offenses	Personal Business Transaction	Fee Dispute	Dissatis-faction	Misc.	Requests for Advice	Attorney in Other Jurisdiction
1964-65	770	23	70	13	71	100	115	65	40	315	182	210	230	179
1965-66	511	22	30	17	52	71	73	50	25	316	168	201	283	201
1966-67	589	14	43	12	73	107	65	25	29	143	158	194	157	240
1967-68	828	12	36	13	73	185	95	41	30	119	99	251	156	238
1968-69	732	10	38	9	78	123	55	24	25	134	75	312	168	209
1969-70	713	14	31	15	89	41	68	25	181	176	181	148	164	315
1970-71	799	12	36	12	96	71	27	58	55	243	124	173	214	294
1971-72	681	17	34	9	77	97	26	48	77	199	122	285	225	286
1972-73	529	17	25	6	41	78	24	47	42	195	117	361	301	513

Note: a.   May 1 - April 30

Source: Association of the Bar of the City of New York, Annual Report of the Committee on Grievances, in The Record (supplement to the October issue)

Table 36a.   Outcomes of Disciplinary Proceedings in New York City, 1958-59 to 1974-75:   Committee on Grievances

Year[a]	Complaints				Disposition						
	Pending from previous year	Filed[b]	Processed	Pending at end of year	Dismissed without hearing	Tried	Dismissed	Admonition	Warning letter	Resigned while pending	Sent to Appellate Division
1958-59	247	1,545	1,792	222	1,510	38	8	14		5	10
1959-60	232	1,702	1,934	230	1,640	44	9	14		5	15
1960-61	234	1,843	2,077		1,841	68	5	31			15
1961-62	156	2,019	2,175		1,841	51	4	30			32
1962-63		2,175				43	7	23			11
1963-64		2,257				47	3	27			10
1964-65		2,383				77	7	19			12
1965-66		2,020	2,040			50	3	18	30	3	13
1966-67		1,914	2,034			55	5	18	64	12	17
1967-68		2,232	2,046			46	3	22	160	13	19
1968-69		1,995	1,907			41	5	15	158	8	13
1969-70		2,031	2,756			47	7	19	144	2	19
1970-71		2,215	2,854			40	3	12	184	5	16
1971-72		2,183				46	1	19	133	3	20
1972-73		2,296							142	5	20
1973-74		2,200	2,800								29
1974-75		2,400	3,000								

Notes: a.   May 1 - April 30
         b.   Between 1944 and 1959 complaints filed and processed ranged between 1,300 and 1,600 annually

Source: Association of the Bar of the City of New York, Annual Report of the Committee on Grievances, in The Record (supplement to the October issue)

Table 36b. Outcomes of Disciplinary Proceedings in New York City, 1958-59 to 1974-75: Appellate Division

Year[a]	Complaints			Disbarment			Suspended			Censured	Dismissed
	Pending from previous year	New	Pending at end of year	After hearing	By consent	On pleading	After hearing	After felony conviction	On pleading		
1958-59[b]	36	15	25	6	4	1	2	4	1	7	1
1959-60	25	13	26	3	5			6		4	1
1960-61	26	18	18	6	3		5	4	1	1	3
1961-62	16	25	26	4	4		1	3	1	4	1
1962-63	26	32	27	2	7	1	1	11	2	6	3
1963-64	27	21	22	3	7		1	2	2	1	4
1964-65	22	15	19	3	5			8	1	3	
1965-66	19	21	23	7	3		2	2		3	
1966-67	48		24	4	5		5	5		2	2
1967-68	54		10	3	5		2	8		3	2
1968-69	56		5	6	6		1	14		3	
1969-70			32	5	3			7			
1970-71			33	3	3			10		2	1
1971-72				4	6		8	7	2	3	1
1972-73			58				4	9		2	
1973-74				6	6		3	9		8	
1974-75				5	6		8	22	3	6	

Notes: a. May 1 - April 30

  b. Between 1944 and 1959 complaints filed and processed ranged between 1,300 and 1,600 annually

Source: Association of the Bar of the City of New York, Annual Report of the Committee on Grievances, in The Record (supplement to the October issue)

Table 37a. Distribution of Lawyers in Practice Settings (percent): Before World War II, Selected Jurisdictions

State, Year and Cohort	Solo Practice	Partner	Associate	Government	Commerce and Industry	Judiciary
Wisconsin, 7-8 years experience 1926	54	25	10	----7----		2
Wisconsin, 1-2 years experience 1936	56	12	24	----7----		
California, year after admission 1932 (N=312)	43	12	32	6	6	
Fifth year after admission 1936 (N=331)	44	19	19	10	8	
Year after admission 1933	43	11.5	32.4	6.4	6.7	
Second year after admission 1934	43.9	12.3	28.7	6.8	8.3	
Fifth year after admission 1937	44.4	18.7	18.7	10.3	7.9	
New York County, 1934	46.7	20.1	17.9	3.3	10.4	0.6
New York City, Jewish lawyers 1937 (N=2,872)	68[a]	15	14	3	3	

Note: a. Includes sole practitioners with lawyer employees

Sources: ABA Special Committee (1938: 48); New York County Lawyers' Association (1936: 12, 27); State Bar of California (1937: 260); Fagen (1939: 96)

Table 37b. Distribution of Lawyers in Practice Settings (percent):
Nationwide, U.S. Census, 1930-70

Year	Private Practice	Government and Judiciary	Commerce and Industry	Nonprofit Associations
1930[a]	86.8	8.0	5.2	N.A.
1940	82.2	11.5	6.3	N.A.
1950	76.7	13.0	10.4	0.8
1960	75.9	13.2	10.9	0.7
1970	72.6	15.9	11.4	1.7

Note: a. Different classification renders figures
noncomparable with later years

Sources: Pashigian (1982: 6); see also Denison (1943: 23)

Table 37c.   Distribution of Lawyers in Practice Settings (percent): Nationwide, Martindale-Hubbell, 1948-80

	1948	1951	1954	1957	1960	1963	1966	1970	1980	% Change of Absolute Numbers Within Category 1951-80
Private Practice										
total	89.2	86.8	85.5	80.1	76.2	74.7	73.5	72.7	68.3	109
solo practice	61.2	59.0	57.5	51.9	46.3	42.1	39.1	36.6	33.2	50
partners	23.6	23.2	23.3	23.3	24.1	26.1	27.1	28.5	26.3	205
associates	4.4	4.6	4.7	4.9	5.8	6.5	7.2	7.6	8.8	391
Private Employ. (excl. educ.)	3.2[a]	5.7	6.9	8.3	9.2	10.2	10.6	11.3	10.9	401
Education		0.6	0.6	0.6	0.7	0.8	0.9	1.1	1.2	445
Govt. (excl. jud.)										
total	8.3	9.8	9.6	10.3	10.2	10.9	10.8	11.1	10.8	195
local	4.7	3.9	3.9	3.3	3.3	2.9	2.6	2.4	5.6	78[b]
state	1.8	1.6	1.7	1.7	1.7	2.4	2.6	2.9	3.7	
federal		4.1	4.1	5.3	5.2	5.6	5.6	5.8	1.5	192[b]
Judicial	4.2	3.6	3.6	3.3	3.2	3.3	3.4	3.2	3.6	156
Retired or Inactive	3.5	3.4	3.0	3.2	4.3	4.5	5.1	5.2	5.3	310
Total										166

Notes: a.   Includes education
           b.   Legal aid-public defender treated as half state/local and half federal

Sources: Sikes et al. (1972: 10-12); Curran et al. (1985)

Table 37d. Distribution of Lawyers in Practice Settings (percent): After World War II, Selected Jurisdictions

State and Year		Solo Practice	Partner	Associate	Government	Commerce and Industry	Judiciary	Not Law
California	1960	36	29	15	--------19----------			
Florida[a]	1963	53	38	9				
	1966	35	47	19				
Colorado	1967	29	35	13	9	7	7	
S. Carolina	1970	40	32.5	6	--------22----------			
Illinois	1975	21	44		8	14	3	10
	1982	16	46		11	16	5	6
Arizona	1976	22.9	38.7	17.4	15	4.2	0.8	

Note: a. Proportions of private practitioners only

Sources: Stevens (1983: 235 n. 23); Field (1960: 2); Bethel (1976: 6,12); Illinois State Bar Association (1983: 127)

Table 38. Lawyer Income by Practice Setting, Selected Jurisdictions, 1933-76 (median or range)

Year	Solo Practice	Partner	Assoc.	House Counsel	Govt.	Jud.	Teaching	Place
1933[a]	2,310	6,490						Manhattan
1947[b]	4,194	10,497						U.S.
1952[c]								
mean	8,900	17,800	6,300	10,400	6,200	7,700	7,800	Ohio
median	7,200	12,900	5,300	7,500	5,500	6,700	6,800	Ohio
1954[m]								
mean	7,315	10,258[aa]	7,786	13,769	7,915	11,616	8,966	U.S.
median	5,485	7,382	6,794	10,330	7,578	11,100	8,429	U.S.
1957[b]	6,550	16,480						U.S.
1965[p]								
mean	18,132	27,341	9,038	14,276	11,042-12,050	19,245	13,305	Florida
median	14,000	22,700	8,000	13,000	10,800-11,200	20,000	14,500	Florida
1965[r]	12,392	18,000	6,350					N. Carolina
1967[e]	13,349	21,521	8,882	14,135	7,439			Colorado
1967[b]	10,850	26,850						U.S.
1967[r]	12,000	23,900	9,000					Georgia
1967[n]	16,000	25,300	10,000	14,800	12,400	23,000		Maryland
1968[d]		39,000						U.S.
		52,000						N.Y.
		60,000						D.C.
1968[q]	16,000	25,000	8,000	15,600	13,000	23,500		S. Carolina
1968[f]		35,095						Virginia
		13,689						Kentucky
1968[l]	11,217	26,395						U.S.
1971[b]	14,170	33,380						U.S.
1972[g]			(13,500-34,800)					All salaried
1972[h]		40,010						U.S.
1973[i]					11,614-31,203			Federal
1974[n]								
mean	34,404	44,206	18,447	27,616	21,911	35,715	26,369	Maryland
median	26,500	40,000	17,500	25,000	21,000	36,750	28,000	Maryland
1975[j]	27,727	47,748	22,439	29,355	21,538	36,596	32,537	Chicago-downtown
1976[k]		55,000						U.S.
		63,000						Calif.
1976[o]	22,000	40,000	16,800	18,000-30,000	19,200	20,200	22,500	Arizona
1976[s]	22,167	55,510	22,014	35,545	25,257	39,107	19,000	Michigan

Note: aa. Solo and partner

Sources:
a. ABF (1958b: 29)
b. Pashigian (1977: 83)
c. Kafoglis (1955: 28)
d. Weil (1972: 10-11)
e. Colorado Bar Association (1968: 11-12)
f. York & Hale (1973: 21)
g. U.S. Dept. of Labor (1972)
h. Green (1976: 64)
i. York & Hale (1973: 18)
j. Illinois State Bar Association (1975: 88)

k. ABAJ (1977)
l. York & Hale (1973: 17-18)
m. Liebenberg (1956: 32-33)
n. Maryland (1975: 6A-7A)
o. Bethel (1976: 7, 12)
p. Cantor (1966)
q. Cantor (1969: 4)
r. Cantor (1969: 6)
s. Henderson & Obst (1977: 924)

Table 39. Distribution of Private Practitioners by Size of Law Firm,
Selected Jurisdictions Between 1960 and 1980 (percent)

Place and Date   Number of Lawyers in Firm

	Solo	2-4	5-14	15-49	$\geq$ 50
Manhattan and Bronx 1960	47	17	15	9	12

Source: Carlin (1966: 18)

	Solo	2	3	4	5	6 $\leq$ 8	
Prairie City[a] 1964	26	15	19	13	5	13	9

Note: a. A midwestern city with a population of 80,000; 120,000
in the greater metropolitan area

Source: Handler (1967: 13)

	2-5	6-10	11-20	21-40	41-100	>100
ABA members 1969[a]	50	20	15	8	5	1

Note: a. Sample of 1,015; 54 percent response

Source: ABAJ (1970)

Illinois[a] 1974	2	3	4	5-9	10-14	15-19	20-49	$\geq$ 50
Chicago	8	12	8	24	8	6	13	21
Suburbs	28	21	12	23	9	4	3	0
Rest of state	11	18	26	33	9	3	1	0

Note: a. Partners only

Source: Illinois State Bar Association (1975: 90-91)

	2-8	9-49	$\geq$ 50
Chicago 1975	27	17	15

Source: Zemans & Rosenblum (1981: 67)

	Solo	2	3	4	5	6-10	11-20	21-50	>50
United States 1980	48.6	8.8	6.1	4.4	3.1	9.0	6.5	6.1	7.3

Source: Curran (1985)

Table 40. Number, Distribution, and Receipts of
Private Practitioners, 1967–82

	1967	1972	1977	1982[a]
Number of law firms	143,069	144,452	167,896	115,435
Sole practitioners	121,930	95,820	124,415	
Partnerships	21,139	25,488	29,234	
Prof. service orgs.		4,574	14,247	
Form unknown		18,570		
Receipts ($000s)	6,333,838	10,938,178	18,695,77	34,325,371
Sole practitioners	2,852,734	2,884,943	4,738,802	
Partnerships	3,481,104	5,910,903	10,093,339	
Prof. service orgs.		1,056,158	3,863,630	
Form unknown		1,086,174		

Note: a. Establishments with payroll

Sources: U.S. Bureau of the Census (1970; 1976; 1981; 1984)

Table 41a. Distribution of Effort in Law Offices: 1967[a]

	Percentage of Specialized Firms with Primary Specialty in:	Percentage of Receipts Earned from Area by All Specialist Firms	Percentage of All Receipts Among Specialist Firms by Those for Whom It is the:	
			Primary Specialty	Other Specialty
Banking and commercial law	5.4	4.5	47.3	16.5
Corporations	14.2	25.7	49.7	13.4
Criminal law	1.5	1.5	64.4	10.4
Domestic relations	1.8	0.8	48.1	17.3
Insurance Law	5.5	5.5	62.5	11.6
Negligence, defendant	13.4	13.2	57.2	11.5
Negligence, plaintiff	15.3	11.0	64.1	9.1
Patent, trademark, and copyright	4.8	6.8	97.8	0.1
Real estate	10.3	7.3	52.6	13.1
Taxation	2.2	2.3	54.8	24.3
Wills, estate planning, probate	15.0	9.8	41.2	16.9
Other	10.5	11.6	65.9	8.3
	N=5,623	N=$1,610,919,000		

Note: a. Offices with four or more employees. Specialization
          defined as earning at least 25% of total receipts

Source: U.S. Bureau of the Census (1970: Table 4)

Table 41b. Distribution of Effort in Law Offices: 1972[a]

	All	Receipts over $1M	Receipts $50,000–99,000	Solo Practice	Partnerships
General practice	58.5	22.0	77.6	74.4	55.8
Specialized fields					
Banking and commercial law	2.8	4.4	1.7	2.2	2.7
Corporations	6.5	20.6	1.7	1.6	8.4
Criminal law	1.3	0.3	1.4	1.8	0.9
Domestic relations	1.2	0.8	1.0	0.7	1.0
Insurance law	1.9	2.9	0.5	0.7	2.2
Negligence, defendant	3.7	6.1	1.0	1.1	4.4
Negligence, plaintiff	3.4	2.3	2.7	2.7	2.7
Patent, trademark, copyright	1.8	3.7	0.6	1.0	2.0
Real estate	4.7	7.0	3.3	3.9	4.7
Taxation	2.9	7.8	1.0	1.1	3.3
Wills, estate planning, probate	4.9	7.4	3.9	4.3	4.9
Other	6.6	14.6	3.5	4.4	7.1
	N=169,882	27,684	29,541	36,812	112,412

Note: a. Establishments open all year, with payroll. Includes
            sole practitioners, partners, associates; specialization
            defined as earning at least 25% of total receipts

Source: U.S. Bureau of the Census (1976: Table 3)

Table 41c. Distribution of Effort in Law Offices: 1977[a]

	All	Receipts over $1M	Receipts $50,000-99,000	Receipts $30,000-49,000	Solo Practice	Partnerships
General practice	60.0	22.0	78.8	85.9	75.6	54.5
Specialized fields						
Banking and commercial law	2.3	4.9	0.8	0.4	1.1	2.7
Corporations	5.8	16.6	1.5	0.4	1.1	7.5
Criminal law	1.9	0.6	1.9	2.1	2.0	1.7
Domestic relations	1.8	1.1	1.4	1.0	1.6	1.4
Insurance law	2.1	4.1	0.4	0.0	0.9	2.3
Negligence, defendant	3.7	7.7	0.6	0.2	1.2	4.1
Negligence, plaintiff	3.3	2.8	1.9	0.8	2.6	2.4
Patent, trademark, copyright	1.6	3.3	0.7	0.3	0.9	1.9
Real estate	4.6	6.7	3.4	2.1	3.8	4.7
Taxation	2.8	6.7	1.0	1.4	1.2	3.1
Wills, estate planning, probate	4.5	6.0	4.4	3.4	4.5	4./
Other	7.8	17.5	2.9	2.2	3.8	8.9
	N=253,565	52,820	36,826	20,052	59,302	148,191

Note : a. Establishments open all year with payroll.
Includes sole practitioners, partners, associates;
specialization defined as earning at least 25% of
total receipts

Source: U.S. Bureau of the Census (1981: Table 8)

Table 42. Concentration Within Private Practice, 1967, 1972, 1977

Type of Firm[c]	1967		1972		1977	
	% firms	% receipts	% firms	% receipts	% firms	% receipts
All firms with receipts > $1 million	3.4	28.0	1.3	24.5	2.6	36.4
All partnerships with receipts > $1 million	3.4	28.0	1.1	21.2	1.9	29.7
All partnerships	72.9	88.5	30.4	61.2	29.7	59.0
All firms with receipts < $50,000	28.8[a]	7.0[a]	46.2	10.2	35.0	5.4
All sole practitioners	27.1	11.5	40.9	18.0	56.1	18.7
All sole practitioners with receipts < $100,000	6.3	1.5	25.2[b]	5.7[b]	30.1[b]	4.6[b]

Notes: a. Less than $100,000
          b. Less than $50,000
          c. Four or more employees 1967; payroll 1972, 1977; operated all year

Sources: U.S. Bureau of the Census (1970: Table 7; 1976: Table 2c; 1981: Table 3)

Table 43.   Labor Force in Private Practice, 1967, 1972, 1977

	1967[a]	1972[c]	1977[c]
All Firms			
Number	9,939	77,282	94,882
Sole practitioners or partners	38,403	129,047	158,368
Associates	22,305	50,763	94,001
Paralegals	b	13,303	32,397
Other employees	77,564	203,085	265,650
Sole practitioners			
Number	1,775	30,856	53,810
Associates	2,939	5,956	N.A.
Paralegals	b	3,018	N.A.
Other employees	8,006	44,634	N.A.
Partnerships			
Number	8,181	23,691	27,237
Partners	36,628	83,680	108,813
Associates	19,366	28,732	39,378
Paralegals	b	7,248	16,639
Other employees	69,558	114,139	141,749

Notes: a.   Firms with four or more employees
          b.   Included in other employees
          c.   Firms with payroll

Sources: U.S. Bureau of the Census (1970: Table 4; 1976:
          Table 2a; 1981: Table 4)

Table 44. Distribution of Effort Within Private Practice Between Individual
and Business Clients, 1967, 1972, 1977 (percentage of receipts)

	1967[c]		1972[d]		1977[d]	
	Indiv.	Business	Indiv.	Business	Indiv.	Business
All establishments	N.A.	N.A.	52.5	42.3	48.5	45.7
All partnerships	N.A.	N.A.	43.3	51.3	38.4	55.6
Partnerships with receipts > $1 million	6.0[b]	77.6	23.1	72.0	20.9	72.9
All sole practitioners	N.A.	N.A.	70.5	24.5	71.2	23.5
Sole practitioners with receipts < $10,000	64.8[a]	19.6[a]	85.6	6.2	76.1[e]	19.1[e]

Notes: a. Sole practitioners with no employee lawyers
        b. Partnerships with 20-49 lawyers
        c. Establishments with at least four employees
        d. Establishments with payroll
        e. Receipts between $50,000-99,000

Sources: U.S. Bureau of the Census (1970: Table 5; 1976: Table 4;
          1981: Table 9)

Table 45.   Growth in Size of Large Law Firms

a.   Ten Largest Chicago Firms in 1979[a]

Year	Total No. Lawyers	Mean No. Lawyers	Range	Median No. Lawyers
1979	1,480	148	97–231	164
1965	555	55.5	44–81	62.5
1950	345	34.5	26–54	40
1935	229	22.9	16–43	29.5

Note: a. Excluding Baker & McKenzie, which is aberrational

Source: Nelson (1981: 105–07, 109)

b.   Fifty Largest U.S. Firms, 1979[a]

1979	9,398	188	131–512	321.5
1950	2,118	44	6–92	49

Note: a. Two of the 1979 firms did not exist in 1950.
Some of the figures for 1950 firm size are
estimates

Source: Nelson (1981: 105–07, 109)

c.   Twenty Largest U.S. Firms, 1968–87

1987	10,533	527	365–946	460
1985	8,284	414	297–755	395
1982	6,350	318	250–622	303
1979	4,681	234	182–512	235
1968	2,568	128	106–169	137.5

Source: Galanter (1982); Lewin (1983); National Law Journal
(1985; 1987)

Table 46. Size of 200 Largest Firms, 1975, 1978-87[a]

Year	Range	Distribution (firms/lawyers)								Totals (firms/lawyers)			
		<100	100-199[b]	200-299	300-399	400-499	500-599	600-699	800-900	Mean	Median	200 Firms	Firms ≥100
1975[c]	41-230	154 9,645	42 5,897	3 661						82	68	199 16,203	45 6,558
1978	53-272	121 8,688	64 8,440	14 3,086						102	86	199 20,214	78 11,526
1979	51-288	111 8,218	78 10,957	10 2,423						109	91	199 21,598	88 13,380
1980	59-312	98 7,624	83 11,306	17 3,961	1 312					117	100	199 23,203	101 15,579
1981	75-330	72 6,050	101 13,445	24 5,536	3 944					130	111	200 25,975	128 19,925
1982	80-343	55 4,904	107 14,542	31 7,159	4 1,330					142	122	197 27,935	142 23,031
1983	94-398	20 1,932	132 17,882	35 8,041	13 4,469					162	141	200 32,324	180 30,392
1984	99-462	1 100	141 19,209	43 10,128	11 3,860	4 1,732				175	150	200 35,029	199 24,929
1985	106-520		131 18,974	51 11,856	8 2,805	6 2,761	1 520			187	161	197 36,916	216 38,860
1986	119-638		109 16,267	62 14,683	17 5,752	4 1,788	3 1,656	2 1,274		210	186	197 41,420	248 46,904
1987	130-828		95 14,847	62 14,997	17 8,986	6 2,545	4 2,232	1 684	2 1,646	233	205	197 45,937	247 51,851

Notes: a. Excludes Baker & McKenzie, always the largest firm but really a consortium of semi-autonomous firms in many countries: 1975--326, 1978--434, 1979--512, 1980--544, 1981--583, 1982--613, 1983--658, 1984--704, 1985--755, 1986--808, 1987--946. Also excludes two legal clinics, which are centrally managed collections of small offices. They were: Jacoby & Meyers: 1980--105, 1981--148, 1982--123, 1983--135, 1984--157, 1985--236, 1986--297, 1987--302; Hyatt Legal Services: 1982--164, 1983--294, 1984--379, 1985--550, 1986--674, 1987--636

b. Among the 250 largest firms there were additional firms with 100-199 lawyers in the following years: 1985: 19 firms with 1,944 lawyers; 1986: 51/5,484; 1987: 50/5,914

c. Based on 1975 data for firms among the top 200 in 1978

Source: National Law Journal, Annual Survey

Table 47.   Geographic Distribution of 100 Largest
Firms by Number, 1978, 1987[a]

City	1978	1987
New York	36	32
Chicago	12	12
District of Columbia	7	3
Philadelphia	7	5
San Francisco	6	8
Houston	5	3
Cleveland	4	4
Los Angeles	3	7
Atlanta	3	1
Boston	3	4
Minneapolis	2	2
Milwaukee	2	1
Richmond	2	2
Detroit	2	2
Columbus	2	2
Pittsburgh	1	2
Omaha	1	1
Rochester, N.Y.	1	1
Dallas		1
Denver		1
St. Louis		1
Seattle		1
Baltimore		1
Uniondale, N.Y.		1

Note: a.   Several firms that said they had no principal office
were categorized by the largest office: Jones Day
(Cleveland), Finley Kumble (N.Y.), Kirkpatrick and
Lockhart (Pittsburgh).   Several firms that listed two
main offices were categorized by the first: McKenna,
Connor & Cunes (D.C.), Sutherland, Asbill & Brennan
(Atlanta), Lillick, McHose & Charles (L.A.).   I
excluded the two legal clinics--Hyatt Legal Services
and Jacoby & Meyers--and Baker & McKenzie (Chicago in
1978, no main office in 1987)

Source: National Law Journal, Annual Survey

Table 48.   Internal Structure of Firms: Ratio of Associates to Partners

a.   Ten Largest New York Firms, 1950-85

	Mean	Range	Median
1985[b]	2.84	2.23-3.54	2.88
1982	2.77	2.01-3.54	2.64
1979	2.36	1.84-3.02	2.43
1960[a]	2.02		
1950[a]	0.63	.09-1.11	0.6

Notes: a. Data represent the four New York firms of the
            fifty largest firms nationwide for which
            actual figures are available
        b. Excludes Finley, Kumble, which has no
            principal office

Sources: Nelson (1981: 105-07); Lewin (1983); National Law
          Journal (1985)

b.   Ten Largest Firms Outside New York, 1950-85

	Mean	Range	Median
1985[b]	1.70	1.36-2.28	1.62
1982	1.51	1.22-1.95	1.49
1979	1.44	1.04-1.93	1.48
1960[a]	1.36		
1950[a]	1.33	0.53-2.25	1.39

Notes: a. Data represent the ten largest firms outside
            N.Y.C. for which actual figures are available.
            Fulbright and Jaworski has been omitted
            because it was temporarily aberrational--a
            ratio of 4.75, which dropped to 1.57 ten years
            later--and the next largest firm has been
            substituted

        b. Excludes Hyatt Legal Services, a clinic with
            4 partners and 546 employed lawyers; and
            Finley, Kumble, which has no principal office

Sources: Nelson (1981: 105-07); Lewin (1983); National Law
          Journal (1985)

c.   A Midwest Firm, 1901, 1953

	Ratio of Associates to Partners	Number of Nonprofessional Staff	Ratio of Salaried Employees to Partners
1953	1.83 (22:12)	42	4.5
1901	0.67 (2:3)	6	2.67

Source: Dodge (1955: 181)

Table 49. Ratios of Associates and Paralegals to Partners
in Large Firms, 1975, 1987

1987[b]

First fifty[a]						Fifth fifty					
Firm size	A/P	PL/P	Firm size	A/P	PL/P	Firm size	A/P	PL/P	Firm size	A/P	PL/P
946	1.80	NA	338	3.06	0.88	130	2.02	0.47	119	0.92	0.34
828	2.04	0.59	334	2.15	0.45	130	1.95	0.66	118	1.57	0.67
818	4.21	2.24	329	0.92	0.48	129	1.74	0.53	117	1.72	0.63
684	1.79	0.58	328	2.90	1.12	129	1.05	0.37	116	1.07	0.79
584	1.83	0.49	323	2.05	0.58	128	1.67	0.65	116	1.58	0.42
579	2.33	1.00	321	1.72	1.14	127	0.84	0.58	115	1.50	1.09
563	1.67	0.59	321	2.73	0.77	126	1.07	0.28	114	1.65	0.51
506	3.48	0.79	318	1.69	0.66	126	0.97	0.45	114	1.53	0.58
477	1.73	0.57	317	2.41	0.52	125	1.31	0.43	114	1.24	0.24
443	3.87	1.00	316	1.39	0.78	125	3.17	1.40	114	1.24	0.47
410	1.34	0.85	312	2.90	0.68	124	1.18	0.42	113	0.82	0.42
406	1.05	0.42	307	1.11	0.67	124	0.88	0.47	113	1.76	0.80
405	1.89	0.55	306	2.26	0.67	123	1.62	0.32	112	1.60	0.33
404	1.36	0.87	303	2.26	0.71	123	1.08	0.32	111	1.60	0.50
375	2.05	0.75	301	1.37	0.56	123	2.84	0.75	111	1.02	0.40
369	1.93	0.97	300	2.90	0.79	123	0.92	0.22	111	1.22	0.38
369	2.24	1.07	294	2.54	0.75	123	2.00	1.02	110	1.00	0.42
366	2.02	0.56	293	1.25	0.37	123	0.84	0.18	110	1.34	0.47
365	1.19	0.35	292	1.03	0.42	122	0.92	0.37	110	1.16	0.49
354	2.44	0.94	290	1.50	0.55	122	1.00	1.48	108	0.86	0.38
345	1.61	0.68	289	0.99	0.26	121	1.81	0.79	108	1.20	0.37
345	1.48	0.47	288	3.57	1.00	121	1.42	0.56	108	1.70	0.68
345	3.01	0.56	282	1.29	0.34	120	2.00	0.82	108	1.60	0.54
341	2.41	0.47	278	2.16	0.57	120	2.63	0.48	108	1.40	0.27
338	2.89	1.46	278	2.48	0.82	119	1.77	0.47	107	0.78	0.13

Table 49.   Ratios of Associates and Paralegals to Partners
in Large Firms, 1975, 1987 (continued)

1975[b]

| First fifty[c] | | | | | | Fourth fifty[e] | | | |
Firm size	A/P	PL/P	Firm size	A/P	PL/P	Firm size	A/P	Firm size	A/P
326	1.26	NA	132	0.97	NA	55	1.12	47	1.35
230	1.47	0.16	130	1.36	0.22	54	1.35	47	1.61
227	2.11	0.53	125	1.36	1.17	54	1.16	46	0.77
204	1.43	0.25	123	2.00	0.15	54	1.08	46	0.71
199	1.46	0.43	120	1.03	0.10	54	0.74	46	1.71
196	1.09	0.19	118	1.51	0.15	54	1.16	46	0.53
186	2.96	0.30	118	0.64	0.32	53	1.04	45	1.81
185	1.37	0.29	117	0.98	0.34	53	0.96	45	0.45
184	1.97	0.37	115	2.48	NA	52	0.58	45	0.88
178	1.14	0.30	114	1.15	NA	52	1.08	45	0.61
174	2.35	0.40	114	1.04	0.12	51	0.82	43	0.72
170	3.05	0.38	114	1.38	0.38	51	0.38	43	0.87
169	0.94	0.10	111	1.47	0.27	51	0.70	43	0.72
167	2.04	0.09	111	1.27	0.49	50	0.79	43	1.53
167	1.93	0.46	106	1.26	0.30	50	1.00	42	0.75
164	1.22	0.27	104	1.21	0.66	50	0.85	42	1.00
164	1.93	0.29	103	1.06	0.42	49	0.22	41	0.46
158	2.51	0.44	103	2.03	0.32	49	0.96	41	0.78
158	1.68	0.25	101	0.98	0.55	49	0.88	40	0.82
155	1.82	0.24	99	1.06	NA	49	0.75	40	1.67
155	0.87	0.33	97	1.06	0.13	48	1.00	40	0.54
152	1.08	0.60	97	2.13	0.32	48	0.81	33	0.74
149	1.98	0.22	96	1.67	0.17	48	2.20	33	0.94
149	0.59	NA	96	1.18	0.30	48	0.92	30	1.72
142	2.09	0.28	96	1.00	0.17	47	1.14	29	0.93

Table 49. Ratios of Associates and Paralegals to
Partners in Large Firms, 1975, 1987 (continued)

A/P Ratio

	Top fifty (mean)			Fourth/fifth fifty (mean)		
	All	N.Y.	Other cities	All	N.Y.	Other cities
1987	2.09	2.76	1.44	1.44	1.97	1.35
1975[d]	1.51	1.99	1.17	0.97	1.20	0.93

PL/P Ratio

	Top fifty (mean)			Fourth/fifth fifty (mean)		
	All	N.Y.	Other cities	All	N.Y.	Other cities
1987	0.72	0.87	0.61	0.51	0.52	0.51
1975[d]	0.32	0.33	0.32			

Notes: a. Excludes Hyatt Legal Services and Jacoby
            & Meyers
        b. Underlined firms have principal office
            in New York
        c. Missing figures for Davis Polk (N.Y.);
            was 200 and 2.85 in 1978
        d. Plunket, Cooney of Detroit (51 lawyers
            in 1975 with a 9.2 A:P ratio) is clearly
            aberrational and has been omitted
        e. Of those in top 200 in 1978

Source: National Law Journal, Annual Survey

Table 50. Growth of Branch Offices Among 100 Largest Firms, 1978, 1987

	Lawyers in Branches		Number of Branches	Number of Firms by Number of Branches																
	Number	Percent		0	1	2	3	4	5	6	7	8	9	10	11	12	13	14	15	16
1978	1,613	12	190	21	30	20	16	4	4	2		1	1				1			
1987	9,597	31	479	3	8	10	17	15	9	18	6	4		1	3	3			1	1

Number of Firms by Percentage of Lawyers in Branches								
	0	0-10	10-20	20-30	30-40	40-50	50-60	60-70	70-80
1978	21	42	17	8	4	6			
1987	3	13	19	17	22	14	8	3	2

Notes: Excludes Baker & McKenzie, which had 330/434 lawyers in 25 branches in 1978 (76 percent) and 798/946 lawyers in 35 offices outside Chicago (which it no longer listed as its main office) in 1987 (84 percent). Also excludes Hyatt Legal Services, which had 636 lawyers in 190 offices in 1987, and Jacoby & Meyers, which had 302 lawyers in 150 offices. Covington & Burling has no branch offices, but 3 lawyers practice both in the District of Columbia and in suburban Virginia

Source: National Law Journal, Annual Survey

Notes

Chapter 2

1. For descriptions of lawyers' work, see Jerome Carlin, Lawyers on Their Own; Hubert O'Gorman, Lawyers and Matrimonial Cases; Douglas Rosenthal, Lawyer and Client; Maureen Cain, "The General Practice Lawyer and the Client"; Kenneth Mann, Defending White Collar Crime; John Griffiths, "What Do Dutch Lawyers Actually Do in Divorce Cases?"; Austin Sarat and William Felstiner, "Law and Strategy in the Divorce Lawyer's Office."

2. Max Weber, Economy and Society; Eliot Freidson, Profession of Medicine; Terence Johnson, Professions and Power; Magali Sarfatti Larson, The Rise of Professionalism.

3. Weber, 1978: 341–42; Frank Parkin, Marxism and Class Theory, p. 44.

4. Karl Polanyi, The Great Transformation.

5. For a recent attempt to synthesize their theoretical frameworks, see James W. Begun, "Economic and Sociological Approaches to Professionalism."

6. Nicholas Abercrombie and John Urry, Capital, Labour and the Middle Classes, pp. 49–51.

7. Emile Durkheim, The Division of Labor In Society; Professional Ethics and Civic Responsibility.

8. Dietrich Rueschemeyer, "Professional Autonomy and the Social Control of Expertise."

9. Daniel Duman, "The Creation and Diffusion of a Professional Ideology in Nineteenth Century England."

10. Erwin O. Smigel, "Trends in Occupational Sociology"; Erwin O. Smigel, Joseph Monane, Robert B. Wood, and Barbara Randall Nye, "Occupational Sociology: A Reexamination"; Richard H. Hall, "Professionalization and Bureaucratization."

11. A. M. Carr-Saunders and P. A. Wilson, The Professions, p. 497; T. H. Marshall, "The Recent History of Professionalism in Relation to Social Structure and Social Policy"; Talcott Parsons, "Social Structure and Dynamic Process: The Case of Modern Medical Practice"; "A Sociologist Looks at the Legal Profession"; "The Professions and Social Structure"; "Professions."

12. Parsons, 1968: 545.

13. See, e.g., Roy Lewis and Angus Maude, Professional People, chap. 4; M. L. Cogan, "Toward a Definition of Profession"; William J. Goode, "Community within a Community: The Professions"; Ernest Greenwood, "Attributes of a Profession"; Bernard Barber, "Some Problems in the Sociology of Professions"; Howard M. Vollmer and Donald L.Mills, eds., Professionalization; D. Hickson and M. Thomas, "Professionalism in Britain: Preliminary Measurement"; Wilbert E. Moore, The Professions: Roles and Rules, pp. 5–6; Philip Elliott, The Sociology of Professions; John B. Cullen, The Structure of Professionalism: A Quantitative Examination; "Professional Differentiation and Occupational Earnings."

14. Royal Commission on Legal Services, Final Report, vol. 1, pp. 28, 30.

15. American Bar Association, Commisssion on Evaluation of Professional Standards, Model Rules of Professional Conduct, pp. 1–2.

16. See, e.g., Julius Roth, Sheryl Ruzek, and Arlene K. Daniels, "Current State of the Sociology of Occupations"; Paul Halmos, "Introduction"; "Professionalisation and Social Change"; Julius Roth, "Professionalism: The Sociologist's Decoy"; Paul Boreham, Alex Pemberton, and Paul Wilson, eds., The Professions in Australia: A Critical Appraisal; Alex Pemberton and Paul Boreham, "Towards a Reorientation of Sociological Studies of the Professions"; Elliott Krause, Power and Illness: The Political Sociology of Health and Medical Care; Eve Spangler and Peter M. Lehman, "Lawyering as Work."

17. Compare Stanley Fish, "Anti-Professionalism," with Drucilla Cornell, "Convention and Critique," and David Luban, "Fish v. Fish or, Some Realism About Idealism."

18. Cf. Barbalet, "Social Closure in Class Analysis: A Critique of Parkin," p. 491.

19. Freidson, 1970: chap. 1

20. Goode, "Encroachment, Charlatanism, and the Emerging Professions: Psychology, Sociology and Medicine," p. 912; Pemberton & Boreham, 1976: 24;

Paul Boreham, "Indetermination: professional knowledge, organization and control," p. 695.

21. James W. Grimm and Carol L. Kronus, "Occupations and Publics: A Framework for Analysis."

22. Eliot Freidson, Professional Powers, p. 225; see also "The Changing Nature of Professional Control."

23. Milton Friedman, Capitalism and Freedom; T. Johnson, 1972: 41. For the emergence of lawyers within the division of labor, see E. Adamson Hoebel, The Law of Primitive Man; Stuart Nagel, "Culture Patterns and Judicial Systems"; Richard Schwartz and James Miller, "Legal Evolution and Societal Complexity"; Katherine S. Newman, Law and Economic Organization.

24. Renee C. Fox, "Training for Uncertainty"; Harold Wilensky, "The Professionalization of Everyone?" p. 148; H. Jamous and B. Peloille, "Professions or Self-Perpetuating Systems? Changes in the French University-Hospital System."

25. John Child and Janet Faulk, "Maintenance of Occupational Control: The Case of Professions."

26. Amitai Etzioni, ed., The Semi-Professions; Larson, 1977.

27. Rue Bucher and Anselm Strauss, "Professions in Process."

28. Pemberton & Boreham, 1976: 28–33.

29. Jamous & Peloille, 1970: 138; Nina Toren, "Deprofessionalization and its Sources."

30. Larson, 1977.

31. Polanyi, 1957; cf. Erich Fromm, Escape from Freedom.

32. Larson, 1977: 135.

33. Max Weber, The Theory of Social and Economic Organization, p. 142; see also 1978: 342; Mike Saks, "Removing the blinkers? A critique of recent contributions to the sociology of professions," p. 5.

34. Allan Parachini, "State Studies Title Licensure Issue."

35. Harris Brotman, "Human Embryo Transplants."

36. See, e.g., Freidson, 1970; John Westergaard and Henrietta Resler, Class in a Capitalist Society, pp. 92, 346; Larson, 1977.

37. Johnson, 1972: 45–46.

38. Frank Parkin, Marxism and Class Theory; see also Abercrombie & Urry, 1983: 90–91.

39. Pierre Bourdieu and Jean-Claude Passeron, Reproduction in Education, Society and Culture; Raymond Murphy, "The Structure of Closure: A Critique and Development of the Theories of Weber, Collins, and Parkin."

40. E.g., Carolyn Tuohy and Alan D. Wolfson, "The Political Economy of Professionalism: A Perspective"; Zenon Bankowski and Geoff Mungham, "A Political Economy of Legal Education"; Robin Luckham, "The Political Economy of Legal Professions: Towards a Framework for Comparison."

41. New York Times, "What Value Education? Study Counts the Ways," citing U.S. Census Bureau, "What's It Worth? Educational Background and Economic Status: Spring 1984."

42. Cf. Michael Young, The Rise of the Meritocracy.

43. Jamous & Peloille, 1970: 113.

44. Victor Merina, "City Seeks to Flag Down 'Bandit' Taxicabs."

45. Max Weber, From Max Weber, pp. 241–42.

46. Parkin, 1979: 104.

47. New York Times, "Circus Work Continues to Draw the Dreamers."

48. Randall Collins, "Functional and Conflict Theories of Educational Stratification"; The Credential Society: An Historical Sociology of Education and Stratification; R. M. Blackburn and M. Mann, The Working Class in the Labour Market; V. Lane Rawlins and Lloyd Ulman, "The Utilization of College-Trained Manpower in the U.S."

49. Ivar Berg, Education and Jobs; K. Kumar, "Continuities and Discontinuities in the Development of Industrial Societies"; Boreham, 1983: 707.

50. Colin M. Campbell, "Lawyers and Their Public," p. 34.

51. Carlin, 1962: 41 n.2, 77.

52. On the first point, see Parkin, 1979: 55; Douglas Klegon, "The Sociology of the Professions: An Emerging Perspective," p. 29. On the second, see Robert K. Merton, George C. Reader, and Patricia Kendell, eds., The Student Physician; Howard S. Becker, Blanche Geer, Everett C. Hughes, and Anselm Strauss, Boys in White; Rue Bucher and Joan Stelling, Becoming Professional. On the third, see Berg, 1970.

53. Sanford A. Marcus, "Too Many Medical Schools in State."

54. Anne C. Roark, "UC May Limit Medical, Dental Students to Cut Spending."

55. Ronald Sullivan, "New York Panel Urges Cut in Doctor Training"; "Hospitals Fight Bid to Limit Doctor Training."

56. Milt Freudenheim, "Organized Medicine Considering Defense Against Glut of Doctors."

57. Parkin, 1979.

58. Terence Johnson, "The State and the Professions: Peculiarities of the British," pp. 198, 205.

59. Freidson, 1986: 64, 77.

60. Geoffrey Millerson, The Qualifying Associations.

61. Larson, 1977: 133.

62. Barbalet, 1982: 488; Freidson, 1986: 76; cf. Carol Kronus, "The Evolution of Occupational Power."

63. Keith M. Macdonald, "Social Closure and Occupational Registration," p. 544.

64. Noel Parry and Jose Parry, "Social Closure and Collective Mobility"; Keith M. Macdonald, "Professional Formation: The Case of Scottish Accountants"; Macdonald, 1985.

65. Johnson, 1972: 52; Macdonald, 1984; Parkin, 1979.

66. For the role of universities in the rise of professionalism in the United States, see Burton J. Bledstein, The Culture of Professionalism. For the balance between academic education and apprentice-

ship in the training of lawyers in civil and common law countries, see Richard L. Abel and Philip S. C. Lewis, eds., Lawyers in Society, vols. 1 and 2.

67. Freidson, 1970; Rosemary Stevens, American Medicine and the Public Interest; Gerald E. Markowitz and David Karl Rosner, "Doctors in Crisis: A Study of the Use of Medical Education Reform to Establish Modern Professional Elitism in Medicine"; Jeffrey L. Berlant, Profession and Monopoly: A Study of Medicine in the United States and Great Britain; Noel Parry and Jose Parry, The Rise of the Medical Profession; Paul Starr, The Social Transformation of American Medicine.

68. Child & Faulk, 1982; Robert A. Rothman, "Deprofessionalization: The Case of Law in America."

69. Harry Nelson, "Many Americans Study Medicine Abroad"; Richard Lyons, "Most Foreign Graduates Failed Test, A.M.A. Is Told"; "Foreign-trained Doctors in for a Thorough Checkup"; Ronald Sullivan, "New York Puts Curb on Medical Students from the Caribbean"; Paul Jacobs, "State Dubious, Will Monitor Caribbean Medical Schools."

70. Richard C. Paddock, "Bills Would Help 2 Get Medical Licenses"; Richard Lyons, "Investigators Check on Thousands for Falsified Degrees as Doctors"; Fred Hechinger, "Study Finds 'Diploma Mills' a Booming Industry"; Gene I. Maeroff, "2 Coaching Concerns Barred from Using S.A.T. Materials"; Fox Butterfield, "Ex-Policeman Tells of Boston Test Thefts"; Joel Brinkley, "28,000 'Doctors' Are Feared Unfit."

71. J. Ben-David, "Professions in the Class System of Present-Day Societies," p. 275; Victor P. Fuchs, The Service Economy; Abercrombie & Urry, 1983: 2–6.

72. Berg, 1970; Ronald Dore, The Diploma Disease.

73. Adam Smith, An Inquiry into the Nature and Causes of the Wealth of Nations, pp. 118–19; see Robert Dingwall, "Introduction," p. 1.

74. E.g., Milton Friedman and Simon Kuznets, Income from Independent Professional Practice; Walter Gellhorn, Individual Freedom and Governmental Restraints; "The Abuse of Occupational Licensing"; Friedman, 1962; Simon Rottenberg, "The Economics of Occupational Licensing"; Occupational Licensure and Regulation; D.S. Lees, The Economic Consequences of the Professions; Alex Maurizi, "Occupational Licensing and the Public Interest"; Philip Slayton and Michael J. Trebilcock, eds., The Professions and Public Policy; Roger D. Blair and Stephen Rubin, eds., Regulating the Professions; Patrick Foley, Avner Shaked, and John Sutton, The Economics of the Professions; John Nieuwenhuysen and Marina Williams-Wynn, Professions in the Marketplace; Daniel P. Hogan, ed., Professional Regulation.

75. E.g., Thomas G. Moore, "The Purpose of Licensing"; George J. Stigler, "The Theory of Economic Regulation"; Richard Posner, "Theories of Economic Regulation"; Sam Peltzman, "Toward a More General Theory of Regulation"; William D.

White, "Dynamic Elements of Regulation: The Case of Occupational Licensure."

76. Sidney L. Carroll and Robert J. Gaston, "New Approaches and Empirical Evidence on Occupational Licensing and the Quality of Service Rendered"; "State Occupational Licensing Provisions and Quality of Service"; "Occupational Licensing and the Quality of Service: An Overview."

77. E.g., R. A. Kessel, "Price Discrimination in Medicine"; "The A.M.A. and the Supply of Physicians"; Arlene S. Holen, "Effects of Professional Licensing Arrangements on Interstate Labor Mobility and Resource Allocation"; Tibor Scitovsky, "An International Comparison of the Trend of Professional Earnings"; M. W. Feldstein, "The Rising Price of Physicians' Services"; E. M. Egleston, "Licensing—Effects on Career Mobility"; H. E. Frech, "Occupational Licensure and Health Care Productivity: The Issues and the Literature"; R. T. Masson and S. Wu, "Price Discrimination for Physicians' Services"; J. Pfeffer, "Some Evidence on Occupational Licensing and Occupational Incomes"; W. Siebert, "Occupational Licensing: The Merrison Report on the Regulation of the Medical Profession"; J. Lipscomb, "Impact of Legal Restrictions on the Future Role of Dental Auxiliaries"; Lawrence Shepard, "Licensing Restrictions and the Cost of Dental Care"; B. Peter Pashigian, "Occupational Licensing and the Interstate Mobility of Professionals"; William D. White, "Why Is Regulation Introduced in the Health Sector? A Look at Occupational Licensure"; "Public Health and Private Gain: The Economics of Licensing Clinical Laboratory Personnel"; "Labor Market Organization and Professional Regulation: A Historical Analysis of Nursing Licensure"; T. R. Muzondo and B. Pazerka, "Occupational Licensing and Professional Incomes in Canada"; James W. Begun, "Professionalism and the Public Interest: Price and Quality in Optometry"; W. Lazarus, Competition Among Health Practitioners: The Impact of the Medical Profession on the Health Manpower Market; Alex R. Maurizi, Ruth L. Moore, and Lawrence Shepard, "Competing for Professional Control: Professional Mix in the Eyeglasses Industry"; D. A. Conrad and G. G. Sheldon, "The Effects of Legal Constraints on Dental Care Prices"; Arthur S. DeVany, Wendy L. Gramm, Thomas R. Saving, and Charles W. Smithson, "The Impact of Input Regulation: The Case of the U.S. Dental Industry"; A. Monheit, "Occupational Licensure and the Utilization of Nursing Labor: An Economic Analysis"; Gerald Larkin, Occupational Monopoly and Modern Medicine.

78. R. J. Arnould, "Pricing Professional Services: A Case Study of the Legal Service Industry"; Richard Freeman, "Legal Cobwebs: A Recursive Model of the Market for New Lawyers"; Robert G. Evans and Michael J. Trebilcock, eds., Lawyers and the Consumer Interest: Regulating the Market for Legal Services.

79. C. M. Lindsay, "Real Returns to Medical Education"; Keith B. Leffler, "Physician Licensure: Competition and Monopoly in American Medicine";

S. T. Mennemeyer, "Really Great Returns to Medical Education"; R. J. Ruffin and D. E. Leigh, "Charity, Competition, and the Pricing of Doctor's Services."

80. E.g., Kenneth Arrow, "Uncertainty and the Welfare Economics of Medical Care"; G. A. Akerlof, "The Market for 'Lemons': Quality Uncertainty and the Market Mechanism"; H. E. Leland, "Quacks, Lemons, and Licensing: A Theory of Minimum Quality Standards"; Carroll & Gaston, 1983; Robert Dingwall and Paul Fenn, " 'A Respectable Profession'? Sociological and Economic Perspectives on the Regulation of Professional Services."

81. Begun, 1986: 122.

82. E.g., Theodore Schultz, "Investment in Human Capital"; Gary Becker, Human Capital: A Theoretical Analysis; B. F. Kiker, The Concept of Human Capital.

83. M. Spence, "Job Market Signalling."

84. E.g., David A. Dodge, "Occupational Wage Differentials, Occupational Licensing and Returns to Investment in Education: An Exploratory Analysis"; G. Psacharapoulos, "Monopoly Elements in Earnings from Education"; Larson, 1977: 212; Brian Riera, Murray Glow, Donald Siddal, and William Klein, Human Capital Analysis: Its Application in the Study of the Consumer Interest in the Professions, chap. 2.

85. Reinhard Kreckel, "Unequal Opportunity Structure and Labour Market Segmentation."

86. Clark Kerr, "The Balkanization of Labor Markets," p. 93; Peter B. Doeringer and Michael J. Piore, Internal Labor Markets and Manpower Analysis; David M. Gordon, Theories of Poverty and Unemployment. On professionals, see Kreckel, 1980: 541.

87. John Creedy, "Professional Labour Markets."

88. Richard A. Posner, "The Social Costs of Monopoly and Regulation"; Gordon Tullock, "The Transitory Gains Gap."

89. Allan Parachini, "Small Towns Benefit from Doctor Glut, Study Says"; "In Near Future, More Doctors May Make Fewer Dollars."

90. Richard Freeman, The Overeducated American; Magali Sarfatti Larson, "Proletarianization and Educated Labor," pp. 151–53.

91. Gene Maeroff, "Enrollment in Professional Schools Declining"; New York Times, "Number in Medical School Off"; "Number Applying to Medical School Drops."

92. Larry Gordon, "U.S. Dental Schools Feel the Crunch."

93. E.g., Robert Dingwall, "Accomplishing Profession"; Saks, 1983: 4–5.

94. Harry Bernstein and Henry Weinstein, "Tests for New Teachers Get Endorsement of AFL-CIO"; Gene Maeroff, "Shanker Urges Teachers Move Past Bargaining"; Dennis Hevesi, "Carnegie Panel Establishes Board to Plan Certification of Teachers"; Carnegie Forum on Education and the Economy, A Nation Prepared: Teachers for the 21st Century.

95. Markowitz & Rosner, 1973: 95, 97; Frech, 1974: 124–25.

96. Ralph Turner, "Models of Social Ascent through Education: Sponsored and Contest Mobility."

97. Macdonald, 1984.

98. Bledstein, 1976; Klegon, 1979: 275.

99. Johnson, 1982: 203.

100. E.g., Mary Frank Fox and Sharlene Hess-Biber, Women at Work.

101. E.g., Stuart Dorsey, The Licensing Queue; Richard Freeman, "The Effect of Occupational Licensure on Black Occupational Achievement."

102. Larson, 1977: 5.

103. Derek Portwood and Alan Fielding, "Privilege and Professions," pp. 759, 765.

104. Andrew Abbott, "Status and Status Strain in the Professions."

105. Lois Timnick, "Psychologists Face Identity Crisis."

106. Weber, 1947: 143.

107. Larson, 1977: 62–63.

108. E.g., Joseph P. Newhouse, "A Model of Physician Pricing"; Joseph P. Newhouse and F. A. Sloan, "Physician Pricing: Monopolistic or Competitive: Reply"; H. E. Frech and Paul B. Ginsberg, "Physician Pricing: Monopolistic or Competitive: Comment"; Lee Benham, "The Effect of Advertising on the Price of Eyeglasses"; Lee Benham and Alexandra Benham, "Regulating Through Professions: A Perspective on Information Control"; J. F. Cady, Drugs on the Market: The Impact of Public Policy on the Retail Market for Prescription Drugs; R. Feldman and James W. Begun, "The Effects of Advertising: Lessons from Optometry"; "Does Advertising of Prices Reduce the Mean and Variance of Prices?"; T. R. Muzondo and B. Pazerka, Professional Licensing and Competition Policy: Effects of Licensing on Rates-of-Return Differentials; Ronald S. Bond, John E. Kwoka, Jr., John J. Phelan, and Ira Taylor, "Self-Regulation in Optometry: The Impact on Price and Quality."

109. Marlene Cimons, "Vision Centers Provide Good Value, FTC Says"; Irwin Molotsky, "State Laws Cost Car Buyers, U.S. Study Says."

110. Tamar Lewin, "Drug Makers Fighting Back Against Advance of Generics."

111. New York Times, "U.S. Judge Finds Medical Group Conspired Against Chiropractors."

112. Jube Shiver, "Low-Cost Health Groups Distress Physician Critics."

113. Daniel Goleman, "Social Workers Vault into a Leading Role in Psychotherapy."

114. Pamela G. Hollie, "New Rx for Pharmacists"; cf. William C. Rempel and Eric Coleman, "Pharmacists Curb Sale of Painkiller"; Harry Nelson, "Dentistry: Offices Need Filling Too"; James Quinn, "Dentists Fail to Halt Plan for Hygienists to Practice on Own"; John Kendall, "Hygienists Countersue in Long Battle with Dentists."

115. Oswald Hall, "Stages of a Medical Career."

116. Larry Green, "Surgical Society's Rules Put Country Doctor in a Dilemma."

117. Goode, 1960; Keith B. Leffler, "Economic and Legal Analysis of Medical Ethics: The Case of Restrictions on Interprofessional Association."

118. Robin Luckham, "The Political Economy of Legal Professions: Towards a Framework for Comparison," p. 325.

119. Terence J. Johnson, "Imperialism and the Professions: Notes on the Development of Professional Occupations in Britain's Colonies and the New States"; Dietrich Rueschemeyer, Lawyers and Their Society; Larson, 1977: 144; Luckham, 1981: 298.

120. Donald Black, The Behavior of Law.

121. New York Times, "A Run on Accountants."

122. Marc Galanter, "Reading the Landscape of Disputes," pp. 51–61.

123. E.g., Robert G. Evans, E. M. A. Parish, and F. Sully, "Medical Productivity and Demand Generation"; Robert G. Evans, "Supplier-Induced Demand: Some Empirical Evidence and Implications"; Penny H. Feldman, "The Impact of Third-Party Payment on Professional Practice: Lessons from the Medical Profession."

124. Warren Berger, "What's New in Cosmetic Dentistry."

125. Garry Abrams, "Dentists Brighten Up Their Marketing Skills."

126. Andrew Feinberg, "Accountants Try to Put a Little Kick in Their Image."

127. John C. Freed, "Glut of Doctors Creating a Patient's Market."

128. Steven A. Meyerowitz, "Marketing the Professions."

129. Tamar Lewin, "Hospitals Pitch Harder for Patients."

130. Allan Parachini, "Hospital Campaigns Aim to Deliver—More Babies."

131. Robert Pear, "Plan for Medicare Forces U.S. to List Approved Doctors"; Robert A. Rosenblatt, "Curb on Medicare Fees of Doctors Pondered."

132. Larry Green, "11 Convicted in Medicaid 'Fraud Mills.'"

133. Los Angeles Times, "Panel Tells Social Security Agency Waste."

134. Michael Seiler, "Audit Finds Physicians Are Overpaid as Witnesses."

135. Johnson, 1972: 77–81.

136. Robert Pear, "For Dishonest Billing by Doctors, a New Rx."

137. Rosenblatt, 1987.

138. Pear, 1987b.

139. Robert Pear, "Rx for Fees. U.S. Outlook"; Fazlur Rahman, "Medicare Makes a Wrong Diagnosis"; Harold P. Lazar, "Doctor, Patient, Bureaucrat"; Richard L. Berke, "A.M.A. Suit Alleges Bias in New Rules on Medicare Fees."

140. Robert Pear, "Companies Tackle Health Costs."

141. Abercrombie & Urry, 1983: 31, 49.

142. Terence J. Johnson, "The Professions in the Class Structure"; "What Is to Be Known?"; Larson, 1977: 213; Al Szymanski, "A Critique and Extension of the PMC"; Charles Derber, "Toward a New Theory of Professionals as Workers: Advanced Capitalism and Postindustrial Labor," p. 200; Abercrombie & Urry, 1983: 77; Boreham, 1983.

143. John Hagan, Marie Huxter, and Patricia Parker, "Class Structure and Legal Practice: Inequality and Mobility Among Toronto Lawyers."

144. G. Carchedi, "On the Economic Identification of the New Middle Class"; Abercrombie & Urry, 1983: 62–63.

145. Nicholas Poulantzas, Classes in Contemporary Capitalism; G. Esland, "Professions and Professionalism."

146. Victor Navarro, Medicine Under Capitalism; Class Struggle, the State and Medicine; David Noble, "The PMC: A Critique," pp. 135–36.

147. Erik Olin Wright, "Intellectuals and the Class Structure of Capitalist Society," p. 201.

148. Erik Olin Wright, Cynthia Costello, David Hachen, and Joey Sprague, "The American Class Structure."

149. Adolf A. Berle and Gardiner C. Means, The Modern Corporation and Private Property. For an argument that lawyers derive their power from their clients rather than from their expertise, see John P. Heinz, "The Power of Lawyers." For an argument that lawyers use their expertise to legitimate their principal client, capital, see James C. Foster, The Ideology of Apolitical Politics. The Elite Lawyers' Response to the Legitimation Crisis in American Capitalism: 1870–1920.

150. E.g., John Kenneth Galbraith, The New Industrial State; Daniel Bell, The Coming of Post-Industrial Society; The Cultural Contradictions of Capitalism; B. Bruce-Biggs, ed., The New Class?; Peter Steinfels, The Neo-Conservatives; Michel Crozier, Strategies for Change; Robert Wuthnow and Wesley Shrum, "Knowledge Workers as a 'New Class': Structural and Ideological Convergence among Professional-Technical Workers and Managers"; Magali Sarfatti Larson, "The Production of Expertise and the Constitution of Expert Power."

151. Alvin Gouldner, The Future of Intellectuals and the Rise of the New Class.

152. George Konrád and Ivan Szelényi, The Intellectuals on the Road to Class Power; see also Ivan Szelényi, "Gouldner's Theory of the 'Flawed Universal Class.'"

153. Parkin, 1979: 58.

154. Gouldner, 1979: 19–20.

155. Barbara Ehrenreich and John Ehrenreich, "The Professional-Managerial Class."

156. E.g., Marie R. Haug, "Deprofessionalization: An Alternative Hypothesis for the Future"; Martin Oppenheimer, "The Proletarianization of the Professional."

157. Charles Derber, "Professionals as New Workers," p. 5.

158. Larson, 1980: 162–71; see generally Stephen Wood, ed., The Degradation of Work? Skill, Deskilling and the Labour Process.

159. Derber, 1982a: 6–7.

160. James O'Connor, The Fiscal Crisis of the State.

161. New York Times, "Doctors In Ontario Strike Over Fee System"; Los Angeles Times, "Ontario Doctors Vote to End Strike, Stage Rotating Halts in Services."

162. Dirk Johnson, "Doctors' Dilemma: Unionizing."

163. Freidson, 1986: chap. 6; see also "The Reorganization of the Professions by Regulation"; "Are Professions Necessary?"

164. Derber, 1982a: 7, 30–31.

165. Freidson, 1986: chap. 6; see also Larson, 1980: 139.

166. Charles Derber, "Managing Professionals: Ideological Proletarianization and Mental Labor," p. 169; see also G. Salaman, Work Organizations: Resistance and Control, p. 139.

167. Derber, 1982d: 196–99; Abercrombie & Urry, 1983: 57, 114–18.

168. Murray L. Schwartz, "The Professionalism and Accountability of Lawyers."

169. Parkin, 1979: 58.

170. E.g., Andre Gorz, Strategy for Labor; "Technology, Technicians and Class Struggle"; Alain Tourraine, The Post-Industrial Society; Serge Mallet, Essays on the New Working Class.

171. Charles Derber, "The Proletarianization of the Professional: A Review Essay," pp. 22–27.

172. E.g., Archie Kleingartner, Professionalism and Salaried Worker Organization; Marie Haug and Marvin Sussman, "Professionalization and Unionization: A Jurisdictional Dispute?"

173. Derber, 1982b: 27–29; 1982d: 204.

174. E.g. John P. Heinz and Edward O. Laumann, Chicago Lawyers, p. 143; Robert L. Nelson, "Ideology, Practice, and Professional Autonomy: Social Values and Client Relationships in the Large Law Firm."

175. Abercrombie & Urry, 1983: chap. 2.

176. E.g., Freidson, 1986: chap. 3.

177. Luckham, 1981: 304–06; Heinz & Laumann, 1982.

178. E.g., R. W. Hodge, P. M. Siegel, and H. Rossi, "Occupational Prestige in the United States, 1925–1963"; Peter Blau and Otis Dudley Duncan, The American Occupational Structure; Donald J. Treiman, Occupational Prestige in Comparative Perspective; A. P. M. Coxon and C. L. Jones, The Images of Occupational Prestige.

179. Larson, 1977: 156–57.

180. Thomas L. Haskell, "Professionalism versus Capitalism: R. H. Tawney, Emile Durkheim, and C. S. Peirce on the Disinterestedness of Professional Communities."

181. Parsons, 1964a: 384.

182. But see Nelson, 1985.

183. John W. Anderson, "How One Company Clamped Down on Doctor Bills."

184. Derber, 1982c: 167.

185. E.g., G. Harries-Jenkins, "Professionals in Organizations"; J. K. Benson, "The Analysis of Bureaucratic/Professional Conflict: Functionalist and Dialectical Approaches"; A. G. Fielding and D. Portwood, "Professions and the State: Towards a Typology of Bureaucratic Professions"; Rueschemeyer, 1983: 52.

186. E.g., Arlene Kaplan Daniels, "The Captive Professional: Bureaucratic Limitations in the Practice of Military Psychiatry"; Barney G. Glaser, Organizational Scientists: Their Professional Careers; William Kornhauser, Scientists in Industry; Simon Marcson, Scientists in Government; Robert Perucci and Joel Gerstl, Profession Without Community: Engineeers in American Society; J. Ben-David, "The Professional Role of the Physician in Bureaucratised Medicine: A Study of Role Conflict"; William G. Rothstein, "Professionalization and Employer Demands: The Cases of Homeopathy and Psychoanalysis in the United States"; Starr, 1982.

187. Peter Blau and Richard A. Schoenherr, The Structure of Organizations; Freidson, 1986: 169.

188. Martha Fay, "Why Your Family Doctor Is a Group," pp. 19–20.

189. Richard W. Stevenson, "Ad Agency Mergers Changing the Business."

190. Joseph A. Raelin, The Clash of Cultures: Managers and Professionals.

191. E.g., Hall, 1968; George Ritzer, "Professionalization, Bureaucratization and Rationalization: The Views of Max Weber"; Derber, 1982b: 16.

192. A. L. Stinchcombe, "Bureaucratic and Craft Administration of Production: A Comparative Survey"; Larson, 1977: 193, 199.

193. Derber, 1982d: 202.

194. Freidson, 1986: 161.

195. E.g., Durkheim, 1957; Goode, 1957.

196. Dietrich Rueschemeyer, "Doctors and Lawyers: A Comment on the Theory of the Professions," p. 17 n.2; Heinz & Laumann, 1982: 206–10.

197. Freidson, 1986: 213.

198. Larson, 1977: 3.

199. T. Johnson, 1972: 59.

200. Bruce Keppel, "Anesthesiologists Most Highly Paid Physicians."

201. Rueschemeyer, 1964: 23–24.

202. Michael Schudson, "The Flexner Report and the Reed Report: Notes on the History of Professional Education in the United States," p. 358.

203. Rueschemeyer, 1964: 19.

204. T. Johnson, 1972: 69.

205. Albert Shanker, "Professionalism under Fire: Power vs. Knowledge in St. Louis."

206. New York Times, "Court Overturns a Schoolbook Ban in 'Humanism' Case."

207. Jonathan Friendly, "Licensing of Latin Journalists Gives Rise to Growing Fears."

208. Michael J. Goodman and Victor Merina, "Lobby Stymies Efforts to Reform Audit Laws."

209. Jon Nordheimer, "Doctors Withhold Service in Insurance Protest."

210. Max Weber, Law in Economy and Society, pp. 202–03.

211. Thorstein Veblen, The Theory of the Leisure Class.

212. Jamous & Peloille, 1970: 141.

213. T. Johnson, 1972: 70; cf. Wilensky, 1964: 152.

214. William J. Goode, "The Protection of the Inept"; Trevor Noble and Bridget Pym, "Collegial Authority and the Receding Locus of Power"; Michael J. Trebilcock, Carolyn J. Tuohy, and Allan D. Wolfson, Professional Regulation: A Staff Study of Accountancy, Architecture, Engineering and Law in Ontario; Marie R. Haug, "The Sociological Approach to Self-Regulation." For physicians, see Robert C. Derbyshire, "How Effective Is Medical Self-Regulation?"; Andrew Dolan and Nicole D. Urban, "The Determinants of the Effectiveness of Medical Disciplinary Boards: 1960–77"; Joel Brinkley, "U.S., Industry and Physicians Attack Medical Malpractice"; "Medical Discipline Laws: Confusion Reigns"; Sidney Wolfe, Henry Bergman, and George Silver, Medical Malpractice: The Need for Disciplinary Reform, not Tort Reform.

215. Joel Brinkley, "State Medical Boards Disciplined Record Number of Doctors in '85."

216. New York Times, "Doctors Called Lax Monitors of Peers in Medicare."

217. Philip Shenon, "Deaver Cites Alcoholism as Perjury Trial Defense."

218. Jerome Carlin, Lawyers' Ethics.

219. Richard L. Abel, "Why Does the ABA Promulgate Ethical Rules?"; Andrew Abbott, "Professional Ethics"; cf. Murray Edelman, Symbolic Uses of Politics.

220. Marie Haug and Marvin Sussman, "Professional Autonomy and the Revolt of the Client"; Child & Faulk, 1982; Eliot Freidson, "Are Professions Necessary?"; 1986: chap. 5. For an argument that these developments do not necessarily signify a loss of autonomy, see Michael Powell, "Developments in the Regulation of Lawyers: Competing Segments and Market, Client, and Government Controls."

221. Jesus Sanchez, "FTC Moves to Overturn Eye-Care Industry Curbs."

222. Robert Pear, "Congress Rethinks Its Hands-Off Policy on Medical Research."

223. Eric N. Berg, "New Auditor Rule to Require Search for Client Fraud."

224. Robert Pear, "Doctors Gain Rights in Medicare Evaluations"; 1987b; 1987c; Robert Reinhold, "Texas Panel Reiterates Vow to Bar Unfit Doctors."

225. Ronald Sullivan, "Health Chief for New York to Act Against Misconduct by Physicians"; "Cuomo's Plan for Testing Doctors Is Part of Growing National Effort"; Jeffrey Schmalz, "Regents Board and Health Dept. Split Over Disciplining of Doctors"; New York Times, "Boston Hospitals vs. State Scrutiny."

226. Robert Pear, "U.S. to Offer Consumers Access to Data on Health Care Quality"; Joel Brinkley, "U.S. Distributing Lists of Hospitals with Unusual Death Rates"; "U.S. Releasing Lists of Hospitals with Abnormal Mortality Rates"; "Key Hospital Accrediting Agency to Start Weighing Mortality Rates."

227. Los Angeles Times, "Doctors and Lawyers Square Off on Legal Records."

Chapter 3

1. These were the Northwest Territories, 1801–02; Georgia, 1807; Tennessee, 1809; South Carolina, 1812; and New Jersey, 1817. See Robert Stevens, Law School, p. 7 nn. 42–43.

2. Robert Stevens, "Two Cheers for 1870," pp. 412–13, 417.

3. Albert J. Harno, Legal Education in the United States, pp. 37–41.

4. Carnegie Foundation, The Study of Legal Education, 1917.

5. R. Stevens, 1983: 7–8; William R. Johnson, Schooled Lawyers, p. 21.

6. James Barr Ames, Annual Address, p. 267; ABA Committee on Legal Education, Report, 1891, pp. 301–04.

7. Of those that required pupillage, seven states demanded two years, seven demanded three, one demanded four and one demanded five. ABA Committee on Legal Education, Report, 1881, pp. 302–04.

8. Ames, 1904, p. 266; R. Stevens, 1971: 427.

9. Harno, 1980: 51–52.

10. William R. Johnson, "Education and Professional Life Styles: Law and Medicine in the Nineteenth Century," p. 185.

11. R. Stevens, 1983: 20 n.2.

12. ABA Committee on Legal Education, Report, 1891, p. 318.

13. Gary Nash, "The Philadelphia Bench and Bar, 1800–1861."

14. ABA Committee on Legal Education, Report, 1891, App. B, Table 2.

15. W. Johnson, 1978: 51–55, 61.

16. Terence Halliday, "Formative Professionalism and the Three Revolutions: Legal Careers in the Chicago Bar, 1850–1900," Table 7.

17. Wayne K. Hobson, "Symbol of the New Profession: Emergence of the Large Law Firm, 1870–1915," p. 14 nn. 31–32.

18. Henry Winthrop Ballantine, "The Place in Legal Education of Evening and Correspondence Schools," p. 369.

19. Wayne K. Hobson, The American Legal Profession and the Organizational Society, 1890–1930, p. 106.

20. Will Shafroth and H. C. Horack, Report of the Committee, p. 5.

21. Joseph A. McClain, Jr., Thomas F. Mc-Donald, and Sidney Post Simpson, Legal Education and Admission to the Bar in California, p. 17.

22. Review of Legal Education, 1923: 47.

23. Marion R. Kirkwood, "Requirements for Admission to Practice Law," pp. 92–94.

24. Letter from Committee of Bar Examiners to Deans of California Law Schools, December 17, 1986.

25. W. Johnson, 1978: 4.

26. Esther Lucille Brown, Lawyers and the Promotion of Justice, pp. 23–24.

27. W. Johnson, 1978: 59–60.

28. Hobson, 1986: 134.

29. W. Johnson, 1978: 56, 71–72, 81, 86. 95, 100.

30. Ames, 1904: 267–68.

31. Ibid.; Lawrence Maxwell, "Chairman's Address," pp. 337–38.

32. Harno, 1980: 51–52.

33. Maxwell, 1905: 337–38; ABA Committee on Legal Education, 1891: 314.

34. W. Johnson, 1978: 75; Alfred Z. Reed, Present-Day Law Schools in the United States and Canada, p. 111.

35. ABA Committee on Legal Education, 1895: 315.

36. Alfred Z. Reed, Training for the Public Profession of the Law, 398.

37. J. R. Woodworth, "Some Influences on the Reform of Schools of Law and Medicine, 1890–1920," pp. 497–500.

38. 1 American Law School Review 20 (1902); 2 American Law School Review 522 (1911).

39. Reed, 1928: 98.

40. Mark W. Granfors and Terence C. Halliday, "Professional Passages: Caste, Class and Education in the 19th Century Legal Profession," Tables 2, 7, and 8.

41. Lawrence M. Friedman, A History of American Law, pp. 561–63; R. Stevens, 1971: 456: George Martin, Causes and Conflicts: The Centennial History of the Bar Association of the City of New York; Herman Kogan, The First Century: The Chicago Bar Association, 1874–1974; Hobson, 1986: 214.

42. E. Brown, 1938: 129; R. Stevens, 1983: 102 n.84.

43. Reed, 1928: 32; J. Willard Hurst, The Growth of American Law: The Law Makers, pp. 287–88; Brown, 1938: 129; Theodore J. Schneyer, "The Incoherence of the Unified Bar Concept: Generalizing from the Wisconsin Case," p. 8; John A. Matzko, " 'The Best Men of the Bar': The Founding of the American Bar Association."

44. Hobson, 1986: 215 n.5, 232–33, 236, 252–53.

45. Martin, 1970: 43, 161, 184, 213, 217, 292.

46. Halliday, 1985: 11, 23; Granfors & Halliday, 1985: 10 n. 6; Terence C. Halliday, Beyond Monopoly: Lawyers, State Crises, and Professional Empowerment, pp. 65–66.

47. Halliday, 1987: 68, 73, Table 5.1.

48. Hobson, 1986: 215 n.4.

49. Field Research Company, Members' Appraisal of the State Bar of California, p. 5.

50. Halliday, 1987: 81, Table 4.5. Only New York fell below this level: 31 percent belonged to the ABCNY and 31 percent to the NYCLA, with some overlap.

51. W. Johnson, 1974: 199–200.

52. Terence C. Halliday, Michael Powell, and Mark W. Granfors, "Minimalist Organizations: Vital Events in State Bar Associations, 1870–1930."

53. Halliday, 1987: 67; Schneyer, 1983: 12.

54. Hurst, 1950: 287–88.

55. Corinne Lathrop Gilb, Self-Regulating Professions and the Public Welfare: A Case Study of the California State Bar, pp. 35–36, 51.

56. Schneyer, 1983: 10; see also Halliday, 1987: Figure 5.1.

57. Schneyer, 1983: 2 n.4; Hobson, 1986: 308–09; Halliday, 1987: Table 3.2.

58. Field Research Company, 1960: 6.

59. Reed, 1928:22–44; Jerold Auerbach, "Enmity and Amity: Law Teachers and Practitioners, 1900–1922"; Hobson, 1986: 368–76.

60. Review of Legal Education, 1921: 101–02.

61. Ibid.; Reed, 1928: 42; Michael Schudson, "The Flexner Report and the Reed Report: Notes on the History of Professional Education in the United States," pp. 350–51.

62. R. Stevens, 1971: 453–56; Harry First, "Competition in the Legal Education Industry (I)," pp. 334 ff.

63. Reed, 1928: 29.

64. John H. Wigmore and Fredric B. Crossley, "A Statistical Comparison of College and High School Education as a Preparation for Legal Scholarship," p. 965.

65. Lloyd Garrison, "A Survey of the Wisconsin Bar," pp. 133–34; see also "Limitation on New York Bar Admissions Recommended," 5 Bar Examiner 115 (1936).

66. 2 Bar Examiner 83–84 (1933); 3 Bar Examiner 23 (1933).

67. 5 Bar Examiner 2 (1935).

68. 18 Bar Examiner 110 (1949).

69. 6 Bar Examiner 32 (1936).

70. Young B. Smith, "Take the Profit Out of Legal Education."

71. See, e.g., New York County Lawyers' Association, Committee on Professional Economics, Survey of the Legal Profession in New York County.

72. R. Stevens, 1983: 102; Garrison, 1935: 138; Schudson, 1974: 349–51.

73. Milton Friedman and Simon Kuznets, Income from Independent Professional Practice, pp. 101, 108–09.

74. M. Louise Rutherford, The Influence of the American Bar Association on Public Opinion and Legislation, p. 50.

75. R. Stevens, 1983: 37 nn. 22, 24.

76. Review of Legal Education, 1925: 53.

77. W. Johnson, 1978: 127, 131.

78. R. Stevens, 1983: 37 nn. 25–26, 196.

79. R. Stevens, 1971: 496–97; Review of Legal Education, 1928.

80. Review of Legal Education, 1923: 46.

81. R. Stevens, 1983: 193–94.

82. Albert P. Blaustein and Charles O. Porter, The American Lawyer, p. 210.

83. R. Stevens, 1983: 207 n. 24.

84. Gerard W. Gawalt, "The Impact of Industrialization on the Legal Profession in Massachusetts, 1870 1900," p. 105.

85. Halliday, 1985: Table 7.

86. ABA Committee on Legal Education, 1891: App. B; Gawalt, 1984: 120.

87. R. Stevens, 1983: 37 n. 22; Joel Seligman, The High Citadel: The Influence of Harvard Law School, pp. 41–42.

88. Jerold Auerbach, Unequal Justice, pp. 94–95; ABA Committee on Legal Education, 1895: Table B.

89. R. Stevens, 1983: 37 n. 22.

90. ABA Committee on Legal Education, 1895: 315.

91. Hobson, 1984: 14 nn. 31–32.

92. Gawalt, 1984: 105.

93. Young B. Smith and James Grafton Rogers, "The Overcrowding of the Bar and What Can be Done About It," p. 569.

94. 3 American Law School Review 622 (1915).

95. Josef E. Gellermann, "Report of a Survey of a Senior Evening Law Class in Washington, D.C.," p. 1074.

96. R. Stevens, 1983: 197 n.55.

97. Jerome E. Carlin, Lawyers' Ethics, p. 21.

98. McClain et al., 1949: 39–41.

99. John G. Hervey, "Pre-Legal Education of Students Admitted to Approved Law Schools—Fall, 1948."

100. Committee of Bar Examiners, Report, pp. 351–52.

101. State Bar of California, Proceedings of the Fifth Annual Meeting, pp. 293–95.

102. McClain et al., 1949: 40.

103. Committee of Bar Examiners, 1930: 351–52; State Bar of California, 1932: 293–95; McClain et al., 1949: 40.

104. New York County Lawyers' Association, 1936: 13.

105. For histories of specific states or institutions, see Robert Stevens, "Law Schools and Legal Education, 1879–1979" (Valparaiso); Stephen E. Kalish, "Legal Education and Bar Admissions" (Nebraska); A. H. Grundman, "Legal Education in Colorado"; see, generally, John Henry Schlegel and Alfred S. Konefsky, "Mirror, Mirror on the Wall: Histories of American Law Schools."

106. Ames, 1904: 267.

107. ABA Committee on Legal Education, 1891: 301–04.

108. Ames, 1904: 268.

109. R. Stevens, 1983. 174.

110. Committee of Bar Examiners, 1930: 351–52; Shafroth & Horack, 1933: 5.

111. James E. Brenner, "A Survey of Employment Conditions among Young Attorneys in California," p. 33.

112. State Bar of California, 1932: 293–95.

113. McClain et al., 1949: 17.

114. Harry H. Platt, "A Survey of Conditions of Law Practice in Michigan," p. 642 (23 percent response rate).

115. Kirkwood, 1952: 95; see also 17 Bar Examiner 32 (1948).

116. Letter from Committee of Bar Examiners to Deans of California Law Schools, December 17, 1986.

117. W. Johnson, 1978: 75, 100, 131–32.

118. U.S. Office of Education, Annual Report, 1872, pp. 814–15.

119. Reed, 1928: 51–52.

120. Reed, 1928: 111; Review of Legal Education, 1922: 66; Horack & Shafroth, 1938: 316.

121. Review of Legal Education, 1928: 42.

122. Review of Legal Education, 1924: 70–71.

123. Morland, 1951: 323.

124. Review of Legal Education.

125. Nor did the emergence of the case method of instruction at Harvard and its rapid spread among full-time law schools. For this reason I do not discuss what has been a preoccupation of historians of American legal education. See Seligman, 1978; R. Stevens, 1983; Anthony Chase, "The Birth of the Modern Law School"; "Origins of Modern Professional Education: The Harvard Case Method Conceived as Clinical Instruction in Law"; "American Legal Education Since 1885: The Case of the Missing Modern"; Hobson, 1986: 318–49. Similarly, I do not discuss the innovations of legal realism in research and teaching and the rivalry between Yale and Harvard in the 1940s and 1950s. See Laura Kalman, Legal Realism at Yale, 1927–1960.

126. Ames, 1904: 265.

127. R. Stevens, 1983: 74.

128. Hobson, 1986: 117–18.

129. 1 American Law School Review 20 (1902); 2 American Law School Review 125 (1907).

130. Reed, 1921: 398.

131. R. Stevens, 1983: 75, 80.

132. Thomas Koenig and Michael Rustad, "The Challenge to Hierarchy in Legal Education: Suffolk and the Night Law School Movement."

133. Shafroth & Horack, 1933: 3.

134. Smith and Rogers, 1932: 568.

135. Jerome E. Carlin, Lawyers on Their Own, p. 22 n. 26.

136. E. Brown, 1938: 170–72.

137. Shafroth & Horack, 1933: 1, 9.

138. Ballantine, 1919: 369.

139. Schudson, 1974: 351–52.

140. Review of Legal Education, 1922: 65.

141. Smith and Rogers, 1932: 569.

142. Koenig & Rustad, 1985.

143. R. Stevens, 1983: 194.

144. Shafroth & Horack, 1933: 1–2.

145. Review of Legal Education, 1932: 29.

146. H. Claude Horack and Will Shafroth, "The Law Schools of Tennessee: Report of the Survey Committee," pp. 313–14.

147. Peter DeL. Swords and Frank Walwer, The Costs and Resources of Legal Education, p. 42.

148. Koenig & Rustad, 1985.

149. John W. Morland, "Legal Education in Georgia," p. 320; see also Committee on Trend of Bar Admissions, Report.

150. 10 Bar Examiner 12 (1941).

151. Review of Legal Education.

152. Albert P. Blaustein, "College and Law School Education of the American Lawyer—A Preliminary Report," pp. 297–98.

153. R. Stevens, 1983: 207.

154. Review of Legal Education, 1979.

155. McClain et al., 1949: 113–15.

156. James W. Brenner and Leon E. Warmke, "Statistically Speaking—," p. 12.

157. McClain et al., 1949, pp. 106–08.

158. State Bar of California, 1932: 293–95.

159. Blaustein & Porter, 1954: 179.

160. Edwin Chen, "The Trials of Low-Budget Law Schools."

161. 9(6) NLJ 4 (October 20, 1986).

162. Harry First, "Competition in the Legal Education Industry (II)," pp. 1076, 1082, 1085; R. Stevens, 1983: 244–45.

163. Jim Mann, "ABA Ends Opposition to Oral Roberts Law School."

164. First, 1979: 1053, 1070 n. 128, 1074.

165. Edward A. Adams, "ABA Denies Accreditation to Three: Western State, Nevada, St. Thomas."

166. Review of Legal Education, 1932: 29.

167. Smith & Rogers, 1932: 567.

168. State Bar of California, 1932: 293–95.

169. New York County Lawyers' Association, 1936: 13.

170. E. Brown, 1938: 50.

171. R. Stevens, 1983: 243 n. 116.

172. AALS Special Committee on Law School Administration and University Relations, Anatomy of Modern Legal Education, pp. 14, 23–24.

173. Joseph T. Tinnelly, Part-Time Legal Education, p. 81.

174. 9(28) NLJ 4 (March 23, 1987).

175. Tinnelly, 1957: 53.

176. Gellerman, 1941: 1074.

177. Lowell S. Nicholson, The Law Schools of the United States, pp. 225–27.

178. W. Johnson, 1978: 132.

179. R. Stevens, 1983: 141 n. 94, 172 n. 5, 197.

180. "Inflation and the Law Schools," 21 Bar Examiner 96–97 (1952).

181. AALS, Special Committee, 1961: 104–05.

182. Swords & Walwer, 1974: 225–26, 228, 254, 264–65.

183. 13(1) AALS Syllabus (Spring 1982).

184. Kenneth A. Pye and John R. Kramer, "Solvency and Survival after the Boom—A Different Perspective," p. 468; XVI(2) AALS Syllabus 2–3 (June 1985).

185. Jim Miskiewicz, "Legal Education Costs Soar."

186. Nicholson, 1958: 230.

187. AALS, Special Committee, 1961: 110–18.

188. Lon H. Fuller, "Legal Education and Admission to the Bar in Pennsylvania."

189. Blaustein & Porter, 1954: 198–99.

190. AALS, Special Committee, 1961: 120–21.

191. Pye and Kramer, 1984: 476.

192. XVI(2) AALS Syllabus 2–3 (June 1985).

193. John Balzar, "Student Loan Defaults Called Alarming: May Exceed 1 Billion for Year; Tougher Rules Planned."

194. E. Brown, 1938: 50.

195. R. Stevens, 1983: 141 n. 93, 160 n. 50, 160–61; Charles E. Clark, "The Selective Process of Choosing Students and Lawyers," pp. 914–15.

196. Albert Crawford, "Use of Legal Aptitude Test in Admitting Applicants to Law School."

197. R. Stevens, 1983: 161 n. 59.

198. Gellerman, 1941: 1074.

199. Morland, 1951: 300.

200. Nicholson, 1958: 218.

201. McClain et al., 1949: 44.

202. Wagner Thielens, Jr., "Some Comparisons of Entrants to Medical and Law School," p. 145.

203. R. Stevens, 1983: 236 n.37.

204. George Neff Stevens, "Better Trained Applicants—An Incentive Approach," p. 82.

205. R. Stevens, 1983: 210 n. 38.

206. R. Stevens, 1983: 236 n. 37.

207. Franklin R. Evans, "Applications and Admissions to ABA Accredited Law Schools," pp. 572–73.

208. Carl A. Auerbach, "Legal Education and Some of Its Discontents," p. 46; Alexander W. Astin, Minorities in Higher Education, p. 84.

209. Evans, 1977: 574.

210. Evans, 1977: 564, 586–89.

211. Review of Legal Education.

212. Richard D. Lyons, "Fake M.D. Degrees Are Put at 10,000"; "House Panel Told of Bogus Doctor Who Left a Patient 'a Vegetable.' "

213. R. Stevens, 1983: 37 n. 22, 160.

214. Stanley T. Wallbank, "The Function of Bar Examiners," p. 37; Koenig & Rustad, 1985.

215. R. Stevens, 1983: 141 n. 93.

216. Review of Legal Education, 1936: 20.

217. McClain et al., 1949: 51.

218. McClain et al., 1949: 48, 50.

219. Thielens, 1957: 146.

220. G. Stevens, 1963: 77.

221. McClain et al., 1949: 48–51.

222. Swords & Walwer, 1974: 333–39.

223. G. Stevens, 1963: 78.

224. For a history of entry barriers in Texas, see Stephen K. Huber, "Admission to the Practice of Law in Texas."

225. Reed, 1928: 11; see also ABA Committee on Legal Education, 1891: 314.

226. R. Stevens, 1983: 27 n. 56.

227. G. Stevens, 1977.

228. Reed, 1928: 11; Fred B. Weil, The 1967 Lawyer Statistical Report, p. 28; R. Stevens, 1983: 98–99, 174 n. 27; Bar Examiner, 1981.

229. Friedman & Kuznets, 1945: 38.

230. R. Stevens, 1983: 25, 94.

231. W. Johnson, 1978: 56.

232. R. Stevens, 1983: 25, 95.

233. ABA Committee on Legal Education, 1881: 302–04.

234. R. Stevens, 1983: 94 n. 21.

235. Reed, 1921: 103.

236. U.S. Office of Education, Annual Report of the Commissioner of Education, 1904, p. 1593.

237. Committee of Bar Examiners, 1930: 359.

238. James E. Brenner, Survey of Bar Examination Procedure in the United States, 1930–1931.

239. E. Brown, 1938: 115–16; Harold Shepherd, "A Survey of Bar Admission Procedures."

240. 1 American Law School Review 57 (1902).

241. William M. Mills, "Development of Requirements for Admission to the Bar in Kansas," p. 81.

242. Fred C. Desmond, "New Hampshire Stops the Leaks," pp. 308–09.

243. Brenner, 1932b.

244. Friedman & Kuznets, 1945: 38.

245. Horack & Shafroth, 1938: 320; Garrison, 1935: 134.

246. E. Brown, 1938: 117.

247. 7 California State Bar Journal 288 (1932).

248. Shafroth & Horack, 1933: 130.

249. James E. Brenner, "Trends in Lawyer Population and the Amount of Legal Business," p. 54; Gilb, 1956: 81; In re Investigation, 1934.

250. Notes on Legal Education 6–7 (July 1933).

251. 10 Bar Examiner 12 (1941).

252. Notes on Legal Education 5, 10 (July 1933).

253. C. Clark, 1933: 918.

254. Brenner, 1935: 54; Friedman & Kuznets, 1945: 38.

255. Philip J. Wickser, "Law Schools, Bar Examiners, and Bar Associations," p. 730; 9 California State Bar Journal 2 (1934).

256. Will Shafroth, "Eventual Success in the Bar Examinations," p. 138.

257. Notes on Legal Education 4–5 (July 1933).

258. Alfred Z. Reed, "Tracking Down the Repeaters," p. 236.

259. Shafroth & Horack, 1933: 121. Between February 1932 and September 1938, the following were the proportion passing and the proportion of all passers: first takers—52%, 72%; second—33%, 18%; third—25%, 6%; fourth—18%, 2%; fifth—13%, 1%; sixth—12%, 0.4%, seventh—1%, 0.3%; eighth—9%, 0.1%; ninth—4%, 0.02%, tenth—6%, 0.02%; four-teen poor souls took the examination eleven, twelve or thirteen times, but none of them passed. 14 California State Bar Journal 66–67 (1939).

260. 2 Bar Examiner 26, 28 (1932).

261. Shafroth, 1936: 138.

262. Friedman & Kuznets, 1945: 38.

263. G. Stevens, 1963: 80–81.

264. American Bar Foundation, The Legal Profession in the United States, p. 28.

265. David A. Kaplan, "Bar Exam: The Rites of Passage Are Getting Tougher."

266. 8(36) NLJ 4 (May 19, 1986).

267. Brenner, 1932b; Committee of Bar Examiners, 1930: 351–52.

268. George F. Baer Appel, "The Pennsylvania System," p. 937; "The Pennsylvania System," p. 23.

269. Horack & Shafroth, 1938: 321–24.

270. Fred C. Desmond, "New Hampshire Applies the Scientific Method," p. 140.

271. John E. Biby, "Bar Examination Statistics and Standards." For comparable figures for both examinations in 1930, see Committee of Bar Examiners, 1930: 351–52; for cumulative figures between 1929 and 1932, see H. Claude Horack and Will Shafroth, "II. Excerpts from the Survey Report," p. 34; Shafroth & Horack, 1933: 5, 118–20. For the August 1933 examination, see 3 Bar Examiner 53 (1934). For cumulative figures 1932–39, see 14 California State Bar Journal 64–65 (1939).

272. 2 Bar Examiner 26–27 (1932).

273. Malcolm K. Benadum, "A Study of Ohio Bar Examinations," pp. 108–10.

274. McClain et al., 1949: 19–20.

275. Chen, 1983; Letter from Committee of Bar Examiners to Deans of California Law Schools, December 17, 1986.

276. Koenig & Rustad, 1985.

277. Loren E. Souers, Jr., "Qualifications of Applicants Seeking to Take a Bar Examination," p. 83.

278. Phillip Cutright, Karen Cutright, and Douglass G. Boschkoff, "Course Selection, Student Characteristics and Bar Examination Peformance: The Indiana University Law School Experience."

279. Los Angeles Times, sec. 1, p. 3 (January 9, 1985).

280. Mary Ann Galante, "Bar Passage Rate Plunges."

281. J. Auerbach, 1971: 585.

282. Milton R. Konvitz, The Alien and the Asiatic in American Law, pp. 190–201.

283. In re Griffiths, 1973.

284. U.S. Office of Education, 1879: CXL.

285. Supreme Court of New Hampshire v. Piper, 1985; Allan Ashman, "Residency Requirements for Admission to the Bar: Gordon and its Progeny"; 71 American Bar Association Journal 64–67 (March 1985).

286. Jonathan Runnells, "Arkansas Changes Its Rules on Residency, Reciprocity"; Alan Cooper, "4th Circuit Upholds Virginia's Tough Reciprocity Rules."

287. Marcia Coyle, "Va. Bar Residency Rule Nixed."

288. 9(12) NLJ 5 (December 1, 1986).

289. J. Auerbach, 1976: 125–28.

290. Deborah L. Rhode, "Moral Character as a Professional Credential," p. 499.

291. Appel, 1933a: 936; Will Shafroth, "The Next Step in the Improvement of Bar Admission Standards," p. 16; Albert L. Moise, "Practical Operation of the Pennsylvania Plan in Philadelphia County."

292. Rhode, 1985a: 501.

293. Appel, 1933a: 936.

294. Wickser, 1933; Will Shafroth, "Character Investigation: An Essential Element of the Bar Admission Process," p. 255.

295. 4 Bar Examiner 301 (1934).

296. Shafroth & Horack, 1933: 7.

297. McClain et al., 1949: 110.

298. Will Shafroth, "A Study of Character Examination Methods in Forty-Nine Commonwealths," p. 197.

299. Shafroth, 1952: 263.

300. 9 Bar Examiner 86 (1940).

301. David A. Kaplan, "Law Schools."

302. Rhode, 1985a: 515.

303. John Moore, "Lawyer Screening: Fact or Fiction?"

304. Rhode, 1985a: 520–22, 530–36.

305. Special Committee on Professional Education, "The Character and Fitness Committee in New York State"; Law Students Civil Rights Research Council, Inc. v. Wadmond, 1971.

306. Sam Roberts, "Bar Panel to Weigh Fitness of Bernardine Dohrn"; John J. Goldman, "Ex-Radical Fights for Bar Status"; Los Angeles Times, sec. 1, p. 13 (December 21, 1985).

307. Fred Leeson, "Ex-Militant Can't Join Bar."

Chapter 4

1. Robert L. Nelson, "The Changing Structure of Opportunity: Recruitment and Careers in Large Law Firms," p. 118.

2. Halliday, 1985: Table 2.

3. Smith & Rogers, 1932: 569.

4. New York County Lawyers' Association, 1936: 94.

5. State Bar of California, Committee for Cooperation, "Economic and Professional Status of California Lawyers During the First Five Years of Practice," p. 260.

6. John P. Heinz and Edward O. Laumann, Chicago Lawyers, pp. 206–08.

7. Garrison, 1935: 140–41.

8. According to another source, the ratio was comparable in 1885 and 1960. See Terence Halliday, "Six Score Years and Ten: Demographic Transitions in the American Legal Profession, 1850–1980."

9. Council on Legal Education, "Report," p. 398.

10. Carnegie Foundation, 1917.

11. 4 American Law School Review 347–49 (1917).

12. Section of Legal Education, "Report of a Meeting, August 1918," p. 382.

13. 4 American Law School Review 404–05 (1919).

14. Carnegie Foundation, 1915–1919.

15. Weinfeld, 1949: 19, 23.

16. Committee on Trend of Bar Admissions, 1948.

17. 10(11) NLJ 2 (November 23, 1987).

18. David H. Vernon and Bruce I. Zimmer, "The Demand for Legal Education: 1984 and the Future," pp. 272–74.

19. Halliday, 1986: 54–58.

20. See also Halliday, 1986; for California, see McClain et al., 1949: 7–10.

21. Halliday, 1986.

22. Bette H. Sikes, Clara N. Carson, and Patricia Gorai, eds., The 1971 Lawyer Statistical Report, pp. 26, 59–61; William L. Blaine, Where to Practice Law in California, p. 3. Several analysts could find no pattern: Garrison, 1935: 137–38; Albert P. Blaustein, "The 1949 Lawyer Count: A Preliminary Statement," p. 371; Halliday, 1986: 58–62.

23. Keith H. Cox, Lawyers, Population, and Society in New York; New York's Main Street and Wall Street Lawyers.

24. E. Brown, 1938: 173.

25. William Weinfeld, "Income of Lawyers, 1929–48," p. 22.

26. Field Research Company, 1960: 4.

27. Friedman & Kuznets, 1945: 180, 184, 289–91.

28. Carlin, 1962: 4–5.

29. Smith & Rogers, 1932: 566; see also Carlin, 1962: 22 n.25.

30. 1 Bar Examiner 273 (1931).

31. U.S. Department of Commerce, Bureau of the Census, Statistical Abstract of the United States, 1982–83, pp. 143, 159, 166.

32. Richard B. Freeman, "Legal 'Cobwebs': A Recursive Model of the Market for New Lawyers," p. 176.

33. Freeman, 1975; B. Peter Pashigian, "The Market for Lawyers: The Determinants of the Demand for and Supply of Lawyers"; "The Number and Earnings of Lawyers: Some Recent Findings"; Halliday, 1986.

34. Eileen Shanahan, "Measuring the Service Economy."

35. Robert L. Weil, "Economically, It's Been a Decade of Running in Place," p. 15.

36. R. Stevens, 1973.

37. Freeman, 1975: 171.

38. Vernon & Zimmer, 1985; David A. Kaplan, "Aggressive Student Recruitment Steps Up as Applications Decline"; 71 ABAJ 47–48 (May 1985).

39. Kaplan, 1985b; 71 ABAJ 36 (September 1985); Wall Street Journal, p. 1, col. 5 (March 18, 1986)

40. 18(4) Syllabus 8 (December 1987); 10(25) NLJ 4 (February 29, 1988). The later account differs from the earlier, reporting a 6.5 percent increase in the number of applicants and a 15 percent increase in the number taking the LSAT between 1985–86 and 1986–87.

41. Vernon & Zimmer, 1985: 278; Gene L. Maeroff, "Enrollment in Professional Schools Declines."

42. New York Times, p. 15 (September 29, 1985).

43. Maeroff, 1985; Vernon & Zimmer, 1985.

44. Heinz & Laumann, 1982: 40; Edwin Chen, "Law Firms' Receipts Soaring, Census Says."

45. Weinfeld, 1949: 19.

46. U.S. Department of Commerce, Bureau of Foreign and Domestic Commerce, "National Income, 1929–32," pp. 148–49.

47. Lloyd K. Garrison, "Results of the Wisconsin Bar Survey," p. 123; 1935: 151–52. But young lawyers in Missouri experienced rising incomes during this period, see Wiley B. Rutledge, "A Survey of the Welfare of the Missouri Bar," p. 131.

48. E. Brown, 1938: 191–92.

49. ABA Special Committee on the Economic Condition of the Bar, The Economics of the Legal Profession, p. 24.

50. New York County Lawyers' Association, 1936: 18.

51. Melvin M. Fagen, "The Status of Jewish Lawyers in New York City," p. 73.

52. Blaustein & Porter, 1954: 24; Freeman, 1975: 172.

53. Garrison, 1935: 139.

54. Robert M. Segal and John Fei, "The Economics of the Legal Profession: An Analysis by States," p. 218.

55. Albert Blaustein, "The Legal Profession in the United States: A 1952 Statistical Analysis," pp. 1009–10; 1950: 371–72.

56. Halliday, 1986.

57. Garrison, 1934: 116–22.

58. Brenner, 1935.

59. Pashigian, 1977: 72; 1978. Pashigian also claims to have found no relationship between the level of government regulation and the demand for legal services; but it seems strange to use the *supply* of lawyers as a surrogate measure of the *demand* for their services, especially when the labor market is so restricted by professially imposed constraints on supply.

60. Chen, 1984.

61. Weinfeld, 1949: 22.

62. Murray L. Schwartz, "The Reorganization of the Legal Profession," p. 1270.

63. Illinois State Bar Association, "1982 Survey of Illinois Lawyers," p. 126.

64. Weinfeld, 1949: 22; Maurice Liebenberg, "Income of Lawyers in the Postwar Period: Factors Affecting the Distribution of Earnings," pp. 33, 36; Barbara A. Curran, "The Legal Profession in the 1980s."

65. Curran, 1986.

66. According to the 1910 Census, 67 percent of lawyers in New York state were under 45, but only 47 percent in Vermont.

67. 3 American Law School Review 622 (1915).

68. Vernon & Zimmer, 1985: 273.

69. Miles Harvey, "Women Outnumber Men on College Campuses."

70. Michael Powell, "Anatomy of a Counter-Bar Association: The Chicago Council of Lawyers."

71. Curran, 1986.

72. Magali Sarfatti Larson, The Rise of Professionalism.

73. Gawalt, 1984: 102–03.

74. Granfors & Halliday, 1985: Tables 4 and 5.

75. Hobson, 1986: 118–19.

76. 1910 Census.

77. 1910 Census; Hobson, 1986: 119.

78. J. Auerbach, 1976; C. Auerbach, 1984: 49.

79. Schudson, 1974: 355; Hobson, 1986: 137–39, 299.

80. Dan A. Oren, Joining the Club; Dirk Johnson, "Yale's Limit on Jewish Enrollment Lasted Until Early 60's, A Book Reveals"; see generally Marcia Synott, The Half-Opened Door: Discrimination and Admission at Harvard, Yale, and Princeton, 1900–1970; Harold S. Wechsler, The Qualified Student: A History of Selective College Admission in America.

81. R. Stevens, 1983: 101

82. J. Auerbach, 1971: 574–75.

83. Carlin, 1962: 22 n. 27; 1966: 20.

84. Koenig & Rustad, 1985.

85. Tinnelly, 1957: 50.

86. New York County Lawyers' Association, 1936: 45.

87. Fagen, 1939: 75.

88. Carlin, 1966: 19, 21.

89. Joseph Zelan, "Social Origins and the Recruitment of American Lawyers," pp. 47–52.

90. C. Auerbach, 1984: 50–51.

91. This occurred in part because immigration from those regions had declined; but this statistic cannot tell us what proportion of the profession were of Irish or central European ancestry. Carlin, 1962: 22 n. 27.

92. Carlin, 1966: 21.

93. Carlin, 1962: 22 n.27.

94. Gawalt, 1984: 104.

95. Fagen, 1939: 81–82.

96. E.g., Dan C. Lortie, "Laymen to Lawmen: Law School, Careers, and Professional Socialization"; Carlin, 1962; Jack Ladinsky, "The Impact of Social Backgrounds of Lawyers on Law Practice and the Law"; "Careers of Lawyers: Law Practice and Legal Institutions"; "The Social Profile of a Metropolitan Bar: A Statistical Survey in Detroit."

97. ABA Special Committee on the Economic Condition of the Bar, 1938: 48, 50; Fagen, 1939: 78, 101.

98. Fagen, 1939: 79.

99. Fagen, 1939: 87, 92.

100. Fagen, 1939: 98, 103.
101. Nelson, 1983: 117.
102. Seymour Warkov and Sharyn L. Roach, "Research on Legal Careers."
103. Seymour Warkov and Sharyn L. Roach, "Social and Academic Origins and Legal Careers."
104. C. Auerbach, 1984: 50–51.
105. Howard S. Erlanger, "The Allocation of Status Within Occupations: The Case of the Legal Profession."
106. Heinz & Laumann, 1982: 65, 183, 193, 205.
107. Gawalt, 1984: 102, 112–13; for Philadelpha, see Nash, 1965: 218.
108. Granfors & Halliday, 1985: Table 3.
109. R. Stevens, 1983: 141 n. 93.
110. Koenig & Rustad, 1985.
111. ABA Special Committee on the Economic Condition of the Bar, 1939: 21–22 and n.12.
112. Gellerman, 1941: 1071–73.
113. Frances K. Zemans and Victor G. Rosenblum, The Making of a Public Profession, p. 34.
114. Heinz & Laumann, 1982: 186.
115. Ronald M. Pipkin, "Moonlighting in Law School: A Multischool Study of Part-Time Employment of Full-Time Students," p. 118.
116. Donald D. Landon, "Lawyers and Localities: The Interaction of Community Context and Professionalism," p. 464.
117. Zelan, 1967: 46; Blaustein & Porter, 1954: 187–88; Thielens, 1957: 135–35; Warkov & Roach, 1987b; Zemans & Rosenblum, 1981: 36; Heinz & Laumann, 1982: 186.
118. Halliday, 1987: Table 5.2.
119. Heinz & Laumann, 1982: 188.
120. Halliday, 1987: Table 5.2.
121. R. Stevens, 1973: 573, 600–01.
122. Zemans & Rosenblum, 1981: 39–40.
123. Charles Cappell and Jessica L. Lynch, "Minorities and Women in Law Schools: New Status Classes?"
124. Evans, 1977: 627–29.
125. Quoted in C. Auerbach, 1984: 48.
126. Astin, 1984: 74.
127. Nelson, 1983: 119.
128. Seymour Warkov, "Employment Expectations of Law Students," p. 229.
129. Heinz & Laumann, 1982: 188.
130. ABA Committee on Legal Education, 1881: 302–04
131. William P. Rogers, "Is Law a Field for Women's Work?" p. 564; see also Gawalt, 1984: 105.
132. R. Stevens, 1983: 83; for first admissions of women by state, see Karen Berger Morello, The Invisible Bar: The Woman Lawyer in America 1638 to the Present, pp. 37–38.
133. Carnegie Foundation, 1919; Ronald Chester, Unequal Access: Women Lawyers in a Changing America, p. 8.
134. Cynthia Fuchs Epstein, Women in Law, pp. 49–51; see generally, Morello, 1986: chaps. 2–4.
135. Chester, 1985.

136. C. Epstein, 1981: 248.
137. Chester, 1985: 10.
138. R. Stevens, 1983: 83.
139. Chester, 1985: 12–13.
140. Gellerman, 1941: 1072.
141. McClain et al., 1949.
142. Carnegie Foundation, 1919. There is some evidence that the absence of men lawyers and particularly law clerks during the Civil War was the impetus for the original entry of women into the profession, Frances Olsen, "From False Paternalism to False Equality," p. 1523.
143. New York County Lawyers' Association, 1936: 9–10.
144. C. Epstein, 1981: 55.
145. C. Epstein, 1981: 56.
146. 10(6) NLJ 4 (October 19, 1987).
147. Harvey, 1984.
148. Andrew Hacker, "Women vs. Men in the Workforce"; see also Mary Durkin and A. Lewis Rhodes, "Shift in Female Participation in the Legal Profession by State: 1960–1970."
149. They increased from 3 percent in Illinois in 1975 to 12 percent in 1982. Illinois State Bar Association, 1983: 126.
150. Vernon & Zimmer, 1985: 271. The same is true in medical schools, New York Times, p. 15 (September 29, 1985).
151. New York County Lawyers' Association, 1936: 9–10, 44.
152. C. Epstein, 1981: 99.
153. 71 ABAJ 25 (July 1985).
154. Jurate Jason, Lizabeth Moody, and James Schuerger, "Women Law Students: The View from the Front of the Classroom."
155. New Jersey Supreme Court Task Force on Women in the Court, Summary Report, pp. 10–12.
156. New York Task Force on Women in the Courts, Report; Jeffrey Schmalz, "New York Courts Cited on Sex Bias"; for Wisconsin, see William Eich, "Gender Bias in the Courtroom." For a review of state studies, see Alberta I. Cook, "Gender Bias: Push Grows for Study, Action." The same problems are found in medicine, see Nadine Brozan, "For Female M.D.'s, Success at a Price."
157. New York County Lawyers' Association, 1936: 18, 92; American Bar Foundation, The Rate of Increase in the Number of Lawyers and Population Growth, p. 25.
158. Illinois State Bar Associaton, "Economics of Legal Services in Illinois: A 1975 Special Bar Survey," pp. 91–92.
159. C. Epstein, 1981: 115.
160. 70 ABAJ 33 (September 1984).
161. Hacker, 1984.
162. Robert Pear, "Women Reduce Lag in Earnings but Disparities with Men Remain."
163. Wall Street Journal, p. 1, col. 5 (November 8, 1983).
164. David Chambers, "Tough Enough: The

Work and Family Experiences of Recent Women Graduates of the University of Michigan Law School," pp. 28–29.

165. Leona M. Vogt, From Law School to Career: Where Do Graduates Go and What Do They Do?, Table D26.

166. National Association of Law Placement, Class of 1983 Employment Report and Salary Survey, p. 108.

167. For the census data, see Andrew Hacker, "Women at Work." For the Boston survey, see Rita Henley Jensen, "Female Lawyers Getting Raw Deal?"

168. Astin, 1984: 84.

169. Ann L. Hussein and Lawrence E. Wightman, "Male-Female LSAT Candidate Study."

170. Evans, 1977: 565.

171. Sharyn Roberts Roach, "The Recruitment of Men and Women Lawyers to In-House Legal Departments: A Study of Organizational Recruitment."

172. 32 Journal of Legal Education 425 (1982); Elyce H. Zenoff and Kathryn V. Lorio, "What We Know, What We Think We Know, and What We Don't Know About Women Law Professors," pp. 893–94; Los Angeles Times, sec. 1, p. 3 (January 9, 1985); but see letter from Committee of Bar Examiners to Deans of California Law Schools, December 17, 1986.

173. Marcia Coyle, "31 New Clerks Begin at Supreme Court."

174. Jill Abramson and Barbara Franklin, Where Are They Now? The Story of the Women of Harvard Law 1974.

175. Stanford Law Review, "Project: Law Firms and Lawyers With Children: An Empirical Analysis of Family/Work Conflict."

176. Women's Law Association, Employment Survey Directory, pp. iii-x.

177. 9(12) NLJ 33 (December 1, 1986).

178. Pear, 1987.

179. For the 1960 and 1970 census data, see C. Epstein, 1981: 330–31. For the 1987 Boston survey, see Jensen, 1988c.

180. William R. Greer, "The Changing Women's Marriage Market."

181. C. Epstein, 1981: 316.

182. D. Chambers, 1987: 126, 128–29.

183. Deborah L. Jacobs, "Part Time: Does It Work?"

184. D. Chambers, 1987: p. 214, Table 87–03.

185. Hishon v. King & Spalding, 1984.

186. D. Chambers, 1987: 30–31 n. 31 and Table 17–01.

187. C. Epstein, 1981: 97.

188. New York County Lawyers' Association, 1936: 27.

189. C. Epstein, 1981: 97.

190. Martha Grossblat and Bette H. Sikes, Women Lawyers, p. 8; Curran, 1986. For Minnesota lawyers, see 70 ABAJ 33 (September 1984).

191. 9(12) NLJ 33 (December 1, 1986).

192. D. Chambers, 1987: 82–83, 173 and Tables 1–01 and 1–02.

193. Vogt, 1986: Table D25.

194. Robert L. Nelson, John P. Heinz, Edward O. Laumann, and Robert H. Salisbury, "Private Representation in Washington."

195. Astin, 1984: 78.

196. D. Chambers, 1987: Table 19–01.

197. Cappell & Lynch, 1986.

198. C. Epstein, 1981: 121–22.

199. Noel J. Augustyn, Summary of Data from Faculty and Administrative Appointments Registers.

200. Curran, 1986

201. Vogt, 1986: Table D25.

202. C. Epstein, 1981: 100.

203. NALP, 1985: 33.

204. D. Chambers, 1987: 221 and Table 87–04.

205. D. Epstein, 1981: 221–22.

206. David Chambers, "Salt Survey of Women in Law School Teaching."

207. Zenoff & Lorio, 1983: 873, 877–78, 880, 883, 887.

208. Richard Chused, "Salt Study on the Hiring and Retention of Minority and Female Faculty."

209. C. Epstein, 1981: 242; see also Morello, 1986: chap. 9.

210. Fund for Modern Courts, The Success of Women and Minorities in Achieving Judicial Office; Alexander Stille, "Election v. Appointment: Who Wins?"; Philip Shenon, "Reagan Is as Intent as Ever on Making Over the Courts"; Eric Lichtblau, "Reagan Record on Naming Women Judges Hit."

211. New York Task Force, 1986: 244–46.

212. 9(50) NLJ 2 (August 24, 1987).

213. New York County Lawyers' Association, 1936: 27.

214. Platt, 1940: 647.

215. Curran, 1986.

216. Bruce Abel, "The Firms—What Do They Want?"

217. Geraldine Segal, Blacks in the Law, pp. 114, 272–75.

218. I calculated these figures from Lisa Hill Fenning and Patricia M. Schnegg, "The Status of Women in L.A.'s Big Firms."

219. XVI(1) Syllabus 1 (March 1985); see also Wall Street Journal, p. 37, col. 3 (November 4, 1986).

220. Curran, 1986; Roach, 1986; but see Vogt, 1986: Table D25.

221. NALP, 1985: 80.

222. Morello, 1986: chap. 8.

223. Smigel, 1969: 46.

224. C. Epstein, 1981: 175–80.

225. G. Segal, 1983: 114, 172–75.

226. Nelson, 1983: 121.

227. Alexander Stille, "Little Room at the Top for Blacks, Hispanics," p. 10.

228. Ivan P.L. Png, David Eaves, and J. Mark Ramseyer, "Sex, Race and Grades: Empirical Evidence of Discrimination in Law-Firm Interviews."

229. D. Chambers, 1987: 49–50.

230. Steven Brill, "The Woman Problem"; David M. Margolick, "Wall Street's Sexist Wall: Barrier to Women Partners"; Abramson & Franklin, 1986.

231. C. Epstein, 1981: 179–80.

232. 7(48) NLJ 2 (August 12, 1985).

233. Fenning & Schnegg, 1983.

234. Doreen Weisenhaus, "Still a Long Way to Go for Women, Minorities," p. 1.

235. National Law Journal (December 20, 1982).

236. Stanford Law Review, 1982: 1263 n. 5.

237. Curran, 1986.

238. Fenning & Schnegg, 1983. These proportions increased to 28 and 6 percent in 1984 and 31 and 8 percent in 1986; in firms with more than 100 lawyers women were 34 percent of associates and 9 percent of partners in 1986. See Vicki Land, "1986 Survey of the Status of Women Lawyers in Los Angeles."

239. C. Epstein, 1981: 175–80; the figures are internally inconsistent.

240. G. Segal, 1983: 114, 272–75.

241. Barbara A. Curran, Katherine J. Rosich, Clara N. Carson, and Mark C. Puccetti, The 1984 Lawyer Statistical Report, p. 10.

242. Jill Abramson and Barbara Franklin, "Are Women Catching Up? Harvard Law '74."

243. D. Chambers, 1987: 207 and Table 10–01.

244. Abramson & Franklin, 1983; see also Fenning & Schnegg, 1983.

245. Trish Beall, "All the Right Lateral Moves," p. 27.

246. Stille, 1985d: 1, 10.

247. Weisenhaus, 1988: 1, 48.

248. Stephen A. Schneider, "Minorities and Women in Law."

249. Reed, 1921: 423–30.

250. 1910 Census.

251. Maxwell Bloomfield, "From Deference to Confrontation: The Early Black Lawyers of Galveston, Texas, 1895–1920," p. 152; Census.

252. Horack & Shafroth, 1938: 324, 326.

253. G. Segal, 1983: 2.

254. G. Segal, 1983: 33, 65–74.

255. G. Segal, 1983: 17, 19.

256. 1930 Census.

257. Jerome Schuman, "A Black Lawyers Study," p. 230 n. 18; Census. Black population includes Indian, Japanese, Chinese, and Philippine in 1940 and 1950. Another source gives 3845 for the last date; there also were 2410 Spanish surname and 288 American Indian lawyers. See Daniel O. Bernstine, "An Empirical Study of the University of Wisconsin Law School Special Admissions Program: A Progress Report," p. 146.

258. G. Stevens, 1969: 1 n. 3.

259. Virginia Law Review, "The Negro Lawyer in Virginia: A Survey"; Schuman, 1971: 303; G. Segal, 1983: 276–77.

260. Sikes et al., 1972; Census.

261. Richard Delgado, Leo Romero, and Cruz Reynoso, "La Raza, the Law and Law Schools," p. 819.

262. Jose Bracamonte, "A Monograph on the Chicano Bar in Texas."

263. Felicienne Ramey, "Minority Lawyers in California: A Survey."

264. Lennox S. Hinds, "Keynote Introduction"; G. Segal, 1983: 6.

265. Bloomfield, 1984: 153–54.

266. R. Stevens, 1983: 195 n. 34, 196 n. 45.

267. Astin, 1982: chap. 9.

268. Leo M. Romero, "An Assessment of Affirmative Action in Law School Admissions After Fifteen Years," p. 431.

269. Evans, 1977: 565.

270. U.S. Bureau of the Census, Educational Attainment in the United States, quoted in New York Times, p. 11 (December 3, 1987).

271. Edward B. Fiske, "Minority Enrollment in Colleges is Declining"; "Enrollment of Minorities in Colleges Stagnating"; New York Times, p. 18 (December 4, 1986).

272. Astin, 1982: chap. 9.

273. New York Times, p. B5 (January 8, 1981); Astin, 1984: 74.

274. Evans, 1977: 565.

275. Kaye, 1980; James C. Hathaway, "The Mythical Meritocracy of Law School Admissions."

276. Evans, 1977: 603.

277. Edward A. Adams, "Law Schools '87."

278. Hacker, 1984: 84.

279. Regents of the University of California v. Bakke, 1978.

280. Steven Shea and Mindy Thompson Fullilove, "Entry of Black and Other Minority Students into U.S. Medical Schools."

281. Ronald Sullivan, "Medical Schools Press Minority Goal."

282. New York Times, p. 16 (November 4, 1987).

283. Michael Rappaport, "The Legal Educational Opportunity Program at UCLA: Eight Years of Experience."

284. Schuman, 1971: 233; Marion S. Goldman, A Portrait of the Black Attorney in Chicago, pp. 12–15.

285. William Boyd, "Legal Education: A Nationwide Survey of Minority Law Students," pp. 530, 544. Financial demands also affected black enrollment in medical school; the National Medical Foundation, which provides financial aid to minorities, cut its grants from $2.3 million in 1974 to $1.5 million in 1981, despite the rapid inflation in educational costs during this period. Shea & Fullilove, 1985.

286. G. Segal, 1983: 69, 266.

287. New York Times (December 4, 1977).

288. Michael D. Rappaport, "Placement Patterns of University of California Los Angeles Law School Minority Graduates," p. 139.

289. Gene Blake, "Minority Group Members Score Lower than Whites on State Bar Examination."

290. Los Angeles Times, sec. 1, p. 3 (January 9, 1985).

291. Letter from Committee of Bar Examiners

to Deans of California Law Schools, December 17, 1986.

292. G. Segal, 1983: 13–15.

293. Wall Street Journal, p. 6, col. 6 (December 24, 1985).

294. Ramey, 1978: 11–18.

295. Romero, 1984: 431.

296. U.S. Department of Commerce, Bureau of the Census, 1982: 26, 388.

297. NALP, 1985: 72.

298. Harry T. Edwards, "A New Role for the Black Law Graduate," p. 30; for comparable figures for other schools see Oliver B. Quinn, "Career Patterns of Black Graduates of Rutgers University School of Law"; James A. Thomas, "Career Patterns of Black Yale Law Graduates."

299. Rappaport, 1974: 517; 1977: 141.

300. Gary A. Muneke, "An Analysis of the Employment Patterns of Minority Law Graduates," p. 155.

301. NALP, 1985: 33, 112.

302. G. Segal, 1983; Charles Cappell, "The Status of Black Lawyers"; Goldman, 1972.

303. Schuman, 1971: 227–28, 236 n. 41, 239, 278–79; cf. Goldman, 1972: 28; Alexander Stille, "A Practice Flourishes in Harlem."

304. Schuman, 1971: 232, 272; cf. Goldman, 1972: 10–11.

305. Martha Melendez, "The Hispanic Bar in Los Angeles."

306. G. Segal, 1983: 79, 84.

307. Wall Street Journal, p. 1, col. 5 (January 1, 1983); p. 1, col. 1 (June 25, 1984).

308. NALP, 1985: 80.

309. 9(9) NLJ 2 (November 10, 1986).

310. 9(11) NLJ 2 (November 24, 1986).

311. Cappell, 1985.

312. B. Abel, 1963.

313. Culp, 1979.

314. NALP, 1985: 80.

315. 9(24) NLJ 4 (February 23, 1987).

316. NALP, 1985: 84; cf. Goldman, 1972: 5–7.

317. Paul Hoffman, Lions in the Street, p. 126.

318. Edwards, 1972: 28; another 27 firms did not respond.

319. Cappell, 1985.

320. Png et al., 1988.

321. G. Segal, 1983: 272–73.

322. C. Epstein, 1981: 183.

323. David M. Margolick, "The Blue-Chip Firms Remain Mostly White."

324. 14(4) Columbia Law Alumni Observer 1 (May 1985).

325. Weisenhaus, 1988: 1, 48.

326. Stille, 1985d: 10; 71 ABAJ 32–33 (April 1985); Margolick, 1985; Weisenhaus, 1988: 1, 48.

327. G. Segal, 1983: 217 n. 30, 235–37.

328. Augustyn, 1985.

329. Review of Legal Education, 1985: 66.

330. Chused, 1987.

331. G. Segal, 1983: 170–71.

332. Fund for Modern Courts, 1985; Stille, 1985–1986; Shenon, 1986; Lichtblau, 1988.

333. Schuman, 1971: 244, 281–82.

334. Illinois State Bar Association, 1975: 91–92.

335. NALP, 1985: 108.

336. Compare C. Epstein, 1981: 255, 259 with Albert P. Melone, Lawyers, Public Policy and Interest Group Politics, pp. 48–49.

337. Goldman, 1972: 36, 38; G. Segal, 1983: 19.

338. G. Segal, 1983: 19.

339. David Ranii, "Black Attorneys Hit Administration."

340. Schuman, 1971: 253.

341. G. Segal, 1983: 95, 97–98.

Chapter 5

1. Barlow F. Christensen, "The Unauthorized Practice of Law," pp. 180–81.

2. Gilb, 1956: 230.

3. Christensen, 1980: 178.

4. Christensen, 1980: 178; Andrew Abbott, "Jurisdictional Conflicts," p. 199; Charles Cappell and Terence Halliday, "Professional Projects of Elite Chicago Lawyers, 1950–1974," pp. 323–27; Halliday, 1987: 69.

5. Halliday, 1987: 77–78.

6. Christensen, 1980: 189–91; Hobson, 1986: 305–06.

7. Christensen, 1980: 190–91.

8. Christensen, 1980: 180–81, 191, 193.

9. Christensen, 1980: 195–96; see also Abbott, 1986: 201; Quintin Johnstone and Dan Hopson, Jr., Lawyers and Their Work, chaps. 5–10.

10. Clyde B. Aitchison, "Practitioners Before the Interstate Commerce Commission"; I.C.C. Report; J. Smith Henley, Admissions of Attorneys to Practice Before Federal Administrative Agencies.

11. Christensen, 1980: 192.

12. Gilb, 1956: 245.

13. Abbott, 1986: 203.

14. Milton Z. Kafoglis, Economic Condition of the Legal Profession in Ohio, pp. 66–69.

15. Gilb, 1956: 230–31, 233–34.

16. Gilb, 1956: 235–40, 242–44, 253.

17. Deborah L. Rhode, "Policing the Professional Monopoly," p. 33.

18. Merton E. Marks, "The Lawyers and the Realtors: Arizona's Experience"; Christensen, 1980: 197.

19. Surety Title Insurance Agency, Inc. v. Virginia State Bar, 1977.

20. Myrna Oliver, "Paralegal to the Rescue."

21. Christensen, 1980: 199.

22. Christensen, 1980: 200; James Podgers, "Statements of Principle: Are They on the Way Out?"

23. E.g., Doug Bandow, "A Brazen System of Self-Enrichment."

24. Wall Street Journal, p. 24, col. 1 (February 23, 1987).

25. See Steven R. Cox and Mark Dwyer, A Report on Self-Help Law, chap. 1.

26. New York Times, p. 15 (February 12, 1984).

27. Yale Law Journal, "Project: The Unauthorized Practice of Law and Pro Se Divorce," p. 110.

28. Eric Freedman, "Non-Lawyers May Represent Clients at Michigan Job Hearings."

29. Donald J. Quigg, "Nonlawyer Practice Before the Patent and Trademark Office"; Jacob M. Wolf, "Nonlawyer Practice Before the Social Security Administration."

30. Jethro K. Lieberman, Crisis at the Bar, p. 124.

31. Jon Nordheimer, "Case Challenges Legal System"; New York Times, p. 23 (November 1, 1984).

32. Oliver, 1986a.

33. John Riley, "Immigration Advice Limited to Lawyers."

34. 71 ABAJ 21 (October 1985).

35. Palmer v. Unauthorized Practice Committee, 1969.

36. Cox & Dwyer, 1987: chap. 2.

37. Cox & Dwyer, 1987: chap. 3.

38. Cox & Dwyer, 1987: 50.

39. B. Peter Pashigian, "Occupational Licensing and the Interstate Mobility of Professionals," pp. 7, 16.

40. Brenner, 1932b.

41. Gilb, 1956: 96–97, citing California Bar Association Proceedings, 1909: 33.

42. Brenner, 1932b.

43. 1 Bar Examiner 273–75 (1932); Alfred L. Bartlett, "Admissions Problems," p. 42.

44. Brenner, 1935: 54; Gilb, 1956: 96–97.

45. "The California Story," 21 Bar Examiner 48 (1952).

46. Goscoe O. Farley, "Admission of Attorneys from Other Jurisdiction," p. 152; see also 20 California State Bar Journal 215 (1945); 24 California State Bar Journal 217 (1949).

47. McClain et al., 1949: 101–05; Charles E. Beardsley, "Admission of Out-of-State Lawyers."

48. Farley, 1952: 157–58.

49. E. Brown, 1938: 160–61; Marjorie Merritt, "The National Conference of Bar Examiners," pp. 475–76.

50. Merritt, 1952: 475–76.

51. Merritt, 1952: 486; Blaustein & Porter, 1954: 232–33.

52. Farley, 1952: 152.

53. McClain et al., 1949: 123.

54. Edward A. Adams, "Multistate Essay Test Renews Controversy."

55. David Lauter, "Waiving Into Another Bar Isn't Always a Real Breeze," p. 32.

56. Blaustein & Porter, 1954: 232–33.

57. 71 American Bar Association Journal 64–67 (March 1985).

58. Supreme Court of New Hampshire v. Piper, 1985.

59. Pashigian, 1979: 20.

60. Runnells, 1985.

61. Cooper, 1985.

62. Frazier v. Heebe, 1987; Supreme Court of Virginia v. Friedman, 1987.

63. 7(51) NLJ 2 (September 2, 1985); see also Gerald M. Stern, The Buffalo Creek Disaster, pp. 34–35.

64. 71 ABAJ 20–21 (December 1985).

65. Hurst, 1950: 323.

66. Halliday, 1987: Table 3.1.

67. ABA Standing Committee on Economics of Law Practice, Statistical Analysis of Recommended Minimum Fees for Selected Legal Services, 1964; 1966.

68. Daniel J. Cantor & Co., The 1966 Survey of the Economics of Florida Law Practice, pp. 43, 62.

69. Colorado Bar Association, Report on the 1967 Economic Survey of the Colorado Bar, p. 6.

70. Daniel J. Cantor & Co., Economic Study of the Lawyers of South Carolina, p. 17.

71. Cantor, 1969: 18; Colorado Bar Association, 1967: 6.

72. Cantor, 1969: 18; Cantor, 1966: App. 24–36; Maryland State Bar Association, 1975 Economic Survey of the Maryland State Bar Association.

73. Richard J. Arnould, "Pricing Professional Services: A Case Study of the Legal Service Industry," pp. 503–04.

74. Goldfarb v. Virginia State Bar, 1975.

75. Harold Hotelling, Jr., Legal Fees after *Goldfarb*, pp. 53, 62, 91–93. Before *Goldfarb*, the fees charged for settling estates also displayed the greatest dispersion in Maryland. See Maryland State Bar Association, 1975.

76. Billie Bethel, " "Economics and the Practice of Law: The 1976 Economic Survey of the State Bar of Arizona," p. 15; but see Stephen R. Cox, Allan C. DeSerpa, and William C. Canby, Jr., "Consumer Information and the Pricing of Legal Services"; compare Illinois State Bar Association, 1983: 148 with Illinois State Bar Association, 1975.

77. ABA Model Rules of Professional Conduct Rule 1.5(a).

78. Lee May, "ABA Sees Risk of Fraud by People Aiding Illegal Aliens"; Joseph Berger, "Brooklyn Bishop Assails High Fees Being Paid by Illegal Aliens."

79. Wall Street Journal, p. 8, col. 4 (January 1, 1985).

80. See, e.g., Bloomfield, 1984: 156, 159.

81. Halliday, 1987: 69, 72 and Table 3.1.

82. Richard L. Abel, "Why Does the ABA Promulgate Ethical Rules?" pp. 660–63.

83. Stuart Taylor, "Senator Baker and the Art of Making Rain."

84. 9(16&17) NLJ 2 (December 29, 1986 & January 5, 1987).

85. Los Angeles Times, sec. 1, p. 2 (January 22, 1985).

86. Amy Tarr, "Are Board Memberships Becoming Too Risky?"

87. Rita Henley Jensen, "Most In-House Marketers Vex Their Firms."

88. Barlow F. Christensen, Lawyers for People of Moderate Means, chaps. 4–5; C. E. Berg, Lawyer Referral Services.

89. Carlin, 1962: chap. 3; Kenneth J. Reichstein, "Ambulance Chasing: A Case Study of Deviation and Control within the Legal Profession."

90. 63 ABAJ 1541 (1977).

91. Bates v. State Bar of Arizona, 1977.

92. ABA Model Rules of Professional Conduct 7.1–2; Lori B. Andrews, "Lawyer Advertising and the First Amendment"; In re R.M.J., 1982; In re Von Wiegen, 1984; Zauderer v. Office of Disciplinary Counsel, 1985; Jim Miskiewicz, "Ad Debate Lingers But Its Focus Shifts." Compare Ohralik v. Ohio State Bar Association, 1978, with In re Primus, 1978. In Shapero v. Kentucky Bar Association, 1988, the Supreme Court extended First Amendment protection to direct mail advertising. See also Marcia Coyle, "Will Another Lawyer Ad Taboo Fail?"

93. Committee on Professional Ethics v. Humphrey, 1985.

94. 8(50) NLJ 4 (August 25, 1986); Chris Mondics, "Court Relaxes N.J. Ad Rules."

95. Gary Taylor, "Showdown Brews on Solicitation in Texas"; "Texas Bar Solicitation Probe Heats Up"; Marcia Coyle, "ATLA Probing Members' Misconduct.' "

96. David Kocieniewski, "Crash Ads Spark Debate."

97. Terence Shimp and Robert Dyer, "How the Legal Profession Views Legal Service Advertising," pp. 77–80; 34 percent response rate. The same correlations were found among Illinois lawyers in 1982, see Illinois State Bar Association, 1983: 163.

98. Donald E. Stem, Jr., Dante Laudadrio, and Jeff T. Israel, "The Effects of Attorney Seniority on Legal Advertising Practice and Attitudes," p. 239.

99. Robert F. Dyer and Terence A. Shimp, "Reactions to Legal Advertising," p. 48; 25 percent response by first group of respondents, 35 percent by second; see also Jeffrey M. Kallis and Dinoo J. Vancr, "Consumer Perceptions of Attorney and Legal Service Advertising"; Larry Lang and Ronald B. Marks, "Consumer Response to Advertisements for Legal Services"; Larry T. Patterson and Robert A. Sherdlow, "Should Lawyers Advertise? A Study of Consumer Attitudes."

100. Donald E. Stem, Jr. and Daniel L. Sisson, "Media and Price Disclosure Effects in Legal Advertising," p. 161; only one year after Bates.

101. Miskiewicz, 1986b.

102. Schneyer, 1983: 12–13.

103. Los Angeles Times, sec. 1, p. 8 (February 19, 1984).

104. 72 ABAJ 53 (May 1986).

105. Patricia Lindenberger and Gene W. Murdock, "Legal Service Advertising."

106. Martha Middleton, "TV Ad Spending Shows Sharp Rise"; 8(7) NLJ 2 (October 28, 1985); Miskiewicz, 1986b.

107. Tamar Lewin, "A Gentlemanly Profession Enters a Tough New Era", Mary Ann Galante, "Firms Find More Value in Marketing."

108. 9(31) NLJ 2 (April 13, 1987).

109. 9(5) NLJ 2 (October 12, 1986).

110. Bill Richards and Barry Meier, "Lawyers Lead Hunt for New Groups of Asbestos Victims."

111. Staff of the Federal Trade Commission, "Improving Consumer Access to Legal Services: The Case for Removing Restrictions on Truthful Advertising"; 71 ABAJ 35 (February 1985); Steven R. Cox, Charles A. Pulaski, Jr., and Morris Axelrod, Lawyers' Fees and Advertising Rules; but see Stewart Macaulay, "Lawyer Advertising: 'Yes, But . . . .' "

112. Herbert M. Kritzer, Austin Sarat, David M. Trubek, Kristin Bumiller, and Elizabeth McNichol, "Understanding the Costs of Litigation: The Case of the Hourly-Fee Lawyer," pp. 588–91.

113. Janet Kiholm Smith and Steven R. Cox, "The Pricing of Legal Services."

114. Charles E. Clark and Emma Corstvet, "The Lawyer and the Public," p. 1288.

115. Committee on the Survey of the Legal Profession for Pennsylvania, "Report," p. 391; only 13 percent response rate; apparently 6 percent had no opinion.

116. Field Research Company, 1960: 2, A-3.

117. U.S. Department of Commerce, Bureau of the Census, Census of Business, 1967: Selected Services: Law Firms, Tables 4 and 8.

118. Cantor, 1969: 13; Cantor, 1966: 58; Colorado Bar Association, 1967: 3–4.

119. Heinz & Laumann, 1982: 53.

120. 68 ABAJ 800 (1982).

121. Heinz & Laumann, 1982: 43–44.

122. Heinz & Laumann, 1982: 48. Ten of the 193 law firms in Wake County, North Carolina, settled more than a third of decedents' estates; twenty settled more than half; thirty settled nearly two thirds; and forty settled nearly three fourths. See Hotelling, 1982: 79.

123. Illinois State Bar Association, 1983: 163; but sole practitioners also favor it.

124. David Fromson, "Let's Be Realistic About Specialization"; David Ranii, "Iowa Justices Delay Decision on Specialization." The fact that thirty-eight states were considering plans in 1980 suggests stagnation. See Schneyer, 1983: 99 n. 578.

125. Alan A. Paterson, "Specialisation and the Legal Profession," p. 722.

126. 8(3) NLJ 9 (September 30, 1985). The Seventh Circuit Court of Appeals upheld the requirement of experience when challenged by a lawyer. See David Ranii, "Novice Lawyers Barred at Trials."

127. Paterson, 1986: 699.

128. In recent years, the Federal Trade Commission has begun to assert its jurisdiction over the professions. Although lawyers maintain that they are sufficiently regulated by the states, this is not likely to immunize their anticompetitive practices from all federal scrutiny. Stuart Taylor, Jr., "Antitrust Policy

Shifts to New Arenas"; 7(34) NLJ 7 (May 6, 1985); First, 1979, 1080–81.

Chapter 6

1. Michael Powell, "Professional Innovation: Corporate Lawyers and Private Lawmaking."
2. Colorado Bar Association, 1967: 18.
3. Robert L. Nelson, "Ideology, Practice, and Professional Autonomy," p. 526.
4. Reginald Heber Smith, Justice and the Poor.
5. ABA Special Committee on the Economic Condition of the Bar, 1939: Part III.
6. Robert D. Abrahams, "Law Offices to Serve Householders in the Lower Income Group"; "The Neighborhood Law Office Experiment"; "The Neighborhood Law Office Plan"; "Twenty-five Years of Service: Philadelphia's Neighborhood Law Office Plan."
7. Barbara A. Curran, The Legal Needs of the Public, pp. 1–9.
8. Curran, 1977: 146–59, 186, 190.
9. Leon H. Mayhew and Albert J. Reiss, Jr., "The Social Organization of Legal Contacts"; Leon H. Mayhew, "Institutions of Representation: Civil Justice and the Public."
10. Curran, 1977: 203; these percentages cannot be added because of multiple uses.
11. Richard L. Abel, "Law Without Politics," pp. 622–25.
12. Curran, 1977: 100.
13. Yale Law Journal, "Project: An Assessment of Alternative Strategies for Increasing Access to Legal Services."
14. Sixty-three percent of those with more than ten years of experience felt obligated, 46 percent of those with less; those rejecting such an obligation had a median of $7916 compared to a statewide median of $13,512. See Colorado Bar Association, 1967: 2, 18.
15. Philip R. Lochner, Jr., "The No-Fee and Low-Fee Legal Practice of Private Attorneys."
16. Dorothy L. Maddi and Frederic R. Merrill, "The Private Practicing Bar and Legal Services for Low-Income People."
17. Lochner, 1975.
18. Joel F. Handler, Ellen Jane Hollingsworth, and Howard S. Erlanger, Lawyers and the Pursuit of Legal Rights, pp. 97–100.
19. 9(9) NLJ 2 (November 10, 1986).
20. Robert T. McCracken, "Report on Observance by the Bar of Stated Professional Standards," pp. 406–07.
21. Handler et al., 1978a: 91–110.
22. D. Weston Darby, Jr., "It's About Time: A Survey of Lawyers' Timekeeping Practices," p. 43. Sixty-six firms responded; the bottom quartile contributed ten hours a year, the top quartile contributed fifty.
23. Nelson, 1985: 540.

24. Illinois State Bar Association, 1983: 165.
25. Alan Ashman, The New Private Practice; Douglas E. Rosenthal, Robert A. Kagan, and Debra Quantrone, Volunteer Attorneys and Legal Services; F. Raymond Marks, Kirk Leswing, and Barbara Fortinsky, The Lawyer, the Public and Professional Responsibility.
26. Kirk Victor, "Pro Bono Work Attracting Some Firms: More Needed."
27. Myrna Oliver, "Pro Bono: Renaissance in Legal Aid."
28. Jim Miskiewicz, "Mandatory Pro Bono Won't Disappear."
29. R. Abel, 1981: 684.
30. State ex rel. Scott v. Roper, 1985; but see Matter of Farrell, 1985.
31. Bridget O'Brian, "New Orleans Pro Bono Battle Centers on a Murder Case."
32. Deborah L. Rhode, "Ethical Perspectives on Legal Practice," p. 610.
33. Miskiewicz, 1987.
34. Johnson v. Zerbst, 1938; Gideon v. Wainwright, 1963; Argersinger v. Hamlin, 1972; see also Johnson v. Avery, 1969.
35. NLADA, The Other Face of Justice, p. 16.
36. Robert Hermann, Eric Single, and John Boston, Counsel for the Poor, p. 1; M. Schwartz, 1980.
37. NLADA, 1973: 83; Paul B. Wice, The Endangered Species: America's Private Criminal Lawyers.
38. David J. Saari, "The Financial Impacts of the Right to Counsel for Criminal Defense of the Poor," pp. 3–4.
39. Richard L. Abel, "Comparative Sociology of Legal Professions," p. 33.
40. County of Fresno v. Superior Court, 1978; Yarbrough v. Superior Court, 1985.
41. Robert Spanenberg, A. David Davis, and Patricia A. Smith, "Contract Defense Systems Under Attack."
42. Mary Ann Galante, "Contract Public Defenders Slammed."
43. Hermann et al., 1977: 35–37, 77, 127.
44. Robert W. Stewart, "County to Probe Payments to Court-Appointed Attorneys."
45. Robert W. Stewart, "Panel Weighs New Rules on Naming Attorneys for Poor."
46. Elizabeth Lu and Carla Rivera, "New Rule Defining Appointed Lawyer Fees Are Circulated"; Paul Feldman, "6 Lawyers Pay $129,500 to Settle Overbilling Claims."
47. Paul Nyden, "West Virginia Bar Claims Attorney Billed a 75–Hour Day."
48. David Ranii, "Appointed Counsel in Michigan Fight Reduction in Trial Fees."
49. Richard L. Abel, "Socializing the Legal Profession: Can Redistributing Lawyers' Services Achieve Social Justice?"
50. Richard L. Abel, "The Sociology of American Lawyers: A Bibliographic Guide, pp. 382–83.

51. Walters v. National Association of Radiation Survivors, 1985.

52. Earl Johnson, Justice and Reform; Jack Katz, Poor People's Lawyers in Transition; R. Abel, 1985a: Table 4.

53. R. Abel, 1985a: 502 n. 163.

54. R. Abel, 1985a: 534, 538.

55. R. Abel, 1985a: 504–05.

56. Katz, 1982: 48.

57. Robert G. Storey, "The Legal Profession Versus Regimentation: A Program to Counter Socialization."

58. E. Johnson, 1974: chap. 3; Harry P. Stumpf, Community Politics and Legal Services.

59. R. Abel, 1985a: Tables 5 and 6.

60. R. Abel, 1985a: 570–79.

61. R. Abel, 1979: 30 n. 31.

62. Dorothy Townsend, "Old Legal Files Hold a Dilemma."

63. R. Abel, 1985a: 508, 547–50.

64. Schneyer, 1983: 100 n. 591; Edwin Chen, "The Poor Still Go Begging for Legal Help"; Carroll v. State Bar of California, 1985.

65. R. Abel, 1985a: 532 n. 365; Ronald B. Taylor, "California Legal Aid Officials Complain of Federal Monitors."

66. 9(24) NLJ 2 (February 23, 1987).

67. R. Abel, 1985a: 556–57.

68 Legal Services Corporation, Delivery Systems Study.

69. Samuel Brakel, Judicare.

70. Council for Public Interest Law, Balancing the Scales of Justice, pp. 30–40.

71. Council for Public Interest Law, 1976: 79–133; Yale Law Journal, "Comment: The New Public Interest Lawyers"; Joel F. Handler, Betsy Ginsberg, and Arthur Snow, "The Public Interest Law Industry"; Burton A. Weisbrod, Joel F. Handler, and Neil K. Komesar, Public Interest Law.

72. Neil K. Komesar and Burton A. Weisbrod, "The Public Interest Law Firm: A Behavioral Analysis"; Burton A. Weisbrod, "Nonprofit and Proprietary Sector Behavior: Wage Differentials Among Lawyers."

73. Ford Foundation, The Public Interest Law Firm: New Voices for New Constituencies.

74. Komesar & Weisbrod, 1978.

75. Lee Epstein, Conservatives in Court.

76. Handler et al., 1978b; Council for Public Interest Law, Survey of Public Interest Law Narrative Reports.

77. Ford Foundation, 1973.

78. Ford Foundation and ABA Special Committee, Public Interest Law: Five Years Later.

79. Marek v. Chesney, 1985; Webb v. County Board of Education, 1985.

80. New York Times, p. 10 (August 19, 1985).

81. Handler et al., 1978b: 116–23; Council for Public Interest Law, 1976: 133–40; Richard L. Abel, "Lawyers and the Power to Change."

82. Christensen, 1970: chap. 5.

83. Schneyer, 1983: 102.

84. Curran, 1977: 241 n. 11.

85. Jack Ladinsky, "The Traffic in Legal Services: Lawyer-Seeking Behavior and the Channeling of Clients"; Richard L. Abel, "Toward a Political Economy of Lawyers," pp. 1148–49.

86. Lillian Deitch and David Weinstein, Prepaid Legal Services: Socioeconomic Impacts, pp. 13–16.

87. Deitch & Weinstein, 1976: 16–17; cf. Eliot Freidson, Profession of Medicine, chap. 2.

88 NAACP v. Button, 1963; BRT v. Virginia, 1964; United Transportation v. State Bar of Michigan, 1971; United Mineworkers v. Illinois State Bar Association, 1976.

89. Freidson, 1970; Paul Starr, The Social Transformation of American Medicine.

90. Deitch & Weinstein, 1976: 21–25.

91. F. Raymond Marks, Robert Paul Hallauer, and Richard R. Clifton, The Shreveport Plan, pp. 67–71.

92. Fredric N. Tulsky, "2 Jurists, 2 Lawyers Indicted in Phila. Legal Services Plot." See also Robert Windrem, "Labor Dept. Investigating Legal Services Plans."

93. Curran, 1977: 248 n. 12.

94. Myrna Oliver, "New Services Plans Ease Burdens of Legal System."

95. Wall Street Journal, p 37, col. 4 (February 24, 1986); American Prepaid Legal Services Institute, Prepaid Legal Service Plans in Profile.

96. 70 ABAJ 48 (December 1984); Emily Couric, "Guardian Angels of the Law"; Tamar Lewin, "Legal Advice: $6.75 a Month"; Oliver, 1987c.

97. Henry Weinstein, "AFL-CIO Starts Legal Services Program."

98. Oliver, 1987c.

99. New York Times, p. 19 (December 29, 1984); Lewin, 1987a.

100. Lewin, 1987a.

101. Sherry Sontag, "By Phone, Legal First Aid for a Fixed Fee."

102. 8(36) NLJ 2 (May 19, 1986); Oliver, 1987c.

103. Couric, 1986b.

104. Timothy J. Muris and Fred S. McChesney, "Advertising and the Price and Quality of Legal Services: The Case of Legal Clinics."

105. C. E. Downey, "Killing Off the Competition"; "The Price Is Right—For Everyone but the California Bar."

106. Bates v. State Bar of Arizona, 1977.

107. Carrie Menkel-Meadow, The American Bar Association Legal Clinic Experiment.

108. Andrews, 1980: 13; Los Angeles Times, sec. 1, p. 9 (February 19, 1984).

109. 8(3) NLJ S-4, S-8 (September 30, 1985).

110. 9(2) NLJ S-4, S-6 (September 22, 1986).

111. 10(3) NLJ S-4, S-8 (September 28, 1987).

112. Los Angeles Times, sec. 1, p. 9 (February 19, 1984); Middleton, 1985a; see also Gerson, "Attorneys Spend $6.15 Million for TV Ads."

113. 8(7) National Law Journal 2 (October 28, 1985).

114. Len Jacoby, "Law Firm's In-House Efforts Work."

115. Carole Gould, "When to Turn to a No-Frills Law Firm."

116. Doug Smith, "Eviction—It's His Key to Success."

117. See Muris & McChesney, 1979; Murdock & White, "Does Legal Service Advertising Serve the Public's Interest?"; Thomas, "Legal Service Advertising."

118. Gould, 1986.

119. Wall Street Journal, p. 1, col. 5 (November 13, 1986).

120. Heinz & Laumann, 1982: 106–07.

121. Curran, 1977: 248 n. 12.

122. Katz, 1982: chap. 1; Andrew Abbott, "Status and Status Strain in the Professions."

123. R. Abel, 1985a: 557 n. 523.

124. David Lauter, "Bill Would Place Cap on U.S. Legal Fees."

125. Curran, 1977: 248 n. 12.

Chapter 7

1. R. Abel, 1981a: 661.

2. W. Johnson, 1974: 191.

3. R. Abel, 1981a: 639–40.

4. Geoffrey C. Hazard, Jr. and W. William Hodes, The Law of Lawyering.

5. E.g., Michael Davis and Frederick A. Elliston, Ethics and the Legal Profession; Georgetown Journal of Legal Ethics, 1987–; Journal of the Legal Profession, 1976–.

6. Standard 302(a)(iii).

7. Carlin, 1966; Ronald M. Pipkin, "Law School Instruction in Professional Responsibility: A Curricular Paradox"; Zemans & Rosenblum, 1981; Stuart C. Goldberg, "1977 National Survey on Current Methods of Teaching Professional Responsibility in Law Schools"; ABA Center for Professional Responsibility, A Survey on the Teaching of Professional Responsibility.

8. Michael J. Patton, "The Student, the Situation and Performance During the First Year of Law School."

9. Albert P. Blaustein, "The Association of the Bar of the City of New York, 1870–1951," p. 265.

10. 33 Proceedings of the Ohio State Bar Association 23–24 (1912).

11. Carlin, 1966: 44–50; Zemans & Rosenblum, 1981.

12. 71 ABAJ 48–49 (February 1985).

13. McCracken, 1951: 415.

14. Steven Pepe, Standards of Legal Negotiations.

15. Rhode, 1985b: 597–98, 628; Wayne D. Brazil, "Views from the Front Lines: Observations by Chicago Lawyers About the System of Civil Discovery"; "Civil Discovery: Lawyers' Views of its Effectiveness, Its Principal Problems and Abuses."

16. Jane Berentson, "Integrity Test: Lawyers Tell Clients to Lie."

17. Nelson, 1985: 534.

18. Robert L. Nelson, John P. Heinz, Edward O. Laumann, and Robert H. Salisbury, "Lawyers and the Structure of Influence in Washington."

19. Reed, "The Lawyer-Client: A Managed Relationship?"

20. Robert A. Kagan and Robert Eli Rosen, "On the Social Significance of Large Law Firm Practice."

21. Robert P. Gandossy, Bad Business: The OPM Scandal and the Seduction of the Establishment; Stewart Macaulay, "Comment: Control, Influence, and Attitudes," pp. 555–56; Rhode, 1985b: 615, 644 n. 173.

22. Nelson, 1985: 530.

23. Jonathan Casper, "Lawyers and Loyalty-Security Litigation"; Lawyers Before the Warren Court; The Politics of Civil Liberties.

24. On contemporary rural practice, see Donald D. Landon, "Clients, Colleagues, and Community: The Shaping of Zealous Advocacy"; David M. Engel, "The Oven Bird's Song: Insiders, Outsiders, and Personal Injuries in an American Community." Only 11.7 percent of lawyers practiced outside Standard Metropolitan Statistical Areas in 1980. Curran et al, 1985: 243. On urban lawyers, see Carlin, 1966: 96–118.

25. Eric H. Steele and Raymond T. Nimmer, "Lawyers, Clients, and Professional Regulation" pp. 962–63.

26. Landon, 1982: 482.

27. Steele & Nimmer, 1976: 973; Carlin, 1966: 153.

28. Kirk Victor, "Firms Facing More Ethical Challenges."

29. Frank J. Prial, "A Year After Settling the Johnson Estate, Lawyers Still Battling Over Ethics."

30. E. R. Shipp, "Court Faults New York Law Firm For Unethical Behavior in a Suit."

31. Carlin, 1966; Philip Shuchman, "Ethics and Legal Ethics: The Propriety of the Canons as a Group Moral Code"; Hobson, 1986: 303.

32. Cappell & Halliday, 1983: 329.

33. Rhode, 1985a: 548; 1985b: 641 n. 168; Curran, 1986: 30.

34. Mills, 1949: 81.

35. Orie L. Phillips and Philbrick McCoy, Conduct of Judges and Lawyers, pp. 90–91.

36. Phillips & McCoy, 1952: 127–29.

37. Blaustein, 1951: 265; Martin, 1970: 184, 201, 213.

38. E. Brown, 1938: 213–14.

39. Blaustein, 1951: 265–66.

40. Sam Roberts, "When Secrecy Seems More Like Professional Courtesy."

41. Schneyer, 1983: 21 n. 122.

42. State Bar of California, Proceedings of the Twelfth Annual Meeting, p. 5; Phillips & McCoy, 1952: 97–98; Blaustein & Porter, 1954: 256.

43. See also E. Brown, 1938: 213–14; Phillips & McCoy, 1952: 97–98; Blaustein & Porter, 1954: 256.

44. Myrna Oliver, "Bar's Disciplinary Policies at Root of Dispute Over Dues."

45. Halliday, 1987: 76–77.

46. Blaustein & Porter, 1954: 257.

47. Phillips & McCoy, 1952: 115; Blaustein & Porter, 1954: 261.

48. Blaustein & Porter, 1954: 258, 60.

49. Phillips & McCoy, 1952: 116. In one other case during this period a special commissioner recommended eight disbarments, eighteen suspensions, and twenty-six dismissals and the court imposed one disbarment and fourteen suspensions and dismissed thirty-seven defendants.

50. San Francisco Examiner, "The Brotherhood: Justice for Lawyers."

51. T. Gest, "Why Lawyers Are in the Doghouse," p. 38.

52. Alberta I. Cook, "Complaints Rise Against Lawyers"; Wall Street Journal, p. 1, col. 5 (November 11, 1986); Martha Middleton, "54,600 Complaints Filed Against Lawyers."

53. Robert C. Fellmeth, Initial Report to the Assembly and Senate Judiciary Committees and Chief Justice of the Supreme Court, Exhibit 19.

54. Steele & Nimmer, 1976: 982; F. Raymond Marks and Darlene Cathcart, "Discipline Within the Legal Profession: Is It Self-Regulation?" p. 215; Gest, 1981: 38.

55. Michael Powell, "Professional Divestiture: The Cession of Responsibility for Lawyer Discipline," p. 46–47.

56. Marks & Cathcart, 1974: 215.

57. Sharon Tisher, Lynn Bernabei, and Mark Green, Bringing the Bar to Justice, p. 97; Steele & Nimmer, 1976: 982.

58. Cook, 1986b.

59. Jeannine Guttman and Brad Bumsted, "Public Access to Disciplinary Hearings Varies."

60. Cook, 1986b.

61. Tisher et al., 1977: 97–98; Cook, 1986b.

62. Steele & Nimmer, 1976: 995.

63. Rhode, 1985a: 549–50.

64. In re Chase, 1985; In re Drakulich, 1985.

65. Chris Mondics, "New Jersey Supreme Court Warns Lawyers on Drug Use."

66. Gail Diane Cox, "Lawyers Who Are Felons."

67. David A. Kaplan, "Clairborne Found Fit to Practice in Nevada."

68. ABA Special Committee on Evaluation of Disciplinary Enforcement, Problems and Recommendations in Disciplinary Enforcement.

69. Phillips & McCoy, 1952: 120, 122, 124.

70. Cook, 1986b.

71. Brad Bumsted and Jeannine Guttman, "N.J. Swings Toward Tough Penalties Against Crooked Lawyers."

72. Brad Bumsted and Jeannine Guttman, "Multiple Licensing Creates Problems in Punishing Rogues."

73. Halliday, 1987: 73.

74. ABA Standing Committee on Professional Discipline, 1978–84.

75. Cook, 1986b; Middleton, 1987e.

76. 7(35) NLJ 9 (May 6, 1985); Los Angeles Times, sec. 1, p. 2 (May 22, 1985).

77. Mary Ann Galante, "Former California Bar Employee Wins Pact Over Firing."

78. Robert C. Fellmeth, "The Discipline System of the California State Bar: An Initial Report," p. 23

79. Robert C. Fellmeth, First Progress Report of the State Bar Discipline Monitor, p. 2.

80. Jennifer Warren, "State Bar Plans to Hike Dues to Pay for Reform."

81. Austin C. Wehrwein, "Is Discipline a 'Major Task' in Minnesota?"

82. ABA Standing Committee on Professional Discipline, Memorandum (March 29, 1983).

83. Mary Ann Galante, "California Bar Enters High Court Fray"; Los Angeles Times, sec 1, p. 3 (November 20, 1985).

84. Powell, 1986: 35; Galante, 1986a; Cook, 1986b.

85. Fellmeth, 1987b: 5–6; 1987c: 25, 39.

86. Fellmeth, 1987b: 6; 1987c: 27.

87. Fellmeth, 1987b: 7.

88. Fellmeth, 1987b: 8, 14, 27.

89. Fellmeth, 1987b: 10; 1987c. 47.

90. Fellmeth, 1987b: 9, 13, 18–19. The salaries of Office of Trial Counsel lawyers were raised to near market levels in 1987, Fellmeth, 1987c: 1.

91. Fellmeth, 1987b: 12.

92. Fellmeth, 1987b: 12, 14 This rule has since been abolished, Fellmeth, 1987c. 47.

93. Fellmeth, 1987b: 12.

94. Fellmeth, 1987b: 25; 1987c: 56.

95. Fellmeth, 1987b: 13; 1987c: 56.

96. Fellmeth, 1987b: 7, 11; 1987c: 2.

97. Fellmeth, 1987b: 9, 19; 1987c: 1, 56.

98. Fellmeth, 1987a: Exhibit 12; 1987b: 6–7.

99. Fellmeth, 1987a: Exhibits 12, 18.

100. Fellmeth, 1987b: 4, 20; 1987c: 11.

101. Fellmeth, 1987b: 12; 1987c: 49.

102. Fellmeth, 1987c: 1, 50.

103. Jeannine Guttman and Brad Bumsted, "Funds Reimburse Victims."

104. Bumsted & Guttman, 1986a; Cook, 1986b; Rorie Sherman, "Big Brother Might Be Watching."

105. Schneyer, 1983: 100. It is important to recognize that significant defaults will reduce the money available for legal aid. See Chapter 5, "The Contested Terrain of Civil Legal Aid."

106. ABA Standing Committee on Client Security Funds, Results of 1981 Survey of State and Local Bars and Bar Associations. Thirty-four jurisdictions reported for 1979 and 1980.

107. Saleeby v. State Bar of California, 1985.

108. ABA Standing Committee on Clients' Security Funds, 1981.

109. Fellmeth, 1987a: Exhibit 29. Elsewhere this source indicates that $3,184,630 was paid in the latter three years, Id. Exhibit 18.

110. Curran, 1977: 230–32; Steele & Nimmer, 1976.

111. Douglas E. Rosenthal, "Evaluating the Competence of Lawyers"; Rick J. Carlson, "Measuring the Quality of Legal Services: An Idea Whose Time Has Not Come."

112. Alfred B. Carlson and Charles E. Werts, "Relationships among Law School Predictors, Law School Performance, and Bar Examination Results."

113. Sidney L. Carroll and Robert Gaston, "Examination Pass Rates as Entry Restrictions into Licensed Occupations."

114. ABA Standing Committee on Professional Discipline, Statistical Report, 1984, pp. 70–71.

115. R. Stevens, 1983: 238 nn. 63–64; Alan S. Kopit, "Trends in Continuing Education."

116. Mark H. Tuohey, III, "Getting CLE Programs Out to Lawyers Who Need Them"; 9(13) NLJ 40 (December 8, 1986).

117. Kopit, 1987.

118. Douglas Shaw Palmer, "How Not to Re-Educate Attorneys."

119. Betsy Stark, "Nine Clinics, Nine Answers: NY Survey Shows Wide Disparities."

120. Martha Middleton, "Are Firms Ready for Peer Review?"

121. Douglas E. Rosenthal, Lawyer and Client: Who's in Charge?; Steele & Nimmer, 1976.

122. Blaustein & Porter, 1954: 258–60.

123. UCLA Law Review, "Comment: Financial Penalties Imposed Directly Against Attorneys in Litigation Without Resort to the Contempt Process."

124. 7(47) NLJ 2 (August 5, 1985).

125. New York Times, p. 10 (January 18, 1986).

126. E. R. Shipp, "108–Year Old Law Firm Under Fire From Court"; see generally Frank Lipsius and Nancy Lisagor, A Law Unto Itself: The Untold Story of Sullivan & Cromwell.

127. New York Times, p. A24 (July 28, 1987); 9(48) NLJ 2 (August 10, 1987).

128. 10(20) NLJ 2 (January 25, 1988).

129. Jeffrey A. Parness, "The New Method of Regulating Lawyers: Public and Private Interest Sanctions During Civil Litigation for Attorney Misconduct."

130. Fred Strasser, "Sanctions: A Sword Is Sharpened"; see also Philip Hager, "Burger Urges Fines for Lawyers Filing Frivolous Suits."

131. Gary Taylor, "Texas Jurists Target Frivolous Suits."

132. 9(24) NLJ 2 (February 23, 1987).

133. George Gombossy, "Excluding Black Jurors Brings Sanction."

134. David Lauter, "Akin Gump Angers Salt Lake City."

135. Marcia Chambers, "Criminal Lawyers in Study Say New Laws Inhibit Case Choices"; Fred Strasser, "Fee-Forfeiture Provisions Illegal, 4th Circuit Says"; "4th Circuit OKs Seizure of Fees."

136. Timothy W. Bingham and Gregory H. Bonenberger, "Lawyers Beware: Small Change in Collection Act Bodes Big Impact."

137. Tulsky, 1986.

138. Blaustein & Porter, 1954: 238; Lieberman 1978.

139. Michelle Galen, "Security More Crucia Than Ever"; 9(7) NLJ 2 (October 27, 1986).

140. Rosenthal, 1974; Murray L. Schwartz and Daniel J. B. Mitchell, "An Economic Analysis of the Contingent Fee in Personal Injury Litigation"; Herbert M. Kritzer, William L. F. Felstiner, Austin Sarat and David M. Trubek, "The Impact of Fee Arrangement on Lawyer Effort"; Herbert M. Kritzer, "Fee Arrangements and Negotiation."

141. Werner Pfennigstorf, "Types and Causes of Lawyers' Professional Liability Claims: The Search for Facts," pp. 255–56.

142. Herbert S. Denenberg, Victor T. Ehre, Jr. and Ronald L. Huling, "Lawyers' Professional Liability Insurance: The Peril, the Protection, and the Price," pp. 391–92.

143. Illinois State Bar Association, 1983: 162 But only 23 percent of government and 41 percent of other (i.e. industry) lawyers purchased insurance.

144. Andrew Blum, "More Judges Turning to Judicial Insurance Policies."

145. Pfennigstorf, 1980: 258. But the author feels these figures are unsubstantiated.

146. Mary Ann Galante, "Malpractice Rates Zoom"; Illinois, 1983: 162. But 12 percent of those in Illinois firms with two to four lawyers had been sued.

147. Rita Henley Jensen, "Is There Life for Firm After Bad Publicity?" p. 29.

148. William H. Gates, "Lawyers' Malpractice Some Recent Data About a Growing Problem," pp. 559–60; Curran, 1986: 28, 37; see also William H Gates, "The Newest Data on Lawyers' Malpractice Claims."

149. Gates, 1986: 561–62.

150. 8 Personal Injury Verdict Review (July 15 1985).

151. Gates, 1986: 563–64.

152. Pfennigstorf, 1980: 258. The author thinks these figures are exaggerated.

153. 8 Personal Injury Verdict Review (July 15 1985).

154. Mary Ann Galante, "$26M Legal Malpractice Judgment Upheld."

155. Mary Ann Galante, "Insurance: Lawyers Face New Fights on Malpractice Coverage"; "Rogers & Wells Will Pay $40M"; "After a $40M Payment It's Not Over Yet for Rogers & Wells"; "Last 'David' Firm Agrees to Pact."

156. Kirk Victor, "Venable Agrees to $27M Accord."

157. Kirk Victor, "Securities Advice Can Pose Risks"; Martha Middleton, "Winston & Strawn t Pay $7.3M in Pact"; 9(43) NLJ 2 (July 6, 1987).

158. William Glaberson, "A Wall St. Firm Breaks Ranks."

159. 10(18) NLJ 2 (January 11, 1988).

160. Galante, 1985a.

161. Mary Ann Galante, "Insurance Costs Soar; Is There Any Way Out?"

162. Galante, 1985b.

163. Pfennigstorf, 1980: 237 n. 8; Galante, 1985b.

164. Galante, 1986c: 7–8; 9(11) NLJ 2 (November 24, 1986).

165. Susan Winchurch, "New Funds for Lawyers Emerge."

166. Robert M. Snider, "Legal Malpractice Insurance"; Galante, 1986b; Robert C. Fellmeth, "The Discipline System of the California State Bar: An Initial Report," pp. 9. 26. In 1986, the governor vetoed a bill that would have mandated malpractice insurance.

167. 71 ABAJ 37 (April 1985).

168. Gail Diane Cox, "Ore. Lawyers Face High Rate of Claims."

169. Robert Wycoff, "The Effects of a Malpractice Suit upon Physicians in Connecticut"; Galante, 1986c: 8.

170. R. Abel, 1981b: 1180.

171. Indiana, South Carolina, New York. See R. Stevens, 1983: 239, 278 n. 96; Heinz & Laumann, 1982: 349 n. 50.

172. Amy Tarr, "Fight Intensifies on Ethics Rules."

173. Texas, Virginia, New Jersey. See Schneyer, 1983: 20 n. 117, 69 n. 400.

174. ABA Center for Professional Responsibility, 1983: 4; Michael Powell, "Professional Self-Regulation: The Transfer of Control from a Professional Association to an Independent Commission"; Rules of the Illinois Supreme Court, 1985.

175. 9(31) NLJ 12 (April 13, 1987).

Chapter 8

1. 10 Bar Examiner 16–17 (1941).

2. Freeman, 1975: 172. It fell more than 30 percent according to another source. See Harold F. Clark, Life Earnings in Selected Occupations in the United States, pp. 7, 240, 247–48.

3. Fagen, 1939: 73.

4. 10 Bar Examiner 72 (1941).

5. 10 Bar Examiner 15–16 (1941).

6. Platt, 1940: 639 (23 percent response rate).

7. American Bar Foundation, Lawyers in the United States: Distribution and Income. Part Two: Income, p. 5. For the income of a sample of fifty Connecticut lawyers in 1938, see Clark & Corstvet, 1938: 1286–87.

8. Edward F. Denison, "Incomes in Selected Professions, Part 2, Legal Service," p. 23.

9. Gawalt, 1984: 98.

10. American Bar Foundation, 1958b: 5. According to another source the percentage increases in the numbers of lawyers and physicians in independent practice were virtually identical between 1929 and 1948. See William Weinfeld, "Income of Physicians, 1929–49," p. 19.

11. American Bar Foundation, 1958a: 3; 1958b: 5; see also H. Clark, 1937: 7; Edward F. Denison, "Incomes in Selected Professions, Part 6, Comparison of Incomes in Nine Independent Professions," p. 15; Garrison, 1934: 124–25; 1935. 156 58.

12. Kafoglis, 1955: 6–8.

13. Weinfeld, 1949: 18, 1951; 11; see also Freeman, 1975: 172; but see H. Clark, 1937: 7.

14. Weinfeld, 1951: 11.

15. Milton Z. Kafoglis, "Commentary," pp. 54–56. But these data aggregate professionals and nonprofessional employees.

16. American Bar Foundation, Recent Statistics on the Income of Lawyers in the United States, p. 2.

17. John W. Oliver, "Big City or Country: Where Start to Practice?" p. 126.

18. Colorado Bar Association, 1967: 2.

19. Liebenberg, 1956: 26–27. Lawyer income grew faster than that of physicians between 1947 and 1948, slower between 1949 and 1951. Weinfeld, 1949: 18 n. 3; Survey of Current Business, "Incomes of Physicians, Dentists, and Lawyers, 1949–51," p. 5.

20. Again this aggregates professionals and nonprofessionals. Kafoglis, 1982: 54–56.

21. John P. Henderson and Norman P. Obst, "The Economic Status of the Michigan Legal Profession in 1976," p. 920.

22. Maryland State Bar Association, 1975: 7A.

23. Illinois State Bar Association, 1983. 128 31.

24. Wall Street Journal, p. 1, col. 5 (July 31, 1984); p. 1, col. 5 (July 16, 1985).

25. D. Weston Darby, Jr., "Are You Keeping Up Financially?" pp. 66–67.

26. Weil, 1986: 16.

27. Wall Street Journal, p. 1, col. 5 (August 30, 1984).

28. Gawalt, 1984: 116.

29. H. Clark, 1937: 8, 245–47.

30. H. Clark, 1937: 252–53 (33 percent return rate).

31. Denison, 1944: 18.

32. Kafoglis, 1955: 26.

33. Michael A. Robinson, "Young Lawyers Find Success Is No Longer a Cinch."

34. Weinfeld, 1951: 18; Liebenberg, 1956: 27.

35. Denison, 1943: 24, 26.

36. Survey of Current Business, 1952: 6.

37. Maryland State Bar Association, 1975: 7A.

38. 10 Bar Examiner 72 (1941).

39. 10 Bar Examiner 19 (1941).

40. ABA Special Committee on the Economic Condition of the Bar, 1939: 16, 18; State Bar of California, Committee for Cooperation, 1937: 260–61.

41. Denison, 1944: 16.

42. Liebenberg, 1956: 34, 36.

43. Illinois State Bar Association, 1983: 128–31.

44. Fagen, 1939: 99.

45. Illinois State Bar Association, 1983: 132–33.

46. Garrison, 1934: 125; 1935: 159; Liebenberg, 1956: 33; Landon, 1982: 473.

47. Dupuy G. Warrick, "Report of Committee on Welfare of the Bar," pp. 224–25.

48. 10 Bar Examiner 72 (1941).

49. Denison, 1943: 25. The correlation may not be strong enough to compensate for the higher living costs in larger cities: South Carolina—Cantor, 1969: 8; Florida—Cantor, 1966: 21; Ohio—Kafoglis, 1955: 30–32.

50. Bethel, 1976: 55.

51. Illinois State Bar Association, 1983: 128–31.

52. Arlene Holen, "Effects of Professional Licensing Arrangements on Interstate Mobility and Resource Allocation."

53. Alex Maurizi, "Occupational Licensing and the Public Interest."

54. Freeman, 1975: 177.

55. Carroll & Gaston, 1977.

56. Malcolm Getz, John Siegfried, and Terry Calvani, "Competition at the Bar: The Correlation Between the Bar Examination Pass Rate and the Profitability of Practice," p. 879.

57. David S. Casey, "We Have Miles to Go, Much to Do."

58. Halliday, 1987: 89–91.

59. 64 ABAJ 41–43 (January 1978); see also Wall Street Journal, p. 1, col. 1 (October 11, 1983).

60. E.g., E. Lee Shepard, "Lawyers Look at Themselves: Professional Consciousness and the Virginia Bar, 1770–1850"; Robert B. Kirtland, "Keep Your Eye on the Bastards! Or sobering reflections on the 150–year record of early Virginia's attitude toward lawyers"; Fredrich Thomforde, Jr., "Public Opinion of the Legal Profession: A Necessary Response by the Bar and the Law School."

61. Marvin W. Mindes and Alan C. Acock, "Trickster, Hero, Helper: A Report on the Lawyer Image," pp. 191–92.

62. Robert W. Hodge, Paul M. Siegel, and Peter H. Rossi, "Occupational Prestige in the United States, 1925–1963," pp. 324, 327; see also Henry S. Drinker, "Views of Laymen on the Competency and Integrity of Lawyers"; Albert P. Blaustein, "What Do Laymen Think of Lawyers?"; Iowa State Bar Association, Lay Opinion of Iowa Lawyers; Phillips & McCoy, 1952: ix.

63. Time, p. 56 (April 10, 1978).

64. David A. Kaplan, "The NLJ Poll Results: Take Heed, Lawyers."

65. Myrna Oliver, "Lawyers Losing the Verdict in the Court of Public Opinion."

66. Heinz & Laumann, 1982: chap. 4; Abbott, 1981.

67. Curran, 1977: 234.

68. Curran, 1977: 229, 231.

69. Curran, 1977: 229–32; see also Clark & Corstvet, 1938: 1281.

70. Curran, 1977: 235.

71. Curran, 1977: 243–50.

72. James W. Meeker, John Dombrink, and Edward Schumann, "Attitudes Towards the Legal Profession: The Poor and the Undocumented."

73. Mindes and Acock, 1982: 191–92.

74. Chase, 1986.

Chapter 9

1. Leona Vogt, From Law School to Career: Where Do Graduates Go and What Do They Do? pp. 11–12.

2. Liebenberg, 1956: 29.

3. Bethel, 1976: 7.

4. Catalyst Legal Resources, 1981–1982 Annual Survey: Compensation of Attorneys in 10 Cities, pp. 72–73.

5. Nelson et al., 1987b; Altman & Weil, Survey of Government Lawyer Salaries, pp. 25, 46.

6. NALP, 1985: 30; 8(26) NLJ 4 (March 10, 1986).

7. Altman & Weil, 1984: 12; Law Office Economics and Management, "Government Lawyer Salaries Compared to Industry and Firms," pp. 117–21; "Associate, Administrative and Support Staff Salaries Survey, p. 124.

8. Altman & Weil, 1984: 13.

9. Vogt, 1986: 62–64 and Table D21.

10. Eve Spangler, Lawyers for Hire, p. 123.

11. Malcolm Spector, "The Rise and Fall of a Mobility Route"; "Secrecy in Job Seeking Among Government Attorneys."

12. Lester Milbrath, The Washington Lobbyists, p. 68; Robert H. Salisbury, John P. Heinz. Edward O. Laumann, and Robert L. Nelson, "Who You Know versus What You Know: The Uses of Government Experience for Washington Lobbyists."

13. Nelson et al., 1987a; 1987b.

14. Vogt, 1986: 14–15 and Table D5.

15. Heinz & Laumann, 1982: 195.

16. Spangler, 1986: 112.

17. Blaustein & Porter, 1954: 59.

18. Schwartz, 1980: 1277.

19. Schwartz, 1980: 1275.

20. Vogt, 1986: 15–16 and Table D6.

21. E.g., Nick Gallucio, "The Rise of the Company Lawyer."

22. B. Peter Pashigian, "Regulation, Preventive Law, and the Duties of Attorneys," pp. 8–9, 20.

23. Edward O. Laumann and John P. Heinz, "Washington Lawyers and Others: The Structure of Washington Representation," Table 2.

24. Spangler, 1986: 74.

25. Pashigian, 1982: 8; Charles Maddock, "The Corporation Law Department"; Halliday, 1986: 66.

26. Robert Bell, "Why Some Corporations Use More Lawyers Than Others."

27. Tom Priest and John Krol, "Lawyers in Corporate Chief Executive Positions: Career Characteristics and 'Inner Group' Membership," pp. 36–37.

28. Pashigian, 1982: 10, 19; Gallucio, 1978.

29. Curran, 1986.

30. Peter W. Bernstein, "Profit Pressures on the Big Law Firm"; Schwartz, 1980: 1275; Marc Galanter,

'Larger than Life: Mega-Law and Mega-Lawyering n the Contemporary United States."

31. Albert F. Lynch, Jr., Thomas S Tilghman, and Robert J. Berkow, National Survey of Corporate Law Departments Compensation and Organization Practices, p. 221.

32. Maddock, 1952.

33. Gallucio, 1978.

34. Gallucio, 1978. The growth is continuing; Mellon National Corp. grew from two to thirty-five between 1981 and 1984. Business Week, "A New Corporate Powerhouse: The Legal Department."

35. Curran et al., 1985; Curran, 1986.

36. Commission on the Corporate Law Departments, National Survey of Corporation Law Compensation and Organization Practices.

37. 9(35) NLJ 2 (May 11, 1987).

38. Antonia Handler Chayes, Bruce C. Greenwald, and Maxine Paisner Winig, "Managing Your Lawyers"; see also Gallucio, 1978; Business Week, 1984; Wall Street Journal, p. 25, col. 4 (March 1, 1982).

39. Lynch et al., 1985: 371–73.

40. Ellen L. Rosen, "It's Not Just a Matter of Time."

41. National Law Journal, "Billing," p. S-1.

42. Abram Chayes and Antonia H. Chayes, 'Corporate Counsel and the Elite Law Firm," pp. 289–93.

43. Mark H. McCormack, The Terrible Truth About Lawyers: How Lawyers Really Work and How to Deal with Them Successfully, as advertised in the New York Times Book Review.

44. Chayes & Chayes, 1985: 294 n. 50.

45. Wall Street Journal, p. 1, col. 5 (November 11, 1986).

46. Pashigian, 1982: 26; Business Week, 1984.

47. Chayes & Chayes, 1985: 279.

48. Wall Street Journal, p. 1, col. 5 (April 5, 1983).

49. Strasser, 1985.

50. Jane Thieberger, "More Graduates Turning to Law Firm Practice."

51. Strasser, 1985; Altman & Weil, "The 1986 Survey of Law Firm Economics," p. 1.

52. 8(45) NLJ 2 (July 21, 1986).

53. Spangler, 1986: 80.

54. Heinz & Laumann, 1982: 195.

55. Lynch et al., 1985: 253–55.

56. Lynch et al., 1985: 264–69.

57. Vogt, 1986: 35.

58. Spangler, 1986: 82.

59. Vogt, 1986: Table D21.

60. Steven Langer, Compensation of Attorneys Non Law Firm), pp. 19, 154, 189, 191–92. For higher figures, see Wall Street Journal, p. 9, col. 3 (July 5, 1985): $31,000 starting; $65,000 general; $68,800 patent; $225,000 chief legal officer. For lower figures that include employees of nonprofit groups, see Wall Street Journal, p. 1, col. 5 (September 17, 1985)— median $56,400.

61. 8(45) NLJ 2 (July 21, 1986); 9(35) NLJ 2 (May 11, 1987).

62. Lynch et al., 1985: 126.

63. Priest & Krol, 1986: 39–40; see also Tom Priest and R. A. Rothman, "Lawyers in Corporate Chief Executive Positions: A Historical Analysis of Careers."

64. 10(10) NLJ 2 (November 16, 1987).

65. Pashigian, 1982: 36–37.

66. R. Abel, 1985c.

67. Stephen Botein, " 'When We All Meet Afterwards in Heaven': Judgeship as a Symbol of Modern American Lawyers."

68. R. Abel, 1985c.

69. Curran et al., 1985; Curran, 1986.

70. National Center for State Courts, Guidelines for the Use of Lawyers to Supplement Judicial Resources; Myrna Oliver, "A Shortcut Through the Legal Muck."

71. Wall Street Journal, p. 52 (September 1, 1981); 71 ABAJ 25–27 (June 1985).

72. R. Stevens, 1983: 63 n.90; Hobson, 1986: 115–16.

73. W. Johnson, 1978: 105, 113, 130–31; cf. John Henry Schlegel, "Between the Harvard Founders and the American Legal Realists: The Professionalization of the American Law Professor."

74. Charles Noble Gregory, "The Wages of Law Teachers," pp. 513–14.

75. W. Johnson, 1978: 105, 113, 130–31.

76. Hobson, 1986: 346–47.

77. ABA Committee on Legal Education, 1891: 315; Review of Legal Education, 1948.

78. Donna Fossum, "Law Professors: A Profile of the Teaching Branch of the Profession," pp. 504–05.

79. Ashbel Green Gulliver, "Effects of the War on the Law Schools," p. 14; Notes on Legal Education (December 31, 1931); Review of Legal Education, 1948; 1984. Fossum and the Review of Legal Education offer inconsistent figures.

80. AALS, Special Committee, 1961: 337.

81. Notes on Legal Education (December 31, 1931).

82. E. Brown, 1938: 107.

83. Benjamin Franklin Boyer, "The Smaller Law Schools: Factors Affecting Their Methods and Objectives," p. 284.

84. Gulliver, 1943: 14.

85. Review of Legal Education, 1948.

86. Review of Legal Education, 1982.

87. Nicholson, 1958: 69. Maxima in California were about twice as high at the elite schools, see McClain et al., 1949: 62.

88. AALS, Special Committee, 1961: 263–64.

89. Boyer, 1941: 284.

90. Swords & Walwer, 1974: 62.

91. John J. Siegfried and Charles E. Scott, "The Economic Status of Academic Lawyers"; Wall Street Journal, p. 52 (September 1, 1981).

92. John J. Siegfried and Charles E. Scott, "The Financial Returns to Law School Faculty."

93. Mara Tapp, "In the Battle of the New Associates Salaries, Could Law Schools End Up Losing Their Faculties?"; Wall Street Journal, p. 1, col. 1 (March 1, 1984).

94. AALS, Special Committee, 1961: 300.

95. Siegfried & Scott, 1976.

96. Zenoff & Lorio, 1983: 882–83.

97. Michael I. Swygert and Nathaniel E. Gozansky, "Senior Law Faculty Publication Study: Comparisons of Law School Productivity," p. 381.

98. Ira Mark Ellman, "A Comparison of Law Faculty Production in Leading Law Reviews," p. 688.

99. D. Chambers, 1983.

100. Elyce H. Zenoff and Lizabeth A. & Moody, "Law Faculty Attrition: Are We Doing Something Wrong?" pp. 210–11, 215.

101. C. Auerbach, 1984: 50–51.

102. Review of Legal Education, 1984: 66.

103. Zenoff & Moody, 1986: 214.

104. David Podmore, Solicitors and the Wider Community, chap. 3.

105. Donald Matthews, The Social Background of Political Decision-Makers, p. 30.

106. Hurst, 1950: 352; see also Matthews, 1954; Charles Y. Chai, "Recruitment Characteristics and Leadership Status of Urban Lawyers in the South: A Case Study of New Orleans"; David R. Derge, "The Lawyer as Decision-maker in the American State Legislature."

107. Justin J. Green, John R. Schmidhauser, Larry L. Berg, and David Brady, "Lawyers in Congress: A New Look at Some Old Assumptions," p. 440; John Brown Mason, "A Study of Legal Education and Training of the Lawyers in the Seventy-Third Congress."

108. David Derge, "The Lawyer in the Indiana General Assembly," p. 19; Heinz Eulau and John D. Sprague, Lawyers in Politics, pp. 11–12.

109. Charles S. Hyneman, "Who Makes Our Laws?" p. 255; Belle Zeller, American State Legislatures, pp. 70–73; Derge, 1959: 410, 423; Paul L. Hair and James E. Piereson, "Lawyers and Politics Revisited: Structural Advantages of Lawyer-Politicans"; Charles M. Moon, Jr., "Careers of Lawyers in Politics: The Case of the Georgia General Assembly."

110. McClain et al., 1949: 11.

111. E.g., Michael Cohen, "Lawyers and Political Careers"; Leonard F. Cormier, "Lawyers and Political Mobility: an alternative to convergence theory"; John Schmidhauser, "The Convergence of Law and Politics Revisited: The Law Firm as a Case Study."

112. Dennis O. Lynch, Legal Roles in Colombia; R. Abel, 1985c.

113. Heinz & Laumann, 1982: 195.

114. Curran et al., 1985: 22.

115. Spector, 1973.

116. Weinfeld, 1949: 19–21. The figures are calculated from tax and census data.

117. Weinfeld, 1949: 20; Liebenberg, 1956: 28.

118. Bethel, 1976: 7.

119. 71 ABAJ 15 (January 1985).

120. A 1939 survey of Michigan lawyers, with a 23 precent response rate, found 93.9 percent in private practice. See Platt, 1940: 632.

121. R. Abel, 1985c.

122. Friedman & Kuznets, 1945: 280. This actually understates the number of sole practitioners.

123. In a 1938 sample of 48 Connecticut lawyers 58 percent were sole practitioners. See Clark & Corstvet, 1938: 1289. In a 1939 survey of Michigan lawyers, with a 23 percent response rate, about 60 percent were sole practitioners. See Platt, 1940: 632.

124. Vogt, 1986: 13 and Table D4.

125. Zemans & Rosenblum, 1981: 67.

126. Illinois State Bar Association, 1983: 127–29.

127. NALP, 1985: 76.

128. Hobson, 1984: 5 n. 9.

129. Weinfeld, 1949: 21.

130. Committee on the Survey, 1952: 383, 385 The response rate was only 13 percent.

131. Liebenberg, 1956: 28–30, 33.

132. Weinfeld, 1949: 21; Curran, 1986.

133. Cantor, 1966: 24.

134. Colorado Bar Association, 1967: 12.

135. Landon, 1982: 463–65.

136. Curran et al., 1985; Curran, 1986.

137. Illinois State Bar Association, 1983: 128.

138. U.S. Department of Commerce, Bureau o the Census, 1972 Census of Selected Service Industries: Summary and Subject Statistics; 1977 Census o Service Industries: Summary and Subject Statistics.

139. Curran, 1986.

140. Bethel, 1976: 11.

141. Illinois State Bar Association, 1983: 127–28.

142. For Florida, Pennsylvania, and New Jersey, see Cantor, 1966: 56. For South Carolina, see Cantor, 1969: 12. For Colorado, see Colorado Ba Association, 1967: 5. For Ohio, see Kafoglis, 1955 57.

143. Rorie Sherman, "For Better or Worse Family Law Is Changing."

144. Curran, 1986: 28.

145. R. Abel, 1985c; Hoffman, 1973; Paul Hoffman, Lions of the Eighties; Erwin O. Smigel, The Wall Street Lawyer; James B. Stewart, The Partners James C. Goulden, The Superlawyers; Mark Green The Other Government; Mark Stevens, Power of Attorney. For novelistic treatments, see the writings o Louis Auchincloss.

146. Hobson, 1984: 19.

147. Halliday, 1985: table 6.

148. Hobson, 1984: 5–7. For histories of individual law firms, see Austin H. Peck, Jr., Bold Beginnings: A Story about the First 50 Years of Latham & Watkins; Otto E. Koegel, Walter S. Carter: Collecto of Young Masters; or, The Progenitor of Many Law Firms; Walter K. Earle, Mr. Shearman and Mr. Sterling and How They Grew; Robert T. Swaine, Th Cravath Firm; Arthur H. Dean, William Nelso Cromwell, 1854–1948: An American Pioneer in Cor

oration, Comparative, and International Law; Henry W. Taft, A Century and a Half of the New York Bar.

149. Robert L. Nelson, Partners With Power, p. 86.

150. Smigel, 1969: 35.

151. Nelson, 1983: 114–15.

152. Schwartz, 1980: 1274.

153. Galanter, 1983.

154. National Law Journal, 1982.

155. National Law Journal, "Annual Survey of the Nation's Largest Law Firms, 1985."

156. R. Stevens, 1983: 267 n. 20; National Law Journal, 1985: S-4.

157. Ellen L. Rosen, "The Large Firm Boom Continues: A 10-Year Look," p. S-2.

158. 10(12) NLJ 2 (November 30, 1987).

159. Martha Middleton, "World's Largest Law Firm Not Through Growing Yet," p. 22.

160. New York Times, p. 25 (July 2, 1987).

161. Ronald J. Gilson and Robert H. Mnookin, "Sharing Among the Human Capitalists: An Economic Inquiry into the Corporate Law Firm and How Partners Split Profits," pp. 324–29.

162. Rita Henley Jensen, "What's Hot, What's Not: A Roundup"; Fred Strasser, "Immigration Law Making Corporate Inroads."

163. Lewin, 1983.

164. Arlene Leibowitz and Robert Tollison, "Free Riding, Shirking, and Team Production in Legal Partnership," p. 383.

165. 9(28) NLJ 2 (March 23, 1987).

166. New York Times, p. 25 (July 2, 1987).

167. Gilson & Mnookin, 1985: 316–18.

168. For Ohio, see Kafoglis, 1955: 63. For Florida, see Cantor, 1966: App. 22.

169. Altman & Weil, The 1985 Survey of Law Firm Economics, pp. 2–6.

170. Robert L. Weil and Robin L. Hegvik, "Small-Firm Poll: Administrative Law Most Lucrative."

171. Rita Henley Jensen, "Partners Work Harder to Stay Even."

172. 9(15) NLJ 2 (December 22, 1986); 10(2) NLJ 2 (September 21, 1987).

173. 9(6) NLJ 2 (October 20, 1986).

174. Michael Powell, "The New Legal Press, the Transformation of Legal Journalism, and the Changing Character of Legal Practice," argues that the growth of the new legal journalism is both a cause and a consequence of this new fluidity.

175. Rita Henley Jensen, "Banking Clients More Willing to Shop for Firms."

176. 10(8) NLJ 2 (November 2, 1987).

177. Barbara Bry, "Finley Kumble Rides a Fast Track"; 7(47) NLJ 2 (August 5, 1985); National Law Journal, "The NLJ 500: Tenth Annual Survey of the Nation's Largest Law Firms," S-4.

178. John C. Metaxas, "Mergers: Working Through the Maze"; National Law Journal, 1987b: S-4.

179. Emily Couric, "Specialities: What's Hot,

What's Not," p. 26; Martha Middleton, "Aggression Pays Off for Chicago Firm."

180. Alexander Stille, "The Megamerger: How Good a Fit?"

181. Rita Henley Jensen, "Look Before Leaping Into Merger."

182. Martha Middleton, "Merger Shock"; 10(14) NLJ 2 (December 14, 1987); 10(19) NLJ 2 (January 18, 1988).

183. For examples of decline, see Gilson & Mnookin, 1985: 314 n.4.

184. Marcia Coyle, "Boutique Shakeout: Merger Can Be an Attractive Option"; "Once-Tranquil Trade Law Hit By New Frenzy"; Emily Couric, "Broadway, Hollywood"; Martha Middleton, "The New Respectability of Breaking Up"; Gary Taylor, "No Apologies Made for the Profit Motive"; Coleman T. Mobley, "Venerable Firm Torn Apart by Modern Pressures"; New York Times, "Lawyers Catch Merger Fever."

185. 10(8) NLJ 2 (November 2, 1987).

186. Bernstein, 1982; Gilson & Mnookin, 1985: 315 n.5.

187. Lewin, 1983; Spangler, 1986: 40; Nelson, 1988: 203.

188. 9(34) NLJ 2 (May 4, 1987).

189. Rita Henley Jensen, "The Rainmakers."

190. Charles H. Carman, "For Rainmakers Here, It Pours."

191. Moore, "Shrunken Leva, Hawes Reels as Lawyers Who Left It Thrive"; see also Weingarten, "Breaking Up."

192. Gilson & Mnookin, 1985.

193. E. J. McMahon, "Old-Fashioned—and Proud of It."

194. 9(33) NLJ 2 (April 27, 1987).

195. Mary Ann Galante, "For Firms, Breaking Up Is Hard to Do"; 8(3) NLJ 2 (September 30, 1985).

196. 9(38) NLJ 2 (June 1, 1987); 9(39) NLJ 2 (June 8, 1987).

197. Albert I. Cook, "The 'Incident at Chappaquiddick.' "

198. Eric Effron, "Public Battle Cracks Firm."

199. John C. Metaxas, "Paying for a Partner's Departure."

200. Nicholas D. Kristof, "The Rush to Hire L.A. Lawyers."

201. 8(19) NLJ 2 (January 20, 1986).

202. E. R. Shipp, "Revamping Is Seen for a Big Law Firm", 10(1) NLJ 2 (September 14, 1987).

203. 10(24) NLJ 2 (February 22, 1988).

204. Lewin, 1983.

205. 8(1) NLJ 2 (September 23, 1985); see also Wall Street Journal, p. 25, col. 4 (January 4, 1987).

206. Alexander Stille, "The Fall of the House of Herrick."

207. 8(29) NLJ 2 (March 31, 1986).

208. Paul Richter, "Antitrust Lawyers Get Less Work as Rules Ease."

209. 9(39) NLJ 2 (June 8, 1987).

210. Mary Ann Galante, "A New Look for Me-

mel Jacobs"; Gail Diane Cox, "End Comes at Last to L.A. Firm."

211. 9(47) NLJ 2 (August 3, 1987).

212. Shipp, 1987b; Rita Henley Jensen and Daniel Wise, "Finley Kumble: The End of an Era"; "Finley Kumble: The Firm's Final Days"; Rita Henley Jensen, "Scenes from a Breakup."

213. Rosen, 1987: S-26.

214. Heinz & Laumann, 1982: 178.

215. Robert M. Snider, "The New Gold Rush: New York Law Firms Advance on L.A.'s Clients," pp. 13–14.

216. Vogt, 1986: 38.

217. National Law Journal, "The NLJ Guide to the Legal Search Profession."

218. New York Times, p. 33 (November 9, 1984).

219. Beall, 1986: 33.

220. Michele Galen, "Innovation Becomes the Norm in the Legal-Recruiting Field."

221. 10(6) NLJ 2 (October 19, 1987).

222. Heinz & Laumann, 1982: 369.

223. Heinz & Laumann, 1982: 369 n. 92.

224. Laumann & Heinz, 1985: 467; Nelson et al., 1987a: n. 1.

225. Rosen, 1987: S-2.

226. Rosen, 1987: S-26.

227. Curran et al., 1985: 53–54, 230.

228. 10(13) NLJ 2 (December 7, 1987).

229. Martha Middleton, "Firms Moving to Virginia Frontier"; Wall Street Journal, p. 1, col. 5 (July 14, 1983).

230. R. Stevens, 1983: 267; 9(34) NLJ 2 (May 4, 1987).

231. 9(38) NLJ 2 (June 1, 1987).

232. Couric, 1986a: 29; Kristof, 1986; Snider, 1986b.

233. Mary Ann Galante, "Westward Expansion"; 9(2) NLJ S-4 (September 22, 1986).

234. Michelle Galen, "Out-of-Town Firms Invade Big Apple."

235. 9(2) NLJ S-14 to S-17 (September 22, 1986); Robert Lever, "American Attorneys in Paris."

236. Marcia Coyle, "Practice in Japan OK'd for U.S. Lawyers"; "A Slow, Steady Japan Push Starts"; Rosen, 1987: S-26.

237. 10(10) NLJ 2 (November 16, 1987).

238. 10(20) NLJ 2 (January 25, 1988).

239. 10(3) NLJ S-4 to S-6 (September 28, 1987).

240. 8(3) NLJ 2 (September 30, 1985).

241. Gail Diane Cox, "A County Beckons Near L.A."

242. Martha Middleton, " 'Corn-Fed' Image Ebbs in St. Louis."

243. Jim Mellowitz, "A Tale of Two Cities: Indianapolis Legal Armies Invade Fort Wayne."

244. 9(2) NLJ 2 (September 22, 1986).

245. 10(5) NLJ 2 (October 12, 1987).

246. Faye A. Silas, "Law Firms Branch Out"; see also Galanter, 1983.

247. Curran et al., 1985: 53–54.

248. Couric, 1986a: 26–27.

249. Galante, 1986f.

250. Illinois State Bar Association, 1983: 127.

251. Zemans & Rosenblum, 1981: 68–19.

252. Altman & Weil, Inc., The 1984 Survey of Law Firm Economics, quoted in 71 ABAJ 17 (May 1985); Altman & Weil, 1985a: 14.

253. U.S. Department of Commerce, Bureau of the Census, 1970: Table 5.

254. Illinois State Bar Association, 1983: 127.

255. John J. Siegfried, "The Effect of Firm Size on the Economics of Legal Practice," p. 26.

256. Siegfried, 1976; Tamar Lewin, "What's New in the Legal Profession."

257. Galanter, 1983.

258. Nelson, 1988: 96–97.

259. Bernstein, 1982.

260. New York Times, p. 25 (July 2, 1987).

261. U.S. Department of Commerce, Bureau of the Census: 1970: Table 10.

262. State Bar of Michigan, Attorney's Desk Book, pp. s.1–5.

263. Altman & Weil, 1985a: 35.

264. Weil & Hegvik, 1987.

265. Ezra Tom Clark, Jr., "Leveraging: Now There's a New Method." For a counterargument, see Arlene Leibowitz and Robert Tollison, "Earning and Learning in Law Firms."

266. Hobson, 1984: 20.

267. Cantor, 1969: 14; Cantor, 1966: 39; Colorado Bar Association, 1967: 3.

268. C. Epstein, 1981: 209.

269. Darby, 1985: 68; cf. Altman & Weil, 1985a: 65.

270. 71 ABAJ 42 (August 1985).

271. Rhode, 1985b: 633 n. 149.

272. 71 ABAJ 42–43 (October 1985); Wall Street Journal, p. 1, col. 5 (October 2, 1984).

273. Altman & Weil, 1985a: 45, 65, 98.

274. Jensen, 1987c; Weil & Hegvik, 1987.

275. Vogt, 1986: 53–54 and Table D18; see also Rossalyn S. Smith, "A Profile of Lawyer Lifestyles."

276. Maryland State Bar Association, 1975: 14A.

277. Leibowitz & Tollison, 1980: 384.

278. Darby, 1985: 66–67.

279. Wall Street Journal, p. 1, col. 5 (October 2, 1984).

280. Median income for all partners was 2. times that of all associates. Altman & Weil, 1985a: 45, 78, 98.

281. Altman & Weil, 1985a: 51, 52, 112.

282. 71 ABAJ 42–43 (October 1985). There also was little difference in Illinois, see Illinois State Bar Association, 1983: 150.

283. 9(10) NLJ 20 (November 17, 1986).

284. Weil & Hegvik, 1987.

285. National Law Journal, 1987c: S-6, S-10.

286. Fred S. McChesney, "Team Production, Monitoring, and Profit Sharing in Law Firms: An Alternative Hypothesis"; Illinois State Bar Association 1983: 153.

287. 9(15) NLJ 2 (December 22, 1986).

288. 9(10) NLJ 21 (November 17, 1986).

289. Maryland State Bar Association, 1975: 12A.

290. Darby, 1978: 41.

291. The medians for the entire category were 1763 for associates and 1599 for partners. Altman & Weil, 1985a: 65, 68. The following year they were 1814 and 1680. See Weil & Hegvllt, 1987.

292. 71 ABAJ 42–43 (October 1985).

293. Jensen, 1987c.

294. Nelson, 1988: 185–86.

295. Alexander Stille and Michelle Galen, "Shakeout Begins Over Pay Hikes."

296. Illinois State Bar Association, 1975: 90.

297. Illinois State Bar Association, 1983: 158.

298. Gilson & Mnookin, 1985: 313 n. 1.

299. Alexander Stille, "Small Firms in America."

300. 71 ABAJ 42 (August 1985).

301. Leibowitz & Tollison, 1980: 383.

302. Altman & Weil, 1985a: 51–52, 88, 92.

303. Stille, 1985a.

304. David Ranii, "A Combative Chicago Firm"

305. Leibowitz & Tollison, 1980: 384.

306. 70 ABAJ 42–43 (August 1984); 71 ABAJ 42 (August 1985).

307. Catalyst Legal Resources, 1982: 71–72.

308. Rebecca E. R. Copeland, "Law Firm Personnel Practices Surveyed: Compensation and Hiring Rates." Part of this is attributable to the fact that associates remain in that status longer in larger firms.

309. Siegfried, 1976: 25.

310. Wall Street Journal, p. 3, col. 3 (October 29, 1986); p. 1, col. 5 (April 9, 1985).

311. Darby, 1985: 68.

312. 71 ABAJ 42 (August 1985); see also Getz, 1981: 872 n. 27.

313. Maryland State Bar Association, 1975: 21A.

314. Daniel Wise, "Psst! Wanna Make Partner?" pp. 32–33.

315. Nelson, 1983: 124.

316. Heinz & Laumann, 1982: 200.

317. Nelson, 1983: 123.

318. American Lawyer, "American Lawyer Guide to Law Firms."

319. Rhode, 1985b: 632 n. 145.

320. Wise, 1987b: 32–33.

321. 9(18) NLJ 2 (January 12, 1987); John C. Metaxas and Ellen L. Rosen, " 'Salary Wars' Still the Talk of New York."

322. 8(50) NLJ 2 (August 25, 1986).

323. Gilson & Mnookin, 1985: 316 n. 7; New York Times, sec. 4, p. 1 (May 29, 1984).

324. Ranii, 1985b.

325. Darby, 1985: 68.

326. Altman & Weil, Compensation Plans for Lawyers and their Staffs: Salaries, Bonuses, and Profit-Sharing Plans, pp. 11–12.

327. Tamar Lewin, "Law Firms Add Second Tier."

328. Cheryl Morrison, "More Firms Turn to 'Temp' Lawyers"; Beall, 1986: 32.

329. Bernstein, 1982.

330. 8(42) NLJ 2 (June 30, 1986).

331. Jensen, 1987c.

332. Mary C. Murphree, "Brave New Office: The Changing World of the Legal Secretary."

333. Ronald W. Staudt, "Large Firms Overwhelmingly Favor IBM and Clones."

334. Jensen, 1987c.

335. U.S. Department of Commerce, Bureau of the Census, 1970: Table 9.B.

336. Altman & Weil, The 1976 Survey of Law Firm Economics.

337. Altman & Weil, 1985a: 2–6.

338. 8(5) NLJ 2 (October 14, 1985).

339. See generally Marvin G. Lathan, "Current Status of Paralegals in Law Offices in the United States as seen by Attorneys, Lawyers, Legal Secretaries, and Paralegals."

340. Bethel, 1976: 60.

341. Illinois State Bar Association, 1983: 152.

342. 7(28) NLJ 23 (March 18, 1985).

343. Quintin Johnstone and John A. Flood, "Paralegals in English and American Law Offices," pp. 155–57.

344. Johnstone & Flood, 1982: 162.

345. Johnstone & Flood, 1982: 157–58.

346. 70 ABAJ 52–53 (December 1984). But there are no significant differences according to Altman & Weil, 1985a.

347. Illinois State Bar Association, 1983: 145.

348. Johnstone & Flood, 1982: 155–57.

349. National Law Journal, 1987b: S-4 to S-6. This list excludes Baker & McKenzie, for which information is unavailable, and Hyatt Legal Services, a legal clinic.

350. Law Office Economics, 1985b: 124.

351. Law Office Economics, 1985b: 123. It was $15,700 according to Copeland, 1985.

352. 9(2) NLJ 2 (September 22, 1986).

353. Murphree, 1984: 144.

354. Altman & Weil, 1985a: 53, 68, 119.

355. 70 ABAJ 52–53 (December 1984). But another survey found no consistent relationship between paralegal:lawyer ratio and lawyer income. See Altman & Weil, 1985a: 31.

356. Siegfried, 1976: 26.

357. Bethel, 1976: 57–58.

358. John A. Jenkins, "Outside the Law: On Lawyers, Nonlawyers, and the Changing Nature of the Business of Law Firms"; Ruth Marcus, "Lawyers Branch Out from the Law."

359. New York Times, p. 10 (April 15, 1985).

360. Los Angeles Times, sec. 4, p. 2 (January 26, 1984).

361. 7(52) NLJ 2 (September 9, 1985); see also Laumann & Heinz, 1985: 500.

362. Michael Siconolfi, "Law Firms Aren't Simply for Law as Attempts to Diversify Begin."

363. Jenkins, 1984; Tamar Lewin, "Law Firms Expanding Scope."

364. 7(48) NLJ 2 (August 12, 1985).
365. 8(50) NLJ 2 (August 25, 1986).
366. 10(8) NLJ 2 (November 2, 1987).
367. 8(26) NLJ 2 (March 10, 1986).
368. Lewin, 1987c.
369. 8(1) NLJ 2 (September 23, 1985).
370. Alexander Stille, "When Law Firms Start Their Own Businesses."
371. 8(29) NLJ 2 (March 31, 1986).
372. Stille, 1985c.
373. Jenkins, 1984.
374. Stille, 1985c.
375. Lewin, 1987c.
376. Smigel, 1969: 210–15; William Delaney and Alan H. Finegold, "Wall Street Lawyer in the Provinces."
377. Cantor, 1966: 29.
378. Bethel, 1976: 61.
379. Galante, 1985c.
380. Jenkins, 1984; New York Times, p. 34 (February 5, 1985); 8(19) NLJ 2 (January 20, 1986); Kenneth Gilpin, "Ex-Corporate Leader Will Manage Law Firm."
381. Beverlee Johnson, "Administration Grows Up."
382. David A. Kaplan, "Want to Invest in a Law Firm?" Compare Gilson & Mnookin, 1985: 329 n. 30 with Eugene F. Fama and Michael C. Jensen, "Separation of Ownership and Control"; "Agency Problems and Residual Claims."
383. Nelson, 1988: 215.
384. Heinz & Laumann, 1982: chap. 10.
385. Joel F. Handler, The Lawyer and His Community, p. 33.
386. Carlin, 1966: 13.
387. Landon, 1982: 465; 1985: 88–89.
388. Bethel, 1976: 14. The same differences separate Baltimore lawyers from the rest of Maryland, see Maryland State Bar Association, 1975: 11A.
389. Barrie Thorne, "Professional Education in Law," pp. 111–12.
390. Edward O. Laumann and John P. Heinz, "Specialization and Prestige in the Legal Profession: The Structure of Deference," p. 155; John P. Heinz and Edward O. Laumann, "The Legal Profession: Client Interests, Professional Roles, and Social Hierarchies," p. 1127.
391. Zemans & Rosenblum, 1981: 71–72.
392. Zemans & Rosenblum, 1981: 73.
393. Laumann & Heinz, 1977: 230–32; Heinz & Laumann, 1978: 1136.
394. Cf. Landon, 1982: 466.
395. Landon, 1985: 88–89.
396. Heinz & Laumann, 1982: 42–43, 64.
397. Denison, 1943: 27; Weinfeld, 1949: 19.
398. Committee on the Survey, 1952: 291 (13 percent response).
399. Weinfeld, 1949: 20; Liebenberg, 1956: 29.
400. Siegfried, 1976: 26.
401. Weil, 1986: 15.
402. Laumann & Heinz, 1977: 225. This is the proportion of aggregate lawyer time, not an average of the proportions devoted by each lawyer. Heinz & Laumann, 1982: 40, revises these figures to 53, 40, and 22 percent, respectively; see also Pashigian, 1978.
403. Heinz & Laumann, 1977: 232, 238–39; Laumann & Heinz, 1978: 1120–22.
404. Carlin, 1966: 13.
405. Heinz & Laumann, 1982: 65.
406. Zemans & Rosenblum, 1981: 75.
407. ABA Special Committee on the Economic Condition of the Bar, 1939: 30–31. The percentages differ slightly depending on date of admission.
408. Carlin, 1966: 12.
409. R. Stevens, 1983: 268 n. 27.
410. Heinz & Laumann, 1978: 1120–22.
411. Illinois State Bar Association, 1983: 139.
412. Landon, 1985: 88–89.
413. Nelson, 1985: 534–35.
414. Spangler, 1986: 47.
415. E.g., Carlin, 1962; 1966; Hubert J. O'Gorman, Lawyers and Matrimonial Cases: A Study of Informal Pressures in Private Professional Practice; Abraham S. Blumberg, "The Practice of Law as a Confidence Game: Organizational Cooptation of a Profession."
416. Rosenthal, 1974: 173.
417. Spangler, 1986: 167.
418. Landon, 1982: 483.
419. Heinz & Laumann, 1982: 64.
420. Heinz & Laumann, 1982: 64.
421. Illinois State Bar Association, 1983: 139.
422. U.S. Department of Commerce, Bureau of the Census, 1970: Table 1c.
423. Heinz & Laumann, 1978: 1120–22; 1982: 65.
424. Heinz & Laumann, 1982: 65.
425. Compare Emily P. Dodge, "Evolution of a City Law Office, Part II: Office Flow of Business," p. 48, with Galanter, 1983; Laumann & Heinz, 1977: 1131; Heinz & Laumann, 1978: 177.
426. Jeffrey S. Slovak, "Working for Corporate Actors: Social Change and Elite Attorneys in Chicago," p. 465; "Giving and Getting Respect: Prestige and Stratification in a Legal Elite," p. 41.
427. Laumann & Heinz, 1977: 177; Heinz & Laumann, 1982: 109–18.
428. Abbott, 1981.
429. Laumann & Heinz, 1977: 177.
430. H. Clark, 1937: 246.
431. New York County Lawyers' Association, 1936: 33.
432. Friedman & Kuznets, 1945: 283.
433. American Bar Foundation, 1958b: 23.
434. U. S. Department of Commerce, Bureau of the Census, 1970: Tables 1b and 8.
435. U.S. Department of Commerce, Bureau of the Census, 1976: Table 1c.
436. Liebenberg, 1956: 29–30, 33; Bethel, 1976: 11.
437. Liebenberg, 1956: 33.
438. Burke A. Parsons, Summary Report of the Virginia Survey of the Economics of Law Practice, p. 29.

439. U.S. Department of Commerce, Bureau of the Census, 1970: Table 8.

440. Weinfeld, 1949: 20; Liebenberg, 1956: 32; Maryland State Bar Association, 1975: 11A; Bethel, 1976: 13–14; U.S. Department of Commerce, Bureau of the Census, 1970: Table 8.

441. Vogt, 1986: 61–62 and Table D21.

442. Illinois State Bar Association, 1975; John C. York and Rosemary D. Hale, "Too Many Lawyers? The Legal Services Industry: Its Structure and Outlook," p. 20; K. Cox, 1977a, 1977b.

443. Illinois State Bar Association, 1975: 86; Garrison, 1934: 126; American Bar Foundation, 1958b: 29.

444. Juris Doctor, "Money Talks: Why It Shouts to Some Lawyers and Whispers to Others."

445. Siegel, "Tackling the Legal Complex."

446. New York Times, p. 19 (January 8, 1984).

447. 71 ABAJ 42 (August 1985).

448. Heinz & Laumann, 1982: 195.

449. Vogt, 1986: figures 36–38.

450. Richard L. Abel, The Legal Profession in England and Wales.

451. Hobson, 1986: chaps. 2 and 7.

452. Halliday, 1987: Tables 5.2–5.4.

453. Ranii, 1985c.

454. New York County Lawyers' Association, 1936: 10, 80.

455. Halliday & Cappell, 1979; Powell, 1979; Jeffrey S. Slovak, "Influence and Issues in the Legal Community: The Role of a Legal Elite," p. 161; J. Auerbach, 1976; John P. Heinz, Edward O. Laumann, Charles L. Cappell, Terence C. Halliday, and Michael H. Schaalman, "Diversity, Representation, and Leadership in an Urban Bar: A First Report on a Survey of the Chicago Bar"; Carlin, 1962: 203.

456. Melone, 1977: 48–49, 59–67, 80–82.

457. Fred Strasser and Eric Effron, "The Bar's Voice."

458. Halliday, 1987: 74, 94–95, 322–26.

459. Heinz & Laumann, 1982: 133.

460. Cappell & Halliday, 1983: 299, 301, 309–10; see also Halliday & Cappell, 1979; Halliday, 1987: Tables 11.1–11.4.

461. Halliday, 1987: 88, 314.

462. Parsons, 1963: 34.

463. Schneyer, 1983: 40.

464. Field Research Company, 1960: 7.

465. Halliday, 1987: 75–76.

466. Richard A. Watson and Randal G. Downing, The Politics of the Bench and Bar.

467. Powell, 1979; Heinz & Laumann, 1982: 235.

468. John C. Metaxas, " 'Educational Feast' Awaiting at ATLA"; Roscoe Pound—American Trial Lawyers Foundation, Ethics and Advocacy; Product Safety in America.

469. Strasser & Effron, 1986.

470. Terence C. Halliday, "The Idiom of Legalism in Bar Politics: Lawyers, McCarthyism, and the Civil Rights Era"; Halliday, 1987.

471. Schneyer, 1983: 81, 83.

472. 9(6) NLJ 9 (October 20, 1986).

473. Fred Strasser, "Justice-ABA Link on Judicial Selection Faces New Challenge."

474. Schneyer, 1983: 3–4; 71 ABAJ 24 (February 1985).

475. Ray Reynolds, "Use of Bar Dues for Lobbying Curtailed"; Dan Morain, "Court Restricts Involvement in Politics by Bar."

476. Schneyer, 1983: 36 n. 203.

477. I. Petersen, "Legal Aid Lawyers and Aides Hold Meeting in Detroit to Organize a National Union"; Bruce J. Stavitsky, "Lawyer Unionization in Quasi-Governmental Public and Private Sectors"; Robert A. Rothman, "Deprofessionalization: The Case of Law in America," p. 198.

478. Myrna Oliver, "Lawyers Who Work on State Bar's Staff Plan to Strike"; 8(38) NLJ 8 (June 2, 1986).

479. Spangler, 1986: 156–57.

Chapter 10

1. See R. Stevens, 1983; Kalman, 1986.

2. Reed, 1928: 251.

3. Seligman, 1978; R. Stevens, 1983.

4. Kalman, 1986: 161 n. 74.

5. G. Andrew H. Benjamin, Alfred Kasniak, Bruce Sales, and Stephen B. Shanfield, "The Role of Legal Education in Producing Psychological Distress Among Law Students and Lawyers"; John Jay Osborn, The Paper Chase; Scott Turow, One L; Duncan Kennedy, Legal Education as Training for Hierarchy; Paul D. Carrington and P. C. James, "The Alienation of Law Students"; Leonard E. Eron and Robert S. Redmount, "The Effect of Legal Education on Attitudes"; Marilyn Heins, Shirley Nichols Fahey, and Roger C. Henderson, "Law Students and Medical Students: A Comparison of Perceived Stress"; R. Stevens, "Law Schools and Law Students"; J. B. Taylor, "Law School Stress and the 'Déformation Professionelle' "; Gregory J. Rathjen, " "Impact of Legal Education on the Beliefs, Attitudes and Values of Law Students"; Ronald M. Pipkin, "Legal Education: The Consumers' Perspective"; Kenneth H. Barry and Patricia A. Connelly, "Research on Law Students: An Annotated Bibliography"; Thomas L. Shaffer and Robert S. Redmount, Lawyers, Law Students, and People.

6. Swords & Walwer, 1974: 48; Reed, 1928: 262.

7. Horack & Shafroth, 1938: 326.

8. Boyer, 1941: 284.

9. Nicholson, 1958: 118, 132.

10. Association of American Law Schools, 1961: 326, 330.

11. Pipkin, 1979; Zemans & Rosenblum, 1981: 168–87.

12. Zemans & Rosenblum, 1981: 36.

13. Paul Van R. Miller, "Personality Differences and Student Survival in Law School"; Shaffer & Redmount, 1977: 95; Lortie, 1958; Wagner Thielens, Jr., The Socialization of Law Students: A Case Study in

Three Parts; Walter W. Steele, Jr., "A Comparison of Attitudes of Freshman and Senior Law Students"; Susan Ann Kay, "Socializing the Future Elite: The Nonimpact of Law School"; Thomas E. Willging and Thomas G. Dunn, "The Moral Development of the Law Student: Theory and Data on Legal Education," p. 350; Carlin, 1966: 143–46.

14. R. Stevens, 1973: 613–14; Howard S. Erlanger and Douglas E. Klegon, "Socialization Effects of Professional School," p. 20.

15. D. Chambers, 1987: 182–83.

16. Joseph Zelan, "Occupational Recruitment and Socialization in Law School," p. 182.

17. Erving Goffman, Asylums.

18. Seligman, 1978.

19. R. Stevens, 1983: 210 n. 46, 213 n. 60.

20. Hobson, 1984: 16.

21. Carlin, 1962.

22. ABA Special Committee, 1938: 48, 50.

23. Brenner, 1932a: 34–35.

24. Warkov, 1965b: 224.

25. C. Auerbach, 1984: 53.

26. Median associate starting salaries in Denver were $6000 in 1965 and $7200 in 1967. Colorado Bar Association, 1967: 14.

27. NALP, 1985: 30; 8(26) NLJ 4 (March 10, 1986); 71 ABAJ 19 (May 1985); Schwartz, 1980: 1274–75; Thieberger, 1987.

28. ABA Special Committee on the Economic Condition of the Bar, 1939: 39.

29. Brenner, 1932a: 34–36.

30. Blaustein & Porter, 1954: 26–27.

31. Blaustein & Porter, 1954: 23–24 (14 percent no answer).

32. Blaustein & Porter, 1954: 26 (50 percent response).

33. Smigel, 1964: 59–61.

34. Blaustein & Porter, 1954: 25.

35. Blaustein & Porter, 1954: 25; 29(2) Law Quadrangle Notes 7–10 (Winter 1985).

36. C. Timothy Corcoran, III, "A Law Firm's View of Student Abuses," p. 16.

37. Howard F. Maltby, "Computers and Hiring: A Brave New World?"

38. 29(2) Law Quadrangle Notes 7–10 (Winter 1985).

39. Corcoran, 1986: 14.

40. 9(29) NLJ 4 (September 29, 1986).

41. Galen, 1986c.

42. Rita Henley Jensen, "Perks: When High Salaries Aren't Enough."

43. Edward A. Adams, " 'Gadfly' Sets Law School Agenda."

44. Myrna Oliver, "L.A.'s Law of Supply and Demand: Courting Interns"; Wall Street Journal, p. 1, col. 4 (August 11, 1983).

45. Edward A. Adams, "Summer Pay Passes $1,000–a-Week Mark."

46. Daniel Wise, "It's A Bull Market for Associates."

47. E.g., American Lawyer, 1984 Summer Associates Survey.

48. Association of American Law Schools, 1961 198.

49. R. Stevens, 1973: 589–90.

50. Pipkin, 1982: 1117, 1124, 1137, 1146–48 1153.

51. Donald N. Zillman and Vickie R. Gregory "Law Student Employment and Legal Education."

52. Vogt, 1986: 27–28.

53. ABA Special Committee on the Economic Condition of the Bar, 1939: 55; New York County Lawyers' Association, 1936: 23, 27.

54. Platt, 1940: 641–42.

55. Fagen, 1939: 97.

56. Blaustein & Porter, 1954: 194–95.

57. H. Clark, 1937: 245–46.

58. Koenig & Rustad, 1985.

59. Blaustein, 1952b: 311–12.

60. Smigel, 1969: 39.

61. Association of American Law Schools, 1969 35, 37.

62. Heinz & Laumann, 1982: 64; see also Zemans & Rosenblum, 1981: 110–19.

63. Catalyst Legal Resources, 1982: 79.

64. Garrison, 1935: 161–64. Data were missing for the war years, 1917–20. See also Association o American Law Schools, 1969: 36.

65. Colorado Bar Association, 1967: 3.

66. Thielens, 1957: 145, 148, 150.

67. 71 ABAJ 35 (May 1985).

68. Martha Middleton, "Lawyer Disbarred; Lied to Employers."

69. Thieberger, 1987; see generally John Bilyeu Oakley and Robert S. Thompson, Law Clerks and the Judicial Process.

70. 8(44) NLJ 4 (July 14, 1986). Cf. Betsy Stark "Stars of '79 Seek Chambers Over Firms."

71. David Lauter, "Clerkships: Picking the Elite."

72. Coyle, 1987g.

73. 8(33) NLJ 2 (April 28, 1986).

74. 8(40) NLJ 2 (June 16, 1986); Tamar Lewin "At Cravath, $65,000 to Start"; Stille & Galen, 1986 Metaxas & Rosen, 1987.

75. 8(41) NLJ 2 (June 23, 1986).

76. 9(36) NLJ 2 (May 18, 1987); 9(38) NLJ 2 (June 1, 1987).

77. National Law Journal, 1987b: S-2.

78. 10(5) NLJ 2 (October 12, 1987).

79. Jensen, 1987a.

80. 9(33) NLJ 2 (April 27, 1987).

81. Metaxas & Rosen, 1987.

82. Tamar Lewin, "Soul-Searching on Salaries" "The Faster Track: Leaving the Law for Wall Street" 9(4) NLJ 4 (October 6, 1986); Wall Street Journal p. 33, col. 4 (June 19, 1986).

83. Kay, 1978: 350; James M. Hedegard, "The Impact of Legal Education: An In-Depth Examination of Career-relevant Interests, Attitudes, and Personality Traits Among First-Year Law Students," pp. 820, 825; "Causes of Career-relevant Interest Changes Among First-Year Law Students: Some Research Data," p. 829; Erlanger & Klegon, 1978

James C. Foster, "The Cooling-Out of Law Students: Facilitating Market Cooptation of Future Lawyers"; "Legal Education and the Production of Lawyers to (Re)Produce Liberal Capitalism"; Robert Granfield, "Legal Education as Corporate Ideology: Student Adjustment to the Law School Experience." There is evidence, however, that commitment to public interest jobs was never high, even in the late 1960s. See Rita J. Simon, Frank Koziol, and Nancy Johnson, "Have There Been Significant Changes in the Career Aspirations and Occupational Choices of Law School Graduates in the 1960's?"

84. D. Chambers, 1987: 151 n. 130.

85. Gilson & Mnookin, 1985: 314 n. 2.

86. NALP, 1985: 30; Thieberger, 1987.

87. D. Chambers, 1987: Tables 87–04 and 87–05.

88. Vogt, 1986: 26–27 and Table D10.

89. Jane Thieberger and Marilyn Tucker, "Influences on Law Student Interview Picks."

90. Fiske, 1986.

91. D. Chambers, 1987: 220.

92. 71 ABAJ 34 (February 1985); Wall Street Journal, p. 1, col. 5 (February 7, 1984).

93. Komesar & Weisbrod, 1978: 83.

94. 9(26) NLJ 4 (March 9, 1987); 10(9) NLJ 4 (November 9, 1987); Fox Butterfield, "Harvard Will Help Some Law Alumni"; Tamar Lewin, "Increasingly, Pro Cash Beats Pro Bono."

95. Thieberger, 1987.

96. Heinz & Laumann, 1982: 206–08.

97. Vogt, 1986: 9–10.

98. E.g., Carlin, 1962; 1966; Katz, 1982; Thomas L. Winfree, Jr., Lawrence Kielich, and Robert E. Clark, "On Becoming a Prosecutor: Observations on the Organizational Socialization of Law Interns."

99. Leonard L. Baird, Alfred B. Carlson, Richard R. Reilly, and Ramon J. Powell, "Defining Competence in Legal Practice: The Evaluation of Lawyers in Large Firms and Organizations," pp. 150–54.

100. David T. Bazelon, "Views from a Law Office Window"; Hoffman, 1973; 1982; Stewart, 1984; David Riesman, "Toward an Anthropological Science of Law and the Legal Profession"; "Law and Sociology: Recruitment, Training and Colleagueship"; "Some Observations on Legal Education." The novels of Louis Auchincloss, a Wall Street law firm partner, also shed light on changes in the experience of associates.

101. 71 ABAJ 19 (May 1985).

102. Heinz & Laumann, 1982: 195.

103. Nelson, 1988: 181–82.

104. 70 ABAJ 42–43 (August 1984); 71 ABAJ 23 (January 1985).

105. Hoffman, 1973: 129; Robert L. Nelson, "Practice and Privilege: Social Change and the Structure of the Large Law Firm," p. 126.

106. Lewin, 1984. On the travails of those who do not make partner, see Wall Street Journal, p. 1, col. 1 (January 3, 1983).

107. Wall Street Journal, p. 1, col. 5 (November 15, 1983).

108. 70 ABAJ 42–43 (August 1984).

109. 70 ABAJ 42–43 (August 1984).

110. Nelson, 1983: 125.

111. Nelson, 1988: 221.

112. Lynn Stephens Strudler and Jane Thieberger, "How to Hire, Retain Lateral Associates"; see also Georgina La Russa, "Portia's Decision: Women's Motives for Studying Law and Their Later Career Satisfaction as Attorneys"; Wall Street Journal, p. 31, col. 4 (April 29, 1982).

113. Robinson, 1984.

114. Vogt, 1986: 28, 32, Figure 35 and Table D15.

115. Alberta I. Cook, "Lawyers Lured by Other Careers, Lifestyles."

Chapter 11

1. ABA Commission on Professionalism, ". . . . In the Spirit of Public Service:" A Blueprint for the Rekindling of Lawyer Professionalism.

2. ABA Commission on Professionalism, 1986: 20–21.

3. ABA Commission on Professionalism, 1986: 9.

4. ABA Special Committee on Economics of Law Practice, Lawyers' Economic Problems and Some Bar Association Solutions 2 (1959), cited in ABA Commission on Professionalism, 1986: 4.

5. ABA Commission on Professionalism, 1986: 32.

6. ABA Commission on Professionalism, 1986: 52.

7. ABA Commission on Professionalism, 1986: 13, 27.

8. ABA Commission on Professionalism, 1986: 28.

9. ABA Commission on Professionalism, 1986: 51.

10. ABA Commission on Professionalism, 1986: 3.

11. ABA Commission on Professionalism, 1986: 53.

12. ABA Commission on Professionalism, 1986: 53.

13. ABA Commission on Professionalism, 1986: 33, 39.

14. ABA Commission on Professionalism, 1986: 3, 27, 36.

15. ABA Commission on Professionalism, 1986: 12, 14, 40.

16. Roscoe Pound, The Lawyer from Antiquity to Modern Times 5 (1953), quoted in ABA Commission on Professionalism, 1986: 10, 12.

17. ABA Commission on Professionalism, 1986: 49.

18. ABA Commission on Professionalism, 1986: 10, 25.

19. ABA Commission on Professionalism, 1986: 12, 13, 15, 18, 23, 26.

20. ABA Commission on Professionalism, 1986: 12, 14, 22, 46.

21. ABA Commission on Professionalism, 1986: 14, 37–38.

22. ABA Commission on Professionalism, 1986: 34–36.

23. ABA Commission on Professionalism, 1986: v (emphasis added).

24. ABA Commission on Professionalism, 1986: 1.

25. ABA Commission on Professionalism, 1986: 3 (footnotes omitted). These conclusions were based on a nonrandom sample of 234!

26. ABA Commission on Professionalism, 1986: 29.

27. ABA Commission on Professionalism, 1986: 15.

28. ABA Commission on Professionalism, 1986: 15.

29. ABA Commission on Professionalism, 1986: 13.

30. ABA Commission on Professionalism, 1986: 30.

31. ABA Commission on Professionalism, 1986: 29.

32. ABA Commission on Professionalism, 1986: 30, 86–97.

33. ABA Commission on Professionalism, 1986: 31.

34. ABA Commission on Professionalism, 1986: 32.

35. ABA Commission on Professionalism, 1986: 23.

36. ABA Commission on Professionalism, 1986: 23.

37. ABA Commission on Professionalism, 1986: 10.

Bibliography

(References in Chapter 2 can be found in the first part of the bibliography; references in Chapters 3 through 11 can be found in the second part.)

THEORIES OF THE PROFESSIONS

Abbott, Andrew. 1981. Status and Status Strain in the Professions. 86 American Journal of Sociology 819.

———. 1983. Professional Ethics. 88 American Journal of Sociology 855.

———. 1986. Jurisdictional Conflicts: A New Approach to the Development of the Legal Profession. 1986 American Bar Foundation Research Journal 187.

Abel, Richard L. 1981. Why Does the ABA Promulgate Ethical Rules? 59 Texas Law Review 639.

Abel, Richard L. and Philip S. C. Lewis, eds. 1988a. Lawyers in Society, vol. 1: The Common Law World. Berkeley: University of California Press.

———. 1988b. Lawyers in Society, vol. 2: The Civil Law World. Berkeley: University of California Press.

Abercrombie, Nicholas and John Urry. 1983. Capital, Labour and the Middle Classes. London: George Allen & Unwin.

Abrams, Garry. 1986. Dentists Brighten Up Their Marketing Skills. Los Angeles Times, sec. 5, p. 1 (February 11).

Akerlof, G. A. 1970. The Market for "Lemons": Quality Uncertainty and the Market Mechanism. 84 Quarterly Journal of Economics 488.

American Bar Association, Commission on Evaluation of Professional Standards. 1981. Model Rules of Professional Conduct (Proposed Final Draft). Chicago: American Bar Association.

Anderson, John W. 1988. How One Company Clamped Down on Doctor Bills. New York Times, sec. 3, p. 10 (January 17).

Arnould, R.J. 1972. Pricing Professional Services: A Case Study of the Legal Service Industry. 38 Southern Economic Journal 495.

Arrow, Kenneth. 1963. Uncertainty and the Welfare Economics of Medical Care. 53 American Economic Review 941.

Bankowski, Zenon and Geoff Mungham. 1978. A Political Economy of Legal Education. 32 New Universities Quarterly 448.

Barbalet, J. M. 1982. Social Closure in Class Analysis: A Critique of Parkin. 16 Sociology 484.

Barber, Bernard. 1963. Some Problems in the Sociology of the Professions. 92 Daedalus 669.

Becker, Gary. 1964. Human Capital: A Theoretical and Empirical Analysis. New York: National Bureau of Economic Research.

Becker, Howard S., Blanche Geer, Everett C. Hughes, and Anselm Strauss. 1961. Boys in White: Student Culture in Medical School. Chicago: University of Chicago Press.

Begun, James W. 1981. Professionalism and the Pubic Interest: Price and Quality in Optometry. Cambridge, MA: MIT Press.

———. 1986. Economic and Sociological Approaches to Professionalism. 13 Work and Occupations 113.

Bell, Daniel. 1974. The Coming of Post-Industrial Society. New York: Basic Books.

———. 1976. The Cultural Contradictions of Capitalism. New York: Basic Books.

Ben-David, J. 1958. The Professional Role of the Physician in Bureaucratised Medicine: A Study of Role Conflict. 11 Human Relations 255.

———. 1963. Professions in the Class System of Present-Day Societies. 12 Current Sociology 249.

Benham, Lee. 1972. The Effect of Advertising on the Price of Eyeglasses. 15 Journal of Law and Economics 337.

Benham, Lee and Alexandra Benham. 1975. Regulating through Professions: A Perspective on

Information Control. 18 Journal of Law and Economics 421.

Benson, J. K. 1973. The Analysis of Bureaucratic/ Professional Conflict: Functionalist and Dialectical Approaches. 14 Sociological Quarterly 376.

Berg, Eric N. 1988. New Auditor Rule to Require Search for Client Fraud. New York Times, p.1 (February 10).

Berg, Ivar. 1970. Education and Jobs: The Great Training Robbery. Harmondsworth: Penguin.

Berger, Warren. 1987. What's New in Cosmetic Dentistry. New York Times, sec. 3, p. 19 (October 11).

Berke, Richard L. 1986. A.M.A. Suit Alleges Bias in New Rules on Medicare Fees. New York Times, p. 1 (December 26).

Berlant, Jeffrey L. 1975. Profession and Monopoly: A Study of Medicine in the United States and Great Britain. Berkeley: University of California Press.

Berle, Adolf A. and Gardiner C. Means. 1933. The Modern Corporation and Private Property. New York: Macmillan.

Bernstein, Harry and Henry Weinstein. 1985. Tests for New Teachers Get Endorsement of AFL-CIO. Los Angeles Times, sec. 1, p. 3 (November 1).

Black, Donald. 1976. The Behavior of Law. New York: Academic Press.

Blackburn, R. M. and M. Mann. 1979. The Working Class in the Labour Market. London: Macmillan.

Blair, Roger D. and Stephen Rubin, eds. 1980. Regulating the Professions: A Public Policy Symposium. Lexington, MA: Lexington Books.

Blau, Peter and Otis Dudley Duncan. 1967. The American Occupational Structure. New York: John Wiley.

Blau, Peter and Richard A. Schoenherr. 1971. The Structure of Organizations. New York: Basic Books.

Bledstein, Burton J. 1976. The Culture of Professionalism: The Middle Class and the Development of Higher Education in America. New York: Norton.

Bond, Ronald S., John E. Kwoka, Jr., John J. Phelan, and Ira Taylor. 1983. Self-Regulation in Optometry: The Impact on Price and Quality. 7 Law and Human Behavior 219.

Boreham, Paul. 1983. Indetermination: professional knowledge, organization and control. 31 Sociological Review 693.

Boreham, Paul, Alex Pemberton, and Paul Wilson, eds. 1976. The Professions in Australia: A Critical Appraisal. St. Lucia: University of Queensland Press.

Bourdieu, Pierre and Jean-Claude Passeron. 1977. Reproduction in Education, Society and Culture. Beverly Hills,CA: Sage Publications.

Brinkley, Joel. 1985a. U.S., Industry and Physicians Attack Medical Malpractice. New York Times, p. 1 (September 2).

———. 1985b. Medical Discipline Laws: Confusion Reigns. New York Times, p. 1 (September 3).

———. 1986a. U.S. Distributing Lists of Hospitals with Unusual Death Rates. New York Times, p. 8 (March 3).

———. 1986b. U.S. Releasing Lists of Hospitals With Abnormal Mortality Rates. New York Times, p. 1 (March 12).

———. 1986c. 28,000 'Doctors' Are Feared Unfit. New York Times, p. 15 (May 3).

———. 1986d. Key Hospital Accrediting Agency to Start Weighing Mortality Rates. New York Times, p. 1 (November 4).

———. 1986e. State Medical Boards Disciplined Record Number of Doctors in '85. New York Times, p. 1 (November 9).

Brotman, Harris. 1984. Human Embryo Transplants. New York Times Magazine, p. 28 (January 8).

Bruce-Biggs, B., ed. 1979. The New Class? New Brunswick, NJ: Transition Books.

Bucher, Rue and Joan Stelling. 1977. Becoming Professional. Beverly Hills, CA: Sage Publications.

Bucher, Rue and Anselm Strauss. 1961. Professions in Process. 66 American Journal of Sociology 325.

Butterfield, Fox. 1987. Ex-Policeman Tells of Boston Test Thefts. New York Times, p. 12 (February 8).

Cady, J. F. 1975. Drugs on the Market: The Impact of Public Policy on the Retail Market for Prescription Drugs. Lexington, MA: Lexington Books.

Cain, Maureen. 1979. The General Practice Lawyer and the Client: Towards a Radical Conception. 7 International Journal of the Sociology of Law 331.

Campbell, Colin M. 1976. Lawyers and Their Public. 1976 Juridical Review 20.

Carchedi, G. 1975. On the Economic Identification of the New Middle Class. 4 Economy and Society 1.

Carlin, Jerome. 1962. Lawyers on Their Own: A Study of Individual Practitioners in Chicago. New Brunswick, NJ: Rutgers University Press.

———. 1966. Lawyers' Ethics: A Survey of the New York City Bar. New York: Russell Sage Foundation.

Carnegie Forum on Education and the Economy. 1986. A Nation Prepared: Teachers for the 21st Century. San Diego: Carnegie Forum on Education and the Economy.

Carr-Saunders, A. M. and P. A. Wilson. 1933. The Professions. Oxford: Clarendon Press.

Carroll, Sidney L. and Robert J. Gaston. 1979a. New Approaches and Empirical Evidence on Occupational Licensing and the Quality of Service Rendered. 7 Industrial Organization Review 1.

———. 1979b. State Occupational Licensing Provisions and Quality of Service: The Real Estate Business. 1 Research in Law and Economics 1.

———. 1983. Occupational Licensing and the Quality of Service: An Overview. 7 Law and Human Behavior 139.

Child, John and Janet Faulk. 1982. Maintenance of Occupational Control: The Case of Professions. 9 Work and Occupations 155–92.

Cimons, Marlene. 1983. Vision Centers Provide Good Value, FTC Says. Los Angeles Times, sec. 1, p. 5 (December 6).

Cogan, M. L. 1953. Toward a Definition of Profession. 23 Harvard Education Review 33.

Collins, Randall. 1977. Functional and Conflict Theories of Educational Stratification. In Jerome Karabel and A. H. Halsey, eds. Power and Ideology in Education. New York: Oxford University Press.

———. 1979. The Credential Society: An Historical Sociology of Education and Stratification. New York: Academic Press.

Conrad, D. A. and G. G. Sheldon. 1982. The Effects of Legal Constraints on Dental Care Prices. 19 Economic Inquiry 51.

Cornell, Drucilla. 1986. Convention and Critique. 7 Cardozo Law Review 679.

Coxon, A. P. M. and C. L. Jones. 1978. The Images of Occupational Prestige. New York: St. Martin's Press.

Creedy, John. 1982. Professional Labour Markets. In John Creedy and Barry Thomas, eds. The Economics of Labour, chap. 7. London: Butterworth Scientific.

Crozier, Michel. 1982. Strategies for Change: The Future of French Society. Cambridge, MA: MIT Press.

Cullen, John B. 1978. The Structure of Professionalism: A Quantitative Examination. New York: Petrocelli Books.

———. 1985. Professional Differentiation and Occupational Earnings. 12 Work and Occupations 351.

Daniels, Arlene Kaplan. 1967. The Captive Professional: Bureaucratic Limitations in the Practice of Military Psychiatry. 10 Journal of Health and Social Behavior 255.

Derber, Charles. 1982a. Professionals as New Workers. In Professionals as Workers: Mental Labor in Advanced Capitalism. Boston: G.K. Hall.

———. 1982b. The Proletarianization of the Professional: A Review Essay. In Professionals as Workers. Boston: G.K. Hall.

———. 1982c. Managing Professionals: Ideological Proletarianization and Mental Labor. In Professionals as Workers. Boston: G.K. Hall.

———. 1982d. Toward a New Theory of Professionals as Workers: Advanced Capitalism and Postindustrial Labor. In Professionals as Workers. Boston: G.K. Hall.

Derbyshire, Robert C. 1983. How Effective Is Medical Self-Regulation? 7 Law and Human Behavior 193.

DeVany, Arthur S., Wendy L. Gramm, Thomas R. Saving, and Charles W. Smithson. 1982. The Impact of Input Regulation: The Case of the U.S. Dental Industry. 25 Journal of Law and Economics 367.

Dingwall, Robert. 1976. Accomplishing Profession. 24 Sociological Review 331.

———. 1983. Introduction. In Robert Dingwall and Philip Lewis, eds. The Sociology of the Professions: Lawyers, Doctors and Others. London: Macmillan.

Dingwall, Robert and Paul Fenn. 1987. 'A Respectable Profession'? Sociological and Economic Perspectives on the Regulation of Professional Services. 7 International Journal of Law and Economics 51.

Dodge, David A. 1972. Occupational Wage Differentials, Occupational Licensing and Returns to Investment in Education: An Exploratory Analysis. In Sylvia Ostry, ed. Canadian Higher Education in the Seventies. Ottawa: Information Canada.

Doeringer, Peter B. and Michael J. Piore. 1971. Internal Labor Markets and Manpower Analysis. Lexington, MA: Lexington Books.

Dolan, Andrew and Nicole D. Urban. 1983. The Determinants of the Effectiveness of Medical Disciplinary Boards: 1960–77. 7 Law and Human Behavior 203.

Dore, Ronald. 1976. The Diploma Disease. London: Allen & Unwin.

Dorsey, Stuart. 1980. The Occupational Licensing Queue. 15 Journal of Human Resources 424.

Duman, Daniel. 1979. The Creation and Diffusion of a Professional Ideology in Nineteenth Century England. 27 Journal of Social History 113.

Durkheim, Emile. 1933. The Division of Labor in Society. New York: Free Press.

———. 1957. Professional Ethics and Civic Responsibility. London: Routledge and Kegan Paul.

Edelman, Murray. 1964. Symbolic Uses of Politics. Urbana: University of Illinois Press.

Egelston, E. M. 1972. Licensing—Effects on Career Mobility. 62 American Journal of Public Health 50.

Ehrenreich, Barbara and John Ehrenreich. 1979. The Professional-Managerial Class. In Pat Walker, ed. Between Labor and Capital. Boston: South End Press.

Elliott, Philip. 1972. The Sociology of Professions. New York: Herder and Herder.

Esland, G. 1980. Professions and Professionalism. In G. Esland and G. Salaman, eds. The Politics of Work and Occupations. Milton Keynes: Open University Press.

Etzioni, Amitai, ed. 1969. The Semi-Professions. New York: Free Press.

Evans, Robert G. 1974. Supplier-Induced Demand:

Some Empirical Evidence and Implications. In Mark Perlman, ed. The Economics of Health and Medical Care. London: Macmillan.

Evans, Robert G., E. M. A. Parish, and F. Sully. 1973. Medical Productivity and Demand Generation. 6 Canadian Journal of Economics 376.

Evans, Robert G. and Michael J. Trebilcock, eds. 1982. Lawyers and the Consumer Interest: Regulating the Market for Legal Services. Toronto: Butterworths.

Fay, Martha. 1987. Why Your Family Doctor Is a Group. New York Times Magazine, p. 16 (June 7).

Feinberg, Andrew. 1987. Accountants Try to Put a Little Kick in Their Image. New York Times, sec. 3, p. 9 (September 27).

Feldman, Penny H. 1980. The Impact of Third-Party Payment on Professional Practice: Lessons from the Medical Profession. In Roger D. Blair and Stephen Rubin, eds. Regulating the Professions. Lexington, MA: Lexington Books.

Feldman, R. and James W. Begun. 1978. The Effects of Advertising: Lessons from Optometry. 13 Journal of Human Resources (Supplement) 247.

———. 1980. Does Advertising of Prices Reduce the Mean and Variance of Prices? 18 Economic Inquiry 487.

Feldstein, M. W. 1970. The Rising Price of Physicians' Services. 52 Review of Economics and Statistics 121.

Fielding, A. G. and D. Portwood. 1980. Professions and the State: Towards a Typology of Bureaucratic Professions. 28 Sociological Review 25.

Fish, Stanley. 1986. Anti-Professionalism. 7 Cardozo Law Review 645.

Foley, Patrick, Avner Shaked, and John Sutton. 1982. The Economics of the Professions: An Introductory Guide to the Literature. London: International Centre for Economics and Related Disciplines, London School of Economics and Political Science.

Foster, James C. 1986. The Ideology of Apolitical Politics. The Elite Lawyers' Response to the Legitimation Crisis in American Capitalism: 1870–1920. Port Washington, NY: Associated Faculty Press, Inc.

Fox, Mary Frank and Sharlene Hess-Biber. 1984. Women at Work. Palo Alto, CA: Mayfield.

Fox, Renee C. 1957. Training for Uncertainty. In Robert K. Merton, George C. Reader, and Patricia Kendell, eds. The Student Physician. Cambridge, MA: Harvard University Press.

Frech, H. E. 1974. Occupational Licensure and Health Care Productivity: The Issues and the Literature. In J. Rafferty, ed. Health Manpower and Productivity, chap. 6. Lexington, MA: Lexington Books.

Frech, H.E. and Paul B. Ginsberg. 1972. Physician Pricing: Monopolistic or Competitive: Comment. 38 Southern Economic Review 573.

Freed, John C. 1985. Glut of Doctors Creating a Patient's Market. New York Times, p. 1 (April 8).

Freeman, Richard. 1975. Legal Cobwebs: A Recursive Model of the Market for New Lawyers. 57 Review of Economics and Statistics 171.

———. 1976. The Overeducated American. New York: Academic Press.

———. 1980. The Effect of Occupational Licensure on Black Occupational Attainment. In Simon Rottenberg, ed. Occupational Licensure and Regulation. Washington, DC: American Enterprise Institute for Public Policy Research.

Freidson, Eliot. 1970. Profession of Medicine. New York: Dodd Mead.

———. 1983. The Reorganization of the Professions by Regulation. 7 Law and Human Behavior 279.

———. 1984. Are Professions Necessary? In Thomas L. Haskell, ed. The Authority of Experts. Bloomington, IN: Indiana University Press.

———. 1984. The Changing Nature of Professional Control. 10 Annual Review of Sociology 1.

———. 1985. The Reorganization of the Medical Profession. 42 Medical Care Review 11.

———. 1986. Professional Powers: A Study of the Institutionalization of Formal Knowledge. Chicago: University of Chicago Press.

Freudenheim, Milt. 1986. Organized Medicine Considering Defense Against Glut of Doctors. New York Times, p. 1 (June 14).

Friedman, Milton. 1962. Capitalism and Freedom. Chicago: University of Chicago Press.

Friedman, Milton and Simon Kuznets. 1945. Income from Independent Professional Practice. New York: National Bureau of Economic Research.

Friendly, Jonathan. 1984. Licensing of Latin Journalists Gives Rise to Growing Fears. New York Times, sec. 1, p. 1 (December 24).

Fromm, Erich. 1941. Escape from Freedom. New York: Farrar and Rinehart.

Fuchs, Victor P. 1968. The Service Economy. New York: National Bureau for Economic Research.

Galanter, Marc. 1983. Reading the Landscape of Disputes: What We Know and Don't Know (and Think We Know) About Our Allegedly Contentious and Litigious Society. 31 UCLA Law Review 4.

Galbraith, John Kenneth. 1967. The New Industrial State. Boston: Houghton Mifflin.

Gellhorn, Walter. 1956. Individual Freedom and Governmental Restraints. Baton Rouge: Louisiana State University Press.

———. 1976. The Abuse of Occupational Licensing. 44 University of Chicago Law Review 6.

Glaser, Barney G. 1964. Organizational Scientists: Their Professional Careers. Indianapolis, IN: Bobbs-Merrill.

Goleman, Daniel. 1985. Social Workers Vault Into a Leading Role in Psychotherapy. New York Times, p. 17 (April 30).

Goode, William J. 1957. Community within a Community: The Professions. 22 American Sociological Review 200.

———. 1960. Encroachment, Charlatanism, and the Emerging Professions: Psychology, Sociology and Medicine. 25 American Sociological Review 902.

———. 1967. The Protection of the Inept. 32 American Sociological Review 5.

Goodman, Michael J. and Victor Merina. 1984. Lobby Stymies Efforts to Reform Audit Laws. Los Angeles Times, sec. 1, p. 3 (June 12).

Gordon, David M. 1972. Theories of Poverty and Unemployment: Orthodox, Radical and Dual Labor Market Perspectives. Lexington, MA: D.C. Heath.

Gordon, Larry. 1987. U.S. Dental Schools Feel the Crunch. Los Angeles Times, sec. 1, p. 1 (October 26).

Gorz, Andre. 1964. Strategy for Labor. Boston: Beacon Press.

———. 1976. Technology, Technicians and Class Struggle. In The Division of Labour: The Labour Process and Class Struggle in Modern Capitalism. London: Harvester Press.

Gouldner, Alvin W. 1979. The Future of Intellectuals and the Rise of the New Class. New York: Seabury Press.

Green, Larry. 1986. 11 Convicted in Medicaid "Fraud Mill." Los Angeles Times, sec. 1, p. 8 (January 23).

———. 1987. Surgical Society's Rules Put Country Doctor in a Dilemma. Los Angeles Times, sec. 1, p. 20 (September 14).

Greenwood, Ernest. 1957. Attributes of a Profession, 2(3) Social Work 44.

Griffiths, John. 1986. What Do Dutch Lawyers Actually Do in Divorce Cases? 20 Law & Society Review 135.

Grimm, James W. and Carol L. Kronus. 1973. Occupations and Publics: A Framework for Analysis. 14 Sociological Quarterly 68.

Hagan, John, Marie Huxter, and Patricia Parker. 1988. Class Structure and Legal Practice: Inequality and Mobility Among Toronto Lawyers. 22 Law & Society Review 9.

Hall, Oswald. 1948. The Stages of a Medical Career. 53 American Journal of Sociology 327.

Hall, Richard H. 1968. Professionalization and Bureaucratization. 33 American Sociological Review 92.

———. 1983. Theoretical Trends in the Sociology of Occupations. 24 Sociological Quarterly 5.

Halmos, Paul. 1973a. Introduction. In Professionalisation and Social Change. Keele: University of Keele (Sociological Review Monographs No. 2).

———, ed. 1973b. Professionalisation and Social Change. Keele: University of Keele.

Harries-Jenkins, G. 1970. Professionals in Organisations. In J.A. Jackson, ed. Professions and Professionalisation. Cambridge: Cambridge University Press.

Haskell, Thomas L. 1984. Professionalism versus Capitalism: R.H. Tawney, Emile Durkheim, and C. S. Peirce on the Disinterestedness of Professional Communities. In Thomas L. Haskell, ed. The Authority of Experts. Bloomington, IN: Indiana University Press.

Haug, Marie R. 1973. Deprofessionalization: An Alternative Hypothesis for the Future. In Paul Halmos, ed. Professionalisation and Social Change. Keele: University of Keele.

———. 1980. The Sociological Approach to Self-Regulation. In Roger D. Blair and Stephen Rubin, eds. Regulating the Professions. Lexington, MA: Lexington Books.

Haug, Marie and Marvin Sussman. 1969. Professional Autonomy and the Revolt of the Client. 17 Social Problems 53.

———. 1973. Professionalization and Unionization: A Jurisdictional Dispute? In Eliot Freidson, ed. The Professions and their Prospects. Beverly Hills, CA: Sage Publications.

Hechinger, Fred. 1985. Study Finds "Diploma Mills" a Booming Industry. New York Times, p. 22 (August 6).

Heinz, John P. 1983. The Power of Lawyers. 17 Georgia Law Review 891.

Heinz, John P. and Edward O. Laumann. 1982. Chicago Lawyers: The Social Structure of the Bar. New York: Russell Sage Foundation and Chicago: American Bar Foundation.

Hevesi, Dennis. 1987. Carnegie Panel Establishes Board To Plan Certification of Teachers. New York Times, p. 1 (May 16).

Hickson, D. and M. Thomas. 1969. Professionalism in Britain: Preliminary Measurement. 3 Sociology 37.

Hodge, R. W., P. M. Siegel, and H. Rossi. 1964. Occupational Prestige in the United States, 1925–1963. In Reinhard Bendix and Seymour Martin Lipset, eds., Class, Status, and Power. New York: Free Press.

Hoebel, E. Adamson. 1954. The Law of Primitive Man. Cambridge, MA: Harvard University Press.

Hogan, Daniel P., ed. 1983. Professional Regulation. 7(2/3) Law and Human Behavior (Special Issue).

Holen, Arlene S. 1965. Effects of Professional Licensing Arrangements on Interstate Labor Mobility and Resource Allocation. 73 Journal of Political Economy 492.

Hollie, Pamela G. 1985. New Rx for Pharmacists. New York Times, sec. 3, p. 1 (October 13).

Jacobs, Paul. 1985. State Dubious, Will Monitor Caribbean Medical Schools. Los Angeles Times, sec. 1, p. 3 (September 13).

Jamous, H. and B. Peloille. 1970. Professions or Self-Perpetuating Systems? Changes in the French University-Hospital System. In J. A. Jackson, ed. Professions and Professionalisation. Cambridge: Cambridge University Press.

Johnson, Dirk. 1987. Doctors' Dilemma: Unionizing. New York Times, p. 24 (July 13).

Johnson, Terence J. 1972. Professions and Power. London: Macmillan.

———. 1973. Imperialism and the Professions: Notes on the Development of Professional Occupations in Britain's Colonies and the New States. In Paul Halmos, ed. Professionalisation and Social Change. Keele: University of Keele.

———. 1977a. The Professions in the Class Structure. In Richard Scase, ed. Industrial Society: Class, Cleavage and Control. London: George Allen & Unwin.

———. 1977b. What Is to Be Known? The Structural Determination of Social Class. 6 Economy and Society 194.

———. 1982. The State and the Professions: Peculiarities of the British. In Anthony Giddens and Gavin Mackenzie, eds. Social Class and the Division of Labour: Essays in Honour of Ilya Neustadt. Cambridge: Cambridge University Press.

Kendall, John. 1988. Hygienists Countersue in Long Battle With Dentists. Los Angeles Times, sec. 1, p. 23 (February 18).

Keppel, Bruce. 1983. Anesthesiologists Most Highly Paid Physicians. Los Angeles Times, sec. 4, p. 2 (November 21).

Kerr, Clark. 1954. The Balkanization of Labor Markets. In E. W. Bakke, ed. Labor Mobility and Economic Opportunity. New York: John Wiley.

Kessel, R. A. 1958. Price Discrimination in Medicine. 1 Journal of Law and Economics 20.

———. 1970. The A.M.A. and the Supply of Physicians. 35 Law and Contemporary Problems 267.

Kiker, B. F. 1966. The Concept of Human Capital. Columbia, SC: University of South Carolina, Bureau of Business and Economic Research.

Klegon, Douglas. 1978. The Sociology of Professions: An Emerging Perspective. 5 Sociology of Work and Occupations 259.

Kleingartner, Archie. 1967. Professionalism and Salaried Worker Organization. Madison: University of Wisconsin, Industrial Relations Research Institute.

Konrád, George and Ivan Szelényi. 1979. The Intellectuals on the Road to Class Power. New York: Harcourt Brace Jovanovich.

Kornhauser, William. 1965. Scientists in Industry. Berkeley: University of California Press.

Krause, Elliott. 1977. Power and Illness: The Political Sociology of Health and Medical Care. New York: Elsevier.

Kreckel, Reinhard. 1980. Unequal Opportunity Structure and Labour Market Segmentation. 14 Sociology 525.

Kronus, Carol. 1976. The Evolution of Occupational Power: An Historical Study of Task Bounda-

ries between Physicians and Pharmacists. 3 Sociology of Work and Occupations 3.

Kumar, K. 1977. Continuities and Discontinuities in the Development of Industrial Societies. In Richard Scase, ed. Industrial Society: Class, Cleavage and Control. London: George Allen & Unwin.

Larkin, Gerald. 1983. Occupational Monopoly and Modern Medicine. London: Tavistock.

Larson, Magali Sarfatti. 1977. The Rise of Professionalism: A Sociological Analysis. Berkeley: University of California Press.

———. 1980. Proletarianization and Educated Labor. 9 Theory and Society 131.

———. 1984. The Production of Expertise and the Constitution of Expert Power. In Thomas L. Haskell, ed. The Authority of Experts. Bloomington: Indiana University Press.

Lazar, Harold P. 1986. Doctor, Patient, Bureaucrat. New York Times, p. 19 (December 20).

Lazarus, W. 1981. Competition Among Health Practitioners: The Impact of the Medical Profession on the Health Manpower Market. Washington, DC: Federal Trade Commission.

Lees, D.S. 1966. The Economic Consequences of the Professions. London: Institute of Economic Affairs.

Leffler, Keith B. 1978. Physician Licensure: Competition and Monopoly in American Medicine. 21 Journal of Law and Economics 165.

———. 1983. Economic and Legal Analysis of Medical Ethics: The Case of Restrictions on Interprofessional Association. 7 Law and Human Behavior 183.

Leland, H. E. 1979. Quacks, Lemons, and Licensing: A Theory of Minimum Quality Standards. 87 Journal of Political Economy 1328.

Lewin, Tamar. 1987a. Hospitals Pitch Harder for Patients. New York Times, sec. 3, p. 1 (May 10).

———. 1987b. Drug Makers Fighting Back Against Advance of Generics. New York Times, p. A1 (July 28).

Lewis, Roy and Angus Maude. 1952. Professional People. London: Phoenix House.

Lindsay, C. M. 1973. Real Returns to Medical Education. 8 Journal of Human Resources 331.

Lipscomb, J. 1978. Impact of Legal Restrictions on the Future Role of Dental Auxiliaries. Springfield, VA: National Technical Information Service.

Los Angeles Times. 1985. Doctors and Lawyers Square Off on Legal Records. Los Angeles Times, sec. 1, p. 11 (December 26).

———. 1986a. Ontario Doctors Vote to End Strike, Stage Rotating Halts in Services. Los Angeles Times, sec. 1, p. 6 (July 5).

———. 1986b. Panel Tells Social Security Agency Waste. Los Angeles Times, sec.1, p. 1 (October 30).

Luban, David. 1986. Fish v. Fish or, Some Realism About Idealism. 7 Cardozo Law Review 693.

Luckham, Robin. 1981. The Political Economy of Legal Professions: Towards a Framework for Comparison. In C. J. Dias, R. Luckham, D. O. Lynch, and J. C. N. Paul, eds. Lawyers in the Third World: Comparative and Developmental Perspectives. Uppsala: Scandinavian Institute of African Studies, and New York: International Center for Law in Development.

Lyons, Richard. 1984a. Investigators Check on Thousands for Falsified Degrees as Doctors. New York Times, p. 1 (March 4).

———. 1984b. Most Foreign Graduates Failed Test, A.M.A. Is Told. New York Times, sec. 1, p. 21 (June 17).

———. 1984c. Foreign-trained Doctors in for a Thorough Checkup. New York Times, sec. 4, p. 24 (June 24).

Macdonald, Keith M. 1984. Professional Formation: The Case of Scottish Accountants. 35 British Journal of Sociology 174.

———. 1985. Social Closure and Occupational Registration. 19 Sociology 541.

Maeroff, Gene I. 1985a. Enrollment in Professional Schools Declining. New York Times, p. 1 (February 10).

———. 1985b. Shanker Urges Teachers Move Past Bargaining. New York Times, p. 1 (April 28).

———. 1985c. 2 Coaching Concerns Barred from Using S.A.T. Materials. New York Times, p. 1 (August 2).

Mallet, Serge. 1975. Essays on the New Working Class. St. Louis, MO: Telos Press.

Mann, Kenneth. 1985. Defending White Collar Crime: A Portrait of Attorneys at Work. New Haven: Yale University Press.

Marcson, Simon. 1966. Scientists in Government. New Brunswick, NJ: Rutgers University Press.

Marcus, Sanford A. 1983. Too Many Medical Schools in State [letter to the Editor]. Los Angeles Times, sec. 2, p. 4 (January 5).

Markowitz, Gerald E. and David Karl Rosner. 1973. Doctors in Crisis: A Study of the Use of Medical Education Reform to Establish Modern Professional Elitism in Medicine. 25 American Quarterly 83.

Marshall, T. H. 1963. The Recent History of Professionalism in Relation to Social Structure and Social Policy. In Sociology at the Cross-Roads and other Essays. London: Heinemann.

Masson, R. T. and S. Wu. 1974. Price Discrimination for Physicians' Services. 9 Journal of Human Resources 63.

Maurizi, Alex. 1974. Occupational Licensing and the Public Interest. 83 Journal of Political Economy 399–413.

Maurizi, Alex R., Ruth L. Moore, and Lawrence Shepard. 1981. Competing for Professional Control: Professional Mix in the Eyeglasses Industry. 24 Journal of Law and Economics 351.

Mennemeyer, S. T. 1978. Really Great Returns to Medical Education. 13 Journal of Human Resources 75.

Merina, Victor. 1986. City Seeks to Flag Down "Bandit" Taxicabs. Los Angeles Times, sec. 2, p. 1 (January 23).

Merton, Robert K., George C. Reader, and Patricia Kendell, eds. 1957. The Student Physician: Introductory Studies in the Sociology of Medical Education. Cambridge, MA: Harvard University Press.

Meyerowitz, Steven A. 1985. Marketing the Professions. New York Times, sec. 3, p. 19 (November 24).

Millerson, Geoffrey. 1964. The Qualifying Associations. London: Routledge and Kegan Paul.

Molotsky, Irwin. 1986. State Laws Cost Car Buyers, U.S. Study Says. New York Times, p. 4 (March 14).

Monheit, A. 1982. Occupational Licensure and the Utilization of Nursing Labor: An Economic Analysis. In R. Scheffler and L. Rossiter, eds. 3 Advances in Health Economics and Heath Services Research 117. Greenwich, CT: JAI Press.

Moore, Thomas G. 1961. The Purpose of Licensing. 4 Journal of Law and Economics 93.

Moore, Wilbert E. 1970. The Professions: Roles and Rules. New York: Russell Sage Foundation.

Murphy, Raymond. 1984. The Structure of Closure: A Critique and Development of the Theories of Weber, Collins, and Parkin. 35 British Journal of Sociology 547.

Muzondo, T. R. and B. Pazerka. 1979. Professional Licensing and Competition Policy: Effects of Licensing on Rates-of-Return Differentials. Ottawa: Consumer and Corporate Affairs Canada.

———. 1980. Occupational Licensing and Professional Incomes in Canada. 13 Canadian Journal of Economics 659.

Nagel, Stuart. 1962. Culture Patterns and Judicial Systems. 16 Vanderbilt Law Review 147.

Navarro, Victor 1976 Medicine Under Capitalism. London: Croom Helm.

———. 1978. Class Struggle, the State and Medicine. London: Martin Robertson.

Nelson, Harry. 1983a. Dentistry: Offices Need Filling Too. Los Angeles Times, sec. 1, p. 1 (March 28).

———. 1983b. Many Americans Study Medicine Abroad. Los Angeles Times, sec. 1, p. 15 (October 17).

Nelson, Robert L. 1985. Ideology, Practice, and Professional Autonomy: Social Values and Client Relationships in the Large Law Firm. 37 Stanford Law Review 503.

New York Times. 1985. Number in Medical School Off. New York Times, p. 15 (September 29).

———. 1986a. Circus Work Continues to Draw the Dreamers. New York Times, p. 28 (March 30).

———. 1986b. Doctors in Ontario Strike Over Fee System. New York Times, sec. 5, p. 2 (June 1).

———. 1986c. A Run on Accountants. New York Times, sec. 3, p. 1 (November 23).

———. 1987a. Boston Hospitals vs. State Scrutiny. New York Times, p. 29 (May 17).

———. 1987b. Number Applying to Medical School Drops. New York Times, sec. 1, p. 11 (August 30).

———. 1987c. U.S. Judge Finds Medical Group Conspired Against Chiropractors. New York Times, p. 11 (August 30).

———. 1987d. Court Overturns a Schoolbook Ban in "Humanism" Case. New York Times, p. 1 (August 27).

———. 1987e. What Value Education? Study Counts the Ways. New York Times, p. 9 (October 3).

———. 1987f. Doctors Called Lax Monitors of Peers in Medicare. New York Times, p. 11 (October 27).

Newhouse, Joseph P. 1970. A Model of Physician Pricing. 37 Southern Economic Journal 174.

Newhouse, Joseph P. and F. A. Sloan. 1972. Physician Pricing: Monopolistic or Competitive: Reply. 38 Southern Economic Journal 577.

Newman, Katherine S. 1983. Law and Economic Organization: A comparative study of preindustrial societies. Cambridge: Cambridge University Press.

Nieuwenhuysen, John and Marina Williams-Wynn. 1982. Professions in the Marketplace: An Australian Study of Lawyers, Doctors, Accountants and Dentists. Melbourne: Melbourne University Press.

Noble, David. 1979. The PMC: A Critique. In Pat Walker, ed. Between Labor and Capital. Boston: South End Press.

Noble, Trevor and Bridget Pym. 1970. Collegial Authority and the Receding Locus of Power. 21 British Journal of Sociology 431.

Nordheimer, Jon. 1986. Doctors Withhold Service in Insurance Protest. New York Times, p. 12 (December 10).

O'Connor, James. 1973. The Fiscal Crisis of the State. New York: St. Martin's Press.

O'Gormon, Hubert J. 1963. Lawyers and Matrimonial Cases: A Study of Informal Pressures in Private Professional Practice. Glencoe, IL: Free Press.

Oppenheimer, Martin. 1973. The Proletarianization of the Professional. In Paul Halmos, ed. Professionalisation and Social Change. Keele: University of Keele.

Paddock, Richard C. 1984. Bills Would Help 2 Get Medical Licenses. Los Angeles Times, sec. 1, p. 3 (March 6).

Parachini, Allan. 1981. State Studies Title Licensure Issue. Los Angeles Times, sec. 5, p. 1 (August 3).

———. 1982. Small Towns Benefit From Doctor Glut, Study Says. Los Angeles Times, sec. 5, p. 1 (May 7).

———. 1985a. In Near Future, More Doctors May Make Fewer Dollars. Los Angeles Times, sec. 5, p. 1 (May 17).

———. 1987. Hospital Campaigns Aim to Deliver—More Babies. Los Angeles Times, sec. 5, p. 1 (September 14).

Parkin, Frank. 1979. Marxism and Class Theory: A Bourgeois Critique. London: Tavistock.

Parry, Noel and Jose Parry. 1976. The Rise of the Medical Profession. London: Croom Helm.

———. 1977. Social Closure and Collective Mobility. In Richard Scase, ed., Industrial Society: Class, Cleavage and Control. London: George Allen & Unwin.

Parsons, Talcott. 1951. Social Structure and Dynamic Process: The Case of Modern Medical Practice. In The Social System. Glencoe, IL: Free Press.

———. 1964a. A Sociologist Looks at the Legal Profession. In Essays in Sociological Theory. New York: Free Press.

———. 1964b. The Professions and Social Structure. In Essays in Sociological Theory. New York: Free Press.

———. 1968. Professions. 12 International Encyclopedia of the Social Sciences 536. New York: Macmillan.

Pashigian, B. Peter. 1979. Occupational Licensing and the Interstate Mobility of Professionals. 22 Journal of Law and Economics 1.

Pear, Robert. 1984. Congress Rethinks Its Hands-Off Policy on Medical Research. New York Times, sec. 4, p. 3 (February 26).

———. 1985a. Companies Tackle Health Costs. New York Times, sec. 3, p. 11 (March 3).

———. 1985b. U.S. to Offer Consumers Access To Data on Health Care Quality. New York Times, p. 9 (April 16).

———. 1985c. Rx for Fees: U.S. Outlook. New York Times, p. 7 (August 24).

———. 1987a. Doctors Gain Rights in Medicare Evaluations. New York Times, p. 1 (May 12).

———. 1987b. Plan for Medicare Forces U.S. to List Approved Doctors. New York Times, p. 1 (October 13).

———. 1987c. For Dishonest Billing by Doctors, a New Rx. New York Times, p. 16 (December 3).

Peltzman, Sam. 1976. Toward a More General Theory of Regulation. 19 Journal of Law and Economics 211.

Pemberton, Alex and Paul Boreham. 1976. Towards a Reorientation of Sociological Studies of the Professions. In Paul Boreham, Alex Pemberton, and P. Wilson, eds. The Professions in Australia: A Critical Approach. St. Lucia: University of Queensland Press.

Perucci, Robert and Joel Gerstl. 1969. Profession Without Community: Engineers in American Society. New York: Random House.

Pfeffer, J. 1974. Some Evidence on Occupational Licensing and Occupational Incomes. 53 Social Forces 102.

Polanyi, Karl. 1957. The Great Transformation. Boston: Beacon Press.

Portwood, Derek and Alan Fielding. 1981. Privilege and Professions. 29 Sociological Review 749.

Posner, Richard A. 1974. Theories of Economic Regulation. 5 Bell Journal of Economics and Management Science 335.

———. 1975. The Social Costs of Monopoly and Regulation. 83 Journal of Political Economy 807.

Poulantzas, Nicholas. 1975. Classes in Contemporary Capitalism. London: New Left Books.

Powell, Michael J. 1985. Developments in the Regulation of Lawyers: Competing Segments and Market, Client, and Government Controls. 64 Social Forces 281.

Psacharapoulos, G. 1975. Monopoly Elements in Earnings from Education. In Earnings and Education in OECD Countries, chap. 5. Paris: OECD.

Quinn, James. 1987. Dentists Fail to Halt Plan for Hygienists to Practice on Own. Los Angeles Times, sec. 2, p. 1 (September 1).

Raelin, Joseph A. 1986. The Clash of Cultures: Managers and Professionals. Boston: Harvard Business School Press.

Rahman, Fazlur 1986. Medicare Makes a Wrong Diagnosis. New York Times, p. 23 (January 23).

Rawlins, V. Lane and Lloyd Ulman. 1974. The Utilization of College-Trained Manpower in the U.S. In Margaret S. Gordon, ed. Higher Education and the Labor Market, chap. 6. New York: McGraw Hill and Carnegie Corp.

Reinhold, Robert 1987, Texas Panel Reiterates Vow to Bar Unfit Doctors. New York Times, p. 8 (June 20).

Rempel, William C. and Eric Coleman. 1986. Pharmacists Curb Sale of Painkiller. Los Angeles Times, sec. 1, p. 1 (July 6).

Riera, Brian, Murray Glow, Donald Siddall, and William Klein. 1977. Human Capital Analysis: Its Application in the Study of the Consumer Interest in the Professions. In Four Aspects of Professionalism. Ottawa: Consumer Research Council.

Ritzer, George. 1975. Professionalization, Bureaucratization and Rationalization: The Views of Max Weber. 53 Social Forces 627.

Roark, Anne C. 1984. UC May Limit Medical, Dental Students to Cut Spending. Los Angeles Times, sec. 1, p. 21 (January 21).

Rosenblatt, Robert A. 1987. Curb on Medicare Fees of Doctors Pondered. Los Angeles Times, sec. 1, p. 14 (October 1).

Rosenthal, Douglas E. 1974. Lawyer and Client: Who's in Charge? New York: Russell Sage Foundation.

Roth, Julius. 1974. Professionalism: The Sociologist's Decoy. 1 Sociology of Work and Occupations 6.

Roth, Julius, Sheryl Ruzek, and Arlene K. Daniels. 1973. Current State of the Sociology of Occupations. 14 Sociological Quarterly 309.

Rothman, Robert A. 1984. Deprofessionalization: The Case of Law in America. 11 Work and Occupations 183.

Rothstein, William G. 1973. Professionalization and Employer Demands: The Cases of Homeopathy and Psychoanalysis in the United States. In Paul Halmos, ed. Professionalisation and Social Change. Keele: University of Keele.

Rottenberg, Simon. 1962. The Economics of Occupational Licensing. In National Bureau of Economic Research, Aspects of Labor Economics. New York: National Bureau of Economic Research.

———. ed. 1980. Occupational Licensure and Regulation. Washington, DC: American Enterprise Institute for Public Policy Research.

Royal Commission on Legal Services. 1979. Final Report, 2 vols. London: Her Majesty's Stationery Office (Cmnd 7648, 7648–1).

Rueschemeyer, Dietrich. 1964. Doctors and Lawyers: A Comment on the Theory of the Professions. 1 Canadian Review of Sociology and Anthropology 17.

———. 1973. Lawyers and Their Society: A Comparative Study of the Legal Profession in Germany and the United States. Cambridge, MA: Harvard University Press.

———. 1983. Professional Autonomy and the Social Control of Expertise. In Robert Dingwall and Philip Lewis, eds. The Sociology of the Professions: Lawyers, Doctors and Others. London: Macmillan.

Ruffin, R. J. and D. F. Leigh. 1973. Charity, Competition, and the Pricing of Doctor's Services. 8 Journal of Human Resources 212.

Saks, Mike. 1983. Removing the blinkers? A critique of recent contributions to the sociology of professions. 31 Sociological Review 1.

Salaman, G. 1979. Work Organizations: Resistance and Control. London: Longman.

Sanchez, Jesus. 1988. FTC Moves to Overturn Eye-Care Industry Curbs. Los Angeles Times, sec. 1, p. 1 (February 11)

Sarat, Austin and William L. F. Felstiner. 1986. Law and Strategy in the Divorce Lawyer's Office. 20 Law & Society Review 93.

Schmalz, Jeffrey. 1986. Regents Board and Health Dept. Split Over Disciplining of Doctors. New York Times, p. 13 (May 23).

Schudson, Michael. 1974. The Flexner Report and the Reed Report: Notes on the History of Professional Education in the United States. 55 Social Science Quarterly 347.

Schultz, Theodore. 1961. Investment in Human Capital. 51 American Economic Review 1.

Schwartz, Murray L. 1978. The Professionalism and Accountability of Lawyers. 66 California Law Review 669.

Schwartz, Richard and James Miller. 1964. Legal Evolution and Societal Complexity. 70 American Journal of Sociology 159.

Scitovsky, Tibor. 1966. An International Comparison

of the Trend of Professional Earnings. 56 American Economic Review 25.

Seiler, Michael. 1985. Audit Finds Physicians Are Overpaid as Witnesses. Los Angeles Times, sec. 2, p. 1 (January 25).

Shanker, Albert. 1986. Professionalism under Fire: Power vs. Knowledge in St. Louis. New York Times, sec. 4, p. 7 (October 26).

Shenon, Philip. 1987. Deaver Cites Alcoholism as Perjury Trial Defense. New York Times, p. 6 (October 3).

Shepard, Lawrence. 1978. Licensing Restrictions and the Cost of Dental Care. 21 Journal of Law and Economics 187.

Shiver, Jube. 1986. Low-Cost Health Groups Distress Physician Critics. Los Angeles Times, sec. 1, p. 1 (December 26).

Siebert, W. 1977. Occupational Licensing: The Merrison Report on the Regulation of the Medical Profession. 15 British Journal of Industrial Relations 29.

Slayton, Philip and Michael J. Trebilcock, eds. 1978. The Professions and Public Policy. Toronto: University of Toronto Press.

Smigel, Erwin O. 1954. Trends in Occupational Sociology: A Survey of Postwar Research. 19 American Sociological Review 398.

Smigel, Erwin O., Joseph Monane, Robert B. Wood, and Barbara Randall Nye. 1963. Occupational Sociology: A Reexamination. 47 Sociology and Social Research 472.

Smith, Adam. 1937. An Inquiry into the Nature and Causes of the Wealth of Nations. New York: Random House.

Spangler, Eve and Peter M. Lehman. 1982. Lawyering as Work. In Charles Derber, ed. Professionals as Workers. Boston: G.K. Hall.

Spence, M. 1973. Job Market Signalling. 87 Quarterly Journal of Economics 355.

Starr, Paul. 1982. The Social Transformation of American Medicine. New York: Basic Books.

Steinfels, Peter. 1979. The Neo-Conservatives. New York: Simon and Schuster.

Stevenson, Richard W. 1986. Ad Agency Mergers Changing the Business. New York Times, p. 1 (May 13).

Stevens, Rosemary. 1971. American Medicine and the Public Interest. New Haven, CT: Yale University Press.

Stigler, George J. 1971. The Theory of Economic Regulation. 2 Bell Journal of Economics and Management Science 3.

Stinchcombe, A. L. 1959. Bureaucratic and Craft Administration of Production: A Comparative Survey. 4 Administrative Science Quarterly 168.

Sullivan, Ronald. 1983. Health Chief for New York to Act Against Misconduct by Physicians. New York Times, sec. 1, p. 1 (April 3).

———. 1985a. New York Puts Curb On Medical Students From the Caribbean. New York Times p. 1 (August 2).

———. 1985b. New York Panel Urges Cut in Doctor Training. New York Times, p. 19 (October 10).

———. 1985c. Hospitals Fight Bid to Limit Doctor Training. New York Times, p. 15 (October 11).

———. 1986. Cuomo's Plan for Testing Doctors Is Part of Growing National Effort. New York Times, p. 1 (June 9).

Szelényi, Ivan. 1982. Gouldner's Theory of the "Flawed Universal Class." 11 Theory and Society 779–99.

Szymanski, Al. 1979. A Critique and Extension of the PMC. In Pat Walker, ed. Between Labor and Capital. Boston: South End Press.

Timnick, Lois. 1981. Psychologists Face Identity Crisis. Los Angeles Times, sec. 1, p. 3 (September 14).

Toren, Nina. 1975. Deprofessionalization and its Sources. 2 Sociology of Work and Occupations 323.

Tourraine, Alain. 1971. The Post-Industrial Society. New York: Random House.

Trebilcock, Michael J., Carolyn J. Tuohy, and Allan D. Wolfson. 1979. Professional Regulation: A Staff Study of Accountancy, Architecture, Engineering and Law in Ontario. Toronto: Province of Ontario, Professional Organizations Committee.

Treiman, Donald J. 1977. Occupational Prestige in Comparative Perspective. New York: Academic Press.

Tullock, Gordon. 1975. The Transitory Gains Gap. 6 Bell Journal of Economics and Management Science 671.

Turner, Ralph. 1960. Models of Social Ascent through Education: Sponsored and Contest Mobility. 25 American Sociological Review 855.

Tuohy, Carolyn and Alan D. Wolfson. 1977. The Political Economy of Professionalism: A Perspective. In Four Aspects of Professionalism. Ottawa: Consumer Research Council.

Veblen, Thorstein. 1915. The Theory of the Leisure Class. New York: Macmillan.

Vollmer, Howard M. and Donald L. Mills, eds. 1966. Professionalization. Englewood Cliffs, N J: Prentice Hall.

Weber, Max. 1947. The Theory of Social and Economic Organization (trans. A. M. Henderson and Talcott Parsons; ed. Talcott Parsons). New York: Free Press.

———. 1954. Law in Economy and Society (trans. Edward Shils and Max Rheinstein; ed. Max Rheinstein). Cambridge, MA: Harvard University Press.

———. 1964. From Max Weber (ed. H. H. Gerth and C. W. Mills). London: Routledge and Kegan Paul.

———. 1978. Economy and Society (2 vols.; ed. Guenther Roth and Claus Wittich). Berkeley: University of California Press.

Westergaard John and Henrietta Resler. 1975. Class in a Capitalist Society. London: Heinemann.

White, William D. 1979a. Why Is Regulation Introduced in the Health Sector? A Look at Occupational Licensure. 4 Journal of Health Politics, Policy, and Law 536.

———. 1979b. Public Health and Private Gain: The Economics of Licensing Clinical Laboratory Personnel. New York: Methuen.

———. 1979c. Dynamic Elements of Regulation: The Case of Occupational Licensure. 1 Research in Law and Economics 15.

———. 1983. Labor Market Organization and Professional Regulation: A Historical Analysis of Nursing Licensure. 7 Law and Human Behavior 157.

Wilensky, Harold L. 1964. The Professionalization of Everyone? 70 American Journal of Sociology 137.

Wolfe, Sidney, Henry Bergman, and George Silver. 1985. Medical Malpractice: The Need for Disciplinary Reform, not Tort Reform. Washington, DC: Public Citizen.

Wood, Stephen, ed. 1982. The Degradation of Work? Skill, Deskilling and the Labour Process. London: Hutchinson.

Wright, Erik Olin. 1979. Intellectuals and the Class Structure of Capitalist Society. In Pat Walker, ed. Between Labor and Capital. Boston: South End Press.

Wright, Erik Olin, Cynthia Costello, David Hachen, and Joey Sprague. 1982. The American Class Structure. 47 American Sociological Review 709.

Wuthnow, Robert and Wesley Shrum. 1983. Knowledge Workers as a "New Class": Structural and Ideological Convergence among Professional-Technical Workers and Managers. 10 Work and Occupations 471.

Young, Michael. 1958. The Rise of the Meritocracy. London: Thames and Hudson.

AMERICAN LAWYERS

Cases

Argersinger v. Hamlin, 407 U.S. 25 (1972).

Bates v. State Bar of Arizona, 433 U.S. 350 (1977).

Brotherhood of Railroad Trainmen v. Virginia, 377 U.S. 1 (1964).

Carroll v. State Bar of California, 116 Cal. App. 3d 1193, 213 Cal. Rptr. 305 (1985), cert. denied, 474 U.S. 848 (1985).

Committee on Professional Ethics v. Humphrey, 377 N.W.2d 643 (Ia. 1985).

County of Fresno v. Superior Court, 82 Cal. App. 3d 191, 146 Cal. Rptr. 880 (1978).

Frazier v. Heebe, 107 Sup. Ct. 2607 (1987).

Gideon v. Wainwright, 372 U.S. 335 (1963).

Goldfarb v. Virginia State Bar, 421 U.S. 773 (1975).

Hishon v. King & Spalding, 467 U.S. 69 (1984).

In re Chase, 299 Ore. 391 (1985).

In re Drukulich, 299 Ore. 417 (1985).

In re Griffiths, 413 U.S. 717 (1973).

In re Investigation of Conduct of Examination for Admission to Practice of Law, 1 Cal 2d 61, 33 P.2d 829 (1934).

In re Primus, 436 U.S. 412 (1978).

In re R.M.J., 455 U.S. 191 (1982).

In re Von Wiegen, 63 N.Y.S.2d 163, 470 N.E.2d 838 (N.Y. 1984), cert. denied, 105 Sup. Ct. 2701 (1985).

Johnson v. Avery, 393 U.S. 483 (1969).

Johnson v. Zerbst, 304 U.S. 458 (1938).

Law Students Civil Rights Research Council, Inc. v. Wadmond, 401 U.S. 154 (1971).

Marek v. Chesney, 473 U.S. 1 (1985).

Matter of Farrell, 127 Misc.2d 350 (1985).

NAACP v. Button, 371 U.S. 415 (1963).

Ohralik v. Ohio State Bar Association, 436 U.S. 447 (1978).

Palmer v. Unauthorized Practice Committee of State Bar, 438 S.W.2d 374 (Tex. Civ. App. 1969).

Regents of the University of California v. Bakke, 438 U.S. 265 (1978).

Saleeby v. State Bar of California, 216 Cal. Rptr. 367 (1985).

Shapero v. Kentucky Bar Association, 100 L Ed 2d 475 (1988).

State ex rel. Scott v. Roper, 688 S.W.2d 757 (Mo. 1985).

Supreme Court of New Hampshire v. Piper, 470 U.S. 275 (1985).

Supreme Court of Virginia v. Friedman, 822 F.2d 423 (4th Cir. 1987), prob. juris. noted 98 L Ed 2d 244 (1987).

Surety Title Insurance Agency, Inc. v. Virginia State Bar, 431 F. Supp. 298 (E.D. Va. 1977), vacated, 571 F.2d 205 (4th Cir.), cert. denied, 436 U.S. 941 (1978).

United Mineworkers, District 12 v. Illinois State Bar Association, 389 U.S. 217 (1976).

United Transportation v. State Bar of Michigan, 401 U.S. 576 (1971).

Walters v. National Association of Radiation Survivors, 473 U.S. 305 (1985).

Webb v. Board of Education of Dyer County, 471 U.S. 234 (1985).

Yarbrough v. Superior Court, 216 Cal. Rptr. 475 (Cal. 1985).

Books, Articles, and Papers

Abbott, Andrew. 1981. Status and Status Strain in the Professions. 86 American Journal of Sociology 819.

———. 1986. Jurisdictional Conflicts: A New Approach to the Development of Legal Professions. 1986 American Bar Foundation Research Journal 187.

Abel, Bruce. 1963. The Firms—What Do They Want?

37(9) Harvard Law Record 9–11 (December 12).

Abel, Richard L. 1979. Socializing the Legal Profession: Can Redistributing Lawyers' Services Achieve Social Justice? 1 Law & Policy Quarterly 5.

———. 1980. The Sociology of American Lawyers: A Bibliographic Guide. 2 Law & Policy Quarterly 335.

———. 1981a. Why Does the ABA Promulgate Ethical Rules? 59 Texas Law Review 639.

———. 1981b. Toward a Political Economy of Lawyers. 1981 Wisconsin Law Review 1117.

———. 1985a. Law Without Politics: Legal Aid Under Advanced Capitalism. 32 UCLA Law Review 474.

———. 1985b. Lawyers and the Power to Change. 7(1) Law & Policy (January) (special issue).

———. 1985c. Comparative Sociology of Legal Professions: An Exploratory Essay. 1985 American Bar Foundation Research Journal 1.

———. 1988. The Legal Profession in England and Wales. Oxford: Basil Blackwell.

Abrahams, Robert D. 1937–38. Law Offices to Serve Householders in the Lower Income Group. 42 Dickinson Law Review 133.

———. 1942. The Neighborhood Law Office Experiment. 9 University of Chicago Law Review 410.

———. 1949. The Neighborhood Law Office Plan. 1949 Wisconsin Law Review 634.

———. 1964. Twenty-five Years of Service: Philadelphia's Neighborhood Law Office Plan. 50 American Bar Association Journal 728.

Abramson, Jill and Barbara Franklin. 1983. Are Women Catching Up? Harvard Law '74. American Lawyer 79 (May).

———. 1986. Where They Are Now. The Story of the Women of Harvard Law 1974. Garden City, NY: Doubleday.

Adams, Edward A. 1986. N.Y. Summer Pay Passes $1,000–a-Week Mark. 8(41) National Law Journal 10 (June 23).

———. 1986–87. Law Schools '87. 9(16 & 17) National Law Journal 20–26 (December 29, 1987–January 5, 1987).

———. 1987a. Multistate Essay Test Renews Controversy. 9(41) National Law Journal 3, 38 (June 22).

———. 1987b. ABA Denies Accreditation to Three: Western States, Nevada, St. Thomas. 9(45) National Law Journal 4 (July 20).

———. 1988. "Gadfly" Sets Law School Agenda. 10(18) National Law Journal 1 (January 11).

Aitchison, Clyde B. 1936. Practitioners Before the Interstate Commerce Commission. 4 I.C.C. Practitioner's Journal 53.

———. 1941. I.C.C. Report. Washington, DC: Government Printing Office.

Altman & Weil, Inc. 1976. The 1976 Survey of Law Firm Economics. Ardmore, PA: Altman & Weil.

———. 1984. Survey of Government Lawyer Salaries. Ardmore, PA.: Altman & Weil.

———. 1985a. The 1985 Survey of Law Firm Economics. Ardmore, PA.: Altman & Weil.

———. 1985b. The 1986 Survey of Law Firm Economics. Ardmore, PA.: Altman & Weil.

———. 1986. Compensation Plans for Lawyers and their Staffs: Salaries, Bonuses, and Profit-Sharing Plans. Chicago: Section of Economics of Law Practice, American Bar Association.

American Bar Association. 1878–1985. Reports, vols. 1–110. Chicago: ABA.

American Bar Association, Center for Professional Responsibility. 1983. 1983 Ethics Committees Operations Survey. Chicago: ABA.

———. 1986. A Survey on the Teaching of Professional Responsibility. Chicago: ABA.

American Bar Association, Commission on Professionalism. 1986. "... In the Spirit of Public Service:" A Blueprint for the Rekindling of Lawyer Professionalism. Chicago: ABA.

American Bar Association, Committee on Legal Education. 1881. Report. 4 American Bar Association Reports 302.

———. 1891. Report. 14 American Bar Association Reports 301.

———. 1895. Report. 18 American Bar Association Reports 315.

American Bar Association, Committee on Legal Education and Admission to the Bar. 1907. Report. 31 American Bar Association Reports 505.

American Bar Association, Special Committee on the Economic Condition of the Bar. 1939. The Economics of the Legal Profession. Chicago: ABA.

American Bar Association, Special Committee on Evaluation of Disciplinary Enforcement. 1970. Problems and Recommendations in Disciplinary Enforcement (Clark Report). Chicago: ABA.

American Bar Association, Standing Committee on Clients' Security Funds. 1981. Results of 1981 Survey of State and Local Bars and Bar Associations. Chicago: National Center for Professional Responsibility.

American Bar Association, Standing Committee on Economics of Law Practice. 1964. Statistical Analysis of Recommended Minimum Fees for Selected Legal Services. Chicago: ABA.

———. 1966. Statistical Analysis of Recommended Minimum Fees for Selected Legal Services. Chicago: ABA.

American Bar Association, Standing Committee on Professional Discipline, and National Center for Professional Responsibility. 1978–1986. Statistical Report Re: Public Discipline of Lawyers by Disciplinary Agencies, 1974–1985. Chicago: ABA.

American Bar Association Journal. 1970. In Search of the Average Lawyer. 56 American Bar Association Journal 1165.

———. 1977. 63 American Bar Association Journal 171.

American Bar Foundation. 1956. Lawyers in the United States: Distribution and Income. Part One: Distribution. Chicago: ABF.

———. 1958a. Lawyers in the United States: Distribution and Income. Part Two: Income. Chicago: ABF.

———. 1958b. The Rate of Increase in the Number of Lawyers and Population Growth. Chicago: ABF (Research Memorandum No. 13).

———. 1960. Recent Statistics on the Income of Lawyers in the United States. Chicago: ABF (Research Memorandum No. 19).

———. 1970. The Legal Profession in the United States. Chicago: ABF.

American Law School Review. 1902–42. vols. 1–10.

American Lawyer. 1982. American Lawyer Guide to Law Firms. New York: AM-LAW Pub. Corp.

——— 1984. 1984 Summer Associates Survey (October).

American Prepaid Legal Services Institute. 1984. Prepaid Legal Service Plans in Profile. Chicago: APLSI.

Ames, James Barr. 1904. Annual Address of the Chairman of the Section of Legal Education of the American Bar Association, 1904. 1 American Law School Review 265.

Andrews, Lori B. 1981. Lawyer Advertising and the First Amendment. 1981 American Bar Foundation Research Journal 967.

Appel, George F. Baer. 1933a. The Pennsylvania System. 7 American Law School Review 928.

———. 1933b. The Pennsylvania System. 3 Bar Examiner 10.

Arnould, Richard J. 1972. Pricing Professional Services: A Case Study of the Legal Service Industry. 38 Southern Economic Journal 495.

Ashman, Allan. 1972. The New Private Practice: A Study of Piper & Marbury's Neighborhood Law Office. Chicago: National Legal Aid and Defender Association.

———. 1982. Residency Requirements for Admission to the Bar: Gordon and its Progeny. 51(1) Bar Examiner 10.

Association of American Law Schools (AALS). 1969. Report on the Study of Part-Time Legal Education. Proceedings of the AALS, Part One, Section II, p. 5.

———. 1980. 80(2) Newsletter (June).

Association of American Law Schools, Special Committee on Law School Administration and University Relations. 1961. Anatomy of Modern Legal Education. St. Paul, MN: West Publishing Co.

Astin, Alexander W. 1982. Minorities in Higher Education. San Francisco: Jossey-Bass.

———. 1984. Prelaw Students—A National Profile. 34 Journal of Legal Education 73.

Auerbach, Carl A. 1984. Legal Education and Some of Its Discontents. 34 Journal of Legal Education 43.

Auerbach, Jerold J. 1971. Enmity and Amity: Law Teachers and Practitioners, 1900–1922. In Donald Fleming and Bernard Bailyn, eds. Law in American History. 5 Perspectives in American History.

———. 1976. Unequal Justice: Lawyers and Social Change in Modern America. New York: Oxford University Press.

Augustyn, Noel J. 1985. Summary of Data from Faculty and Administrative Appointments Registers. Washington, DC: Association of American Law Schools.

Baird, Leonard L., Alfred B. Carlson, Richard R. Reilly, and Ramon J. Powell. 1979. Defining Competence in Legal Practice: The Evaluation of Lawyers in Large Firms and Organizations. 4 Reports of Law School Admissions Council Sponsored Research 125. Newton, PA: Law School Admission Services, Inc. (LSAC-79-1).

Ballantine, Henry Winthrop. 1919. The Place in Legal Education of Evening and Correspondence Schools. 4 American Law School Review 369.

Balzar, John. 1985. Student Loan Defaults Called Alarming: May Exceed 1 Billion for Year; Tougher Rules Planned. Los Angeles Times, sec. 1, p. 8 (August 30).

Bandow, Doug. 1987. A Brazen System of Self-Enrichment. New York Times, sec. 3, p. 2 (March 15).

Bar Examiner. 1931–87. vols. 1–56.

Barry, Kenneth H. and Patricia A. Connelly. 1978. Research on Law Students: An Annotated Bibliography. 1978 American Bar Foundation Research Journal 751.

Bartlett, Alfred L. 1932. Admissions Problems. Proceedings of the Fifth Annual Meeting of the State Bar of California 38.

Bazelon, David T. 1969. Views from a Law Office Window. In Nothing But a Fine Tooth Comb, chap. 7. New York: Simon & Schuster.

Beall, Trish. 1986. All the Right Lateral Moves. 9(7) Los Angeles Lawyer 27 (October).

Beardsley, Charles E. 1946. Admission of Out-of-State Lawyers. 15 Bar Examiner 10.

Bell, Robert. 1985. Why Some Corporations Use More Lawyers Than Others. Paper presented at the annual meeting of the Law and Society Association, San Diego, June.

Benadum, Malcolm K. 1933. A Study of Ohio Bar Examinations. 2 Bar Examiner 100.

Benjamin, G. Andrew H., Alfred Kasniak, Bruce Sales, and Stephen B. Shanfield. 1986. The Role of Legal Education in Producing Psychological Distress Among Law Students and Lawyers. 1986 American Bar Foundation Research Journal 225.

Berentson, Jane. 1980. Integrity Test: Lawyers Tell Clients to Lie. 2 American Lawyer 15 (May).

Berg, C. E. 1979. Lawyer Referral Services. In Legal Services for the Middle Class. Chicago: American Bar Association.

Berger, Joseph. 1987. Brooklyn Bishop Assails High

Fees Being Paid by Illegal Aliens. New York Times, p. 20 (May 5).

Bernstein, Peter W. 1982. Profit Pressures on the Big Law Firms. 195(8) Fortune 84 (April 19).

Bernstine, Daniel O. 1981. An Emprical Study of the University of Wisconsin Law School Special Admissions Program: A Progress Report. 7 Black Law Journal 146.

Bethel, Billie. 1976. Economics and the Practice of Law: The 1976 Economic Survey of the State Bar of Arizona. 12(3) Arizona State Bar Journal 4 (October).

Biby, John E. 1930. Bar Examination Statistics and Standards. 7 American Law School Review 17.

Bingham, Timothy W. and Gregory H. Bonenberger. 1986. Lawyers Beware: Small Change In Collection Act Bodes Big Impact. 9(7) National Law Journal 26 (October 27).

Blaine, William L. 1976. Where to Practice Law in California: Statistics on Lawyers' Work. Berkeley, CA: Continuing Legal Education of the Bar.

Blake, Gene. 1980. Minority Group Members Score Lower than Whites on State Bar Examination. Los Angeles Times, sec. 1, p. 2 (March 8).

Blaustein, Albert P. 1950. The 1949 Lawyer Count: A Preliminary Statement. 36 American Bar Association Journal 370.

———. 1951. The Association of the Bar of the City of New York, 1870–1951. 6 The Record 261.

———. 1952a. The Legal Profession in the United States: A 1952 Statistical Analysis. 38 American Bar Association Journal 1006.

———. 1952b. College and Law School Education of the American Lawyer—A Preliminary Report. 4 Journal of Legal Education 284.

———. 1952c. What Do Laymen Think of Lawyers? 38 American Bar Association Journal 39.

Blaustein, Albert P. and Charles O. Porter. 1954. The American Lawyer: A Summary of the Survey of the Legal Profession. Chicago: University of Chicago Press.

Bloomfield, Maxwell. 1984. From Deference to Confrontation: The Early Black Lawyers of Galveston, Texas, 1895–1920. In Gerard W. Gawalt, ed. The New High Priests: Lawyers in Post-Civil War America. Westport, CT: Greenwood Press.

Blum, Andrew. 1987. More Judges Turning to Judicial Insurance Policies. 10(10) National Law Journal 10 (November 16).

Blumberg, Abraham S. 1967. The Practice of Law as a Confidence Game: Organizational Cooptation of a Profession. 1 Law & Society Review 15.

Botein, Stephen. 1983. "When We All Meet Afterwards in Heaven": Judgeship as a Symbol for Modern American Lawyers. In Gerald L. Geison, ed. Professions and Professional Ideologies. Chapel Hill: University of North Carolina Press.

Boyd, William. 1974. Legal Education: A Nationwide Survey of Minority Law Students 1974. 4 Black Law Journal 527.

Boyer, Benjamin Franklin. 1941. The Smaller Law Schools: Factors Affecting Their Methods and Objectives. 20 Oregon Law Review 281.

Bracamonte, Jose. 1987. A Monograph on the Hispanic Bar in Texas (unpublished).

Brakel, Samuel J. 1974. Judicare: Public Funds, Private Lawyers, and Poor People. Chicago: American Bar Foundation.

Brazil, Wayne D. 1980a. Views from the Front Lines: Observations by Chicago Lawyers About the System of Civil Discovery. 1980 American Bar Foundation Research Journal 217.

———. 1980b. Civil Discovery: Lawyers' Views of Its Effectiveness, Its Principal Problems and Abuses. 1980 American Bar Foundation Research Journal 787.

Brenner, James E. 1932a. A Survey of Employment Conditions among Young Attorneys in California. Proceedings of the Fifth Annual Meeting of the State Bar of California 32.

———. 1932b. Survey of Bar Examination Procedure in the United States, 1930–1931. San Francisco: State Bar of California, Committee of Bar Examiners.

———. 1935. Trends in Lawyer Population and the Amount of Legal Business. 11 Los Angeles Bar Association Bulletin 53.

Brenner, James E. and Leon E. Warmke. 1942. Statistically Speaking-. 11 Bar Examiner 8.

Brill, Steven. 1983. The Woman Problem. 5(2) American Lawyer 1 (February).

Brown, Esther Lucille. 1938. Lawyers and the Promotion of Justice. New York: Russell Sage Foundation.

Brozan, Nadine. 1986. For Female M.D.'s, Success at a Price. New York Times, p. 21 (April 16).

Bry, Barbara. 1983. Finley-Kumble Rides a Fast Track. Los Angeles Times, sec. 4, p. 1 (April 11).

Bumsted, Brad and Jeannine Guttman. 1986a. N.J. Swings Toward Tough Penalties Against Crooked Lawyers. Cincinnati Enquirer, p. E-3 (October 21).

———. 1986b. Multiple Licensing Creates Problems in Punishing Rogues. Cincinnati Enquirer, p. E-3 (October 21).

Business Week. 1984. A New Corporate Powerhouse: The Legal Department. Business Week, p. 66 (April 9).

Butterfield, Fox. 1987. Harvard Will Help Some Law Alumni. New York Times, p. 21 (February 22).

Campbell, Cleopatra. 1967. The Attitudes of First-Year Law Students at the University of New Mexico. 20 Journal of Legal Education 71.

Campbell, Don G. 1981. Real Estate/Legal Service Combined. Los Angeles Times, sec. 4, p. 1 (December 20).

Cantor, Daniel J. & Company. 1966. The 1966 Survey of the Economics of Florida Law Practice. Tallahassee: Florida Bar.

———. 1969. Economic Study of the Lawyers of South Carolina. Charleston, SC: Committee on the Economics of the Profession, South Carolina State Bar and South Carolina Bar Association.

Cappell, Charles L. 1980. The Reproduction of Status Hierarchies Within the Legal Profession. Paper presented at the annual meeting of the Law and Society Association, Madison, June 5–8.

———. 1985. The Status of Black Lawyers. Paper presented at the annual meeting of the Law and Society Association, San Diego, June.

Cappell, Charles L. and Terence C. Halliday. 1983. Professional Projects of Elite Chicago Lawyers, 1950–1974. 1983 American Bar Foundation Research Journal 291.

Cappell, Charles and Jessica L. Lynch. 1986. Minorities and Women in Law Schools: New Status Classes? Paper presented at the annual meeting of the Law and Society Association, Chicago, June.

Carlin, Jerome E. 1962. Lawyers on Their Own. New Brunswick, NJ: Rutgers University Press.

———. 1966. Lawyers' Ethics. New York: Russell Sage Foundation.

Carlson, Alfred B. and Charles E. Werts. 1976. Relationships among Law School Predictors, Law School Performance, and Bar Examination Results. 3 Reports of Law School Admissions Council Sponsored Research 211. Princeton, N.J.: Law School Admission Council.

Carlson, Rick J. 1976. Measuring the Quality of Legal Services: An Idea Whose Time Has Not Come. 11 Law & Society Review 287.

Carman, Charles H. 1987. For Rainmakers Here, It Pours. 9(19) National Law Journal 1 (January 19).

Carnegie Foundation for the Advancement of Teaching. 1915–1919. The Study of Legal Education (excerpt from the annual report of the president). New York: Carnegie Foundation.

Carrington, Paul D. and J. C. James. 1977. The Alienation of Law Students. 75 Michigan Law Review 887.

Carroll, Sidney L. and Robert Gaston. 1977. Examination Pass Rates as Entry Restrictions into Licensed Occupations. In Occupational Licensing, app. VII (unpublished).

———. 1981. A Note on the Quality of Legal Services: Peer Review and Disciplinary Service. 3 Research in Law and Economics 251.

Casey, David S., 1975. We Have Miles to Go, Much to Do. 50 California State Bar Journal 455.

Casper, Jonathan. 1969. Lawyers and Loyalty-Security Litigation. 3 Law & Society Review 575.

———. 1972a. Lawyers Before the Warren Court. Urbana: University of Illinois Press.

———. 1972b. The Politics of Civil Liberties. New York: Harper & Row.

Catalyst Legal Resources. 1982. 1981–1982 Annual Survey: Compensation of Attorneys in 10 Cities. New York: Catalyst Legal Resources.

Chai, Charles Y. 1974. Recruitment Characteristics and Leadership Status of Urban Lawyers in the South: A Case Study of New Orleans. 48 Tulane Law Review 239.

Chambers, David. 1983. Salt Survey of Women in Law School Teaching. 1983(1) Salt Newsletter 1 (July).

———. 1987. Tough Enough: The Work and Family Experiences of Recent Women Graduates of the University of Michigan Law School (unpublished draft, July 7).

Chambers, Marcia. 1985. Criminal Lawyers in Study Say New Laws Inhibit Case Choices. New York Times, p. 10 (November 21).

Chase, Anthony. 1979. The Birth of the Modern Law School. 23 American Journal of Legal History 329.

———. 1981. Origins of Modern Professional Education: The Harvard Case Method Conceived as Clinical Instruction in Law. 5 Nova Law Journal 323.

———. 1985. American Legal Education Since 1885: The Case of the Missing Modern. 30 New York Law School Law Review 519.

———. 1986. Lawyers and Popular Culture: A Review of Mass Media Portrayals of American Attorneys. 1986 American Bar Foundation Research Journal 281.

Chayes, Abram and Antonia H. Chayes. 1985. Corporate Counsel and the Elite Law Firm. 37 Stanford Law Review 277.

Chayes, Antonia Handler, Bruce C. Greenwald, and Maxine Paisner Winig. 1983. Managing Your Lawyers. 61 Harvard Business Review 84.

Chen, Edwin. 1983. The Trials of Low-Budget Law Schools. Los Angeles Times, sec. 1, p. 1 (February 4).

———. 1984a. The Poor Still Go Begging for Legal Help. Los Angeles Times, sec. 1, p. 1 (February 19).

———. 1984b. Law Firms' Receipts Soaring, Census Says. Los Angeles Times, sec. 1, p. 20 (June 14).

Chester, Ronald. 1985. Unequal Access: Women Lawyers in a Changing America. South Hadley, MA: Bergin & Garvey.

Christensen, Barlow F. 1970. Lawyers for People of Moderate Means. Chicago: American Bar Foundation.

——— 1980. The Unauthorized Practice of Law: Do Good Fences Really Make Good Neighbors— or Even Good Sense? 1980 American Bar Foundation Research Journal 159.

Chused, Richard. 1987. Salt Study on the Hiring and Retention of Minority and Female Faculty (unpublished memorandum, October 22).

Clark, Charles E. 1933. The Selective Process of Choosing Students and Lawyers. 7 American Law School Review 913.

Clark, Charles E. and Emma Corstvet. 1938. The Lawyer and the Public: An A.A.L.S. Survey. 47 Yale Law Journal 1272.

Clark, Ezra Tom, Jr. 1987. Leveraging: Now There's a New Method. 9(52) National Law Journal 15 (September 7).

Clark, Harold F. 1937. Life Earnings in Selected Occupations in the United States. New York: Harper & Bros.

Cohen, Michael. 1969. Lawyers and Political Careers. 3 Law & Society Review 563.

Colorado Bar Association. 1967. Report on the 1967 Economic Survey of the Colorado Bar. Denver: Colorado Bar Association, Economics of Law Practice Committee.

Commission on the Corporate Law Departments, Association of the Bar of the City of New York and Arthur Young & Co. 1983. National Survey of Corporation Law Compensation and Organization Practices (6th ed.). New York: Association of the Bar of the City of New York.

Committee of Bar Examiners. 1930. Report. 5 California State Bar Journal 351.

Committee on the Survey of the Legal Profession for Pennsylvania. 1952. Report. 23 Pennsylvania Bar Association Quarterly 381.

Committee on Trend of Bar Admissions. 1948. Report. 17 Bar Examiner 137.

Cook, Alberta I. 1986a. Gender Bias: Push Grows for Study, Action. 8(36) National Law Journal 1 (May 19).

———. 1986b. Complaints Rise Against Lawyers. 9(7) National Law Journal 1 (October 27).

———. 1987a. Lawyers Lured by Other Careers, Lifestyles. 9(23) National Law Journal 1 (February 16).

———. 1987b. The "Incident at Chappaquiddick." 9(21)National Law Journal 1 (February 2).

Cooper, Alan. 1985. 4th Circuit Upholds Virginia's Tough Reciprocity Rules. 7(45) National Law Journal 5 (July 22).

Copeland, Rebecca E. R. 1985. Law Firm Personnel Practices Surveyed: Compensation and Hiring Rates. 8(12) National Law Journal 14 (December 2).

Corcoran, C. Timothy, III. 1986. A Law Firm's View of Student Abuses. 8(29) National Law Journal 14 (March 31).

Cormier, Leonard F. 1982. Lawyers and Political Mobility: an alternative to convergence theory. Ph.D. dissertation, political science, University of Southern California.

Council for Public Interest Law. 1976. Balancing the Scales of Justice: Financing Public Interest Law in America. Washington, DC: Council for Public Interest Law.

———. 1980. Survey of Public Interest Law Narrative Reports. Washington, DC: Council for Public Interest Law.

Council on Legal Education. 1919. Report. 4 American Law School Review 394.

Couric, Emily. 1985. Firms Adapt to New Era: The Move In-House. 7(43) National Law Journal 1 (July 8).

———. 1986a. Specialities: What's Hot, What's Not. 8(21) National Law Journal 1 (February 3).

———. 1986b. "Guardian Angels" of the Law. 9(10) National Law Journal 1 (November 17).

———. 1986c. Broadway, Hollywood. 9(7) National Law Journal 1 (October 27).

Cox, Gail Diane. 1987a. Ore. Lawyers Face High Rate of Claims. 9(22) National Law Journal 3 (February 9).

———. 1987b. End Comes at Last to L.A. Firm. 9(23) National Law Journal 3 (February 16).

———. 1987c. A County Beckons Near L.A. 9(43) National Law Journal 1 (July 6).

———. 1987d. Lawyers Who Are Felons. 10(9) National Law Journal 1 (November 9).

Cox, Keith H. 1977a. Lawyers, Population and Society in New York. Ithaca, NY: Department of Rural Sociology, Cornell University (Bulletin No. 86).

———. 1977b. New York's Main Street and Wall Street Lawyers. Ithaca, NY: Department of Rural Sociology, Cornell University (Bulletin No. 87).

Cox, Steven R., Allan C. DeSerpa, and William C. Canby, Jr. 1982. Consumer Information and the Pricing of Legal Services. 30 Journal of Industrial Economics 305.

Cox, Steven R. and Mark Dwyer. 1987. A Report on Self Help Law: Its Many Perspectives. Chicago: American Bar Association Special Committee on the Delivery of Legal Services.

Cox, Steven R., Charles A. Pulaski, Jr., and Morris Axelrod. 1982–83. Lawyers' Fees and Advertising Rules. Tempe: Arizona State University (Working Paper EC 82/83–5).

Coyle, Marcia. 1987a. ATLA Probing Members' "Misconduct." 9(37) National Law Journal 3 (May 25).

———. 1987b. Va. Bar Residency Rule Nixed. 9(42) National Law Journal 3 (June 29).

———. 1987c. Practice in Japan OK'd for U.S. Lawyers. 9(27) National Law Journal 3 (March 16).

———. 1987d. A Slow, Steady Japan Push Starts. 9(36) National Law Journal 1 (May 18).

———. 1987e. Boutique Shakeout: Merger Can Be an Attractive Option. 9(25) National Law Journal 1 (March 2).

———. 1987f. Once-Tranquil Trade Law Hit By New Frenzy. 9(32) National Law Journal 1 (April 20).

———. 1987g. 31 New Clerks Begin at Supreme Court. 10(5) National Law Journal 3 (October 12).

———. 1988. Will Another Lawyer Ad Taboo Fall? 10(25) National Law Journal 3 (February 29).

Crawford, Albert. 1932. Use of Legal Aptitude Test

in Admitting Applicants to Law School. 1 Bar Examiner 151.

Culp, Jerome. 1981. Blacks in Prestigious Law Firms. 7 Black Law Journal 159.

Curran, Barbara A. 1977. The Legal Needs of the Public. Chicago: American Bar Foundation.

———. 1986. The Legal Profession in the 1980s: Selected Statistics from the 1984 Lawyer Statistical Report. 20 Law & Society Review 19.

Curran, Barbara A., Katherine J. Rosich, Clara N. Carson, and Mark C. Puccetti. 1985. The 1984 Lawyer Statistical Report: A Profile of the Legal Profession in the 1980s. Chicago: American Bar Foundation.

Cutright, Phillip, Karen Cutright, and Douglass G. Boshkoff. 1975. Course Selection, Student Characteristics and Bar Examination Performance: The Indiana University Law School Experience. 27 Journal of Legal Education 127.

Darby, D. Weston, Jr. 1978. It's About Time: A Survey of Lawyers' Timekeeping Practices. 4(3) Legal Economics 39 (fall).

———. 1985. Are You Keeping Up Financially? 71 American Bar Association Journal 66 (December).

Davis, Michael and Frederick A. Elliston. 1986. Ethics and the Legal Profession. Buffalo: Prometheus Books.

Dean, Arthur H. 1957. William Nelson Cromwell, 1854–1948: An American Pioneer in Corporation, Comparative, and International Law. New York: Ad Press

Deitch, Lillian and David Weinstein. 1976. Prepaid Legal Services: Socioeconomic Impacts. Lexington, MA: Lexington Books.

Delaney, William and Alan H. Finegold. 1970. Wall Street Lawyer in the Provinces. 15 Administrative Science Quarterly 191.

Delgado, Richard, Leo Romero, and Cruz Reynoso. 1975. La Raza, the Law and Law Schools. 1975 University of Toledo Law Review 810.

Denenberg, Herbert S., Victor T. Ehre, Jr., and Ronald L. Huling. 1970. Lawyers' Professional Liability Insurance: The Peril, the Protection, and the Price. 1970 Insurance Law Journal 389.

Denison, Edward F. 1943. Incomes in Selected Professions, Part 2, Legal Service. 23(8) Survey of Current Business 23 (August).

———. 1944. Incomes in Selected Professions, Part 6, Comparison of Incomes in Nine Independent Professions. 24(5) Survey of Current Business 15 (May).

Derge, David R. 1959. The Lawyer as Decision-maker in the American State Legislature. 21 Journal of Politics 408.

———. 1962. The Lawyer in the Indiana General Assembly. 6 Midwest Journal of Political Science 19.

Desmond, Fred C. 1933. New Hampshire Stops the Leaks. 2 Bar Examiner 306.

———. 1934. New Hampshire Applies the Scientific Method. 3 Bar Examiner 134.

Dodge, Emily P. 1955. Evolution of a City Law Office, Part I: Office Organization. 1955 Wisconsin Law Review 180.

———. 1956. Evolution of a City Law Office, Part II: Office Flow of Business. 1956 Wisconsin Law Review 35.

Downey, C. E. 1975. Killing Off the Competition. Juris Doctor 29 (October).

———. The Price is Right — For Everyone but the California Bar. Juris Doctor 31 (June).

Drinker, Henry S. 1952. Views of Laymen on the Competency and Integrity of Lawyers. 22 Tennessee Law Review 371.

Durkin, Mary and A. Lewis Rhodes. 1979. Shift in Female Participation in the Legal Profession by State: 1960–1970. 65(4) Women Lawyers Journal 11.

Dyer, Robert F. and Terence A. Shimp. 1980. Reactions to Legal Advertising. 20(2) Journal of Advertising Research 43 (April).

Earle, Walter K. 1963. Mr. Shearman and Mr. Sterling and How They Grew. New York: no publisher.

Edwards, Harry T. 1972. A New Role for the Black Law Graduate. 2 Black Law Journal 21.

Effron, Eric. 1986. Public Battle Cracks Firm. 8(32) National Law Journal 1 (April 21).

Eich, William. 1986. Gender Bias in the Courtroom. 59 Wisconsin Bar Bulletin 22 (June).

Elliott, Shelden D. 1952. Administration, Preparation, and Grading of Bar Examinations. In ABA Survey of the Legal Profession, Reports of Consultant and the Advisory and Editorial Committee on Bar Examinations and Requirements for Admission to the Bar. Colorado Springs: Shepard's Citations (originally published in 19 Bar Examiner 126 [1950]).

Ellman, Ira Mark. 1983. A Comparison of Law Faculty Production in Leading Law Reviews. 33 Journal of Legal Education 681.

Engel, David M. 1984. The Oven Bird's Song: Insiders, Outsiders, and Personal Injuries in an American Community. 18 Law & Society Review 583.

Epstein, Cynthia Fuchs. 1981. Women in Law. New York: Basic Books.

Epstein, Lee. 1985. Conservatives in Court. Knoxville: University of Tennessee Press.

Erlanger, Howard S. 1980. The Allocation of Status Within Occupations: The Case of the Legal Profession. 58 Social Forces 882.

Erlanger, Howard S. and Douglas A. Klegon. 1978. Socialization Effects of Professional School. 13 Law & Society Review 11.

Eron, Leonard E. and Robert S. Redmount. 1957. The Effect of Legal Education on Attitudes. 9 Journal of Legal Education 431.

Eulau, Heinz and John D. Sprague. 1964. Lawyers in Politics. Indianapolis, IN: Bobbs-Merrill.

Evans, Franklin R. 1977. Applications and Admissions to ABA Accredited Law Schools: An Analysis of National Data for the Class Entering in the Fall of 1976. 3 Reports of Law School Admission Council Sponsored Research 551. Princeton, NJ: LSAC.

Fagen, Melvin M. 1939. The Status of Jewish Lawyers in New York City. 1 Jewish Social Studies 73.

Fama, Eugene F. and Michael C. Jensen. 1983a. Separation of Ownership and Control. 26 Journal of Law and Economics 301.

———. 1983b. Agency Problems and Residual Claims. 26 Journal of Law and Economics 327.

Farley, Goscoe O. 1952. Admission of Attorneys from Other Jurisdictions. In ABA Survey of the Legal Profession, Reports of Consultant and the Advisory and Editorial Committees on Bar Examinations and Requirements for Admission to the Bar. Colorado Springs: Shepard's Citations (originally published in 19 Bar Examiner 227 [1950]).

Feldman, Paul. 1986. 6 Lawyers Pay $129,500 to Settle Overbilling Claims. Los Angeles Times, sec. 2, p. 10 (May 23).

Fellmeth, Robert C. 1987a. Initial Report to the Assembly and Senate Judiciary Committees and Chief Justice of the Supreme Court: A Report on the Performance of the Disciplinary System of the California State Bar (unpublished).

———. 1987b. The Discipline System of the California State Bar: An Initial Report. 7(3) California Regulatory Law Reporter 1.

———. 1987c. First Progress Report of the State Bar Discipline Monitor (unpublished, November).

Fenning, Lisa Hill and Patricia M. Schnegg. 1983. The Status of Women in L.A.'s Big Firms. 6(8) Los Angeles Lawyer 27 (November).

Field Research Company. 1960. Members' Appraisal of the State Bar of California and the Present and Proposed Public Relations Programs. San Francisco: Field Research Company.

First, Harry. 1978. Competition in the Legal Education Industry (I). 53 NYU Law Review 311.

———. 1979. Competition in the Legal Education Industry (II): An Antitrust Analysis. 54 NYU Law Review 1049.

Fiske, Edward B. 1985. Minority Enrollment in Colleges is Declining. New York Times, p. 1 (October 27).

———. 1986. Student Debt Reshaping. New York Times, sec. 12, p. 34 (August 3).

———. 1987. Enrollment of Minorities in Colleges Stagnating. New York Times p. 1 (April 19).

Flegal, Frank F. 1982. Discovery Abuse: Causes, Effects and Reform. 3 Review of Litigation 1.

Ford, Peyton, Clive W. Palmer, and David Reich. 1952. The Government Lawyer. Englewood Cliffs, NJ: Prentice Hall.

Ford Foundation. 1973. The Public Interest Law Firm: New Voices for New Constituencies. New York: Ford Foundation.

Ford Foundation and American Bar Association, Special Committee on Public Interest Practice.

1976. Public Interest Law: Five Years Later. Chicago: ABA and New York: Ford Foundation.

Fossum, Donna. 1980a. Law Professors: A Profile of the Teaching Branch of the Profession. 1980 American Bar Foundation Research Journal 501.

———. 1980b. Women Law Professors. 1980 American Bar Foundation Research Journal 903.

Foster, James C. 1981. The Cooling Out of Law Students: Facilitating Market Cooptation of Future Lawyers. In Richard A. C. Gambitta, Marlynn L. May, and James C. Foster, eds. Governing through the Courts. Beverly Hills, CA: Sage Publications.

———. 1985. Legal Education and the Production of Lawyers to (Re)Produce Liberal Capitalism. 9(2) Legal Studies Forum 179.

Freedman, Eric. 1985. Non-Lawyers May Represent Clients at Michigan Job Hearings. 7(46) National Law Journal 11 (July 25).

Freeman, Richard B. 1975. Legal "Cobwebs": A Recursive Model of the Market for New Lawyers. 57 Review of Economics and Statistics 171.

Freidson, Eliot. 1970. Profession of Medicine. A Study of the Sociology of Applied Knowledge. New York: Harper & Row.

Friedman, Lawrence M. 1973. A History of American Law. New York: Simon & Schuster.

Friedman, Milton and Simon Kuznets. 1945. Income from Independent Professional Practice. New York: National Bureau of Economic Research.

Fromson, David. 1977. Let's Be Realistic About Specialization. 63 American Bar Association Journal 74 (January).

Fuller, Lon H. 1952. Legal Education and Admissions to the Bar in Pennsylvania. 25 Temple Law Quarterly 249.

Fund for Modern Courts, Inc. 1985. The Success of Women and Minorities in Achieving Judicial Office. New York: Fund for Modern Courts, Inc.

Galante, Mary Ann. 1985a. Malpractice Rates Zoom. 7(38) National Law Journal 1 (June 3).

———. 1985b. Insurance: Lawyers Face New Fights on Malpractice Coverage. 7(51) National Law Journal 3 (September 2).

———. 1985c. For Firms, Breaking Up Is Hard to Do. 7(50) National Law Journal 1 (August 26).

———. 1985d. $26M Legal Malpractice Judgment Upheld. 7(50) National Law Journal 11 (August 26).

———. 1985e. Bar Passage Rate Plunges in Wash. 8(9) National Law Journal 3 (November 11).

———. 1985f. California Bar Enters High Court Fray. 8(5) National Law Journal 3 (October 14).

———. 1985g. Firms Finding More Value in Marketing. 8(10) National Law Journal 1 (November 18).

———. 1986a. Former California Bar Employee Wins Pact Over Firing. 8(22) National Law Journal 16 (February 10).

————. 1986b. Rogers & Wells Will Pay $40M. 8(25) National Law Journal 3 (March 3).

————. 1986c. Insurance Costs Soar; Is There Any Way Out? 8(26) National Law Journal 1 (March 10).

————. 1986d. Contract Public Defenders Slammed. 8(29) National Law Journal 3 (April 7).

————. 1986e. After a $40M Payment, It's Not Over Yet for Rogers & Wells. 8(31) National Law Journal 1 (April 14).

————. 1986f. Westward Expansion. 8(50) National Law Journal 1 (August 25).

————. 1986g. A New Look for Memel Jacobs. 9(2) National Law Journal 1 (September 22).

————. 1987. Last "J. David" Firm Agrees to Pact. 9(31) National Law Journal 3 (April 13).

Galanter, Marc. 1983. Larger than Life: Mega-Law and Mega Lawyering in the Contemporary United States. In Robert Dingwall and Philip Lewis, eds. The Sociology of the Professions: Lawyers, Doctors, and Others. London: Macmillan.

Galen, Michelle. 1986a. Security More Crucial Than Ever. 8(42) National Law Journal 10 (June 30).

————. 1986b. Out-of-Town Firms Invade Big Apple. 8(49) National Law Journal 6 (August 18).

1986c. Innovation Becomes the Norm In the Legal Recruiting Field. 9(13) National Law Journal 1 (December 8).

Gallucio, Nick. 1978. The Rise of the Company Lawyer. 122 Forbes 168 (September 18).

Gallup, George. 1978. Honesty/Ethical Standards. 150 Gallup Opinion Index 7 (January).

Gandossy, Robert P. 1985. Bad Business: The OPM Scandal and the Seduction of the Establishment. New York: Basic Books.

Garrison, Lloyd K. 1934. Results of the Wisconsin Bar Survey. 8 American Law School Review 116.

————. 1935. A Survey of the Wisconsin Bar. 20 Wisconsin Law Review 131.

Gates, William H. 1984. The Newest Data on Lawyers' Malpractice Claims. 70 American Bar Association Journal 78 (April).

————. 1986. Lawyers' Malpractice: Some Recent Data About a Growing Problem. 37 Mercer Law Review 559.

Gawalt, Gerard W. 1984. The Impact of Industrialization on the Legal Profession in Massachusetts, 1870–1900. In Gerard W. Gawalt, ed. The New High Priests: Lawyers in Post-Civil War America. Westport, CT: Greenwood Press.

Gellerman, Josef E. 1941. Report of a Survey of a Senior Evening Law Class in Washington, D.C. 9 American Law School Review 1970.

Georgetown Journal of Legal Ethics. 1987–.

Gerson. 1982. Attorneys Spend $6.15 Million for TV Ads. 4 National Law Journal 2 (April 26).

Gest, T. 1981. Why Lawyers Are in the Doghouse. U.S. News and World Report 38 (May 11).

Getz, Malcolm. John Siegfried, and Terry Calvani.

1981. Competition at the Bar: The Correlation Between the Bar Examination Pass Rate and the Profitability of Practice. 67 Virginia Law Review 863.

Gilb, Corinne Lathrop. 1956. Self-Regulating Professions and the Public Welfare: A Case Study of the California State Bar. Ph.D. thesis, history, Radcliffe College.

Gilpin, Kenneth N. 1985. Ex-Corporate Leader Will Manage Law Firm. New York Times, p. 34 (February 5).

Gilson, Ronald J. and Robert H. Mnookin. 1985. Sharing Among the Human Capitalists: An Economic Inquiry into the Corporate Law Firm and How Partners Split Profits. 37 Stanford Law Review 313.

Glaberson, William. 1987. A Wall St. Firm Breaks Ranks. New York Times, sec. 3, p. 1 (April 12).

Goffman, Erving. 1961. Asylums: Essays on the social situation of mental patients and other inmates. Garden City, NY: Doubleday.

Goldberg, Stuart C. 1979. 1977 National Survey on Current Methods of Teaching Professional Responsibility in Law Schools. In Patrick A. Keenan, Stuart C. Goldberg, and G. Griffith Dick, eds. Teaching Professional Responsibility: Materials and Proceedings from the National Conference. Detroit: University of Detroit Law School.

Goldman, John J. Ex-Radical Fights for Bar Status. Los Angeles Times, sec. 1, p. 4 (November 11).

Goldman, Marion S. 1972. A Portrait of the Black Attorney in Chicago. Chicago: American Bar Foundation.

Goldstein, Tom. 1977. Law, Fastest Growing Profession, Many Find Prosperity Precarious. New York Times, sec. 1, p. 1 (May 16).

Gombossy, George. 1987. Excluding Black Jurors Brings Sanction. 9(9) National Law Journal 3 (November 10).

Gould, Carole. 1986. When to Turn to a No-Frills Law Firm. New York Times, sec. 3, p. 15 (November 9).

Goulden, James C. 1972. The Superlawyers: The Small and Powerful World of the Great Washington Law Firms. New York: Weybright & Talley.

Granfield, Robert. 1986. Legal Education as Corporate Ideology: Student Adjustment to the Law School Experience. 1 Sociological Forum 514.

Granfors, Mark W. and Terence C. Halliday. 1985. Professional Passages: Caste, Class and Education in the 19th Century Legal Profession. Paper presented at the annual meeting of the Social Science History Association, Chicago, November 22.

Grant, W. Vance and Leo J. Eiden. 1980. Digest of Education Statistics 1980. Washington, DC: Government Printing Office.

Green, Justin J., John R. Schmidhauser, Larry L.

Berg, and David Brady. 1973. Lawyers in Congress: A New Look at Some Old Assumptions. 26 Western Political Quarterly 440.

Green, Mark J. 1975. The Other Government: The Unseen Power of Washington Lawyers. New York: Grossman.

———. 1976. The Gross Legal Product: "How Much Justice Can You Afford?" In Ralph Nader and Mark Green, eds. Verdicts on Lawyers. New York: Crowell.

Greer, William R. 1986. The Changing Women's Marriage Market. New York Times, p. 16 (February 22).

Gregory, Charles Noble. 1897. The Wages of Law Teachers. 20 American Bar Association Reports 511.

Grossblatt, Martha and Bette H. Sikes. 1973. Women Lawyers: Supplemental Data to the 1971 Lawyer Statistical Report. Chicago: American Bar Foundation.

Grundman, A. H. 1983. Legal Education in Colorado: The Formative Years. 54 University of Colorado Law Review 555.

Gulliver, Ashbel Green. 1943. Effects of the War on the Law Schools. 12 Bar Examiner 10.

Guttman, Jeannine and Brad Bumsted. 1986a. Funds Reimburse Victims. Cincinnati Enquirer, p. E-3 (October 21).

———. 1986b. Public Access to Disciplinary Hearings Varies. Cincinnati Enquirer, p. E-6 (October 21).

Hacker, Andrew. 1984. Women vs. Men in the Workforce. New York Times Magazine 124 (December 9).

———. 1986. Women at Work. 33(13) New York Review of Books 26 (August 14).

Hager, Philip. 1985. Burger Urges Fines for Lawyers Filing Frivolous Suits. Los Angeles Times, sec. 1, p. 7 (December 30).

Hair, Paul L. and James E. Piereson. 1975. Lawyers and Politics Revisited: Structural Advantages of Lawyer-Politicians. 19 American Journal of Political Science 41.

Halliday, Terence C. 1982. The Idiom of Legalism in Bar Politics: Lawyers, McCarthyism, and the Civil Rights Era. 1982 American Bar Foundation Research Journal 913.

———.1985. Formative Professionalism and the Three Revolutions: Legal Careers in the Chicago Bar, 1850–1900. Paper presented at the Joint Academic Colloquium of the Institute of United States Studies and the American Bar Foundation, London, July 17.

———. 1986. Six Score Years and Ten: Demographic Transitions in the American Legal Profession, 1850–1980. 20 Law & Society Review 53.

———. 1987. Beyond Monopoly: Lawyers, State Crises, and Professional Empowerment. Chicago: University of Chicago Press.

Halliday, Terence C. and Charles L. Cappell. 1979. Indicators of Democracy in Professional Associations: Elite Recruitment, Turnover, and

Decisionmaking in a Metropolitan Bar Associaton. 1979 American Bar Foundation Research Journal 697.

Halliday, Terence C., Michael Powell, and Mark W. Granfors. 1987. Minimalist Organizations: Vital Events in State Bar Associations, 1870–1930. 52 American Sociological Review 456.

Handler, Joel F. 1967. The Lawyer and His Community. Madison: University of Wisconsin Press.

Handler, Joel F., Betsy Ginsberg, and Arthur Snow. 1978b. The Public Interest Law Industry. In Burton A. Weisbrod, Joel F. Handler, and Neil K. Komesar, eds. Public Interest Law: An Economic and Institutional Analysis. Berkeley: University of California Press.

Handler, Joel F., Ellen Jane Hollingsworth, and Howard S. Erlanger. 1978a. Lawyers and the Pursuit of Legal Rights. New York: Russell Sage Foundation.

Harno, Albert J. 1980. Legal Education in the United States. Westport, CT: Greenwood Press (originally published 1953).

Harvey, Miles. 1984. Women Outnumber Men on College Campuses. Los Angeles Times, sec. 1, p. 5 (October 18).

Hathaway, James C. 1984. The Mythical Meritocracy of Law School Admissions. 34 Journal of Legal Education 86.

Hazard, Geoffrey C., Jr. and W. William Hodes. 1985. The Law of Lawyering: A Handbook on the Model Rules of Professional Conduct. Clifton, NJ: Law & Business, Inc.

Hedegard, James M. 1979. The Impact of Legal Education: An In-Depth Examination of Career-relevant Interests, Attitudes, and Personality Traits Among First-Year Law Students. 1979 American Bar Foundation Research Journal 791.

———. 1982. Causes of Career-relevant Interest Changes Among First-Year Law Students: Some Research Data. 1982 American Bar Foundation Research Journal 789.

Heins, Marilyn, Shirley Nichols Fahey, and Roger C. Henderson. 1983. Law Students and Medical Students: A Comparison of Perceived Stress. 33 Journal of Legal Education 511.

Heinz, John P. and Edward O. Laumann. 1978. The Legal Profession: Client Interests, Professional Roles, and Social Hierarchies. 76 Michigan Law Review 1111.

———. 1982. Chicago Lawyers: The Social Structure of the Bar. New York: Russell Sage Foundation and Chicago: American Bar Foundation.

Heinz, John P., Edward O. Laumann, Charles L. Cappell, Terence C. Halliday, and Michael H. Schaalman. 1976. Diversity, Representation, and Leadership in an Urban Bar: A First Report on a Survey of the Chicago Bar. 1976 American Bar Foundation Research Journal 717.

Henderson, John P. and Norman P. Obst. 1977. The

Economic Status of the Michigan Legal Profession in 1976. 56 Michigan State Bar Journal 920.

Henley, J. Smith. 1957. Admissions of Attorneys to Practice Before Federal Administrative Agencies: An Analysis and Recommendation. Washington, DC: Office of Administrative Procedure, Office of Legal Counsel, U.S. Department of Justice.

Hermann, Robert, Eric Single, and John Boston. 1977. Counsel for the Poor: Criminal Defense in Urban America. Lexington, MA: Lexington Books.

Hervey, John G. 1949. Pre-Legal Education of Students Admitted to Approved Law Schools—Fall, 1948. 1 Journal of Legal Education 443.

Hinds, Lennox S. 1977. Keynote Introduction. 5 Black Law Journal 123.

Hobson, Wayne K. 1984. Symbol of the New Profession: Emergence of the Large Law Firm, 1870–1915. In Gerard W. Gawalt, ed. The New High Priests: Lawyers in Post-Civil War America. Westport, CT: Greenwood Press.

———. 1986. The American Legal Profession and the Organizational Society, 1890–1930. New York: Garland Publishing.

Hodge, Robert W., Paul M. Siegel, and Peter H. Rossi. 1966. Occupational Prestige in the United States, 1925–1963. In Reinhard Bendix and Seymour Martin Lipset, eds., Class, Status, and Power: Social Stratification in Comparative Perspective (2d ed.). New York: Free Press.

Hoffman, Paul. 1973. Lions in the Street: The Inside Story of the Great Wall Street Law Firms. New York: New American Library.

———. 1982. Lions of the Eighties: The Inside Story of the Powerhouse Law Firms. Garden City, NY: Doubleday.

Holen, Arlene. 1965. Effects of Professional Licensing Arrangements on Interstate Mobility and Resource Allocation. 73 Journal of Political Economy 492.

Horack, H. Claude and Will Shafroth. 1933. II. Excerpts from the Survey Report. 3 Bar Examiner 30.

———. 1938. The Law Schools of Tennessee: Report of the Survey Committee. 15 Tennessee Law Review 311.

Hotelling, Harold, Jr. 1982. Legal Fees after *Goldfarb:* Settling Estates in Wake County, North Carolina, 1971–77. Ph.D. dissertation, economics, Duke University.

Huber, Stephen K. 1980. Admission to the Practice of Law in Texas: A Critique of Current Standards and Procedures. 17 Houston Law Review 687.

Hurst, J. Willard. 1950. The Growth of American Law: The Law Makers. Boston: Little, Brown.

Hussein, Ann L. and Lawrence E. Wightman. 1971. Male-Female LSAT Candidate Study. 2 Reports of Law School Admission Council Sponsored Research 125. Princeton, NJ: Law School Admission Council.

Hyneman, Charles S. 1959. Who Makes Our Laws? In J. C. Wahlke and Heinz Eulau, eds. Legislative Behavior. Glencoe, IL: Free Press.

Illinois State Bar Association. 1975. Economics of Legal Services in Illinois: A 1975 Special Bar Survey. 1975 Illinois Bar Journal 73 (October).

——— 1983. 1982 Survey of Illinois Lawyers. 72 Illinois Bar Journal 115 (November).

Iowa State Bar Association. 1949. Lay Opinion of Iowa Lawyers, Courts and Laws. Ames: Iowa State Bar Association.

Jacobs, Deborah L. 1986. Part Time: Does It Work? 8(25) National Law Journal 1 (March 3).

Jacoby, Len. 1987. Law Firm's In-House Efforts Work. 9(37) National Law Journal 19 (May 25).

Jason, Jurate, Lizabeth Moody, and James Schuerger. 1975. Woman Law Students: The View from the Front of the Classroom. 24 Cleveland State Law Review 223.

Jenkins, John A. 1984. Outside the Law: On Lawyers, Nonlawyers, and the Changing Nature of the Business of Law Firms. TWA Ambassador 14 (August).

Jensen, Rita Henley. 1987a. Perks: When High Salaries Aren't Enough. 9(41) National Law Journal 1 (June 22).

———. 1987b. Look Before Leaping Into Merger. 9(44) National Law Journal 1 (July 13).

———. 1987c. Partners Work Harder to Stay Even. 9(48) National Law Journal 12 (August 10).

———. 1987d. Is There Life for a Firm After Bad Publicity? 9(47) National Law Journal 1 (August 3).

———. 1987e. The Rainmakers. 10(4) National Law Journal 1 (October 5).

———. 1987f. What's Hot, What's Not: A Roundup. 10(8) National Law Journal 1 (November 2).

———. 1987g. Most In-House Marketers Vex Their Firms. 10(12) National Law Journal 1 (November 30).

———. 1988a. Banking Clients More Willing to Shop for Firms. 10(19) National Law Journal 1 (January 18).

———. 1988b. Scenes from a Breakup. 10(22) National Law Journal 1 (February 8).

———. 1988c. Female Lawyers Getting Raw Deal? 10(25) National Law Journal 9 (February 29).

Jensen, Rita Henley and Daniel Wise. 1987a. Finley Kumble: The End of an Era. 10(11) National Law Journal 1 (November 23).

———. 1987b. Finley Kumble: The Firm's Final Days. 10(15) National Law Journal 3 (December 21).

Johnson, Beverlee. 1986. Administration Grows Up. 8(33) National Law Journal 17 (April 28).

Johnson, Dirk. 1986. Yale's Limit on Jewish Enrollment Lasted Until Early 60's, A Book Reveals. New York Times, p. 18 (March 4).

Johnson, Earl, Jr. 1974. Justice and Reform: The

Formative Years of the OEO Legal Services Program. New York: Russell Sage Foundation.

Johnson, Earl, Jr., Steven A. Bloch, Ann Drew, William L. F. Felstiner, E. Wayne Hansen, and Georges Sabagh. 1977. A Comparative Analysis of the Statistical Dimensions of the Justice Systems of Seven Industrial Democracies. Los Angeles: Social Science Research Institute, University of Southern California.

Johnson, William R. 1974. Education and Professional Life Styles: Law and Medicine in the Nineteenth Century. 14 History of Education Quarterly 185.

———. 1978. Schooled Lawyers: A Study in the Clash of Professional Cultures. New York: New York University Press.

Johnstone, Quintin and John A. Flood. 1982. Paralegals in English and American Law Offices. 2 Windsor Yearbook of Access to Justice 152.

Johnstone, Quintin and Dan Hopson, Jr. 1967. Lawyers and their Work: An Analysis of the Legal Profession in the United States and England. Indianapolis: Bobbs-Merrill.

Juris Doctor. 1972. Money Talks: Why It Shouts to Some Lawyers and Whispers to Others. 2 Juris Doctor 55 (January).

Kafoglis, Milton Z. 1955. Economic Condition of the Legal Profession in Ohio. Columbus: Ohio State Bar Association.

———. 1982. Commentary. In Wiliam J. Carney, ed. The Changing Role of the Corporate Attorney. Lexington, MA: Lexington Books.

Kagan, Robert A. and Robert Eli Rosen. 1985. On the Social Significance of Large Law Firm Practice. 37 Stanford Law Review 399.

Kalish, Stephen E. 1976. Legal Education and Bar Admissions: a history of the Nebraska experience. 55 Nebraska Law Review 596.

Kallis, Jeffrey M. and Dinoo J. Vanier. 1983. Consumer Perceptions of Attorney and Legal Service Advertising: A Managerial Approach to the Delivery of Legal Services. 14 Akron Business and Economics Review 42.

Kalman, Laura. 1986. Legal Realism at Yale, 1927–1960. Chapel Hill: University of North Carolina Press.

Kaplan, David A. 1985a. Bar Exam: The Rites of Passage Are Getting Tougher. 7(38) National Law Journal 1 (June 3).

———. 1985b. Aggressive Student Recruitment Steps Up as Applications Decline. 8(3) National Law Journal 4 (September 30).

———. 1985c. Law Schools. 7(41) National Law Journal 4 (June 24.

———. 1986. The NLJ Poll Results: Take Heed, Lawyers. 8(49) National Law Journal S-2 (August 18).

———. 1987a. Want to Invest in a Law Firm? 9(19) National Law Journal 1 (January 19, 1987).

———. 1987b. Clairborne Found Fit to Practice in

Nevada. 10(14) National Law Journal 9 (December 14).

Katz, Jack. 1982. Poor People's Lawyers in Transition. New Brunswick, NJ: Rutgers University Press.

Kay, Susan Ann. 1978. Socializing the Future Elite: The Nonimpact of a Law School. 59 Social Science Quarterly 347.

Kaye, David. 1980. Searching for Truth About Testing. 90 Yale Law Journal 431.

Kennedy, Duncan. 1982. Legal Education as Training for Hierarchy. In David Kairys, ed. The Politics of Law. New York: Pantheon.

———. 1983. Legal Education and the Reproduction of Hierarchy: A Polemic Against the System. Cambridge, MA: AFAR.

Kirkwood, Marion R. 1952. Requirements for Admission to Practice Law: Statutes, Rules, Regulations, and Correspondence Schools, Law Office Study, Private Study, In ABA Survey of the Legal Profession, Reports of Consultant and the Advisory and Editorial Committee on Bar Examinations and Requirements for Admisssion to the Bar. Colorado Springs: Shepard's Citations (originally published in 20 Bar Examiner 18 [1951]).

Kirtland, Robert B. 1983. Keep Your Eye on the Bastards! Or sobering reflections on the 150–year record of early Virginia's attitude toward lawyers. 14 University of Toledo Law Review 685.

Kocieniewski, David. 1987. Crash Ads Spark Debate. 9(52) National Law Journal 11 (September 7).

Koegel, Otto E. 1953. Walter S. Carter: Collector of Young Masters; or, The Progenitor of Many Law Firms. New York: Round Table Press.

Koenig, Thomas and Michael Rustad. 1985. The Challenge to Hierarchy in Legal Education: Suffolk and the Night Law School Movement. 7 Research in Law, Deviance and Social Control 189.

Kogan, Herman. 1974. The First Century: The Chicago Bar Association, 1874–1974. Chicago: Rand McNally.

Komesar, Neil K. and Burton A. Weisbrod. 1978. The Public Interest Law Firm: A Behavioral Analysis. In Burton A. Weisbrod, Joel F. Handler, and Neil K. Komesar, eds. Public Interest Law: An Economic and Institutional Analysis. Berkeley: University of California Press.

Konvitz, Milton R. 1946. The Alien and the Asiatic in American Law. Ithaca, NY: Cornell University Press.

Kopit, Alan S. 1987. Trends in Continuing Education. 9(24) National Law Journal 15 (February 23).

Kristof, Nicholas D. 1986. The Rush to Hire L.A. Lawyers. New York Times, sec. 3, p. 14 (September 21).

Kritzer, Herbert M. 1987. Fee Arrangements and Negotiation. 21 Law & Society Review 341.

Kritzer, Herbert M., William L. F. Felstiner, Austin

Sarat, and David M. Trubek. 1984a. The Impact of Fee Arrangement on Lawyer Effort. Madison: University of Wisconsin Law School (Disputes Processing Research Program Working Paper 1984-3).

ritzer, Herbert M., Austin Sarat, David M. Trubek, Kristin Bumiller, and Elizabeth McNichol. 1984b. Understanding the Costs of Litigation: The Case of the Hourly-Fee Lawyer. 1984 American Bar Foundation Research Journal 559.

ubey. Craig. 1976. Three Years of Adjustment: Where Your Ideals Go. 6(11) Juris Doctor 34 (December).

adinsky, Jack. 1963a. The Impact of Social Backgrounds of Lawyers on Law Practice and the Law. 16 Journal of Legal Education 127.

———. 1963b. Careers of Lawyers: Law Practice and Legal Institutions. 28 American Sociological Review 47.

———. 1964. The Social Profile of a Metropolitan Bar: A Statistical Survey in Detroit. 43 Michigan State Bar Journal 12.

———. 1976. The Traffic in Legal Services: Lawyer-Seeking Behavior and the Channeling of Clients. 11 Law & Society Review 207.

and, Vicki E. 1986. 1986 Survey of the Status of Women Lawyers in Los Angeles. 9(8) Los Angeles Lawyer 12 (November).

andon, Donald D. 1982. Lawyers and Localities: The Interaction of Community Context and Professionalism. 1982 American Bar Foundation Research Journal 459.

———. 1985. Clients, Colleagues, and Community: The Shaping of Zealous Advocacy. 1985 American Bar Foundation Research Journal 81.

ang, Larry and Ronald B. Marks. 1980. Consumer Response to Advertisements for Legal Services: An Empirical Analysis. 8 Journal of the Academy of Marketing Science 357.

anger, Steven. 1984. Compensation of Attorneys (Non Law Firm) (6th ed.). Crete, IL: Abbott, Langer & Associates.

arson, Magali Sarfatti. 1977. The Rise of Professionalism: A Sociological Analysis. Berkeley: University of California Press.

aRussa, Georgina. 1977. Portia's Decision: Women's Motives for Studying Law and Their Later Career Satisfaction as Attorneys. 1 Psychology of Women Quarterly 350.

athan, Marvin G. 1980. Current Status of Paralegals in Law Offices in the United States as seen by Attorneys, Lawyers, Legal Secretaries, and Paralegals, with implications for four-year college and university curriculums. Ed.D. dissertation, University of Southern Mississippi.

aumann, Edward O. and John P. Heinz. 1977. Specialization and Prestige in the Legal Profession: The Structure of Deference. 1977 American Bar Foundation Research Journal 155.

———. 1985. Washington Lawyers and Others: The Structure of Washington Representation. 37 Stanford Law Review 465.

Lauter, David. 1985. Bill Would Place Cap on U.S. Legal Fees. 7(51) National Law Journal 3 (September 2).

———. 1986a. Waiving Into Another Bar Isn't Always a Real Breeze. 8(27) National Law Journal 1 (March 17).

———. 1986b. Akin Gump Angers Salt Lake City. 9(14) National Law Journal 3 (December 15).

———. 1987. Clerkships: Picking the Elite. 9(22) National Law Journal 1 (February 9).

Law Office Economics and Management. 1985a. Government Lawyer Salaries Compared to Industry and Firms. 26 Law Office Economics and Management 117.

———. 1985b. Associate, Administrative and Support Staff Salaries Survey. 26 Law Office Economics and Management 123.

Law Student. 1923-1929. vols. 1-6.

Leary, John C. and Michael B. Douty. 1958. Compilation of Published Statistics on Law School Enrollments and Admissions to the Bar, 1889-1957 (preliminary draft). Chicago: American Bar Foundation (Research Memorandum No. 15).

Leeson, Fred. 1987. Ex-Militant Can't Join Bar. 9(36) National Law Journal 14 (May 18).

Legal Services Corporation. 1980. Delivery Systems Study. Washington, DC: Legal Services Corporation.

Leibowitz, Arlene and Robert Tollison. 1978. Earning and Learning in Law Firms. 7 Journal of Legal Studies 65.

———. 1980. Free Riding, Shirking, and Team Production in Legal Partnership. 18 Economic Inquiry 380.

Lever, Robert. 1987. American Attorneys in Paris. 9(41) National Law Journal 1 (June 22).

Lewin, Tamar. 1983. A Gentlemanly Profession Enters a Tough New Era. New York Times, sec. 3, p. 1 (January 16).

———. 1984. What's New in the Legal Profession. New York Times, sec. 3, p. 17 (June 3).

———. 1986a. At Cravath, $65,000 to Start. New York Times, p. 33 (April 18).

———. 1986b. Soul-Searching on Salaries. New York Times, p. 26 (May 27).

———. 1986c. The Faster Track: Leaving the Law For Wall Street. New York Times Magazine, p. 14 (August 10).

———. 1987a. Legal Advice: $6.75 a Month. New York Times, p. 27 (February 3).

———. 1987b. Increasingly, Pro Cash Beats Pro Bono. New York Times, sec. 4, p. 28 (March 22).

———. 1987c. Law Firms Expanding Scope. New York Times, p. 25 (February 11).

———. 1987d. Law Firms Add Second Tier. New York Times, p. 29 (March 11).

Lichtblau, Eric. 1988. Reagan Record on Naming

Women Judges Hit. Los Angeles Times, sec. 1, p. 4 (February 3).

Liebenberg, Maurice. 1956. Income of Lawyers in the Postwar Period: Factors Affecting the Distribution of Earnings. 36(12) Survey of Current Business 26 (December).

Lieberman, Jethro K. 1978. Crisis at the Bar: Lawyers' Unethical Ethics and What To Do About It. New York: Norton.

Lindenberger, Patricia and Gene W. Murdock. 1982. Legal Service Advertising: Wyoming Attorney Attitudes Compared with Consumer Attitudes. 17 Land & Water Law Review 209.

Lipsius, Frank and Nancy Lisagor. 1988. A Law Unto Itself: The Untold Story of Sullivan & Cromwell. New York: William Morrow & Co.

Lochner, Philip R., Jr. 1975. The No-Fee and Low-Fee Legal Practice of Private Attorneys. 9 Law & Society Review 431.

Lortie, Dan C. 1958. Laymen to Lawmen: Law School, Careers, and Professional Socialization. 29 Harvard Education Review 352.

Lu, Elizabeth and Carla Rivera. 1985. New Rules Defining Appointed Lawyer Fees Are Circulated. Los Angeles Times, sec. 2, p. 1 (August 1).

Lynch, Albert F., Jr., Thomas S. Tilghman, and Robert J. Berkow. 1985. National Survey of Corporate Law Departments Compensation and Organization Practices. New York: Committee on Corporate Law Departments, Association of the Bar of the City of New York.

Lynch, Dennis O. 1981. Legal Roles in Colombia. Uppsala: Scandianaian Institute of African Studies, and New York: International Center for Law in Development.

Lyons, Richard D. 1984a. Fake M.D. Degrees Are Put at 10,000. New York Times, p. 11 (December 12).

———. 1984b. House Panel Told of Bogus Doctor Who Left a Patient "a Vegetable." New York Times, p. 11 (December 8).

Macaulay, Stewart. 1985a. Lawyer Advertising: "Yes, But . . . ." Madison: University of Wisconsin Law School (Working Paper No. 2).

———. 1985b. Comment: Control, Influence, and Attitudes. 37 Stanford Law Review 553.

Maddi, Dorothy L. and Frederic R. Merrill. 1971. The Private Practicing Bar and Legal Services for Low-Income People. Chicago: American Bar Foundation.

Maddock, Charles S. 1952. The Corporation Law Department. 30 Harvard Business Review 119.

Maeroff, Gene L. 1985. Enrollment in Professional Schools Declines. New York Times, p. 1 (February 10).

Maltby, Howard F. 1987. Computers and Hiring: A Brave New World? 10(12) National Law Journal 14 (November 30).

Mann, Jim. 1981. ABA Ends Opposition to Oral Roberts Law School. Los Angeles Times, sec. 1, p. 15 (August 13).

Mann, Kenneth. 1985. Defending White-Collar Crime: A Portrait of Attorneys at Work. New Haven, CT: Yale University Press.

Marcus, Ruth. 1986. Lawyers Branch Out from the Law. Washington Post, p. A1 (March 13).

Margolick, David M. 1980. Wall Street's Sexist Wall Barrier to Women Partners. 2 National Law Journal 1 (August 4).

———. 1983. The Blue-Chip Firms Remain Mostly White. New York Times, sec. 4, p. 18 (February 13).

Marks, F. Raymond and Darlene Cathcart. 1974. Discipline Within the Legal Profession: Is It Self Regulation? 1974 Illinois Law Forum 193.

Marks, F. Raymond, Robert Paul Hallauer, and Richard R. Clifton. 1974. The Shreveport Plan: An Experiment in the Delivery of Legal Services. Chicago: American Bar Foundation.

Marks, F. Raymond, Kirk Leswing, and Barbara Fortinsky. 1972. The Lawyer, the Public and Professional Responsibility. Chicago: American Bar Foundation.

Marks, Merton E. 1963. The Lawyers and the Realtors: Arizona's Experience. 49 American Bar Association Journal 139.

Martin, George. 1970. Causes and Conflicts: The Centennial History of the Bar Association of the City of New York. Boston: Houghton Mifflin.

Maryland State Bar Association, Young Lawyers Section. 1975. 1975 Economic Survey of the Maryland State Bar Association. 9(2) Maryland Bar Journal 1A (June).

Mason, John Brown. 1934. A Study of Legal Education and Training of the Lawyers in the Seventy-Third Congress. 3 Bar Examiner 254.

Matthews, Donald. 1954. The Social Background of Political Decision-Makers. New York: Random House.

Matzko, John A. 1984. "The Best Men of the Bar": The Founding of the American Bar Association. In Gerard W. Gawalt, ed. The New High Priests: Lawyers in Post-Civil War America. Westport, CT: Greenwood Press.

Maurizi, Alex. 1974. Occupational Licensing and the Public Interest. 82 Journal of Political Economy 399.

Maxwell, Lawrence, Jr. 1905. Chairman's Address, Section of Legal Education of the American Bar Association, 1905. 1 American Law School Review 337.

May, Lee. 1986. ABA Sees Risk of Fraud by People Aiding Illegal Aliens. Los Angeles Times, sec. 1, p. 6 (November 4).

Mayhew, Leon H. 1975. Institutions of Representation: Civil Justice and the Public. 9 Law & Society Review 401.

Mayhew, Leon H. and Albert J. Reiss, Jr. 1969. The Social Organization of Legal Contacts. 34 American Journal of Sociology 309.

McChesney, Fred S. 1982. Team Production, Monitoring, and Profit Sharing in Law Firms: An

Alternative Hypothesis. 11 Journal of Legal Studies 379.

McClain, Joseph A., Jr., Thomas F. McDonald, and Sidney Post Simpson. 1949. Legal Education and Admission to the Bar in California: Report of the Special Survey Board. San Francisco: State Bar of California.

McCormack, Mark H. 1987. The Terrible Truth About Lawyers: How Lawyers Really Work and How to Deal with Them Successfully. New York: William Morrow.

McCracken, Robert T. 1951. Report on Observance by the Bar of Stated Professional Standards. 37 Virginia Law Review 399.

McMahon, E. J. 1988. Old-Fashioned—and Proud of It. 10(21) National Law Journal 1 (February 1).

Meeker, James W., John Dombrink, and Edward Schumann. 1986. Attitudes Towards the Legal Profession: The Poor and the Undocumented. 6 Windsor Yearbook of Access to Justice 141.

Melendez, Martha. 1987. The Hispanic Bar in Los Angeles: A Study of the Availability of Legal Services for the Spanish-Speaking (unpublished).

Mellowitz, Jim. 1987. A Tale of Two Cities: Indianapolis Legal Armies Invade Fort Wayne. 9(30) National Law Journal 1 (April 6).

Melone, Albert P. 1977. Lawyers, Public Policy and Interest Group Politics. Washington, DC: University Press of America.

Menkel-Meadow, Carrie. 1979. The American Bar Association Legal Clinic Experiment: An Evaluation of the 59th Street Legal Clinic, Inc. Chicago: American Bar Association.

Merritt, Marjorie. 1952. The National Conference of Bar Examiners. In ABA Survey of the Legal Profession, Reports of Consultant and the Advisory and Editorial Committee on Bar Examinations and Requirements for Admission to the Bar. Colorado Springs: Shepard's Citations (originally publshed in 18 Bar Examiner 135 [1949]).

Mctaxas, John C. 1985a. "Educational Feast" Awaiting at ATLA. 7(46) National Law Journal 3 (July 29).

———. 1985b. Mergers: Working Through the Maze. 8(3) National Law Journal 1 (September 30).

———. 1986a. Paying for a Partner's Departure. 8(23) National Law Journal 1 (February 17).

———. 1986b. Number of Applicants Rises Again: Final Effect on Enrollment Unclear. 8(29) National Law Journal 4 (April 7).

Metaxas, John C. and Ellen L. Rosen. 1987. "Salary Wars" Still the Talk of New York. 9(26) National Law Journal 1 (March 9).

Middleton, Martha. 1985a. TV Ad Spending Shows Sharp Rise. 7(29) National Law Journal 3 (March 25).

———. 1985b. Firms Moving to the Virginia Frontier. 8(8) National Law Journal 1 (November 1).

———. 1986a. World's Largest Law Firm Not Through Growing Yet. 8(27) National Law Journal 1 (March 17).

———. 1986b. "Corn-Fed" Image Ebbs In St. Louis. 9(1) National Law Journal 1 (September 15).

———. 1986c. Aggression Pays Off for Chicago Firm. 9(4) National Law Journal 1 (October 6).

———. 1986d. Lawyer Disbarred; Lied to Employers. 9(7) National Law Journal 3 (October 27).

———. 1987a. The New Respectability of Breaking Up. 9(35) National Law Journal 1 (May 11).

———. 1987b. Winston & Strawn to Pay $7.3M in Pact. 9(36) National Law Journal 3 (May 18).

———. 1987c. Are Firms Ready for Peer Review? 9(50) National Law Journal 1 (August 24).

———. 1987d. Merger Shock. 10(7) National Law Journal 1 (October 26).

———. 1987e. 54,600 Complaints Filed Against Lawyers. 10(13) National Law Journal 19 (December 7).

Milbrath, Lester. 1963. The Washington Lobbyists. Chicago: Rand McNally.

Miller, Paul Van R. 1967. Personality Differences and Student Survival in Law School. 19 Journal of Legal Education 460.

Mills, William M., Jr. 1949. Development of Requirements for Admission to the Bar in Kansas. 18 Bar Examiner 75.

Mindes, Marvin W. and Alan C. Acock. 1982. Trickster, Hero, Helper: A Report on the Lawyer Image. 1982 American Bar Foundation Research Journal 177.

Miskiewicz, Jim. 1986a. Legal Education Costs Soar. 9(6) National Law Journal 34 (October 20).

———. 1986b. Ad Debate Lingers But Its Focus Shifts. 9(14) National Law Journal 1 (December 15).

———. 1987. Mandatory Pro Bono Won't Disappear. 9(28) National Law Journal 1 (March 23).

Mobley, Coleman T. 1986. Venerable Firm Torn Apart by Modern Pressures. 8 Legal Times 6 (May 26).

Moise, Albert L. 1939. Practical Operation of the Pennsylvania Plan in Philadelphia County. 8 Bar Examiner 38.

Mondics, Chris. 1986. Court Relaxes N.J. Ad Rules. 9(15) National Law Journal 14 (December 22).

———. 1987. New Jersey Supreme Court Warns Lawyers on Drug Use. 9(33) National Law Journal 24 (April 17).

Moon, Charles M., Jr. 1977. Careers of Lawyers in Politics: The Case of the Georgia General Assembly. Ph.D. dissertation, political science, Georgia State University.

Moore. 1984. Shrunken Leva, Hawes Reels as Lawyers Who Left It Thrive. 6 Legal Times 1 (January 30).

Moore, John H. 1984. Lawyer Screening: Fact or Fiction? XV(3) Association of American Law Schools Syllabus 1 (September).

Morain, Dan. 1986. Court Restricts Involvement in Politics by Bar. Los Angeles Times, sec. 1, p. 1 (May 24).

Morello, Karen Berger. 1986. The Invisible Bar: The Woman Lawyer in America 1638 to the Present. New York: Random House.

Morland, John W. 1951. Legal Education in Georgia. 2 Mercer Law Review 291.

Morrison, Cheryl. 1986. More Firms Turn to "Temp" Lawyers. 8(46) National Law Journal 1 (July 28).

Munneke, Gary A. 1981. An Analysis of the Employment Patterns of Minority Law Graduates. 7 Black Law Journal 153.

Murdock and White. 1985. Does Legal Service Advertising Serve the Public's Interest? A Study of Lawyer Ratings and Advertising Practices. 8 Journal of Consumer Policy 153.

Muris, Timothy J. and Fred S. McChesney. 1979. Advertising and the Price and Quality of Legal Services: The Case of Legal Clinics. 1979 American Bar Foundation Research Journal 179.

Murphree, Mary C. 1984. Brave New Office: The Changing World of the Legal Secretary. In Karen Brodkin Sacks and Dorothy Remy, eds. My Troubles Are Going to Have Trouble With Me: Everyday Trials and Triumphs of Women Workers. New Brunswick, NJ: Rutgers University Press.

Nash, Gary. 1965. The Philadelphia Bench and Bar, 1800-1861. 7 Contemporary Studies in Society and History 203.

National Association of Law Placement (NALP). 1985. Class of 1983 Employment Report and Salary Survey (10th ed.). Washington, DC: NALP.

National Center for State Courts. 1984. Guidelines for the Use of Lawyers to Supplement Judicial Resources. Williamsburg, VA: NCSC.

National Law Journal. 1982. National Law Firm Survey. 5(1) National Law Journal 14 (September 13), 5(2) National Law Journal 13 (September 20).

———. 1985. Annual Survey of the Nation's Largest Law Firms. 8(3) National Law Journal S-1 (September 30).

———. 1987a. The NLJ Guide to the Legal Search Profession. 9(40) National Law Journal S-1 (June 15).

———. 1987b. The NLJ 500: Tenth Annual Survey of the Nation's Largest Law Firms. 10(3) National Law Journal S-1 (September 28).

———. 1987c. Billing. 10(11) National Law Journal S-1 (November 23).

National Legal Aid and Defender Association (NLADA). 1973. The Other Face of Justice. Chicago: NLADA.

Nelson, Robert L. 1981. Practice and Privilege: Social Change and the Structure of the Large Law Firm. 1981 American Bar Foundation Research Journal 95.

———. 1983. The Changing Structure of Opportunity: Recruitment and Careers in Large Law Firms. 1983 American Bar Foundation Research Journal 109.

———. 1985. Ideology, Practice, and Professional Autonomy: Social Values and Client Relationships in the Large Law Firm. 37 Stanford Law Review 503.

———. 1988. Partners With Power: The Social Transformation of the Large Law Firm. Berkeley: University of California Press.

Nelson, Robert L., John P. Heinz, Edward O. Laumann, and Robert H. Salisbury. 1987. Private Representation in Washington: Surveying the Structure of Influence. 1987 American Bar Foundation Research Journal 141.

Nelson, Robert L., John P. Heinz, with Edward O. Laumann and Robert H. Salisbury. 1988. Lawyers and the Structure of Influence in Washington. 22 Law & Society Review 237.

New Jersey Supreme Court Task Force on Women in the Court. 1983. Summary Report. Parsippany: New Jersey Judicial College.

New York County Lawyers' Association, Committee on Professional Economics. 1936. Survey of the Legal Profession in New York County. New York: New York County Lawyers' Association.

New York Task Force on Women in the Courts. 1986. Report. Albany: New York Unified Court System, Office of Court Administration.

New York Times. 1987. Lawyers Catch Merger Fever. New York Times, p. 27 (August 25).

Nicholson, Lowell S. 1958. The Law Schools of the United States. Baltimore: Lord Baltimore Press.

Nordheimer, Jon. 1984. Case Challenges Legal System. New York Times, p. 16 (August 12).

Notes on Legal Education. 1930-37. Denver: Section of Legal Education and Admissions to the Bar, American Bar Association.

Nyden, Paul J. 1987. West Virginia Bar Claims Attorney Billed a 75-Hour Day. 9(47) National Law Journal 13 (August 3).

Oakley, John Bilyeu and Robert S. Thompson. 1980. Law Clerks and the Judicial Process: Perceptions of Qualities and Functions of Law Clerks in American Courts. Berkeley: University of California Press.

O'Brian, Bridget. 1987. New Orleans Pro Bono Battle Centers on a Murder Case. 9(41) National Law Journal 10 (June 22).

O'Gorman, Hubert J. 1963. Lawyers and Matrimonial Cases: A Study of Informal Pressures in Private Professional Practice. Glencoe, IL: Free Press.

Oliver, John W. 1948. Big City or Country: Where Start to Practice? 4 Journal of the Missouri Bar 113.

Oliver, Myrna. 1985a. L.A.'s Law of Supply and Demand: Courting Interns. Los Angeles Times, sec. 1, p. 1 (May 8).

———. 1985b. Bar's Disciplinary Policies at Root of Dispute Over Dues. Los Angeles Times, sec. 1, p. 3 (December 16).

———. 1986a. Paralegal to the Rescue. Los Angeles Times, sec. 1, p. 3 (March 26).

———. 1986b. Lawyers Who Work on State Bar's Staff Plan to Strike. Los Angeles Times, sec. 2, p. 1 (April 25).

———. 1987a. Pro Bono: Renaissance in Legal Aid. Los Angeles Times, sec. 1, p. 1 (April 7).

———. 1987b. Lawyers Losing the Verdict in the Court of Public Opinion. Los Angeles Times, sec. 1, p. 3 (October 19).

———. 1987c. New Services Plans Ease Burdens of Legal System. Los Angeles Times, sec. 1, p. 3 (December 21).

———. 1987d. A Shortcut Through the Legal Muck. Los Angeles Times, sec. 1, p. 1 (February 18).

Olsen, Frances. 1986. From False Paternalism to False Equality: Judicial Assaults on Feminist Community, Illinois 1869-1895. 84 Michigan Law Review 1518.

Oren, Dan A. 1986. Joining the Club. New Haven, CT: Yale University Press.

Osborn, John Jay. 1971. The Paper Chase. Boston: Houghton Mifflin.

Palmer, Douglas Shaw. 1986-87. How Not to Re-Educate Attorneys. 9(16 & 17) National Law Journal 15 (December 29, 1986 and January 5, 1987).

Parness, Jeffrey A. 1987. The New Method of Regulating Lawyers: Public and Private Interest Sanctions During Civil Litigation for Attorney Misconduct. 47 Louisiana Law Review 1305.

Parsons, Burke A. 1963. Summary Report of the Virginia Survey of the Economics of Law Practice. Richmond: Virginia State Bar.

Pashigian, B. Peter. 1977. The Market for Lawyers: The Determinants of the Demand for and Supply of Lawyers. 20 Journal of Law and Economics 53

———. 1978. The Number and Earnings of Lawyers: Some Recent Findings. 1978 American Bar Foundation Research Journal 51

———. 1979. Occupational Licensing and the Interstate Mobility of Professionals. 22 Journal of Law and Economics 1.

———. 1982. Regulation, Preventive Law, and the Duties of Attorneys. In William J. Carney, ed. The Changing Role of the Corporate Attorney. Lexington, MA: Lexington Books.

Paterson, Alan A. 1986. Specialisation and the Legal Profession. 136 New Law Journal 697-99, 721-23 (July 25, August 1).

Patterson, Larry T. and Robert A. Sherdlow. 1982. Should Lawyers Advertise? A Study of Consumer Attitudes. 10 Journal of the Academy of Marketing Science 314.

Patton, Michael J. 1968. The Student, the Situation and Performance During the First Year of Law School. 21 Journal of Legal Education 10.

Pear, Robert. 1987. Women Reduce Lag in Earnings but Disparities with Men Remain. New York Times, p. 1 (September 4).

Peck, Austin H., Jr. 1984. Bold Beginnings: A Story about the First 50 Years of Latham & Watkins. Los Angeles: Latham & Watkins.

Pepe, Steven. 1983. Standards of Legal Negotiations: Summary of Preliminary Findings. Ann Arbor: University of Michigan Law School.

Petersen, I. 1978. Legal Aid Lawyers and Aides Hold Meeting in Detroit to Organize a National Union. New York Times, p. 25 (June 11).

Pfennigstorf, Werner. 1980. Types and Causes of Lawyers' Professional Liability Claims: The Search for Facts. 1980 American Bar Foundation Research Journal 255.

Phillips, Orie L. and Philbrick McCoy. 1952. Conduct of Judges and Lawyers: A Study of Professional Ethics, Discipline and Disbarment. Los Angeles: Parker and Company.

Pipkin, Ronald M. 1976. Legal Education: The Consumers' Perspective. 1976 American Bar Foundation Research Journal 1161.

———. 1979. Law School Instruction in Professional Responsibility: A Curricular Paradox. 1979 American Bar Foundation Research Journal 247.

———. 1982. Moonlighting in Law School: A Multi-school Study of Part-Time Employment of Full-Time Students. 1982 American Bar Foundation Research Journal 1109.

Platt, Harry H. 1940. Survey of Conditions of Law Practice in Michigan. 19 Michigan State Bar Journal 631.

Png, Ivan P. L., David Eaves, and J. Mark Ramseyer. 1989. Sex, Race and Grades: Empirical Evidence of Discrimination in Law-Firm Interviews. 6 Law & Inequality (1989).

Podgers, James. 1980. Statements of Principle: Are They on the Way Out? 66 American Bar Association Journal 129 (February).

Podmore, David. 1980. Solicitors and the Wider Community. London: Heinemann.

Powell, Michael J. 1976. Professional Self-Regulation: The Transfer of Control from a Professional Association to an Independent Commission. Paper presented to the annual meeting of the American Sociological Association, New York, August.

———. 1979. Anatomy of a Counter-Bar Association: The Chicago Council of Lawyers. 1979 American Bar Foundation Research Journal 501.

———. 1985. The New Legal Press, the Transformation of Legal Journalism, and the Changing Character of Legal Practice. Paper presented at the annual meeting of the Law and Society Association, San Diego, June.

———. 1986. Professional Divestiture: The Cession of Responsibility for Lawyer Discipline. 1986 American Bar Foundation Research Journal 31.

———. 1987. Professional Innovation: Corporate Lawyers and Private Lawmaking (unpublished).

Prial, Frank J. 1987. A Year After Settling the Johnson Estate, Lawyers Still Battling Over Ethics. New York Times, p. 18 (May 7).

Priest, Tom and John Krol. 1086. Lawyers in Corporate Chief Executive Positions: Career Characteristics and "Inner Group" Membership. 14 International Journal of the Sociology of Law 33.

Priest, Tom and R. A. Rothman. 1985. Lawyers in Corporate Chief Executive Positions: A Historical Analysis of Careers. 12 Work and Occupations 131.

Pye, A. Kenneth and John R. Kramer. 1984. Solvency and Survival after the Boom—A Different Perspective. 34 Journal of Legal Education 462.

Quigg, Donald J. 1985. Nonlawyer Practice Before the Patent and Trademark Office. 37 Administrative Law Review 409.

Quinn, Oliver B. 1977. Career Patterns of Black Graduates of Rutgers University School of Law, Newark, New Jersey. 7 Black Law Journal 127.

Raelin, Joseph A. 1986. The Clash of Cultures: Managers and Professionals. Boston: Harvard Business School Press.

Ramey, Felicenne H. 1978. Minority Lawyers in California: A Survey. 78—11 Los Angeles Daily Journal Report (November 17).

Ramsey, Henry, Jr. 1980. Affirmative Action at American Bar Association Approved Law Schools: 1979-1980. 30 Journal of Legal Education 377.

Ranii, David. 1985a. Iowa Justices Delay Decision on Specialization. 7(29) National Law Journal 9 (April 8).

———. 1985b. A Combative Chicago Firm. 7(42) National Law Journal 1 (July 1).

———. 1985c. Black Attorneys Hit Administration. 7(47) National Law Journal 5 (August 5).

———. 1985d. Appointed Counsel in Michigan Fight Reduction in Trial Fees. 7(49) National Law Journal 4 (August 19).

———. 1985e. Novice Lawyers Barred at Trials. 8(6) National Law Journal 3 (October 21).

Rappaport, Michael D. 1974. The Legal Educational Opportunity Program at UCLA: Eight Years of Experience. 4 Black Law Journal 506.

———. 1977. Placement Patterns of University of California—Los Angeles Law School Minority Graduates. 7 Black Law Journal 137.

Rathjen, Gregory J. 1976. Impact of Legal Education on the Beliefs, Attitudes and Values of Law Students. 44 Tennessee Law Review 85.

Reed, Alfred Zantzinger. 1921. Training for the Public Profession of the Law. New York: Carnegie Foundation (Bulletin Number 15).

———. 1926. Recent Progress in Legal Education. 5 American Law School Review 695.

———. 1928. Present-Day Law Schools in the United States and Canada. New York: Carnegie Foundation (Bulletin No. 21).

———. 1933. Tracking Down the Repeaters. 2 Bar Examiner 235.

Reed. 1972. The Lawyer-Client: A Managed Relationship? In C. Bryant, ed., The Social Dimensions of Work.

Reichstein, Kenneth J. 1965. Ambulance Chasing: A Case Study of Deviation and Control within the Legal Profession. 13 Social Problems 3.

Review of Legal Education. Chicago: ABA Section of Legal Education and Admissions to the Bar.

Reynolds, Ray. 1986. Use of Bar Dues for Lobbying Curtailed. 9(5) National Law Journal 3 (October 13).

Reynoso, Cruz, Jose Alvarez, Albert F. Moreno, Mario Olmos, Anthony Quintero, and William Soria. 1970. La Raza, the Law, and the Law Schools. 1970 University of Toledo Law Review 809.

Rhode, Deborah L. 1981. Policing the Professional Monopoly: A Constitutional and Empirical Analysis of Unauthorized Practice Prohibitions. 34 Stanford Law Review 1.

———. 1985a. Moral Character as a Professional Credential. 94 Yale Law Journal 491.

———. 1985b. Ethical Perspectives on Legal Practice. 37 Stanford Law Review 589.

Richards, Bill and Barry Meier. 1987. Lawyers Lead Hunt For New Groups Of Asbestos Victims. Wall Street Journal, p. 1 (February 18).

Richter, Paul. 1986. Antitrust Lawyers Get Less Work as Rules Ease. Los Angeles Times, sec. 1, p. 11 (March 24).

Riesman, David. 1951. Toward an Anthropological Science of Law and the Legal Profession. 57 American Journal of Sociology 121.

———. 1957. Law and Sociology: Recruitment, Training and Colleagueship. 9 Stanford Law Review 643.

———. 1968. Some Observations on Legal Education. In Arthur Sutherland, ed. The Path of the Law from 1967. Cambridge, MA: Harvard University Press.

Riley, John. 1985. Immigration Advice Limited to Lawyers. 7(38) National Law Journal 3 (June 3).

Roach, Sharyn Roberts. 1986. The Recruitment of Men and Women Lawyers to In-House Legal Departments: A Study of Organizational Recruitment. Paper presented at the annual meeting of the Law and Society Association, Chicago, June.

Roberts, Sam. 1985a. Bar Panel to Weigh Fitness of Bernardine Dohrn. New York Times, p. 13 (August 26).

———. 1985b. When Secrecy Seems More Like Professional Courtesy. New York Times, sec 4, p. 8 (December 1).

Robinson, Michael A. 1984. Young Lawyers Find Success Is No Longer a Cinch. San Francisco Examiner, sec. E, p. 1 (November 11).

Rogers, William P. 1901. Is Law a Field for Women's Work? 24 American Bar Association Reports 548.

Romero, Leo M. 1984. An Assessment of Affirmative

Action in Law School Admissions After Fifteen Years: A Need for Recommitment. 34 Journal of Legal Education 430.

Roscoe Pound-American Trial Lawyers Foundation. 1978. Ethics and Advocacy. Washington, DC: Roscoe Pound-American Trial Lawyers Foundation.

———. 1985. Product Safety in America. Washington, DC: Roscoe Pound-American Trial Lawyers Foundation.

Rosen, Ellen L. 1986. It's Not Just a Matter of Time. 9(10) National Law Journal 17 (November 17).

———. 1987. The Large-Firm Boom Continues: A 10-Year Look. 10(3) National Law Journal S-2 (September 28).

Rosenthal, Douglas E. 1974. Lawyer and Client: Who's in Charge? New York: Russell Sage Foundation.

———. 1976. Evaluating the Competence of Lawyers. 11 Law & Society Review 257.

Rosenthal, Dougles E., Robert A. Kagan, and Debra Quantrone. 1971. Volunteer Attorneys and Legal Services: New York's Community Law Office Program. New York: Russell Sage Foundation.

Rothman, Robert A. 1984. Deprofessionalization: The Case of Law in America. 11 Work and Occupations 183.

Roy, Paul D. 1983. Income Statistics of Law Firms—From the IRS. 23 Law Office Economics and Management 447.

Runnels, Jonathan. 1985. Arkansas Changes Its Rules on Residency, Reciprocity. 7(46) National Law Journal 8 (July 29).

Rutherford, M. Louise. 1937. The Influence of the American Bar Association on Public Opinion and Legislation. Philadelphia: Foundation Press.

Rutledge, Wiley B. 1934. A Survey of the Welfare of the Missouri Bar. 8 American Law School Review 128.

Saari, David J. 1979. The Financial Impacts of the Right to Counsel for Criminal Defense of the Poor. Paper presented at the annual meeting of the Law and Society Association, San Francisco, May 10–12.

Salisbury, Robert H., with John P. Heinz, Edward O. Laumann, and Robert L. Nelson. 1986. Who You Know versus What You Know: The Uses of Government Experience For Washington Lobbyists. Paper presented at the annual meeting of the Midwest Political Science Association, Chicago, April.

San Francisco Examiner. 1985. The Brotherhood: Justice for Lawyers (March 25–29).

Schlegel, John Henry. 1985. Between the Harvard Founders and the American Legal Realists: The Professionalization of the American Law Professor. 35 Journal of Legal Education 311.

Schlegel, John Henry and Alfred S. Konefsky. 1982. Mirror, Mirror on the Wall: Histories of American Law Schools. 95 Harvard Law Review 833.

Schmalz, Jeffrey. 1986. New York Courts Cited on Sex Bias. New York Times, p. 1 (April 20).

Schmidhauser, John. 1983. The Convergence of Law and Politics Revisited: The Law Firm as a Case Study. 1 Journal of Law and Politics 133.

Schneider, Stephen A. 1977. Minorities and Women in Law. In The Availability of Minorities and Women for Professional and Managerial Positions, 1970–1985. Philadelphia: Industrial Research Unit, Wharton School.

Schneyer, Theodore J. 1983. The Incoherence of the Unified Bar Concept: Generalizing from the Wisconsin Case. 1983 American Bar Foundation Research Journal 1.

Schudson, Michael. 1974. The Flexner Report and the Reed Report: Notes on the History of Professional Education in the United States. 55 Social Science Quarterly 547.

Schuman, Jerome. 1971. A Black Lawyers Study. 16 Howard Law Journal 225.

Schwartz, Murray L. 1980. The Reorganization of the Legal Profession. 58 Texas Law Review 1269.

Schwartz, Murray L. and Daniel J. B. Mitchell. 1970. An Economic Analysis of the Contingent Fee in Personal Injury Litigation. 22 Stanford Law Review 1125.

Section of Legal Education, American Bar Association. 1919. Report of a Meeting, August 1918. 4 American Law School Review 378.

Segal, Geraldine R. 1983. Blacks in the Law: Philadelphia and the Nation. Philadelphia: University of Pennsylvania Press.

Segal, Robert M. 1957. A New Look: the Economics of the Profession. 43 American Bar Association Journal 789, 853.

Segal, Robert M. and John Fei. 1953. The Economics of the Legal Profession: An Analysis by States. 39 American Bar Association Journal 110, 216, 258.

Seligman, Joel. 1978. The High Citadel: The Influence of Harvard Law School. Boston: Houghton Mifflin.

Shaffer, Thomas L. and Robert S. Redmount. 1977. Lawyers, Law Students, and People. Colorado Springs: Shepard's.

Shafroth, Will. 1934. A Study of Character Examination Methods in Forty-Nine Commonwealths. 3 Bar Examiner 195.

———. 1936a. The Next Step in the Improvement of Bar Admission Standards. 1935 Annual Review of Legal Education 13. Chicago: American Bar Association.

———. 1936b. Eventual Success in the Bar Examinations. 5 Bar Examiner 136.

———. 1952. Character Investigation: An Essential Element of the Bar Admission Process. In ABA Survey of the Legal Profession, Reports of Consultant and the Advisory and Editorial Committee on Bar Examinations and Requirements for Admission to the Bar. Colorado Springs: Shepard's Citations (originally published in 18 Bar Examiner 194 [1949]).

Shafroth, Will and H. C. Horack. 1933. Report of the Committee Appointed by the State Bar of California to Make a Survey of Legal Education and Admissions to the Bar in that State. San Francisco: State Bar of California.

Shanahan, Eileen. 1985. Measuring the Service Economy. New York Times, sec. 3, p. 4 (October 27).

Shea, Steven and Mindy Thompson Fullilove. 1985. Entry of Black and Other Minority Students Into U.S. Medical Schools. Historical Perspectives and Trends. 313(15) New England Journal of Medicine 933 (October).

Shenon, Philip. 1986. Reagan Is As Intent As Ever on Making Over the Courts. New York Times, sec. 5, p. 5 (June 1).

Shepard, E. Lee. 1981. Lawyers Look at Themselves: Professional Consciousness and the Virginia Bar, 1770–1850. 25 American Journal of Legal History 1.

Shepard, Harold. 1937. A Survey of Bar Admission Procedures. 6 Bar Examiner 19.

Sherman, Rorie. 1987. For Better or Worse, Family Law Is Changing. 10(10) National Law Journal 1 (November 16).

———. 1988. Big Brother Might Be Watching. 10(23) National Law Journal 1 (February 15).

Shimp, Terence and Robert Dyer. 1978. How the Legal Profession Views Legal Service Advertising. 42(3) Journal of Marketing 74 (July).

Shipp, E.R. 1987a. Court Faults New York Law Firm For Unethical Behavior in a Suit. New York Times, sec. 1, p. 20 (June 28).

———. 1987b. Revamping Is Seen for a Big Law Firm. New York Times, p. 1 (November 11).

———. 1987c. 108-Year Old Law Firm Under Fire From Court. New York Times, p. 16 (December 18).

Shuchman, Philip. 1968. Ethics and Legal Ethics: The Propriety of the Canons as a Group Moral Code. 37 George Washington Law Review 244.

Siconolfi, Michael. 1985. Law Firms Aren't Simply for Law As Attempts to Diversify Begin. Wall Street Journal, p. 37 (November 11).

Siegel. 1978. Tackling the Legal Complex. Los Angeles Times, sec. 1, p. 1 (August 31).

Siegfried. John J. 1976. The Effect of Firm Size on the Economics of Legal Practice. 2(3) Legal Economics 23 (fall).

Siegried, John J. and Charles E. Scott. 1976. The Economic Status of Academic Lawyers. 1(4) Legal Economics 26 (Winter).

———. 1981. The Financial Returns to Law School Faculty. 31 Journal of Legal Education 466.

Sikes, Bette H., Clara N. Carson, and Patricia Gorai, eds. 1972. The 1971 Lawyer Statistical Report. Chicago: American Bar Foundation.

Silas, Faye A. 1985. Law Firms Branch Out. 71 American Bar Association Journal 44 (June).

Simon, Rita J., Frank Koziol, and Nancy Johnson 1973. Have There Been Significant Changes the Career Aspirations and Occupation Choices of Law School Graduates in th 1960's? 8 Law & Society Review 95.

Slovak, Jeffrey S. 1979. Working for Corporate A tors: Social Change and Elite Attorneys in Ch cago. 1979 American Bar Foundatic Research Journal 465.

———. 1980. Giving and Getting Respect: Prestig and Stratification in a Legal Elite. 1980 American Bar Foundation Research Journal 31.

———. 1981. Influence and Issues in the Legal Com munity: The Role of a Legal Elite. 1981 American Bar Foundation Research Journal 141.

Smigel, Erwin O. 1969. The Wall Street Lawye Bloomington: Indiana University Press.

Smith, Doug. 1985. Eviction—It's His Key to Succes Los Angeles Times, sec. 1, p. 1 (June 10).

Smith, Janet Kiholm and Steven R. Cox. 1985. Th Pricing of Legal Services: A Contractual So lution to the Problem of Bilateral Opportun ism. 14 Journal of Legal Studies 167.

Smith, Reginald Heber. 1919. Justice and the Poo New York: Carnegie Foundation.

Smith, Rossalyn S. 1984. A Profile of Lawyer Life styles. 70 American Bar Association Journa 50 (February).

Smith, Young B. 1937. Take the Profit Out of Leg Education. 6 Bar Examiner 57.

Smith, Young B. and James Grafton Rogers. 193 The Overcrowding of the Bar and What Ca be Done About It. 7 American Law Schoc Review 565.

Snider, Robert M. 1986a. Legal Malpractice Insu ance. Los Angeles Lawyer 18 (February).

———. 1986b. The New Gold Rush: New York La Firms Advance on L.A.'s Clients. 9(5) Los Ar geles Lawyer 10 (July/August).

Sontag, Sherry. 1985. By Phone, Legal First Aid fc a Fixed Fee. New York Times, p. 18 (Augu 3).

Souers, Loren E., Jr. 1962. Qualifications of Appl cants Seeking to Take a Bar Examination. 3 Bar Examiner 79.

Spanenberg, Robert, A. David Davis, and Patricia A Smith. 1982. Contract Defense Systems Unde Attack: Balancing Cost and Quality. 39(1 NLADA Briefcase 5 (Fall).

Spangler, Eve. 1986. Lawyers for Hire. New Haver CT: Yale University Press.

Special Committee on Professional Education an Admissions, Association of the Bar of the Cit of New York, and Committee on Legal Edu cation and Admissions to the Bar, New Yor State Bar Association. 1978. The Characte and Fitness Committees in New York State 33 The Record 20.

Spector, Malcolm. 1972. The Rise and Fall of a Mc bility Route. 20 Social Problems 173.

————. 1973. Secrecy in Job Seeking Among Government Attorneys: Two Contingencies in the Theory of Subculture. 2 Urban Life and Culture 211.

taff of the Federal Trade Commission. 1984. Improving Consumer Access to Legal Services: The Case for Removing Restrictions on Truthful Advertising. Washington, DC: Federal Trade Commission.

tanford Law Review. 1982. Project: Law Firms and Lawyers With Children: An Empirical Analysis of Family/Work Conflict. 34 Stanford Law Review 1263.

tark, Betsy. 1979a. Stars of '79 Seek Chambers Over Firms. 1(1) American Lawyer 3 (February).

————. 1979b. Nine Clinics, Nine Answers: NY Survey Shows Wide Disparities. 1 American Lawyer 12 (August).

tarr, Paul. 1982. The Social Transformation of American Medicine. New York: Basic Books.

tason, E. Blythe, John C. Leary, Donald M. McIntyre, and Donald A. Strickland. 1960. Lawyers Migrations. Chicago: American Bar Foundation (Research Memorandum No. 18).

tate Bar of California. 1932. Proceedings of the Fifth Annual Meeting 293. San Francisco: State Bar of California.

————. 1939. Proceedings of the Twelfth Annual Meeting. San Francisco: State Bar of California.

tate Bar of California, Committee for Cooperation Between the Law Schools and the State Bar. 1937. Economic and Professional Status of California Lawyers During the First Five Years of Practice. 12 California State Bar Journal 259.

tate Bar of Michigan. 1967. Attorney's Desk Book. Ann Arbor: Institute of Continuing Legal Education.

taudt, Ronald W. 1987. Large Firms Overwhelmingly Favor IBM and Clones. 10(5) National Law Journal 14 (October 12).

tavitsky, Bruce J. 1980. Lawyer Unionization in Quasi-Governmental Public and Private Sectors. 17 California Western Law Review 55.

teele, Eric H. and Raymond T. Nimmer. 1976. Lawyers, Clients, and Professional Regulation. 1976 American Bar Foundation Research Journal 917.

teele, Walter W., Jr. 1970. A Comparison of Attitudes of Freshman and Senior Law Students. 23 Journal of Legal Education 318.

tem, Donald E., Jr. and Daniel L. Sisson. 1979. Media and Price Disclosure Effects in Legal Advertising. 7 Journal of Contemporary Business 149.

tem, Donald E., Jr., Dante Laudadrio, and Jeff T. Israel. 1981. The Effects of Attorney Seniority on Legal Advertising Practice and Attitudes. In Kenneth Bernhardt, Ira Dolich, Michael Etzel, William Kehoe, Thomas Kinnear, William Perreault, Jr., and Kenneth Roering. The Changing Marketing Environment: New Theories and Applications. Chicago: American Marketing Association.

Stern, Duke and Nordlinger. 1979. Causes of Attorney Malpractice Claims. 3 Professional Liability Reporter 199.

Stern, Gerald M. 1976. The Buffalo Creek Disaster. New York: Vintage.

Stevens, George Neff. 1963. Better Trained Applicants—An Incentive Approach. 32 Bar Examiner 74.

————. 1969. Bar Examination Success of Minority Group Applicants: A Report and Some Suggestions. Washington, DC: Association of American Law Schools (Bar Examination Study Project, Memorandum No. 6).

————. 1977. Appendix to Diploma Privilege, Bar Examination or Open Admission. 46 Bar Examiner 71.

Stevens, Mark. 1987. Power of Attorney: The Rise of the Giant Law Firms. New York: McGraw-Hill.

Stevens, Robert B. 1971. Two Cheers for 1870: The American Law School. In Donald Fleming and Bernard Bailyn, eds. Law in American History, 5 Perspectives in American History 405.

————. 1973. Law Schools and Law Students. 59 Virginia Law Review 551.

————. 1980. Law Schools and Legal Education, 1879–1979: Lectures in Honor of 100 years of Valparaiso Law School. 14 Valparaiso University Law Review 179.

————. 1983. Law School: Legal Education in America from the 1850s to the 1980s. Chapel Hill: University of North Carolina Press.

Stewart, James B. 1984. The Partners: Inside America's Most Powerful Law Firms. New York: Warner Books.

Stewart, Robert W. 1985a. County to Probe Payments to Court-Appointed Attorneys. Los Angeles Times, sec. 2, p. 1 (January 9).

————. 1985b Panel Weighs New Rules on Naming Attorneys for Poor. Los Angeles Times, sec. 1, p. 3 (May 2).

Stille, Alexander. 1985a. Small Firms in America. 7(43) National Law Journal 1 (July 8).

————. 1985b. A Practice Flourishes in Harlem. 8(1) National Law Journal 1 (September 16).

————. 1985c. When Law Firms Start Their Own Business. 8(6) National Law Journal 1 (October 1).

————. 1985d. Little Room at the Top for Blacks, Hispanics. 8(15) National Law Journal 1 (December 23).

————. 1985–86. Election v. Appointment: Who Wins? 8(16 & 17) National Law Journal 7 (December 30, 1985 and January 6, 1986).

————. 1986a. The Megamerger: How Good a Fit? 8(19) National Law Journal 3 (January 20).

————. 1986b. The Fall of the House of Herrick. 8(24) National Law Journal 6 (February 24).

Stille, Alexander and Michelle Galen. 1986. Shakeout

Begins Over Pay Hikes. 8(37) National Law Journal 1 (May 26).

Storey, Robert G. 1951. The Legal Profession Versus Regimentation: A Program to Counter Socialization. 37 American Bar Association Journal 100.

Strasser, Fred. 1985. Sanctions: A Sword is Sharpened. 8(9) National Law Journal 1 (November 11).

———. 1986. Justice-ABA Link on Judicial Selection Faces New Challenge. 9(9) National Law Journal 5 (November 10).

———. 1987a. Fee-Forfeiture Provisions Illegal, 4th Circuit Says. 9(28) National Law Journal 11 (March 23).

———. 1987b. Immigration Law Making Corporate Inroads. 10(10) National Law Journal 1 (November 16).

———. 1988. 4th Circuit OKs Seizure of Fees. 10(21) National Law Journal 3 (February 1).

Strasser, Fred and Eric Effron. 1986. The Bar's Voice. 8(49) National Law Journal 52 (August 18).

Strudler, Lynn Stephens and Jane Thieberger. 1986. How to Hire, Retain Lateral Associates. 8(42) National Law Journal 16 (June 30).

Stumpf, Harry P. 1975. Community Politics and Legal Services: The Other Side of the Law. Beverly Hills, CA.: Sage Publications.

Sullivan, Ronald. 1985a. New York Panel Urges Cut in Doctor Training. New York Times, p. 19 (October 10).

———. 1985b. Hospitals Fight Bid to Limit Doctor Training. New York Times, p. 15 (October 11).

———. 1986. Medical Schools Press Minority Goal. New York Times, p. 15 (October 6).

Survey of Current Business. 1952. Incomes of Physicians, Dentists, and Lawyers, 1949–51. 32(7) Survey of Current Business 5 (July).

Swaine, Robert T. 1946–48. The Cravath Firm, 3 vols. New York: privately published.

Swords, Peter DeL. and Frank K. Walwer. 1974. The Costs and Resources of Legal Education: A Study in the Management of Educational Resources. New York: Council on Legal Education for Professional Responsibility.

Swygert, Michael I. and Nathaniel E. Gozansky. 1985. Senior Law Faculty Publication Study: Comparisons of Law School Productivity. 35 Journal of Legal Education 373.

Synott, Marcia G. 1979. The Half-Opened Door: Discrimination and Admissions at Harvard, Yale, and Princeton, 1900–1970. Westport, CT: Greenwood Press.

Taft, Henry W. 1930. A Century and a Half at the New York Bar. New York: privately printed.

Tapp, Mara. 1986. In the Battle of the New Associates Salaries, Could Law Schools End Up Losing Their Faculties? 15 Student Lawyer 9 (December).

Tarr, Amy. 1985a. Are Board Memberships Becoming Too Risky? 7(40) National Law Journal 1 (June 17).

———. 1985b. Fight Intensifies on Ethics Rules. 8(13) National Law Journal 3 (December 9).

Taylor, Gary. 1986a. Showdown Brews on Solicitation in Texas. 9(8) National Law Journal 3 (November 3).

———. 1986b. Texas Jurists Target Frivolous Suits. 9(5) National Law Journal 3 (October 13).

———. 1987a. Texas Bar Solicitation Probe Heats Up. 9(39) National Law Journal 3 (June 8).

———. 1987b. No Apologies Made for the Profit Motive. 9(29) National Law Journal 1 (March 30).

Taylor, J. B. 1975. Law School Stress and the "Déformation Professionelle." 27 Journal of Legal Education 251.

Taylor, Ronald B. 1985. California Legal Aid Officials Complain of Federal Monitors. Los Angeles Times, sec. 1, p. 3 (November 11).

Taylor, Stuart, Jr. 1984. Senator Baker and the Art of Making Rain. New York Times, p. 8 (December 11).

———. 1985. Antitrust Policy Shifts to New Arenas. New York Times, p. 15 (January 20).

Thieberger, Jane. 1987. More Graduates Turning to Law Firm Practice. 9(29) National Law Journal 14 (March 30).

Thieberger, Jane and Marilyn Tucker. 1987. Influences on Law Student Interview Picks. 9(51) National Law Journal 20 (August 31).

Thielens, Wagner, Jr. 1957. Some Comparisons of Entrants to Medical and Law School. In Robert K. Merton, George G. Reader, and Patricia L. Kendall, eds. The Student Physician: Introductory Studies in the Sociology of Medical Education. Cambridge, MA: Harvard University Press.

———. 1965. The Socialization of Law Students: A Case Study in Three Parts. Ph.D. dissertation, sociology, Columbia University.

Thomas, James A. 1977. Career Patterns of Black Yale Law Graduates: From Young Blacks to Old Blues. 7 Black Law Journal 131.

Thomas. 1985. Legal Service Advertising—A Comment on the Paper by Murdock and White. 8 Journal of Consumer Policy 165.

Thomforde, Fredrich, Jr. 1974. Public Opinion of the Legal Profession: A Necessary Response by the Bar and the Law School. 41 Tennessee Law Review 503.

Thorne, Barrie. 1973. Professional Education in Law. In Everett C. Hughes, Barrie Thorne, Agostino M. DeBaggis, Arnold Gurin, and David Williams. Education for the Professions of Medicine, Law, Theology and Social Welfare. New York: McGraw Hill.

Tinnelly, Joseph T. 1957. Part-Time Legal Education. Brooklyn: Foundation Press.

Tisher, Sharon, Lynn Bernabei, and Mark Green. 1977. Bringing the Bar to Justice: A Comparative Study of Six Bar Associations. Washington, DC: Public Citizen.

Townsend, Dorothy. 1986. Old Legal Files Hold a Dilemma. Los Angeles Times, sec. 2, p. 1 (March 3).

Tulsky, Fredric N. 1986. 2 Jurists, 2 Lawyers Indicted in Phila. Legal-Services Plot. 9(9) National Law Journal 8 (November 10).

Tuohy, Mark H., III. 1985. Getting CLE Programs Out to Lawyers Who Need Them. 7(28) National Law Journal 15 (March 19).

Turow, Scott. 1977. One L. New York: Putnam.

UCLA Law Review. 1979. Comment: Financial Penalties Imposed Directly Against Attorneys in Litigation Without Resort to the Contempt Process. 26 UCLA Law Review 855.

U.S. Department of Commerce, Bureau of Foreign and Domestic Commerce, Division of Economic Research. 1933. National Income, 1929–32. Washington, DC: Government Printing Office (Senate Document 124, 73rd Cong., 2d Sess.).

U.S. Department of Commerce, Bureau of the Census. 1970. Census of Business, 1967: Selected Services: Law Firms. Washington, DC: Government Printing Office (BC67–SS5).

———. 1975. Historical Statistics of the United States, Colonial Times to 1970, 2 vols. Washington, DC: Government Printing Office.

———. 1976. 1972 Census of Selected Service Industries: Summary and Subject Statistics. Washington, DC: Government Printing Office (SC72–5–4).

———. 1981. 1977 Census of Service Industries: Summary and Subject Statistics. Washington, DC: Government Printing Office.

———. 1982. Statistical Abstract of the United States, 1982–83 (103d ed.). Washington, DC: Government Printing Office.

———. 1984a. 1982 Census of Service Industries: Geographic Area Series: United States. Washington, DC: Government Printing Office.

———. 1984b. 1982 Census of Service Industries: Preliminary Report: Industry Series: Legal Services. Washington, DC: Government Printing Office (SC82–A-52).

U.S. Department of Labor, Bureau of Labor Statistics. 1972. National Survey of Professional, Administrative, Technical, and Clerical Pay. Washington, DC: Government Printing Office.

U.S. Office of Education. 1868–1919. Annual Report of the Commissioner of Education. Washington, DC: Government Printing Office.

Van Alstyne, Scott. 1982. Ranking the Law Schools: The Reality of the Illusion. 1982 American Bar Foundation Research Journal 649.

Vernon, David H. and Bruce I. Zimmer. 1985. The Demand for Legal Education: 1984 and the Future. 35 Journal of Legal Education 261.

Victor, Kirk. 1985. Pro Bono Work Attracting Some Firms: More Needed. 7(26) National Law Journal 1 (March 3).

———. 1986a. Securities Advice Can Pose Risks. 9(5) National Law Journal 1 (October 13).

———. 1986b. Firms Facing More Ethical Challenges. 9(12) National Law Journal 1 (December 1).

———. 1987. Venable Agrees to $27M Accord. 9(37) National Law Journal 3 (May 25).

Virginia Law Review. 1962. The Negro Lawyer in Virginia: A Survey. 51 Virginia Law Review 521.

Vogt, Leona M. 1986. From Law School to Career: Where Do Graduates Go and What Do They Do? A Career Paths Study of Seven Northeastern Area Law Schools. Cambridge, Mass.: Harvard Law School Program on the Legal Profession.

Wallbank, Stanley T. 1931. The Function of Bar Examiners. 1 Bar Examiner 27.

Warkov, Seymour. 1965a. Lawyers in the Making. Chicago: Aldine.

———. 1965b. Employment Expectations of Law Students. 6 Sociological Quarterly 222.

Warkov, Seymour and Sharyn L. Roach. 1987a. Research on Legal Careers: Integrating Survey and Professional Directory Data. Paper presented at the annual meeting of the Law and Society Association, Chicago, May 30, 1986.

———. 1987b. Social and Academic Origins and Legal Careers: An Overview of Findings. Paper presented at the annual meeting of the Law and Society Association, Washington, DC, June 14.

Warren, Jenifer. 1988. State Bar Plans to Hike Dues to Pay for Reform. Los Angeles Times, sec. 1, p. 34 (January 23).

Warrick, Dupuy G. 1934. Report of Committee on Welfare of the Bar. 5 Missouri Bar Journal 223.

Watson, Richard A. and Randal G. Downing. 1969. The Politics of the Bench and Bar. New York: John Wiley.

Wechsler, Harold S. 1977. The Qualified Student: A History of Selective College Admission in America. New York: John Wiley.

Wehrwein, Austin C. 1985. Is Discipline a "Major Task" in Minnesota? 7(45) National Law Journal 8 (July 29).

Weil, Fred B. 1968. The 1967 Lawyer Statistical Report. Chicago: American Bar Foundation.

Weil. 1972. The Census of Law Firms.

Weil, Robert L. 1986. Economically, It's Been a Decade of Running in Place. 8(22) National Law Journal 15 (February 10).

Weil, Robert L. and Robin L. Hegvik. 1987. Small-Firm Poll: Administrative Law Most Lucrative. 10(4) National Law Journal 14 (October 5).

Weinfeld, William. 1949. Income of Lawyers, 1929–48. 29(8) Survey of Current Business 18 (August).

———. 1951. Income of Physicians, 1929–49. 31(7) Survey of Current Business 9 (July).

Weingarten. 1981. Breaking Up. National Law Journal 26 (June 1).

Weinstein, Henry. 1987. AFL-CIO Starts Legal Services Program. Los Angeles Times, sec. 1, p. 17 (February 17).

Weisbrod, Burton A. 1983. Nonprofit and Proprietary Sector Behavior: Wage Differentials Among Lawyers. 1 Journal of Labor Economics 246.

Weisbrod, Burton A., Joel F. Handler, and Neil K. Komesar, eds. 1978. Public Interest Law: An Economic and Institutional Analysis. Berkeley: University of California Press.

Weisenhaus, Doreen. 1988. Still a Long Way to Go For Women, Minorities. 10(22) National Law Journal 1 (February 8).

White, Thomas O. 1984. LSAC/LSAS: A Brief History. 34 Journal of Legal Education 369.

Wice, Paul B. 1978. The Endangered Species: America's Private Criminal Lawyers. Beverly Hills, CA.: Sage Publications.

Wickser, Philip J. 1933. Law Schools, Bar Examiners, and Bar Associations. 7 American Law School Review 725.

Wigmore, John H. 1915. Should the Standard of Admission to the Bar Be Based on Two Years or More of College Grade Education? It Should. 4 American Law School Review 30.

Wigmore, John H. and Fredric B. Crossley. 1909. A Statistical Comparison of College and High School Education as a Preparation for Legal Scholarship. 34 American Bar Association Reports 941.

Willging, Thomas E. and Thomas G. Dunn. 1981. The Moral Development of the Law Student: Theory and Data on Legal Education. 31 Journal of Legal Education 306.

Winchurch, Susan. 1987. New Funds for Lawyers Emerge. 10(3) National Law Journal 3 (September 28).

Windrem, Robert. 1979. Labor Dept. Investigating Legal Services Plans. 1(2) American Lawyer 12 (April).

Winfree, L. Thomas, Jr., Lawrence Kielich, and Robert E. Clark. 1984. On Becoming a Prosecutor: Observations on the Organizational Socialization of Law Interns. 11 Work and Occupations 207.

Wise, Daniel. 1987a. It's a Bull Market for Associates. 9(48) National Law Journal 3 (August 10).

———. 1987b. Psst! Wanna Make Partner? 10(7) National Law Journal 1 (October 26).

Wolf, Jacob M. 1985. Nonlawyer Practice Before the Social Security Administration. 37 Administrative Law Review 413.

Women's Law Association, Harvard Law School. 1985. Employment Survey Directory. Cambridge. MA: Women's Law Association.

Woodworth, J. R. 1973. Some Influences on the Reform of Schools of Law and Medicine, 1890–1920. 14 Sociological Quarterly 496.

Wycoff, Robert. 1962. The Effects of a Malpractice Suit upon Physicians in Connecticut. In Albert Averbach and Melvin Belli, eds. 2 Tort and Medical Handbook. Indianapolis, IN: Bobbs-Merrill.

Yale Law Journal 1970. Comment: The New Public Interest Lawyers. 79 Yale Law Journal 1069.

———. 1976. Project: The Unauthorized Practice of Law and Pro Se Divorce: An Empirical Analysis. 86 Yale Law Journal 104.

———. 1980. Project: An Assessment of Alternative Strategies for Increasing Access to Legal Services. 90 Yale Law Journal 122.

York, John C. and Rosemary D. Hale. 1973. Too Many Lawyers? The Legal Services Industry: Its Structure and Outlook. 26 Journal of Legal Education 1.

Zelan, Joseph. 1967. Social Origins and the Recruitment of American Lawyers. 18 British Journal of Sociology 45.

———. 1968. Occupational Recruitment and Socialization in Law School. 21 Journal of Legal Education 182.

Zeller, Belle, ed. 1954. American State Legislatures. New York: Crowell.

Zemans, Frances K. and Victor G. Rosenblum. 1981. The Making of a Public Profession. Chicago: American Bar Foundation.

Zenoff, Elyce H. and Kathryn V. Lorio. 1983. What We Know, What We Think We Know, and What We Don't Know About Women Law Professors. 25 Arizona Law Review 869.

Zenoff, Elyce H. and Lizabeth A. Moody. 1986. Law Faculty Attrition: Are We Doing Something Wrong? 36 Journal of Legal Education 209.

Zillman, Donald N. and Vickie R. Gregory. 1986. Law Student Employment and Legal Education. 36 Journal of Legal Education 390.

Index

Page numbers in *italic* refer to tables.